Baseball Meets the Law

Baseball Meets the Law

*A Chronology of Decisions,
Statutes and Other Legal Events*

ED EDMONDS *and*
FRANK G. HOUDEK

McFarland & Company, Inc., Publishers
Jefferson, North Carolina

LIBRARY OF CONGRESS CATALOGUING-IN-PUBLICATION DATA

Names: Edmonds, Edmund P., author. | Houdek, Frank G., author.
Title: Baseball meets the law : a chronology of decisions, statutes and other legal events / Ed Edmonds and Frank G. Houdek.
Description: Jefferson, North Carolina : McFarland & Company, Inc., 2017. | Includes bibliographical references and index.
Identifiers: LCCN 2017003949 | ISBN 9781476664385 (softcover : acid free paper) ∞
Subjects: LCSH: Baseball—Law and legislation—United States.
Classification: LCC KF3989.2 .E36 2017 | DDC 344.73/099—dc23
LC record available at https://lccn.loc.gov/2017003949

BRITISH LIBRARY CATALOGUING DATA ARE AVAILABLE

ISBN (print) 978-1-4766-6438-5
ISBN (ebook) 978-1-4766-2906-3

© 2017 Ed Edmonds and Frank Houdek. All rights reserved

No part of this book may be reproduced or transmitted in any form or by any means, electronic or mechanical, including photocopying or recording, or by any information storage and retrieval system, without permission in writing from the publisher.

Front cover image © 2017 studiocasper/iStock

Printed in the United States of America

*McFarland & Company, Inc., Publishers
Box 611, Jefferson, North Carolina 28640
www.mcfarlandpub.com*

To my loving wife, Brigid,
who has endured many things including
our first trip to Cooperstown near the end
of our honeymoon. Her support has
always been unwavering.—EE

To my children Patrick, Jason, Katy, and Lizzie
for always understanding that Dad's head
in a baseball book does not mean he loves them any
less. And especially for Susan, ever there when
I need her, which means most of the time.—FGH

Table of Contents

Introduction   1

1. Baseball Origins and Club Teams, 1791–1865   13
Introduction 13; *September 5, 1791*: Pittsfield Bylaw Bans Ball Playing Near Meeting House 14; *April 22, 1794*: Pennsylvania Blue Law Bans Sunday Baseball 14; *June 6, 1816*: Cooperstown Ordinance Bans Baseball on Future Site of Hall of Fame 14; *December 7, 1837*: Olympic Town Ball Club Adopts Constitution 15; *March 8, 1841*: Oliver Wendell Holmes, Jr., Is Born in Boston 15; *September 23, 1845*: Lawyer Wheaton Codifies Rules of New York Knickerbockers 15; *September 1, 1850*: "Orator" O'Rourke, Hall of Fame Player and Lawyer, Is Born 15; *March 10, 1858*: Formation of National Association of Base Ball Players in NYC 16; *July 20, 1858*: Fashion Race Course All-Star Contest First to Charge Admission Fee 16; *March 3, 1860*: Ward, Hall of Fame Player, Lawyer, and Brotherhood Founder, Is Born 17; *September 28, 1865*: First Known Fixed Game, Mutuals vs. Eckfords at Elysian Fields 17

2. Professionalization and the Rise of Leagues, 1866–1902   18
Introduction 18; *July 23, 1866*: Red Stockings Formed in Cincinnati Law Office as Resolute Base Ball Club 19; *November 20, 1866*: Birth of Kenesaw Mountain Landis, Baseball's First Commissioner 19; *March 16, 1867*: Birth of George Wharton Pepper, Lawyer for Organized Baseball 20; *August 20, 1867*: First Patent for a Baseball-Themed Board Game Issued 20; *October 18, 1867*: All-Black Pythian Club Rejected for Membership by NABBP 21; *November 22, 1867*: First Judicial Ruling with Reference to Baseball 21; *December 17, 1867*: First Patent for the Game of Baseball Issued 21; *April 2, 1869*: Hughie Jennings, Hall of Fame Player and Lawyer, Is Born 22; *May 4, 1869*: All-Professional Cincinnati Red Stockings Play First Game 22; *September 3, 1869*: First Known Game Between Organized Black and White Teams 22; *March 17, 1871*: National Association Formed, First League of Professional Baseball Teams 23; *December 5, 1874*: Davy Force Contract Dispute 23; *May 26, 1875*: Bechtel and Craver Sold for $1,500, First Sale of a Player 24; *July 27, 1875*: First Patent for a Baseball Issued 24; *December 14, 1875*: Patent for "Ding Dong" Base with Attached Bell 24; *February 2, 1876*: Founding of the National League 24; *April 25, 1877*: New York Antipooling Act Addresses Gambling Ills 25; *October 30, 1877*: Louisville Game-Fixing Scandal 25; *February 12, 1878*: Thayer Receives First Patent for a Catcher's

(Professionalization... *continued*)

Mask 26 *June 21, 1879*: William Edward White Is First African American Major League Player 26; *September 29, 1879*: National League Establishes First Reserve Rule 27; *September 2, 1880*: Jones Sues Boston for Back Pay After Suspension by Soden 27; *October 6, 1880*: National League Expels Cincinnati Over Beer and Sunday Baseball 27; *November 2, 1881*: American Association Forms, Reserve Clause Banned 28; *December 20, 1881*: Branch Rickey, Pioneering Executive and Lawyer, Is Born 28; *January 22, 1882*: Organized Baseball's First Use of Court System to Settle Dispute 29; *April 10, 1882*: National League Founder William Hulbert Dies 29; *November 18, 1882*: Charlie Bennett and Baseball's First Contract Litigation 29; *March 12, 1883*: Harmony Conference Leads to First National Agreement 30; *September 12, 1883*: Union Association Founded, Bans Use of Reserve Clause 30; *March 25, 1884*: Patent for Inflatable, Padded Chest Protector 31; *November 3, 1884*: Supreme Court Issues Its First Opinion Related to Baseball 31; *May 27, 1885*: John Montgomery Ward Graduates from Columbia Law School 31; *September 8, 1885*: Rawlings Receives First Patent for Baseball Glove 32; *October 18, 1885*: New National Agreement Contains First-Ever Salary Cap 32; *October 22, 1885*: Brotherhood Is Formed, Baseball's First Player Union 32; *April 22, 1886*: Court Allows Property Owner to Build Grandstand Next to Stadium 33; *November 15, 1886*: First Player Trade Between Major League Teams 33; *June 7, 1887*: Reach Patents Catcher's Mask with Inflatable Padding 33; *December 7, 1887*: Richter's Millennium Plan Proposes Reserve for Minor Leagues 34; *January 10, 1888*: Patent Issued for Open View Catcher's Mask 34; *December 15, 1888*: National League Adopts Brush Salary Classification Scheme 34; *November 4, 1889*: Brotherhood Forms the Players' League 34; *January 28, 1890*: Reserve Clause Held Unenforceable in Ward Case 35; *February 3, 1890*: Larry MacPhail, Baseball Executive and Lawyer, Is Born 35; *March 15, 1890*: Contract Lacks Mutuality, Court Allows Hallman to Jump to Players' League 36; *March 25, 1890*: Court Won't Enforce Reserve Clause, Allows Ewing to Jump to Players' League 36; *April 19, 1890*: Players' League Begins Its First and Only Season 36; *May 5, 1890*: Court Prevents Pickett from Revolving to Players' League 37; *June 7, 1890*: Court Allows Frank Grant to Play with Integrated Team 37; *July 2, 1890*: Harrison Signs Sherman Antitrust Act 37; *January 16, 1891*: New National Agreement Creates System for Trades, Abolishes Blacklist 38; *February 14, 1891*: Alleghenys Become "Pirates" After Contract Squabbles Over Stovey, Bierbauer and Mack 38; *February 17, 1891*: American Association Withdraws from National Agreement, Board Declares Open Season on AA Players 38; *April 26, 1891*: Nebraska Supreme Court Upholds Statutory Prohibition Against Sunday Baseball 39; *December 15, 1891*: Peace Agreement Results in NL Takeover of Four Teams, Demise of American Association 39; *June 6, 1892*: Harrison Becomes First President to Attend Major League Game 40; *April 28, 1896*: Giants Suspend Baseball Labor Leader Fred Pfeffer 40; *May 16, 1897*: Ohio Supreme Court Upholds Sunday Baseball Law 40; *June 19, 1898*: Spiders Fail in Challenge to Ohio Sunday Baseball Ban 41; *July 5, 1898*: Lizzie Arlington Becomes First Woman to Play in Minor League Game 41; *August 17, 1898*: Ad Gumbert Loses Legal Challenge to Reserve Clause 41; *June 10, 1900*: Formation of Players Protective Association, Second Player Union 42; *November 20, 1900*: American League Formed, Declares Itself a Major League 42; *September 5, 1901*: National

Association Established to Govern Minor Leagues 43; *April 21, 1902*: Lajoie Enjoined from Playing for American League's Athletics 43

3. The National Commission Era, 1903–1920   44

Introduction 44; *January 10, 1903*: American and National Leagues Reach Peace Agreement 45; *September 11, 1903*: New National Agreement Creates National Commission, Reestablishes Reserve System 45; *September 16, 1903*: Agreement Signed for First Modern World Series 46; *October 9, 1903*: O'Malley, Lawyer and Dodger Owner, Is Born 46; *June 18, 1904*: Judge Upholds Ban on Sunday Baseball in New York 47; *January 24, 1905*: Patent for Pneumatic Head Protector, the First Batting Helmet 47; *May 7, 1905*: Peter Seitz, Messersmith-McNally Arbitrator, Is Born 47; *March 30, 1906*: Ty Cobb's Mother Acquitted in Killing of Her Husband 48; *April 9, 1907*: First-Ever Patent for a Batting Cage Issued 48; *December 30, 1907*: Mills Commission Declares Doubleday Baseball's Founder 48; *May 2, 1908*: Copyright Issued to Composers of "Take Me Out to the Ballgame" 49; *October 7, 1908*: Attempt to Bribe Umpires of Cubs-Giants Pennant Decider Fails 49; *November 12, 1908*: Harry Blackmun, Author of *Flood v. Kuhn* Case, Is Born 50; *March 4, 1909*: John Tener Is First Former Player to Serve in U.S. Congress 50; *June 15, 1909*: Shibe Patents First Cork-Centered Baseball 51; *July 16, 1909*: Democrats Prevail in First-Ever Congressional Baseball Game 51; *April 14, 1910*: Taft Begins Tradition of Opening Day Presidential First Pitch 51; *July 18, 1910*: John Montgomery Ward Wins Libel Suit Against Ban Johnson 52; *October 9, 1910*: O'Connor Fired After Chalmers Batting Race Incident, Sues for Breach of Contract 52; *March 24, 1911*: Helene Britton Becomes First Female Major League Owner 53; *March 11, 1912*: Congressman Seeks Investigation of "Baseball Trust" 53; *May 18, 1912*: Tigers Stage First-Ever Players Strike to Protest Cobb Suspension 53; *May 20, 1912*: Britton Enjoins Cardinals President, Secures Team Ownership 54; *September 6, 1912*: Players' Fraternity Becomes Baseball's Third Union 54; *October 16, 1912*: Supreme Court Receives World Series Updates While in Session 54; *October 22, 1912*: Bresnahan Sues Cardinals Owner After Dismissal as Manager 55; *February 17, 1913*: Assumption of Risk a Defense Against Injury from Foul Ball 55; *March 8, 1913*: Federal League Formed, Challenges AL and NL for Players 55; *January 6, 1914*: Players' Fraternity Achieves Victory with "Cincinnati Agreement" 56; *April 10, 1914*: Judge Holds Reserve Clause Unenforceable in Killefer Case 56; *April 23, 1914*: Court Refuses to Stop "Chief" Johnson's Jump to Federal League 57; *June 22, 1914*: Temporary Injunction Stops Marsans from Jumping to Federal League 57; *July 21, 1914*: Hal Chase's White Sox Contract Lacks Mutuality and Is Unenforceable 57; *January 5, 1915*: Federal League Files Antitrust Suit Against Organized Baseball 58; *January 9, 1915*: National Commission Voids Contract Sisler Signed as Minor 58; *December 17, 1915*: Peace Agreement Between Federal League and Organized Baseball 59; *February 7, 1916*: Landis Dismisses Federal League's Suit Against Organized Baseball 59; *March 4, 1916*: Bresnahan Settles Dispute with Cubs Over Managerial Contract 60; *March 29, 1916*: Baltimore Feds Sue Organized Baseball Over Peace Agreement 60; *April 14, 1917*: Future MLBPA Executive Director Marvin Miller Is Born 60; *June 17, 1918*: A's Enjoin National Commission from Interfering with Scott Perry Sale 61; *July 19, 1918*: Baseball Ruled Nonessential Occupation, Players Must Serve During World War 61;

Table of Contents

(National Commission... *continued*)
January 31, 1919: Jackie Robinson Is Born in Georgia 62; *April 19, 1919*: Local Option Law Leads to First "Legal" Sunday Games in New York 62; *July 13, 1919*: Court Order Halts Suspension of Carl Mays by Ban Johnson 62; *February 10, 1920*: AL Owners Defy Ban Johnson, Uphold Mays Trade to Yankees 63; *February 13–14, 1920*: Negro National League Founded with Rube Foster as President 63; *April 14, 1920*: Magee Loses Suit Against Cubs When He Admits Role in Fixing Game 64; *August 7, 1920*: John McGraw Arrested After Lambs Club Brawl 64; *September 15, 1920*: Babe Ruth Loses Court Battle Over Use of His Image in Films 64; *September 19, 1920*: Ruth Pursues Breach of Contract Claim Against Movie Producer 65; *September 28, 1920*: Cicotte and Jackson Admit Black Sox Role to Grand Jury 65; *October 29, 1920*: Grand Jury Indicts Players and Gamblers in Black Sox Scandal 66; *November 12, 1920*: Kenesaw Mountain Landis Is First Baseball Commissioner 66

4. Landis in Charge, 1921–1944   67

Introduction 67; *January 12, 1921*: New National Agreement Establishes Powers of Commissioner 68; *February 21, 1921*: Congressman Welty Proposes Impeachment of Judge Landis 68; *February 21, 1921*: Christy Walsh Inks Babe Ruth, Becomes First Player Agent 69; *April 7, 1921*: Landis Permanently Suspends Benny Kauff Despite Acquittal in Criminal Trial 69; *May 16, 1921*: "Reuben's Rule" Leads to Change in Stadium Foul Ball Policy 70; *June 27, 1921*: Black Sox Criminal Trial Begins in Chicago 70; *August 2, 1921*: Jury Acquits Black Sox Players, Landis Banishes Them Anyway 70; *December 5, 1921*: Landis Suspends Ruth and Others for Post-World Series Play 71; *April 26, 1922*: Banned Black Sox Players File Civil Suits Against White Sox 71; *May 29, 1922*: Supreme Court Establishes Antitrust Exemption in *Federal Baseball* 71; *June 8, 1922*: Richter Analyzes *Federal Baseball* Decision for *Sporting News* 72; *July 1, 1922*: Illinois Enacts Sports Anti-Corruption Statute After Black Sox Scandal 73; *August 22, 1922*: Doak Patents First Fielder's Glove with Webbing 73; *August 26, 1922*: Cannon Seeks Players for National Baseball Players Association 73; *December 16, 1922*: Ed Bolden Leads Formation of Eastern Colored League 74; *March 15, 1923*: Paternity Suit Against Babe Ruth Dropped as "Frame-Up" 74; *March 20, 1923*: Former Ump Johnstone Patents Improved Mask 74; *February 14, 1924*: Joe Jackson Arrested for Perjury, Loses Civil Suit 75; *October 4, 1924*: Coolidge Becomes First Sitting President to Attend World Series Opening Game 75; *November 28, 1924*: Negro National League Formally Chartered in Illinois 75; *October 28, 1926*: Future Lawyer and Baseball Commissioner Bowie Kuhn Is Born 76; *December 3, 1926*: Midge Donahue Is MLB's First Female Front-Office Executive 76; *June 25, 1927*: Pennsylvania Supreme Court Upholds Ban Against Sunday Baseball 76; *November 6, 1928*: Boston Approves Sunday Games After Referendum Allows Local Option 77; *May 19, 1929*: Yankee Stadium Fan Stampede Blamed on Ruth's Failure to Hit Home Run 77; *May 27, 1929*: Muddy Ruel Admitted to Practice Before U.S. Supreme Court 78; *January 28, 1930*: "Baby Ruth" Defeats Babe Ruth in Trademark Dispute 78; *March 8, 1930*: $80K Contract for the Babe, Tops President's Salary 79; *April 2, 1931*: Jackie Mitchell Is First Woman to Sign Professional Contract 79; *April 21, 1931*: Commissioner's Powers Upheld in Ruling Over Bennett Contract 79; *December 1, 1931*: Burglary

Haul Includes a Dozen Babe Ruth Home Run Candy Bars 80; *June 30, 1932*: Rogers Hornsby Loses Tax Case 80; *July 6, 1932*: Former Beau Violet Popovich Shoots the Cubs' Billy Jurges 81; *April 8, 1934*: Philadelphia Last City to Host "Legal" Sunday Baseball Game 81; *May 12, 1934*: Joe Judge, *Damn Yankees* Inspiration, Plays Last Game 81; *June 17, 1935*: Landis Approves Signing of Alabama Pitts, Former Sing Sing Prisoner 82; *July 15, 1935*: Court Ends Dispute Between Rival Companies Over Autograph Bats 82; *December 10, 1936*: Landis Rules Against Des Moines, Feller Remains with Indians 83; *March 23, 1938*: Landis Rules That Cardinals Farmhands Are Free Agents 83; *April 4, 1938*: Bart Giamatti, Future Commissioner of Baseball, Is Born 84; *August 8, 1938*: Pirates Prevail Over KQV in Dispute Over Radio Broadcasts 84; *November 28, 1938*: Copyright Issued for Baseball's Centennial Logo 84; *March 1, 1939*: New Agreement Creates Unified Program for Radio Broadcasting 84; *June 12, 1939*: In Cooperstown, Landis First Purchaser of Centennial Postage Stamp 85; *January 14, 1940*: Landis Declares Tiger Minor Leaguers Free Agents 85; *September 9, 1940*: Gehrig Sues Columnist Jimmy Powers for Defamation 86; *November 5, 1940*: Walter Johnson Loses in Maryland Congressional Bid 86; *January 15, 1942*: FDR "Green Lights" Baseball to Continue Play During the War 86; *February 2, 1943*: New York Legislative Resolution Opposes Baseball's Color Line 87; *February 7, 1943*: Landis Says Players Won't Seek Exemption from Military Draft 87; *August 2, 1944*: Jackie Robinson Cleared of Insubordination Charge in Court-Martial 87

5. Owners on Top, 1945–1965   89

Introduction 89; *April 24, 1945*: Happy Chandler Elected as Second Baseball Commissioner 90; *April 26, 1945*: Congressman Seeks Investigation of Baseball's Color Line 91; *October 23, 1945*: Jackie Robinson Signs Contract to Play for Montreal Royals 91; *December 12, 1945*: Pacific Coast League Unsuccessful in Bid to Become Third Major League 91; *April 17, 1946*: Robert Murphy Forms American Baseball Guild to Represent Players 92; *May 20, 1946*: Yankees Enjoin Pasquel Brothers from Inducing Players to Jump to Mexican League 92; *May 31, 1946*: Dodgers Fail in Injunction Attempt Against Mexican League Poaching 92; *June 7, 1946*: Pirates Strike Vote Fails, American Baseball Guild Soon Follows Suit 93; *October 10, 1946*: Truman Presents Moe Berg with Medal of Freedom for Wartime Service 93; *February 28, 1947*: Dodgers Become First Team to Televise All Home Games 93; *April 9, 1947*: Chandler Suspends Dodger Manager Leo Durocher for a Year 94; *April 10, 1947*: Jackie Robinson Plays for Dodgers, Breaks Unwritten Color Line 94; *July 5, 1947*: Larry Doby Debuts for Indians, Integrates American League 94; *August 26, 1947*: Dan Bankhead Becomes First Black Pitcher in Major Leagues 95; *January 18, 1948*: Don Fehr, Lawyer and MLBPA Executive Director, Is Born 95; *February 7, 1949*: DiMaggio Signs MLB's First $100,000 Contract 96; *February 9, 1949*: Second Circuit Questions Reserve Clause in *Gardella* Decision 96; *June 5, 1949*: Chandler Lifts Ban on Players Who Jumped to Mexican League 96; *June 14, 1949*: Steinhagen Shoots Eddie Waitkus, Inspires Malamud's *The Natural* 97; *July 18, 1949*: Jackie Robinson First Major League Player to Testify Before Congress 97; *October 12, 1949*: Parolee Returns to Baseball After Serving Time in San Quentin 98; *December 29, 1950*: Hugh Casey Loses Paternity Suit, Commits Suicide 98; *March 12, 1951*: Chandler Loses

Table of Contents

(Owners... *continued*)

Owners' Support, Resigns as Commissioner 98; *April 10, 1951*: Wage Board Limits Player Salaries, Musial a Big Loser 98; *June 26, 1951*: Court Dismisses Injured Pitcher's Negligence Suit Against Cubs 99; *July 30, 1951*: Congressional Committee Investigates Baseball's Antitrust Exemption 99; *August 19, 1951*: Midget Pinch-Hits for Browns After Signing Contract with Bill Veeck 99; *October 23, 1951*: Ford Frick First Commissioner to Testify Before Congress 100; *June 20, 1952*: Future President Portrays Real-Life Pitcher Named for Former President in Hollywood Biopic 100; *June 21, 1952*: Eleanor Engle Is Second Woman Signed to Minor League Contract 101; *January 28, 1953*: Saigh Convicted of Income Tax Evasion, Forced to Sell Cardinals 101; *February 16, 1953*: Court Creates Right of Publicity in Suit Between Baseball Card Companies 101; *November 9, 1953*: Supreme Court's *Toolson* Decision Upholds Antitrust Exemption 102; *April 8, 1954*: Garagiola Supports Reserve Clause Before Congress 102; *May 18, 1954*: Olympic and Baseball Star Buried in Towns Renamed for Jim Thorpe 103; *July 12, 1954*: Major League Baseball Players Association Formed 103; *October 27, 1954*: Joe DiMaggio and Marilyn Monroe Are Divorced 103; *July 5, 1955*: Doctor Sues O'Malley Over Comments About Campy's Wrist Surgery 104; *January 20, 1956*: Topps Settles Baseball Card Suit, Acquires Bowman's Trademarks 104; *July 16, 1956*: Louisiana Anti-Mixing Law Causes Demise of Minor League Teams 105; *February 2, 1957*: Owners Won't Raise Minimum Salary but Increase Pension Benefits 105; *June 3, 1958*: LA Voters Approve Plan to Provide Land for Dodger Stadium 105; *July 9, 1958*: Casey Stengel Testifies Before Congress About Antitrust Exemption 106; *July 21, 1959*: Pumpsie Green Debuts for Red Sox, Last Team to Integrate 106; *July 27, 1959*: Continental League Announced, MLB Responds by Adding Teams 106; *July 30, 1959*: Portland Beavers Sue MLB Over Revenue Lost Because of Television 107; *May 17, 1960*: Furillo Sues Dodgers After Release While Injured 107; *November 3, 1960*: A Player Named "Law"—Vernon—Wins Cy Young Award 107; *April 29, 1962*: Roseboro Sues Rawlings Over Injury Caused by Defective Mask 108; *May 29, 1962*: Buck O'Neil Becomes First African American Coach in MLB 108; *October 2, 1963*: Koufax's Mastery of Yankees Inspires "Baseball and the Law" Poem 109; *April 17, 1964*: Shea Stadium Opens, Only Ballpark Named for a Lawyer 109; *May 28, 1964*: Spahn's Suit Creates Cause of Action for False Praise 110; *July 16, 1964*: Congress Approves Little League's Charter of Incorporation 110; *September 1, 1964*: Murakami Debuts with Giants, First Japanese Player in Majors 110; *August 22, 1965*: Roseboro Sues Marichal After Bat Attack 111

6. MLBPA and the Rise of the Players, 1966–1995   112

Introduction 112; *February 23, 1966*: Koufax and Drysdale Holdout Together, Seek $1 Million Contract 113; *March 5, 1966*: MLBPA Elects Marvin Miller as Its Executive Director 114; *April 11, 1966*: Emmett Ashford Is First African American Umpire in MLB History 114; *April 18, 1966*: Monsanto's Patented Artificial Turf First Used in Astrodome 114; *July 27, 1966*: Wisconsin Supreme Court Clears Braves for Move to Atlanta 115; *June 19, 1967*: Father's Coaching Accepted as Business Expense for Tax Purposes 115; *February 19, 1968*: First-Ever Basic Agreement Establishes Grievance Arbitration 115; *August 7, 1968*: Cepeda Loses

Suit for Unauthorized Use of His Name by Advertiser 116; *September 16, 1968*: Umpire Firing Leads to Antitrust Suit and NLRB Claim 116; *November 18, 1968*: MLBPA's Baseball Card Licensing Agreement with Topps 116; *February 4, 1969*: Bowie Kuhn Succeeds William Eckert as Commissioner 117; *May 14, 1969*: Maury Wills Found Guilty of Income Tax Deficiencies 117; *December 15, 1969*: NLRB Rules MLB Is Subject to Its Jurisdiction 118; *December 24, 1969*: Curt Flood Attacks Reserve Clause in Suit Over Trade 118; *February 19, 1970*: Kuhn Suspends Denny McLain for Gambling Activities 118; *March 4, 1970*: District Court Favors MLB in Flood Antitrust Suit 119; *May 12, 1970*: Second Basic Agreement Creates Grievance Arbitration Panel 119; *June 28, 1970*: Law School Built on Former Site of Forbes Field 120; *August 25, 1970*: Video Games Must Have License to Use Player Names and Stats 120; *October 1, 1970*: Lawyer Lewis Gill Named First Impartial Grievance Arbitrator 120; *October 3, 1970*: Umpires Win Concessions After One-Day Strike During LCS 120; *September 1, 1971*: Pirates Use First-Ever All-Minority Starting Lineup 121; *September 28, 1971*: Arbitrator Overturns Kuhn's Suspension of Alex Johnson 121; *December 28, 1971*: Ruling Over Compensation Owed PCL for MLB's Expansion 122; *April 1, 1972*: Pension Dispute Leads to First-Ever League-Wide Strike 122; *June 19, 1972*: Supreme Court Upholds Reserve Clause and Antitrust Exemption in *Flood* 122; *February 8, 1973*: Salary Arbitration Added by New Basic Agreement 123; *March 5, 1973*: Yankee Pitchers Swap Wives and Families 123; *June 19, 1973*: Mill Valley Withholds Use of Field Until Little League Accepts Girls 124; *March 29, 1974*: New Jersey Requires Little League to Allow Participation by Girls 124; *August 23, 1974*: Kuhn Suspends Steinbrenner After Campaign Misconduct Conviction 124; *December 13, 1974*: Arbitrator Makes Catfish Hunter a Free Agent Because of Finley Contract Breach 125; *April 8, 1975*: Frank Robinson Is First African American Manager 125; *August 12, 1975*: Al Campanis Patents "Target Glove" for Catchers 126; *December 23, 1975*: Seitz Ends Reserve System in Messersmith-McNally Arbitration Decision 126; *January 13, 1976*: Court Blocks Sale of Giants, Halts Move to Toronto 126; *March 1, 1976*: Kuhn Ends Spring Training Lockout by Owners 126; *March 9, 1976*: Court Supports Arbitrator's Jurisdiction in Messersmith-McNally 127; *June 15, 1976*: Kuhn Voids Finley Sale of Prospective Free Agents 127; *September 6, 1976*: Patent for Catcher's Mask with "Billy Goat" Throat Protector 127; *January 3, 1977*: Congressional Committee Wants Antitrust Exemption Eliminated 128; *May 19, 1977*: Federal Court Supports Kuhn's Suspension of Ted Turner for Tampering 128; *December 29, 1977*: Suit Seeks Access for Female Reporters to Clubhouses 128; *April 7, 1978*: Court Upholds Kuhn's Disapproval of Finley's Player Fire Sale 129; *April 5, 1979*: Law Professor Compares Players to Supreme Court Justices 129; *May 18, 1979*: Umpires' Strike Ends with Significant Concessions for Union 129; *July 26, 1979*: Paul Hits First Out-of-Park HR in Congressional Game 130; *October 26, 1979*: Kuhn Bans Mays and Mantle Because of Casino Jobs 130; *November 19, 1979*: Contract Makes Nolan Ryan Baseball's First Million-Dollar Player 130; *March 4, 1980*: In-Season Strike Averted, New CBA Reached 131; *August 25, 1980*: Ferguson Jenkins Arrested for Drug Possession 131; *September 30, 1980*: House Committee Holds Hearing on Violence in Sports 132; *January 5, 1981*: Owners Unilaterally Adopt System for Free Agent Compensation 132; *May 29, 1981*: Court Won't Enjoin Owners, Leads to First-Ever Mid-Season Strike 133; *July 31,*

(MLBPA... continued)

1981: Seven-Week Strike Ends with Free Agent Compensation Pact 133; *August 6, 1981*: Split-Season Format for Determining Playoffs Adopted 133; *August 25, 1981*: Licensing Agreements for Topps Baseball Cards Don't Violate Antitrust Laws 134; *February 19, 1983*: Valenzuela First to Win $1 Million Salary Arbitration Award 134; *December 8, 1983*: Lawyer Donald Fehr Elected MLBPA Executive Director 134; *July 27, 1984*: Brewers Owner Selig Wins Tax Case in Opinion Filled with Baseball References 135; *August 6, 1985*: Players Stage One-Day Mid-Season Strike Over Salary Arbitration 135; *September 20, 1985*: Pittsburgh Drug Trials End with Guilty Verdict 135; *February 28, 1986*: Ueberroth Suspends Players from Pittsburgh Drug Trials 136; *October 29, 1986*: Court Rules That MLB Owns Copyright to Game Telecasts 136; *July 23, 1987*: Steinbrenner's Criticism of Umpire Is "Razzing," Not Libel 136; *September 8, 1987*: Maryland Court Nixes Referendum Against Acquiring Land for Camden Yards 137; *September 21, 1987*: Arbitrator Finds Owners Guilty of Collusion Against Free Agents 137; *March 28, 1988*: Woman Loses Discrimination Suit to Play High School Baseball 138; *June 3, 1988*: "Casey at the Bat" Read Into *Congressional Record* on Its Centennial 138; *August 31, 1988*: Arbitrator Again Holds Owners Guilty of Collusion Against Free Agents 138; *September 28, 1988*: Canseco Is First Player Publicly Accused of Steroid Use 139; *February 3, 1989*: Bill White Named NL President, First Black to Head League 139; *August 24, 1989*: Giamatti Brokers Rose's Banishment for Gambling on Baseball 140; *August 31, 1989*: $10.5 Million Awarded to Victims of Collusion After 1985 Season 140; *January 29, 1990*: Court Holds Trademark in Ruth's Name Doesn't Cover Photos 140; *February 15, 1990*: "Super Twos" Created in Resolving Dispute Over Salary Arbitration Eligibility 141; *April 20, 1990*: Pete Rose Imprisoned for Filing False Tax Returns 141; *July 18, 1990*: Arbitrator Focuses on Owners' Information Bank in Finding Collusion 141; *November 29, 1990*: Federal Act Adds Steroids to List of Controlled Substances 142; *December 21, 1990*: MLB Settles Collusion Grievances for $280 Million 142; *June 4, 1991*: Patent Granted for Chest Protector with Hinged Shoulder Flap 143; *June 7, 1991*: Steroids on List of Substances Banned by Baseball's Drug Policy 143; *July 17, 1992*: Umpire Pam Postema Sues Baseball for Discrimination 143; *July 23, 1992*: Commissioner Enjoined from Moving Cubs to NL East 144; *August 6, 1992*: *Piazza* Holds that Antitrust Exemption Limited to Reserve System 144; *September 7, 1992*: Vincent Resigns as Commissioner After No Confidence Vote 145; *September 24, 1992*: Illinois Enacts Nation's First "Foul Ball" Legislation 145; *April 6, 1993*: LA Dodgers Lose Trademark Battle Against Brooklyn Bar 145; *March 1, 1994*: Antitrust Exemption Held to Cover Minor League Franchise Transfer Rules 146; *March 10, 1994*: Newcombe Sues Beer Maker for Misuse of His Likeness in Ad 146; *May 8, 1994*: All-Female Silver Bullets Play First Game 147; *May 15, 1994*: First Woman Pitcher to Start Game in Major League Stadium 147; *July 28, 1994*: Owners Withhold Pension Payment Over Salary Cap Dispute, Players Strike 147; *August 18, 1994*: Act to Remove Antitrust Exemption Introduced During Strike 147; *October 6, 1994*: Court Rules Antitrust Exemption Does Not Cover Sale and Location of Franchises 148; *November 23, 1994*: Vincent Halts "Tell-All" Bio, Co-Author Sues for Contract Breach 148; *April 3, 1995*: Sotomayor Ends Strike by Enjoining Owners from Unilaterally Adopting New CBA 149; *July 26, 1995*:

Table of Contents   xv

Players' Right of Publicity Prohibits Use of Mets Team Photo on Clothing 149; *November 2, 1995*: Antitrust Exemption Covers Entirety of Business of Baseball 149

7. Selig, Steroids and Baseball Prosperity   151

Introduction 151; *September 30, 1996*: Jethroe Suit Leads to Pension Benefits for Negro Leaguers 152; *January 20, 1997*: Curt Flood Dies After Fight Against Throat Cancer 153; *July 1, 1997*: Mascot Distraction Not an Assumed Risk for Fan Hit by Foul Ball 153; *October 27, 1998*: Congress Passes Curt Flood Act 153; *December 12, 1998*: Kevin Brown Signs $105 Million Contract 154; *February 8, 1999*: Neumeier First Woman to Serve as Baseball Arbitrator 154; *April 29, 1999*: Court Rules Antitrust Exemption Covers Entirety of Baseball Business 154; *July 15, 2000*: First Baseball Card to Sell for More Than $1 Million 155; *September 6, 2000*: Law Firm Transfers Its Internet Domain Name to MLB 155; *April 17, 2001*: Supreme Court Resolves Tax Issue Rising from Collusion Settlement Payments 156; *May 14, 2001*: Arbitrator's Decision in Garvey Claim Against Collusion Settlement Upheld 156; *October 2, 2001*: Trademark Dispute Over Use of Mascot Name Settled 156; *October 7, 2001*: Court Battle Over Bonds Home Run Ball Concludes 157; *December 10, 2001*: MLB's Use of Player Names and Images Protected by First Amendment 157; *January 22, 2002*: League Contraction Thwarted by Minnesota Supreme Court 157 *June 3, 2002*: Ken Caminiti Admits Steroid Use During MVP Season 158; *August 7, 2002*: MLBPA Agrees to Random Testing for PEDs 158; *November 13, 2003*: Mandatory Random Testing and Penalties for PED Use Adopted 159; *September 13, 2004*: Player Faces Criminal Charge and Civil Suit for Throwing Chair at Fan 159; *March 17, 2005*: Players Testify at Congressional Hearing About PED Use in Baseball 159; *May 8, 2005*: Court Rejects Male Fan's Discrimination Claim in Dispute Over Mother's Day Giveaway 160; *September 12, 2005*: Roberts Compares Judges to Umpires in Confirmation Hearing 160; *November 15, 2005*: "Three-Strikes-and-You're Out" Penalty for PED Use Announced 160; *March 13, 2006*: Insurance Co. Denies Claim for Bagwell Disability 161; *October 16, 2007*: First Amendment Protects Fantasy League Use of Names and Stats 161; *December 13, 2007*: Mitchell Report Details PED Use in Baseball 161; *February 13, 2008*: Clemens Indicted for Congressional Hearing Statements 162; *April 3, 2008*: Pitcher Brocail Loses Suit Against Tigers for Arm Injuries 162; *February 12, 2009*: Suspended Pitcher Challenges NCAA No-Agent Rule 163; *May 26, 2009*: Obama Nominates Sotomayor to U.S. Supreme Court 163; *June 22, 2009*: Donald Fehr Retires from MLBPA, Replaced by Michael Weiner 163; *January 27, 2010*: Uecker Defends Defamation Suit by Alleged Stalker 164; *June 26, 2012*: Court Resolves Copyright Dispute Over Yankee's Top Hat Logo 164; *December 19, 2012*: *A League of Their Own* Added to National Film Registry 165; *February 8, 2013*: Yankees Win Trademark Dispute Over Use of "Evil Empire" 165; *March 22, 2013*: MLB Sues Biogenesis for Facilitating PED Use by Players 165; *May 22, 2014*: Obama First Sitting President to Visit Hall of Fame 166; *June 24, 2014*: Assumption of Risk Defense Rejected for Fan Injury Caused by Object Thrown by Mascot 166; *July 9, 2014*: Jury Verdict for Fan Injured in Dodger Stadium Attack 167; *July 27, 2014*: La Russa—Manager and Lawyer—Inducted into Hall of Fame 167; *August 14, 2014*: Lawyer Manfred Selected New Baseball Commissioner 167; *October 23,*

xvi Table of Contents

(**Prosperity…** *continued*)
2014: Thorpe's Body Remains in Pennsylvania, Native American Graves Act Not Applicable 168; *December 12, 2014*: First Major League Player to Serve as a U.S. Ambassador 168; *January 15, 2015*: Court Rules Antitrust Exemption Covers Franchise Relocations 168; *March 18, 2015*: Settlement Reached in McNamee-Clemens Defamation Suit 169; *April 1, 2015*: Rooftop Businesses Unable to Halt Erection of Wrigley Video Board 169; *July 21, 2015*: Bonds Obstruction of Justice Conviction Overturned 170; *August 17, 2015*: Fan Caught Sleeping on Camera Loses Defamation Suit 170; *September 22, 2015*: Inspiration for "Jurisprudence of Yogi Berra" Dies at 90 170; *December 14, 2015*: Manfred Denies Pete Rose Reinstatement Request 171

Appendix A: A Selective List of Lawyers Involved with Baseball   173

Appendix B: A Selective Chronology of the Black Sox Scandal   199

Appendix C: A Selective Black Sox Bibliography   206

Chapter Notes   210

Bibliography   258
   Books 258; Chapters in Books 268; Periodical Articles 271; Newspaper Articles 275; Websites and Blogs 285; Government Documents 289; Miscellaneous 290

Index of Cases and Statutes   293
   Cases 293; Statutes and Regulations 295

Subject Index   297

Introduction

This is a book of nearly 400 individual accounts that, taken together, give a much clearer picture of the profound effect that law in its many forms has had, and continues to have, on baseball.

Well into the second decade of the twenty-first century, the statement that baseball and law are intimately intertwined comes as no surprise to even the most casual observer of the national pastime. Reports of court hearings, criminal charges, protracted contract negotiations, labor-management clashes, congressional hearings—the list goes on and on—make daily appearances in the sporting press and broadcast media. What some might not know, however, is that this is not a new phenomenon. It is not simply a byproduct of the rise of the Major League Baseball Players Association in the 1960s and 1970s, the increasing presence of immensely wealthy owners, the ascension of player agents in the 1980s, or whatever else on which one might choose to lay "blame." In fact, as this book seeks to document, the intersection of baseball and law is not a recent development at all. It can be found at the very beginnings of the sport in America—including a 1791 ordinance that prevented ball playing near the Pittsfield, MA, meeting house and a 1794 Pennsylvania statute that barred ball playing on Sundays—and thereafter almost continuously to the present day.

More important, this intersection has influenced baseball's development, often, we think, for its betterment, although sometimes that might be arguable. In any case, we believe that a deeper understanding of the sport, both on and off the field, demands at least some knowledge of when and how baseball and law have come together. Our hope is that this book can be a starting point for a reader interested in acquiring that knowledge.

Before proceeding further, let us briefly explain how we determined the "identity" of our "protagonists," baseball and law. For each, we used a broad definition and tended to err on the side of inclusion, rather than exclusion. So while most of the situations we share in the book focus on some aspect of professional baseball at the major league level—for example, the founding of the National League or the criminal trial of the Black Sox players—we also cover matters concerning minor league, amateur, and even Little League baseball. Readers will learn about the founding of the National Association of Professional Baseball Leagues, the governing body of the minor leagues, in 1901; a 2009 case challenging the NCAA's rule that limits a college player's use of an agent; and the federal chartering of the Little League in 1964. Similarly, while there are many instances of on-field action with a legal connection, including liability for foul ball injuries and the arrest of players defying Sunday baseball laws, there are even more about off-field matters that, ultimately, had a significant effect on the game (the adoption of the reserve rule in 1879, for example). And law-related accounts of individuals who might seem only tangentially connected to baseball are told throughout the pages of the book. The 1906 murder acquittal of Amanda Cobb, the mother of Hall of Famer Ty, for the killing of her husband, provides one example. Another involves a Supreme Court justice whose interest in the game was so great he made his clerk deliver World Series updates to him while court was in session.

We used an equally broad definition when determining whether there was a sufficient legal connection in an event to justify its telling in this book. So while we had no hesitation in writing about baseball situations in which a statute, court decision, administrative ruling, legislative hearing, presidential action, or legal document such as a contract played a part, or in which a lawyer or government official took a critical role, in some circumstances the legal nexus may not be nearly as obvious. This was particularly true for baseball matters involving discrimination and segregation, for often they were the result of rigid custom and unwritten, extra-legal rules, rather than actual legal pronouncements or instruments. Nonetheless, it is our view that ultimately such behavior is appropriately seen as violating legal prohibitions, and certainly many of the efforts to address it invoked the law directly. Witness legislative resolutions against baseball's color line introduced during the 1940s, and gender discrimination lawsuits brought by female players and umpires in the 1970s and 1980s. But even without a direct legal connection, we think the documentation of baseball's racial, ethnic, and gender barriers and how they were overcome must be included in a book about the law's intersection with the game. In particular, we relate specific instances of baseball's integration, whether or not a legal solution was involved, such as the first recorded game between organized black and white teams, the Pythians vs. the Olympics in Philadelphia in 1869, and the selection of Bill White as National League president in 1989, the first African American to head a major professional sports league.

Bottom line, this book is a collection of anecdotes about baseball. But not baseball alone. Baseball in combination with law, broadly defined. To be more precise, it is filled with baseball happenings in which law, in some form

Introduction

or fashion, makes an appearance. That appearance is often a starring one, but sometimes it is only as a bit player. But one way or the other, law and baseball come together in each of the individual events we chronicle in this book.

To perhaps better explain both the subject matter we cover and our goal in doing so, let us tell you about our experience at a relatively meaningless Cactus League game that we attended on March 12, 2016, at Surprise Stadium in Surprise, Arizona. We were in Arizona for the annual Nine Spring Training Conference on the Historical and Sociological Impact of Baseball, so admittedly we may have been primed for what happened. Anyway, for those keeping score, the host Texas Rangers beat the Oakland Athletics, 14–5, in a sloppy game (the A's had five errors and walked eight batters and there were five wild pitches between the two teams). For most fans, this and the great weather were the sum total of their day. But not for us because, ultimately, we viewed the game from a different lens.

Our version begins with a sign we saw affixed to nearly every pillar as we walked along the wide concourse before the game looking for the perfect ballpark food. The sign read, in all caps, "CAUTION: BEWARE OF OBJECTS LEAVING THE FIELD." It included a cartoon image of a baseball in flight, presumably heading right toward anyone sitting, standing, or walking outside the chalk lines defining the field of play. Having spent the preceding three-plus years researching and writing this book, we immediately nodded knowingly and said aloud, "Spectators sitting in the stands assume the risk of injury from a foul ball under the long-established 'baseball rule' of negligence law, but what about people walking on the concourse trying to choose between Italian sausage and barbecue?" The proverbial light bulb flashed on. Liability for injuries to spectators is a theme that runs throughout baseball history, from the nineteenth century to the present. (In 2014, a Missouri Supreme Court had to decide whether a fan who suffered a detached retina when he was struck in the eye by a hot dog tossed into the stands by Sluggerrr, the mascot of the Kansas City Royals, was barred from suing the team for damages by the assumption of the risk defense.) Because of this sign, an account of our day suddenly went from hits, runs, and errors to watching the baseball and law themes of this book literally come to life before our eyes.

For instance, in the gift shop we found baseball cards, magnets, jerseys, jackets, and other souvenirs for sale, all replete with team colors and insignia, not to mention player names and numbers. For most that's a great shopping opportunity, but for us it represented the legal questions surrounding licensing and control of image that have been a part of baseball since the late nineteenth century, and thus frequently appear in the book. And it's just a step from that to thinking about a great character from the Golden Age of Sports, Christy Walsh, a lawyer who became baseball's first player agent by inking a contract with Babe Ruth in 1921 and then proceeding to make his client a marketing behemoth. Which reminded us of an another prominent theme of this book: the importance of lawyers to baseball and the frequency of their involvement, from the very beginning of the sport (lawyer William Wheaton was the codifier and scribe of the Knickerbocker rules formally adopted in 1845) to the present (Commissioner Rob Manfred is a lawyer who served as MLB's chief labor negotiator from 1998 to 2013).

Thinking about Christy Walsh and the Babe's multiple endorsements quickly led us to recall Ruth's 1930 trademark battle with the Curtiss Candy Company, a great anecdote about a candy bar "war" (Ruth's Home Run Candy Bar vs. Curtiss's Baby Ruth bar), a president's tragically deceased daughter, and, tangentially, a 1929 Missouri burglary that netted items worth only $7.15 (but included a dozen of the Babe's candy bars that would soon be off the market because of the dispute). More important, intellectual property protection, through copyright, trademark, and patent law, is a constant in the history of baseball, including the early patenting of baseball-themed games (a patent was issued in 1867 for a board game called "Base-Ball Table") and equipment (the first catcher's mask was patented in 1878); a copyright for baseball's centennial logo in 1938; and, down to the present, a 2013 trademark dispute over use of the phrase "evil empire" to describe the New York Yankees. These and other examples of the interplay of baseball and intellectual property law are featured throughout the book.

Having exhausted the possibilities offered by the concourse, we made our way to our seats (they were outside the protection of the home plate screen, so we kept a sharp eye out for foul balls and flying bats). As we scanned the field, we saw players for both teams warming up. One of us is a great baseball card collector and fantasy sports player, so he does better than the other in spotting familiar players, but still, there were many names and numbers. One thing was apparent to both of us, however. Although the Rangers assigned uniform numbers as low as 1 (Elvis Andrus) and as high as 99 (Tom Wilhelmsen), and the A's had numbers between 1 (Billy Burns) and 73 (J.B. Wendelken), no one on either team wore number 42. Jackie Robinson of the Brooklyn Dodgers carried that number on his back when, on April 15, 1947, he became the first African American to play in the major leagues in the twentieth century, breaking baseball's unwritten but rigidly enforced color line. Fifty years later Major League Baseball honored that incredibly important moment, both for the sport and American society, by permanently retiring Robinson's number for all teams. It is now conspicuously displayed in MLB ballparks, serving as a constant reminder not only of Robinson's courage but also the game's long history of rampant discrimination and, eventually, its move toward integration and inclusiveness. As indicated earlier, the barriers as well as the steps taken to remove them are described in many of the events related in this book.

Introduction

Because this was 2016 and we had smart phones, it was not long before we pulled up the rosters of both teams as well as Baseball-Reference.com, quickly acquiring an incredible amount of information about each of the 50 players we would see over the next three-and-a-half hours. Since it is hard not to think of money when you are watching major league ballplayers (after all, the *minimum* salary mandated by the current collective bargaining agreement, signed in 2012, is $507,500, and the *average* salary in 2015 was $4,250,000), we took a quick look to see who among the players on these two teams was paid the most. No one who has read Michael Lewis's *Moneyball* about the Oakland A's will be surprised to learn that all of the highest paid players were members of the Rangers: Josh Hamilton at $25 million per year led the way, followed by Prince Fielder ($24 million), Cole Hamels ($23.5 million), Shin-Soo Chin ($20 million), Adrian Beltre ($18 million), and Elvis Andrus ($15.33 million). (The highest-paid A's player was Coco Crisp at $11 million.) Digging a little deeper, we found that several of these players utilized the free agent status to which they were entitled under the various collective bargaining agreements negotiated by the Major League Baseball Players Association since the landmark Messersmith-McNally arbitration ruling in December 1975 to achieve substantial salary increases. For instance, Fielder jumped from $15.5 million per year to $23 million when he left the Milwaukee Brewers and signed with the Detroit Tigers in January 2012, and Beltre went from $9 million to $14 million after leaving the Red Sox and signing with the Rangers for the 2011 season. Chin almost doubled his salary, going from $7.37 million to $14 million, by leaving the Cincinnati Reds after the 2013 season and signing with the Rangers.

This "research" brought to mind the off-field "game" that has been played right alongside the on-field game ever since the Cincinnati Red Stockings—initially formed as the Resolute Base Ball Club in a Cincinnati law office in 1866—played its inaugural game as the first openly all-professional team in 1869. Anecdotes about the off-field game, pitting labor against management and played with as much zeal as any contest on the field, may be the single most recurring theme in this book. The reserve clause, player unions, work stoppages, blacklists, contract-jumping, salary disputes, arbitration, and collective bargaining—they are constant fodder for the never-ending nexus between baseball and law described herein. Fans today think of baseball as highly litigious, with examples too numerous to mention here, but the number of lawsuits involving players and owners that were filed and carried to conclusion during the late nineteenth and early twentieth centuries is remarkable, not to mention the fact that the names of some of those involved is a veritable Hall of Fame roster, including John Montgomery Ward, Buck Ewing, and Napoleon Lajoie.

Minutes before the start of the game, a local dignitary tossed a ceremonial first pitch from the mound to a backup catcher set up behind the plate. This now commonplace occurrence was much more of a rarity when William Howard Taft became the first American president to offer an opening day first "pitch" at American League Park in Washington, D.C., on April 14, 1910. The effort we saw at Surprise symbolized for us how frequently federal and other government officials, including not only presidents, but also members of Congress, Supreme Court justices, state judges and legislators, and city mayors and alderman, appear in the accounts of baseball and law we tell in this book. Not to mention the ballplayers, such as John Tener, Vinegar Bend Mizell, and Jim Bunning, who became officials themselves once their playing careers were over.

With the Rangers leading 9–2 by the 4th inning, the story of the game for many fans was already almost written. But ours continued as we reflected on the provenance of the participating teams. The visiting Oakland Athletics have a long history, starting as a charter member of the American League in 1901 when they were called the Philadelphia Athletics and managed by the legendary Connie Mack. The franchise shifted to Kansas City in 1955, and then again to Oakland in 1968. The Texas Rangers are a much younger team, beginning 60 years after the A's, in 1961, as an American League expansion team called the Washington Senators (not to be confused with the Washington franchise that started in the American League in 1901 but moved to Minneapolis in 1961, becoming the Minnesota Twins). These teams exemplify another trend that frequently appears in the pages of our book—the myriad court cases, statutes, legislative hearings, and the like directed at the establishment of new franchises, the movement of existing franchises, or both. Among other events this includes the acquisition of four franchises of the defunct American Association by the National League in an 1891 "peace" agreement, increasing the size of the survivor to 12 clubs; the legal maneuvering that made Dodger Stadium and Camden Yards possible; and thwarted attempts to move the Giants from San Francisco to Toronto or later to St. Petersburg, Florida.

It seems fitting that we should end in the bottom of the 7th inning with what has become, thanks primarily to Cubs broadcaster Harry Caray, *de rigeur* in virtually every ballpark in the country, no matter amateur or professional: the singing of "Take Me Out to the Ball Game." The legal connection here goes back to one of the themes mentioned earlier, intellectual property law. On May 2, 1908, composer Albert Von Tilzer and lyricist Jack Norworth submitted two copies of their new song to the U.S. Copyright Office. It remained protected by copyright law until 1983 when it finally entered the public domain. In 2011, James Billington, Librarian of Congress, selected a 1908 recording of the song for the National Recording Registry, itself created by a federal statute, the National Recording Preservation Act of 2000.

Introduction 7

The copyright and preservation of a baseball song may not equal the importance of decades-long litigation over the reserve clause or breaking the color line, but it does represent yet another characteristic of this book, a predilection for including whimsical baseball and law connections right along with the serious ones. Readers will discover, for instance, that only four players in major league history have had "Law" as a surname (two are father and son) and an even smaller number, one, has been named "Judge" (he was the inspiration for Joe Hardy of *Damn Yankees* fame). Another "lighter" anecdote is the source for a great trivia question: who is the only future American president to portray a real-life Hall of Fame pitcher named for another president in a Hollywood biopic?

So after the 7th inning we stopped looking for baseball and law connections and returned to "normal" fandom. We had peanuts and Cracker Jack to eat, souvenirs to buy, and the final out to see. For most of those in attendance, the story of the game could be found in the box score—hits, runs, errors, and so on. But for us, it had been different because we watched the game from a different perspective. Even in a relatively inconsequential spring training contest, we found evidence for and reminders of almost all of the major legal themes that weave in and out of these pages: liability for spectator injuries; licensing, merchandising, and control of images; the near constant involvement of lawyers in many aspects of the sport, both off-field and on; the role of intellectual property protections, including copyright, patent, and trademark; the presence of discrimination and the slow move toward integration and inclusiveness; the struggle between labor and management; the frequent involvement of government officials, both federal and state, in the game; franchise movement and the frequent expansion or contraction of professional leagues; and, finally, the whimsical connections between baseball and law. There are a few others we didn't "see" that day—the impact of gambling and game-fixing and the role of broadcasting come to mind—but the truth is that baseball and law connections are on display in any ballpark on any given day if one knows what to look for. It is our hope that this book will sharpen the observational skills of its readers to these connections, thereby enhancing their appreciation for what is happening on the field and has happened off it.

There is one more explanation to provide before bringing this introduction to a close. And that's the why and how of this book.

Its genesis—the why—lies in the fact that we both are inveterate collectors and that much, though not all, of our collecting pertains to baseball. Baseball cards, signed balls, mini-bats, jerseys and caps, batting helmets, player figures and bobbleheads (*not* "dolls" as one author's spouse unkindly calls them), Wheaties boxes, photographs and posters, jigsaw puzzles, and books ... many, many books. So identifying, researching, writing, and bringing together a large *collection* of baseball-related happenings was very appealing to us.

Add to the mix that we are both trained as lawyers and have for many years taught classes at our employing law schools, including legal research and sports law courses, and it is easy to see why the collection is composed not just of baseball anecdotes but of baseball anecdotes in which law, in some form, played a part. Lastly, for the past four decades, our primary profession has been as law librarians, necessarily using (and in some cases creating) a wide range of research tools and materials for which we have great respect and appreciation. With this background, we wanted to create a collection of write-ups about baseball and law that would serve as both an informative and (we hope) entertaining contribution to baseball literature and as a useful reference volume for those interested in exploring one or more aspects of the intersection of baseball and law, both broadly defined. Thus, we saw this book as not merely the end point of one's research about the Brotherhood of Professional Base Ball Players and its leader John Montgomery Ward, but also as a tool which could lead the researcher to more sources and, ultimately, a much deeper understanding of them. Fortunately, our experience in producing and editing legal academic scholarship fit neatly with this latter goal. As a result, readers will find notes with each entry that provide sources for virtually every factual assertion and quotation offered in this book.

Turning now to the "how," there were various approaches we could have used to describe baseball's intersection with the law, each of which is exemplified by several worthy predecessors. For instance, we could have explored each of our major themes by offering an illustrative event that highlighted the legal issues to which it gave rise. Roger I. Abrams made effective use of this method in his path-breaking study *Legal Bases: Baseball and the Law* (Temple University Press, 1998). Or we could have presented an in-depth study of a single event so rich in fact and nuance that it alone raised many of the issues we wished to consider. Daniel R. Levitt did just this with *The Battle That Forged Modern Baseball: The Federal League Challenge and Its Legacy* (Ivan R. Dee, 2012). In a similar vein, we could have developed an intensive study of a particular baseball entity or activity in which the law played an important role. Charles P. Korr's *The End of Baseball As We Knew It: The Players Union, 1960–81* (University of Illinois Press, 2002) used this approach. Alternatively, perhaps a book that examined not a single entity, but rather a single legal issue. Two recent and excellent examples of this approach considered the same subject: Stuart Banner, *The Baseball Trust: A History of Baseball's Antitrust Exemption* (Oxford University Press, 2013), and Nathaniel Grow, *Baseball on Trial: The Origin of Baseball's Antitrust Exemption*

(University of Illinois Press, 2014). What about a biographical approach, concentrating on the life of an individual who was intimately involved in the intersection of baseball and the law? There are many outstanding examples, but two which we frequently relied on in preparing this book are Lee Lowenfish, *Branch Rickey: Baseball's Ferocious Gentleman* (University of Nebraska Press, 2007), and David Pietrusza, *Judge and Jury: The Life and Times of Judge Kenesaw Mountain Landis* (Diamond Communications, 1998). Finally, how about a casebook, traditionally used as the main teaching device in law schools since its introduction in the 1870s by Harvard's Christopher Columbus Langdell? But Louis H. Schiff and Robert M. Jarvis recently did that exact thing with *Baseball and the Law: Cases and Materials* (Carolina Academic Press, 2016).

While each of these books, and many more that we could mention, are outstanding in both approach and execution, we decided to take another route into our subject by preparing a chronology—that is, a work with material presented in order by date rather than subject or some other method of arrangement—that is heavily annotated, rich with cited sources, and wide not only in the time span covered but also in the range of topics presented. To our knowledge, this book is unique in its use of this approach for law and baseball, although there certainly are other chronologies that cover baseball generally (for instance, the Protoball and BaseballChronology.com websites) and at least one excellent chronology that focuses on one of our themes, labor-management relations in major league baseball (Ross E. Davies, "Along Comes the Players Association: The Roots and Rise of Organized Labor in Major League Baseball," in the 2013 volume of the *NYU Journal of Legislation and Public Policy*).

Using an annotated chronology allows us to address two different but, we hope, overlapping audiences. The first includes readers interested in baseball generally who we think will enjoy being introduced to material that is outside their usual purview. Readers who are familiar with Ty Cobb's batting and base stealing, but may not know that his attack on a fan led to the first player's strike. Readers who may have been Pirates fans their entire lives but don't know that the team's nickname stems from its involvement with an 1891 contract squabble that included a young ballplayer named Connie Mack. These readers can peruse the book from front to back or jump in on any page and, either way, find something that will leave them shaking their head.

Although we hope all readers will fall into this first group, we believe that some also will be part of a second group, those interested in beginning more in-depth research on a particular person, event, or subject with a baseball and law connection. They can use our work as a starting point for their project, developing an initial understanding from the book's entries and following the multiple references provided with the entries to explore additional resources. To find relevant entries, these readers will use the table of contents, which provides a short subject descriptor for every entry, or, more likely, the very detailed subject index that offers numerous access points into the body of the book. They may also consult the table of cases and statutes if they seek material on either of these types of legal authorities. The comprehensive bibliography, arranged by type of material (e.g., book, chapter in book, journal or magazine article, newspaper article), also will be useful for those embarking on in-depth research.

We have included three appendices that we hope will be of interest to readers. The first is a lengthy but selective annotated list of attorneys who in some significant way have been involved with baseball from the nineteenth century to the present. While many on the list also appear in individual entries in the book (use the index to find them), there are some who do not. The other two appendices address the Black Sox Scandal, a standout event in the intersection of baseball and law. The first of these is a time line covering many of the complicated events that, taken together, comprise the story of the scandal. Some of the items in the time line also appear in more detail as entries in the body of the book but, as with the lawyers list, there are many aspects of the scandal that are given only here. We readily acknowledge our heavy reliance on William F. Lamb's *Black Sox in the Court Room: The Grand Jury, Criminal Trial and Civil Litigation* (McFarland, 2013) in preparing this time line. The second scandal-related appendix is a selective bibliography of writings on the topic that we hope will be useful to the researcher embarking on a Black Sox research project.

Before closing, it is appropriate to mention a couple of challenges we faced along the way. First, we committed in the very beginning to entries that would not exceed about 300 words. To do otherwise would doom any chance at achieving our goal of covering baseball and the law from the very beginning to the present. The obvious difficulty of this limitation is trying to encapsulate often highly complex legal issues and fact situations in such a limited space. It required us to identify and then stay focused on the most important aspects of each story; often it meant excising details which we longed to tell but could not (though, in the tradition of legal scholarship, some of this ended up in the endnotes). Second, this was a chronology of full dates (month-day-year) and we occasionally were hard-pressed to identify a date for a particular story we thought should be included in the book. Sometimes that required some creative thinking on our part. Readers wondering why a story is listed under a particular date might look to this as the reason. On a related note, most, if not all, stories actually are comprised of multiple dates. Another early choice was that for most topics, we would not have multiple entries covering each event but, rather, we would incorporate later aspects of the story into the single entry. There are exceptions to this practice (e.g., the Black Sox scandal, *Flood v. Kuhn*), but for the most part we resisted that impulse. We did, however, provide numerous cross-references in the form of "see entry for [date]" when we thought a reader might wish to immediately consult related entries (e.g., all the court decisions which ruled on whether the reserve clause could be used to prevent players from jumping to the Federal League are tied together with these cross-references).

The final challenge to preparing a book that strives to cover the entire field of baseball's intersection with law is simply the overwhelming number of stories that fit within its parameters. As collectors our first inclination, of course, was to be complete. But that was quickly abandoned. We shifted to a goal of making sure that we included all the "must have" stories (adopting Justice Potter Stewart's famous "I know it when I see it" definition of obscenity for determining which events and individuals met that criterion). Even that proved extremely difficult, although we did our best. Ultimately, we resigned ourselves to publishing a *selective* chronology of baseball and law, using a cutoff date of December 31, 2015, with the tacit understanding that our readers would tell us what we missed. So while we hope you find much to enjoy about *Baseball Meets the Law*, we invite your suggestions if we left out your favorite law-related baseball story (or baseball-related law story).

CHAPTER 1

Baseball Origins and Club Teams, 1791–1865

Introduction

Bat-and-stick games have fascinated humans throughout history, with different cultures creating their own specific variations. In colonial America, games with British origins were common, including cricket, rounders, trap ball, and one-old-cat, but the nineteenth-century version of town ball began to emerge as a dominant form in New York, Pennsylvania, and New England in the 1840s.

The intersection of these games with law, however, predates the 1840s. In the late eighteenth and early nineteenth centuries, local towns and state assemblies began to pass ordinances and laws restricting where "base ball" could be played and even prohibiting it altogether on Sundays. By the mid-nineteenth century, clubs formed for playing the sport began to establish rules for the game. Many of these clubs adopted constitutions establishing the responsibilities of members and coordinating the loose arrangement of the game. Prominent clubs of the period, like the Olympic Ball Club of Philadelphia and the Knickerbockers of New York, vied for power and began to focus on the game's attraction to spectators. In March 1858, New York City's strongest clubs came together to create the National Association of Base Ball Players. The NABBP established itself as the initial arbiter of the game and implemented enduring rules changes while advancing the "New York Game" over the competing Massachusetts version.

As the game gathered momentum in the north and overshadowed its development in the south, the Civil War provided such a boost to base ball that it would become, by war's end, the acknowledged "national game" as Union and Confederate soldiers enjoyed the diversion it provided to the regimented nature of camp life. Post-war opportunities to make money from the game created two major themes which are highlighted in this book. First, although it started as an amateur sport, the professional game soon became dominant, producing conflict between labor and management that still exists today. Second, gambling and the opportunity for crooked behavior emerged. In September 1865, Tammany Hall corruption touched the game when the first acknowledged bribery scheme prompted the NABPP to expel three members of the New York Mutuals for accepting money to "heave" a game against the Brooklyn Eckfords.

1791

September 5, 1791: Pittsfield Bylaw Bans Ball Playing Near Meeting House

The town of Pittsfield, Massachusetts, enacts a bylaw which bans playing with bats and balls within 80 yards of the newly constructed meeting house.[1] In 2004, baseball historian John Thorn will find references to the bylaw in an 1869 book on Pittsfield's history[2]; a librarian will then find the actual document in a vault at the Berkshire Athenaeum library. Later, the National Baseball Hall of Fame will recognize the bylaw as the first known reference to the game and honor Pittsfield with a plaque.

1794

April 22, 1794: Pennsylvania Blue Law Bans Sunday Baseball

The Pennsylvania General Assembly passes "An Act for the Prevention of Vice and Immorality, and of Unlawful Gaming, and to Restrain Disorderly Sports and Dissipation,"[3] a "blue law" that will make it illegal to, among other things, play baseball in the Commonwealth of Pennsylvania on Sunday. The statute will remain in effect until 1933, when the General Assembly will pass legislation allowing local jurisdictions to determine, by voter ballot, whether Sunday sports can take place within their jurisdictions (see entry for April 8, 1934).[4]

1816

June 6, 1816: Cooperstown Ordinance Bans Baseball on Future Site of Hall of Fame

Trustees of the Village of Cooperstown, New York, enact an ordinance prohibiting any person from "play[ing] at Ball in Second or West Street [now Pioneer and Main Streets], in this village, under a penalty of one dollar, for each and every offence."[5] The intersection is about half a block from 25 Main

Street, the future site of the National Baseball Hall of Fame and Museum, called the National Baseball Museum when it was dedicated on June 12, 1939.[6]

1837

December 7, 1837: Olympic Town Ball Club Adopts Constitution

The Olympic Ball Club of Philadelphia adopts a written constitution, the first town ball team known to do so.[7] The constitution covers the responsibilities and duties of the board of directors, the members, and the recorder, who is charged with keeping an "accurate account of all the games played on Club days, date of the same, names of the players, the number of points made by each, and the ground used on each occasion."[8] The constitution, along with the club's bylaws and membership roster, will be published in 1838 and, within a few years, the club will grow to include about a hundred members.[9]

1841

March 8, 1841: Oliver Wendell Holmes, Jr., Is Born in Boston

Oliver Wendell Holmes, Jr., who as an associate justice of the United States Supreme Court will author baseball's most famous court decision, *Federal Baseball Club v. National League*[10] (see entry for May 29, 1922), is born in Boston, Massachusetts.[11] Ironically, Holmes will have no interest in baseball; in fact, one of his clerks will say of him, "there was nothing that did not interest him except athletics."[12]

1845

September 23, 1845: Lawyer Wheaton Codifies Rules of New York Knickerbockers

New York City lawyer William R. Wheaton, first vice president of the Knickerbocker Base Ball Club of New York, plays a prominent role in the club's formal adoption of playing rules, serving as codifier and scribe of the 20 provisions (the first six actually cover the privileges and duties of Knickerbocker membership) which "are later seen as the basis for the game we now call baseball."[13] That Wheaton served in this capacity is no surprise; in 1837, he also wrote down the rules for New York's Gotham Club which, he would state later in his life, were adopted by the Knickerbockers with few changes.[14] On October 6, 1845, at Hoboken's Elysian Fields, Wheaton will continue his pioneering ways by serving as the umpire of the first recorded game played under the new rules.[15]

1850

September 1, 1850: "Orator" O'Rourke, Hall of Fame Player and Lawyer, Is Born

Destined to become a Hall of Fame player and minor league baseball executive, James Henry O'Rourke is born in Bridgeport, Connecticut.[16] O'Rourke's long professional career will begin with the Middletown Mansfields of the National Association in 1872. On April 22, 1876, as a member of the Boston Red Caps, O'Rourke will stroke a single to left field off Philadelphia Athletics pitcher Alonzo "Lon" Knight, the first base hit in the new National League's history.[17] His graduation from Yale Law School in 1887 not only will make him an anomaly among his largely uneducated immigrant teammates, but his "law school background and flowery language" will earn O'Rourke the nickname "Orator."[18] When O'Rourke and George Wright revolve[19] to the Providence Grays for the 1879 season, Red Caps owner Arthur Soden will convince his fellow National League owners to create the reserve clause (see entry for September 29, 1879). A longtime advocate for the rights of players, O'Rourke will join with John Montgomery Ward to help form the Brotherhood of Professional Base Ball Players (see entry for October 22, 1885) and the Players' League (see entry for November 4, 1889). He also will help found the National Association of Professional Baseball Leagues, a minor-league protective organization, in 1901 (see entry for September 5, 1901).

1858

March 10, 1858: Formation of National Association of Base Ball Players in NYC

While the groundwork for its formation was begun at a meeting of 14 area clubs at Smith's Hotel on Broome Street in New York City on January 22, 1857,[20] the National Association of Base Ball Players (NABBP) is officially established as a permanent body at a convention held the following year at 298 Bowery, the headquarters of the New York Gothams, with representatives of 22 organized clubs in the metropolitan area in attendance.[21] Although hardly "national" in its makeup despite its name—"participants: came from no further south than New Brunswick, New Jersey, or any further west and north than Manhattan and the Bronx"—the nation's only formal baseball organization at the time will serve to advance the widespread adoption of the "New York Game" over the "Massachusetts game" played in New England, town ball played in Philadelphia, and cricket still played in many areas.[22] A major tenet of the new association is a rule forbidding the compensation of players, but an increase in teams charging admission fees (see entry for July 20, 1858) and paying players, albeit under the table and by deceptive means, eventually will lead the NABPP to legalize professionalism in 1868.[23]

July 20, 1858: Fashion Race Course All-Star Contest First to Charge Admission Fee

Players chosen from various club teams in the cities of New York and

Brooklyn square off at the Fashion Race Course, a horse racing track near the village of Flushing on Long Island, in what is not only the first all-star contest, but also the first documented instance in which an admission fee is charged to attend a baseball game.[24] The fact that it also is the first game played on an enclosed grounds facilitates the collection of the admission fee. Playing before a crowd estimated at between 4,000 and 10,000, the New Yorkers defeat the Brooklynites, 22–18. Within a few months, the all-star squads will complete the three-game series, with Brooklyn taking the second, 29–8, on August 17, and New York the rubber match, 29–18, on September 10.[25]

1860

March 3, 1860: Ward, Hall of Fame Player, Lawyer, and Brotherhood Founder, Is Born

John Montgomery Ward, future Hall of Fame pitcher and shortstop, Columbia-trained lawyer (see entry for May 27, 1885), and founder of the Brotherhood of Professional Baseball Players (see entry for October 22, 1885), is born in Bellefonte, Pennsylvania[26]

1865

September 28, 1865: First Known Fixed Game, Mutuals vs. Eckfords at Elysian Fields

Third-baseman Edward Duffy, shortstop Thomas Devyr, and catcher William Wansley of the New York Mutuals—led by William M. "Boss" Tweed of the notoriously corrupt Tammany Hall[27]—conspire to "heave" a game against the Brooklyn Eckfords at Elysian Fields in Hoboken, New Jersey, in "the first fixed game."[28] The first four innings are "splendidly played and closely contested on both sides," leaving the Mutuals on top, 5–4, but sloppy defensive play by the Mutuals allows the Eckfords to score 11 runs in the bottom of the fifth and eventually win the game, 23–11. Immediately afterward, the Mutuals charge Wansley, who had two missed catches, six passed balls, and four wild throws, with "willful and designed inattention." On October 20, after an investigation by the team, Wansley will offer a full confession at the club's offices.[29] The 18-year-old Devyr will confess in writing that Duffy and Wansley offered him $300 to "stand with" them in throwing the game.[30] All three soon will be expelled from the National Association of Base Ball Players, but Devyr will be brought back by the Mutuals in 1867, triggering multiple protests. He eventually will be reinstated by a 453–143 vote at the NABBP convention on December 11, 1867. By 1870, all three will have been reinstated.[31]

CHAPTER 2

Professionalization and the Rise of Leagues, 1866–1902

Introduction

In the aftermath of the Civil War, baseball quickly established itself as a professional venture at the top end. When the Cincinnati Red Stockings won all 57 of its contests in 1869 with a salaried lineup, like-minded teams banded together two years later to form the National Association of Professional Base Ball Players, the first professional league. Soon, the frequency of players ignoring their contracts and jumping to other teams ("revolving") prompted William Hulbert of Chicago to establish the eight-team National League of Professional Base Ball Clubs with restrictions on player mobility.

Hulbert's untimely death in 1882 coincided with the rise of rival leagues challenging the National League for equal major league status, leading Arthur Soden of Boston to forge an agreement over a reserve system. The reserve system, with its multiple components producing a perpetual hold that binds players to one team, became the foundation of the relationship between labor and management for nearly a century. Nonetheless, the new system of player restraint is unsuccessful in creating labor peace for the next two decades, years highlighted by the rise and fall of new leagues and unsuccessful attempts to unionize the players.

By 1883, the American Association reached detente with the National League through the adoption of a National Agreement at the same time that a new league, the Union Association, made an unsuccessful attempt to join the top echelon. Continuing labor unrest produced Francis Richter's Millennium Plan and John Brush's salary classification scheme, but neither proposal prevented the establishment of the Brotherhood of Professional Base Ball Players nor the Players' League later formed by this union. Although stars Buck Ewing and John Montgomery Ward joined lesser known players Bill

Hallman and John Pickett to amass an impressive string of legal victories for these player-led ventures, the new league was not a commercial success and folded after only a single season. With labor unrest escalating again in 1891, the National League and the American Association agreed to implement a new peace agreement, but it failed to prevent the demise of four American Association franchises. When the remaining twelve teams joined together for the remainder of the decade, a seemingly stable "big league" produced a fixed pitching distance, a 154-game schedule, the infield fly rule, gloves and full catcher's gear. However, after the 1899 season, the National League shrunk by buying out the Baltimore, Cleveland, Louisville, and Washington franchises.

The sudden increased supply of major league talent and the commercial success of the 1899 National League season provided an opening for Western League president Ban Johnson. After renaming his minor league circuit as the American League, Johnson openly challenged the National League's status as the lone major league. Two years of fierce fighting that saw higher player salaries and the landmark *Philadelphia Ball Club, Ltd. v. Lajoie* case finally culminated in peace between the leagues. Among its important provisions, the National Agreement of 1903 created a new governance mechanism, a three-person National Commission that would now serve as Organized Baseball's final arbiter.

1866

July 23, 1866: Red Stockings Formed in Cincinnati Law Office as Resolute Base Ball Club

The team that a few years later will become baseball's first openly all-professional team (see entry for May 4, 1869) is organized at the Cincinnati law office of Tilden, Sherman & Moulton as the Resolute Base Ball Club of Cincinnati. The name soon will be simplified to the Cincinnati Base Ball Club, and two years later the club will become known as the Red Stockings because of the color of the hose worn by its players. Its formation in a law office is not accidental, since many of the team's first players are Cincinnati-area attorneys and the club's president, eventually responsible for paying the salaries of the players, is Aaron Burt Champion, a lawyer active in local politics.[1]

November 20, 1866: Birth of Kenesaw Mountain Landis, Baseball's First Commissioner

Kenesaw Mountain Landis is born in Millville, Ohio, the sixth child of Dr. Abraham and Mary Kumler Landis.[2] The future federal judge and commissioner of baseball is named for the Civil War battle in which his father's left leg was badly shattered by a Confederate cannon ball that bounced off a tree before striking the regimental surgeon.[3] On March 18, 1905, President Theodore Roosevelt will nominate Landis to fill a vacant judicial position on the United States District Court for the Northern District of Illinois; Landis is confirmed on the same day. Landis soon will become nationally famous for fining Standard Oil and John D. Rockefeller more than $29 million for antitrust violations.[4] Given his trust-busting reputation, the Federal League will choose Landis to preside over its antitrust action against Organized Baseball (see entry for January 5, 1915). Several years later, the owners will respond to the Black Sox scandal by dismantling the National Commission ruling triumvirate and hiring the judge as the initial commissioner of baseball (see entry for November 12, 1920). Although a Chicago jury determines that the eight members of the White Sox are not guilty, Landis will ban them all from Organized Baseball for life (see entry of August 2, 1921). Landis will die on November 5, 1944; on December 10, a special committee chaired by Stephen C. Clark, president of the National Baseball Hall of Fame, will select Landis for induction.[5]

1867

March 16, 1867: Birth of George Wharton Pepper, Lawyer for Organized Baseball

George Wharton Pepper, who will represent Organized Baseball during the first decades of the twentieth century and remain a prominent lawyer until his death in 1961,[6] is born in Philadelphia to a prominent family.[7] A multi-sport star and scholar as an undergraduate at the University of Pennsylvania, Pepper will graduate from its law school in 1889.[8] During the Federal League-Major League Baseball litigation wars, Pepper will represent Organized Baseball in *Weegham v. Killefer* (see entry for April 10, 1914) and in the numerous trials involving the Baltimore baseball club that ultimately establishes baseball's antitrust exemption in 1922 (see entries for March 29, 1916, and May 29, 1922).[9] Later that year, Pepper will be appointed to Pennsylvania's vacant United States Senate seat, a position he will hold until 1927 when he returns to private practice.[10]

August 20, 1867: First Patent for a Baseball-Themed Board Game Issued

William Buckley of New York City receives the first-ever patent for a board game based on baseball as U.S. patent 67,951 is issued for "Base-Ball Table," essentially a pinball style game in which "a marble-sized ball is rolled by the mechanical 'pitcher' toward a spring-activated bat that would drive the ball into the field of play."[11] Although there is no evidence that Buckley's game was ever actually produced, the same can't be said for Francis Sebring's "Parlor Base Ball," which was described and illustrated with a woodcut of adults and children enjoying the game in *Leslie's Illustrated Newspaper* on December 8, 1866. Sebring of Hoboken, New Jersey, will receive the second patent for a baseball board game on February 4, 1868, when U.S. patent 74,154 is issued for "Parlor Base-Ball," also a pinball style game, though it uses a cent piece rather than a ball to initiate the action.[12]

October 18, 1867: All-Black Pythian Club Rejected for Membership by NABBP

During the Pennsylvania State Convention of Base Ball Players, the all-black Pythian Base Ball Club, led by field captain and manager Octavius V. Catto, suffer "the first recorded baseball act of segregation"[13] when, despite an invitation from the Athletics, Philadelphia's premier white team, and its vice president, E. Hicks Hayhurst, also the convention's presiding officer, procedural maneuvering forces the team to withdraw its application to join the state's association of amateur baseball clubs.[14] At its December 1867 annual meeting in Philadelphia, the National Association of Base Ball Players also will refuse to admit the Pythians based upon its decision to reject "any club which may be composed of one or more colored persons."[15] Although the team will persevere, participating in the first known match game between black and white baseball teams (see entry for September 3, 1869), tragically, Catto, an early civil rights advocate who worked for the passage of the Fifteenth Amendment and helped desegregate Philadelphia's trolley systems, will be shot and killed on October 10, 1871, during Election Day rioting in Philadelphia.[16]

November 22, 1867: First Judicial Ruling with Reference to Baseball

A Kentucky Court of Appeals case involving the relationship of a secular court to an ecclesiastical tribunal becomes the first published judicial ruling to include a reference to baseball (including "baseball," "base ball," or "base-ball").[17] In dissenting, Judge Williams takes the court's majority to task for "putting the constitution, laws, usages, courts, and tribunals of a great body of Christians [i.e., the Presbyterian Church]: upon a par with the voluntary association of an insignificant base-ball club."[18]

December 17, 1867: First Patent for the Game of Baseball Issued

The United States Patent Office issues Letters Patent No. 72,355 to Henry A. Alden of Matteawan, New York, for an "improvement in the manufacture of base-balls," specifically to substitute the use of yarn wound around a rubber cone and covered with a leather casing with a process where "the body of the ball [consists] of a rubber compound" which, once vulcanized, can be used with or without a leather cover "for a base-ball [or] for a cricket-ball."[19] This is not only the first patent for the manufacture of the ball used in the game of baseball, but also for the sport itself.[20]

1869

April 2, 1869: Hughie Jennings, Hall of Fame Player and Lawyer, Is Born

Future Hall of Fame player and one of only eight major league managers to either earn a law degree or pass a bar examination,[21] Hugh Ambrose "Hughie" Jennings is born in Pittston, Pennsylvania.[22] Jennings, who as a youngster works as a breaker boy in the nearby coal mines, will become a star for the National League Baltimore Orioles in the 1890s playing alongside John McGraw. When the National League drops four teams and numerous jobs for players in 1900, Jennings will help found the Players Protective Association, baseball's second union (see entry for June 10, 1900). Although not graduating, Jennings will complete enough courses at Cornell Law School to sit for the bar examination and be admitted to the Maryland bar in 1905 and the Pennsylvania bar in 1907.[23] Hired to manage the Ty Cobb–led Detroit Tigers in 1907, he will lead the team to three consecutive American League pennants (1907–1909) during his 14 years at the helm, all accentuated by his famous "EE-yah!" whoop from the third-base coaching box.

May 4, 1869: All-Professional Cincinnati Red Stockings Play First Game

The Cincinnati Red Stockings, first formed as the Resolute Base Ball Club and now baseball's first openly all-professional team (see entry for July 23, 1866), play their initial game against a team in the National Association of Base Ball Players (NABBP), a 45–9 victory over the Great Westerns of Cincinnati.[24] Organized and managed by English-born William Henry (Harry) Wright, who also plays center field, the Red Stockings have ten players under salary for eight months, March to November.[25] Harry's brother George Wright is the star shortstop for a team that will post an undefeated season, 57–0, against other teams in the NABBP.[26] Both Wrights will subsequently be enshrined in the National Baseball Hall of Fame.

September 3, 1869: First Known Game Between Organized Black and White Teams

At its home field located at 25th and Jefferson Streets, the Olympics, Philadelphia's oldest ball club (see entry for December 7, 1837) defeat the all-black Pythians, also of Philadelphia (see entry for October 18, 1867) in a three-hour match game by a score of 44 to 23.[27] Described as "the first known baseball contest between organized black and white teams,"[28] the game results from a challenge issued to the Olympics by the Pythians and the "mediation" of Col. Thomas Fitzgerald, founding president of the Athletic Base Ball Club of Philadelphia in 1860 and publisher of the *City Item* newspaper which he used to promote both baseball and equality before the law, who even serves as umpire of the game.[29] A rematch was scheduled but there is no record of it being played. The Pythians did defeat Fitzgerald's all-white *City Item* team by a score of 27 to 17 in a game played on September 16 at the Athletics field on Columbia Avenue.[30]

1871

March 17, 1871: National Association Formed, First League of Professional Baseball Teams

The National Association of Professional Base Ball Players (NAPBBP), the first league of professional baseball teams—indeed, the first professional sports organization in the United States—is founded.[31] The league, however, will lack stability,[32] fielding 24 teams during its five years of existence, half of them for only one year and many from small towns which produced small crowds that were unappealing to teams from larger cities.[33] In another sign of disorder, players known as "revolvers" will jump from team to team depending upon who makes the best offer.[34]

1874

December 5, 1874: Davy Force Contract Dispute

Diminutive shortstop Davy Force (he stood 5-foot-4) signs to play for the Philadelphia Athletics of the National Association of Professional Base Ball Players in 1875 despite having already signed two contracts with the NAPBBP's Chicago White Stockings for the same season (the first violated an association rule because it was signed during the 1874 season). The association's Judiciary Committee will initially favor Chicago in its resolution of the dispute over Force, but Charles Spering, president not only of the NAPBBP but also the Athletics, will assemble another committee that rules in his team's favor.[35] Anger over both the decision and the biased makeup of the committee—it included two other individuals with Philadelphia connections—will fuel Chicago president William Hulbert's resolve to find an alternative to the poorly run association and, a little more than a year later, he will lead the move to create the National League (see entry for February 2, 1876).[36] As a result, after hitting over .300 for the NAPBBP's Athletics in 1875, "Wee Davy" Force will go on to spend two-thirds of his 15-year major league career (1871–86) in the National League, most of them with the Buffalo Bisons.

1875

May 26, 1875: Bechtel and Craver Sold for $1,500, First Sale of a Player

In what is generally considered the first sale of a baseball player, the Philadelphia Centennials of the National Association of Professional Base Ball Clubs sell George Bechtel and Bill Craver to the NA's Philadelphia Athletics for $1,500. The money paid for the players is designed to induce the Centennials to disband and, in fact, the team will immediately fold, having played only 14 games during its sole season of existence.[37] Bechtel, while playing for the National League's Louisville Grays the following season, will become the first player banned for life by that league for fixing games.[38] Similarly, Craver will be expelled from the National League for his involvement in the Louisville Scandal (see entry for October 30, 1877).

July 27, 1875: First Patent for a Baseball Issued

John Giblin of Boston receives what is identified by one commentator as the first patent for a baseball—though not the first baseballs, most of which were handmade until John Van Horn of New York and Harvey Rose of Brooklyn became the first manufacturers of balls in the 1850s.[39] Giblin's "improvement" uses a center made of palm leaves, encased by wound woolen yarn and cotton thread and a rubber cover. According to its inventor, the waterproof covered ball "will outlast very many of the leather-covered balls, and, having no seams or sewing as they have, is not so liable to injure the hands of a player."[40]

December 14, 1875: Patent for "Ding Dong" Base with Attached Bell

The United States Patent Office issues U.S. patent 171,038 to John C. O'Neill of St. Louis for an "improved" base-ball base that features a hidden, attached bell designed to ring when a player steps on it ("mechanism to sound the [bell] upon sudden and forcible pressure of its top").[41] The ringing is supposed to help umpires decide whether a runner is safe or out, but O'Neill apparently forgot that the bell would also ring when the first baseman planted his foot on the base.[42]

1876

February 2, 1876: Founding of the National League

Under the leadership of William Hulbert who, in a letter dated January 23, 1876, had invited four clubs from the National Association of Professional Base Ball Clubs to attend a meeting at which the "formation of a new association" might be considered,[43] the National League of Professional Base Ball Clubs (National League) is formed in New York City.[44] The organizational meeting is held at the Grand Central Hotel on Broadway.[45] The constitution for the new league is drafted by C. Orrick Bishop.[46] One of the main features of the new league is adherence to restraints on player movements primarily through the blacklist.[47] The eight charter member franchises of the National League are Boston, Chicago, Cincinnati, Hartford, Louisville, New York, Philadelphia, and St. Louis.[48] Morgan Bulkeley, "a well-known Connecticut politician," is chosen as the new league's first president.[49] Although he will leave the position within a year and never again be involved with Organized Baseball, except for his participation on the Mills Commission which in 1907 will conclude that baseball was "invented" in Cooperstown, New York, by Alexander Doubleday in 1839 (see entry for December 30, 1907), he will enter the National Baseball Hall of Fame as part of the 1939 induction class.

1877

April 25, 1877: New York Antipooling Act Addresses Gambling Ills

The New York state legislature passes an anti-pooling law[50] to address the complicated system of "pool-selling" that occurs in saloons and billiard parlors where the proprietor collects the money wagered in bets, keeps records of the transactions, pays the winners and "receive[s] a percentage of each bet."[51] The act takes particular aim at the ills of gambling connected to horse racing and elections, but it also covers problems caused by betting on baseball games through pools located away from the ballpark. Despite the legislation, the press will expose suspicious activities surrounding National League players and crooked pool room operators early in the 1877 season, even before the Louisville Grays scandal breaks later in the year (see entry for October 30, 1877).[52]

October 30, 1877: Louisville Game-Fixing Scandal

Directors of the Louisville Grays of the National League pass resolutions expelling substitute Alfred "Slippery Elm" Nichols, outfielder and team captain "Gentleman" George Hall, and pitcher James A. "Terror" Devlin from the team for "selling games, conspiring to sell games, and tampering with players"; and shortstop William "Butcher" Craver for "general misconduct and suspicious play."[53] Although leading the league on August 13, the team had managed to lose seven and tie one on a subsequent eastern road trip, raising suspicion about the team's play. The four claim they never threw anything but exhibition games, but sportswriter John A. Haldeman of the *Louisville Courier-Journal*, the son of team owner Walter Haldeman and nephew of club official Charles Chase who was responsible for the day-to-day operations of the team, had uncovered evidence of "hippodroming" by the quartet.[54] Seizing a chance to demonstrate its commitment to clean play, the National League will ratify the Grays' action and ban the players from

Organized Baseball for life at its annual meeting in December.[55] Albert Spalding will later declare the resolution of the scandal the "first great victory won over gambling and the gamblers."[56]

1878

February 12, 1878: Thayer Receives First Patent for a Catcher's Mask

The United States Patent Offices issues the first patent for a baseball catcher's mask to Frederick W. Thayer of Waverly, Massachusetts.[57] On January 15, 1878, Thayer, former manager of the Harvard University baseball team, had applied for a patent on the face guard he had crafted from a fencing mask, first used by Crimson player James Alexander Tyng on April 12, 1877, in a game between Harvard and the Live Oaks, a semipro team from Lynn, Massachusetts.[58] The complex design included padded rests for the player's chin and forehead; one problem was that the bar in the center of the mask obscured the vision of its wearer. Nonetheless, with patent 200,358 in hand, the "Thayer Catcher's Mask" will be advertised for $3 in the 1878 Spalding catalog and improvements will soon follow to what quickly becomes an essential piece of baseball equipment.[59]

1879

June 21, 1879: William Edward White Is First African American Major League Player

William Edward White, a student at Brown University and a member of its baseball team which claimed the 1879 college championship, replaces injured Joe Start at first base for the National League's Providence Grays in its game against the Cleveland Blues. Although White singles in the game, scores a run, and flawlessly fields 12 chances at first base, his is a one-game career.[60] Future Hall of Famer Jim O'Rourke, the Grays regular right fielder, will cover the remaining games for "Old Reliable" Start until he returns from the broken finger he suffered on June 19. Nevertheless, in playing for the Grays on this day, White arguably becomes the first African American player in big-league history. Born in 1860 to Andrew J. White, a Georgia businessman and slave owner who was white, and his mulatto house servant Hannah White, William Edward White was partially African American. However, federal census research indicates that White consistently self-identified as white and there are no contemporary materials, including Brown University records, newspaper accounts, and his 1937 death certificate, which indicate otherwise.[61] Thus, although "[b]y the retroactive application of genetic rules, [he] is the first known black man to play major-league baseball," the truth is that "if White ... said he was white and he was not challenged, he was white in his time and circumstances."[62]

September 29, 1879: National League Establishes First Reserve Rule

At a meeting at the Palace Hotel in Buffalo, New York, National League owners establish the first reserve rule.[63] After two of his stars, future Hall of Famers George Wright and James "Orator" O'Rourke, jump to the Providence Grays for the 1879 season,[64] Boston Red Caps owner Arthur H. Soden convinces his fellow owners of the need for each team to reserve five players.[65] Under Soden's plan, the players would not be informed they had been "reserved," they would just discover that no other team would sign them.[66] Present at the meeting are William A. Hulbert and Nicholas E. Young, National League President and Secretary, respectively, and owners J. Ford Evans (Cleveland), T. Gardner Earl and C. L. Deforest (Troy), Henry J. Root (Providence), John B. Sage (Buffalo), and Soden. Hulbert represents the interests of both the Chicago and Cincinnati teams.

1880

September 2, 1880: Jones Sues Boston for Back Pay After Suspension by Soden

During a road trip to Cleveland, Charley Jones, a home run-hitting star for the National League's Boston Red Stockings, asks manager Harry Wright for his August salary of $378, as well as $128 still owed on his July salary. When his request is denied, Jones refuses to play the scheduled afternoon game against the Cleveland Blues. This prompts Boston owner Arthur Soden to suspend Jones and impose a fine of $100 for making the request and his "poor play and insubordination."[67] On September 7, Soden will release Jones under a provision of the league constitution calling for the expulsion of "any player under contract with a League club who shall, without the written consent of such club, leave its service...."[68] When Boston takes the position that it is not required to honor the back salary demands of a player no longer eligible to participate in the National League, Jones will sue his former team in the Cleveland Court of Common Pleas, winning a judgment that he will be able to collect only by attaching Boston's share of the gate receipts for a game played in Cleveland. Procedural and legal maneuvering, including the American Association's initial decision to honor the National League's blacklist, will prevent Jones from playing for two years, but he finally will join the Association's Cincinnati Red Stockings in 1883.[69]

October 6, 1880: National League Expels Cincinnati Over Beer and Sunday Baseball

At the urging of National League President William A. Hulbert, seven of the league's eight teams pledge to approve a rule at their December meeting which will ban stadium beer sales and Sunday games.[70] William H. Kennett, president of the Cincinnati Reds, a charter member of the league in 1876, refuses to sign the pledge because of the revenue that will be lost without Sunday rentals of Bank Street Grounds and the knowledge that most of the city's largely German immigrant fan base desire a brew while watching a game.[71] The other owners respond by officially expelling the Reds from the league; the Detroit Wolverines will fill the opening in the 1881 season.[72] Cincinnati will not be without major league baseball for long, however; within a few years, under the guidance of *Cincinnati Enquirer* sports editor Oliver Perry "O. P." Caylor, a new franchise calling itself the Reds will become a founding member of the American Association (see entry for November 2, 1881).

1881

November 2, 1881: American Association Forms, Reserve Clause Banned

Following a less than successful attempt at an organizational meeting instigated by Horace B. Phillips of the Philadelphia Athletics in Pittsburgh on October 10, 1881, the American Association is formed at the plush Gibson House hotel in Cincinnati. Harmer Denny McKnight, founding owner of the Pittsburgh Alleghenys, is chosen as president; J.H. Pank, executive with the Kentucky Malting Company and organizer of the Louisville Eclipse, vice-president.[73] Significantly, the Association's player contracts will not include a reserve clause, although signed contracts will be honored while in force.[74] Other policies in direct conflict with those of the incumbent National League are its allowance of Sunday games; beer sales; and admission for 25 cents, half the price charged by its rival (see entry for October 6, 1880).[75] The charter members of the Association, dubbed by its critics as the "Beer and Whiskey Circuit" because of its liberal rules and heavy backing by liquor interests, are the Baltimore Orioles (which replaced the Brooklyn Atlantics prior to the start of the season), Cincinnati Red Stockings, Louisville Eclipse (later the Colonels), Philadelphia Athletics, Pittsburgh Alleghenys (later the Pirates), and St. Louis Brown Stockings (later the Browns and Cardinals).[76]

December 20, 1881: Branch Rickey, Pioneering Executive and Lawyer, Is Born

Wesley Branch Rickey, who will post a mediocre record as a major league player (4 years, 120 games, .239 BA, 3 HRs) but reach the Hall of Fame in 1967 as an astute and path-breaking executive, is born in Little California (soon renamed Stockdale), Ohio.[77] After his modest playing career, he will earn a law degree from the University of Michigan before returning to the big leagues as manager of the St. Louis Browns (1913–15) and St. Louis Cardinals (1919–25). He will also serve as general manager of four clubs: Browns

(1913–15, 1919), Cardinals (1919–42), Dodgers (1943–50), and Pirates (1951–55[78]). Among his many accomplishments in baseball, Rickey is best known for helping to break the color line in MLB by signing Jackie Robinson to play for the Brooklyn Dodgers (see entries for October 23, 1945, and April 10, 1947)[79] and for creating the modern farm system.[80]

1882

January 22, 1882: Organized Baseball's First Use of Court System to Settle Dispute

The *Boston Daily Globe* reports that despite signing a contract "some time ago" with the Cincinnati Red Stockings of the newly established American Association, infielder Samuel Washington "Sam" Wise has decided to "revolve" to the National League's Boston Red Stockings, rather than the league's Providence Grays run by Harry Wright, because its offer is the "most liberal" of the two.[81] The *Globe* opines that Washington, a native of Akron, Ohio, who played one game for the NL's Detroit Wolverines in 1881, "will pay no attention whatever to the contract he made with Cincinnati" but will instead pack "his gripsack preparatory to a pilgrimage to the Hub." Fighting back in what Harold Seymour and Dorothy Seymour Mills identify as "the first time professional baseball went into the courts to settle a dispute," Cincinnati applies to a Massachusetts court for an injunction "on the plea that [Wise's] loss was irreparable and could not be calculated financially."[82] The court refuses to grant the injunction, however, and Wise will enjoy seven seasons playing for New England's version of the Red Stockings before spending the 1890 season in the Players' League and the following year in the American Association.[83]

April 10, 1882: National League Founder William Hulbert Dies

William A. Hulbert, lauded as the "savior of baseball" for his role in the formation of the National League in 1876 (see entry for February 2, 1876), dies of heart disease.[84] He will be buried in Graceland Cemetery in Chicago, with a most appropriate grave marker—a big, carved baseball inscribed with the names of the inaugural National League teams.[85] More than a century will pass before Hulbert is finally elected to the National Baseball Hall of Fame by the Veterans Committee in 1995.[86]

November 18, 1882: Charlie Bennett and Baseball's First Contract Litigation

In what one writer has referred to as "baseball's first instance of contract litigation"[87] and another as the "earliest litigation regarding the reserve clause,"[88] Judge Marcus W. Acheson of the United States Circuit Court for the Western District of Pennsylvania denies a request by the Allegheny Base-

Ball Club for a preliminary injunction to compel Charlie Bennett to sign a contract with the team for the 1883 season.[89] Bennett, a fine fielding and hitting catcher, played in 1882 for the National League's Detroit Wolverines and then signed a document in which he promised to jump to the Pittsburgh Alleghenys of the American Association in 1883. But when he reversed his plans and said he would stay with Detroit, the Alleghenys sought to prevent him from returning to his former team by suing for breach of contract. However, Judge Acheson determines that there was no mutual agreement as to "essential terms, stipulations, and conditions," and thus "the present bill for an injunction … will not lie for the reason the contract is a mere preliminary arrangement and not a final agreement."[90]

1883

March 12, 1883: Harmony Conference Leads to First National Agreement

At the Victoria Hotel in New York, National League president A.G. Mills—who in later years will chair the commission which concludes baseball was "invented" by Abner Doubleday in Cooperstown (see entry for December 30, 1907)—convenes a "Harmony Conference" of the three main professional leagues, the National League, the American Association, and the minor Northwestern League.[91] Seeking to end the turmoil between the warring leagues, characterized by rampant "revolving" and contract breaking, and to regulate and control players and their salaries, they adopt the National (also known as Tripartite) Agreement of Professional Base Ball Clubs, the first such agreement for baseball.[92] Modeling the pact after a proposal from Mills, the three leagues agree to respect each other's contracts, as well as their suspensions and expulsions; blacklist players outside of the system; maintain a minimum salary of $1,000 ($750 for Northwestern League players); have an 11-man reserve list (thereby extending the reserve to the American Association, which had explicitly excluded its use upon formation of the league in 1881; see entry for November 2, 1881); and create a mechanism to resolve disputes.[93] At least one commentator has called the National Agreement "the beginning of what is called Organized Baseball,"[94] while another observed that "if Hulbert made the National League possible, Mills made organized baseball possible."[95]

September 12, 1883: Union Association Founded, Bans Use of Reserve Clause

St. Louis millionaire and trolley-car magnate Henry Van Noye Lucas founds the Union Association at a meeting at the Monongahela House in Pittsburgh.[96] In an effort to attract players from its established rivals, the National League and the American Association, the new league bans the use of the reserve clause in its contracts.[97] Striking back, the incumbent leagues will blacklist any of their players who jump contract or reservation to join the brash upstart.[98] The Union Association will begin play on April 17, 1884, but only five of the 12 teams will finish the season. "[U]nderfinanced, informally run, and clearly of lower quality than either [of its rivals],"[99] the Association will fold after one year when Lucas accepts an invitation for his St. Louis Maroons to join the National League.[100] Despite its short life span and various failures, all baseball encyclopedias dating from the first in 1922 (*The Baseball Cyclopedia* by Ernest Lanigan) will classify the Union Association as a major league, as will MLB's Special Baseball Records Committee in its rulings of 1968–69 (see entry for March 17, 1871).[101]

1884

March 25, 1884: Patent for Inflatable, Padded Chest Protector

The U.S. Patent Office issues a patent to William Gray of Hartford, Connecticut, who had "used the same principle as the then-new pneumatic tire" to create an "inflatable, padded protector that shielded the catcher's entire chest and groin without obstructing his movement."[102] Gray stated that the protector would help the player whose position "exposes him to painful blows from the ball unexpectedly turned from its course, as by a 'foul tip.'"[103] Marketed as "Gray's Patent Body Protector" by A.G. Spalding & Company, in 1891 the device will sell for $10, twice the price of its competitors which use stuffed canvas or leather rather than the rubber-bladder ribs of Gray's design.[104]

November 3, 1884: Supreme Court Issues Its First Opinion Related to Baseball

The United States Supreme Court renders its first—but certainly not its last—decision related to baseball.[105] In *Mahn v. Harwood*,[106] the court rules that the assignor of a patent is not entitled to a reissue of the original patent simply to enlarge the claims of the invention. In this instance, James Osgood had received a patent on May 21, 1872, for "improvements in modes of covering rounded articles with leather," which he noted were "suitable for the manufacture of base-balls and other similar articles." The invention featured Osgood's "double herring-bone secured stitch" to ensure that only one stitch of the ball's covering could be broken at a time.[107] Osgood assigned his rights to Louis H. Mahn, who was reissued the patent on April 11, 1876. However, the descriptions and drawings were identical, leading the court to void the reissue of the patent and dismiss Mahn's claims against an alleged infringer.[108]

1885

May 27, 1885: John Montgomery Ward Graduates from Columbia Law School

During his eighth season in the National League, 25-year-old John Montgomery Ward graduates from Columbia Law School.[109] Armed with organizational and communication skills honed by his legal education, Ward soon will mobilize players to fight for their rights, principally by guiding the formation of the Brotherhood of Professional Base Ball Players (see entry for October 22, 1885) and the Players' League (see entry for November 4, 1889). And in one of the earliest but most enduring attacks on the reserve system, he will effectively articulate the concerns of professional ballplayers in an August 1887 article for *Lippincott's Magazine*, "Is the Base-Ball Player a Chattel?"[110]

September 8, 1885: Rawlings Receives First Patent for Baseball Glove

The U.S. Patent Office issues a patent for a short-fingered buckskin glove intended for use by "base-ball players and cricketers." It consists of two layers of felt and one of rubber designed to prevent "the bruising of the hands when catching the ball."[111] Although there is no consensus as to the identity of the first player to use a glove for fielding purposes,[112] it is clear that two names familiar to sporting good users are involved in this first patent issued for a baseball glove.[113] Albert G. Spalding, important to the development of the national pastime in so many ways, helped make gloves acceptable when he became a first baseman during the final year of his playing career in 1877.[114] And a few years later, George H. Rawlings, founder with his brother Alfred of the company which marketed the famous Bill Doak model glove that made modern fielding possible (see entry for August 22, 1922), bases his design of the glove for which he receives the first patent on that used by Spalding.[115]

October 18, 1885: New National Agreement Contains First-Ever Salary Cap

The National League and American Association sign a new National Agreement. Salaries are restricted to between $1,000 and $2,000 per season organized baseball's first-ever salary cap—and the reserve list is expanded to 12 players per club.[116]

October 22, 1885: Brotherhood Is Formed, Baseball's First Player Union

A group of National League players, led by John Montgomery Ward, shortstop of the New York Gothams and a recent graduate of Columbia Law School (see entry for May 27, 1885), form the Brotherhood of Professional Base Ball Players, baseball's first union.[117] While organized baseball's first salary cap, adopted a few days earlier in the new national agreement (see entry for October 18, 1885), is "the straw that broke the camel's back," the players also object to such abuses as buying and selling players without their permission, blacklisting to force players to accept bad contract terms, and lending players to other teams without their consent.[118] The players agree to keep the union secret for the first year. By early summer 1886, a majority of players on seven of the eight National League teams will join the Brotherhood. And by the fall, all eight teams will have chapters and the Brotherhood more than a hundred members, constituting nearly 90 percent of the players in the National League.[119]

1886

April 22, 1886: Court Allows Property Owner to Build Grandstand Next to Stadium

Holding that "courts cannot limit the extent, up or down, to which a man may enjoy his property," the Michigan Supreme Court rules in favor of John Deppert, Jr., who had erected grandstands on top of his barn across from Recreation Park, the home of the National League's Detroit Wolverines.[120] Although the team attempted to thwart Deppert's efforts with boards and cloth screens, their enterprising neighbor kept building higher to provide his paying customers a view of future Hall of Famers Dan Brouthers, Ned Hanlon, and Sam Thompson while also hawking apples, nuts, and lemonade.[121]

November 15, 1886: First Player Trade Between Major League Teams

Cincinnati Red Stockings manager Gus Schmelz presents a document to St. Louis Browns owner Chris Von der Ahe in which he agrees to give $350 and rookie catcher Jack Boyle to the Browns in exchange for the release of outfielder Hugh Nicol, "conditional on Nicol's signing with the Cincinnati B.B. Club."[122] Thus the two American Association teams consummate what amounts to the first trade of players between major league clubs.[123] An earlier trade between a major and minor league team had occurred on August 29, 1885, when the Louisville Colonels of the American Association sent 23-year-old pitcher John Connor to the Chattanooga Lookouts of the Southern League, a minor league, for 20-year-old pitcher Thomas "Toad" Ramsey.[124]

1887

June 7, 1887: Reach Patents Catcher's Mask with Inflatable Padding

Robert (Bob) Reach, a former ballplayer and brother of Al Reach, himself a player for the Philadelphia Athletics and founder of what was for a time the country's largest sporting goods manufacturer,[125] receives a patent for a new catcher's mask from the U.S. Patent Office.[126] In addition to using loops that interlock with the wires of the mask to create a sturdy construction better able to withstand balls which strike the mask, Reach's innovation offers inflatable padding to make it more comfortable.[127]

December 7, 1887: Richter's Millennium Plan Proposes Reserve for Minor Leagues

Francis Richter, editor of the *Sporting Life*, publishes the details of his "Millennium Plan" in which he proposes a system for the Minor Leagues that will allow teams to reserve eleven players. The plan will be endorsed by the National League and the American Association the following season.[128]

1888

January 10, 1888: Patent Issued for Open View Catcher's Mask

The U.S. Patent Office issues Letters Patent No. 376,278, to George Barnard of Chicago, Illinois, for his "open view" catcher's mask, a wire-basket cage designed to provide better visibility and greater protection for its wearers.[129] According to the specifications filed by Barnard in his patent application, the "object of this invention is to construct an effectual guard and protection at [the catcher's neck]; and its nature consists in providing an extension of the mask proper to come below the chin of the wearer...."[130] As with other nineteenth-century baseball inventions (see entry for February 12, 1878), Barnard assigns his rights to A.G. Spalding & Brothers, the Chicago sporting goods magnate.[131]

December 15, 1888: National League Adopts Brush Salary Classification Scheme

The National League adopts a salary classification scheme proposed by Indianapolis owner John T. Brush whereby the league classifies players into five categories, A to E. Each category provides for a specific salary: A, $2,500; B, $2,250; C, $2,000; D, $1,750; and E, $1,500. On-field and off-field performance both are to be considered in determining a player's classification.[132] Brotherhood President John Montgomery Ward and other union members will be livid when they finally hear of the Brush Plan in February 1989 while traveling abroad as members of A.G. Spalding's worldwide baseball tour.[133] Although the classification scheme will not be strictly enforced—hardly any player with an existing salary exceeding $2,500 will be cut—its very existence will contribute to a growing resolve among players over the next year to form their own league (see entry for November 4, 1889).[134]

1889

November 4, 1889: Brotherhood Forms the Players' League

At 7:00 p.m., following a day-long meeting of its chapter representatives at the Fifth Avenue Hotel in New York City, President John Montgomery Ward of the Brotherhood of Professional Base Ball Players presents to the press a document later to be known as the Brotherhood Manifesto that announces the formation of the Players' League.¹³⁵ The Brotherhood's action is sparked by the belief that the owners will never meet player demands and thus the only way for players to achieve their goals is by forming a league of their own.¹³⁶ Key features of the new league include profit-sharing among teams, no reserve rule, no player classification or blacklist, and a prohibition against trading or selling players without their consent.¹³⁷ By mid–December, nearly a hundred players will have joined the Players' League, with eighty coming from the National League and the rest from the American Association. The National League, threatened by loss of so many of its marquee players, will respond in familiar fashion, seeking to restrain player movement by using the courts to enforce the reserve rule (see entries for January 28, 1890, March 15, 1890, March 25, 1890, and May 5, 1890).¹³⁸

1890

January 28, 1890: Reserve Clause Held Unenforceable in Ward Case

In *Metropolitan Exhibition Co. v. Ward*,¹³⁹ Judge Morgan J. O'Brien of the New York State Supreme Court rules that the reserve clause in the New York Giants' contract with its star shortstop, John Montgomery Ward, lacks mutuality and refuses to grant the Giants' request to temporarily enjoin Ward from playing for any team other than the Giants.¹⁴⁰ The *Sporting Life* calls the decision a "signal victory for the Players' League" and, conversely, "a mortifying and costly [defeat] for the [National] League, inasmuch as it destroys its prestige, ... lays its entire line of policy open to severest criticism, ... undermines the loyalty of its players and reduces it to a secondary position in the estimation of the fickle public...."¹⁴¹

February 3, 1890: Larry MacPhail, Baseball Executive and Lawyer, Is Born

Leland Stanford "Larry" MacPhail, Sr., lawyer and Hall of Fame baseball executive, is born in Cass City, Michigan, to a prosperous banking family.¹⁴² After graduating from George Washington University Law School in 1910, MacPhail will join the Chicago law firm of Davis and Rankin, but have no success defending the Union Pacific Railroad from claims related to the 1906 San Francisco earthquake and fail to make partner. MacPhail will launch his baseball career in 1931 as president of the Columbus Red Birds, but clashes with owner Branch Rickey will lead him to the Cincinnati Reds in 1933 as the team's general manager. With Cincinnati, MacPhail will pioneer night baseball in the major leagues and hire Red Barber for his first baseball broadcasting job.¹⁴³ Moving to the Brooklyn Dodgers as executive vice-president in 1938, he will champion televised baseball and be selected Sporting News Executive of the Year in 1939. As president and part-owner of the New York Yankees after World War II, MacPhail will chair an owners committee that proffers a few small concessions to players in response to their efforts to form a union (see entry for June 7, 1946). When Lee MacPhail, a longtime executive for the Yankees and Orioles and president of the American League (1974–84), is inducted in 1998, he and Larry will become the only father and son members of the National Baseball Hall of Fame.

March 15, 1890: Contract Lacks Mutuality, Court Allows Hallman to Jump to Players' League

When the Philadelphia County Court of Common Pleas refuses to grant the injunction requested by the Philadelphia Quakers, Bill Hallman, who had played shortstop for the National League's Quakers in 1889, is free to jump to the Philadelphia Athletics of the new Players' League for the 1890 season. Judge M. Russell Thayer states that Hallman's contract with the Quakers "is so wanting in mutuality that no court of equity would lend aid to compel compliance with it."[144] In particular, the ten-day notice clause allowed the National League team to set a player "adrift at the beginning or in the middle of a season, at home or two thousand miles from it, sick or well, at the mere arbitrary discretion of the plaintiffs."[145]

March 25, 1890: Court Won't Enforce Reserve Clause, Allows Ewing to Jump to Players' League

In another case involving a National League player's attempt to jump to the newly formed Players' League, Federal judge William P. Wallace immediately establishes the heart of the matter: "This action is brought to restrain a threatened breach of contract for the performance of personal services which require special aptitude, skill, and experience."[146] In this case, the jumper is catcher William "Buck" Ewing, a future Hall of Famer and a leader of the Brotherhood of Professional Base Ball Players, who has bolted from the New York Giants to the Players' League team of the same name. In denying the motion for an injunction, Wallace cites earlier decisions involving John Montgomery Ward (see entry for January 28, 1890) and Bill Hallman (see entry for March 15, 1890) to support his decision that the reservation in Ewing's contract with the NL's Giants is "in a legal sense ... merely a contract to make a contract if the parties can agree."[147]

April 19, 1890: Players' League Begins Its First and Only Season

The new Players' League, formed by the Brotherhood of Professional Base Ball Players (see entry for November 4, 1889), begins its first season of play with games involving all eight of the league's teams in four cities, three in direct competition with a National League game: Philadelphia Quakers at New York Giants, Chicago Pirates at Pittsburgh Burghers, and Brooklyn Wonders at Boston Reds. With the game at Brotherhood Park in New York leading the way with 12,013 spectators, the 32,000 who attend the four games help the league open "in a blaze of glory and with great enthusiasm."[148] On the PL's opening day, it outdraws the NL by a 3 to 1 margin in the cities where it directly competes against the established league, a pattern that will continue throughout the season.[149] Unfortunately, despite this auspicious start, the new league will last only one season, as the National League is successful in dividing the players from their financial backers, causing the Players' League to go out of business by late November 1890.[150] With the ratification of a new National Agreement soon after the new year (see entry for January 16, 1891), the league will officially cease to exist.[151]

May 5, 1890: Court Prevents Pickett from Revolving to Players' League

After John Pickett, a backup outfielder for the 1889 Kansas City Cowboys of the American Association, breaks his 1890 contract with the team and jumps ("revolves") to the Philadelphia Athletics of the Players' League, Judge Michael Arnold of the Court of Common Pleas in Philadelphia enjoins the Athletics from using Pickett.[152] Relying on the famous 1852 English precedent *Lumley v. Wagner* in supporting Kansas City's bill, Judge Arnold states that Pickett's "ingratitude is shown to be equal to his bad faith. While we cannot punish him for his ingratitude, we can restrain him from deriving any benefit from his breach of contract."[153] Despite the ruling, one month later Pickett will purchase his release from Kansas City and play in 100 games for Philadelphia during the 1890 season.[154]

June 7, 1890: Court Allows Frank Grant to Play with Integrated Team

Concluding that his contract with the all-black Cuban Giants (known as the York Monarchs when admitted to the Eastern Interstate League to represent York, Pennsylvania) lacks mutuality because only the Giants/Monarchs had the right to cancel it at any time, a Pennsylvania court refuses to grant an injunction that would prevent African American second baseman Ulysses "Frank" Grant from playing with the integrated Harrisburg Ponies during the 1890 season.[155] Described by Sol White as a "base ball marvel [whose] 'playing was a revelation to his fellow team mates, as well as the spectators,'"[156] Grant will be inducted into the National Baseball Hall of Fame in 2006.[157]

July 2, 1890: Harrison Signs Sherman Antitrust Act

President Benjamin Harrison signs the Sherman Antitrust Act,[158] named for its author, Senator John Sherman (R–Ohio), thereby enacting the first federal statute to limit cartels and monopolies. Its purpose is to protect consumers by limiting business activities that reduce competition and raise prices.

1891

January 16, 1891: New National Agreement Creates System for Trades, Abolishes Blacklist

National League President Nicholas E. Young, American Association President Allan W. Thurman, and Western Association President Louis C. Krauthoff sign a new National Agreement in a public meeting of 75 individuals described as the "greatest assemblage of base-ball men ever gathered together in this country." The compact, designed to govern relations between the leagues, abolishes the blacklist and creates a system of advancement for players in lower classifications. The three presidents describe the new system of in-season player transfers as requiring an increased salary for the consenting player that "destroys all criticism upon the 'reserve rule,' and forever ends the existence of what has been called the 'sales system.' The corner-stone grievance claimed by the brotherhood is thus carefully and judiciously met." The new agreement also establishes a three-person board to resolve important "controversies and grievances" arising among and between the participant leagues, including the approval of all contracts with managers and players.[159]

February 14, 1891: Alleghenys Become "Pirates" After Contract Squabbles Over Stovey, Bierbauer, and Mack

After the American Association's Philadelphia Athletics fail to properly reserve Harry Stovey and Louis Bierbauer by the October 10, 1890, deadline, Allan Thurman, AA president and chair of the National Board, only recently created by the National Agreement of 1891 between the National League, the AA, and the Western Association (see entry for January 16, 1891), announces the Board's decision ratifying Stovey's contract with the NL's Boston Beaneaters and Bierbauer's with the NL's Pittsburgh Alleghenys. The Board also rules in favor of the contract Connie Mack signed with Pittsburgh in January 1891 over one he signed with the Boston Reds of the AA in December 1890, invalidating the earlier contract because the Reds had not yet been admitted into the league at the time of its execution.[160] When the Pittsburgh actions resulting in the acquisition of Bierbauer and Mack are described as "piratical," the club will gladly adopt "Pirates" as their nickname for the 1891 season.[161]

February 17, 1891: American Association Withdraws from National Agreement, Board Declares Open Season on AA Players

Still stinging from the National Board's decision regarding the contractual status of Harry Stovey, Louis Bierbauer, and Connie Mack (see entry for February 14, 1891), American Association owners meeting at the Murray Hill Hotel in Manhattan vote to withdraw from the new 1891 National Agreement.[162] Allan Thurman, who as chair of the National Board had decided against the Association and in favor of the National League in each instance, is deposed as president, and Louis Kramer, an attorney from Cincinnati, is elected to the consolidated offices of president, secretary, and treasurer.[163] Responding to the AA's withdrawal, the National Board will declare that all AA players are freed from reservation and thus available for signing by any club of the National League or Western Association, the other parties to the agreement and participants in the National Board.[164]

April 26, 1891: Nebraska Supreme Court Upholds Statutory Prohibition Against Sunday Baseball

A crowd of more than 3,000 spectators "riot" when the county sheriff tries to break up a Sunday afternoon professional baseball game at Lincoln Park in Nebraska City, Nebraska. Players and fans surround the sheriff, "roughing" him up and stealing his revolver. After restoring calm, the sheriff issues tickets to the Nebraska City players and manager Tim O'Rourk for violating the state's "blue law" which prohibits, among other things, any person 14 years or older from "sporting, rioting, quarreling, hunting, fishing, or shooting" on Sunday.[165] Although the county judge will throw the case out, it will be appealed all the way to the Nebraska Supreme Court, which will conclude that "playing baseball comes within the term 'sporting'" and, thus, is an activity prohibited by the statute.[166] After a long discourse on the Christian requirement of "a day of rest" on the Sabbath, the court will conclude that failure to enforce the law will "lead to infamy and ruin" for the participants and "a tendency to break down the moral sense, and make them less worthy citizens."[167] Sunday baseball in Nebraska won't become legal until 1913, when the statute is amended to leave the decision up to individual cities and counties.

December 15, 1891: Peace Agreement Results in NL Takeover of Four Teams, Demise of American Association

A peace agreement between the warring National League and the American Association is reached in Indianapolis. With most of its teams at or near bankruptcy, the American Association had folded at the conclusion of the 1891 season. As part of the agreement, the National League purchases four of the American Association teams—Baltimore, Louisville, St. Louis, and Washington—for $130,000, thereby expanding the League to 12 teams. The surviving owners spend $131,000 to shut down Association franchises in Boston, Chicago, Columbus, Milwaukee, and Philadelphia. Players coming from defunct American Association clubs will be allocated by the National League and must play for the team to which they are assigned or be blacklisted.[168]

1892

June 6, 1892: Harrison Becomes First President to Attend Major League Game

Benjamin Harrison, the 23rd President of the United States, becomes the first to attend a Major League baseball game when he watches the National League's Washington Senators lose in 11 innings to the Cincinnati Reds, 7–4, at Boundary Field in Washington, D.C.[169] President Harrison will attend one more game during his term in office (March 4, 1889–March 4, 1893), on June 25, 1892, with the Senators again losing, this time to the Philadelphia Phillies, 9–2.[170] The result is not surprising, as the Senators will finish the season in tenth place in the 12-team National League, with a record of 58–93, 44½ games behind the pennant-winning Boston Beaneaters.[171]

1896

April 28, 1896: Giants Suspend Baseball Labor Leader Fred Pfeffer

The New York Giants suspend second-baseman Fred Pfeffer, claiming that he is not "in fit condition to play ball."[172] In reality, it is likely that Giants owner Andrew Freedman was attempting to blacklist Pfeffer, once a member of the famed "stonewall infield" of the 1880s Chicago Nationals and, more important, a prominent leader in the Brotherhood of Professional Base Ball Players (see entry for October 22, 1885), the Players' League (see entry for November 4, 1889), and the attempt to form a new American Association as a challenge to the National League in 1894.[173] Pfeffer will refuse to back down, hiring his Brotherhood colleague John Montgomery Ward, now an attorney, to sue Freedman. Although it will take 11 years before the case is finally resolved by the New York Court of Appeals in 1907, Pfeffer will be awarded $800 in back pay and costs, a relatively small amount but a victory in a fight that was more about "principle rather than capital."[174]

1897

May 16, 1897: Ohio Supreme Court Upholds Sunday Baseball Law

In an effort to increase profits for both his baseball team and streetcar interests, Cleveland Spiders owner Frank Robison flaunts Ohio state law by scheduling a Sunday game against the Washington Senators at League Park.[175] The game is halted in the first inning when all 18 players and umpire Tim Hurst are arrested for violating the law which prohibits playing baseball or exhibiting "any baseball playing" on Sunday. Rookie pitcher Jack Powell, who starts at first base for the Spiders, is designated to be the sole defendant in a test case that by design will reach the Ohio Supreme Court.[176] Found guilty by a jury in police court, the verdict against Powell is reversed on July 9 by the court of common pleas when Judge Walter Ong holds the Sunday law unconstitutional, thereby freeing the Spiders to play six more well-attended Sunday games over the remainder of the season.[177] On April 19, 1898, however, the Ohio Supreme Court upholds the state law prohibiting playing baseball on Sunday, rejecting the argument that the statute violates the constitutional separation of church and state.[178]

1898

June 19, 1898: Spiders Fail in Challenge to Ohio Sunday Baseball Ban

The marshal of Collinwood, Ohio, acting on warrants sworn out by a local Congregational minister, halts a game between the Cleveland Spiders and the Pittsburgh Pirates in the eighth inning when he arrests all the Spiders players for violating the state law prohibiting the playing of baseball on Sunday.[179] Spiders owner Frank Robison had hoped to escape the impact of the Ohio Supreme Court's recent decision upholding the law (see entry for May 16, 1897) by relocating his team's scheduled Sunday home games to Euclid Beach Park in nearby Collinwood, a community beyond the Cleveland city limits, surmising that town officials would not object to Sunday crowds from the popular local amusement park moving on to a baseball game played there.[180] Although the justice of the peace will fine each player only $1 and costs, it will become clear to Robison that "Sunday games ... cannot be played in or near Cleveland,"[181] leading him to relegate the Spiders to playing all but three of its remaining home games for the 1898 season on the road.[182]

July 5, 1898: Lizzie Arlington Becomes First Woman to Play in Minor League Game

Playing under the name of Lizzie Arlington, twenty-two-year old Elizabeth Stroud of Mahanoy City, Pennsylvania, becomes the first woman to play in a regulation minor league game, pitching a scoreless ninth inning for Reading of the Atlantic League against Allentown.[183] Despite the praise offered in contemporary newspaper accounts,[184] the assessment of league president Ed Barrow that she "could really pitch ... with plenty of stuff and control," and the ballyhoo accorded her presence, the game draws a disappointing thousand spectators and Arlington is quickly released, never to pitch again in Organized Baseball although she continues to barnstorm for years with women's traveling teams.[185]

August 17, 1898: Ad Gumbert Loses Legal Challenge to Reserve Clause

In Pittsburgh, Federal District Court Judge Joseph Buffington upholds the reserve clause when he rules against Addison Courtney "Ad" Gumbert in his suit against the Chicago National League Baseball Club for damages and wages lost during the period in 1893 when the pitcher/outfielder held out after the Colts' Cap Anson offered him a contract for 1893 at $1,800, a significant cut from his 1892 contract at $2,700.[186] After being traded to Pittsburgh on June 26, 1893, for pitcher Bert Abbey,[187] Gumbert sued his former team for $2,250 plus interest, arguing that the reserve clause had prevented him from finding employment with a different major league team. Five years later, when the court rules in the club's favor, Chicago President James A. Hart characterizes the decision as "the most important ruling ever made in which baseball figures."[188]

1900

June 10, 1900: Formation of Players Protective Association, Second Player Union

National League players meeting at the Sturtevant House in New York form the Protective Association of Professional Baseball Players (also known as the Players Protective Association), baseball's second labor union. With three representatives from each League team in attendance, the group chooses as its officers Pittsburgh catcher Charley "Chief" Zimmer, president; Cubs pitcher Clark Griffith,[189] vice-president; Brooklyn first-baseman Hughie Jennings, secretary; and Boston catcher Bill Clarke, treasurer. At a second meeting in late July attended by almost a hundred players, the Association will adopt a constitution drafted by its legal counsel, Buffalo attorney Harry Leonard Taylor, formerly a player for Louisville in both the American Association in 1890–91 and the National League in 1892 before concluding his major league career with the National League Baltimore Orioles in 1893.[190] Among other things, the new union champions the right of players to receive half the sale price when they are sold to another team.[191] However, in the wake of the American League's successful plundering of National League rosters, which will eventually lead to a peace pact between the two warring leagues (see entry for January 10, 1903), the association will collapse by the end of the 1902 season.[192]

November 20, 1900: American League Formed, Declares Itself a Major League

Under the leadership of Byron Bancroft "Ban" Johnson, a former Cincinnati newspaperman who in 1894 became president of a regional minor league then called the Western League, representatives of the recently renamed American League of Professional Base Ball Clubs sign a contract asserting the league's standing as a major league. In doing so, the American League rejects the existing National Agreement, stating that it will operate "independent of, but not antagonistic to any other Professional Base Ball organization."[193] The eight charter teams which will participate in the inaugural 1901 season are the Baltimore Orioles, Boston Americans, Chicago White Stockings, Cleveland Blues, Detroit Tigers, Milwaukee Brewers, Philadelphia Athletics, and Washington Senators.[194]

1901

September 5, 1901: National Association Established to Govern Minor Leagues

In an effort to create peace between competing minor leagues over markets and players and to establish a better relationship with the National Commission and the National League, representatives of the strongest minor league circuits meet at the Leland Hotel in Chicago to establish the National Association of Professional Baseball Leagues.[195] Pat Powers, president of the Eastern League, is selected as the first president. The organization's structure and leadership will be finalized in New York City on October 25, with the announcement of a new 10-year National Agreement between the minor leagues. It reestablishes the reserve system, implements salary limitations, and creates a National Board of Arbitration to resolve grievances and dispense sanctions on violators.[196] Nearing its centennial, the NAPBL will officially change its name to Minor League Baseball in 1999.

1902

April 21, 1902: Lajoie Enjoined from Playing for American League's Athletics

Justice William P. Potter of the Pennsylvania Supreme Court rules in favor of the National League's Philadelphia Phillies and owner John I. Rogers in their suit to restrain Napoleon Lajoie from playing for the American League's Philadelphia Athletics.[197] Lajoie, a hard-hitting infielder who began his major league career with the Phillies in 1896, had jumped to the Athletics for the 1901 season, becoming an immediate star in the new league by winning the batting triple crown.[198] Justice Potter reverses the decision of the Philadelphia County Court of Common Pleas allowing Lajoie to play for the Athletics, determining that the Phillies will suffer irreparable damage because his services are "of peculiar and special value to the plaintiff, and not easily replaced.... He may not be the sun in the baseball firmament, but he is certainly a bright particular star."[199] The court concludes that while it cannot force Lajoie to play for the Phillies, it can prevent him from playing for any other team. But negotiations with Rogers will break down and Lajoie, barred from playing in Pennsylvania for any team other than the Phillies, will instead sign with the AL's Cleveland Bronchos.[200] With the injunction still hanging over him, Lajoie will avoid the reach of Pennsylvania courts by spending his days in Atlantic City, New Jersey, when Cleveland plays in Philadelphia during the 1902 season.[201]

CHAPTER 3

The National Commission Era, 1903–1920

Introduction

After two years of intense competition, Cincinnati Reds president Garry Herrmann helped broker the historic 1903 National Agreement that created a new governing body for Organized Baseball, the National Commission, and recognized the American League as an equal partner with its well-established counterpart, the National League. It also created a new reserve system and paved the way for relocation of the American League's Baltimore Orioles to New York. The 16 franchises, divided equally between each league, remained geographically stable for the next 54 years.

In 1907, the Mills Commission issued its report claiming that baseball was invented by Abner Doubleday, a future Union general during the Civil War, in Cooperstown, New York, in 1839. Although the myth of a single moment and locus of creation for the national pastime was later debunked, the connection of the game to this New York village endured.

Another connection, that existing between the federal government and baseball, was strengthened in 1909 when Republicans and Democrats took to the diamond in the first Congressional Baseball Game. And in the very next year, William Howard Taft began the tradition of the president throwing a ceremonial first pitch on Opening Day.

A decade of major league stability and labor peace was shattered in 1914 when the Federal League emerged as a rival to the American and National leagues. The battle in the courts produced victories for the new league over Organized Baseball's reserve system, but losses in the economic battle for fan support led it to pursue an antitrust action against the two established leagues in early 1915. Federal district court judge Kenesaw Mountain Landis, noted for his large antitrust damages award against oil magnate John D. Rockefeller, presided over the case, but when he refused to enter a ruling during the 1915 season, the Federal League dissolved in December with a deal that satisfied all but the leadership of the league's Baltimore Terrapins. When a special committee failed to offer a satisfactory solution, the Baltimore stockholders brought multiple lawsuits that eventually led to the historic 1922 Supreme Court decision that refused to extend the coverage of the Sherman Antitrust Act to professional baseball.

The deadball era produced some exciting on-field action, but attendance dropped precipitously as the United States became embroiled in Europe's world war. Team owners' diminishing confidence in the National Commission's ability to effectively govern the sport prompted calls for reform, but the greatest threat to the game was the pernicious influence of gamblers. When rumors that members of the Chicago White Sox had fixed the outcome of 1919 World Series erupted into a full-blown scandal in 1920, the structure of baseball's hierarchy toppled. The owners again sought the help of Chicago's white-haired jurist, but Judge Landis demanded absolute power before accepting their offer to become the game's first commissioner. The desperate owners acceded to his demands, and the national pastime prepared for a stunning recovery.

1903

January 10, 1903: American and National Leagues Reach Peace Agreement

After two days of intense negotiations expertly managed by Cincinnati Reds president August "Garry" Herrmann, committees for both the National and American leagues meeting in conference at the St. Nicholas Hotel in Cincinnati hammer out a peace agreement to end the struggle which had placed the economic survival of major league baseball at risk. The agreement provides for the use of a reserve rule, allows the American League to move its Baltimore franchise to New York, and resolves numerous contractual disputes over players, largely to the benefit of American League teams. The two leagues further agree that their presidents, Ban Johnson and Harry Pulliam, will work with Pat Powers, president of the National Association of Professional Baseball Leagues, to create a national agreement that carries out the terms of this peace pact (see entry for September 11, 1903).[1]

September 11, 1903: New National Agreement Creates National Commission, Reestablishes Reserve System

At Cincinnati, Ohio, a new "National Agreement for the Government of Professional Base Ball Clubs," comprised for the most part of provisions agreed upon earlier in the year (see entry for January 10, 1903), is signed by representatives of the National League, American League, and National Association of Professional Baseball Leagues (representing the minor leagues).[2] With "protection of the property rights of those engaged in base ball as a business" among the objects listed in the agreement's preamble, the document requires that each of its signatories "honor the reserve clause and refuse to employ players under contract with other member-teams."[3] It also creates a National Commission, consisting of the presidents of the National and American leagues and a third member who will serve as its chair.[4] The commission will serve as baseball's governing body until its demise in November 1920 when Kenesaw Mountain Landis is chosen as the sport's first commissioner (see entry for November 11, 1920).

September 16, 1903: Agreement Signed for First Modern World Series

Barney Dreyfuss, president and owner of the Pittsburgh Pirates of the National League, and Henry Killilea, owner of the Boston Americans (also known as the Pilgrims or Puritans) of the American League, sign a bilateral agreement in which they commit to represent their leagues in a championship series to be played after the completion of the 1903 season.[5] Since there is no official league sanction for what will become the first World Series of the modern era, Dreyfuss and Killilea establish their own rules, including a best-of-nine format, games to be played in the home parks of the teams rather than on a neutral field, and eligibility limited to players on the team's roster as of September 1.[6] Despite the peace agreement between the National and American leagues (see entry for January 10, 1903) and the creation of the National Commission as Organized Baseball's governing body (see entry for September 11, 1903), it will not be until February 1905 that the leagues and commission officially adopt the "Rules and Regulations Governing the Contest for the Professional Base Ball Championship of the World" (also known as the "Brush Rules" after its principal architect, Giants owner John T. Brush), mandating an annual best-of-seven post-season World Series between the champions of each league.[7]

October 9, 1903: O'Malley, Lawyer and Dodger Owner, Is Born

Walter O'Malley, who will be inducted into the National Baseball Hall of Fame in 2008 as an executive, is born in the Bronx, New York.[8] He will earn a law degree from Fordham University in 1930, and eventually become the senior partner of O'Malley & Wilson, concentrating on bankruptcy work during the Great Depression.[9] As part of his legal work, O'Malley will forge a strong relationship with George V. McLaughlin, president of the Brooklyn Trust Company which represents the estates of Charles Ebbets and Edward McKeever, deceased co-owners of the Brooklyn Dodgers. After years of doing legal work for the Dodgers, O'Malley will purchase an ownership interest in the Dodgers in the mid–1940s; on October 26, 1950, he will acquire a controlling interest in the team and become its president. Later in the decade, O'Malley will tangle with New York City Parks Commissioner Robert Moses over plans to build a new stadium in the borough, and ultimately decide to move the Dodgers to Los Angeles in 1958.[10] When O'Malley dies in August 1979, the *Sporting News* will note that he is "said by many to have been the most powerful man in baseball."[11]

1904

June 18, 1904: Judge Upholds Ban on Sunday Baseball in New York

Reversing the position he took in an April test case of New York's criminal prohibition against playing baseball on Sunday, New York Supreme Court Magistrate and future New York major William Jay Gaynor refuses to dismiss a complaint against Brooklyn Dodgers pitcher Ed Poole who was arrested on May 29 for participating in a Sunday baseball game at Washington Park between the Dodgers and their intra-city rival, the New York Giants.[12] In the earlier matter, Gaynor had chastised members of the Sabbath Observance Association for failure to allege that the game disturbed the peace.[13] In the case against Poole, however, Gaynor states that "the present game is different. The complaint is ... of a game ... to which an admission fee was charged. Is such a game prohibited by statute? I think it is."[14] Assessing the import of the Poole case, baseball historian Charlie Bevis will write that it "became an oft-cited precedent in the two-decade-long-battle to legalize Sunday baseball in New York"[15] (see entry for April 19, 1919).

1905

January 24, 1905: Patent for Pneumatic Head Protector, the First Batting Helmet

Philadelphia inventor Frank Mogridge's "Pneumatic Head Protector," the first headgear designed to protect batters in baseball games, is patented by the A.J. Reach Company.[16] To use the primitive, inflatable device, a teammate had to blow into a small tube after the batter placed the protector on his head.[17] Future Hall-of-Famer Roger Bresnahan, who in 1907 will also pioneer the use of shin guards by catchers,[18] will become the first player to use the head protector in a major league game after returning from a hospital stay caused by a beaning.[19]

May 7, 1905: Peter Seitz, Messersmith-McNally Arbitrator, Is Born

Peter Seitz, the arbitrator who will render baseball's reserve clause obsolete in his 1975 decision over grievances filed on behalf of Andy Messersmith of the Los Angeles Dodgers and Dave McNally of the Montreal Expos (see entry for December 23, 1975), is born. Baseball lawyer and arbitrator Roger

I. Abrams will label Seitz an arbitration "superstar" and call his work "legendary."[20]

1906

March 30, 1906: Ty Cobb's Mother Acquitted in Killing of Her Husband

After deliberating for only an hour, a jury in Lavonia, Georgia, finds Amanda Cobb, mother of future Hall of Famer Ty Cobb, not guilty of murdering her husband and Ty's father, Professor W.H. Cobb.[21] Amanda fatally shot Cobb's father, a former Georgia state senator and Franklin County School Commissioner, during the early morning of August 9, 1905, allegedly mistaking him for a burglar. However, the circumstances of the shooting and the relationship between Cobb's parents remain unsettled, including the speculation that W.H. was trying to surprise Amanda with a supposed lover when he was shot.[22] The impact of the shooting on Cobb's life and his relationship with his father, who originally discouraged his son's interest in a professional baseball career but ultimately inspired Ty by telling him not to "come home a failure," is still hotly debated in numerous publications.[23]

1907

April 9, 1907: First-Ever Patent for a Batting Cage Issued

The first-ever patent for a portable batting cage—a "base ball back stop" on wheels—is issued to Wellington Stockton Titus of Glenmore, New Jersey.[24] Titus, a postmaster, house builder and mover, civil engineer, and farm foreman who also played third base for the town team in nearby Hopewell, had previously jury-rigged a cage using pipes and chicken wire to help train his cousin, George Titus Wells, later captain of the Princeton nine in 1908. On February 26, 1907, contingent to receiving the patent, Titus executed a memorandum of agreement with A.G. Spalding and Brothers for the manufacture and sale of his batting cage.[25] With its capability of being moved to and used from anywhere on the field, Titus's invention will serve as the prototype of the batting cage still used today throughout professional baseball.

December 30, 1907: Mills Commission Declares Doubleday Baseball's Founder

Abraham G. Mills, chair of the special commission formed in 1905 by Albert G. Spalding to resolve his dispute with Henry Chadwick over the origins of baseball, writes an eight-paragraph letter to James E. Sullivan, president of the Amateur Athletic Union and secretary to the commission, in which he declares that "according to the best evidence obtainable to date, [baseball] was devised by Abner Doubleday at Cooperstown, N.Y. in 1839."[26]

Although Mills, president of the National League from 1882 to 1884 and the architect of baseball's first National Agreement (see entry for March 12, 1883), was an 1869 graduate of Columbian Law School (now George Washington University), he primarily relies on a single piece of detailed but undocumented "evidence." This is a letter written by Abner Graves, a 71-year-old mining engineer, to Sullivan, which was immediately published as an article in the *Akron Beacon Journal* on April 4, 1905, under the title "Abner Doubleday Invented Base Ball."[27] Despite never investigating Graves's claim that, as a five-year-old boy in Cooperstown, he saw and heard future Civil War general Doubleday sketch out a diagram of a diamond, create player positions, and explain how the game was played,[28] Mills's short letter eventually will constitute the commission's full report when it is published in the *Spalding Guide* in March 1908.[29] Not surprisingly, the report favors Spalding's view of baseball as American born, rather than Chadwick's theory that it evolved from the English game of rounders.

1908

May 2, 1908: Copyright Issued to Composers of "Take Me Out to the Ballgame"

Albert Von Tilzer, composer and manager of the York Music Company of New York, and lyricist Jack Norworth submit two copies of their new song, "Take Me Out to the Ball Game," to the U.S. Copyright Office. Vaudeville star Norworth, also the writer of "Shine On Harvest Moon," later claimed that despite never having attended a professional baseball game, he was inspired to write the song after seeing a "gaudy, lithographed poster of a silk-hosed baseball player standing with a bat" while riding the subway.[30] There is some uncertainty as to when the story of Katie Casey, a girl mad with baseball fever, was first sung in public, although evidence points to its debut occurring at the Grand Opera House in Brooklyn in late April 1908.[31] But there is no doubt that it quickly will become a success and today, though the original version entered the public domain in 1983, it "remains the most popular baseball song of all time."[32] This is due, at least in part, to broadcaster Harry Caray, called by some "the most important figure in the song's history" after Von Tilzer and Norworth, who in the late 1970s will popularize the singing of "Take Me Out to the Ball Game" during the home team's seventh-inning stretch.[33] In 2011, a 1908 recording of the song by Edwin Meeker and the Edison Orchestra will be selected for the National Recording Registry by James H. Billington, Librarian of Congress.[34]

October 7, 1908: Attempt to Bribe Umpires of Cubs-Giants Pennant Decider Fails

One day prior to the makeup game scheduled to decide the National

League pennant, necessitated by the infamous base-running blunder of Giants rookie Fred Merkle on September 23 that ultimately led to the game between the Chicago Cubs and New York Giants being declared a tie, Umpires Bill Klem and James Johnstone inform National League Secretary John Heydler of separate attempts to give them money to throw the game in favor of the Giants.[35] Leery of damaging baseball's reputation, the National League will not publicly acknowledge the attempted bribery until December 10 when President Harry Pulliam announces the formation of a committee to investigate the affair, chaired by Giants president John T. Brush.[36] The bribery case will never be tried in either criminal or civil court, with Brush declaring that New York law applied only to bribes of public officials, but in April the National Commission will ban for life Giants team physician Dr. Joseph M. Creamer from entering any major league ballpark, making him the only person ever sanctioned for the bribe effort.[37]

November 12, 1908: Harry Blackmun, author of *Flood v. Kuhn* Case, Is Born

Harry Blackmun is born in Nashville, Illinois, but will grow up in Saint Paul, Minnesota.[38] The 1932 Harvard Law School graduate will serve on the United States Court of Appeals for the Eighth Circuit until President Richard Nixon nominates him to the U.S. Supreme Court on April 14, 1970, following the failure of two previous nominees to gain Senate approval.[39] A lifelong baseball fan who kept a copy of the *Baseball Encyclopedia* close to his desk, Justice Blackmun will write the majority opinion in *Flood v. Kuhn* (see entry for June 19, 1972). Law professor Roger Abrams will describe part I of the opinion as "a paean to baseball and the men who played the game," as it includes an "extraordinary list of 88 ballplayers and baseball business figures.... There is nothing like Blackmun's list anywhere else in the hallowed tomes of American judicial opinions."[40]

1909

March 4, 1909: John Tener Is First Former Player to Serve in U.S. Congress

Republican John Kinley Tener, formerly a pitcher for the Chicago White Stockings (National League, 1888–89) and Pittsburgh Burghers (Players League, 1890), becomes the first major league player to serve in the United States Congress[41] when he begins his term in the House as the representative of Pennsylvania's 24th Congressional District. His stay will be short-lived as he will resign on January 16, 1911, to take office as the newly elected governor of Pennsylvania. Unanimously elected the eighth president of the National League on December 9, 1913—thereby becoming the first former Major League player to serve as president of either league—he will serve in both capacities until his term as governor expires in January 1915, and then continue as league president until his resignation on August 6, 1918.[42]

June 15, 1909: Shibe Patents First Cork-Centered Baseball

Benjamin F. Shibe, an original owner of the Philadelphia Athletics along with Connie Mack, receives a patent for the first cork-centered baseball.[43] Known as the "Edison of Baseball" for his many patents related to baseballs, Shibe says in his application that he wants to increase "strength and durability,"[44] replacing the solid rubber-centered core with one consisting of ground up cork covered by India rubber around which strands of yard are tightly wound.[45] But use of the ball—quietly during the 1910 season and World Series and then openly throughout the 1911 season—will lead to an "offensive explosion, extending base hits from singles to doubles, and doubles to triples."[46] Although the "dead-ball era" will continue through the decade, the combination of Shibe's cork-centered ball and various rule changes will eventually lead to a new "live-ball era" during the 1920 season.

July 16, 1909: Democrats Prevail in First-Ever Congressional Baseball Game

The Democrats prevail over the Republicans, 26 to 16, in the first-ever Congressional Baseball Game, played at American League Park in northwest Washington, D.C.[47] It is organized by Representative John K. Tener of Pennsylvania just months after he becomes the first former major league player to serve in Congress (see entry for March 4, 1909).[48] The Democrats will win the first six of what will become an annual contest in which members of Congress, including a number of former professional baseball players (see entry for July 26, 1979), put on uniforms and spikes to play baseball and raise money for local District of Columbia charities.[49]

1910

April 14, 1910: Taft Begins Tradition of Opening Day Presidential First Pitch

As the Washington Senators prepare to meet the Philadelphia Athletics at American League Park II in Washington, D.C., William Howard Taft becomes the first United States President to throw out a ceremonial first pitch on opening day at a major-league game when he tosses a ball supplied to him by umpire Billy Evans to Walter Johnson, the Senators starting pitcher.[50] This act, coupled with his brother Charles's financial interests in Major League Baseball (he was a majority owner of the Chicago Cubs from 1914 to 1916), may explain why Major League owners will offer Taft the position of commissioner of baseball in November 1918.[51] But Taft refuses, thereby making him available when later called upon to serve as chief justice of the U.S. Supreme Court, a position he will hold from 1921 to 1930.

July 18, 1910: John Montgomery Ward Wins Libel Suit Against Ban Johnson

John Montgomery Ward, former leader of the Brotherhood of Professional Base Ball Players (see entry for October 22, 1885) and now a practicing lawyer in New York City, files a defamation lawsuit against American League President Ban Johnson. Ward is seeking $50,000 in damages for statements allegedly made by Johnson to Ring Lardner regarding Ward's candidacy to replace John A. Heydler as National League president, as reported in the November 28, 1909, edition of the *Chicago Tribune* under Lardner's byline and then repeated in a Newspaper Enterprise Association (NEA) wire service release by Ernest Stout.[52] Johnson's characterization of Ward as a trickster and statements that he "refused to sit on the national commission with Ward" and "would not stand for him" form the basis of Ward's complaint.[53] During the May 1911 trial of the case in the courtroom of Federal District Court Judge Learned Hand, the famed jurist will dismiss four of Ward's five counts but the jury, after deliberating for 75 minutes, returns a $1,000 award for Ward on the final count, accepting Stout's testimony that Johnson's signature affixed to the bottom of the draft NEA release after his review of the piece is not a forgery and concluding that Johnson's trickster statement is libelous.[54]

October 9, 1910: O'Connor Fired After Chalmers Batting Race Incident, Sues for Breach of Contract

In a season-ending doubleheader against the St. Louis Browns, Napoleon "Larry" Lajoie of the Cleveland Naps records eight hits in eight at-bats to seemingly overtake Ty Cobb for the American League batting title and win the new touring car offered by the Chalmers Motor Company as a prize for the batting champion of the major leagues.[55] But the hits are suspect—after a fly ball falls untouched in front of the center fielder for a triple, the positioning of the left side of the infield literally invites Lajoie to lay down eight consecutive bunts (seven are scored as hits, one as an error and a sacrifice).[56] Many in the press accuse Browns manager John O'Connor of turning the game into a "hippodrome" by ordering rookie third baseman John "Red" Corriden to play the hard-hitting but slow-footed Lajoie near or on the outfield grass.[57] In November, Browns owner Robert Lee Hedges will dismiss O'Connor because of his alleged role in the affair, leading "Rowdy Jack" to file suit against the team for breach of contract on October 12, 1911.[58] The case will go to trial in St. Louis on May 12, 1913, resulting in a unanimous jury verdict and an award of $5000 in damages for O'Connor.[59] Finally, on January 4, 1916, the Missouri Court of Appeals will uphold the verdict, concluding that whether O'Connor had failed to manage the Browns in good faith by favoring Lajoie in the batting contest with Cobb was a question of fact for the jury to decide.[60]

1911

March 24, 1911: Helene Britton Becomes First Female Major League Owner

Thirty-two-year-old Helene Hathaway Robison Britton, a mother of two, becomes the first female owner of a major league team when she inherits 75 percent of the St. Louis Cardinals upon the death of her bachelor uncle, M. Stanley Robison. The remaining 25 percent is bequeathed to Sarah Robison, Britton's mother. Stanley Robison and his brother Frank deHaas Robison, Helene Britton's father, acquired the team in 1898 in the aftermath of Chris Von der Ahe's financial and legal woes. They changed the team's name to Cardinals in 1900, and Stanley became sole owner when Frank died of a stroke on September 25, 1908.[61]

1912

March 11, 1912: Congressman Seeks Investigation of "Baseball Trust"

In what one commentator has called the beginning of "[b]aseball's decade-long antitrust crisis,"[62] Illinois Congressman Thomas Gallagher introduces House Resolution 450 requesting the creation of a special committee to consider the behavior of "the Baseball Trust," which is described as "the most audacious and autocratic trust in the country," enslaving players by forcing them "to accept salaries and terms or be forever barred from playing."[63] While acknowledging that baseball is "under the direction of an autocratic trust," John Montgomery Ward, organizer of baseball's first player union (see entry for October 22, 1885), will write in response that "it is a good thing that it is. I think that Congress is no place to discuss Base Ball."[64] The resolution will die in the House Committee on Rules.

May 18, 1912: Tigers Stage First-Ever Players Strike to Protest Cobb Suspension

The Detroit Tigers stage baseball's first-ever players strike in response to American League President Ban Johnson's indefinite suspension of Ty Cobb for attacking Highlanders fan Claude Lueker—"a one-handed loudmouth who had a violent hatred of Cobb" which he expressed through continued and obscene abuse of the Tiger star[65]—in the stands at New York's Hilltop Park on May 15.[66] To avoid a forfeit and the mandatory $5000 fine, Tigers manager Hughie Jennings cobbles together a substitute team, comprised of a dozen retired, semipro, and college players at $10 each, to face the Philadelphia Athletics.[67] The Athletics overwhelm "Tiger" pitcher Aloysius

S. Travers, a seminarian who will later become a Catholic priest,[68] and win 24 to 2. Another "Tiger" recruit is local prizefighter Billy Maharg,[69] better known to baseball historians as an important figure in the 1919 World Series scandal. At Cobb's urging and to support owner Frank Navin who they fear will suffer financially if the strike continues, the "regular" Tigers will return to action minus Cobb on Monday, May 21, in Washington. On May 25, Johnson, who had attended the game involving the fight,[70] will fix Cobb's suspension at 10 days and fine him $50; he also will fine each member of the Tigers $100.[71]

May 20, 1912: Britton Enjoins Cardinals President, Secures Team Ownership

Helene Britton, known to the press as "Lady Bee,"[72] secures her position as the first female owner of a major league ball club when she successfully enjoins Edward Steininger, president of the St. Louis Cardinals, from voting or transferring stock belonging to Britton and her mother, Sarah Robison. Britton had inherited control of the Cardinals in 1911 on the death of her uncle, M. Stanley Robison (see entry for March 24, 1911). Steininger, administrator of Stanley's estate, had sought to control the team by voting the stock inherited by Britton (75 percent) and her mother (25 percent) against Lady Bee's interests. But Britton heads him off when Circuit Court Judges Grimm and Hitchcock permanently enjoin Steininger from voting or transferring the stock and order him to issue new certificates for the stock that Britton owns.[73]

September 6, 1912: Players' Fraternity Becomes Baseball's Third Union

The Fraternity of Professional Baseball Players of America (referred to publicly as the Players' Fraternity) is chartered in New York, becoming the third baseball labor union, after the Brotherhood of Professional Base Ball Players (1885–91) and Protective Association of Professional Baseball Players (1900–02) (see entries for October 22, 1885, and June 10, 1900, respectively). David L. Fultz, a seven-year major league veteran (1898–1905) who represents players in his post-playing career law practice, serves as president; four players, two each from the American and National leagues, as vice-presidents; and one player as secretary. The fraternity quickly signs up 288 players, each paying $18 annual dues, and will reach a membership of 1,100, many of them minor leaguers, by 1914.[74] Fultz soon will delineate the fraternity's goals in an article published in *Baseball Magazine*.[75]

October 16, 1912: Supreme Court Receives World Series Updates While in Session

In an act of "unprecedented procedure,"[76] a court page slips notes on the progress of the final game of the World Series between the Red Sox and Giants to U.S. Supreme Court Justice William R. Day, the Court's "First Fan of Baseball,"[77] during oral arguments in the Bathtub Trust case.[78] Per Day's instruction, the bulletins are delivered to the court "inning by inning" and "passed along the bench from Justice to Justice,"[79] which will lead some observers to wonder whether "the Bathtub Trust was forgotten,"[80] at least temporarily. There is no extant report as to whether Day and his colleagues are pleased with the 3-2 Red Sox victory at Boston's new Fenway Park which secures the team's second World Series championship.

October 22, 1912: Bresnahan Sues Cardinals Owner After Dismissal as Manager

St. Louis Cardinals owner Helene Britton, baseball's first female owner (see entries for March 24, 1911, and May 20, 1912), fires Cardinals manager Roger Bresnahan after he unleashes a profanity-laced tirade against her for questioning his leadership to the press.[81] With four years remaining on a five-year, $10,000 a year contract (plus 10 percent of the profits) signed after the Cardinals' success in the 1911 season, Bresnahan will file suit against Britton after his dismissal.[82] Although the Chicago Cubs will purchase Bresnahan on June 8, 1913,[83] the litigation will continue for more than two years before Bresnahan accepts $20,000 to settle the suit.[84] In the meantime, Britton will replace Bresnahan as manager of the Cardinals with Miller Huggins, the team's second-baseman, thereby setting the erstwhile lawyer on a path that will eventually lead him to the National Baseball Hall of Fame.[85]

1913

February 17, 1913: Assumption of Risk a Defense Against Injury from Foul Ball

Judge J.M. Johnson of the Missouri Court of Appeals decides that the owners of the Kansas City Blues of the American Association are not liable in negligence for the injuries suffered by S.J. Crane when struck by a foul ball during a game at the Blues' Association Park.[86] Crane sought $100 and costs in damages, but Johnson determines that he assumed the risk of injury and also was contributorily negligent when he chose a seat in the unscreened grandstands beyond third base. The case appears to be the first appellate court opinion to consider a tort action involving an injury to a spectator resulting from a foul ball at a professional baseball game.[87]

March 8, 1913: Federal League Formed, Challenges AL and NL for Players

The Federal League of Professional Baseball Clubs (Federal League), an outgrowth of two failed 1912 ventures, the Columbian and the United States leagues, is formed in Indianapolis with six franchises and a goal of becoming a third major league.[88] Using former major league stars such as Cy Young

(Cleveland Green Sox) as managers and minor league and semipro stars as players, the league will manage to successfully complete its inaugural 1913 season. But in 1914, feeling that Organized Baseball's reserve clause is legally unenforceable, the upstart league will embark on a campaign to attract established major league players from the American and National leagues to the venture.[89] The effort will spawn numerous lawsuits, with the outcome of several favoring the Federal League (see entries for April 23, 1914 (George "Chief" Johnson), June 22, 1914 (Armando Marsans), and July 21, 1914 (Hal Chase), but the league will fold after the 1915 season (see entry for December 17, 1915). Further litigation involving the Baltimore Federal League franchise ultimately will lead to a decision by the United States Supreme Court which establishes an antitrust exemption for major league baseball (see entry for May 29, 1922).

1914

January 6, 1914: Players' Fraternity Achieves Victory with "Cincinnati Agreement"

Just 16 months after its birth (see entry for September 6, 1912), the Players' Fraternity achieves a "huge victory" in what will become known as the "Cincinnati Agreement" when the National Commission, during its annual meeting at the Sinton Hotel in Cincinnati, accedes to a majority of the 17 demands for changes in player contracts contained in a petition signed by nearly 500 players and submitted by the Fraternity to the commission on November 8, 1913.[90] Many of the proposals adopted in whole or part by the commission cover communications and working conditions, but it also accepts a recommendation that a ten-year veteran should become a free agent if he is waived and not claimed (dubbed the Brown Rule in honor of Mordecai "Three-Finger" Brown).[91] The Cincinnati Agreement will be hailed as evidence that the Fraternity "is now a reality" and that the players have "really united and ... [are] a power to be considered."[92] However, just three years later, the Fraternity's position will have been so weakened by a failed strike attempt and the collapse of the Federal League that the National Commission will revoke the Agreement on February 13, 1917, and sever its relationship with the union.[93]

April 10, 1914: Judge Holds Reserve Clause Unenforceable in Killefer Case

Federal District Court Judge Clarence W. Sessions rules the reserve clause in the 1913 contract between the National League's Philadelphia Phillies and catcher William "Reindeer Bill" Killefer is unenforceable in equity because it lacks "the necessary qualities of definiteness, certainty and mutuality." The team could "terminate [the contract] at anytime upon 10 days notice," which, according to Judge Sessions, made it "nothing more than a contract to enter into a contract, in the future, if the parties can agree to contract."[94] Nevertheless, the judge refuses to grant the injunction sought by Charles Weeghman to prevent Reindeer Bill from returning to the Phillies despite signing a three-year contract with Weeghman's Chicago Federal League team, ruling that the Whales owner lacks "clean hands," having "induced [Killefer] to repudiate his obligation to his employer [the Phillies]" by offering him a contract with a "longer term of employment and a much larger compensation."[95] Edward Gates, general counsel of the Federal League, characterizes the decision as a "victory" because of the repudiation of the reserve clause, but George Wharton Pepper, representing Killefer and the Phillies, is "publicly pleased" with the outcome.[96]

April 23, 1914: Court Refuses to Stop "Chief" Johnson's Jump to Federal League

Judge Charles M. Foell of the Cook County, Illinois, Superior Court grants a preliminary injunction sought by the Cincinnati Reds of the National League against the club's former pitcher, George H. "Chief" Johnson,[97] to stop him from playing for the Kansas City Packers (or Kawfeds) of the Federal League.[98] Foell will sustain the preliminary injunctions on June 6,[99] but on July 16, the Illinois Appellate Court will reverse Foell's decision and find for Johnson based on a lack of mutuality in the ten-day release clause.[100] Johnson will return to the mound for Kansas City on July 25 in Buffalo.[101]

June 22, 1914: Temporary Injunction Stops Marsans from Jumping to Federal League

A week after Armando Marsans jumped from the Cincinnati Reds to the St. Louis Terriers of the Federal League for a three-year, $21,000 deal, federal judge Walter H. Sanborn issues a temporary injunction preventing him from playing for the Federal League team.[102] Sanborn reasons that "the court may issue an injunction to prevent him from violating the negative covenant [not to play for another team] in order to induce him to perform his contract."[103] In a major blow to the Federal League, the hearing on the permanent injunction, originally set for July 8, will be postponed until after the end of the season. The Cuban-born outfielder will remain sidelined for more than a year until federal judge David Dyer lifts the temporary injunction on August 19, 1915, freeing Marsans to play for the Terriers.[104] But the loss of playing time will dull his skills, and Marsans will end his career during the abbreviated 1918 season as a part-time player for the New York Yankees.[105]

July 21, 1914: Hal Chase's White Sox Contract Lacks Mutuality and Is Unenforceable

Citing cases involving John Montgomery Ward, Buck Ewing, and Napoleon Lajoie (see entries for January 28, 1890, March 25, 1890, and April

21, 1902) as precedent, New York Supreme Court Judge Herbert Bissell decides in favor of Hal Chase in a suit brought by the Chicago White Sox to prevent its star first baseman from jumping to the Buffalo Blues of the Federal League.[106] Believing that the 10-day cancellation clause in the standard contract required by the National Commission should be available to the player as well as the team, Chase had notified the White Sox on June 15 of his intention to become a free agent, causing it to seek to enjoin "Prince Hal" from playing for any team other than the Pale Hose. Since the clause gave only the team, not the player, the option of cancelling the contract with 10 days notice, Bissell determines that the contract lacks mutuality and renders a player chattel, stating that "the quasi peonage of baseball players under the operations of this plan and agreement is contrary to the spirit of American institutions, and ... the Constitution of the United States."[107] But Chase's contention that Organized Baseball is in violation of the Sherman Antitrust Act fails, Bissell concluding that players are not "commodities or articles of merchandise" and therefore rejecting "the proposition that the business of baseball for profit is interstate trade or commerce."[108] Nonetheless, the defense's "novel argument," as termed by Judge Bissell, constituted what one author identifies as "the first challenge to baseball which involved the antitrust laws."[109]

1915

January 5, 1915: Federal League Files Antitrust Suit Against Organized Baseball

The Federal League files suit against Organized Baseball and members of the National Commission in federal district court in Chicago for conspiring to restrain trade in violation of federal antitrust statutes by interfering with its attempts to sign major league players no longer under contract to a National or American League team (though still bound by the reserve clause of their prior contract).[110] Later in the month, on January 20–23, a four-day hearing is held before Judge Kenesaw Mountain Landis who will then withhold judgment in the case for more than a year.[111] In early 1916, Landis will dismiss the suit at the request of the parties after they finalize negotiations in the "Cincinnati Peace Agreement" of December 1915 (see entries for February 7, 1916, and December 17, 1915, respectively).

January 9, 1915: National Commission Voids Contract Sisler Signed as Minor

With Cincinnati president and part owner August "Garry" Herrmann casting the deciding vote,[112] the National Commission rules that the contract signed in 1910 by George Sisler to play for the Akron Champs of the Ohio & Pennsylvania League, subsequently purchased by Pittsburgh Pirates owner Barney Dreyfuss, is void because it lacks the signature of the then 17-year-old high school student's father. After the commission makes him a free agent, Sisler, now 22 and a University of Michigan graduate, will sign with the St. Louis Browns, managed by Branch Rickey, his college coach and a licensed attorney who first took the case to the commission on his player's behalf. Dreyfuss will contest the signing on the grounds of alleged tampering and interference by Rickey but, a year later on June 10, 1916, the National Commission will reject his grievance and declare Sisler's contract with St. Louis legitimate.[113]

December 17, 1915: Peace Agreement Between Federal League and Organized Baseball

At the Biltmore Hotel in New York, Federal League President James A. Gilmore announces to a group of club executives that he and Harry Sinclair, owner of the Newark franchise, have reached a tentative peace agreement with Organized Baseball that will end the Federal League.[114] The agreement will be finalized at the Sinton Hotel in Cincinnati on December 22.[115] It will allow Charles Weeghman, the Chicago Federal League owner, to purchase the National League Cubs, and grant Philip Ball, primary financier of the Federal League's St. Louis Terriers, an option to purchase the American League St. Louis Browns. Brooklyn Federal League owner Robert Ward will be paid $400,000 over twenty years, and the Pittsburgh Federal League team will accept $50,000. The agreement grants amnesty to former Federal League players and both sides agree to drop the federal antitrust lawsuit currently awaiting the decision of Judge Landis (see entry for February 7, 1916).[116] The Baltimore Federal club is unsuccessful in gaining satisfactory concessions, however, so a seven-person committee is charged with resolving the remaining issues (see entry for March 29, 1916).[117]

1916

February 7, 1916: Landis Dismisses Federal League's Suit Against Organized Baseball

During a proceeding at which he dismisses "without prejudice" the antitrust case brought by the Federal League against the National and American Leagues in light of the settlement reached between the parties in December 1915 (see entry for December 17, 1915), Federal District Court Judge Kenesaw Mountain Landis explains why he failed to render a decision in the case for nearly 13 months after presiding at a single, four-day hearing in January 1915 (see entry for January 5, 1915). Landis states that he would have been compelled to find in favor of the Federal League, an outcome that "would have been if not destructive, vitally injurious to the subject matter of the litigation" (i.e., Organized Baseball).[118] Instead, he chose to postpone deciding the case until the parties were forced to negotiate a settlement.

March 4, 1916: Bresnahan Settles Dispute with Cubs Over Managerial Contract

After threatening to file a lawsuit to enforce the two remaining years on his managerial contract with the Chicago Cubs,[119] Roger Bresnahan agrees with new Cubs owner Charles Weeghman to accept a $10,000 settlement in lieu of managing the club. Bresnahan also is to receive financial assistance in purchasing a controlling interest in his hometown Toledo franchise in the American Association.[120] Weeghman, who won the right to purchase the Cubs as a result of the peace agreement that dissolved the Federal League (see entry for December 17, 1915), had wanted Whales manager Joe Tinker at the helm of his new team—not Bresnahan—after the peace agreement allowed him to combine the rosters of the Federal League Whales and the National League Cubs.[121]

March 29, 1916: Baltimore Feds Sue Organized Baseball Over Peace Agreement

After an appointed committee fails to resolve issues lingering after the December 1915 peace agreement between Organized Baseball and the Federal League (see entry for December 17, 1915), the latter's Baltimore club files an antitrust suit in federal district court in Philadelphia against the American and National Leagues, the National Commission, and ex-Federal Leaguer executives Jim Gilmore, Charles Weeghman, and Harry Sinclair, seeking damages of $300,000 that would be trebled to $900,000.[122] The trial will begin on June 11, 1917, but on June 15, Stuart Janney, Baltimore's counsel as well as a shareholder in the team, feeling that the case is not developing properly, will surprise the court and the defendants by requesting that the court allow him to "formally file a motion of discontinuance" without reaching a settlement.[123] The club will later resume the lawsuit and the U.S. Supreme Court ultimately renders a decision in which it establishes baseball's antitrust exemption, impacting the sport for decades to come (see entry for May 29, 1922).

1917

April 14, 1917: Future MLBPA Executive Director Marvin Miller Is Born

Described by Studs Terkel as "the most effective union organizer since John L. Lewis," Marvin Miller, future executive director of the Major League Baseball Players Association, is born in a small apartment on Beck Street in the Bronx, New York.[124] After growing up a Dodger fan in Flatbush, Brooklyn, Miller will graduate from New York University in 1938 with a degree in economics.[125] During World War II, he will work for the War Production Board, the War Manpower Commission, and the National War Labor Board.[126] Following post-war stints with the International Association of Machinists and United Auto Workers, Miller will join the United Steelworkers in 1950, eventually becoming its principal economic adviser and chief contract negotiator.[127] He will work alongside Arthur Goldberg,[128] later a justice of the U.S. Supreme Court and the lead attorney in *Flood v. Kuhn* (see entries for December 24, 1969, March 4, 1970, and June 19, 1972). In 1966, Miller will be elected executive director of the Major League Baseball Players Association (see entry for March 5, 1966).

1918

June 17, 1918: A's Enjoin National Commission from Interfering with Scott Perry Sale

In the Court of Common Pleas in Cleveland, Connie Mack and the Philadelphia Athletics of the American League seek and receive an injunction restraining the National Commission, baseball's ruling body, from interfering with their title to, and use of, the services of pitcher Scott Perry.[129] The Commission had awarded Perry to the National League's Boston Braves on June 12, conditioned on a payment of $2,000 the team owed to the Southern Association's Atlanta Crackers in a previous dispute over Perry. After failing to receive payment, the Crackers had sold Perry to Mack during spring training in 1918, engendering the dispute between the Braves and the A's. National League owners angered by Mack's defiance of the Commission—it was the first time any team challenged a Commission decision in court[130]—are convinced that American League president Ban Johnson is behind the action. Nonetheless, they will refuse to break relations with the American League, leading NL president John Tener to resign on August 6, 1918. Within a few months, in October 1918, the teams will settle the Perry matter when the A's agree to pay $2,500 to the Braves.[131]

July 19, 1918: Baseball Ruled Nonessential Occupation, Players Must Serve During World War

When Washington Senators catcher Eddie Ainsworth appeals the decision of his local board to cancel his deferred classification under new work-or-fight regulations effective July 1, 1918, Secretary of War Newton D. Baker declares that baseball is a nonessential occupation and thus players are not exempt from military service in World War I.[132] In responding to the assertion that placing the continuation of the national game in jeopardy will "work a social and industrial harm far out of proportion to the military loss involved by the exemption of the limited number of players in question," Baker notes that "the times are not normal, ... we all must make sacrifices, ... [and] our people are resourceful enough to find other means of recreation and relaxation if there be not enough persons beyond the useful military age ... to perform such functions...."[133] With team rosters slashed by so many players having to choose between military service or employment in war-related industries, the season will be cut short by five weeks, ending on Labor Day, September 2, 1918, resulting in the cancellation of about 25 games for each team.[134]

1919

January 31, 1919: Jackie Robinson Is Born in Georgia

Jack (John) Roosevelt Robinson, who will go on to break the color line in Organized Baseball (see entries for October 23, 1945, and April 10, 1947), is born in Cairo, Georgia, although his mother will move the family to Pasadena, California, in 1920, after his father Jerry abandons the family.[135] Robinson will attend John Muir Technical High School and Pasadena Community College before transferring to the University of California, Los Angeles.[136] In his years at UCLA, 1939–1941, he will become the only athlete in the school's history to letter in four sports—baseball, football, basketball, and track—and will excel in others as well, such as swimming and tennis.[137]

April 19, 1919: Local Option Law Leads to First "Legal" Sunday Games in New York

New York Governor Al Smith, a future presidential candidate, signs the "Sunday Baseball Law" permitting cities, towns, or villages to pass an ordinance allowing the playing of baseball after 2:00 pm on Sundays.[138] Senator James J. "Jimmy" Walker, who will use the support of Tammany Hall to become mayor of New York in 1926, introduced the bill that overcame more than a decade of frustration for proponents of Sunday games in New York City.[139] The city's Board of Alderman will quickly respond by passing an enabling ordinance on April 29, and five days later, on May 4, the New York Giants will draw 35,000 to the Polo Grounds and the Brooklyn Dodgers 25,000 to Ebbets Field for the first "legal" Sunday games.[140]

July 13, 1919: Court Order Halts Suspension of Carl Mays by Ban Johnson

In a game against the Chicago White Sox at Comiskey Park, Boston Red Sox pitcher Carl Mays stalks off the field in the second inning, declaring, "I'll never pitch for this club again!" He was struck in the back of the head by a throw to second base from his own catcher, Wally Schang, the last straw in a series of events that causes Mays to leave the team, telling reporters he needs to make a fresh start with a new team.[141] American League President Ban Johnson orders club owners not to discuss a trade for Mays with Boston owner Harry Frazee.[142] Despite the edict, New York Yankees owners Colonel Tillinghast L'Hommedieau Hustin and Jacob Ruppert will complete a deal on July 29 with Frazee that brings Mays to New York.[143] Johnson will respond by suspending Mays and directing league umpires not to allow him to play in any games.[144] But the New York Supreme Court will grant the Yankee owners' request to enjoin Johnson from preventing the participation of Mays in any games, and the submarine style pitcher will take the mound against the St. Louis Browns on August 7 after umpires are served with a court order on the field at the Polo Grounds.[145] Finally, on October 25, 1919, New York Supreme Court Judge Robert F. Wagner will permanently enjoin Johnson from suspending Mays.[146]

1920

February 10, 1920: AL Owners Defy Ban Johnson, Uphold Mays Trade to Yankees

In a meeting at the Congress Hotel in Chicago which stretches until the early hours of the following morning, American League owners craft an agreement that upholds the trade of Carl Mays from the Red Sox to the Yankees (see entry for July 13, 1919), which had been challenged by League President Ban Johnson, and creates a two-man committee (comprised of Yankees co-owner Jacob Ruppert and Senators owner Clark Griffith) to review any fines over $100 and suspensions over 10 days imposed by Johnson.[147] In return, the Yankees agree to withdraw their lawsuits against Johnson and other league officials, but when the dust settles it is clear that Yankee co-owners Ruppert and Tillinghast L'Hommedieau Huston now control the American League owners group. The hiring of Judge Kenesaw Mountain Landis as commissioner later in the year (see entry for November 12, 1920) will further diminish Johnson's control, a pattern that will continue until he is finally replaced in 1927.[148]

February 13–14, 1920: Negro National League Founded with Rube Foster as President

The Negro National League—officially called the National Association of Colored Professional Base Ball Clubs—is founded at the Paseo YMCA, located at 1824 Paseo Boulevard in the Jazz District of Kansas City, Missouri. The new league includes the American Giants (Chicago), Cuban Stars (although based in Harlem under the direction of Alex Pompez, they lacked a playing site and essentially were a permanent road team for much of their existence[149]), Indianapolis ABCs, Dayton Marcos, Detroit Stars, Kansas City Monarchs, and St. Louis Giants. A future member of the National Baseball Hall of Fame, Andrew "Rube" Foster, is elected president, and attorney Elisha Scott of Topeka, Kansas, and journalists Elwood Knox (*Indianapolis Freeman*), Cary B. Lewis (*Chicago Defender*), and Dave Wyatt (*Indianapolis Ledger*) draft the league's constitution.[150]

April 14, 1920: Magee Loses Suit Against Cubs When He Admits Role in Fixing Game

Unconditionally released by the Chicago Cubs in winter 1920, Lee Magee, a former Federal League star (he hit .323 for the Brooklyn Tip Tops in 1915), files a civil damages suit for breach of contract against the team in the Court of Common Pleas, Hamilton County (Cincinnati); the suit is later removed to federal district court on diversity of citizenship grounds.[151] Over the course of the litigation, evidence will show that on February 20, 1920, Magee had confessed to Cubs owner William L. Veeck, Sr., and National League President John Heydler his involvement, along with Cincinnati Reds teammate Hal Chase, in a plan to fix the game between the Reds and Boston Braves on July 25, 1918.[152] Despite Magee's testimony that he had intended to bet on, not against, the Reds and was double-crossed by Chase, the jury will find in favor of the Cubs after deliberating for only 44 minutes.[153] Commissioner Kenesaw Mountain Landis will ban Magee from baseball for life after he takes office later in the year (see entry for November 12, 1920).

August 7, 1920: John McGraw Arrested After Lambs Club Brawl

Following his team's 5–2 loss to the Chicago Cubs, New York Giants manager John McGraw engages in a night of drinking with actor William Boyd and others, ending at the Lambs Club on West 44th Street. In the early morning hours, a brawl breaks out with the heavily intoxicated Muggsy at its center. In the end, McGraw severely beats comedian James Slavin who makes the mistake of helping the manager home.[154] With no witnesses willing to testify, McGraw will be indicted on October 29, but only for illegal possession of alcohol. Represented by William "The Great Mouthpiece" Fallon, famed Manhattan defense attorney who later will help Arnold Rothstein avoid indictment by the Black Sox grand jury (see entry for October 29, 1920), McGraw will be acquitted by a jury in less than five minutes when the case finally goes to trial in May 1921.[155]

September 15, 1920: Babe Ruth Loses Court Battle Over Use of His Image in Films

Justice Charles Guy of the New York Supreme Court refuses to grant a permanent injunction sought by Babe Ruth against Educational Films Corporation, which had spliced together newsreel footage of the popular Yankee slugger into a series of one-reel "Babe Ruth Instructional Films." Ruth sought to prevent the showing of the films in New York without his approval and also filed a $1 million civil damages suit based on the state's civil rights law regarding use of an individual's image. This led to a countersuit by Educational Films for defamation of character.[156] In denying the injunction, Justice Guy rules the civil rights law does not apply and that Ruth's image and actions are current news and thus appropriate subjects for pictures taken without his permission.[157] With this ruling, later affirmed by the court's appellate division,[158] all parties will drop their suits and countersuits.

September 19, 1920: Ruth Pursues Breach of Contract Claim Against Movie Producer

Headin' Home, a baseball-themed motion picture starring Yankee slugger Babe Ruth filmed in early August in New Jersey and on location in New York City (Ruth was on set in the mornings, at the Polo Grounds in the afternoon), premieres at Madison Square Garden to a crowd variously estimated at 6,000 to 10,000, garnering a decent review from the *New York Times*.[159] The film is financed in part by gambler Abe Attell, soon to be indicted for his role in the Black Sox World Series-fixing scandal (see entry for October 29, 1920).[160] Promised $50,000 in the contract he signed with producer William Shea in June 1920, Ruth received a check for $15,000 while making the film, but a second check for $35,000 given to Ruth at its completion will prove worthless when the film company collapses.[161] Claiming breach of contract, Ruth will file a civil rights claim in October to enjoin Shea and the film's distributor, but the New York State Supreme Court will find the argument inappropriate. In November, Shea's company will file for bankruptcy, thereby removing any chance of Ruth collecting the money owed to him.[162]

September 28, 1920: Cicotte and Jackson Admit Black Sox Role to Grand Jury

In testimony under oath before the Cook County Grand Jury, White Sox players Eddie Cicotte and Joe Jackson admit accepting payments to fix the 1919 World Series between the Sox and the Cincinnati Reds.[163] Earlier in the morning the players had made the same admission to White Sox legal counsel Alfred Austrian and Assistant State's Attorney Hartley Replogle during separate meetings in Austrian's law office. Neither confesses to making a deliberate misplay, however, despite press reports to the contrary.[164] White Sox owner Charles A. Comiskey immediately responds, suspending indefinitely seven of the eight players accused of fixing the 1919 World Series: Eddie Cicotte, Oscar "Happy" Felsch, Joe Jackson, Fred McMullin, Charles "Swede" Risberg, George "Buck" Weaver, and Claude "Lefty" Williams. The eighth, Chick Gandil, was already suspended in the spring for failing to report to the team.[165] A day later, on September 29, Williams, the losing pitcher in three of the games, will admit his part in the conspiracy to fix the 1919 World Series, first to Austrian and then in testimony before the grand jury. Like his teammates, he will claim not to have done anything wrong on the diamond, but unlike Cicotte and Jackson, he also will identify by name some of the gamblers who were at the meetings at which the fix was discussed prior to the series.[166]

October 29, 1920: Grand Jury Indicts Players and Gamblers in Black Sox Scandal

In Chicago, at the conclusion of proceedings which included testimony by National Commission chairman and Cincinnati Reds President Garry Herrmann, American League President Ban Johnson, and gambler Arnold Rothstein among others, the Cook County Grand Jury formally returns indictments against various individuals for their alleged role in conspiring to fix the 1919 World Series between the Chicago White Sox and the Cincinnati Reds. Charged with five counts of conspiracy to obtain money by false pretenses, means of a confidence game, or both, are eight White Sox players (Cicotte, Jackson, Weaver, Gandil, Risberg, Williams, Felsch, and McMullin); four gamblers (Bill "Sleepy" Burns, Joseph "Sport" Sullivan, Rachael Brown, and Abe Attell); and fix intermediary, the notorious Hal Chase. Not indicted is Rothstein, the reputed mastermind of the conspiracy.[167]

November 12, 1920: Kenesaw Mountain Landis Is First Baseball Commissioner

In the wake of the growing scandal over allegations of a 1919 World Series fix, Kenesaw Mountain Landis, a federal judge for the Northern District of Illinois, accepts the offer by team owners to become the first commissioner of baseball, replacing the three-man National Commission which has governed the sport since 1903. Landis takes the position for seven years at a salary of $50,000, on the condition he can retain his position as a judge.[168] Landis will reign as commissioner for 24 years until his death from a heart attack on November 25, 1944, five days after his 78th birthday. Two weeks later he will be voted into the National Baseball Hall of Fame by a special vote.

CHAPTER 4

Landis in Charge, 1921–1944

Introduction

Judge Landis moved quickly to consolidate his power as baseball's new commissioner. While fending off a Congressional impeachment attempt because he remained an active federal judge while engaged in his new role in baseball, Landis acted boldly to finally bring an end to the long history of gambling's influence on the game. In his very first year in office, he acted decisively in imposing a lifetime ban on all eight members of the Black Sox despite their acquittal by a Chicago jury. Even the transcendent, home-run hitting Babe Ruth, viewed by some as baseball's savior, was not immune from the judge's reach. Landis fined and suspended the Bambino and two teammates for violating the major league rule prohibiting World Series participants from barnstorming after the season.

Less worthy of commendation was the game's continuing ill treatment of African American players. Yet, despite Major League Baseball's rigid though unwritten ban against their participation, this period saw the establishment of parallel professional circuits. The Negro National League was founded in 1920, followed two years later by the creation of the Eastern Colored League and, in 1924, the first Negro World Series. Still, African American players remained outside of Major League Baseball for the remainder of Landis's reign.

Intense interest in baseball, as well as boxing, football, golf, horse racing, and tennis, served to mark the 1920s as the Golden Age of Sports. The New York Yankees emerged as the game's dominant franchise, with the larger-than-life Ruth extending his influence—and contact with the law—far outside the diamond. But even in this boom period for the sport, tensions over the governance of the game remained. Ban Johnson's criticism of the commissioner for not dealing harshly with Ty Cobb and Tris Speaker over a fixed game in 1919 forced a showdown with Landis, who was able to successfully undermine the power of the longtime American League president. Johnson was forced out by American League owners after the 1927 season. A broken man, Johnson died in 1931.

The economic health of the game was exemplified by rising salaries. By the beginning of the 1930s, Ruth's salary exceeded that of President Herbert Hoover. Landis continued to control the game. For instance, over the objections of the minor league Des Moines Demons, he declared that teenager Bob Feller would remain the property of the Cleveland Indians. In separate rulings, he awarded free agent status to nearly 200 minor league farmhands of the St. Louis Cardinals and Detroit Tigers because of practices he deemed harmful to the sport's health. At the start of World War II, President Roosevelt responded to Landis's query about whether baseball should continue by granting the "Green Light" to provide the American people with both recreation and a diversion. At Roosevelt's suggestion, night baseball expanded. Landis also declared that Organized Baseball would not seek any exemptions from the military draft for its players.

In August 1944, a young African American Army lieutenant named Jack Roosevelt Robinson, charged with insubordination for refusing a bus driver's demand that he move to the back of the bus, was found not guilty by a court-martial board of nine judges at Camp Hood, Texas. Robinson's strength and courage will play a crucial role in Organized Baseball's post-war era which would commence a few months later when, after 24 years as the sport's first commissioner, Kenesaw Mountain Landis died while still in office on November 25, 1944, five days after his 78th birthday.

1921

January 12, 1921: New National Agreement Establishes Powers of Commissioner

The National and American leagues and the owners of their constituent clubs adopt a new national agreement which officially creates, and establishes the primacy of, the office of Commissioner, and designates Kenesaw M. Landis as the first commissioner.[1] The final language is drafted by a committee of four lawyers: George Wharton Pepper, John Conway Toole, James C. Jones, and Landis himself.[2] It details the powers of the commissioner, including the ability to declare a player "temporarily or permanently ineligible" for "conduct detrimental to base ball."[3] In a side agreement, the owners pledge their loyalty to Landis and agree not to criticize him in public.[4]

February 21, 1921: Congressman Welty Proposes Impeachment of Judge Landis

During a U.S. House Judiciary Committee hearing, Congressman Benjamin Welty of Ohio submits a proposed impeachment of Kenesaw Mountain Landis as a federal district judge.[5] Welty and others are angered that Landis has continued to serve as a federal judge in Chicago after his appointment as the first commissioner of Major League Baseball in 1920. They are concerned that he is neglecting his judicial duties in favor of his work as commissioner and about the conflict of interest inherent in holding both positions. The committee fails to impeach Landis, but the controversy will continue to fester for a year, until Landis finally submits his resignation as a federal judge to President Warren G. Harding on February 18, 1922.[6]

February 21, 1921: Christy Walsh Inks Babe Ruth, Becomes First Player Agent

With a single, typed sheet signed at New York's Penn Station as Babe Ruth prepares to leave for Hot Springs, Arkansas, Christy Walsh becomes baseball's first player agent by contracting to syndicate ghost-written articles in Ruth's name ("By Babe Ruth") for 50 percent of the gross receipts. Trained as a lawyer, Walsh had worked as a sports cartoonist and ghostwriter for world war flying ace Eddie Rickenbacker before cadging a meeting with Ruth by volunteering to deliver a case of bootleg beer to the slugger at his apartment in the Ansonia Hotel.[7] In addition to becoming Ruth's friend, business manager, and booking agent, Walsh will go on to represent many of sport's greatest figures, including Lou Gehrig, Knute Rockne, John McGraw, and Ty Cobb.[8]

April 7, 1921: Landis Permanently Suspends Benny Kauff Despite Acquittal in Criminal Trial

Commissioner Kennesaw Mountain Landis indefinitely suspends New York Giants outfielder Benny Kauff pending resolution of criminal charges against him for car theft and receiving stolen property. Although he will be acquitted by a jury on May 13, 1921, Landis still refuses to reinstate him, setting a precedent he will follow a few months later when dealing with the eight players found not guilty in the Black Sox criminal trial (see entry for August 2, 1921).[9] As Landis will explain in a letter to Kauff on August 25, 1921, "your mere presence in the lineup would inevitably burden patrons of the game with grave apprehensions as to its integrity."[10] Now on the permanently ineligible list, Kauff will secure a temporary injunction against Landis and the National League, but on January 17, 1922, Justice Edward Whitaker will reject Kauff's request to make it permanent, concluding that the New York State Supreme Court has no grounds to act on the request despite noting that "an apparent injustice has been done the plaintiff [Kauff]."[11] Kauff, known as the "Ty Cobb of the Feds" after leading the Federal League in hitting and stolen bases during its two seasons of existence (1914–15), will remain on the "permanently ineligible" list even after his death in 1961, at the age of 71.

May 16, 1921: "Reuben's Rule" Leads to Change in Stadium Foul Ball Policy

While attending a game between the New York Giants and the Cincinnati Reds at the Polo Grounds in New York, Reuben Berman, a 31-year-old stockbroker catches a foul ball hit into the stands. Like many teams in Major League Baseball at the time, the Giants' policy is that foul balls must be returned to the team. But Berman refuses to do so—in fact, he throws the ball into the stands rather than give it back to the attendant—and eventually the Giants remove him from the ballpark, although they refund his ticket. Not content with this outcome, on August 12, 1921, Berman will file suit against the Giants, alleging that the team unlawfully detained, imprisoned, and threatened him; he will ask for $20,000 to cover the humiliation, mental and bodily distress, and loss of reputation he claims to have suffered. When the case goes to trial, the jury will find for Berman but only award him $100.[12] Nonetheless, "Reuben's Ruling," as it will become known, will lead the Giants to change its policy about foul balls, and other major league teams will soon follow suit.[13]

June 27, 1921: Black Sox Criminal Trial Begins in Chicago

The case of *State of Illinois v. Cicotte et al.* commences in the Chicago court room of Judge Hugo Friend. Jury selection will begin on July 5 and conclude on July 16, resulting in a panel of 12 "mostly working class white men, ... none of whom professed to being much of a baseball fan."[14] State's Attorney George Gorman, the lead prosecutor, will deliver his opening statement to the jury on July 18, detailing the plot to fix the 1919 World Series and describing the role of the indicted Black Sox figures, both players and gamblers, as well as others who were involved but not defendants in the current prosecution (such as Arnold Rothstein and Abe Attell).[15]

August 2, 1921: Jury Acquits Black Sox Players, Landis Banishes Them Anyway

After deliberating for less than three hours and taking a single ballot, a Chicago jury returns a verdict of not guilty for each defendant on all charges in the Black Sox criminal trial.[16] Despite the acquittal, on the very next day, August 3, Commissioner Kenesaw Mountain Landis will announce that he is banishing the eight Chicago White Sox players implicated in the plot to fix the 1919 World Series from baseball for life: Eddie Cicotte, Oscar "Happy" Felsch, Arnold "Chick" Gandil, "Shoeless" Joe Jackson, Fred McMullin, Charles "Swede" Risberg, George "Buck" Weaver, and Claude "Lefty" Williams.[17] They will never be reinstated.

December 5, 1921: Landis Suspends Ruth and Others for Post-World Series Play

Commissioner Kenesaw Mountain Landis suspends three standout New York Yankees players, Babe Ruth, Bob Meusel, and Bill Piercy, from the beginning of the 1922 season through May 20, and fines each the amount of their 1921 World Series winnings for flagrantly violating the major league rule which prohibits series participants from barnstorming after the season.[18] Landis declares that "this case resolves itself into a question of who is the biggest man in baseball, the Commissioner or the player who makes the most home runs."[19] With the commissioner's power secure, the owners will later alter the rule to allow World Series players to seek permission from the commissioner to participate in post season exhibitions. Following this change, Landis will allow the Babe to barnstorm after the Giants defeat the Yankees in the 1922 World Series.[20]

1922

April 26, 1922: Banned Black Sox Players File Civil Suits Against White Sox

Former White Sox center fielder Oscar "Happy" Felsch, expelled from Organized Baseball by Commissioner Landis for his role in the Black Sox scandal (see entry for August 2, 1921), files a civil suit against the Chicago White Sox in the Circuit Court of Wisconsin, Milwaukee County, seeking back pay and bonuses withheld by the team. Represented by Milwaukee attorney Raymond J. Cannon, Felsch will later amend the complaint to specify four claims: balance due on his 1920 contract; a withheld World Series bonus from 1917; injury to his professional reputation; and restraint on his livelihood caused by conspiracy to blacklist him.[21] A few weeks later, on May 12, Cannon will file civil actions against the White Sox on behalf of two more Black Sox players, Swede Risberg and Joe Jackson, in the Milwaukee circuit court. Risberg's claims are the same as those raised in the Felsch suit, but Jackson will allege breach of contract based on the three-year, $8,000 per-season pact he signed with the club in February 1920 and for which he had not been paid since owner Charles Comiskey voided it in March 1921. In addition to the unpaid wages and 1917 World Series bonus, Jackson also will ask for the same $100,000 defamation and restraint on livelihood damages sought by Felsch and Risberg.[22]

May 29, 1922: Supreme Court Establishes Antitrust Exemption in Federal Baseball

In a unanimous decision written by Justice Oliver Wendell Holmes, the U.S. Supreme Court renders a decision in *Federal Baseball Club v. National*

League of Professional Baseball Clubs that will come to be read as according Organized Baseball an exemption from federal antitrust laws.[23] The litigation resulted from the demise of the Federal League after the 1915 season based upon a peace agreement brokered between Federal League officials and representatives of the American and National leagues (see entry for December 17, 1915). Dissatisfied with its treatment under the agreement, the Baltimore Terrapins of the Federal League instituted a suit in federal court alleging that Organized Baseball was in violation of the Sherman Antitrust Act (see entry for March 29, 1916). Six years later, in finally deciding the case, the Supreme Court was faced with determining whether the Sherman Act could be applied to baseball. While many later commentators will focus on what they believe was the court's erroneous conclusion that baseball was not a form of interstate commerce and therefore not subject to the Act,[24] in fact the court saw the overriding issue as whether baseball was even commerce to begin with. In concert with a view commonly held at the time that it was not (see entry for June 8, 1922), Holmes will write that "the exhibition [of baseball], although made for money, would not be called trade or commerce in the commonly accepted use of those words. As it is put by the defendants, personal effort not related to production is not a subject of commerce. That which in its consummation is not commerce does not become commerce among the States because the transportation that we have mentioned takes place."[25] Years later, George Wharton Pepper, the National League's primary counsel in the case, will reiterate that his primary argument to the court was that "personal effort not related to production ... is not a subject of commerce; that the attempt to secure all the skilled service needed for professional baseball is not an attempt to monopolize commerce or any part of it; and that Organized Baseball, not being commerce, and therefore not interstate commerce, does not come within the scope of the prohibitions of the Sherman Act."[26]

June 8, 1922: Richter Analyzes *Federal Baseball* Decision for *Sporting News*

Francis C. Richter, editor of the weekly *Sporting Life* from its founding in 1883 until its demise in 1917, analyzes the recently decided Supreme Court case, *Federal Baseball Club v. National League of Professional Baseball Clubs* (see entry for May 29, 1922), for his one-time rival, the *Sporting News*. Focusing on an aspect of the case that will be long overlooked by subsequent courts and commentators, Richter writes that "the decision affirms that Organized Ball is not in any way a trust within the meaning of the law, that baseball, though played for money, is not trade or commerce, that it is a game entirely of personal effort, not related to production, and therefore not a subject of commerce...." He also notes a point frequently emphasized in later critiques of the Holmes opinion, that traveling between states by the teams does not provide the element necessary to subject Organized Baseball to the Constitution's interstate commerce clause.[27]

July 1, 1922: Illinois Enacts Sports Anti-Corruption Statute After Black Sox Scandal

The Illinois sports anti-corruption statute adopted in the wake of the Black Sox scandal becomes effective. The new statute makes it illegal to accept money, a bribe, or anything of value in return for failing to use one's best efforts in a professional or amateur athletic contest.[28] Although enacted on July 13, 1921, the prosecution in the Black Sox criminal trial had been unable to apply it retroactively to establish that the object of the alleged conspiracy—fixing the World Series—was an unlawful act in itself. Consequently, the prosecution had to "shoehorn" the fix charges into "some form of criminal fraud, such as obtaining money by false pretenses or via a confidence game," a gambit which was attacked by defense lawyers but eventually allowed by trial court judge Hugo Friend.[29]

August 22, 1922: Doak Patents First Fielder's Glove with Webbing

William L. Doak of Pittsburgh patents an improved fielder's glove that, for the first time, provides a webbing connecting the thumb and fingers of the glove.[30] In so doing, "Spittin' Bill," who will use his spitball to win 169 games as a pitcher for the Cardinals and Dodgers between 1913 and 1929, gives birth to the modern baseball glove, creating a pocket by which a player can catch balls away from the palm and one-handed, using the glove as a net of sorts to scoop the ball from the ground.[31] St. Louis-based Rawlings Sporting Goods will sell the "Premier Players' Glove," the first based on this revolutionary design, for $10 in 1920; the Bill Doak model glove will be a best-seller for years, still in production when its inventor passes away in Bradenton, Florida, on November 26, 1954.[32]

August 26, 1922: Cannon Seeks Players for National Baseball Players Association

Raymond J. Cannon, a Milwaukee attorney and former semi-professional baseball player who represented several Black Sox players in their civil suits against Charles Comiskey and the Chicago White Sox (see entry for April 26, 1922), sends a letter to all major and minor league players seeking their pledge to join the newly formed National Baseball Players Association.[33] Headed by Cannon, who will later represent Wisconsin in the U.S. Congress from 1933 to 1939 and whose son, Robert, will serve as a legal advisor to the Major League Baseball Players Association in the early 1960s (see entry for March 5, 1966), the NBPA is the fourth attempt to create a players' union (see entries for October 22, 1885, June 10, 1900, and September 6, 1912).[34] But it too will be unsuccessful, dissolving in the summer of 1923 "[u]nder a barrage of threats and promises from the owners."[35]

December 16, 1922: Ed Bolden Leads Formation of Eastern Colored League

Ed Bolden, owner of the Philadelphia-area Hilldale Daisies, an independent Negro team formed in 1910, is the guiding force behind the formation of the Eastern Colored League (Mutual Association of Eastern Colored Baseball Clubs) at the Christian Street YMCA in Philadelphia.[36] Owners of the league's six founding franchises—the Atlantic City Bacharach Giants (Thomas Jackson), Baltimore Black Sox (Charles Spedden), Brooklyn Royal Giants (Nat Strong), New York Cuban Stars (Alex Pompez), Hilldale (Bolden), and New York Lincoln Giants (James Keenan)—elect Bolden chairman of the commission which will run the league.[37] The ECL will directly compete with the Negro National League (NNL), formed in 1920 (see entry for February 13–14, 1920). The rival leagues eventually will reach a truce and establish the Negro World Series, first played in October 1924 between Bolden's Hilldale club and the Kansas City Monarchs of the NNL.[38]

1923

March 15, 1923: Paternity Suit Against Babe Ruth Dropped as "Frame-Up"

After Yankee outfielder and "home run king" Babe Ruth declines to reach an out-of-court settlement, attorney George Feinberg files a complaint in New York Supreme Court seeking $50,000 plus costs on behalf of a pregnant Dolores Dixon, who claims that Ruth is the father the child.[39] Dixon, a 19-year-old department store saleswoman, claims that she had regularly gone for rides with Ruth in his automobile and that he assaulted her on a yacht in Freeport, Long Island.[40] The lawsuit will be withdrawn on April 27 when Hyman Bushel, Ruth's attorney, announces in court that he has a signed confession from Dixon admitting that the "suit was the result of a frameup in which several persons were involved."[41]

March 20, 1923: Former Ump Johnstone Patents Improved Mask

The U.S. Patent Office issues a patent to James E. "Jim" Johnstone of Newark, New Jersey, for his "improved baseball mask."[42] Inventor Johnstone combined the knowledge of field conditions he acquired as a minor league pitcher (1894–1900) and umpire in three major leagues (American, National, and Federal, 1902–15) with the skills he developed as a metal molder and patternmaker in the offseason to create and manufacture the "Original Full Vision Mask."[43] Also referred to as the "platform mask," Johnstone's invention employs one-piece aluminum casting and horizontal crossbars instead of the soldered mesh of the earlier masks used by catchers and umpires.[44]

1924

February 14, 1924: Joe Jackson Arrested for Perjury, Loses Civil Suit

Judge John J. Gregory startles a Milwaukee courtroom by ordering the arrest of Joe Jackson just as the jury in the former White Sox star's breach of contract action against Charles Comiskey (see entry for April 26, 1922) retires to consider "ten special interrogatories ... designed to guide the jurors through the various issues ... and help them reach a just and rational verdict."[45] Gregory's unhappiness about Jackson's testimony prompts the jurist to declare that Jackson is "guilty of perjury, rank perjury ... in connection with the testimony he gave under oath before the Chicago grand jury."[46] When the jury returns an $18,000 verdict in Jackson's favor, Gregory is indignant and sets aside the verdict, "specifying fraud and perjured testimony" as grounds.[47] After a Jackson appeal, the Wisconsin Supreme Court dismisses Jackson's appeal on October 20, 1925, ultimately leaving the Black Sox scandal as one of the most remembered and oft-discussed events in Major League Baseball history.[48]

October 4, 1924: Coolidge Becomes First Sitting President to Attend World Series Opening Game

Although not really a baseball fan,[49] Calvin Coolidge becomes the first sitting American President to attend the opening game of a World Series when he throws out a ceremonial (and "wildly errant") first pitch at Game One between the Washington Senators and the New York Giants at Griffith Stadium in Washington, D.C.[50] On October 9, 1915, at the Baker Bowl in Philadelphia, Woodrow Wilson had launched a ceremonial pitch at the second game of the World Series between the Phillies and the Boston Red Sox, thereby becoming the first U.S. chief executive to attend a Series game.[51]

November 28, 1924: Negro National League Formally Chartered in Illinois

Although formed four years earlier (see entry for February 13–14, 1920), the Negro National League is formally chartered with $2,500 in common stock at $25 per share when its articles of incorporation are filed with the office of the Illinois Secretary of State. The five directors are Walter M. Farmer, Rube Foster, Willie Foster, Russell Thompson, and J.L. Wilkinson. The league's stated object is "the organizing, equipped [sic] and maintaining Baseball Clubs, composed of Colored Professional baseball players, sufficient to constitute and form a Circuit for the playing of championship games among the clubs belonging to The Negro National League of Professional Baseball Clubs." The league will officially dissolve on June 5, 1929.[52]

1926

October 28, 1926: Future Lawyer and Baseball Commissioner Bowie Kuhn Is Born

Bowie Kuhn, who will become the fifth commissioner of major league baseball, is born in Tacoma Park, Maryland.[53] After graduating from the University of Virginia School of Law in 1950, Kuhn will join the Wall Street law firm of Willkie Owen Farr Gallagher & Walton, counsel for the National League.[54] Soon after his election as commissioner in 1969 (see entry for February 4, 1969), Kuhn and others will be sued by Curt Flood in a case which solidifies baseball's antitrust exemption (see entries for December 24, 1969, March 4, 1970, and June 19, 1972). Over his tenure as commissioner, Kuhn will duel with owners Charlie Finley of the Oakland Athletics (see entries for June 14–15, 1976, and April 7, 1978) and Ted Turner of the Atlanta Braves (see entry for May 19, 1977), and ban legends Willie Mays and Mickey Mantle from the game for casino connections (see entry for October 26, 1979). Despite successes which include dramatic increases in attendance and revenue (particularly from television), realignment of leagues into divisions, and World Series games played at night, Kuhn ultimately angers owners over his stances on players' drug use and the labor unrest that produces the 1981 strike, and he will lose a protracted reelection bid in 1983.[55] Nonetheless, he will be selected to the National Baseball Hall of Fame in 2008.

December 3, 1926: Midge Donahue Is MLB's First Female Front-Office Executive

Margaret "Midge" Donahue becomes the first female front-office executive in Major League Baseball who is not also an owner when the Board of Trustees of the Chicago Cubs promotes her to the position of corporate secretary.[56] Donahue, who started with the club in 1919 when president William Veeck, Sr., hired her as a stenographer, will continue with the Cubs until her retirement as a vice-president in 1958.[57] Along the way, she will help Veeck popularize the weekly Ladies' Day at the Cubs' park; originate season tickets, off-site ticket sales (using Western Union offices), and discounted tickets for children; and come to be known as "the leading expert on baseball waiver transactions."[58]

1927

June 25, 1927: Pennsylvania Supreme Court Upholds Ban Against Sunday Baseball

Justice William Schaeffer and the Pennsylvania Supreme Court uphold the state's 1794 law banning "any worldly employment or business whatsoever on the Lord's day" (see entry for April 22, 1794), ruling that "we cannot imagine in this sense anything more worldy or unreligious in the way of employment than the playing of professional baseball as it is played today."[59] The court's opinion results from a decision by Athletics owners Connie Mack, John Shibe, and Tom Shibe to play a test game on Sunday, August 22, 1926, against the Chicago White Sox at Shibe Park. Lefty Grove pitched the A's to a 3–2 victory during a steady rain. The owners challenged the law in part to cover large expenditures for signing then minor leaguers Grove and Mickey Cochrane and to take advantage of the 1925 addition of a second deck at their ballpark.[60] Sunday baseball at Pennsylvania's three major league stadiums will not become legal until the legislature enacts a local option law in 1933 (see entry for April 25, 1933).

1928

November 6, 1928: Boston Approves Sunday Games After Referendum Allows Local Option

After the legislature consistently blocks attempts to enact a statute reversing the state's seventeenth-century Puritan blue law,[61] Massachusetts voters overwhelmingly approve a referendum providing communities the option of approving the playing of baseball and other sports on Sunday.[62] When the Boston City Council delays voting on an enabling ordinance, Braves owner Emil "Judge" Fuchs and vice president Charles Adams charge City Councilman William Lynch with requesting a $5,000 bribe for himself and each of 12 of his colleagues on November 23 in Fuchs's suite at the Copley Plaza Hotel. The Boston Finance Committee launches an investigation that largely undermines the position of Fuchs and Adams. Nonetheless, on January 29, 1929, the council finally passes a Sunday Sports Ordinance—officially "An Ordinance Concerning Professional Outdoor Sports on the Lord's Day"—which includes ten requirements.[63] One of the requirements, that no game can be held within a thousand feet of a church, will prevent the Boston Red Sox from playing Sunday games in Fenway Park for three seasons.[64]

1929

May 19, 1929: Yankee Stadium Fan Stampede Blamed on Ruth's Failure to Hit Home Run

Seventeen-year old Hunter College student Eleanor Pierce and 60 year-old truck driver Joseph Carter are killed and 62 are injured when "the sky suddenly open[s] up and a solid sheet of water, so dense as to obscure from sight objects only a few score feet away, roar[s] down" on the 9,000 fans sitting in Ruthville, the right-field bleacher area at Yankee Stadium, causing a stampede toward an exit during the fifth inning of a game with the Boston Red Sox.[65] Despite a determination by District Attorney John N. McGeehan that the deaths and injuries were not due to negligence by the Yankees but rather "a wild rush of people down a narrow chute without apparent reason,"[66] the heirs of Pierce and Carter and 30 of those injured will sue the Yankees, arguing that Babe Ruth's failure to hit a home run was partly to blame because fans only rushed toward the inadequate exits after the Bambino grounded out to first.[67] But on February 16, 1932, Supreme Court Justice Edward J. Gavegan will set aside a verdict awarding $960,000 in damages because the jury had found that both the Yankees and the plaintiffs were negligent.[68] The matter will finally conclude on December 15, 1932, when the Yankees agree to settle the claims for $45,000.[69]

May 27, 1929: Muddy Ruel Admitted to Practice Before U.S. Supreme Court

Herold D. "Muddy" Ruel, a catcher for the Washington Senators, is admitted to practice before the United States Supreme Court, becoming the first, and to date only, major league player accorded this right. A graduate of Washington University Law School in St. Louis, Ruel previously was admitted to practice in Missouri in January 1923, after passing that state's bar examination on December 20, 1922. Ruel will complete his playing career with the Chicago White Sox in 1934, going on to serve as the team's bullpen coach for 11 seasons, 1935–45. In November 1945, Ruel will be hired by Commissioner Happy Chandler to serve as his executive assistant, a position he holds for two years until leaving to become manager of the St. Louis Browns in 1947.[70]

1930

January 28, 1930: "Baby Ruth" Defeats Babe Ruth in Trademark Dispute

Commissioner William Kinnan of the U.S. Trade Mark Interferences Trial and Appeal Board rules in favor of the Curtiss Candy Company in its suit opposing the trademark granted in 1926 to the George H. Ruth Candy Company for its "Ruth's Home Run" candy bar, featuring the Yankee slugger's signature on its wrapper. Curtiss contends that its own candy bar, peanuts covered with nougat and chocolate, was named for President Grover Cleveland's popular daughter Ruth, born in 1891, despite the fact that she had been dead for 16 years when the company changed the name of its "Kandy Kate" bar to "Baby Ruth" in 1920, the year George Herman Ruth obliterated the single season home run record with 54 roundtrippers.[71] Nonetheless, Kinnan holds that "Baby Ruth" and "Babe Ruth" are "confusingly similar" and would produce confusion in trade. Since Curtiss had registered its name in 1924, conducted an extensive advertising, and had a lengthy history of high sales compared to those of the new company, Kinnan rules that doubt must be resolved against the latter.⁷² When the decision is ultimately affirmed on appeal by the Court of Patents and Customs on May 27, 1931, the Babe will respond, "Well, I ain't eatin' your damned candy bar anymore."⁷³

March 8, 1930: $80K Contract for the Babe, Tops President's Salary

Babe Ruth ends his salary holdout by signing a two-year contract with the Yankees for $80,000 per year, an increase over the $70,000 per year he had received for the preceding three seasons, but less than the three-year deal at $85,000 per year he sought when he opened negotiations with owner Jacob Ruppert and general manager Ed Barrow on January 7.⁷⁴ Still, the new contract will maintain Ruth's status as baseball's highest paid player, and eventually engender the probably apocryphal story of the Babe's response to a query about whether it was right for him to earn more than President Hoover's $75,000 in 1931: "Why not? I had a better year than he did."⁷⁵

1931

April 2, 1931: Jackie Mitchell Is First Woman to Sign Professional Contract

Jackie Mitchell, a 17-year-old left-handed pitcher who was coached by Dazzy Vance and attended Kid Elberfeld's baseball school in Atlanta, causes a "media sensation" when she strikes out Babe Ruth and Lou Gehrig in the first inning of an exhibition game between the New York Yankees and the Chattanooga Lookouts of the Class A Southern Association.⁷⁶ Although there will be speculation that the Yankee sluggers cooperated in a publicity stunt engineered by Lookouts owner and president Joe Engel, there is no doubt that he had signed Mitchell to play for the team and added her to its roster.⁷⁷ By doing so, she became the "first woman to ever sign a professional baseball contract."⁷⁸ Unfortunately, before she has a chance to play in a league game for the Lookouts, Baseball Commissioner Kenesaw Mountain Landis will void her contract, stating that "baseball life was too strenuous for a woman."⁷⁹ Although Mitchell will continue to play baseball, it will be with semipro teams outside the commissioner's jurisdiction, including the House of David; it will take more than two decades before another woman, Eleanor Engle, will sign a minor league contract (see entry for June 21, 1952).⁸⁰

April 21, 1931: Commissioner's Powers Upheld in Ruling Over Bennett Contract

In a suit in which the Milwaukee Brewers of the American Association and the St. Louis Browns of the American League sought to enjoin Commissioner Kenesaw Mountain Landis from dissolving their optional contract covering the services of outfielder Fred Bennett, Judge Walter C. Lindley of the U.S. District Court for the Northern District of Illinois rules that Landis had the authority to arbitrate the matter and that his decision to grant Bennett free agent status was final under the applicable rules.[81] Lindley also notes that the Major-Minor League Agreement "disclose(d) a clear intent upon the part of the parties to endow the commissioner with all the attributes of a benevolent but absolute despot and all the disciplinary powers of the proverbial pater familias."[82]

December 1, 1931: Burglary Haul Includes a Dozen Babe Ruth Home Run Candy Bars

Finding no error in either the procedural aspects of the trial or the sufficiency of the evidence, the Missouri Supreme Court upholds the verdict of a Ripley County jury finding Floyce Reed guilty of burglarizing John Wright's store in the village of Tucker on the night of November 20, 1929. Mr. Wright discovered the break-in on reopening the store after attending a pie supper at the school house to accommodate a customer. Seeing the back window up and a window pane broken, Mr. Wright found that cans of Prince Albert tobacco, cigarettes, cigarette papers, and "about a dozen bars of Babe Ruth [Home Run] candy" had been taken from a show case; he later found that three or four pocket knives also were missing. Mr. Wright estimated that the value of the "stuff" taken was $7.15, which included about 60 cents for the Babe's candy bars, which sold for a nickel apiece. Mr. Reed will serve a two-year sentence in the penitentiary for what he himself admitted was an act of "just pure damned meanness."[83]

1932

June 30, 1932: Rogers Hornsby Loses Tax Case

Future Hall of Famer Rogers Hornsby loses his case at the U.S. Board of Tax Appeals when the court determines that he did not have a legal domicile in Texas for the 1926 and 1927 taxable years and, thus, was not entitled to use Texas community property law to split his income with his wife Jeanette for those years. While earlier in his career the native Texan resided in the off-season at a home he owned in Fort Worth, he deeded that property to his former wife when they divorced in 1923. After remarrying in 1924, Hornsby and Jeanette lived year-round in St. Louis while playing for the Cardinals through 1926, then in a rented apartment in New York after being traded to the New York Giants prior to the 1927 season. He and Jeanette bought a permanent home outside St. Louis in 1928.[84] Judge Ernest Van Fossan also determines that Jeanette's forgetting to file their tax return in a timely fashion is not "reasonable cause" sufficient to relieve the couple of a penalty for delinquent filing.[85]

July 6, 1932: Former Beau Violet Popovich Shoots the Cubs' Billy Jurges

In an incident that will echo 17 years later when love-struck Ruth Ann Steinhagen shoots Eddie Waitkus (see entry for June 14, 1949), Violet Popovich, a showgirl who uses the stage name Violet Valli, confronts her former beau Billy Jurges, the Cubs' 24-year-old shortstop, at the Hotel Carlos, just a few blocks north of Wrigley Field.[86] A struggle ensues after she takes a .25 caliber pistol from her purse—police will later find a suicide note in her hotel room[87]—and three shots are fired, two striking Billy and one hitting Violet, breaking her wrist. As with Waitkus, Jurges escapes serious injury and will return to the playing field in late July.[88] Popovich is arrested and charged with intent to kill, but Jurges will decline to testify against her, causing Judge John Sbarbaro to dismiss the case "for want of prosecution, and I hope no more Cubs get shot."[89] Popovich will soon return to the cabaret circuit with a 22-week contract in clubs throughout Chicago, billed as "Violet 'What I Did for Love' Valli, the Most Talked-about Girl in Chicago," while Jurges will go on to a 17-year playing career for the Cubs and Giants, and will be the manager in 1959 when Pumpsie Green joins the Boston Red Sox and completes the integration of the major leagues (see entry for July 21, 1959).[90]

1934

April 8, 1934: Philadelphia Last City to Host "Legal" Sunday Baseball Game

Philadelphia becomes the final city to host a legally sanctioned game[91] between major league teams played on a Sunday when a crowd of 15,000 sees the Phillies defeat the Athletics, 8–1, at Shibe Park.[92] The game was made possible on April 25, 1933, when, after substantial lobbying efforts by Athletics owner Connie Mack, Pennsylvania Governor Gifford Pinchot signed into law a statute modifying the state's "blue law" (see entry for April 22, 1794) so that local jurisdictions could choose whether to allow baseball or football games to be played on Sunday.[93] In November 1933, Philadelphians took advantage of the option provided in the statute and voted by referendum in favor of Sunday sports, setting the stage for the Athletics-Phillies exhibition game the following April.[94]

May 12, 1934: Joe Judge, *Damn Yankees* Inspiration, Plays Last Game

Thirty-nine-year old Joe Judge—the only judge, surname-wise, in Major League Baseball history[95]—plays the last of his 2,129 big league games when he pinch hits for the Boston Red Sox against the Cleveland Indians in a game at Fenway Park. An outstanding first baseman who led the American League in fielding six times and finished second another five, Judge spent most of his 20-year career in the nation's capital with the Washington Senators (1916–32). Retiring with a lifetime batting average of .298, slugging percentage of .420, and 1,034 RBIs, Judge served as the head coach of the Georgetown University baseball team from 1934 to 1957, except for 1945–46 when he coached the Senators under manager Ossie Bluege.[96] According to his grandson, as a result of Judge's friendship with the author, he became the inspiration for the character of Joe Hardy in Douglass Wallop's novel, *The Year the Yankees Lost the Pennant*,[97] which later was adapted into the hit stage play and motion picture, *Damn Yankees*.[98]

1935

June 17, 1935: Landis Approves Signing of Alabama Pitts, Former Sing Sing Prisoner

Bowing to public pressure, Commissioner Kenesaw Mountain Landis overturns the ruling of President W.G. Bramham and the executive committee of the National Association of Professional Baseball Leagues, the governing body of the minor leagues, who had refused to approve the May 22, 1935, signing of Edwin "Alabama" Pitts, incarcerated for armed robbery at the infamous Sing Sing Prison in Ossining, New York, by the International League's Albany Senators.[99] While confined, Pitts had become a national sensation, batting .500 with eight home runs in 21 games for the prison baseball team while also serving as captain of the Black Sheep, the football squad coached by former Notre Dame star John Law.[100] Freed to play by Landis after his June 1935 parole, Pitts will manage only 43 games for Albany in a 1935 season marred by injury; in total he will play only 171 minor-league games before completing his career in 1940 for the Hickory Rebels of the Class D Tar Heel League.[101] Pitts will die tragically at the age of 31 from a knife wound inflicted during a late night roadhouse altercation on June 6, 1941, in Valdese, North Carolina.

July 15, 1935: Court Ends Dispute Between Rival Companies Over Autograph Bats

In a patent, trademark, and unfair competition dispute between competing manufacturers of baseball bats—newcomer Hanna Manufacturing Company and Hillerich & Bradsby Company, "an old and the largest manufacturer of bats"[102]—the United States Circuit Court of Appeals for the Fifth Circuit addresses the use of the names and signatures of famous Major League players to create "autograph" or "player's name" bats.[103] The district court had enjoined Hanna's use of the names of any players who had granted exclusive right of use to Hillerich and Bradsby. Writing for the circuit court, however, Judge Samuel H. Sibley holds that "it is the trade rather than the names and likenesses which the law will protect as property."[104] The court modifies the injunction so Hanna can produce bats with the names of players under agreement with Hillerich and Bradsby as long as it puts the word "style" or "shape" together with the player's name.[105]

1936

December 10, 1936: Landis Rules Against Des Moines, Feller Remains with Indians

In what one writer will call "the most important player decision since the old National Commission awarded George Sisler to the St. Louis Browns in 1915" (see entry for January 9, 1915),[106] Commissioner Kenesaw Mountain Landis issues a meandering mimeographed opinion during baseball's winter meetings announcing that Bob Feller, who already had made his major league debut on July 19, 1936, at the age of 17, will remain the property of the Cleveland Indians.[107] Lee Keyser, owner of the Des Moines Demons of the Class A Western League, had filed a complaint with Landis alleging that the Indians violated the Major-Minor League Agreement by secretly hiding Feller on the roster of Class D Fargo-Moorhead Twins of the Northern League.[108] At a hearing, Rapid Robert and his father Bill stated that the teenager only wanted to pitch for the Indians and would file a civil suit if Landis held otherwise.[109] In resolving the dispute, Landis rules in favor of the Indians but requires the team to pay Keyser $7,500, the amount the Des Moines owner had offered to the teenager from nearby Van Meter, Iowa, to sign with his team.

1938

March 23, 1938: Landis Rules That Cardinals Farmhands Are Free Agents

Fearing that the minor leagues would be destroyed by the innovative farm system created by Branch Rickey, general manager of the St. Louis Cardinals, Commissioner Kenesaw Mountain Landis issues a 5,000-word decision that frees 74 minor leaguers controlled by the extensive collection of teams with which the Cardinals have "working agreements," citing the team for violating the rule that no major league team can control two clubs in the same minor league.[110] The released players are from six midwestern teams, many with a connection to the Class A Western League's Cedar Rapids Raiders. Team owners are fined a total of $2,176.[111] Although most of the new free agents will never rise above the low minors, "Pistol Pete" Reiser will become an all-star center fielder for the Brooklyn Dodgers before missing three full seasons to the Army during World War II, not to mention numerous games because of injury (he had a predilection for running into outfield walls).[112]

April 4, 1938: Bart Giamatti, Future Commissioner of Baseball, Is Born

A. Bartlett Giamatti, the seventh commissioner of Major League Baseball, is born in Boston, Massachusetts. A classics professor who will also serve as president of his alma mater, Yale University, from 1978 to 1986, and president of the National League from 1986 to 1989, Giamatti may be best known for his handling of the Pete Rose gambling affair (see entry for August 23, 1989).[113]

August 8, 1938: Pirates Prevail Over KQV in Dispute Over Radio Broadcasts

The Pittsburgh Pirates prevails in its action to enjoin KQV Broadcasting Company from delivering play-by-play descriptions of games played in Forbes Field on the radio.[114] Although the Pirates had contracted with General Mills, which negotiated with the National Broadcasting Company to allow KDKA and WWSW to broadcast Pirates home games, KQV was paying individuals to report game information from vantage points outside the ballpark.[115] In granting the injunction, the federal district court finds that KQV's behavior "is a violation of the property rights of the plaintiffs," and notes that the team has "a legitimate right to capitalize on the news value of their games by selling exclusive broadcasting rights to companies which value them as affording advertising mediums for their merchandise."[116]

November 28, 1938: Copyright Issued for Baseball's Centennial Logo

The U.S. Copyright Office issues a copyright for a Baseball Centennial logo created by Marjori Bennett, a New York artist,[117] for a contest dreamed up by Steve Hannagan, public relations guru of the National Baseball Centennial Commission. Bennett's winning design—red, white, and blue and featuring a batter encircled by a baseball and set against the background of a diamond and four bases—will be used on a wide range of items produced or licensed by the Commission to commemorate the centennial of the alleged "invention of baseball" by Abner Doubleday in 1839 (see entry for December 30, 1907). It also will be used on the first-ever commemorative sleeve patch worn by every Major League club when all major and minor league players wear the patch on their left sleeve throughout the 1939 season—with the exception of the St. Louis Browns, who wear it on their right sleeve because the left is already used for the team logo.[118]

1939

March 1, 1939: New Agreement Creates Unified Program for Radio Broadcasting

After years when many major league teams, including the Yankees,

Dodgers, and Giants in New York, prohibited local radio stations from broadcasting their games,[119] representatives of each of the 16 clubs of the National and American leagues sign the "Major League Broadcasting Agreement" which establishes a unified program governing broadcasting of games by radio and telephone. Among its provisions, the document prevents a team from broadcasting its games on a station located within 50 miles of another team's stadium; in cities with two teams, prevents a team from broadcasting an away game when the other team is playing a home game; lifts the longstanding moratorium on New York's local radio broadcasts; and allows broadcasting between 550 and 1600 on the AM band, but forbids shortwave or other high frequency stations.[120]

June 12, 1939: In Cooperstown, Landis First Purchaser of Centennial Postage Stamp

At the United States Post Office in Cooperstown, New York, located on Main Street directly across from the new National Baseball Museum, Commissioner Kenesaw Mountain Landis purchases the first stamp marking baseball's centennial from U.S. Postmaster General Jim Farley.[121] Bedecked in red, white, and blue caps sporting the copyrighted centennial logo (see entry for November 28, 1938), Landis and Farley have come to the village to celebrate the grand opening of the Hall of Fame. Following Farley's endorsement of the plan to issue a baseball commemorative stamp, artist William Roach of the Bureau of Engraving developed a design depicting youngsters watching and playing a sandlot game in a small village setting modeled on Milford, Delaware.[122] The first of at least 60 stamps devoted to the game which the United States eventually will issue is hugely popular on its release, with more than 450,000 stamps and as many first-day covers sold in one day, second at the time only to the nearly 600,000 New York World's fair first-day covers sold earlier in the year.[123]

1940

January 14, 1940: Landis Declares Tiger Minor Leaguers Free Agents

Commissioner Kenesaw Mountain Landis declares 91 players affiliated with the Detroit Tigers' farm system free agents as a result of the team's violation of MLB rules involving working agreements and control of multiple teams in the same minor league.[124] Landis also requires the Tigers to pay 15 Detroit farm hands a total of $47,250.[125] Jack Zeller, the Tigers general manager and chief target of Landis's wrath, attempts to shield Detroit owner Walter Briggs by accepting full responsibility, but Briggs declares that "the cost of this is mine and will be properly taken care of."[126] Landis also fines the Chicago Cubs and St. Louis Browns for tampering with Benny McCoy and Roy Cullenbine by negotiating with the Tiger major leaguers before he declared them free agents.[127] McCoy, the most valuable of the lot, prompts a 12-team bidding war that will be won by the Philadelphia Athletics, who sign the middle infielder for $45,000 plus two years at $10,000 per year.[128]

September 9, 1940: Gehrig Sues Columnist Jimmy Powers for Defamation

Lou Gehrig files a $1 million defamation lawsuit in New York state supreme court against Jimmy Powers, sports editor of the *New York Daily News*, and the News Syndicate Company, based on the writer's assertion in an August 18 article that the Yankees' poor on-field performance was the result of Gehrig's communicable polio disease having spread among his teammates.[129] Shortly after the article appeared, the Yankees' Iron Horse had stated: "As it is now I am a pariah who many people shun. I might just as well have been marked with leprosy."[130] After the *News* issues a retraction on September 26, Gehrig will settle the suit for $17,500. The effects of Gehrig's actual disease, amyotrophic lateral sclerosis (ALS), will be readily apparent when he can barely sign the settlement agreement on December 19.[131] Gehrig will succumb to the disease on June 2, 1941.

November 5, 1940: Walter Johnson Loses in Maryland Congressional Bid

Lauded as one of the great pitchers of all time, Walter Johnson loses his election bid for Maryland's Sixth Congressional District seat to incumbent William Byron, a Democrat.[132] Despite modest campaigning, the "Big Train" receives 52,258 (47 percent) votes to Byron's 60,037 (53 percent), even as President Franklin D. Roosevelt is reelected for a third term in a landslide over Wendell Willkie, the Republican who launched his campaign in Johnson's hometown of Coffeyville, Kansas.[133] Ty Cobb, honored along with Johnson and other first-time inductees at the opening of the National Baseball Museum and Hall of Fame in Cooperstown, New York (see entry for June 12, 1939), had endorsed his old foe in a letter to the *Bethesda Journal*: "I think so highly of the man's integrity that I can't resist recommending him to the voters of his district."[134] Johnson had won his first political campaign in 1938 when he was the lone Republican elected to the five-person Board of Commissioners of Montgomery County, Maryland.

1942

January 15, 1942: FDR "Green Lights" Baseball to Continue Play During the War

Responding to a January 14 letter from Commissioner Kenesaw Mountain Landis asking whether the president thought professional baseball should be played in what "are not ordinary times," President Franklin D. Roosevelt gives what will come to be known as the "Green Light" for baseball to continue despite the disruption of World War II. Acknowledging that the final decision rests with baseball club owners, Roosevelt writes to Landis "that it would be best for the country to keep baseball going. There will be fewer people unemployed and everybody will work longer hours and harder than ever before. And that means that they ought to have a chance for recreation and for taking their minds off their work even more than before."[135] Baseball will not only continue to be played throughout the war, the owners will even follow Roosevelt's suggestion to play more night games so as to give "an opportunity to the day shift to see a game occasionally."[136]

1943

February 2, 1943: New York Legislative Resolution Opposes Baseball's Color Line

Senator Charles D. Perry, a New York City Democrat, introduces a resolution in the New York State Legislature which, if approved, will inform Commissioner Kenesaw Mountain Landis and presidents Ford Frick of the National League and William Harridge of the American League of the state's opposition to professional baseball's "unwritten law" which bars "certain people because of their race" as players in violation of New York's anti-discrimination laws.[137]

February 7, 1943: Landis Says Players Won't Seek Exemption from Military Draft

Barely a year after receiving the "Green Light" from President Roosevelt for professional baseball to continue despite the ongoing world war (see entry for January 15, 1942), Commissioner Kenesaw Mountain Landis declares that Organized Baseball will not seek any special favors by asking that its players be exempted from the draft. Landis tells the New York Baseball Writers' Association at its annual dinner that "[w]e do not want baseball exempt from the liabilities of common life in America.... When I give thought to the statutes ruling our lives in war, I think of those fellows in New Guinea crawling in trenches and those fellows in Africa. They have complied with those statutes.... I don't want any man in the stands to think that any man on the field is exempt from any law or statute."[138]

1944

August 2, 1944: Jackie Robinson Cleared of Insubordination Charge in Court-Martial

After a four-hour hearing, a court-martial board of nine judges at Camp Hood, Texas, finds U.S. Army Lieutenant Jack R. Robinson not guilty of insubordination toward superior officers. A month earlier, on July 6, Robinson, a former UCLA All-American football player who in 1947 will break the Major League Baseball color barrier (see entry for April 10, 1947), had refused to obey the order of the driver to move to the back of an army bus at Camp Hood, an action which ultimately led to his arrest. Although all charges related to his encounter with the bus driver, a bus dispatcher, and a white female passenger were dropped prior to the hearing, Robinson still faced a court-martial on two lesser charges of insubordination based on his aggressive confrontation with the officers investigating the matter.[139]

CHAPTER 5

Owners on Top, 1945–1965

Introduction

Two weeks before World War II ended in Europe, major-league owners looked again to a federal government official to serve as baseball's second commissioner. As they prepared for the return of war veterans to the diamond, the owners selected Albert "Happy" Chandler, a member of the United States Senate from Kentucky, to succeed Kenesaw Mountain Landis who had died in November 1944. The most dramatic and transcendent decision, however, occurred in Brooklyn, New York, when Dodgers general manager Branch Rickey signed African American Jackie Robinson to a contract and placed him on the roster of the club's AAA-affiliate Montreal Royals for the 1946 season. A year later, on April 15, 1947, Robinson appeared in the season opener against the Boston Braves, bringing the longstanding, though unwritten, color barrier to an end. Later in July, Larry Doby integrated the American League when he debuted for the Cleveland Indians. In barely a decade, by 1958, African Americans comprised 10 percent of the players on major league rosters; by 1965, it was 20 percent.

The years immediately following the end of the war gave rise to several significant challenges which the owners were able to overcome, at least in the short term. In the area of labor relations, another attempt at organizing players, the American Baseball Guild, provided a glimpse of the future for those prescient enough to see it, but for the time being the owners avoided the Guild's goals of increased benefits and salaries, free agency, and salary arbitration by quickly destroying the nascent union. The effort achieved some small measure of success, including the creation of the first-ever player pension system, a minimum salary and maximum pay cut percentage, and payment for spring training expenses (known thereafter as "Murphy money" for the Guild's founder, Robert F. Murphy), but it would take more than two decades before the players made real inroads into the owner's stranglehold on the conditions under which they worked and their ability to choose where they played.

In another threat to Organized Baseball, the Pasquel brothers, Jorge and Bernardo, sought to lure major league players to their reinvigorated Mexican League with promises of high salaries and excellent working conditions. The owners successfully fought back, often through court-granted injunctions, but at least one case, that involving a challenge to the reserve clause by blacklisted Giants outfielder Danny Gardella, provided another glimpse of the future when a federal circuit court declared the clause violated antitrust law. But Gardella chose to settle rather than continue the litigation, opening the door for the U.S. Supreme Court to solidify baseball's antitrust exemption a few years later in *Toolson v. New York Yankees* despite a broad-based investigation of the game's practices by a committee chaired by Brooklyn Congressman Emanuel Celler.

In the early 1950s, a half-century of franchise stability was shattered by the relocation of the Boston Braves to Milwaukee and the Philadelphia Athletics to Kansas City. This was followed by a more seismic shift later in the decade when the Brooklyn Dodgers moved to Los Angeles and the New York Giants to San Francisco, finally bringing major league baseball to the West Coast (and sealing the fate of the existing Pacific Coast League which had long sought such status for itself). The New York City exodus opened the door for Branch Rickey and New York lawyer William Shea to unveil plans in 1959 for an east coast-centered Continental League as a third major league. Although it never played a game, the threat of a new competitor finally pushed Major League Baseball to expand from the 16 franchises it had fielded since 1901 to 20, two new teams for each league.

During these two decades, strong ownership, led in particular by the Dodgers' Walter O'Malley, oversaw all aspects of the game by controlling commissioners Chandler and Ford Frick and maintaining the upper hand with players. This domination was about to change.

1945

April 24, 1945: Happy Chandler Elected as Second Baseball Commissioner

On the second ballot, major-league owners elect Albert Benjamin "Happy" Chandler, current United States senator and a former governor of Kentucky (1935–39; he will later serve a second term, 1955–59), as the second commissioner of baseball. He replaces Kenesaw Mountain Landis, who died on November 25, 1944.[1] Chandler is given a seven-year term and will be installed in office on July 12, 1945.[2] Similar to Landis's decision to remain on the federal bench when he was selected commissioner in 1920 (see entries for November 12, 1920, and February 21, 1921), Chandler will continue in the Senate until resigning his seat on November 1, 1945.[3]

April 26, 1945: Congressman Seeks Investigation of Baseball's Color Line

Representative Vito Marcantonio, a member of the American Labor Party whose district includes East Harlem in New York City, introduces House Joint Resolution 173 which directs the Secretary of Commerce "to investigate the employment policy and practices of baseball clubs affiliated with the National and American Leagues ... to determine the extent of discrimination in employment of baseball players because of race, color or creed."[4] Although the resolution merely calls for an inquiry, Marcantonio's overriding goal is the elimination of baseball's longstanding color line.[5]

October 23, 1945: Jackie Robinson Signs Contract to Play for Montreal Royals

Jackie Robinson, an African American shortstop on the roster of the Kansas City Monarchs of the Negro American League, officially signs a contract tendered by Branch Rickey, president and general manager of the Brooklyn Dodgers, to play for the Montreal Royals, the Dodgers triple-A minor league farm club during the 1946 season.[6] In so doing, the two initiate the process that will lead to the fall of major league baseball's unspoken color line when Robinson joins the Dodgers in 1947 (see entry for April 10, 1947). While most in the black community are supportive of Robinson's signing, Monarch owners J.L. Wilkinson and Thomas Baird will object to Rickey's failure to compensate them for signing their ballplayer. He had argued that Robinson was not bound by any agreement, oral or written, to stay with the Monarchs, but Wilkinson and Baird will consider suing Rickey for stealing their property before Negro League officials persuade them against such action for fear it will appear that they are standing in the way of black players advancement.[7]

December 12, 1945: Pacific Coast League Unsuccessful in Bid to Become Third Major League

During baseball's annual winter meetings, major league owners unanimously deny the Pacific Coast League's request to be recognized as a third major league.[8] In explaining the owners' refusal, National League President Ford Frick and American League President Will Harridge issue a joint statement declaring "that promotion of the Pacific Coast League to major status would react unfairly to players," since teams in the PCL "could not pay top major league salaries." PCL president Clarence "Pants" Rowland presciently responds that the "men who control major league baseball are merely postponing the inevitable."[9] Nonetheless, even writers from cities with PCL franchises point to the inadequate seating capacities of most of the league's ballparks as reason enough for rejecting its advancement to major league status at this time.[10]

1946

April 17, 1946: Robert Murphy Forms American Baseball Guild to Represent Players

Robert Francis Murphy, a labor relations attorney who formerly served as an examiner for the National Labor Relations Board, formally establishes the American Baseball Guild as a labor organization by registering it in Suffolk County, Massachusetts. The organization seeks to represent major league players, calling for a minimum salary of $7500, impartial arbitration of salary and contract disputes, payment of 50 percent of the sale price to a player who is sold to another team, creation of spring training and insurance benefits, and "the replacement of the reserve clause with long-term contracts featuring annual renegotiable financial terms."[11]

May 20, 1946: Yankees Enjoin Pasquel Brothers from Inducing Players to Jump to Mexican League

After Mexican League vice-president Bernardo Pasquel declares that he will not leave New York City without signing "one of the 'biggest name players of the Yankees,'"[12] the team successfully petitions for a temporary injunction restraining Bernardo and three other defendants from inducing players currently under contract with the Yankees from breaking their contracts to play in the Mexican League.[13]

May 31, 1946: Dodgers Fail in Injunction Attempt Against Mexican League Poaching

Judge Rubey M. Hulen of the St. Louis federal district court refuses to grant an injunction sought by the Brooklyn Dodgers to prevent *St. Louis Star-Times* sportswriter Ray Gillespie from conspiring with Jorge and Bernardo Pasquel to induce baseball players to break their major league contracts to jump to the Mexican League because there is no evidence he has done so. The Dodgers contend that Gillespie's participation in the signing of former Dodger catcher Mickey Owen to play ball in Mexico is sufficient evidence, but the court finds that though the reporter was an agent of the Pasquel brothers for a specific purpose, this did not support the alleged conspiracy.[14] Hulen also refuses to grant injunctive relief involving the Pasquel brothers and two other defendants because they are non-residents.[15]

June 7, 1946: Pirates Strike Vote Fails, American Baseball Guild Soon Follows Suit

Prior to a home game against the New York Giants, the Pittsburgh Pirates players, coaches, and trainers vote 20–16 in favor of refusing to play the game in support of the recently formed American Baseball Guild (see entry for April 7, 1946), but this fails to meet the required two-thirds majority and so a strike is averted. The vote will sound the death knoll for the Guild and its creator, Robert Murphy, but the owners, responding to the close call in Pittsburgh and threats from the Pasquel brothers and the Mexican League, will follow the recommendations of the secret August 27, 1946, report of their Major League Steering Committee, chaired by Larry MacPhail, and pledge to create the first-ever players pension, set a minimum salary of $5000,[16] fix the maximum pay cut at 25 percent, and pay spring training expenses of $25 a week (hereinafter referred to as "Murphy money" by ballplayers with little or no knowledge of Robert Murphy or the short-lived American Baseball Guild).[17]

October 10, 1946: Truman Presents Moe Berg with Medal of Freedom for Wartime Service

President Harry S. Truman awards Moe Berg, a 1930 graduate of Columbia Law School who played 15 years (1923, 1926–39) in the Major Leagues, primarily as a catcher for the White Sox, Senators, and Red Sox, the Medal of Freedom for his wartime service as a member of the Secret Intelligence branch of the Office of Strategic Services from 1943 to 1945.[18] On December 12, however, Berg will decline to accept the award "with due respect for the spirit with which it is offered."[19] After his death in 1972, his sister Ethel will finally accept the award on his behalf and donate it to the Hall of Fame in 1974.[20]

1947

February 28, 1947: Dodgers Become First Team to Televise All Home Games

The Columbia Broadcasting System (CBS) announces that Ford Motor Company and General Foods will alternate daily as advertisers on the television broadcasts of the 77 home games the Brooklyn Dodgers will play in the 1947 season, making it the first major league team to televise all of its home games with commercial sponsorship.[21] President Branch Rickey of the Dodgers and President Frank Stanton of CBS had announced in November 1946 that the team was breaking new ground in the MLB by assigning exclusive television rights for all of its 1947 home games to the broadcaster, which had televised 18 Dodger games in 1946 as an experiment.[22] For the Dodgers,

Rickey worked on the general structure of these deals, while Walter O'Malley, chief legal counsel and part owner of the Dodgers, negotiated the details of the contracts.[23]

April 9, 1947: Chandler Suspends Dodger Manager Leo Durocher for a Year

Major League Baseball Commissioner A.B. "Happy" Chandler informs the Brooklyn Dodgers that he is suspending manager Leo Durocher from baseball for one year for "conduct detrimental to baseball."[24] Although Durocher will long deny knowing the reason for the suspension,[25] Chandler identifies an "accumulation of unpleasant incidents," certainly referring to gambling debts, association with known gamblers, and his courtship of actress Larraine Day, married to another at the time, which had led the Brooklyn Catholic Youth Organization to withdraw its support for the team's Knothole Club on March 1, 1947, effectively declaring a boycott of Dodger games at Ebbets Field.[26] Though not expressly mentioned at the time, it is likely that continuing tension between Dodger owner and general manager Branch Rickey and Yankee owner Larry MacPhail also plays a large role in the commissioner's action.[27]

April 10, 1947: Jackie Robinson Plays for Dodgers, Breaks Unwritten Color Line

Arthur Mann, assistant to Branch Rickey, president of the Brooklyn Dodgers, distributes an announcement to press box reporters during the sixth inning of an exhibition game between the Dodgers and Montreal Royals at Ebbets Field: "The Brooklyn Dodgers today purchased the contract of Jackie Roosevelt Robinson from the Montreal Royals. He will report immediately." In the Dodgers dressing room, Robinson is given a uniform with the number 42.[28] The following day, he will sign a contract with the Dodgers for the major-league minimum salary of $5,000.[29] On Tuesday, April 15, he will become the first African American to play in the Major Leagues in the twentieth century by starting at first base for the Dodgers in the season opener against the Boston Braves, thereby breaking Major League Baseball's unwritten but rigidly enforced color line.[30] Robinson will be selected as the National League's Rookie of the Year in 1947 and its Most Valuable Player Award in 1949, and become the first African American inducted into the National Baseball Hall of Fame in 1972.[31]

July 5, 1947: Larry Doby Debuts for Indians, Integrates American League

Less than three months after Jackie Robinson made history with the Dodgers as the first African American to play in the Major Leagues in the twentieth century (see entry for April 10, 1947), 23-year-old Larry Doby debuts with the Cleveland Indians as a pinch-hitter, thereby integrating the American League and becoming the second black player in the majors.[32] Doby had signed with the Indians a few days earlier, after owner Bill Veeck purchased his contract from the Newark Eagles of the Negro National League, paying $10,000 to owner and chief operating officer Effa Manley, with a promise of $5,000 more if Doby stuck with the Tribe.[33] Following a 13-year playing career and seven All-Star game selections, Doby will serve as a coach for the Expos, Indians, and White Sox from 1969 to 1977, before finally becoming the second black manager in major league history after Frank Robinson (see entry for April 8, 1975), when Veeck hires him to replace Bob Lemon as manager of the White Sox on June 30, 1978.[34] Nineteen years later, on July 5, 1997, the Indians will retire Doby's number 14 on the 50th anniversary of his major league debut, and in 1998 he will be elected to the National Baseball Hall of Fame by the Veteran's Committee.[35]

August 26, 1947: Dan Bankhead Becomes First Black Pitcher in Major Leagues

With Brooklyn already trailing Pittsburgh, 4–0, Dan Bankhead relieves Dodger starting pitcher Hal Gregg in the top of the second inning, thereby becoming the first African American to pitch in a Major League game.[36] In dire need of better pitching, Brooklyn's Branch Rickey had purchased Bankhead's contract from the Memphis Red Sox of the Negro American League for $15,000 only a few days prior to his historic appearance.[37] Bankhead is ineffective, giving up 10 hits and 8 runs in 3⅓ innings, but he does hit a home run in his first at bat.[38] Bankhead will appear in only three more games in 1947, and a total of 52 in his three-year career, compiling a record of 9 wins and 4 losses in 1950, his best year in the majors.[39]

1948

January 18, 1948: Don Fehr, Lawyer and MLBPA Executive Director, Is Born

Donald Fehr, future Executive Director of the Major League Baseball Players Association, is born in Prairie Village, Kansas. While an attorney at the Kansas City law firm of Jolley, Moran, Walsh, Hager & Gordon, the University of Missouri–Kansas City law graduate will successfully represent MLBPA when Major League Baseball appeals the Messersmith-McNally free agency decision by arbitrator Peter Seitz (see entries for December 23, 1975, and March 9, 1976).[40] After replacing Richard Moss as MLBPA's general counsel in 1977, Fehr will eventually become the association's second executive director upon the retirement of Marvin Miller (see entry for December 8, 1983). As director, Fehr will successfully lead the union's challenge to ownership collusion (see entries for September 21, 1987, August 31, 1988, and July 18, 1990); negotiate with ownership over franchise expansion, interleague play, and revenue sharing; and resist the imposition of a salary cap. He also will fight efforts to institute mandatory drug testing during the steroid era, a stance for which he will receive much criticism.[41]

1949

February 7, 1949: DiMaggio Signs MLB's First $100,000 Contract

Joe DiMaggio signs the first player contract providing for an annual salary of $100,000.[42] The Yankee Clipper inks the pact with President Dan Topping and General Manager George Weiss at the Yankees' Fifth Avenue offices. Neither side discloses the terms to the media gathered for the event, with DiMaggio simply calling the new deal "the best of the eleven contracts I have signed to date with the Yankees."[43] It is only later that the actual amount is verified and claims that Hank Greenberg was the first $100,000 player are disproved.[44]

February 9, 1949: Second Circuit Questions Reserve Clause in *Gardella* Decision

Judges Learned Hand and Jerome Frank of the U.S. Court of Appeals for the Second Circuit join in a 2–1 decision granting former N.Y. Giants outfielder Danny Gardella the right to sue Major League Baseball to collect treble damages for antitrust violations under the Sherman and Clayton Acts.[45] After rejecting the Giants contract offer of $5000 for the 1946 season, Gardella had signed a five-year deal to play in the Mexican League; on February 22, 1946, he became the first American player to arrive in Mexico.[46] Commissioner A.B. "Happy" Chandler quickly banned Gardella and the others who had jumped leagues from Organized Baseball.[47] Even after the Mexican League faltered, sending most Americans back to the states, Chandler refused to lift the ban, leading Gardella to challenge the reserve clause in a federal antitrust suit in which he sought $300,000 in damages.[48] Although the Second Circuit decision presents a serious challenge to the reserve clause,[49] on October 7, 1949, one month prior to the scheduled November 1949 trial date, Gardella will accept an out-of-court settlement which includes the purchase of his Giants contract by the Cardinals and "a $60,000 payment to Gardella and his lawyer," Frederic A. Johnson.[50]

June 5, 1949: Chandler Lifts Ban on Players Who Jumped to Mexican League

At a special press conference in Washington, D.C., Commissioner Happy Chandler, "tempering justice with mercy," lifts the ban on all former players who jumped to the Mexican League and grants them amnesty.[51] Any player who submits a written request for reinstatement will be granted "automatic" approval.[52] As a result of Chandler's action, in August formerly suspended Cardinal pitchers Max Lanier and Fred Martin will drop their $2.5 million lawsuit against Major League Baseball and Giant pitcher Sal Maglie will decide not to initiate the legal action he had been contemplating. Danny Gardella, however, will continue to pursue his case against MLB (see entry for February 9, 1949).[53]

June 14, 1949: Steinhagen Shoots Eddie Waitkus, Inspires Malamud's *The Natural*

Ruth Ann Steinhagen, a 19-year-old typist for an insurance company, shoots Phillies first-baseman Eddie Waitkus in the chest with a .22 caliber rifle after using a cryptic note to lure him to a 12th-floor room at the Edgewater Beach Hotel in Chicago.[54] Although they had never met, Steinhagen had become obsessed with the handsome Waitkus when he played for the Cubs from 1946 to 1948. Just 17 days after the shooting, on June 30, Judge James McDermott of the Cook County Criminal Court will declare Steinhagen insane and strike her indictment for assault with intent to commit murder.[55] Waitkus will experience a "near miraculous" recovery, returning a year later to play for the 1950 Phillies National League champion "Whiz Kids" and posting a lifetime .285 batting average by the time he completes his 11-year career in 1955 at the age of 35.[56] When Steinhagen is ruled sane and released from Kankakee State Prison after three years in 1952, Waitkus will refuse to bring charges against her, saying he wants to forget the incident. Though Steinhagen herself will quickly fade into obscurity, not to reemerge until after her death at age 83 on December 29, 2012,[57] the story of obsession, insanity, and a fallen ballplayer will inspire a 1952 novel, *The Natural* by Bernard Malamud, and a later film version starring Robert Redford in the iconic role of Roy Hobbs and Barbara Hershey as the stalker who shoots him.[58]

July 18, 1949: Jackie Robinson First Major League Player to Testify Before Congress

In the earliest instance of a major league baseball player appearing before Congress,[59] Jackie Robinson testifies at a House Un-American Activities Committee (HUAC) hearing in Washington, D.C., about Communist infiltration of minority groups.[60] Georgia Congressman John S. Wood, HUAC chair, had invited Robinson to appear as a witness so he could "give the lie to statements by Paul Robeson" regarding blacks and the Soviet Union.[61] Although Robinson disputes Robeson's alleged statement that blacks would refuse to fight in a war against the Soviet Union, he focuses most of his attention on racial discrimination and civil rights.[62]

October 12, 1949: Parolee Returns to Baseball After Serving Time in San Quentin

Ralph Richard "Blackie" Schwamb, who pitched in 12 games for the St. Louis Browns as a 21-year-old rookie in 1948, brutally beats Long Beach, California, physician Donald Buge to death during a robbery.[63] After a December trial, Schwamb will be sentenced to life in prison and sent to San Quentin.[64] While behind bars at San Quentin and Folsom, Schwamb will become a legendary pitcher; according to his own record-keeping, he posts 131 wins against only 35 losses and fashions a 1.80 ERA.[65] Schwamb will be paroled on January 5, 1960, and, in 1961, at the age of 34, pitch in six games for the Hawaii Islanders of the Pacific Coast League.

1950

December 29, 1950: Hugh Casey Loses Paternity Suit, Commits Suicide

In a paternity suit the New York Special Sessions Court concludes that Hugh Casey, a relief pitching ace for the Brooklyn Dodgers from 1939 through 1948, is the father of a baby boy born to 25-year old Brooklyn salesgirl Hilda Weissman on November 2, 1949.[66] The court orders Casey to pay $20-per-week in child support plus $102 in lying-in expenses.[67] Casey's problems will increase on January 31, 1951, when a $6,759.36 tax lien is levied against him for unpaid income taxes, threatening his ownership of the popular Hugh Casey's Steak and Chop House bar on Flatbush Avenue.[68] On July 3, 1951, the 38-year-old Casey will commit suicide by shooting himself in the throat with a 16-gauge shotgun at the Atlantan Hotel in his native Atlanta while his estranged wife Kathleen tries to talk the "Fireman" out of it over the phone at the same time that Casey's close friend Gordon McNabb and his wife are rushing to his room.[69]

1951

March 12, 1951: Chandler Loses Owners' Support, Resigns as Commissioner

During their spring meeting at the Shoremede Hotel ballroom in Miami Beach, major-league owners deliver a crushing blow to the future of A.B. "Happy" Chandler, the sport's second commissioner. Needing the support of three-fourths of the owners to retain his position, Chandler can only muster a 9 to 7 vote in his favor.[70] On June 15, 1951, Chandler will announce his resignation, effective a month later on July 15, 1951.[71]

April 10, 1951: Wage Board Limits Player Salaries, Musial a Big Loser

The Wage Stabilization Board, an independent federal agency charged with controlling wages in the aftermath of the surge in inflation at the start of the Korean War in June 1950, rules that baseball salaries are subject to government control. A club may not pay any player more than the salary of its highest paid player during the 1950 season.[72] The new policy will have the greatest impact on Stan Musial, whose 1951 contract called for an increase of up to $35,000 more than the $50,000 he received in 1950 as the highest paid Cardinal player.[73] After months of appeals and negotiation by representatives of Organized Baseball, on January 16, 1952, the Board will change its policy, abolishing salary ceilings on individual players in favor of club payroll ceilings. Teams can use as their ceiling a figure 10 percent more than the highest annual payroll paid during the period 1946–1950, or the amount paid in 1951. The new policy also allows teams to pay held-up 1951 raises to individual stars; within a few weeks, the Cardinals will issue a check to Musial for $20,001 ($25,000 increase, less withholding taxes).[74]

June 26, 1951: Court Dismisses Injured Pitcher's Negligence Suit Against Cubs

Boyd Tepler, a left-handed pitcher in the Cubs organization, sues Organized Baseball, the Chicago Cubs, and owner William Wrigley in federal court for $450,000, alleging that the injury he suffered to his pitching arm was the result of negligence by managers who failed to correct his pitching style. He also contends that the reserve clause made it impossible for him to get proper advice which might have prevented permanent injury to his arm. On May 1, 1953, the U.S. Court of Appeals for the Second Circuit will affirm the decision of the lower court dismissing his complaint for failure to state a cause of action.[75]

July 30, 1951: Congressional Committee Investigates Baseball's Antitrust Exemption

Brooklyn Congressman Emanuel Celler, chairman of the Subcommittee on Monopoly Power of the House Judiciary Committee,[76] begins a wide-ranging hearing on monopolies that will investigate, among other topics, whether the antitrust exemption granted to professional baseball by the U.S. Supreme Court's 1922 *Federal Baseball v. National League* decision should continue. On this opening day of the hearing, Hall of Famer Ty Cobb testifies that the reserve clause does not violate players' rights.[77]

August 19, 1951: Midget Pinch-Hits for Browns After Signing Contract with Bill Veeck

Eddie Gaedel, a three-foot, seven-inch, 65-pound midget, makes his major league debut for the St. Louis Browns when he pinch hits for rookie outfielder Frank Saucier in the bottom of the first inning of the second game of a doubleheader against the Detroit Tigers.[78] To legitimize the publicity stunt, part of a celebration to mark the 50th anniversary of the American League, Browns owner Bill Veeck had the previous day signed Gaedel to a contract for $15,400, or $100 a day, the minimum wage scale for a midget act.[79] Veeck mailed the contract to American League headquarters the night before the Sunday game, but retained a second copy which manager Zack Taylor shows to umpire Ed Hurley when Gaedel, wearing number ⅛[80] and carrying a toy bat, strides to the plate. With proof in hand that Gaedel is on the Browns' roster, Hurley instructs the Tigers to play ball. Faced with a strike zone of about an inch and a half, Bob Cain serves up four straight balls and Gaedel earns a walk in his first and only major league at-bat.[81] Two days later, on August 21, American League President Will Harridge will void Gaedel's contract on the grounds that it is not in the best interests of baseball.[82]

October 23, 1951: Ford Frick First Commissioner to Testify Before Congress

Less than a week into his new job, Ford Frick becomes the first commissioner of baseball to testify before Congress when he appears as a witness at the ongoing hearing investigating baseball's antitrust exemption (see entry for July 30, 1951).[83] Future Supreme Court Associate Justice John Paul Stevens, then serving as counsel for the subcommittee conducting the hearing, handles most of Frick's testimony, starting with questions and answers on "the rape of the Red Sox" between 1919 and 1921.[84] Stevens also asks Frick about the commissioner's role in representing "the players, the public, and the owners," and the new commissioner agrees that the question places his constituencies in the correct order.[85]

1952

June 20, 1952: Future President Portrays Real-Life Pitcher Named for Former President in Hollywood Biopic

The Winning Team, a "Hollywoodization" of the life of Hall of Fame pitcher Grover Cleveland Alexander who had died on November 4, 1950, at the age of 63, premieres at the Mayfair Theater in New York City.[86] The Warner Brothers film, which will gross $1.7 million during its run and later become a staple on late night television, stars Ronald Reagan as "Old Pete" and Doris Day as his wife Aimee. In addition to climaxing with Alexander's heroic strikeout of Yankee slugger Tony Lazzeri to clinch the 1926 World Series title for the Cardinals (in reality, the strikeout occurred in the 7th inning), the film also chronicles Alexander's early life as a telephone company lineman and amateur ballplayer, a career path he chose over his father's wish that he study law and become a lawyer.[87] Reagan's performance as Alexander gives rise to the "ultimate trivia question" about baseball and presidents:

"Name the only pitcher named for a U.S. President who was played by another one in the movies."[88]

June 21, 1952: Eleanor Engle Is Second Woman Signed to Minor League Contract

Twenty-six-year-old softball player Eleanor Engle, who works as a stenographer for the Pennsylvania Public Utilities Commission, is signed to a contract by the Harrisburg (Pennsylvania) Senators of the Interstate League, a class B minor league.[89] The second woman signed as a minor league player—pitcher Jackie Mitchell, by the class A Chattanooga Lookouts, in 1931, is the first (see entry for April 2, 1931)—Engle will participate in pre-game drills the next day but never get into a game. George M. Trautman, president of the National Association of Professional Baseball Leagues (the minor leagues), immediately declares her contract null and void, calling it a "travesty" on baseball.[90] With the support of Major League Baseball Commissioner Ford Frick, he also rules against any further signing of female players, declaring in a bulletin sent to all minor league teams that "no such contract will be approved and that any club which undertakes to enter into such a contract … will be subject to severe disciplinary action."[91]

1953

January 28, 1953: Saigh Convicted of Income Tax Evasion, Forced to Sell Cardinals

Fred Saigh, a tax and corporate lawyer and the owner of the St. Louis Cardinals, is sentenced to 15 months in federal prison and fined $15,000 for income tax evasion. As a result of the criminal conviction, Major League Baseball, led by Commissioner Ford Frick and National League President Warren Giles, will force Saigh to sell the team. Despite higher offers from groups in Milwaukee and Houston, Saigh will sell the Cardinals to Anheuser-Busch, Inc., for $3,750,000, partly in return for Gussie Busch's commitment to keep the team in St. Louis. Together with St. Louis businessman Robert Hannegan, Saigh had purchased the team from Sam Breadon in 1947 for $4 million; he later bought out Hannegan and became sole owner of the Cardinals in 1949.[92] Ironically, despite a long-standing disagreement with Anheuser-Busch over who deserved credit for keeping the team in St. Louis, Saigh began purchasing A-B shares soon after his release from prison in November 1953 (he served six months) and "was said to have become the largest single owner of the brewery's stock outside the Busch family," with holdings valued at about $60 million.[93]

February 16, 1953: Court Creates Right of Publicity in Suit Between Baseball Card Companies

In litigation involving rival chewing gum companies—Topps of Brooklyn and Bowman, owned by Haelan Laboratories of Philadelphia—fighting over the use of photographs of leading players on their respective baseball cards, Judge Jerome Frank of the United States Court of Appeals for the Second Circuit creates a new legal right involving personality and control of an image. He determines that "a man has a right in the publicity value of his photograph, i.e., the right to grant the exclusive privilege of publishing his picture" and that this is "independent of the right of privacy." Judge Frank even provides the name for this new right when he notes that it "might be called a 'right of publicity.'"[94] The "sleepless rivalry to sign up the baseball players" will be deemed newsworthy enough to be featured in the very first issue of a new magazine, *Sports Illustrated*, complete with a six-page gatefold containing 27 full-color reproductions of 1954 Topps baseball cards, including future Hall of Famers Willie Mays, Jackie Robinson, Duke Snider, Eddie Mathews, and Richie Ashburn.[95] It will be nearly three years after Frank's decision before the Topps-Bowman dispute is finally resolved by an out-of-court settlement (see entry for January 20, 1956).

November 9, 1953: Supreme Court's *Toolson* Decision Upholds Antitrust Exemption

The United States Supreme Court issues its decision in *Toolson v. New York Yankees*,[96] upholding professional baseball's antitrust exemption first granted by the Court's 1922 *Federal Baseball* decision (see entry for May 29, 1922) and rejecting a challenge to the reserve clause. The Court notes that "Congress has had the ruling under consideration but has not seen fit to bring such business [of providing public baseball games for profit between professional baseball players] under these laws by legislation having prospective effect."[97] Justice Harold Burton, joined by Justice Stanley Reed, dissents from the per curiam majority decision, concluding that "it is a contradiction in terms to say that the defendants ... are not now engaged in interstate trade or commerce...."[98]

1954

April 8, 1954: Garagiola Supports Reserve Clause Before Congress

Joe Garagiola, a 28-year-old reserve catcher for the Chicago Cubs, appears before the Subcommittee on Antitrust and Monopoly Legislation of the House Judiciary Committee to describe the difficulties he has experienced in trying to retire from the game to work as a radio broadcaster.[99] The subcommittee is considering legislation to make baseball teams owned by alcoholic beverage companies, such as Anheuser-Busch and the St. Louis Cardinals, subject to antitrust laws. After engaging in a lengthy discussion of baseball's tampering rules with Colorado Senator Edwin C. Johnson, also the president of the Western League, Garagiola, who eventually will become a renowned broadcaster and receive the Ford C. Frick Award from the Hall of Fame in 1991, declares that in spite of the confusion it may have engendered for his post-career plans, "you have to have the reserve clause."[100]

May 18, 1954: Olympic and Baseball Star Buried in Towns Renamed for Jim Thorpe

Voters of Mauch Chunk and East Mauch Chunk, Pennsylvania, approve a consolidation of their towns under a new name, Jim Thorpe. Hoping tourism will resurrect the struggling community, officials of the new municipality will the next day enter into a contract with Patricia "Patsy" Thorpe, third wife and widow of the Olympic legend and former outfielder who played 289 major league games between 1913 and 1919, mostly for the New York Giants, in which she agrees to allow his body to remain buried there as long as the towns "are officially known and designated as 'Jim Thorpe.'" Thorpe's body actually had been moved from Tulsa to Pennsylvania in February 1954, 11 months after his death on March 28, 1953, in Lomita, California, but it will be more than three years later, on May 30, 1957, when the 20-ton red marble Jim Thorpe Memorial Mausoleum, featuring a baseball player at bat among its medallion images, is finally dedicated a short distance outside of the renamed town.[101]

July 12, 1954: Major League Baseball Players Association Formed

In Cleveland one day before the All-Star game (won by the American League, 11–9), player representatives from each major league team form the Major League Baseball Players Association. Attorney J. Norman Lewis, previously retained to oversee negotiations over the pension plan, is hired to assist the new organization.[102] Ralph Kiner of the Chicago Cubs and Allie Reynolds of the New York Yankees will continue to serve in their elected roles as League Player Representatives until July 1955, when all 16 teams will elect representatives; they in turn will elect the league representatives. Shirley Povich heralds the efforts of Kiner and Reynolds, noting their refusal "to be bluffed or intimidated by the prospect of retaliation from the owners" and acknowledging that it was they "who pushed through the project for legal counsel for the players."[103] Despite the gains signified by its formation and survival, later commentators will characterize the MLBPA, at least until it elects Marvin Miller as its executive director (see entry for March 5, 1966), as a "'House Union' guided by a member of the Commissioner's office and the most influential owner [Walter O'Malley of the Dodgers] of that time."[104]

October 27, 1954: Joe DiMaggio and Marilyn Monroe Are Divorced

After a brief hearing in a Santa Monica, California, court, Judge Orlando H. Rhodes grants actress Marilyn Monroe an interlocutory decree of divorce from husband Joe DiMaggio, the retired Yankee Clipper, on the grounds of mental cruelty.[105] On October 6, 1954, a mere ten months after their January 14, 1954, marriage by a Municipal Court judge at San Francisco City Hall,[106] a teary-eyed Monroe, with Hollywood defense lawyer Jerry Geisler ("attorney to the stars") at her side, had publicly announced their separation in front of their North Palm Beach home.[107] The divorce will become official one year after the interlocutory decree is granted; the marriage lasted 286 days.

1955

July 5, 1955: Doctor Sues O'Malley Over Comments About Campy's Wrist Surgery

Neurosurgeon Samuel Shenkman files a $500,000 slander lawsuit against Walter O'Malley over a statement issued to the press by the Dodger owner upon receipt of the $9,500 bill Shenkman submitted for the surgery he had performed on catcher Roy Campanella's hand.[108] In May 1954, after Campanella jammed his left wrist while sliding in a spring training game, Dr. Herbert Fett surgically removed an inch-long bone chip fragment which he said had become entangled with a nerve. But Campy suffered through a poor 1954 season, batting only .207 with 19 home runs and 51 RBIs, prompting him to undergo a second operation on the hand, performed by Shenkman on October 20, 1954.[109] While Campanella returned to form in 1955, winning his third MVP award, the Dodgers refused to pay Shenkman's fee, leading the surgeon to sue Campanella and the Dodgers in May 1955.[110] A New York trial jury will resolve the litigation over the fee by awarding Shenkman $5,000 for his services in February 1956, and a year later, in November 1957, O'Malley will settle the separate slander suit for $15,000.[111]

1956

January 20, 1956: Topps Settles Baseball Card Suit, Acquires Bowman's Trademarks

After acquiring Haelan Laboratories—producer of Bowman baseball cards—in a merger, Connelly Containers settles litigation with rival Topps Chewing Gum over the use of photographs on baseball cards produced by both companies (see entry for February 16, 1953). Topps agrees to pay $200,000 for the rights to Bowman's trademarks and player contracts plus a five-year non-competition agreement.[112] Topps will later perfect the monopoly that Bowman unsuccessfully attempted and convince the Federal Trade Commission, in the face of a 1965 challenge by the Frank H. Fleer Corporation of Philadelphia,[113] that its practices in gaining control of the baseball card industry were legal.

July 16, 1956: Louisiana Anti-Mixing Law Causes Demise of Minor League Teams

Louisiana Governor Earl K. Long signs an act passed unanimously by the state legislature which prevents racial mixing in sporting events, stating that "the comment I've had over the state has run about 4 to 1 in favor of it."[114] Dick Butler, president of the double-A Texas League, had asked the governor to veto the bill, suggesting that the Shreveport Sports, the league's only Louisiana team, would be "seriously, if not conclusively affected" by its passage. In fact, without a major league affiliation due to the ban and a significant drop in attendance, the Sports will fold after the 1957 season.[115] On November 28, 1958, Justice John Minor Wisdom, ruling in a challenge brought by African American boxer Joe Dorsey, will declare the antimixing law "unconstitutional insofar as ... [it] attempt[s] to prohibit athletic contests between negroes and whites based solely on the contestants' race or color."[116] A five-year boycott by once-loyal African-American fans will force the New Orleans Pelicans of the double-A Southern Association to surrender its franchise to the league on March 15, 1960; Little Rock is immediately assigned the team.[117]

1957

February 2, 1957: Owners Won't Raise Minimum Salary but Increase Pension Benefits

At a mid-winter gathering of players at New York's Hotel Commodore, Major League owners reject a request from the players, represented by J. Norman Lewis, to increase the minimum salary from $6000 to $7500. The owners also decline the players' request to permit an inactive player, the recently retired Bob Feller, to serve on the four-man pension plan committee. Feller is allowed to complete his two-year term, but without voting rights. The owners do agree, however, to increase pension plan benefits, setting the minimum monthly check at $88 and the maximum at $550.[118]

1958

June 3, 1958: LA Voters Approve Plan to Provide Land for Dodger Stadium

Los Angeles County voters pass Proposition B, the "Dodger referendum," by a narrow margin—24,293 out of the 666,577 votes cast.[119] With this vote, the electorate affirm the agreement approved by the Los Angeles City Council on October 7, 1957, in which the city agreed to provide Dodger owner Walter O'Malley with approximately 300 acres in Chavez Ravine in exchange for, among other things, Wrigley Field, a minor league stadium sitting on nine acres near downtown Los Angeles,[120] and a commitment by the team to build a new major league ballpark on the property provided by the city.[121]

July 9, 1958: Casey Stengel Testifies Before Congress About Antitrust Exemption

New York Yankees manager Casey Stengel testifies as an expert witness at a hearing conducted by the Subcommittee on Antitrust and Monopoly of the U.S. Senate Committee of the Judiciary to consider bills seeking to exempt professional baseball from federal antitrust laws. Questioned by Chairman Estes Kefauver as to why Organized Baseball wants the bills enacted into law, Stengel "launch[es] into a rambling stream of consciousness and disjoined observations that were typical of the speech patterns dubbed Stengelese. By the time he finish[es], the whole room [is] in an uproar."[122]

1959

July 21, 1959: Pumpsie Green Debuts for Red Sox, Last Team to Integrate

At Chicago's Comiskey Park, Elijah Green, Jr., an African American infielder better known as Pumpsie who has just been called up from the Minneapolis Millers, debuts for the Boston Red Sox, entering the game against the White Sox in the eighth inning as a pinch runner and finishing up at shortstop. By doing so, Green completes the process begun by Jackie Robinson 12 years earlier when he broke baseball' s color line (see entry for April 10, 1947) as the Red Sox become the last major league team to integrate. Green will play more than 300 games for the Red Sox in four years with the team, 1959 to 1962, and then complete his five-year MLB career with the New York Mets in 1963 after being traded to the National League expansion team on December 11, 1962.[123]

July 27, 1959: Continental League Announced, MLB Responds by Adding Teams

William A. Shea, an attorney serving as chairman of the Mayor's Baseball Committee of the City of New York, issues a press release announcing the formation of a third major league. Called the Continental League, it intends to begin play with a minimum of eight teams in 1961.[124] Within a month, Branch Rickey will be announced as president of the new league and MLB owners, wary of pressure from Congress to provide more major league teams, will indicate their support of a new league as long as various conditions are met (e.g., indemnifying owners whose territory is violated).[125] However, hardly more than a year later, on August 1, 1960, Shea and Rickey will announce the cessation of the Continental League in light of the National and American leagues agreeing to expand to ten clubs each.[126] The National League will keep its promise by accepting two Continental League franchise groups, Houston and New York, as expansion teams for the 1962 season, but the American League will ignore Continental League investors and instead add teams in Los Angeles and Washington for the 1961 season.[127]

July 30, 1959: Portland Beavers Sue MLB Over Revenue Lost Because of Television

The Pacific Coast League's Portland Beavers sue Major League Baseball in federal district court for $1.8 million, claiming a substantial loss of revenue due to the televising of major league games and seeking to break up a major league monopoly on players and to prevent "unfair competition through television." The Beavers contend that MLB's "monopolistic practices" could bring the downfall of the minor leagues.[128] A year later, on September 13, 1960, the U.S. Court of Appeals for the Ninth Circuit will uphold the district court's judgment for MLB, holding that "if professional baseball is to be brought within the pale of federal antitrust laws, the Congress must do it."[129]

1960

May 17, 1960: Furillo Sues Dodgers After Release While Injured

General manager Buzzie Bavasi ends Carl Furillo's 15-year career with the Dodgers by giving the 38-year-old right fielder his unconditional release after he has appeared in only eight games for the season, due at least in part to a calf injury. Furillo will sue the Dodgers for breach of contract to recover the remaining $21,000 of his 1960 salary of $33,000, relying on a provision in his contract providing for full payment of salary for a disability resulting from injury.[130] Within a few months of his release, the Dodgers promise to pay the full salary for 1960, but Furillo subsequently contends that his continuing injuries obligate the team to pay him for 1961 as well, and that Organized Baseball has blacklisted him.[131] On July 13, 1961, a month after conducting a day-long hearing at his office in New York, MLB Commissioner Ford Frick rules that Furillo is entitled to his full 1960 salary, but not his 1961 salary, finding that the Dodgers terminated his contract "due to insufficient playing ability," not injury. He will later state that "[t]here is no such thing as a baseball black list."[132]

November 3, 1960: A Player Named "Law"—Vernon—Wins Cy Young Award

Capping the greatest season of his 16-year-career, Vernon Law of the Pittsburgh Pirates is selected as the winner of the Cy Young Award as baseball's best pitcher of 1960.[133] The most successful of the four players named Law who have played in the big leagues,[134] Deacon[135] posted a record of 20 wins, 9 losses, 3.08 ERA, and a league-leading 18 complete games in 1960. He also won two games for the Pirates in their World Series victory over the New York Yankees that October. Although arm troubles will lead him to retire in August 1963, Law returns and in 1965 he will be named Comeback Player of the Year when he finishes 17–9 with a 2.15 ERA. He will retire for good in 1967 with 162 career victories, all for the team that used a scouting tip from future U.S. senator Herman Welker to his Gonzaga University friend and Pirates part-owner Bing Crosby to help recruit the 18-year-old Law for the Bucs in the spring of 1948.[136]

1962

April 29, 1962: Roseboro Sues Rawlings Over Injury Caused by Defective Mask

Los Angeles Dodgers catcher John Roseboro is injured during the second game of a doubleheader between the Dodgers and Pittsburgh Pirates at Dodger Stadium when a foul ball off the bat of Pirates slugger Dick Stuart cracks the weld in his face mask and hits him above the right eye. Roseboro is removed on a stretcher, treated in the clubhouse, and transferred to Daniel Freeman Hospital for overnight observation and x-rays.[137] Although Roseboro will return to the lineup in less than two weeks, he will continue to have bad headaches for the remainder of the season. He will later sue the Rawlings Manufacturing and Sporting Goods companies on a theory of strict liability for the manufacture and distribution of an allegedly defective mask. On October 20, 1967, a Los Angeles Superior Court jury will award Roseboro $20,000 in damages,[138] but two years later, on July 23, 1969, the California Court of Appeals will uphold a motion to grant a new trial because Roseboro's theory of strict liability required him to prove that "the mask was defective when it was delivered" and the evidence on that point was conflicting. In addition, the court finds that the damages award was excessive.[139]

May 29, 1962: Buck O'Neil Becomes First African American Coach in MLB

The Chicago Cubs, in the midst of its unique "college of coaches" experiment, sign 50-year-old John "Buck" O'Neil as the first African American coach in major league history. He becomes the eleventh member of the Cubs' coaching staff, but General Manager John Holland indicates that he will serve as an instructor and won't be a member of the head coaching rotation which will consist of El Tappe, Lou Klein, and Charlie Metro.[140] O'Neil had previously played for and managed the Kansas City Monarchs of the Negro American League from 1938 until the team folded in 1955.[141] Having employed him as a part-time scout since 1953, the Cubs made him full-time in 1955, and in that capacity he signed Lou Brock for the team in 1960 and mentored such players as Ernie Banks, Billy Williams, and George Altman.[142] After his tenure as a coach ends, he will return to scouting full-time in 1964 and remain in that capacity until retiring after 32 years with the Cubs in 1988. Buck O'Neil will become a self-described "overnight star" at age 82 in 1994 when he plays a starring on-screen role in Ken Burns's nine-part PBS documentary, *Baseball*.[143] He will remain in the public eye thereafter, including serving as chairman of the Negro Leagues Baseball Museum in Kansas City, Missouri, until his death in 2006 at the age of 94.[144]

1963

October 2, 1963: Koufax's Mastery of Yankees Inspires "Baseball and the Law" Poem

Dodger pitcher Sandy Koufax sets a World Series record by striking out 15 Yankees in Game One of the fall classic, a 5–2 victory for Los Angeles.[145] Edward R. Ward will be so inspired by the future Hall of Famer's domination of the Bronx Bombers that he will include a mock caption of a "lawsuit" (Tony Kubek, Bobby Richardson, Tom Tresh, Mickey Mantle, Roger Maris, et al. vs. Sandy Koufax) dated October 2, 1963, in a poem titled "Baseball and the Law" that he publishes years later in the *Baseball Research Journal*.[146] Equally impressed after Koufax finishes the Dodgers 4–0 sweep of its longtime rival by pitching another complete game victory on October 6, Yankee player-coach Yogi Berra will say, "I can see how he won twenty-five games. What I can't see is how he lost five."[147]

1964

April 17, 1964: Shea Stadium Opens, Only Ballpark Named for a Lawyer

Lawyer William A. Shea, instrumental in the return of National League baseball to the city of New York through his chairmanship of Mayor Robert Wagner's Baseball Committee and formation of the Continental League as a potential rival of the National League (see entry for July 27, 1959), throws out the first pitch on the inaugural opening day at the Flushing, New York, stadium named in his honor.[148] Shea Stadium, a multi-purpose facility built at a cost of $29.5 million which will serve as the home of the New York Mets from 1964 through 2008, and the New York Jets from 1964 to 1983, is the only major-league stadium named for a lawyer.[149] In addition to a near capacity crowd of 50,312, eight members of the National Baseball Hall of Fame (Luke Appling, Max Carey, Red Faber, Frank Frisch, Burleigh Grimes, Heinie Manush, Bill Terry, and Zack Wheat) are on hand to witness the stadium's first game, a 4–3 defeat of the home team Mets, managed by future Hall of Famer Casey Stengel, by the Pirates.[150] The stadium will be demolished in 2009 to provide parking for nearby Citi Field, the new home of the Mets, where a logo with Shea's name on it hangs on the left-field wall alongside uniform numbers retired by the Mets (Stengel's 37, Gil Hodges's 14, Tom Seaver's 41, and Jackie Robinson's 42).[151]

May 28, 1964: Spahn's Suit Creates Cause of Action for False Praise

In a case described as "like no other ... in the history of American law,"[152] New York Supreme Court Judge Jacob Markowitz grants Warren Spahn, a Hall of Fame inductee in 1973 and the all-time leader in wins by a left-handed pitcher, $10,000 in damages and an injunction preventing the further distribution of *The Warren Spahn Story*, a 1958 biography for children written by Milton Shapiro and published by Julian Messner, Inc. Spahn had sought $175,000 in damages under New York's right to privacy law, claiming that Shapiro, who never met with the ballplayer, his family, friends, or any of Spahn's Milwaukee Brave teammates and used newspaper and magazine articles and general reference books as his only sources, manufactured facts and dialogue, obscuring the true facts of his life including his relationship with his wife, father, and son.[153] More than four years later and after multiple appeals, Spahn will agree to settle the case by foregoing the damages and injunctive relief for a book that is now more than ten years old.[154] Nevertheless, the case will stand alone as establishing the existence of a false light privacy cause of action based on false praise rather than defamatory statements.[155]

July 16, 1964: Congress Approves Little League's Charter of Incorporation

Twenty-five years after its first game on June 6, 1939—Lundy Lumber beat Lycoming Dairy, 23–8, on a field laid out in Williamsport, Pennsylvania, by founder Carl E. Stotz[156]—Little League's federal charter of incorporation is approved by unanimous act of both houses of the U.S. Congress and signed by President Lyndon B. Johnson.[157] Ten years later, on December 26, 1974, the act will be amended to remove barriers preventing girls from playing Little League baseball.[158]

September 1, 1964: Murakami Debuts with Giants, First Japanese Player in Majors

Nearly 40,000 spectators at Shea Stadium witness the debut of Masanori "Mashi"[159] Murakami, a 20-year-old left-handed pitcher for the San Francisco Giants, who becomes the first Japanese player in the major leagues when he takes the mound in the 8th inning against the New York Mets, giving up a hit but no runs, and striking out two in one inning of work.[160] Murakami was available only because his Japanese team, the Nankai Hawks, had signed an agreement with the Giants on January 6, 1964, which allowed the National League team to sign the pitcher for their Fresno farm club for the 1964 season. Murakami will be so successful in his September call-up, recording a 1.80

ERA over 9 games and 15 innings, that in October the Giants will exercise the option provided in the agreement with the Hawks to purchase the pitcher's contract from Nankai for $10,000.[161] Seeking to regain Murakami's services for the 1965 season, the Hawks will dispute the validity of the option as well as the contract Murakami had signed with the Giants in November, but a compromise eventually will be reached in late April 1965 which allows him to pitch for the Giants in 1965, then choose whether to stay with the Giants or return to the Hawks in 1966.[162] Loyalty to his Japanese baseball mentor and family pressure will bring Murakami back to Japan after the 1965 season, where he will continue to pitch until his retirement in 1982.

1965

August 22, 1965: Roseboro Sues Marichal After Bat Attack

While batting in the third inning against Dodger ace Sandy Koufax, Giants hurler Juan Marichal strikes Dodger catcher Johnny Roseboro in the forehead with his bat, opening up a two-inch gash and setting off a 14-minute brawl.[163] Roseboro will later accept blame for provoking the incident, admitting to buzzing a return throw to Koufax past the head of the Giants pitcher in retaliation for the brushback pitches Marichal had thrown at two Dodger batters earlier in the game.[164] On September 1, 1965, Roseboro will sue Marichal for assault and battery, seeking $110,000 in damages but eventually settling out of court in February 1970, reportedly for $7,500.[165] The two combatants eventually will reconcile and become friends, with Roseboro supporting Marichal's election to the National Baseball Hall of Fame in 1983 and Marichal serving as a pallbearer and speaker at Roseboro's 2002 funeral.[166]

CHAPTER 6

MLBPA and the Rise of the Players, 1966–1995

Introduction

Dodger pitchers Don Drysdale and Sandy Koufax staged a joint holdout in 1966 in their quest for a three-year, $1,000,000 pact. Although they failed to reach their goal, the effort produced two important outcomes. For the players, they broke the $100,000 annual salary barrier for pitchers. For Marvin Miller, the new executive director of the Major League Baseball Players Association (MLBPA), he gained a wedge which he used ten years later to convince owners fearful of similar combined player negotiations to accept reciprocal anti-collusion language in the 1976 basic agreement. Before that, however, Miller successfully negotiated the first collective bargaining agreement between MLB and the MLBPA in 1968. When the National Labor Relations Board asserted jurisdiction over Major League Baseball the following year, the stage was set for labor to achieve its greatest advances yet in the struggle with management over working conditions in baseball.

Although the Supreme Court's decision in *Flood v. Kuhn* handed the owners a significant victory in 1972 by solidifying MLB's antitrust exemption and failing to outlaw the reserve clause, in truth the means to its end already existed in the form of a collectively-bargained arbitration panel with an impartial chair which in 1970 replaced the commissioner as the device for resolving grievances. The long sought alteration to the perpetual reserve system finally occurred in 1975 with a favorable arbitration decision involving the contract rights of Dave McNally and Andy Messersmith. In various collective bargaining efforts, Miller negotiated other significant concessions from management, including increasing the minimum salary and establishing salary arbitration with the right of access to salary information. Nonetheless, concessions did not come without a price, as the 1970s were marred with labor stoppages in 1972, 1973, and 1976, and an equal number in the following decade (1980, 1981, and 1985). Worse yet, in the mid-to-late 1980s, owners sought to destroy the gains of the players and their union by colluding for three consecutive years to avoid signing free agents. In each instance, arbitrators found they had violated the very provision they had earlier inserted into the basic agreement. The resulting damage award was $180,000,000.

The period is not just about labor-management issues however. The passage of Title IX by Congress in 1972 helped create opportunities for girls to play Little League and youth baseball, although the regulations solidified softball as an alternative for high school and collegiate players. In another of baseball's halting steps toward increased diversity, Frank Robinson finally broke the color barrier for managers when he took the helm for the Cleveland Indians in 1975. Still the percentage of African Americans in the majors leveled off while players from Latin America began to rise.

By the mid–1980s, Organized Baseball was challenged by player use of street drugs. The 1985 Pittsburgh drug trials brought significant notoriety to the issue, although a decade later this would be eclipsed by the dramatic rise in the use of steroids. Gambling also resurfaced as a major issue when Pete Rose, baseball's all-time hit leader, was banned from the game by Commissioner Bart Giamatti.

After more than two decades of labor contentiousness, the nadir was reached in 1994 when an August players' strike shut down the game for the remainder of the season, including the World Series. The strike significantly impacted fan interest and the sport seemed to be in trouble as its new leader, Acting Commissioner Allan "Bud" Selig, sought ways to solidify his power and forge a more effective labor-management relationship. No one could have predicted the level of success that would be achieved.

1966

February 23, 1966: Koufax and Drysdale Holdout Together, Seek $1 Million Contract

The *Los Angeles Times* breaks the news that Don Drysdale and Sandy Koufax will ask the Dodgers for a combined three-year pact of $1,000,000, equally split between the two aces of the Los Angeles pitching staff.[1] Ginger Drysdale had proposed the joint effort to her husband and Koufax when the two stars expressed their frustration with General Manager Buzzie Bavasi's negotiating tactics.[2] The duo will engage noted entertainment lawyer J. William Hayes to represent them. With California's so-called de Havilland Law[3] prohibiting personal service contracts from exceeding seven years as a potentially more effective weapon in a court challenge than an attack on a reserve clause protected by baseball's antitrust exemption, Hayes eventually will be able to broker a compromise between the Dodgers and the pitchers, both of whose tenure with the club is well past seven years.[4] Under their new one-year contracts, they will become the first hurlers to break the $100,000 barrier: Koufax will receive $125,000 for what will turn out to be his last season, while Drysdale will be paid $110,000.[5] Beyond this historic breakthrough, their efforts will provide Marvin Miller with the leverage to negotiate for the inclusion of anti-collusion language for both players and teams in the 1976 collective bargaining agreement (see entry for September 21, 1987).[6]

March 5, 1966: MLBPA Elects Marvin Miller as Its Executive Director

The Executive Committee of the Major League Baseball Players Association elects Marvin Miller as full-time executive director of the association after negotiations with Robert C. Cannon, the MLBPA's legal advisor since 1959 and the committee's original choice, falter due to Cannon's additional demands.[7] Following the committee's action, Miller will tour spring training camps in Arizona and Florida, responding to player concerns and questions and, ultimately, winning their support of his selection in a 489–136 vote.[8] As executive director from 1962 to 1982, Miller will turn the "House Union" (see entry for July 12, 1954) into a powerful force for the players, increasing salaries, negotiating important concessions from owners, and supporting the Messersmith-McNally arbitration grievance that creates free agency (see entries for December 23, 1975, and March 9, 1976).

April 11, 1966: Emmett Ashford Is First African American Umpire in MLB History

After 15 years as a minor league umpire, including 12 in the triple-A Pacific Coast League,[9] 52-year-old Emmett Ashford becomes the first African American umpire in major league history as he works third base during the traditional American League season opener at Washington's D.C. Stadium, a 5–2 victory for the Cleveland Indians over the Washington Senators.[10] The stylish Ashford ("I'm not exactly without color" he said of himself) will work five years in the major leagues, including the 1967 All-Star game and the 1970 World Series, before retiring in 1970, one year past the mandatory retirement age of 55 which had been waived for him.[11]

April 18, 1966: Monsanto's Patented Artificial Turf First Used in Astrodome

In their first home game of the season, the Houston Astros take on the Los Angeles Dodgers at the Astrodome which, for the first time ever, sports an infield covered in "Astroturf," a synthetic surface created by Monsanto Industries under the name of ChemGrass.[12] In July 1967, Monsanto's James Faria and Robert Wright will receive a patent for their invention of a "grass-like turf useful both indoors and outdoors for a variety of recreational and sports activities."[13] By then, the Astrodome field, now completely covered with Astroturf, will be regularly used by both the Astros and the NFL's Houston Oilers.[14]

July 27, 1966: Wisconsin Supreme Court Clears Braves for Move to Atlanta

Resolving Wisconsin's suit against the National League and its ten teams for allowing the Milwaukee Braves to relocate to Atlanta beginning with the 1966 season, the Wisconsin Supreme Court reverses the May 5, 1966, decision of Judge Elmer W. Roller of the Circuit Court for Milwaukee County which enjoined the Braves franchise from playing its home games any place other than Milwaukee County Stadium unless and until the National League granted approval for a new Milwaukee franchise for the 1967 season.[15] The Supreme Court determines that baseball's antitrust exemption and the commerce and supremacy clauses of the United States Constitution bar using Wisconsin state antitrust law to prevent the Braves from relocating or force the league to grant an expansion franchise to Milwaukee.

1967

June 19, 1967: Father's Coaching Accepted as Business Expense for Tax Purposes

In a Tax Court decision, Judge Austin Hoyt determines that it is appropriate for Chicago Cubs catcher Randy Hundley to allocate $11,000, one-half of his annual $22,000 bonus payment,[16] as a business expense deduction for valuable services performed by his father Cecil in coaching his son.[17] In particular, Cecil, a former semipro ballplayer, taught Randy the then-novel one-handed catching style, an "unorthodox technique" requiring "an inordinate amount of time and effort by the teacher and the pupil."[18] Cecil also improved Randy's power hitting capability and worked with the media to promote his son's potential and garner a significant signing bonus.

1968

February 19, 1968: First-Ever Basic Agreement Establishes Grievance Arbitration

The first-ever Basic Agreement between Major League Baseball (MLB) and the Major League Baseball Players Association (MLBPA) is reached through collective bargaining. Among its key provisions, the agreement provides players with the right to have an impartial arbitrator from outside MLB decide grievances (art. III and schedule C of the Basic Agreement), increases the minimum salary from $7,000 to $10,000,[19] and establishes a study committee to consider "possible alternatives to the reserve clause as now constituted" (art. VIII).[20]

August 7, 1968: Cepeda Loses Suit for Unauthorized Use of His Name by Advertiser

In *Cepeda v. Swift & Company*, Judge John K. Regan of the United States District Court for the Eastern District of Missouri grants summary judgment for defendant companies Swift and Wilson against Orlando Cepeda, who sought actual and punitive damages for the "'unauthorized use of his name, photograph, reputation and signature' for advertising purposes."[21] Cepeda had signed an exclusive agreement which gave Wilson the right to make and sell baseballs with his name, as well as to license others to do so. Judge Regan disagrees with Cepeda's contention that the latter provision did not allow Wilson, a sporting goods manufacturer, to license the use of his name by Swift in connection with its meat products.

September 16, 1968: Umpire Firing Leads to Antitrust Suit and NLRB Claim

American League president Joe Cronin informs veteran umpires Al Salerno and Bill Valentine by phone that they are fired, effective immediately. The umpires assert that the dismissal is in response to their efforts to form a union for AL umpires, including a meeting on September 12 with National League umpires and their union's lawyer (NL umpires had successfully organized in 1963 and now had higher salaries and better pension benefits).[22] Cronin, however, will tell the press that the two were "inefficient umpires who were never first-class at any one time" and that he had "'no knowledge' of any umpire-organizing activities."[23] Reacting to the firing, the umpires union (now including AL umps) will file an unfair-labor-practice claim with the NLRB in January 1969 (see entry for December 15, 1969), and Salerno and Valentine will sue MLB, Joe Cronin, and the AL for $4 million in September 1969, alleging antitrust violations and defamation of character. But the NLRB will rule against the umpires in November 1970, claiming they had not proven the firing was because of union activities,[24] and the U.S. Court of Appeals for the Second Circuit will affirm a lower court's dismissal of the lawsuit, noting that only the Supreme Court could overturn its previous decisions holding that professional baseball was not subject to antitrust laws.[25]

November 18, 1968: MLBPA's Baseball Card Licensing Agreement with Topps

Marvin Miller and the Major League Baseball Players Association reach a new agreement with Topps Chewing Gum, Inc., on the licensing of images of players on trading cards. Soon after his election as MLBPA executive director (see entry of March 5, 1966), Miller noted the numerous copies of signed contracts in the office files, contracts with a "structure [that] ... was unconscionable."[26] After forcing the issue with Topps by convincing players not to sign renewal agreements, Miller is able to double the annual individual fee to players from $125 to $250 in the first year, and $500 in 1969.[27] More important, for the first time, players are guaranteed a royalty payment of 8 percent of Topps' sales up to $4 million and 10 percent for sales over $4 million.[28] Royalties in the first year of the new agreement will be $320,000; over the next 25 years, this figure will rise to $50 million from Topps and four other companies.[29] The Players Association eventually will use the licensing revenue strategically to build a substantial strike fund for use during work stoppages.[30]

1969

February 4, 1969: Bowie Kuhn Succeeds William Eckert as Commissioner

At a meeting at the Americana Hotel in Bal Harbour, Florida, baseball owners unanimously elect forty-two-year-old Bowie Kuhn, a partner in the New York City law firm of Willkie Farr & Gallagher, as commissioner pro tempore for a one-year term at a salary of $100,000. With previous experience as legal counsel for Major League Baseball, Kuhn succeeds William D. "Spike" Eckert, forced by the owners to resign in December 1968.[31] After receiving a long-term contract in August 1969, Kuhn will serve as Major League Baseball's fifth commissioner for 15 years, until the owners deny him a third term and unanimously elect Peter Ueberroth as commissioner on March 3, 1984.[32] Since Ueberroth is not available until he completes his duties as organizer of the 1984 Olympic Games in Los Angeles, Kuhn will continue in office until September 30, 1984.[33]

May 14, 1969: Maury Wills Found Guilty of Income Tax Deficiencies

A federal court of appeals finds Montreal Expos shortstop Maury Wills guilty of income tax deficiencies for 1962 and 1963, when he played for the Los Angeles Dodgers. The court affirms the decision of the commissioner of internal revenue that Wills's "tax home" was Los Angeles, not Spokane where he had a personal residence but spent little time during the years in question, and therefore he could not deduct travel expenses while in the City of Angels.[34] The court also rejects Wills's argument that the fair market value of the MG automobile ($1,731) he received as the "Most Popular Dodger" and the S. Rae Hickok Belt ($6,038) he was presented as the outstanding professional athlete of 1962 should be exempt as awards given in "recognition of religious, charitable, scientific, educational, artistic, literary, or civic achievement," rather than taxable as personal income from a prize or award.[35]

December 15, 1969: NLRB Rules MLB Is Subject to Its Jurisdiction

In a decision that will have a major effect on the relationship between Major League Baseball and the unions representing both players and umpires, the National Labor Relations Board rules that the MLB is subject to the jurisdiction of the NLRB.[36] In so ruling, the Board rejects the American League's contention that the NLRB lacks jurisdiction to handle a dispute with two umpires, Al Salerno and Bill Valentine (see entry for September 16, 1968), because of baseball's antitrust exemption and because the umpires are "supervisors" and thus not eligible to appeal to the NLRB.

December 24, 1969: Curt Flood Attacks Reserve Clause in Suit Over Trade

Objecting to his trade from the St. Louis Cardinals to the Philadelphia Phillies in October 1969,[37] Curt Flood writes a letter to Commissioner Bowie Kuhn asking that he be allowed to avoid the reserve clause and determine for himself where to play by seeking offers from other major league teams. He states: "After twelve years in the major leagues, I do not feel that I am a piece of property to be bought and sold irrespective of my wishes. I believe that any system which produces that result violates my basic rights as a citizen and is inconsistent with the laws of the United States and of the several states."[38] On December 30, 1969, Kuhn will deny the three-time All-Star's request, agreeing with Flood that he is not a piece of property but finding the point inapplicable to the player trade in question.[39] With the backing of the Major League Baseball Players Association, former Supreme Court Associate Justice Arthur Goldberg will file suit on Flood's behalf on January 16, 1970, in the United States District Court for the Southern District of New York against Kuhn, the presidents of the American and National leagues, and all 24 MLB teams. Seeking a preliminary injunction to stop enforcement of the trade and $1 million in damages, the suit will allege that the enforcement of the reserve clause violates the Sherman Act, state antitrust laws, and certain civil rights statutes, and subjects him to involuntary servitude in violation of the Thirteenth Amendment.[40]

1970

February 19, 1970: Kuhn Suspends Denny McLain for Gambling Activities

Acting in response to advance notice of a *Sports Illustrated* cover story about "Baseball's Big Scandal," Commissioner Bowie Kuhn indefinitely suspends Detroit Tigers pitcher Denny McLain, who won 31 games in 1968, for "involvement in 1967 bookmaking activities and his associations at that time."[41] The suspension will be converted to three months on April 1; McLain will pitch his first game on July 1, but will win only three of eight decisions over the season. In 1985, McLain will be convicted of racketeering, extortion, and conspiracy to distribute cocaine and sentenced to 23 years in jail, but when a federal appeals court grants him a new trial in August 1987, McLain will be released from the Federal Correctional Facility in Talladega, Alabama, having spent less than three years in jail.[42] McLain later will accept a plea bargain and be sentenced to five years of probation on December 16, 1988.[43] Troubles will return for McLain in 1996, when he and his business partner will be convicted for embezzlement and money-laundering $3 million from their company's employee pension fund. With the company forced into bankruptcy, nearly 200 employees will be put out of work. McLain will be sentenced to eight years in prison and required to pay $2.5 million in restitution.[44]

March 4, 1970: District Court Favors MLB in Flood Antitrust Suit

Responding to plaintiff Curt Flood's request for a preliminary injunction that is designed to allow him to play the 1970 season without reporting to the Philadelphia Phillies to whom he was traded by the Cardinals in October 1969 (see entry for December 24, 1969), Judge Irving Ben Cooper of the United States District Court for the Southern District of New York rules that not only has Flood failed to show the irreparable harm required for granting the injunction, but to do so would provide Flood with the ultimate relief he seeks, free agency.[45] The actual trial, which commences on May 19 and concludes on June 10,[46] will feature former players Jim Brosnan, Hank Greenberg, and Jackie Robinson testifying on Flood's behalf, but no current players come to his defense or even attend the trial.[47] In deciding the case on August 12, Cooper will rule against Flood's contention that enforcing the reserve clause violates antitrust and civil rights statutes, as well as the 13th Amendment's involuntary servitude provision.[48] He not only finds that "[c]learly the preponderance of credible proof does not favor elimination of the reserve clause," but also that "[s]ince baseball remains exempt from the antitrust laws unless and until the Supreme Court or Congress holds to the contrary, we have no basis for proceeding to the underlying question of whether baseball's reserve system would or would not be deemed reasonable if it were in fact subject to antitrust regulation."[49] Cooper's decision will be affirmed by a federal appeals court on April 7, 1971,[50] setting the stage for the case to make its way to the United States Supreme Court (see entry for June 19, 1972).

May 12, 1970: Second Basic Agreement Creates Grievance Arbitration Panel

Major League Baseball and the Major League Baseball Players Association reach accord on the second Basic Agreement, with provisions retroactive to January 1, 1970. The new agreement raises the minimum salary to $12,000, recognizes the MLBPA as exclusive bargaining agent for the players, reduces the maximum salary cut to 20 percent, establishes the right to representation by an agent, and, in a "significant breakthrough, ... [creates] a tripartite grievance arbitration panel with a permanent impartial chairman,"[51] thereby eliminating the power of the commissioner of baseball to rule on disputes over the interpretation of the collective bargaining agreement.[52]

June 28, 1970: Law School Built on Former Site of Forbes Field

Almost 61 years to the day after the Pittsburgh Pirates lost to the visiting Chicago Cubs, 3–2, on June 30, 1909, in the first game played at Forbes Field, one of the first steel and concrete ballparks, the Pirates again play the Cubs in the last game at the now venerable ballpark (a 4–1 Pirates victory, completing a doubleheader sweep[53]). Two fires will damage the park before it is finally demolished in July 1971. The University of Pittsburgh had purchased Forbes Field in 1958, and after its demolition, the university will erect, among other structures, the Barco Law Building, home to the University of Pittsburgh School of Law, on the site where Forbes was located. A section of the outfield wall will stand beside the university's business school, and home plate, encased in Plexiglas, is set into the lobby floor of the Forbes Quadrangle building.[54]

August 25, 1970: Video Games Must Have License to Use Player Names and Stats

Judge Philip Neville of the United States District Court for the District of Minnesota grants an injunction against Keith and Kent Henricksen, manufacturers and sellers of "Negamco's Major League Baseball" and "Big League Manager Baseball" games, for failing to pay a licensing fee when using the names and statistics of hundreds of major league players in the games.[55] Neville determines that the players possess a proprietary or property interest that the game manufacturers had misappropriated by using the names and data while refusing to enter into a licensing agreement.

October 1, 1970: Lawyer Lewis Gill Named First Impartial Grievance Arbitrator

Lewis M. "Lew" Gill, a 1936 graduate of the University of Pennsylvania School of Law and a veteran arbitrator and mediator for the federal government,[56] is named by the Major League Baseball Players Association and the clubs of the American and National leagues as the first permanent impartial grievance arbitrator under article X of the second basic agreement between MLB and the MLBPA (see entry for May 12, 1970).[57]

October 3, 1970: Umpires Win Concessions After One-Day Strike During LCS

Unhappy with stalled talks about higher salaries and supported by the Teamsters and the Building Services unions, American and National League umpires strike during the opening games of the League Championship Series in Pittsburgh and Minnesota. Amateur umpires are used as replacements.[58] The action follows a tumultuous year and a half in which American League President Joe Cronin had dismissed umpires Al Salerno and Bill Valentine for "incompetence," leading to an unfair-labor-practice claim with the NLRB and a suit by the fired umps (see entry for September 16, 1968). And in December 1969, American and National League umpires had voted favorably in an NLRB-certified election to be represented by a single bargaining agent, the renamed Major League Umpires Association (previously the Umpires Association).[59] In quickly settling the one-day walkout, John Reynolds, attorney for the umpires, will gain concessions from a management negotiating team led by National League President Chub Feeney, including increases in compensation for working the All-Star Game, the League Championship Series, and the World Series.[60]

1971

September 1, 1971: Pirates Use First-Ever All-Minority Starting Lineup

With 11,278 in attendance at Three Rivers Stadium in Pittsburgh, another barrier drops in the long fight to integrate baseball when the Pirates field an all-minority starting lineup against the Philadelphia Phillies, a first in Major League history. The Pirates use all African American and dark-skinned Latin American players in the following batting order: Rennie Stennett, 2B; Gene Clines, CF; Roberto Clemente, RF; Willie Stargell, LF; Manny Sanguillen, C; Dave Cash, 3B; Al Oliver, 1B; Jackie Hernandez, SS; Dock Ellis, P.[61] After the game, a 10–7 victory for the Bucs, Pirates manager Danny Murtaugh denies even being aware of the makeup of the starting nine when he handed his lineup card to umpire Stan Landes, let alone its historical significance.[62] Although fans, players, and even the media may initially share Murtaugh's view, years later the game will be called "one of the most significant milestones in the racial history of major league baseball."[63]

September 28, 1971: Arbitrator Overturns Kuhn's Suspension of Alex Johnson

Arbitrator Lewis Gill overturns Commissioner Bowie Kuhn's placement of Alex Johnson on the "restricted list," ruling that the troubled Angels outfielder was "emotionally incapacitated" during the events that led the team to suspend him without pay or service credit for 30 days on June 16 for "failure to give his best efforts toward the winning of the club's baseball games." Prior to the suspension, the Angels had fined him on 29 separate occasions. As a result of Gill's decision, Johnson is placed on the disabled list with full pay and credit for service retroactive to the date of the suspension, although his fines of $3750 are upheld. Required to pay his full $30,000 salary, the Angels trade Johnson to the Cleveland Indians at the end of the 1971 season.[64]

December 28, 1971: Ruling Over Compensation Owed PCL for MLB's Expansion

The Portland Baseball Club, former owner of the Portland Beavers of the Pacific Coast League, sued Commissioner Bowie Kuhn, the American and National leagues, and all their individual teams, claiming a breach of contract under Rule 1(a) of the Professional Baseball Rules. Portland Baseball Club alleged that defendants had refused to pay just compensation to the PCL and its clubs—required by Rule 1(a) when MLB expands into a minor league's market—after the Seattle Pilots and San Diego Padres expansion franchises drafted two PCL club territories in 1968.[65] Pursuant to Rule 1(a) procedure, the amount of compensation was decided by an arbitration panel in March 1969.[66] In the subsequent litigation contesting the arbitration determined amount, Federal District Court Judge Gus J. Solomon rules that the monetary award belonged to the PCL or the new owners of the Portland franchise, not the former owner, and that, in any case, "the constitution of the arbitration panel was proper and … the award was neither fraudulent nor corrupt."[67]

1972

April 1, 1972: Pension Dispute Leads to First-Ever League-Wide Strike

Following a strike authorization vote of 47–0 (with one abstention) by player representatives of the Major League Baseball Players Association on March 31—subsequently approved by the entire union membership, 663–10—players begin not only the first league-wide strike in Major League history, but also the "first industry-wide work stoppage in American professional sports."[68] Before the dispute over the pension fund is settled on April 13, the strike will cause the elimination of the final week of spring training and result in the loss of 86 regular-season games, costing owners "an estimated $5.2 million" and players "about $600,000."[69] Play for the 1972 season, which will range from 153 games for some teams to 156 for others, with division winners determined by won-loss percentage, will begin on April 15.[70]

June 19, 1972: Supreme Court Upholds Reserve Clause and Antitrust Exemption in *Flood*

Justice Harry Blackmun, writing for a 5–3 majority, rules against Curt Flood, the veteran St. Louis Cardinals center fielder who sued Organized Baseball and Commissioner Bowie Kuhn in an effort to eliminate the game's longstanding reserve clause after being traded to the Philadelphia Phillies (see entries for December 24, 1969, and March 4, 1970).[71] After considering the Court's earlier *Federal Baseball* and *Toolson* opinions (see entries for May 29, 1922, and November 9, 1923), as well as others involving professional sports and theater, Blackmun relies on stare decisis to rule in favor of Kuhn and uphold both the reserve clause and baseball's antitrust exemption.[72] Justice William O. Douglas writes a stinging dissent, claiming that "this Court's decision in *Federal Baseball* ... is a derelict in the stream of the law that we, its creator, should remove. Only a romantic view of a rather dismal business account over the last 50 years would keep that derelict in midstream."[73] Justice Thurgood Marshall also dissents, correctly identifying what will come to be the accepted legal view that "the reserve system is now part and parcel of the collective-bargaining agreement and that because it is a mandatory subject of bargaining, the federal labor statutes are applicable, not the federal antitrust laws."[74] Perhaps ironically, the lead section of *Flood v. Kuhn*, titled "The Game," beginning with the June 19, 1846, New York Nine victory over the Knickerbockers, concluding with references to poems about the game, and containing in the middle Blackmun's carefully chosen list of 88 baseball luminaries,[75] will become as well known and talked about as the outcome of the case itself.

1973

February 8, 1973: Salary Arbitration Added by New Basic Agreement

Hoping to gain leverage in their negotiations with the Major League Baseball Players Association over a new basic agreement, team owners tell their 960 players that spring training, scheduled to commence on February 14, will not open until the ongoing dispute over working conditions is resolved.[76] After many months of talks, the owners and players will bring an end to the lockout on February 25 when they reach a tentative three-year agreement. Most important, the new basic agreement that both sides quickly ratify will establish salary arbitration for the first time in baseball history. It also raises the minimum salary to $15,000, sets new limits on salary cuts, and creates a five-and-ten year rule nicknamed the "Curt Flood Rule."[77] The latter will allow a player with ten years of major league experience and five consecutive years with the same club to veto a proposed trade.[78]

March 5, 1973: Yankee Pitchers Swap Wives and Families

New York Yankees pitchers Mike Kekich and Fritz Peterson hold separate press conferences to announce that they have agreed to swap wives and families. The two had agreed to consider the idea in July 1972 and began the arrangement in October after the season ended. Susanne Kekich, her two daughters Kristen and Reagan, and the family terrier joined Peterson at his home, while Marilyn "Chip" Peterson, her two sons Gregg and Eric, and a poodle moved in with Kekich. Kekich and Marilyn's relationship will not last, but Peterson and Susanne will marry in 1974 and have four children of their own together.[79] As for the baseball careers of the two lefties, Peterson will pitch one more season for the Yankees, then be traded to the Indians. He will post a 133–131 record and 3.30 ERA over his 11-year career. Kekich will pitch only five more games for the Yankees before being traded to the Indians on June 12, 1973; his record will stand at 39–51, with a 4.59 ERA when he finishes his nine-year career in 1977.

June 19, 1973: Mill Valley Withholds Use of Field Until Little League Accepts Girls

The Mill Valley, California, City Council refuses to allow the town's only public ball field to be used for Little League baseball in the coming year unless girls are allowed to participate. The Council's action is prompted by the refusal of league officials to let ten-year-old Jenny Fuller try out for a team during the previous two seasons. Fuller had even sought the assistance of the White House, writing to President Nixon to no avail.[80]

1974

March 29, 1974: New Jersey Requires Little League to Allow Participation by Girls

The Appellate Division of New Jersey Superior Court upholds the order of the New Jersey Division on Civil Rights that "Little League Baseball, Inc. and all local baseball leagues chartered by it in [New Jersey must] admit girls aged 8 to 12 to participation in their baseball programs conducted in [New Jersey]."[81] The agency's order was based on the findings and recommendations of its hearing officer, Sylvia Pressler, entered on November 7, 1973, in a gender discrimination claim filed by the Exxex chapter of the National Organization for Women on behalf of 12-year-old Maria Pepe, who in 1972 had been removed from her Hoboken little league team after only three games.[82] Little League officials from Williamsport, Pennsylvania, had threatened to revoke Hoboken's Little League charter unless it banned girls from participating in the league.[83]

August 23, 1974: Kuhn Suspends Steinbrenner after Campaign Misconduct Conviction

Two weeks after President Richard M. Nixon resigns from office, Yankees owner George Steinbrenner pleads guilty to one count of conspiracy to violate federal campaign contribution laws, a felony, and one count of aiding and abetting obstruction of an investigation, a misdemeanor, both stemming from his illegal contribution of $100,000 to Nixon's 1972 re-election campaign. The "Boss" will avoid jail time when Federal District Court Judge Leroy Contie,

Jr., fines him $15,000, and his company, American Shipbuilding, an additional $20,000.[84] Two months later, on November 27, Commissioner Bowie Kuhn, troubled particularly by the obstruction of justice conviction, will suspend Steinbrenner from baseball for two years.[85] Nevertheless, Kuhn will reinstate him after only 15 months, on March 1, 1976, in time for Opening Day. And on January 19, 1989, in one of his final acts in office, President Ronald Reagan will pardon Steinbrenner's felony conviction.[86]

December 13, 1974: Arbitrator Makes Catfish Hunter a Free Agent Because of Finley Contract Breach

Arbitrator Peter Seitz rules in favor of future Hall of Fame hurler Jim "Catfish" Hunter in his grievance against Oakland Athletics owner Charles O. Finley. Seitz finds that Finley breached Hunter's two-year contract by failing to make required installment payments on a $50,000 insurance annuity (designed to defer salary until Hunter retired), and declares the pitching ace, a 20-game winner in each of the previous four seasons, a free agent.[87] Declaring that Seitz has given "a life sentence to a pickpocket," Commissioner Bowie Kuhn initially will seek to block teams from negotiating with Hunter, but will relent when MLBPA chief Marvin Miller threatens to file suit for collusive restraint in violation of the Basic Agreement.[88] Finley, however, will file suit in Alameda County Superior Court, seeking to have the arbitration decision overturned.[89] Finley will lose his request for a restraining order on January 3, 1975, when Judge George W. Phillips, Jr., concludes that Seitz's ruling was within the parameters of the subject presented to him and thus not "grossly irrational," a decision that is ultimately upheld by the California Supreme Court.[90] On December 31, 1974, Catfish Hunter, the "first big-money free agent," will sign a five-year contract with the Yankees with a value variously reported between $3.35 million and $3.75 million; in any case, it is the "largest in baseball history at that time."[91]

1975

April 8, 1975: Frank Robinson Is First African American Manager

Major League Baseball finally responds to Jackie Robinson's frequent criticism about the lack of blacks in off-field roles when 39-nine-year-old Frank Robinson becomes the first African American to manage a regular season game, leading the Cleveland Indians to a 5–3 victory over the New York Yankees in the Tribe's season opener at Municipal Stadium.[92] Signed as the team's player-manager on October 3, 1974,[93] Robinson, a triple-crown winner in 1966 and the only player to win MVP awards in both leagues, contributes a home run in his first at bat in the bottom of the first inning as the club's designated hitter.[94] Robinson will go on to helm four teams for a total of 16 years, compiling a record of 1065–1176 and receiving the American

League Manager of the Year Award in 1989 for his leadership of the Baltimore Orioles.[95]

August 12, 1975: Al Campanis Patents "Target Glove" for Catchers

Al Campanis, a former second baseman who played seven games for the Brooklyn Dodgers in 1943 and later served as the team's general manager in Los Angeles from 1968 to 1987, receives a patent for devising a catcher's mitt with a fluorescent orange stripe surrounding the pocket of the glove. The "target glove" is intended "to keep the eyes of a player throwing a baseball at the glove riveted on the glove, and especially the pocket of the catching side of the glove."[96]

December 23, 1975: Seitz Ends Reserve System in Messersmith-McNally Arbitration Decision

Arbitrator Peter Seitz renders his decision in grievances filed on behalf of Andy Messersmith of the Los Angeles Dodgers and Dave McNally of the Montreal Expos by the Major League Baseball Players Association. Seitz concludes that major league players become free agents if they play for one year for their team without a contract, despite the existence of a reserve clause in their previous contracts. The decision, in effect, ends the reserve system in Major League Baseball which had existed since the 1880s. Baseball lawyer and arbitrator Roger I. Abrams will call it "perhaps the most important labor arbitration award ever issued. Its impact still reverberates throughout the multibillion-dollar sports industry."[97] Nonetheless, Seitz is promptly fired after issuing his decision.[98]

1976

January 13, 1976: Court Blocks Sale of Giants, Halts Move to Toronto

When the city of San Francisco sues the San Francisco Giants for breaching its agreement to play all of its home games at Candlestick Park until 1995, Superior Court Judge Robert J. Drewes grants a court order temporarily blocking the sale of the Giants by owner Horace Stoneham to a Toronto group headed by the Labatt Brewing Company.[99] The proposed purchase included relocation of the team to Toronto. On March 21, the American League will grant an expansion franchise to Toronto to balance its earlier decision to add a franchise in Seattle and five days later, on March 26, the league will approve Labatt as the owner of the expansion Blue Jays, eliminating any further discussion of selling the Giants to the Canadian group.[100]

March 1, 1976: Kuhn Ends Spring Training Lockout by Owners

Owners lockout players as negotiations on a new collective bargaining agreement stall in the aftermath of the arbitration decision by Peter Seitz granting Dave McNally and Andy Messersmith free agency status (see entry for December 23, 1975).[101] On March 17, with Opening Day three weeks away, Commissioner Bowie Kuhn will use his authority to act in the best interest of baseball and order owners to open spring training camps after an 18-day delay, the third time in the past eight years the preseason period had been disrupted by labor issues.[102] On July 12, the owners and players will reach a new four-year basic agreement that grants free agency to players with six years of major league service, continues salary arbitration for players with two years of service, increases pension funding by 29 percent, and establishes a new minimum salary of $18,000.[103]

March 9, 1976: Court Supports Arbitrator's Jurisdiction in Messersmith-McNally

In *Kansas City Royals Baseball Corp. v. Major League Baseball Players Ass'n.*,[104] the United States Court of Appeals for the Eighth Circuit rules that arbitrator Peter Seitz had jurisdiction to render an arbitration decision in the disputes involving the free agent status of Andy Messersmith and Dave McNally (see entry for December 23, 1975) because the arbitration panel had been established through collective bargaining between the parties.

June 15, 1976: Kuhn Voids Finley Sale of Prospective Free Agents

With the trading deadline of midnight, June 15, looming, Oakland A's owner Charlie Finley, reaches agreements to sell players Joe Rudi and Rollie Fingers to the Boston Red Sox for $2 million, and former Cy Young Award winner Vida Blue to the New York Yankees for $1.5 million.[105] Finley is seeking recompense for players he fears he will lose to free agency at the end of the 1976 season. Several days later, on June 18, Commissioner Bowie Kuhn will void both sales as "not in the best interests of baseball." Finley, in turn, will file a $10 million restraint of trade suit against Kuhn, whom he called "the village idiot," on June 26.[106] The litigation won't be completed until 1978 (see entry for April 7, 1978).

September 6, 1976: Patent for Catcher's Mask with "Billy Goat" Throat Protector

At San Diego's Jack Murphy Stadium, shards from the broken bat of batter Bill Russell puncture the throat of Dodger catcher Steve Yeager in the on-deck circle. Despite the fact that one of the splinters narrowly misses piercing a major artery, Yeager will return to the lineup in just three weeks.[107] Inspired by the near tragedy, Dodger trainer Bill Buhler will develop and patent a throat protector device for the masks worn by catchers and umpires.[108] The plastic shield hangs from the bottom of the mask and thus becomes known as a "billy goat" by its legion of users.[109] The innovative Buhler, who spent 44 years with the Dodgers and was their lead trainer from 1960 until his retirement in 1995, also patented a lightweight baseball catcher's chest protector and developed special exercise equipment used by Tommy John while rehabilitating from the eponymous reconstructive elbow procedure developed by Frank Jobe in 1974.[110]

1977

January 3, 1977: Congressional Committee Wants Antitrust Exemption Eliminated

The House Select Committee on Professional Sports, formed in May 1976 after Major League Baseball refused to place a team in the nation's capital while approving expansion teams for Seattle and Toronto, issues its final report in which it concludes that "adequate justification does not exist for baseball's special exemption from the antitrust laws and that its exemption should be removed in the context of over-all sports antitrust reform."[111] Instead of calling for a full House vote, however, the committee requests additional study in the next Congress.[112] Chaired by B. F. "Bernie" Sisk of California, the committee had held hearings from June through September of 1976.[113]

May 19, 1977: Federal Court Supports Kuhn's Suspension of Ted Turner for Tampering

Federal District Court Judge B. Avant Edenfield upholds Baseball Commissioner Bowie Kuhn's use of the "best interests of baseball" clause to suspend Atlanta Braves owner Ted Turner for one year after Turner, in an effort to lure Giants outfielder Gary Matthews to Atlanta, disregarded Kuhn's multiple directives to avoid contacting or discussing potential free agents prior to the November reentry draft.[114] Judge Edenfield, however, refuses to uphold Kuhn's decision to take away Atlanta's first round draft choice in the June 1977 amateur free agent draft because "denial of a draft choice is simply not among the penalties authorized for this offense."[115]

December 29, 1977: Suit Seeks Access for Female Reporters to Clubhouses

Melissa Ludtke, a female sportswriter for *Sports Illustrated*, files suit in Manhattan federal court against Commissioner Bowie Kuhn and the New York Yankees for denying her access to the team's clubhouse during the 1977 World Series.[116] On September 25, 1978, the court will decide that the actions of the commissioner, including a letter sent to all teams on April 2, 1975, in which Kuhn indicated that all teams should take a "unified stand" against the admission of women reporters to major league clubhouses, and the Yankees "unreasonably interferes with plaintiff Ludtke's fundamental right to pursue her profession in violation of the due process clause of the Fourteenth

Amendment." It will enjoin the Yankees from denying "accredited women sports reporters" access to its clubhouse.[117]

1978

April 7, 1978: Court Upholds Kuhn's Disapproval of Finley's Player Fire Sale

In *Finley v. Kuhn*,[118] the United States Court of Appeals for the Seventh Circuit affirms the opinion of the District Court for the Northern District of Illinois upholding Commissioner Bowie Kuhn's use of the "best interests of baseball" clause of the Major League Agreement[119] to disapprove the Oakland A's attempts to sell Joe Rudi and Rollie Fingers to the Boston Red Sox and Vida Blue to the New York Yankees (see entry for June 15, 1976). A's owner Charles O. Finley claimed in his suit that the commissioner's action was beyond his authority, "arbitrary and capricious," and procedurally unfair. But the court determines that Kuhn acted in good faith and had the authority to make his ruling.[120]

1979

April 5, 1979: Law Professor Compares Players to Supreme Court Justices

Yale Law Professor Robert Cover offers "Your Law-Baseball Quiz" in the *New York Times* in which he asks readers to solve his multiple-choice quiz by identifying the baseball player who "bears the same relationship to baseball as a particular U.S. Supreme Court justice bears to the law." For instance, Cover finds that among Yogi Berra, Roberto Clemente, Tris Speaker, and Willie Mays, Chief Justice Earl Warren is most like Berra because "both ... were enormously effective performers on teams with many stars. Despite the presence of players such as Mantle, Maris, Frankfurter, Douglas and Black in the same lineup.... Berra and Warren were the truly most valuable players. Both would frequently swing at bad pitches, but both were capable of hitting them for extra bases, especially in the clutch."[121]

May 18, 1979: Umpires' Strike Ends with Significant Concessions for Union

The third strike by umpires in major league history—the first occurred during the 1970 League Championship Series (see entry for October 3, 1970) and the second was a one-day walkout on August 25, 1978, which was quickly ended by injunction[122])—ends after seven weeks when an agreement between Major League Baseball and the Major League Umpires Association, is formally signed. The umpires' union, led by attorney Richie Phillips, achieves significant concessions, including a fixed salary scale of $22,000 to $55,000, based on years of service; annual no-cut contracts; an increase in per diem while traveling; rotation of postseason assignments; and a two-week in-season vacation.[123] The latter will exacerbate the ill will developed during the lengthy work stoppage, which began on Opening Day, between the striking umpires and their replacements, minor league umpires and others who were willing to cross the picket lines. Part of the agreement includes retaining eight of the replacements after the conclusion of the strike, primarily to make the bargained for vacations feasible.[124]

July 26, 1979: Paul Hits First Out-of-Park HR in Congressional Game

Representative Ron Paul (R–Tex) launches a slow curveball from Representative Ron Mottl (D–Ohio) over the left-field wall at Alexandria's Four Mile Run Park for the "first out-of-the-park home run" ever hit in the Congressional Baseball Game.[125] Despite Paul's heroics, the Democrats and Mottl, who pitched in nine games for the Class D Pony League Bradford Phillies in 1955, win the annual charity game, first played in 1909 (see entry for July 16, 1909), 7–3.[126] More than 30 years later, Paul, sporting the distinctive multicolored Houston Astros throwback jersey, will be inducted into the Roll Call Congressional Baseball Hall of Fame on June 28, 2012.[127]

October 26, 1979: Kuhn Bans Mays and Mantle Because of Casino Jobs

Commissioner Bowie Kuhn sends a telegram to Willie Mays telling him that because of concerns over potential contact with gamblers, he will have to choose between his position as a batting coach with the New York Mets and an offer of a high-paying public relations job with Bally's Park Place Casino in Atlantic City. When financial considerations lead Mays to choose the position with Bally's, Kuhn will ban him from any official association with the game on October 29, less than three months after his August 5 induction into the Hall of Fame.[128] In 1983, Kuhn will issue a similar edict against another Hall of Famer, Mickey Mantle, when the former Yankee slugger and current batting coach takes a position with Del Webb's Claridge Casino Hotel in Atlantic City, also for financial reasons.[129] Both players will remain outside baseball until March 18, 1985, when Kuhn's successor, Peter Ueberroth, reverses Kuhn's rulings, concluding that "[i]t was in the best interest of baseball that two of its greatest stars be reinstated."[130]

November 19, 1979: Contract Makes Nolan Ryan Baseball's First Million-Dollar Player

After playing eight years (and tossing four no-hitters) for the California Angels, free agent Nolan Ryan more than quadruples his $200,000 annual salary and becomes baseball's first million-dollar-year player when he signs a four-year contract with the Houston Astros for $4.5 million, the richest pact in baseball history to date.[131] The contract negotiated for Ryan by lawyer Dick Moss, MLBPA general counsel from 1967 to 1977, will pay Ryan a salary of $1 million a year, plus a $250,000 signing bonus and a $250,000 retirement payment.[132] Ryan will go on to pitch nine years for the Astros, winning 106 games and striking out 1,866 batters, before ending his 27-year major league career in 1993 after five years with the Texas Rangers. He will be elected to the Hall of Fame in his first year of eligibility in 1999.

1980

March 4, 1980: In-Season Strike Averted, New CBA Reached

Meeting at a Tampa motel, the executive board of the Major League Baseball Players Association, frustrated by a lack of "constructive negotiating by the owners for a new basic agreement," votes 27–0 in support of a resolution authorizing a players strike on or after April 1.[133] On that date, the board will vote to strike the remaining eight days of spring training exhibition games, open the season on time, but then initiate a strike of the regular season on May 23 unless significant progress has been made on a new collective bargaining agreement.[134] On May 23, Marvin Miller, MLBPA's executive director, and Ray Grebey, MLB's chief negotiator, will reach a tentative four-year agreement on all issues except free agency, thereby averting the in-season strike. In the new basic agreement, the owners commit to increasing their pension benefits contribution from $8.3 million to $15.5 million; raising the minimum salary from $21,000 to $30,000, with an escalation to $35,000 by 1984; and broadening eligibility for salary arbitration. Both sides also agree to create a joint study committee, consisting of two players and two general managers, and charge it with issuing a report on compensation issues pertaining to free agency by January 1, 1981, with the proviso that owners may insert their own proposal on the matter if differences are not resolved by February 15, 1981 (see entry for January 5, 1981).[135]

August 25, 1980: Ferguson Jenkins Arrested for Drug Possession

Texas Rangers Pitcher Ferguson Jenkins is arrested after cocaine, hashish, and marijuana are found in his luggage at the Toronto airport.[136] Within a few days, Commissioner Bowie Kuhn will suspend Jenkins indefinitely for refusing to cooperate with MLB's investigation, but two weeks later arbitrator Raymond Goetz will order the suspension lifted with back pay at a grievance hearing requested on his behalf by the MLBPA. Then, on December 18, Canadian judge Gerald Young will find Jenkins guilty of three counts of cocaine possession but give him an "absolute discharge, meaning no fine, no jail term and no record of conviction."[137] Jenkins will deny his guilt, writing in his autobiography: "I did not put drugs in my suitcase, and I did not know what was going on.... I have contended that I was set up for this arrest and that I committed no crimes. I am pretty sure I know who did it, but that is not something I will reveal publicly."[138] Jenkins will be elected to the Hall of Fame in 1991—to date the only Canadian so honored—but this incident may explain why it took three years of eligibility to select a pitcher who had seven 20-victory seasons and 284 career wins.[139]

September 30, 1980: House Committee Holds Hearing on Violence in Sports

Michigan Congressman John Conyers, Jr., chair of the Subcommittee on Crime of the House Judiciary Committee, convenes the first of two days of hearings on excessive violence in professional sports. The hearings are prompted by the introduction on July 31, 1980, of the Sports Violence Act of 1980[140] by Congressman Ron Mottl (D–Ohio), a former collegiate and minor league pitcher (see entry for July 26, 1979). Mottl's "bill would make it a federal crime for professional players to use during-the-game force that creates a significant risk of injury, when that force has no reasonable relationship to the competitive goals of the sport, is unreasonably violent, and could not be reasonably foreseen or consented to by the intended victim."[141] Baltimore General Manager Hank Peters, appearing on behalf of Commissioner Bowie Kuhn, states that "we feel while the bill under consideration is a well intended one, it is totally unnecessary as it applies to our sport. Baseball is a nonviolent sport."[142] The bill fails to make it out of committee, but generates significant scholarly interest.

1981

January 5, 1981: Owners Unilaterally Adopt System for Free Agent Compensation

A special joint study committee of players (Bob Boone, Philadelphia Phillies, and Sal Bando, Milwaukee Brewers) and general managers (Frank Cashen, New York Mets, and Harry Dalton, Milwaukee Brewers) meets for the last time in an effort to resolve a dispute over compensation for teams that lose free agents (see entry for March 4, 1980). The committee's failure to do so triggers a provision that gives owners the option, between February 15 and 19, to insert their own system for free agent compensation into the Basic Agreement; should they do so, the players then have the right to call a strike.[143] On February 19, Ray Grebey, director of the owners' Player Relations Committee, will inform MLBPA executive director Marvin Miller that the owners are exercising their option. The existing system provides a draft pick to a team that loses a free agent; under the owners' proposal, professional compensation will be given for the top one-half of available free agents.[144] Fearing that this will limit the bargaining power of free agents and depress salaries, the players will respond on February 26 by establishing a May 29 strike date.

May 29, 1981: Court Won't Enjoin Owners, Leads to First-Ever Mid-Season Strike

The MLPBA agrees to postpone its strike while Daniel Silverman, New York regional director of the National Labor Relations Board, requests an injunction from Judge Henry F. Werker of the U.S. District Court, Southern District of New York, requiring owners to open their books to the union. A finding that the owners had committed an unfair labor practice would allow the players to recover lost wages and cause the owners to lose the value of their strike insurance.[145] But on June 10, 1981, Judge Werker will refuse to grant the injunction and instead send the matter back to collective bargaining. Two days later, on June 12, Major League players will go on strike, the first mid-season walkout in the sport's history.[146]

July 31, 1981: Seven-Week Strike Ends with Free Agent Compensation Pact

Seven weeks after the players walkout, Ray Grebey and Marvin Miller meet one-on-one to hammer out an agreement on free agent compensation, ending "the first strike with a season in progress in the history of major league American sport"[147] and the longest stoppage in baseball history to date. More than 700 games have been cancelled as a result of the strike, nearly 40 percent of the season. The loss in salaries by players is approximately $28 million, while the owners' losses are estimated at $116 million. Their net loss—less strike insurance of $44,000,000—is $72 million.[148] At the heart of the complicated solution which brings an end to the strike is the creation of two categories of ranking free agents based on a two-year statistical analysis by position, with the top 20 percent assigned to the Type A category and the next 10 percent to the Type B category. A team that loses a Type A free agent will be able to select a player from a compensation pool and an amateur draft choice. For the loss of a Type B free agent, the team will receive two amateur draft choices. The compensation pool consists of all the players that remain after teams protect either 24 players if they sign a ranking free agent or 26 if they do not sign such a player.[149]

August 6, 1981: Split-Season Format for Determining Playoffs Adopted

After consulting with the MLBPA, the National League votes 9–3 and the American League 12–2 to approve a split-season format for determining the playoffs. The Athletics, Yankees, Dodgers, and Phillies, are declared the first-half champions.[150] They will play against the four second-half champions

(Expos, Astros, Brewers, and Royals), with the Dodgers eventually winning the 1981 World Series in six games over the Yankees.

August 25, 1981: Licensing Agreements for Topps Baseball Cards Don't Violate Antitrust Laws

In a case involving rival manufacturers of baseball cards,[151] Judge James Hunter III of the federal Court of Appeals for the Third Circuit rules that neither Topps' licensing agreements with individual players nor its group agreement with the Major League Baseball Players Association violate sections one or two of the Sherman Antitrust Act. With respect to the section one claim, Hunter determines that "[m]erely because Topps, through individual contracts with every minor league player, managed to obtain license agreements with all major league players does not make the aggregation of these contracts an unlawful combination in restraint of trade."[152] Hunter refuses to find Topps or MLBPA in violation of section two because neither could prevent other competitors from entering the market by negotiating deals with minor league players. Competition was not foreclosed by the actions of either Topps or MLBPA.[153]

1983

February 19, 1983: Valenzuela First to Win $1 Million Salary Arbitration Award

Fernando Valenzuela, the Mexican-born Los Angeles "folk hero" who inspired "Fernandomania" with his superlative pitching in 1981 and went on to win Rookie of the Year and Cy Young awards in the same season, becomes the first player to win a $1 million award at a salary arbitration hearing.[154] Arbitrator Tom Roberts, who later will rule on claims of owner collusion (see entries for August 31, 1989, and May 14, 2001), chooses Valenzuela's figure over the offer of $750,000 by the Dodgers. Valenzuela's representatives, Tony DeMarco, Steve Fehr, and Dick Moss, presented data showing a substantial increase in attendance at Dodger home games when the young southpaw took the mound, a key factor in the award which will make him the only pitcher other than Nolan Ryan to make $1 million a year (see entry for November 19, 1979).[155] Valenzuela held out in 1982, when he compiled a 19–13 win-loss record with a 2.87 ERA, and played under a renewed contract of $350,000. The award breaks the previous record of $700,000 awarded in 1980 to future Hall-of-Famer and Chicago Cubs reliever Bruce Sutter.

December 8, 1983: Lawyer Donald Fehr Elected MLBPA Executive Director

Donald M. Fehr, general counsel of the Major League Baseball Players Association since 1977, is elected acting executive director by the association's executive board at its meeting in Maui, Hawaii. Fehr had first become involved with the players union when he worked on the landmark Messersmith-McNally free agency case (see entry for December 23, 1975).[156] Fehr will assume the executive director position on a permanent basis in December 1985.[157] Over his 26 years as MLBPA's leader, the average player salary will increase from $289,000 in 1983 to $3.24 million in 2009.[158]

1984

July 27, 1984: Brewers Owner Selig Wins Tax Case in Opinion Filled with Baseball References

In an opinion replete with references and quotations from baseball history, Judge William J. Bauer of the 7th U.S. Court of Appeals affirms a district court opinion allowing Brewers owner Bud Selig to allocate $10.2 million of the $10.8 million purchase price of the Seattle Pilots to the value of the 149 player contracts acquired by the Milwaukee club in the 1970 sale. In 1979, the Internal Revenue Service disallowed the entire allocation by determining that the value of the players' contracts were zero, creating a tax liability of "a little more than $141,000."[159] In a fight between the government and Selig's appraisers, Judge Bauer upholds the lower court's determination that Selig has the stronger argument. Judge Bauer ends his opinion by paraphrasing Ernest L. Thayer's "Casey at the Bat" (see entry for June 3, 1988), concluding that "there should be joy somewhere in Milwaukee—the district court's judgment is affirmed."[160] As a result, Selig will receive a $151,609 refund from the federal government.[161]

1985

August 6, 1985: Players Stage One-Day Mid-Season Strike Over Salary Arbitration

With salary arbitration as the major obstacle separating the parties, players go on strike for the second time at mid-season. The debate involves service time. The owners want to require three years for eligibility while the players want a two-year requirement.[162] The strike is settled the very next day, August 7, when Lee MacPhail, the primary negotiator for the owners as head of the Player Relations Committee, retreats from his demand for a 100 percent cap on salary increases in arbitration awards. In turn, the players agree to accept a delay in eligibility from two years to three years.[163]

September 20, 1985: Pittsburgh Drug Trials End with Guilty Verdict

In what will become known as the "Pittsburgh Drug Trials," a trial jury in the Federal District Court for the Western District of Pennsylvania finds Curtis Strong, a former Philadelphia Phillies clubhouse chef, guilty on 11 counts of distributing cocaine to major league baseball players.[164] The 14-day trial was a media sensation as seven current or former major leaguers—Keith Hernandez, Dave Parker, Jeffrey Leonard, John Milner, Dale Berra, Lonnie Smith, and Enos Cabell, all granted immunity from prosecution—testified about the rampant use of cocaine and amphetamines in baseball.[165]

1986

February 28, 1986: Ueberroth Suspends Players from Pittsburgh Drug Trials

Baseball Commissioner Peter Ueberroth conditionally suspends 11 players involved with cocaine admissions stemming from the 1985 Pittsburgh Drug Trials (see entry for September 20, 1985), seven for a year (Keith Hernandez, Dave Parker, Jeffrey Leonard, Dale Berra, Lonnie Smith, Enos Cabell, and Joaquin Andujar), four for 60 days. Ueberroth agrees to waive the suspensions of the former if they contribute 10 percent of their 1986 salaries to drug programs in their cities, the latter, 5 percent. All must perform at least 100 hours of drug-related community service and undergo drug testing for the rest of their careers, along with ten other players named in testimony during the drug trials.[166]

October 29, 1986: Court Rules That MLB Owns Copyright to Game Telecasts

In a battle over control of the immense revenue potential represented by telecast rights to major league baseball games, Federal Circuit Court Judge Jesse E. Eschbach decides in favor of Major League Baseball and its teams in a suit against the Major League Baseball Players Association in which they sought a declaratory judgment that they owned all rights to MLB games, including the right to license telecasts of them.[167] The players argued that the common law right of publicity gave them control over their individual performances such that MLB could not contract with broadcasters to televise games without first acquiring express authorization from the players performing in them. Since this had not been done, telecasts of MLB games violated the property rights of the players.[168] Eschbach, however, rules that the performances are "works for hire" under copyright law, since completed within the scope of the players' employment, and thus MLB and its teams, as the employer, own the copyrights to the telecasts.[169] Furthermore, the players' publicity rights in their performances are preempted under federal copyright law by the owners' exclusive copyright in the telecasts.[170]

1987

July 23, 1987: Steinbrenner's Criticism of Umpire Is "Razzing," Not Libel

Noting that former American League umpire Dallas Parks's action for defamation against New York Yankees owner George Steinbrenner requires consideration of "one of the most colorful of American traditions—the razzing of the umpire," New York Appellate Division Justice Betty Weinberg Ellerin dismisses the complaint on the ground that the press release to which Parks objects was a "constitutionally protected expression of pure opinion."[171] Steinbrenner responded to Parks ejecting two Yankee players, Roy Smalley and Oscar Gamble, in consecutive games against the Toronto Blue Jays by issuing a press release on August 29, 1982, in which he lambasted the ejections as "ludicrous" and noted that "my people tell me he is not a capable umpire."[172] Ellerin states that in determining whether a statement expresses actionable facts or protected opinion, a court must look at the "broader social context" for any customs or traditions which might indicate to a reader whether the statement is fact or opinion. In this instance, she relies on such baseball luminaries as Albert G. Spalding and Ned Hanlon, as well as General Douglas MacArthur (reported to have said when returning to America that "he was proud to have protected American freedoms, like the freedom to boo the umpire"), to find ample evidence for the "venerated American tradition of 'baiting the umpire.'"[173] Seen in this light, the average reader would regard Steinbrenner's remarks as merely "venting his frustrations" over the Yankees' poor performance by razzing the umpire, not as statements of fact, and thus not actionable.

September 8, 1987: Maryland Court Nixes Referendum Against Acquiring Land for Camden Yards

In a suit brought to force the secretary of state to accept referendum petitions opposing statutes authorizing acquisition of land for and the building of new baseball and football stadiums in Baltimore, the Maryland Court of Appeals rules that the bill funding the stadium authority was an "appropriations bill" and thus, under Maryland law, cannot be challenged by referendum.[174] One commentator has noted that with the determination by the court that the "private citizens of Maryland ... had no power to challenge the expenditure of funds, ... the door was opened. The stadium [Oriole Park at Camden Yards] would be a reality."[175]

September 21, 1987: Arbitrator Finds Owners Guilty of Collusion Against Free Agents

Arbitrator Tom Roberts rules in favor of the Major League Baseball Players Association in Grievance 86–2, filed in early 1986, in which it claimed that baseball's owners had acted in concert after the 1985 season to produce what Roberts characterizes as "the sudden and abrupt termination of all efforts to secure the services of free agents from other clubs."[176] Roberts finds that the owners violated the provision of the Basic Agreement forbidding either clubs or players from acting in concert which, ironically, was included in 1976 at the behest of owners who were concerned about the implications of the joint holdout and negotiations of Los Angeles Dodgers pitchers Don Drysdale and Sandy Koufax (see entry for February 23, 1966).[177] Roberts declares that Kirk Gibson and six other players should receive a "free-look" chance again as free agents in the ruling that will become known as "Collusion I,"[178] since it will be followed by two other arbitration decisions that also find the owners guilty of colluding against free agents (see entries for August 31, 1988, and July 18, 1990). Roberts will later award more than $10 million in damages to the players represented in this case by the MLBPA (see entry for August 31, 1989).

1988

March 28, 1988: Woman Loses Discrimination Suit to Play High School Baseball

A federal district court judge refuses to award damages and denies the injunction sought by 17-year-old high school senior Julie Croteau in the sexual discrimination lawsuit she brought to secure a position on the all-male varsity baseball team at Osbourn Park High School in Manassas, Virginia. Judge Tim Ellis III rules that the tryout in which Croteau participated was fair and free of gender bias and that "there is no constitutional or statutory right to play any position on any athletic team."[179] Croteau's passion for baseball will not lapse, however, and on March 17, 1989, as an 18-year-old freshman, she will play first base for five innings for St. Mary's College of Maryland in a Division III game against Spring Garden College, thereby becoming the first woman to play in an NCAA college baseball game.[180] After playing professionally for the Colorado Silver Bullets in its inaugural season (see entry for May 8, 1994), she will become the first woman to coach a men's NCAA Division I baseball team, the University of Massachusetts in 1995–96.[181]

June 3, 1988: "Casey at the Bat" Read Into *Congressional Record* on Its Centennial

On the centennial of the original publication of "Casey at the Bat" in William Randolph Hearst's San Francisco daily newspaper, the *Examiner*, on June 3, 1888,[182] Representative Tom Lantos of California requests that Ernest Lawrence Thayer's famous poem, "one of the highlights of American Culture" according to the congressman, be included in the record of the day's proceedings. With no objections, Speaker Pro Tem John Murtha orders that it be printed in the Congressional Record.[183]

August 31, 1988: Arbitrator Again Holds Owners Guilty of Collusion Against Free Agents

Arbitrator George Nicolau issues his decision in the grievance filed against the owners by the Major League Baseball Players Association on behalf of players who became free agents or filed for arbitration after the 1986 season. Filed on February 20, 1987, MLBPA contended that the owners violated a provision in the collective bargaining agreement which prevents clubs from acting "in concert with other clubs."[184] In the ruling, which will become known as "Collusion II" to distinguish it from similar rulings (see entries for September 21, 1987, and July 18, 1990), Nicolau concludes that major league owners and league executives, including Commissioner Peter Ueberroth, American League president Bobby Brown, and Barry Rona of the owners' Player Relations Committee, acted intentionally and together to ensure that the players who were free agents after the 1986 season were not signed by any team.[185]

September 28, 1988: Canseco Is First Player Publicly Accused of Steroid Use

Appearing on the CBS late night news program *Nightwatch*, *Washington Post* columnist Tom Boswell becomes the first to publicly accuse a ballplayer of using steroids when he tells host Charlie Rose that Oakland outfielder José Canseco is "the most conspicuous example of a player who has made himself great with steroids."[186] Although Canseco, who would finish the season as the first player ever to record 40 home runs and 40 steals and then win the American League Most Valuable player award, denies Boswell's claim,[187] Red Sox fans will mercilessly barrage the A's slugger ("Ster-oids! "Ster-oids!") when the teams face off at Fenway Park in the AL championship series the following week.[188] Canseco will finally admit to using steroids during a *60 Minutes* interview with Mike Wallace on February 13, 2005, a day before the release of his tell-all book, *Juiced*, which will go on to become a *New York Times* bestseller.[189]

1989

February 3, 1989: Bill White Named NL President, First Black to Head League

Fifty-five-year-old Bill White, a 13-year major league veteran who played first base and outfield for the St. Louis Cardinals and Philadelphia Phillies, is chosen to become the 13th president of the National League following a unanimous recommendation by the search committee, chaired by Peter O'Malley of the Los Angeles Dodgers, and the 12 league owners.[190] After finishing his playing career in 1969, the five-time All-Star became the first African American broadcaster for a major-league team when he teamed with Phil Rizzuto to cover the New York Yankees for 18 years (1971–89).[191] When he succeeds Bart Giamatti as NL president on April 1—Giamatti becomes commissioner of baseball on the same day—White will be the first African American to head a major professional sports league, as well as the first former player to head the National League since John Tener in 1913–18 (see entry for March 4, 1909).[192]

August 24, 1989: Giamatti Brokers Rose's Banishment for Gambling on Baseball

On the day after the birth of his daughter Cara Chea, Pete Rose, the all-time leader in base hits and manager of the Cincinnati Reds, signs a five-page document in which he voluntarily accepts permanent placement on baseball's ineligible list as a result of allegations of gambling documented in a report prepared by lawyer John Dowd for Major League Baseball.[193] In return, MLB agrees to make no formal finding as to the allegations.[194] At 9 a.m. the next day, Commissioner Bart Giamatti will fax a copy of the agreement to every team; he then will issue a press release and hold a press conference announcing Rose's banishment from baseball.[195] Just a few days later, on September 1, Giamatti will succumb to a heart attack which he suffers on Martha's Vineyard in Massachusetts.

August 31, 1989: $10.5 Million Awarded to Victims of Collusion After 1985 Season

Arbitrator Thomas Roberts awards $10,528,086.71 in salary shortfall damages to the 139 players, including Kirk Gibson, Carlton Fisk, Phil Niekro, Tommy John, and Don Sutton, represented by the Major League Baseball Players Association in the grievance it filed over collusion by owners against free agents after the 1985 season (see entry for September 21, 1987).[196] The award, determined only after Roberts spent more than a year consulting economic experts about the amount lost by players because of the collusion, covers only damages sustained in 1986 but not those from the loss of long-term contracts and bonuses, which are yet to be determined, along with interest and attorney's fees.[197] Also to be determined is how the money will be distributed among the players, since the decision does not give awards to specific individuals.[198]

1990

January 29, 1990: Court Holds Trademark in Ruth's Name Doesn't Cover Photos

Dorothy Ruth Pirone and Julia Ruth Stevens, Babe Ruth's two daughters, lose their federal circuit court appeal against publishing behemoth Macmillan for its use of three pictures of the Sultan of Swat in "The 1988 Macmillan Baseball Engagement Calendar." Although the women hold a trademark in the words "Babe Ruth," Judge Irving Kaufman rules that their rights do not extend to the photographs of the Bambino that Macmillan used, along with those of others such as Lou Gehrig and Mickey Mantle, to identify him as a great baseball star. This wasn't a trademark use and therefore there was no infringement.[199] Their right of publicity claim also fails because New York's privacy law applies only to living individuals.[200] Finally, the court rules that Macmillan's efforts did not constitute unfair competition.

February 15, 1990: "Super Twos" Created in Resolving Dispute Over Salary Arbitration Eligibility

In a dispute largely over salary arbitration eligibility, the owners lockout players before the beginning of spring training.[201] On March 18, both sides will agree to a new four-year Basic Agreement that ends the 32-day stalemate without losing any in-season games, although Opening Day will be delayed a week until April 9. Under the new agreement, eligibility for salary arbitration, which increased from two years to three years in 1985, also will now include the top 17 percent of players with more than two but less than three years of service time ("Super Twos"[202]). In addition, the minimum salary will increase from $68,000 to $100,000, and the owners' contribution to the pension plan from $34 million per season to $55 million.[203] Commissioner Fay Vincent, who is much more involved in these negotiations than were previous commissioners in earlier disputes, will contribute the basic framework for the compromise on salary arbitration.[204]

April 20, 1990: Pete Rose Imprisoned for Filing False Tax Returns

Already banned from baseball for alleged gambling on Major League Baseball games (see entry for August 23, 1989), Pete Rose pleads guilty in federal district court to two felony counts of filing false income tax returns for 1985 and 1987, charges stemming from his failing to declare income from baseball card shows.[205] By doing so, Rose escapes prosecution for income tax evasion when prosecutors agree to drop charges that he failed to report more than $25,000 in gambling winnings in those years. On July 19, Judge S. Arthur Spiegel will sentence Rose to five months incarceration at the Federal Prison Camp in Marion, Illinois; three months at the Talbert Halfway House in Cincinnati; one thousand hours of community service; and a fine of $50,000.[206] Rose will begin his prison sentence in Marion on August 8 and be released on January 7, 1991, just three days before a special committee formed by the Baseball Hall of Fame's Board of Directors supports the addition of a clause to the Hall's voting regulations: "Persons on the ineligible list cannot be eligible candidates."[207]

July 18, 1990: Arbitrator Focuses on Owners' Information Bank in Finding Collusion

Arbitrator George Nicolau rules in favor of the Major League Baseball

Players Association in its grievance over free agents after the 1987 season, dubbed Collusion III after two previous decisions concerning collusion by baseball owners (see entries for September 21, 1987, and August 31, 1988).[208] Nicolau focuses his attention on the owners' use of a salary offer information bank, created through the owners' Player Relations Committee after the first collusion decision, which made available to all clubs any offers made to free agents. While the clubs argued that they had a right to share information on free agents, Nicolau finds that it was basically intended to affect free agent salaries.[209] He points out that "the bank's message was plain—if we must go out into that market and bid, then let's quietly cooperate by telling each other what the bids are. If we do that, prices won't get out of line and no club will be hurt too much."[210]

November 29, 1990: Federal Act Adds Steroids to List of Controlled Substances

President George H.W. Bush, a former captain and first baseman for the Yale University baseball team (for which he played in the first two College World Series in 1947 and 1948), signs into law S. 3266, the Crime Control Act of 1990. Title XIX of this omnibus bill contains the Anabolic Steroids Control Act, under which steroids are for the first time classified as Schedule III controlled substances, along with amphetamines, methamphetamines, opiates, and morphine. With the passage of this Act, it is now illegal for anyone other than a registrant under the Act to prescribe, dispense, or distribute anabolic steroids.[211]

December 21, 1990: MLB Settles Collusion Grievances for $280 Million

Donald Fehr, executive director of the Major League Baseball Players Association and Chuck O'Connor, chief labor negotiator for major league team owners, use a fax machine to formally sign a $280 million settlement of the three grievances filed by the MLBPA against the owners for their alleged collusion against free agents after the 1985, 1986, and 1987 seasons (see entries for September 21, 1987, August 31, 1988, and July 18, 1990).[212] The settlement was first announced on November 3, 1990, when 16 players who were free agents after the 1987 season, including Jack Morris, Jack Clark, and Gary Gaetti, were granted new-look-free agent status.[213] The six-week delay in formalizing the earlier "handshake agreement" is necessary to finalize when and how the damages will be distributed and the tax implications of the damage payments to players, although it eventually will require a decision by the U.S. Supreme Court to determine how they are treated for tax purposes (see entry for April 17, 2001).[214] In fact, the final distribution won't occur until May 2004, 18 years after the cases began and 13 years after the damages award is established at $280 million. The years of delay caused by appeals and arbitration decisions will allow a Nashville money manager to increase the funds ultimately paid out to more than 650 players to $434 million.[215] Bob Horner will receive the largest amount, $7.03 million, followed by Lance Parrish ($5.8 million), Jack Clark ($4.4 million), and Doyle Alexander ($4.06 million). MLBPA, with the responsibility of determining who receives what, will reject about 3,800 claims, including that of Steve Garvey (see entry for May 14, 2001).

1991

June 4, 1991: Patent Granted for Chest Protector with Hinged Shoulder Flap

Mark Neuhalfen patents a chest protector with a removable, hinged shoulder flap, thus allowing the catcher freedom of motion when throwing the ball while offering additional protection for the shoulder of the throwing arm against foul balls or errant throws which hit the player's upper body. This protection is not available in existing chest protectors which have only a single shoulder pad to protect the upper portion of the non-throwing arm; the throwing arm is left unprotected so as to limit the restrictions on mobility.[216]

June 7, 1991: Steroids on List of Substances Banned by Baseball's Drug Policy

Baseball Commissioner Fay Vincent issues a memorandum to all Major League Clubs in which he becomes the first commissioner to explicitly include anabolic steroids among the substances prohibited under the sport's drug policy.[217] He acts in apparent response to the passage of the Anabolic Steroids Control Act of 1990 in which Congress added steroids to the list of Schedule III controlled substances (see entry for November 29, 1990).[218]

1992

July 17, 1992: Umpire Pam Postema Sues Baseball for Discrimination

Ruling on several motions in long-time minor league umpire Pam Postema's employment discrimination suit against both major leagues and the association of minor league clubs, federal district court Judge Robert P. Patterson, Jr., refuses to grant summary judgment against Postema because a material issue of fact exists as to whether defendant American League was involved in her termination by the Triple-A Alliance minor league.[219] Postema, "the "fourth woman ever to umpire a professional baseball game ... [and] the first woman to ever umpire ... game above the Class A level,"[220] had been discharged and unconditionally released from her AAA contract on November

6, 1989, on the ground that neither major league was interested in considering her for an umpire position.[221] Postema eventually will reach an out-of-court settlement in which she agrees not to reveal the amount she receives and to no longer apply for umpiring positions in any league affiliated with Major League Baseball.[222]

July 23, 1992: Commissioner Enjoined from Moving Cubs to NL East

Judge Suzanne B. Conlon of the United States District Court for the Northern District of Illinois issues a preliminary injunction preventing MLB Commissioner Fay Vincent from moving the Chicago Cubs to the National League's Eastern Division from the Western Division.[223] Judge Conlon determines that "the Commissioner lacked authority to unilaterally abrogate the Chicago Cubs' rights under Section 9.4 and 16.1 of the National League Constitution."[224] In less than two months, however, Vincent will be forced to resign by baseball's owners (see entry for September 7, 1992), whereupon Judge Conlon will issue an order on September 24, 1992, withdrawing and vacating the findings of fact, conclusions of law and order, and dissolving the preliminary injunction.

August 6, 1992: *Piazza* Holds That Antitrust Exemption Limited to Reserve System

Intending to relocate the team to St. Petersburg, Florida, Philadelphia businessmen Vince Piazza, father of Dodger rookie catcher Mike Piazza who will be inducted into the Hall of Fame in 2016, and Vincent Tirendi, along with four Florida investors, execute a letter of intent to purchase the San Francisco Giants from Bob Lurie for $115 million.[225] On September 10, Major League Baseball's Ownership Committee will claim that a background check has raised questions about Piazza and Tirendi; on November 10, MLB will formally reject the proposal to move the Giants to Florida.[226] Piazza and Tirendi, alleging damage to their reputations, will sue MLB for violating rights granted them by the Constitution and federal antitrust and civil rights statutes. On August 4, 1993, Judge John R. Padova of the Eastern District of Pennsylvania will dismiss the constitutional claims but allow the civil rights and antitrust claims to survive summary judgment, holding "that the [antitrust] exemption created by *Federal Baseball* is inapplicable here because it is limited to baseball's 'reserve system'"[227] (see entry for May 29, 1922). Judge Padova reasons that the Supreme Court in *Flood v. Kuhn* "stripped from *Federal Baseball* and *Toolson* any precedential value those cases may have had beyond the particular facts there involved, i.e., the reserve clause"[228] (see entries for November 9, 1953, and June 19, 1972). Although subsequent litigants seek to rely on Padova's opinion, most courts will hold that the exemption applies to the entire business of baseball and is not limited to the reserve clause (see entries for March 1, 1994, November 2, 1995, April 29, 1999, and January 15, 2015).[229]

September 7, 1992: Vincent Resigns as Commissioner After No Confidence Vote

In the face of an 18 to 9 vote of no confidence orchestrated by the "Great Lakes Gang"[230] a few days earlier on September 3 in Rosemont, Illinois,[231] Fay Vincent resigns as major league baseball's eighth commissioner. Although Vincent had initially vowed to fight his ouster, he agrees to step down in the "best interests of baseball." At the same time, he notes that "People have said, 'You're the last commissioner.' Well, if I'm the last commissioner, that's a sad thing."[232]

September 24, 1992: Illinois Enacts Nation's First "Foul Ball" Legislation

Illinois Governor Jim Edgar signs the nation's first "foul ball" legislation, the Baseball Facility Liability Act.[233] The act prevents fans injured by a ball hit into the stands (or a bat thrown into the stands) from suing the owner of the stadium unless the injury is the result of a protective screen that is defective because of the negligence of the owner or is due to the "willful and wanton conduct" of the owner or its manager, coach, or players.[234] Chicago's Cubs and White Sox supported passage of the legislation after two Illinois court decisions reversed the long-established legal trend that denied plaintiffs any recourse when injured by foul balls.[235] Arizona, Colorado, and New Jersey will eventually pass similar laws.[236]

1993

April 6, 1993: LA Dodgers Lose Trademark Battle Against Brooklyn Bar

Residents of Brooklyn get "a small measure of revenge" against the team which in 1957 abandoned the borough for greener pastures when a Manhattan federal district court judge rules that the Brooklyn Dodger Sports Bar and Restaurant can keep its name despite an attempt by the Los Angeles Dodgers to cut off its use, primarily to protect the sales of merchandise bearing the team's logo.[237] The Dodgers had brought a trademark and unfair competition action against the owners of the three New York establishments bearing the "offending" name. Judge Constance Baker Motley concludes that the Dodgers failed to establish actual confusion or a likelihood of confusion, thus failing to show trademark infringement or unfair competition.[238] She also rules that the team had abandoned use of the mark, particularly because of its failure to make any commercial trademark use of "Brooklyn Dodgers" between 1958 and 1981.[239] On May 4, 1994, the decision will be vacated pursuant to a settlement agreement reached between the parties.

1994

March 1, 1994: Antitrust Exemption Held to Cover Minor League Franchise Transfer Rules

Federal district court judge Martin Feldman grants a motion for summary judgment on plaintiff's federal and state antitrust claims in a suit brought by a group whose bid to purchase and transfer the Charlotte Knights, a Double A Southern League franchise, to the New Orleans market was unsuccessful.[240] Instead, the defendant, the National Association of Professional Baseball Leagues, allowed the Denver Zephyrs, a Triple A International League franchise, to relocate to New Orleans, in part because of its rules which gave priority to a league or club of higher classification. While refusing to grant defendant's motions for summary judgment on the plaintiff's other claims—arbitrary and capricious conduct, specific performance, damages—Judge Feldman accepts the argument that baseball's antitrust exemption covers the entirety of the business of baseball, not just the player reserve system as was held in *Piazza v. Major League Baseball*,[241] stating that "although *Piazza* presents an impressive dissent from [U.S. Supreme Court] precedent, this Court associates itself with the weight of authority."[242]

March 10, 1994: Newcombe Sues Beer Maker for Misuse of His Likeness in Ad

Don Newcombe, winner of the National League Rookie of the Year Award in 1949 and the Most Valuable Player and Cy Young awards in 1956, files a $100 million lawsuit in Los Angeles County Superior Court against the Adolf Coors Co., Time, Inc., and advertising agency Foote Cone and Belding over a Killian's Irish Red beer advertisement appearing in the February 14, 1994, swimsuit edition of *Sports Illustrated* magazine.[243] Newcombe claims that the drawing of a baseball pitcher in the ad, though unnamed, is a depiction of him in his distinctive windup motion, apparently an adaptation of a newspaper photograph of Newcombe pitching in the 1949 World Series for the Brooklyn Dodgers against the New York Yankees. He contends that, as a recovering alcoholic who has served as a spokesperson for the National Institute on Alcohol Abuse and the National Clearinghouse for Alcohol Information,[244] the drawing is defamatory and a commercial misappropriation of his likeness, and constitutes intentional infliction of emotional distress. The case is removed to federal court and a defense motion for summary judgment is granted by the trial court. On appeal, Ninth Circuit Chief Judge Proctor Hug decides that, as to the misappropriation claim, it is "a triable issue of fact ... as to whether Newcombe is readily identifiable as the pitcher in the advertisement,"[245] but affirms the lower court's dismissal of Newcombe's libel, emotional distress, and negligent publication claims.

May 8, 1994: All-Female Silver Bullets Play First Game

On Mother's Day, the Colorado Silver Bullets plays its inaugural game against the Northern League All-Stars, losing 19–0. Formed after the success of *A League of Their Own*, the 1992 movie based on the All-American Girls Professional Baseball League, the Bullets are the first all-female professional baseball team since the demise of the AAGPBL in 1954, and the first to be officially recognized by the National Association of Professional Baseball Leagues. Coors Brewing Company commits to an annual sponsorship of $2.6 million—hence naming the team after the company's light beer. The Bullets are managed by future Hall of Fame pitcher Phil Niekro and feature firstbaseman Julie Croteau, the first woman to play NCAA college baseball (see entry for March 28, 1988), and pitcher Gina Satriano, the first girl to play Little League baseball in California (see entry for May 15, 1994). During its four-year existence (1994–97), the team will barnstorm around the country, playing nearly 200 games against a collection of men's amateur and professional teams.[246]

May 15, 1994: First Woman Pitcher to Start Game in Major League Stadium

On leave from her position as a deputy district attorney for Los Angeles County, 28-year-old Gina Satriano becomes the first woman pitcher to start a game in a major league stadium when she takes the mound for the Colorado Silver Bullets against the Northern California Junior College All-Stars before 8,000 fans at Candlestick Park, home of the San Francisco Giants.[247] Satriano, the daughter of former major league catcher Tom Satriano, first became a trailblazer for women's baseball in 1973 when, as a 7-year-old, she was the first girl to play Little League baseball in California after her mother Sherry threatened to sue unless the league allowed her to participate.[248]

July 28, 1994: Owners Withhold Pension Payment Over Salary Cap Dispute, Players Strike

After negotiations stall on a new collective bargaining agreement, the executive committee of the Major League Baseball Players Association unanimously votes to establish a strike date of August 12.[249] On August 1, upset over the players' refusal to accept a salary cap they feel is needed because of their financial difficulties, team owners decline to make a $7.8 million pension plan payment. This provokes MLBPA to charge the owners with an unfair labor practice charge. As a consequence, the strike begins as planned on August 12.[250]

August 18, 1994: Act to Remove Antitrust Exemption Introduced During Strike

Reacting quickly to the players strike (see entry for July 28, 1994)—the eighth work stoppage in 23 years—Representative Mike Synar (D–OK) introduces the Baseball Fans and Communities Protection Act in Congress.[251] Co-sponsored by Jim Bunning (R–KY), a future member of the National Baseball Hall of Fame, the bill seeks to amend the Clayton Act to partially remove the judicially created antitrust law exemption for major league baseball franchises.[252] It will not be passed, nor will it bring an end to the crippling strike that causes the cancellation of the World Series and is not settled until well into 1995 (see entry for April 3, 1995),[253] but the goal of the act—to require the application of federal antitrust laws to major league baseball—will finally be achieved four years later with the passage of the Curt Flood Act of 1998 (see entry for October 27, 1998).

October 6, 1994: Court Rules Antitrust Exemption Does Not Cover Sale and Location of Franchises

The Florida Supreme Court allows Florida Attorney General Robert Butterworth to proceed with his antitrust civil investigative demands against National League President Bill White over the failed attempt by investors to purchase the San Francisco Giants and to relocate the team to Tampa Bay. In responding to a certified question from the Fifth District Court of Appeal as to whether baseball's antitrust exemption protects all decisions about the sale and location of franchises from antitrust action, the Court adopts the rationale of *Piazza v. Major League Baseball*[254] in concluding that "baseball's antitrust exemption extends only to the reserve system" (see entry for August 6, 1992). The Court acknowledges "that *Piazza* is against the great weight of federal cases regarding the scope of the exemption," but chooses to follow it because "none of the other cases have engaged in such a comprehensive analysis of *Flood* and its implications."[255]

November 23, 1994: Vincent Halts "Tell-All" Bio, Co-Author Sues for Contract Breach

Fay Vincent tells David Kaplan, a senior *Newsweek* writer, that he is halting publication of their jointly written "tell-all" book about his years as baseball's commissioner (1989–92) despite the fact that the manuscript is 90 percent complete.[256] Problems between the two men were exacerbated when the *New York Times* published an article in March 1994 which quoted from the 40-page book proposal then circulating among publishing houses and eventually accepted by Little, Brown & Co., that included descriptions of acting commissioner Bud Selig as "a small-town schlepper" and Chicago White Sox owner Jerry Reinsdorf as "the emblem of baseball's decline."[257] On September 10, 1996, federal district court Judge Barrington D. Parker, Jr., will rule that Kaplan does not have a breach of contract claim based upon the publishing agreement, nor can he recover on quasi contract grounds for the work he completed. However, he also concludes that a trial is necessary to determine promissory estoppel, fraud in the inducement, and intention of both parties to be joint authors.[258] Kaplan never publishes his work, but Vincent will finally publish a more sanitized memoir in 2002.[259]

1995

April 3, 1995: Sotomayer Ends Strike by Enjoining Owners from Unilaterally Adopting New CBA

Concluding that there is reasonable cause to believe that MLB owners committed unfair labor practices when they unilaterally rescinded the free-agent bidding, salary arbitration, and anticollusion provisions of the expired collective bargaining agreement on February 6, 1995, U.S. District Court Judge Sonia Sotomayor grants the NLRB's request for a temporary injunction against Major League Baseball owners.[260] The ruling prevents the owners from unilaterally implementing a new collective bargaining agreement and using replacement players to begin the 1995 MLB season. With the owners deciding two days later not to lock out the players, the decision effectively ends the labor impasse which lasted 232 days and led to the cancellation of the 1994 World Series.[261]

July 26, 1995: Players' Right of Publicity Prohibits Use of Mets Team Photo on Clothing

Members of the 1969 World Series champion New York Mets[262] prevail in their lawsuit against a manufacturer of clothing that features a group portrait of the team, as well as individual drawings and statistical facts, in violation of the players' right of publicity under New York's Civil Rights Law. Recognizing that under the statute, the players have a right to commercially exploit their identities, Supreme Court Justice Martin Schoenfeld concludes that Garan, Inc., "is attempting to cash in on plaintiffs' skill and renown on the baseball diamond. Without plaintiffs' consent, that is something defendant simply may not do."[263] He also finds that the players' right of publicity is not preempted by federal copyright law, distinguishing the present case based on commercial exploitation of identity, from *Baltimore Orioles v. Major League Baseball Players Association*, where publicity rights in a particular performance were preempted (see entry for October 29, 1986).[264]

November 2, 1995: Antitrust Exemption Covers Entirety of Business of Baseball

Concluding that Yogi Berra might describe the case as "deja vu all over again," Federal District Court Judge Carolyn R. Dimmick resolves an antitrust action brought against baseball owners because of their alleged unfair labor practices during the 1994 players' strike by granting the defendants' motion to dismiss on the basis of baseball's antitrust exemption.[265] Noting the failure of Congress to modify it through legislation, Judge Dimmick rules that the exemption covers the entire business of baseball, refusing to follow earlier cases which had restricted applicability of the exemption solely to issues involving the reserve clause (see entries for August 6, 1992, and October 6, 1994). The court also determines that the businesses near the stadiums and disgruntled fans who sued the owners lack standing to challenge the antitrust exemption.[266]

CHAPTER 7

Selig, Steroids and Baseball Prosperity

Introduction

Twenty-six years after the Supreme Court's ruling in *Flood v. Kuhn*, and nearly two years after Flood himself passed away, the United States Congress finally responded to judicial pleas for a legislative solution to baseball's unique antitrust status by passing the Curt Flood Act in 1998. The statute altered the game's exemption by granting players the same rights enjoyed by those in other sports. But the Act left unanswered the scope of the exemption beyond labor issues, and this issue was the subject of litigation on several occasions.

With Major League Baseball concerned about decreased revenue, particularly with small market clubs, team owners voted after the 2001 season to decrease the number of clubs by at least two. The Minnesota Twins and Montreal Expos were the teams most likely to be eliminated, but Minnesota courts blocked these attempts by construing the Twins' stadium lease to require the team to play the forthcoming season in the Metrodome. By delaying the scheduled actions of multiple teams, the contraction plans fell apart.

The prevalence of performance enhancing drugs became baseball's defining issue. In June 2002, Ken Caminiti revealed that he had used steroids during his 1996 MVP season. That revelation, along with startling charges from José Canseco, forced the Players Association to agree to "survey testing" in 2003. When the results showed that more than 5 percent of players failed the tests, it triggered a provision in the collective bargaining agreement that instituted mandatory random "program testing" and stiff penalties for violators. In March 2005, a number of current and former high profile players appeared before the House Committee on Government Reform, providing testimony that proved frustrating to the legislators and fanned the ire of the public. This was exacerbated in December 2007 by the release of a damning report by former U.S. Senator George Mitchell that named 89 players who had used steroids or drugs, including such familiar names as Barry Bonds, Kevin Brown, Roger Clemens, Jason Giambi, Rafael Palmeiro, and Andy Pettitte.

Many members of the Baseball Writers Association of America showed their disdain for players suspected of using PEDs steroids when casting their votes for the National Baseball Hall of Fame. Beginning in 2007 with Mark McGwire, players who had once been considered sure inductees found themselves with vote totals far short of that needed for election. In 2013, another PED-related scandal broke involving Biogenesis, a South Florida anti-aging clinic, which eventually led MLB to suspend a number of players, including former National League MVP Ryan Braun and three-time American League MVP Alex Rodriguez. Barry Bonds, the all-time career home-run leader, and Roger Clemens, the only pitcher to win seven Cy Young Awards, also were tainted by court actions stemming from their alleged involvement with performance enhancing drugs.

Despite overwhelmingly negative fan reaction, first to the disastrous 1994–95 strike that led to a cancelled World Series, and then to round after round of revelations about PED use, MLB Commissioner Bud Selig proved an effective leader, not just reviving interest in the game but sparking a remarkable renaissance. The owners relationship with the Players Association finally stabilized, leading to more than two decades of successful negotiations for new collective bargaining agreements without rancor or work stoppages. Major League Baseball Advanced Media embraced the internet and parlayed regional network regular season rights into an enormously successful and lucrative venture. The launching of the MLB Network provided unprecedented coverage of the game, both in and out of season. Thus, when Selig stepped down from his post on January 24, 2015, to be replaced by Rob Manfred, a lawyer and longtime MLB executive, it could hardly be denied that baseball's ship was righted and on course for a bright future.

1996

September 30, 1996: Jethroe Suit Leads to Pension Benefits for Negro Leaguers

Federal District Court Judge Sean McLaughlin dismisses a suit brought by Sam Jethroe against Major League Baseball and the Players Association to secure compensation for pension payments which he alleged were denied because baseball's color line prevented him from reaching the majors in time to accumulate the four years of playing time required for pension eligibility prior to 1980.[1] Jethro, the oldest player ever to win rookie of the year honors, was 33 years old when he debuted for the Boston Braves on April 18, 1950, but he had already starred in the Negro Leagues for the Cleveland Buckeyes since the early 1940s. He went on to play a total of three years and 17 days for the Braves and the Pirates before finishing his career in 1958 with the Toronto Maple Leafs of the triple-A International League at the age of 41.[2] A few months after the suit's dismissal, Major League Baseball will adopt a "Negro League Supplemental Income Plan" providing for an annual $10,000 payment to Jethroe and others who played in the Negro Leagues prior to 1948 and were shut out of the MLB pension plan.[3]

1997

January 20, 1997: Curt Flood Dies After Fight Against Throat Cancer

Curtis Charles Flood[4] dies at the UCLA Medical Center after a prolonged fight against throat cancer. Flood had challenged Major League Baseball's reserve clause by filing suit in 1969 after being traded from the St. Louis Cardinals to the Philadelphia Phillies (see entry for December 24, 1969). Three years later, in a majority opinion written by Justice Harry Blackmun that was laced with the names of baseball greats, the U.S. Supreme Court found for MLB, upholding baseball's exemption to the federal antitrust law in *Flood v. Kuhn* (see entry for June 19, 1972).[5]

July 1, 1997: Mascot Distraction Not an Assumed Risk for Fan Hit by Foul Ball

The California Court of Appeals reverses a summary judgment granted to the owners of the Rancho Cucamonga Quakes of the Class A California League by the trial court in an action brought by a spectator who suffered serious facial injuries when he was struck by a foul ball while attending a game at "The Epicenter," home of the Quakes.[6] Plaintiff John Lowe contended that he was distracted by Tremor, the seven-foot dinosaur mascot of the Quakes, when he was repeatedly struck by Tremor's tail. After looking behind him to discover what was striking him on the shoulder, Lowe was hit by a line drive as he turned back to the game. The appellate court determined that the doctrine of primary assumption of risk did not apply because the "defendants had a duty *not to increase* the inherent risks to which spectators at professional baseball games are regularly exposed and which they assume."[7]

1998

October 27, 1998: Congress Passes Curt Flood Act

The 105th Congress passes the Curt Flood Act of 1998,[8] finally responding to the U.S. Supreme Court's plea in its *Toolson* (see entry for November 9, 1953) and *Flood* (see entry for June 19, 1972) decisions for a legislative solution to the antitrust exemption established for baseball by the Court itself in its 1922 *Federal Baseball Club* opinion (see entry for May 29, 1922). The impetus for the legislation is Article XXVIII of the 1996 collective bargaining agreement which provided that Major League Baseball and the Players Association would lobby Congress to "clarify that Major League Baseball Players are covered under the antitrust laws" similarly to football and basketball players. With substantial penalties in place if legislation is not enacted, the lobbying efforts are successful but only after satisfying many Congressional delegations that the act will not change the nature of minor league baseball by prohibiting those players from using it to alter the existing labor relationship.[9]

December 12, 1998: Kevin Brown Signs $105 Million Contract

Represented by lawyer and player agent Scott Boras, free agent pitcher Kevin Brown signs a seven-year, $105 million contract with the Los Angeles Dodgers, making him major league baseball's first $100 million player. The largest contract in total value prior to Brown's is catcher Mike Piazza's seven-year deal with the Mets for $91 million signed in October 1998. Brown, who will turn 34 in March 1999, is to receive a $5-million signing bonus and a $10-million salary in 1999, and salaries of $15 million annually for the remainder of the contract.[10] Brown will ultimately pitch five years for Los Angeles, winning 58 games and posting a 2.83 ERA, before he is traded to the New York Yankees in December 2003. It will become common wisdom that the contract is a bad deal for the Dodgers, but at least one commentator will contend that the team "paid Brown $73.6 million, and got $63.5 million back from the market value of his performance and the profits from trading him," a relatively small deficit in comparison with the many disastrous free agent deals that followed his.[11]

1999

February 8, 1999: Neumeier First Woman to Serve as Baseball Arbitrator

In the 410th case to be heard since salary arbitration was introduced for the 1974 season after its inclusion in the 1973 Basic Agreement (see entry for February 8, 1973),[12] Elizabeth Neumeier, a professional arbitrator from Gloucester, Mass., and graduate of Boston University School of Law, becomes the first woman to serve on a baseball salary arbitration panel when she hears the case of Boston Red Sox outfielder Midre Cummings. The Red Sox prevail when the panel rejects Cummings's request that his salary be raised from $250,000 to $725,000, instead selecting the team's proposal of $450,000.[13]

April 29, 1999: Court Rules Antitrust Exemption Covers Entirety of Baseball Business

The Supreme Court of Minnesota concludes that Minnesota Attorney General Michael Hatch doesn't have the authority to enforce civil investigative demands related to possible state antitrust violations arising from the proposed sale of the Minnesota Twins by owner Carl Pohlad to Donald Beaver and the relocation of the team to North Carolina.[14] In so doing, the Court reverses lower court decisions in the case that had adopted the rationale in *Piazza v. Major League Baseball*[15] which limited the scope of baseball's antitrust exemption to matters pertaining solely to the reserve system. Rejecting *Piazza*, the Court declares that it will follow the majority of opinions which have found that the exemption covers the entirety of the business of professional baseball and therefore the sale and relocation of a franchise falls within its scope.[16]

2000

July 15, 2000: First Baseball Card to Sell for More Than $1 Million

Brian Seigel, a 40-year-old businessman from Santa Ana, California, becomes the first person to spend more than a million dollars for a baseball card when he pays nearly $1.27 million to win an online auction conducted by eBay and Robert Edward Auctions for a tobacco advertising card he calls the "Mona Lisa of baseball cards," the Gretzky T-206 Wagner.[17] Produced by the American Tobacco Company for its 1909 set, the card depicts future Hall of Fame shortstop Honus Wagner on the front and an advertisement for Piedmont cigarettes on the back. It became "the most valuable and coveted trading card of all time" after Wagner refused to grant the company permission to use his image—forcing it to pull the card from circulation after only a few hundred had been produced—either because he didn't want children to associate him with tobacco use or, more likely, he wanted compensation for his likeness.[18] The near mint version of the card purchased by Seigel came on the market in 1986 and was sold over the years for increasing amounts, including for a then record $451,000 in 1991 to hockey great Wayne Gretzky and Los Angeles Kings owner Bruce McNall.[19]

September 6, 2000: Law Firm Transfers Its Internet Domain Name to MLB

In a joint press release, Major League Baseball and Morgan, Lewis and Bockius LLP announce that the law firm has transferred the internet domain name it registered in 1994—mlb.com—to MLB. Neither the transfer nor the apparent lack of compensation is a surprise given the longstanding relationship between MLB and the Philadelphia firm.[20] In October 1987, the Player Relations Committee had hired Morgan, Lewis to represent management in its dealings with the Major League Baseball Players Association, and the firm continued to serve MLB well into the twenty-first century.[21] And in late 2014,

Robert D. "Rob" Manfred, Jr., a former partner at Morgan, Lewis who had worked full-time in the commissioner's office since 1998, will be elected baseball's tenth commissioner, to succeed Bud Selig in January 2015 (see entry for August 14, 2014).

2001

April 17, 2001: Supreme Court Resolves Tax Issue Rising from Collusion Settlement Payments

In a dispute between the Cleveland Indians and the Internal Revenue Service growing out of the December 1990 settlement of the grievance by the Major League Baseball Players Association over collusion against free agents after the 1985, 1986, and 1987 seasons (see entry for December 21, 1990), the Supreme Court sides with the government when it decides that salary damages classified as wages should be taxed at the 1994 rates, the year in which the damages were paid to 22 players, instead of 1986 and 1987 rates, the years in which the players should have been paid higher salaries.[22] The court denies the team's claim for a refund of the higher tax amounts they paid the government in 1994 and 1995 (about $100,000 on more than $2 million in back salary), and the players are forced to pay higher taxes because the rates for Social Security, Medicare and federal unemployment taxes were higher in 1994 than in 1986 or 1987.[23]

May 14, 2001: Arbitrator's Decision in Garvey Claim Against Collusion Settlement Upheld

The United States Supreme Court issues a per curiam opinion[24] reversing the decision of the United States Circuit Court of Appeals for the Ninth Circuit[25] which had rejected the decision of arbitrator Thomas Roberts to disallow Steve Garvey's claim against the global settlement agreement that resolved Major League Baseball's collusion against free agents after the 1985, 1986, 1987 seasons (see entry for December 21, 1990). Garvey had filed a claim for damages under the Agreement, alleging that the San Diego Padres failed to offer him a contract extension for the 1988 and 1989 seasons because of the collusion. Roberts concluded that Garvey's evidence of this was not credible, but the Court of Appeals disagreed. The Supreme Court, however, rules that it was inappropriate for the Ninth Circuit to decide the case on the merits and to vacate the arbitrator's decision.

October 2, 2001: Trademark Dispute Over Use of Mascot Name Settled

The Salt Lake Stingers, a triple-A affiliate of the Anaheim Angels in the Pacific Coast League, settle a three-year long trademark infringement suit brought by Georgia Tech, home of the "Yellow Jackets," over rights to the use of the school's name for its mascot, "Buzz." In a settlement filed in the U.S. District Court in Atlanta, the Stingers, known from 1994 to 2000 as the Buzz, agree to pay Georgia Tech $600,000 and refrain from using Buzz in the team's name, on its website, or for merchandising purposes. Salt Lake owner Joe Buzas had moved his Portland Beavers to Utah in 1993 and renamed the team the Salt Lake Buzz in a nod to the old Salt Lake Bees, the original PCL franchise which played in Salt Lake City from 1915 to 1926.[26] In 2006, the Stingers will officially change its name to the Salt Lake Bees.

October 7, 2001: Court Battle Over Bonds Home Run Ball Concludes

Batting in the first inning of the last game of the season, Barry Bonds of the San Francisco Giants hits his 73rd and final round tripper of the 2001 campaign off Dodger knuckleball pitcher Dennis Springer, establishing the all-time single-season home run record.[27] Fourteen months later, on December 18, 2002, California Superior Court Judge Kevin McCarthy will rule that neither Alex Popov, who claimed to have caught the Bonds home run, nor Patrick Hayashi, who ended up with it after a scrum of fans piled on Popov, can claim sole ownership of the historic ball. He rules that the ball must be sold and the proceeds split between the two men.[28] Although memorabilia experts predicted $1 million, the Bonds ball will sell to toy manufacturer and *Spawn* comic book creator Todd McFarlane for only $450,000 ($517,500 with commissions) in a four-minute auction conducted at the ESPN Zone restaurant in Times Square on June 25, 2003.[29]

December 10, 2001: MLB's Use of Player Names and Images Protected by First Amendment

In a lawsuit brought by several retired players who played between 1932 and 1948, including Frankie Crosetti, Dolph Camilli, and Al Gionfriddo, against Major League Baseball, the court rules that the First Amendment defeats their claim that the use of their names, likenesses, and photographs in print and on video is commercial speech and therefore protected by California's common law and statutory right of publicity. Because their participation in baseball was noteworthy and of public interest,[30] Justice Mark B. Simons writes that "the uses at issue [e.g., in All-Star and World Series programs, on MLB website, in films produced by MLB] are entitled to receive the full constitutional protection accorded to noncommercial speech."[31]

2002

January 22, 2002: League Contraction Thwarted by Minnesota Supreme Court

The Minnesota Court of Appeals affirms the November 16, 2001, decision of Hennepin County District Judge Harry S. Crump to grant a temporary injunction forcing the Minnesota Twins to play its home games for the 2002 season at the Hubert H. Humphrey Metrodome, pursuant to the existing use agreement between the Twins and plaintiff Metropolitan Sports Facilities Commission.[32] The decision will prove critical in thwarting Major League Baseball's efforts to eliminate the Twins and another franchise (presumed to be the Montreal Expos); MLB will drop its plans for contraction in the 2002 season on February 5, 2002, the day after the Minnesota Supreme Court refuses to consider an appeal of the Court of Appeals decision.[33]

June 3, 2002: Ken Caminiti Admits Steroid Use During MVP Season

In what is characterized as "the first public admission of steroid use—without remorse—by a prominent former player," Ken Caminiti is quoted by an article in *Sports Illustrated* as admitting that he used steroids purchased from a pharmacy in Tijuana, Mexico, during the 1996 season in which he won the National League Most Valuable Player Award.[34] In response, on June 18, 2002, the U.S. Senate will conduct a hearing on steroids in professional baseball, barely two weeks after publication of Caminiti's admission. Rob Manfred, MLB executive vice president, labor and human resources, will testify about the substantial increase in the number of players going on the disabled list and the belief that steroid use was an important contributing factor, while Donald Fehr, executive director of the MLBPA, will indicate that steroid testing of players would be an issue for the next collective bargaining agenda.[35] In fact, within two months, the players and owners will agree to a new drug program that for the first time provides for anonymous testing of players (see entry for August 7, 2002).

August 7, 2002: MLBPA Agrees to Random Testing for PEDs

After revelations of rampant steroid use in baseball, particularly those involving MVPs Ken Caminiti (see entry for June 3, 2002) and José Canseco (see entry for September 28, 1988), lead to a shift in public opinion, the Major League Baseball Players Association drops its opposition to testing for performance-enhancing drugs, proposing that random testing on a trial basis begin in 2003.[36] After this breakthrough, the players association and MLB will reach accord on a new collective bargaining agreement on August 30 that not only avoids a labor stoppage but also establishes a joint drug prevention and treatment program (the first since 1985) that includes for the first time ever mandatory random drug testing. Anonymous "survey testing" will be conducted in 2003, with all players randomly tested for illegal steroids. If more than 5 percent of the players test positive during the survey year, mandatory random testing will occur in 2004 and 2005, with disciplinary measures taken against those who test positive (see entry for November 13, 2003).[37]

2003

November 13, 2003: Mandatory Random Testing and Penalties for PED Use Adopted

Major League Baseball announces that from 5 to 7 percent of the 1,438 random drug tests conducted in 2003 during its first-ever "survey testing" program were positive for steroids. All 40 players on each team's roster were randomly tested at unannounced times, while 240 randomly selected players were tested a second time. With the percentage exceeding 5 percent, "program testing" will be instituted over the next two years under the terms of the 2002 collective bargaining agreement between MLB and the Major League Baseball Players Association (see entry for August 7, 2002).[38] This stricter regimen will include mandatory random testing and, for the first time, the imposition of penalties against offenders. First-time offenders will be placed in a treatment program, but not publicly identified. However, players who subsequently test positive will be named and subject to suspensions ranging from 15 days to one year or fines from $10,000 to $100,000.[39]

2004

September 13, 2004: Player Faces Criminal Charge and Civil Suit for Throwing Chair at Fan

Late in a game at Network Associates Coliseum in Oakland between the Texas Rangers and the Oakland Athletics, heckling by fans sitting in the field box seats near the Rangers' bullpen provokes a brawl between players and fans that culminates when rookie reliever Frank Francisco throws a plastic chair into the stands, breaking the nose of spectator Jennifer Bueno. Police arrest Francisco on a felony charge of aggravated battery and take him to jail, where he is later released on $15,000 bond.[40] Bob Watson, baseball's vice president in charge of discipline, will suspend Francisco for the remainder of the season, a total of 15 games.[41] In 2005, Francisco will plead no contest to a misdemeanor charge of assault for which he will serve 20 days in a work program and take anger management classes. In April 2005, Bueno will file a civil lawsuit against Francisco, two of his teammates, and the Rangers, with the Rangers countersuing Bueno's husband, Craig, who was one of the hecklers. On January 11, 2007, the Rangers will reach a cash settlement with Bueno and all litigation will be dismissed.[42]

2005

March 17, 2005: Players Testify at Congressional Hearing About PED Use in Baseball

Current and former players Jim Bunning, José Canseco, Sammy Sosa,

Mark McGwire, Rafael Palmeiro, Curt Schilling, and Frank Thomas testify about steroid use, problems, and policies in Major League Baseball at a hearing on performance enhancing drugs in baseball conducted by the U.S. House Committee on Government Reform.[43] McGwire refuses to answer questions about his own use of steroids, noting that he is "not here to talk about the past."[44] And although he defiantly denies using steroids ("I have never used steroids. Period."), four months later Palmeiro will be suspended by MLB for violating baseball's anti-drug policy.[45]

May 8, 2005: Court Rejects Male Fan's Discrimination Claim in Dispute Over Mother's Day Giveaway

Arriving at a Tigers-Angels game at Angel Stadium on Mother's Day, Michael Cohn and two friends are denied a tote bag intended as a giveaway available only to women over the age of 18. He will later sue both the Angels and Corinthian Colleges, sponsor of the tote bag portion of the Mother's Day celebration, for violating California's Unruh Civil Rights Act. But the court will reject Cohn's allegation that limiting the bags to women constituted "intentional discrimination that [was] unreasonable, arbitrary, or invidious," concluding that the Act's "power and efficacy" should not be denigrated by applying it to "manufactured injuries" such as those asserted by Cohn.[46]

September 12, 2005: Roberts Compares Judges to Umpires in Confirmation Hearing

John Roberts invokes the image of a baseball umpire in his opening statement to the Senate Judiciary Committee during his confirmation hearing to be chief justice of the U.S. Supreme Court. Roberts notes that "Judges are like umpires. Umpires don't make the rules; they apply them. The role of an umpire and a judge is critical. They make sure everybody plays by the rules. But it is a limited role. Nobody ever went to a ball game to see the umpire."[47]

November 15, 2005: "Three-Strikes-and-You're Out" Penalty for PED Use Announced

In the face of Congressional pressure—including the threat of federal steroid legislation, particularly the Integrity in Professional Sports Act introduced by Senator (and Hall of Fame pitcher) Jim Bunning on November 3, 2005[48]—Commissioner Bud Selig and MLBPA Executive Director Donald Fehr announce a joint agreement to establish a "three-strikes-and-you're out" steroid policy, effective with the 2006 season.[49] The new policy provides for much stiffer penalties for offenses involving the use of PEDs (i.e., 50-game suspension for first positive test, 100 games for second, lifetime ban for third) than did the drug-testing agreement reached by the players and owners less than a year earlier, on January 13, 2005 (i.e., 10-day suspension for first positive test, 30 days for second, 60 days for third, one year for 4th).[50] The new agreement also requires random testing for amphetamines and establishes penalties for offenders.[51]

2006

March 13, 2006: Insurance Co. Denies Claim for Bagwell Disability

Connecticut General Life Insurance Company (CIGNA) denies the Houston Astros insurance claim for $15.6 million of Jeff Bagwell's guaranteed $17 million dollar salary for 2006. The team asserts that the player's arthritic right shoulder has left him unable to play, but CIGNA argues that the Astros "claim [does] not support a finding of total disability" since the "injury prevent[s] him from throwing, but [does] not prevent him from hitting."[52] Since the signing of Bagwell's five-year contract on December 19, 2000, the Astros had paid $2.4 million in premiums on a policy from CIGNA to cover payments on the contract in case the All-Star first-baseman and former MVP became disabled during the term of his deal.[53] On January 12, 2006, prior to the January 31 expiration date of the policy, noted orthopedic surgeon James Andrews examined Bagwell and determined that he was disabled. Bagwell appeared in spring training camp despite this pronouncement, but he quickly noted that his throwing ability was a "joke" and stopped playing because of "the tremendous amount of pain that I couldn't deal with anymore."[54] The Astros will file a breach of contract suit on May 2 against CIGNA, but in December Bagwell, not having played a game in 2006, will announce his retirement after a 15-year major league career and the two parties will reach a confidential settlement before the case goes to trial.[55]

2007

October 16, 2007: First Amendment Protects Fantasy League Use of Names and Stats

In *C.B.C. Distribution & Marketing, Inc. v. Major League Baseball Advanced Media, L.P.*,[56] the U.S. Court of Appeals for the Eighth Circuit allows a fantasy baseball league operator to use the names and statistical information of actual players on the ground that the operator's First Amendment right takes precedence over the players' rights to be protected from unauthorized publicity.

December 13, 2007: Mitchell Report Details PED Use in Baseball

Fulfilling the charge he received when Commissioner Bud Selig appointed him to investigate performance-enhancing drug use in Major League Baseball on March 30, 2006, George Mitchell, a former United States senator and federal district court judge from Maine, releases a 409-page report about the use of anabolic steroids and human growth hormone that is immediately called the Mitchell Report.[57] It names 89 major league players from all 30 teams who are alleged to have used steroids or drugs, including such familiar names as Barry Bonds, Kevin Brown, Roger Clemens, Jason Giambi, Rafael Palmeiro, and Andy Pettitte. During the 20-month investigation which cost a reported $20 million, Mitchell examined 115,000 pages of documents and interviewed more than 700 people, including 60 former players but only two active ones, Giambi and Frank Thomas, known for his outspoken opposition to steroids.[58] The "star witness" in the Mitchell Report, however, is Kirk Radomski, a batboy and clubhouse attendant for the New York Mets from 1985 to 1995, who had pled guilty in federal district court on April 27, 2007, to "distributing performance-enhancing drugs to dozens of former and current Major League Baseball players" but avoided a heavy jail sentence through a plea bargain that included cooperating with Mitchell and the federal government.[59] In addition to documenting what he terms "baseball's steroids era" which started in 1988, Mitchell offers 20 recommendations, including an independent drug-testing program, public reporting of results, and a unit within the commissioner's office to investigate reports of PED use by players.[60]

2008

February 13, 2008: Clemens Indicted for Congressional Hearing Statements

In testimony before a congressional committee investigating the illegal use of steroids in major league baseball, Roger Clemens vehemently denies ever using such substances while Brian McNamee, a former New York City policeman and Clemens's trainer when he played for the Toronto Blue Jays and New York Yankees, claims that he repeatedly injected the seven-time Cy Young award winner with performance-enhancing drugs.[61] Clemens's statement also contradicts a sworn affidavit provided to the committee by Andy Pettitte, a teammate of Clemens on the Yankees and Houston Astros. As a result of the inconsistencies in Clemens's testimony, on August 19, 2010, a grand jury will indict him for making false statements to Congress, obstructing Congress, and perjury. A first trial will result in a mistrial in July 2011, but Clemens will be acquitted at a second trial on June 18, 2012.[62]

April 3, 2008: Pitcher Brocail Loses Suit Against Tigers for Arm Injuries

Pitcher Doug Brocail loses his multiple-claims lawsuit (including allegations of negligence, fraud, fraudulent concealment, and breach of contract) against the Detroit Tigers for injuries suffered to his pitching arm when Justice Eva Guzman affirms a lower court determination that his claims are barred under the federal Labor-Management Relations Act, the Michigan Workers Disability Compensation Act, and the Michigan statute of frauds.[63]

In particular, Brocail is unsuccessful in his claim that the Tigers were guilty of an intentional tort that would overcome the exclusive application of the workers' compensation law. After experiencing elbow pain in June 2000 and being treated by team physicians, Brocail was placed on the disabled list and eventually underwent arthroscopic surgery. After a December 2000 trade to the Houston Astros, Brocail suffered another injury that was diagnosed as a medial collateral ligament tear and a partial tear of the flexor tendon. Recovery from the surgery costs Brocail the 2002 and 2003 seasons, but he will resume his career in 2004 and pitch until 2009 when he retires at the age of 42.

2009

February 12, 2009: Suspended Pitcher Challenges NCAA No-Agent Rule

In a suit for a declaratory judgment and injunctive relief brought by Oklahoma State University pitcher Andy Oliver against the National Collegiate Athletic Association, Judge Tygh M. Tone of the Court of Common Pleas of Erie County, Ohio, declares the NCAA's "no-agent" rule (Bylaw 12.3.2.1) invalid as "arbitrary and capricious."[64] With his lawyer and sports advisor Tim Baratta present in the family home, Oliver turned down an offer from the Minnesota Twins, who had selected him in the 17th round of the 2006 draft, to attend Oklahoma State on a full scholarship. Oliver later switched agents from Robert and Tim Baratta to Scott Boras. In 2008, the NCAA suspended Oliver after the Barattas notified the organization of their involvement in the player's negotiations with the Twins. Despite the court's declaration, the NCAA will keep its bylaw intact when Judge Tone approves a $750,000 settlement for Oliver on October 7, 2009, halting a trial on damages and vacating his order banning the NCAA from enforcing the no-agent rule.[65]

May 26, 2009: Obama Nominates Sotomayor to U.S. Supreme Court

Noting that "[s]ome say Judge Sotomayor saved baseball," a reference to the injunction she issued as a federal district court judge which led to the end of the 1994–95 baseball strike (see entry for April 3, 1995), President Barack Obama announces his selection of Sonia Sotomayor to replace retiring Justice David Souter on the United States Supreme Court.[66] The nomination of Sotomayor, presently serving on the U.S. Court of Appeals for the Second Circuit, will be formally submitted to the Senate on June 1, 2009; it will confirm her on August 6, 2009, by a 68–31 vote. Chief Justice John Roberts will administer the oath of office on August 8, 2009.

June 22, 2009: Donald Fehr Retires from MLBPA, Replaced by Michael Weiner

Sixty-year-old Donald Fehr announces his intention to step down as Executive Director of Major League Baseball Players Association no later than March 2010. In fact, he will retire in December 2009 and be replaced by the individual he tabbed as his successor, Michael Weiner, a lawyer like Fehr, who served as a staff attorney for the MLBPA from 1988 to 2004, and then as its general counsel from 2004. During Fehr's 26-year tenure, he guided the union through many contentious battles with management, causing him to be described as "the most powerful man" in baseball and considered "one of the most successful union leaders in the country."[67] As only the fifth executive director in the association's history, Weiner also will achieve success, particularly with a new five-year basic agreement concluded in November 2011 that includes "the most comprehensive drug-testing program of any pro sports league in North America." Sadly, Weiner's tenure will be all too brief as he succumbs to brain cancer at age 51 on November 21, 2013.[68]

2010

January 27, 2010: Uecker Defends Defamation Suit by Alleged Stalker

Bob Uecker, longtime Milwaukee Brewers announcer and "Mr. Baseball" according to Johnny Carson,[69] successfully defends against a defamation suit brought by "devoted fan" Ann Ladd when a Wisconsin court rules that her claims are barred by the statute of limitations. Uecker was granted a four-year restraining order against Ladd in 2006 after claiming in an affidavit that she had stalked and harassed him for many years, resulting in "repeated and serious invasions of my personal privacy."[70] After the affidavit was published by smokinggun.com, a website specializing in posting legal documents, arrest records, mug shots, and similar material, Ladd filed a "sprawling pro se complaint" alleging that Uecker had defamed her by claiming she was a stalker.[71] In affirming the case's dismissal, the court adopts the single-publication rule for Internet postings, so that each viewing of a website does not constitute a new publication that triggers the statute of limitations. The court also says it is "unpersuaded that Uecker's factual statements amount to defamation in the first instance, despite negative fallout to Ladd.... [E]ven if untrue, statements made in judicial proceedings are absolutely privileged."[72]

2012

June 26, 2012: Court Resolves Copyright Dispute Over Yankee's Top Hat Logo

The United States Court of Appeals for the Second Circuit affirms the decision of Federal District Court Judge Deborah A. Batts dismissing Tanit Buday's complaint against the New York Yankees which claimed that her uncle, Kenneth Timur, was not paid for designing the team's iconic top hat logo in the 1930s (and revising it in 1947).⁷³ The court concludes that "unfortunately for Buday ... the allegations in the complaint conclusively establish that she has no such copyright."⁷⁴ The court also finds that Buday lacks a copyright interest and, even if she did have one, the logo was covered by the "work for hire" doctrine.⁷⁵

December 19, 2012: A League of Their Own Added to National Film Registry

Twenty years after its 1992 release, *A League of Their Own* is added to the National Film Registry of the Library of Congress, the first baseball-specific film to be so honored.⁷⁶ The registry was created by the National Film Preservation Act of 1988 to preserve and recognize films that are "culturally, historically, or aesthetically significant."⁷⁷ Each year the Librarian of Congress names 25 films to the registry. The movie, based upon the All-American Girls Professional Baseball League (AAGPBL) founded by Cubs owner Philip K. Wrigley and operated in midwestern cities near Chicago,⁷⁸ was directed by Penny Marshall for Columbia Pictures and stars Tom Hanks, Geena Davis, Madonna, Rosie O'Donnell, Lori Petty, Jon Lovitz, and David Strathairn.

2013

February 8, 2013: Yankees Win Trademark Dispute Over Use of "Evil Empire"

Trademark Trial and Appeal Board administrative law judge Thomas Shaw rules in favor of the New York Yankees in a dispute with Evil Enterprises, Inc., over the right to control the use of "Baseball's Evil Empire."⁷⁹ In opposing the granting of a trademark to Evil Enterprises, which planned to use the phrase on apparel and other merchandise, the Yankees offered numerous newspaper articles, blog posts, and other materials as evidence that it was closely associated with the team and its use would be confusing to consumers. Both sides agree that this association occurred when Larry Lucchino, president of the rival Boston Red Sox, characterized the Yankees as the "evil empire" after its swift signing of free agent pitcher José Contreras following his October 2002 defection from Cuba.⁸⁰ In refusing to grant Evil Enterprises a trademark, Shaw states that "the record shows that there is only one EVIL EMPIRE in baseball and it is the New York Yankees. Accordingly, we find that opposer has a protectable trademark right in the term EVIL EMPIRE as used in connection with baseball."⁸¹

March 22, 2013: MLB Sues Biogenesis for Facilitating PED Use by Players

Major League Baseball files suit in the 11th judicial circuit in Miami-

Dade County, Florida, against Anthony Bosch and five others connected to Biogenesis, a South Florida anti-aging clinic which allegedly provided performance enhancing drugs to numerous baseball players, an allegation first reported by the *Miami New Times* in January 2013.[82] The suit charges that the defendants participated in a scheme to induce players to obtain and use PEDs in violation of MLB's Joint Drug Prevention and Treatment program. After Bosch cooperates in an MLB investigation that culminates in the suspension of 14 players, including Ryan Braun for 65 games and Alex Rodriguez for a record 211-game ban (later reduced to 162 games by arbitrator Fredric Horowitz[83]), MLB will drop the lawsuit in February 2014.[84]

2014

May 22, 2014: Obama First Sitting President to Visit Hall of Fame

As the National Baseball Hall of Fame and Museum celebrates its 75th anniversary, President Barack Obama becomes the first sitting American President to visit baseball's shrine in Cooperstown.[85] With Hall of Fame President Jeff Idelson and Hall of Fame outfielder Andre Dawson as tour guides, the President hefts a Babe Ruth bat, handles the ball used by William Howard Taft in 1910 as the first President to toss an Opening Day pitch (see entry for April 14, 1910), and salutes his favorite team, the Chicago White Sox, by trying on the 2005 World Series ring and visiting their locker display. He also donates the Sox jacket he wore when he threw out the opening pitch at the 2009 All-Star Game in St. Louis. His comment in Hall guest book: "Go Sox!" He uses the Hall visit to promote international tourism and the benefits it generates for the nation.[86]

June 24, 2014: Assumption of Risk Defense Rejected for Fan Injury Caused by Object Thrown by Mascot

The Missouri Supreme Court rejects a trial court decision for the Kansas City Royals in a negligence suit brought by John Coomer, an "ardent" fan of the team who suffered a detached retina when he was struck in the eye by a hot dog tossed into the stands by Sluggerrr, the team's mascot, during the between innings hot dog launch, a Royals staple since 2000.[87] The court holds that the trial judge erred in instructing the jury to decide whether being hit by a hot dog was an inherent risk of attending a baseball game. The court concludes that the "risk of being injured by Sluggerrr's hotdog toss ... is not an unavoidable part of watching the Royals play baseball" and therefore the team cannot use the assumption of the risk doctrine as a defense. The only issues for the jury are to decide if Coomer was injured by the mascot's action and whether that constituted negligence.[88] After a two-day retrial in June 2015, the jury will find that neither the Royals nor Coomer were negligent.[89]

July 9, 2014: Jury Verdict for Fan Injured in Dodger Stadium Attack

A jury in Los Angeles Superior Court awards San Francisco Giants fan Bryan Stow nearly $18 million for lost wages, pain and suffering, and medical costs, past and present, in the negligence suit he brought against the Los Angeles Dodgers. Stow was permanently disabled as a result of a severe beating by Los Angeles Dodger fans Louie Sanchez and Marvin Norwood in a Dodger Stadium parking lot on Opening Day, March 31, 2011. Stow was hospitalized for two years while recovering from his injuries.[90] After 20 days of testimony and 9 days of deliberation, the jury determined that both Sanchez and Norwood, who plead guilty to the attack, were each 37.5 percent at fault while the Dodgers were 25 percent at fault for failure to provide proper lighting and security.[91] The jury absolved former Dodgers owner Frank McCourt of any wrongdoing.

July 27, 2014: La Russa—Manager and Lawyer—Inducted into Hall of Fame

Tony La Russa, who earned a law degree from Florida State University College of Law in 1978, was admitted to the Florida Bar in 1979, and for a time practiced commercial and real estate law during the offseason in Sarasota, Florida,[92] is inducted into the National Baseball Hall of Fame before an estimated crowd of 48,000, the third largest in history.[93] After a middling playing career (parts of 6 years with 3 MLB teams, career batting average of .199), in 1979 the 34-year-old La Russa began a 33-year career as a major league manager that would take him to Cooperstown. Along the way he secured four Manager of the Year Awards while winning 12 division titles, 6 pennants, 3 World Series titles, and 2,728 games (third all-time, behind only Connie Mack and John McGraw).[94] La Russa is one of only eight major league managers to have earned a law degree or passed a state bar exam (see entry for April 2, 1869); remarkably, he is the sixth to become a member of the Hall of Fame, after Hughie Jennings (inducted in 1945), James "Orator" O'Rourke (1945), Miller Huggins (1964), John Montgomery Ward (1964), and Branch Rickey (1967).[95]

August 14, 2014: Lawyer Manfred Selected New Baseball Commissioner

After six rounds of voting over a two-day span of meetings, major league owners elect Robert D. "Rob" Manfred, Jr., MLB's chief operating officer and a former partner at the Philadelphia law firm of Morgan, Lewis & Bockius LLP, to succeed his boss, Allan H. "Bud" Selig as the tenth commissioner of Major League Baseball. Manfred began his relationship with MLB as outside counsel, but joined the commissioner's office on a full-time basis in 1998 when he became executive vice-president of labor relations, a position he held until 2013 when he was appointed COO. Manfred was MLB's lead negotiator during the discussions which culminated in new collective bargaining agreements in 2002, 2006, and 2011.[96]

October 23, 2014: Thorpe's Body Remains in Pennsylvania, Native American Graves Act Not Applicable

The United States Court of Appeals for the Third Circuit rules that the body of Jim Thorpe, a Native American of Sauk heritage and a member of the Sac and Fox Nation, should remain in Jim Thorpe, Pennsylvania, where it has been interred since 1954 (see entry for May 18, 1954).[97] In resolving an action brought by several children of the famous Olympian and former New York Giant outfielder seeking to rebury his body on Sac and Fox tribal land in Oklahoma, the court determines that the U.S. federal district court had misapplied the Native American Graves Protection and Repatriation Act[98] in concluding that the borough of Jim Thorpe was a "museum" under the act. Museums holding Native American human remains must return them to descendants upon a request for repatriation, but the Third Circuit rules that finding the Borough to be a museum would lead to "a clearly absurd result and ... [be] contrary to Congress's intent to protect Native American burial sites."[99]

December 12, 2014: First Major League Player to Serve as a U.S. Ambassador

The United States Senate confirms the appointment of Mark Gilbert, an outfielder who played seven games for the Chicago White Sox in July 1985, as ambassador to New Zealand. Gilbert becomes the first former major league player to serve as a credentialed United States ambassador, although former Texas Rangers president Tom Schieffer was ambassador to Australia (2001–05) and Japan (2005–09). Following his retirement from baseball after the 1985 season, Gilbert, a graduate of Florida State University, worked as a banking executive with Drexel Burnham Lambert, Goldman Sachs, and Lehman Brothers (now Barclays Wealth).[100]

2015

January 15, 2015: Court Rules Antitrust Exemption Covers Franchise Relocations

Concluding that "like Casey, San Jose has struck out here," Judge Alex Kozinski of the United States Court of Appeals for the Ninth Circuit rules in *City of San José v. Office of the Commissioner of Baseball* that baseball's antitrust exemption continues to apply in franchise relocation cases.[101] The city had alleged that the commissioner and Major League Baseball violated the Sherman and Clayton Acts by failing to approve relocation of the Oakland

Athletics to a site offered to the team by San José for a new stadium. Noting that San José is within the territorial rights held by the San Francisco Giants, Kozinski agrees with MLB's contention that the location (and relocation) of franchises to designated geographic areas falls squarely within the "business of baseball" and therefore its 92-year old antitrust exemption requires the court to dismiss the city's antitrust claims. Kozinski also relies on Congress's explicit exclusion of franchise location or relocation from coverage by the Curt Flood Act of 1998 to support his ruling.[102]

March 18, 2015: Settlement Reached in McNamee-Clemens Defamation Suit

In negotiations conducted before U.S. Magistrate Judge Cheryl L. Pollak in Brooklyn, a settlement is reached in the defamation suit brought by Brian McNamee in 2008 against Roger Clemens.[103] The seven-time Cy Young Award winning pitcher had called his former trainer a liar and mentally unstable after McNamee claimed that he had provided Clemens and teammate Andy Pettitte with performance-enhancing drugs (see entry for February 13, 2008). In return for dropping the suit, McNamee will receive an unspecified payment from insurer AIG with whom Clemens has a homeowner's policy which includes defamation claims. Clemens's lawyers stress that no admission of wrongdoing is involved in the settlement.[104]

April 1, 2015: Rooftop Businesses Unable to Halt Erection of Wrigley Video Board

U.S. District Court Judge Virginia Kendall denies Edward McCarthy's request for a preliminary injunction to block the installation of a 2,250 square foot right-field video board in Wrigley Field, home of the Chicago Cubs.[105] McCarthy, the owner of two Sheffield Avenue rooftop businesses (Skybox on Sheffield and Lakeview Baseball Club), claims the video board will destroy his businesses and that the installation violates a decade-old licensing agreement granting the team 17 percent of the revenue of businesses on Wakeland and Sheffield avenues that provide a view of Cubs games because it is not an "expansion" of the ballpark as provided for in the agreement. In denying the preliminary injunction, Kendall finds there to be little likelihood of success on the merits of these claims.[106] On September 30, Judge Kendall will dismiss all nine counts of McCarthy's complaint, determining that the improvements approved by Chicago's City Council and the Commission on Chicago Landmarks fall within the definition of "any expansion" in the rooftop owners' contract with the Cubs. She finds that the Cubs are protected against McCarthy's claim that the team is engaged in a monopoly by baseball's antitrust exemption.[107]

July 21, 2015: Bonds Obstruction of Justice Conviction Overturned

Although perhaps convicted in the court of public opinion and in the minds of Hall of Fame voters,[108] the legal odyssey of Barry Bonds and the use of performance-enhancing drugs ends without a felony conviction attached to his name when the Department of Justice announces that Solicitor General Donald B. Verrilli, Jr., will not seek Supreme Court review of the 9th Circuit Court of Appeals decision overturning his 2011 conviction for obstruction of justice.[109] Bonds had been convicted for providing a "meandering" answer to a 2003 federal grand jury when asked whether his personal trainer ever gave him a substance which required a syringe for self-injection.[110] In rejecting that statement as the basis for a conviction, Judge Alex Kozinski writes: "The most one can say ... is that it was non-responsive and thereby impeded the investigation to a small degree by wasting the grand jury's time and trying the prosecutors' patience. But real-life witness examinations, unlike those in movies and on television, invariably are littered with non-responsive and irrelevant answers."[111]

August 17, 2015: Fan Caught Sleeping on Camera Loses Defamation Suit

Judge Julia Rodriguez of the Bronx County, New York Supreme Court, dismisses a $10 million lawsuit brought by Yankee fan Andrew Rector in July 2014 against MLB, the Yankees, ESPN, and the latter's announcers, Dan Shulman and John Kruk, for defamation and intentional infliction of emotional distress. The suit stemmed from a brief segment of the televised broadcast of an April 13, 2014, Yankees-Red Sox game which showed Rector asleep in the stands, leading to some jocular remarks by the announcers. A portion of the 81-second segment was later posted to MLB.com and YouTube, leading to several online comments. Judge Rodriguez rules that the announcers' comments were not defamatory or false, nor were they sufficiently extreme and outrageous to support a claim for intentional infliction of emotional distress. She also concludes that there is no legal basis for holding the defendants liable for the online comments of third parties.[112]

September 22, 2015: Inspiration for "Jurisprudence of Yogi Berra" Dies at 90

Exactly 69 years after his major league debut for the New York Yankees on September 22, 1946, Lawrence Peter "Yogi" Berra passes away from natural causes at the age of 90. "Arguably the greatest catcher in baseball history and inarguably the greatest winner the game has ever known,"[113] Yogi's witty observations—actual and apocryphal "Berraisms"—also inspired scholars in a great many fields, including law. Thus, in 1997, 39 authors contributed to "The Jurisprudence of Yogi Berra," a wide-ranging essay that included such topics as constitutional law, torts, civil procedure, and property. It sought to "demonstrate the parallels between judges' and legislators' comments and what Yogi said; only Yogi said it better."[114]

December 14, 2015: Manfred Denies Pete Rose Reinstatement Request

Commissioner Rob Manfred denies Pete Rose's request that he be reinstated from baseball's permanently ineligible list on which he was placed in 1989 for violating Major League Baseball's Rule 21 prohibition against gambling.[115] In his four-page written decision, the commissioner cites a notebook taken from Michael Bertolini in October 1989 but not available to John Dowd when he prepared the report which comprised the primary evidence against Rose in 1989 (see entry for August 23, 1989). It shows that Rose bet on the Cincinnati Reds in 1986 while he was the team's player-manager.[116] Furthermore, during an interview with Manfred on September 24, 2015, Rose initially denied that he had continued to bet on horse racing and professional sports, including baseball, but later clarified that he did in fact gamble legally in his new place of residency, Las Vegas, Nevada.[117] Ultimately, Manfred decides that Rose's behavior falls "well short" of the requirements for reinstatement, including that the applicant "has fundamentally changed his life and that, based on such changes, the applicant does not pose a risk for violating Rule 21 in the future."[118]

Appendix A: A Selective List of Lawyers Involved with Baseball

(At the end of many entries are citations to recommended reading)

ALDERSON, RICHARD ("SANDY") (November 22, 1947–)
- Graduate, Harvard Law School, 1976
- Team Executive:
    Oakland A's: General Counsel, 1981–83; General Manager, 1983–97
    San Diego Padres: CEO, 2005–09
    New York Mets: General Manager, 2011–
- MLB Official: executive vice president for baseball operations, 1998–2005
- General Manager for Oakland during successful period in which A's won four division titles, three pennants and the 1989 World Series

ALLEN, MEL (February 14, 1913–June 16, 1996)
- Graduate, University of Alabama School of Law, 1937
- Broadcaster:
    New York Yankees and New York Giants (home games only), 1939–43
    New York Yankees, 1946–64, 1976–85 (limited role)
    22 World Series on radio and television, including 18 in a row from 1946 to 1963; also broadcast 24 All-Star games
    hosted *This Week in Baseball* syndicated TV series from its inception in 1977 to his death in 1996
- Inducted into National Sportscasters and Sportswriters Association Hall of Fame, 1972; American Sportscasters Association Hall of Fame, 1985; National Radio Hall of Fame, 1988
- One of first two recipients (with Red Barber) of Ford C. Frick Award from National Baseball Hall of Fame, 1978

Allen, Mel, and Ed Fitzgerald. *You Can't Beat the Hours: A Long, Loving Look at Big-League Baseball, Including Some Yankees I Have Known.* New York: Harper & Row, 1964.

Borelli, Stephen. *How About That! The Life of Mel Allen*. Champaign, IL: Sports Publishing LLC, 2005.
Smith, Curt. *The Voice: Mel Allen's Untold Story*. Guilford, CT: Lyons Press, 2007.

ANGELOS, PETER G. (July 4, 1929–)
- Graduate, University of Baltimore School of Law, 1961
- Private practice, 1961–
- Team Executive:
    Owner, Baltimore Orioles, 1993–present
    Chairman of the Board and CEO of Orioles
    Member, Executive Council of Major League Baseball
- Member of Baltimore City Council, 1959–63

AUSTRIAN, ALFRED S. (June 15, 1870–January 26, 1932)
- Graduate, Harvard Law School, 1891
- Partner, Mayer, Meyer, Austrian, and Platt, Chicago, 1905–1932
- Attorney for Charles Comiskey and Chicago White Sox during Black Sox litigation period

BERG, MOE (March 2, 1902–May 29, 1972)
- Graduate, Columbia Law School, 1930
- Major League Baseball Player, 1923, 1926–39
- Rumored to be American spy during 1934 visit of AL all-stars to Japan, but no evidence exists to substantiate claim
- Served with the Office of Strategic Services (OSS) during World War II, 1943–45; awarded the Presidential Medal of Freedom on October 10, 1945, but he rejected the award. Some years after his death, the award was accepted on his behalf by his sister.

Dawidoff, Nicholas. *The Catcher Was a Spy: The Mysterious Life of Moe Berg*. New York: Vintage, 1994.
Dawidoff, Nicholas. "Scholar, Lawyer, Catcher, Spy." *Sports Illustrated* (March 23, 1992): 76–86.
Kaufman, Louis, Barbara Fitzgerald, and Tom Sewell. *Moe Berg: Athlete, Scholar, Spy*. Boston: Little, Brown, 1974.

BLACKMUN, HARRY A. (November 12, 1908–March 4, 1999)
- Graduate, Harvard Law School, 1932
- Private practice: Dorsey and Whitney, 1934–50; Resident Counsel, Mayo Clinic, 1950–59
- Judge, U.S. Court of Appeals, 8th Cir., 1959–70
- Justice, U.S. Supreme Court, 1970–94
- Wrote opinion for 5–3 majority in *Flood v. Kuhn* (1972), in which U.S. Supreme Court upheld baseball's antitrust exemption and refused to rule that baseball's reserve system violated federal antitrust laws; the opinion included an "extraordinary list of 88 ballplayers and baseball business figures"

Abrams, Roger I. "Blackmun's List." *Virginia Sports and Entertainment Law Journal* 6 (2007): 181–207.
Greenhouse, Linda. *Becoming Justice Blackmun: Harry Blackmun's Supreme Court Journey*. New York: Times Books, 2005.

Yarbrough, Tinsley E. *Harry A. Blackmun: The Outsider Justice*. New York: Oxford University Press, 2008.

BORAS, SCOTT (November 2, 1952–)
- Graduate, University of Pacific, McGeorge School of Law, 1982
- Admitted to practice, California, 1983
- Player Agent
- 1st agent to negotiate contracts larger than $50 million (Greg Maddux) and $100 million (Kevin Brown)
- In December 2000, negotiated what was then the largest contract in professional sports history (Alex Rodriguez, $252 million/10 years)

BRAMHAM, WILLIAM G. ("Judge") (July 13, 1874–July 8, 1947)
- Admitted to practice, North Carolina, 1905
- Private practice, Durham, NC
- League President: North Carolina State League, 1916–17; Piedmont League, 1920–32; South Atlantic League, 1924–30; Virginia League, 1925–28; Eastern Carolina League, 1928–29
- President, National Association of Professional Baseball Leagues (NAPBL) (governing body for minor leagues), 1933–46
- Largely responsible for the creation of the Durham Bulls baseball team in 1902
- As third president of NAPBL, created financial stability in minor leagues despite Great Depression; inherited 14 leagues and 102 clubs, but turned over 52 leagues and 388 clubs to George M. Trautman in 1947
- "Bramham carried his judicial title despite never having sat upon a bench. His law school classmates bestowed it to honor his dignified manner...." [David Pietrusza, *Baseball's Canadian-American League: A History of Its Inception, Franchises, Participants, Locales, Statistics, Demise and Legacy* (McFarland, 1990), 2]

Pietrusza, David. "Judge Bramham: Czar of the Minor Leagues." In *Minor Miracles: The Legend & Lure of Minor League Baseball*, 42–48. South Bend, IN: Diamond Communications, 1995.

Sumner, Jim L. "William G. Bramham: The Czar of Minor League Baseball." *Carolina Comments* 37 (1989): 116–22.

CANNON, RAYMOND J. (August 26, 1894–November 25, 1951)
- Graduate, Marquette University Law School, 1914
- Admitted to practice, Wisconsin, 1914
- Private practice in Milwaukee, 1914–29, 1932–33, 1942–51
- Member, U.S. House of Representatives, 1933–39
- As sports lawyer, represented Jack Dempsey among other clients
- Semi-pro baseball pitcher, 1908–22
- Represented Happy Felsch in suit against Charles Comiskey and Chicago White Sox for back pay, World Series share, and damages; also represented other Black Sox players (Weaver, Jackson, Risberg)
- In 1922, formed the National Baseball Players Association, the fourth attempt to form a players union
- Father of Robert C. Cannon (see below)

CANNON, ROBERT C. (June 10, 1917–October 22, 2008)
- Graduate, Marquette University Law School, 1941
- Admitted to practice, Wisconsin, 1941
- Special assistant U.S. district attorney
- Judge: Milwaukee Civil Court, 1946–53; Milwaukee Circuit Court, 1953–78; Wisconsin Court of Appeals, 1978–81
- Part-time Legal Advisor, MLBPA, 1959–1966 (helping to achieve increase in pension benefits, with player pension fund receiving 95% of ticket sales and radio/TV fees for All-Star game, and 60–40 split of World Series ticket sales and radio/TV fees
- Candidate to succeed Ford Frick as MLB commissioner, reportedly lost by one vote to William Eckert
- As Vice-President of Milwaukee Brewers Inc., organization established to return baseball to Milwaukee after Braves moved to Atlanta, he played important role in bringing Seattle Pilots to Milwaukee; later served as Vice-President of Milwaukee Brewers
- Son of Raymond J. Cannon (see above)

McKenna, Brian. "Robert Cannon." Society for American Baseball Research, SABR Baseball Biography Project. Accessed March 2, 2013. http://sabr.org/bioproj/person/a7414ea2.

CARROLL, LOUIS F. (May 31, 1905–October 25, 1971)
- Graduate of University of Iowa Law School, 1930
- Admitted to practice, New York, 1930
- Attorney at Willkie, Farr and Gallagher, New York City, 1930–71
- Served as outside counsel to National League for 35 years, known as "The Wise Man" of baseball; frequently testified before Congress on behalf of Organized Baseball in antitrust hearings; represented National League in *Flood v. Kuhn*

CELLER, EMANUEL (May 6, 1888–January 15, 1981)
- Graduate, Columbia University Law School, 1912
- Admitted to practice, New York, 1912
- Practiced law, NYC
- Member, U.S. House of Representatives, 1923–73, fourth longest tenure in history
- In 1951–52, as chair of Subcommittee on Monopoly Power of the House Judiciary Committee, conducted hearings on baseball's antitrust exemption; he continued to lead fight against exemption, including introducing bills
- "They [organized baseball] want exemption from antitrust laws. Well, they're not going to get it. I am going to fight it tooth and nail." Quoted in "They Said It," *Sports Illustrated*, February 2, 1959, 18.

Celler, Emanuel. *You Never Leave Brooklyn: The Autobiography of Emanuel Celler*. New York: John Day Co., 1953.

CHAMPION, AARON BURT (February 9, 1842–September 1, 1895)
- Studied law under Francis Collins, Columbus, OH
- Admitted to practice, Ohio, 1863
- 1865–188?, partner, Wilson and Champion law firm, Cincinnati
- Co-organizer of Union Cricket Club in Cincinnati, 1865

- Co-organizer and first president of the Cincinnati Base Ball Club, 1866, which eventually becomes known as Cincinnati Red Stockings in 1868; remained as president of Red Stockings when it became first openly all-professional team in 1869
- President, Ohio State Base-Ball Association, 1868

Faber, Charles F. "Aaron Burt Champion." SABR Baseball Biography Project, accessed June 13, 2014, http://sabr.org/node/24735.

CHANDLER, A.B. ("HAPPY") (July 14–1898–June 15, 1991)
- Graduate, University of Kentucky Law School, 1924
- Admitted to practice, Kentucky, 1925
- Second Commissioner of Baseball (April 24, 1945–July 15, 1951), succeeding Landis
- As commissioner: imposed 5-year ban on players jumping to Mexican League; player pension fund was created during his tenure; presided over MLB when it integrated in 1947, supporting Jackie Robinson and integration of baseball (contending that owners secretly voted 15–1 against integration, but he refused to support it)
- Inducted into National Baseball Hall of Fame as pioneer/executive, 1982
- Twice served as governor of Kentucky, 1935–39, 1955–59; served as United States senator from Kentucky, 1939–45

Chandler, A.B., with John Underwood. "How I Jumped from Clean Politics into Dirty Baseball." *Sports Illustrated* (April 26, 1971): 73–86.

Chandler, A.B., with John Underwood. "Gunned Down by the Heavies." *Sports Illustrated* (May 3, 1971): 52–58.

Chandler, A.B., with Vance Trimble. *Heroes, Plain Folks, and Skunks: The Life and Times of Happy Chandler—An Autobiography*. Chicago: Bonus Books, 1989.

CLARK, STEPHEN CARLTON (August 29, 1882–September 17, 1960)
- Graduate, Columbia Law School, 1907
- Admitted to practice, New York
- Founder of National Baseball Hall of Fame, Cooperstown, NY: Born in Cooperstown, he wanted to display the "Doubleday baseball" in his home town. He placed it and other baseball paraphernalia in room in the village library building in 1937. At encouragement of NL President Ford Frick, he then donated funds for a building to serve as permanent hall to commemorate baseball, which was established in 1939.
- Grandson of Edward Clark, a founder of the Singer Sewing Machine Company
- Member of the New York State Assembly (Otsego Co.) in 1910
- Also founded Farmers Museum in Cooperstown in 1942

CLENDENON, DONN A. (July 15, 1935–September 17, 2005)
- Graduate, Duquesne Law School, 1978
- Legal positions: Lawyer, Legal Department, Mead Corporation; Montgomery County Public Defenders Office, Dayton, OH; Founding Partner, Bostick, Guerren and Clendenon, Dayton, OH; Clendenon, Henney and Hoy, Minnesota; Carlsen, Carter, Hoy and Eirinberg, PC, Sioux Falls, SD
- Major League Player, 1961–72 (Pirates, Expos, Mets, Cardinals); MVP of 1969 World Series

- Inducted into Georgia Sports Hall of Fame, 2005
- Author of *Miracle in New York: The Story of the 1969 Mets Through the Eyes of Donn Clendenon, World Series MVP* (Sioux Falls, SD: Penmarch Publishing, 1999)

Hoyt, Ed. "Donn Clendenon." Society for American Baseball Research, SABR Baseball Biography Project. Accessed July 19, 2013. http://sabr.org/bioproj/person/d9b9b223.

CLINE, WILLIAM A. (July 21, 1910–June 12, 2012)
- Graduate, Cumberland Law School, Tenn., 1931
- Admitted to practice, Texas; practiced law in Wharton, Texas, until 2006
- Represented Jackie Robinson in 1944 court martial for insubordination arising from confrontation with officers after Ft. Hood army bus incident

COONELLY, FRANK (March 31, 1960–)
- Graduate, Catholic University, Columbus School of Law, 1986
- Partner, Morgan, Lewis and Bockius, Wash., DC
- Represented MLB as outside counsel
- MLB Official: Senior Vice-President and General Counsel of Labor, Office of Commissioner, 1998–2000
- Team Executive: President, Pittsburgh Pirates, 2007–present
- For Pirates, responsible for the day-to-day operations of the organization
- In commissioners office, responsible for arbitration hearings and draft bonuses; negotiated and administered CBAs with MLBPA

DALE, FRANCIS L. (July 13, 1921–November 28, 1993)
- Graduate, University of Virginia School of Law, 1948
- Partner, Frost and Jacobs, Cincinnati; practice focused on antitrust law
- President and Majority Owner, Cincinnati Reds, 1967–73; as president, supporter of building downtown Riverfront Stadium
- June 3, 1970: testified for defense at Curt Flood trial, supporting "uniqueness" of baseball as justification for baseball's exemption from federal antitrust laws [Neil F. Flynn, *Baseball's Reserve System—The Case and Trial of Curt Flood v. Major League Baseball* (2006), 190–98]
- President, Ohio State Bar Association, 1965
- Publisher, *Cincinnati Enquirer*, 1965–73; *Los Angeles Herald Examiner*, 1977–85
- U.S. representative to European Office of the United Nations in Geneva, with rank of ambassador, 1973–76
- Commissioner, Major Indoor Soccer League, 1985–86

DEWITT, WILLIAM O., SR. (August 3, 1902–March 4, 1982)
- Graduate, Washington University School of Law
- Team Owner and Executive:
    St. Louis Cardinals: treasurer and farm director
    St. Louis Browns: served as General Manager and minority owner (1936–48), and majority owner (1948–51)
    New York Yankees: Assistant General Manager (1954–58)
    Detroit Tigers: president and General Manager (1959–60)
    Cincinnati Reds: General Manager (1960–66) and Owner (1962–66)
    Chicago White Sox: Chairman (1975–81)

- For Browns: Recipient of *Sporting News Executive of the Year Award* (1944), when Browns won their only pennant; as General Manager and minority owner, on July 17, 1947, DeWitt purchased Hank Thompson and Willard Brown from KC Monarchs; on 7/17/47, Thompson became second to integrate AL (after Larry Doby of Indians on 7/5/47); on 7/19/47, Brown became third
- With Tigers, traded for Norm Cash, Rocky Colavito, and manager Joe Gordon (for whom he traded Detroit's manager, Jimmy Dykes, to Cleveland)
- With Reds, traded Frank Robinson to Orioles (calling him "an old 30")

Isgrig, Dwayne. "Bill DeWitt." In *The 1934 St. Louis Cardinals: The World Champion Gas House Gang*, edited by Charles F. Faber, 243–49. Phoenix: Society for American Baseball Research, 2014.

DOWD, JOHN M. (February 11, 1941–)
- Graduate, Emory University School of Law, 1965
- Attorney, Tax Division of U.S. Department of Justice, and chief of an Organized Crime Strike Force, Criminal Div., DOG
- Partner, Akin Gump Strauss Hauer and Feld, Washington, D.C.
- Special Counsel to Commissioners Peter Ueberroth, Bart Giamatti and Fay Vincent
    Investigator and author of 225-page "Dowd Report" (May 1989) which described Pete Rose's betting on baseball and which precipitated his lifetime banishment
    Also investigated George Steinbrenner, Don Zimmer, and Len Dykstra

DUPUY, ROBERT A. (1947–)
- Graduate, Cornell University Law School, 1973
- Admitted, New York and Wisconsin
- Foley and Lardner, Milwaukee, WI, 1973–98 (partner in 1980)
- Foley and Lardner, NYC, sports industry team, 2011–present
- Outside counsel for MLB, 1989–98, including principal outside counsel to commissioner and executive council, 1992–98
- MLB Official: Executive Vice-President of Administration and Chief Legal Officer, 1998; President and Chief Operating Officer, 2002–10
- As Executive VP, oversaw consolidation of AL and NL into Central Offices and led formation of Major League Baseball Advanced Media
- As President, responsible for all phases of baseball's Central Offices
- As outside counsel, helped negotiate $280 million collusion settlement with the MLBPA in 1990

EPSTEIN, THEO NATHANIEL (December 29, 1973–)
- Graduate, University of San Diego School of Law, 2000
- Team Executive:
    San Diego Padres: Director of Baseball Relations, 1997–2002
    Boston Red Sox: General Manager, 2002–11
    Cubs: President of Baseball Operations, 2011–present
- Youngest general manager in history of baseball when hired by Boston Red Sox in Nov. 2002 at age of 28
- GM of World Series winning Red Sox (2004, 2007) and Cubs (2016) teams

FEENEY, CHARLES STONEHAM ("CHUB") (August 31, 1921–January 10, 1994)
- Graduate, Fordham Law School
- Team Executive: New York and San Francisco Giants: Vice President, 1950–69; San Diego Padres: President, 1987–88
- President, National League, 1970–86
- Grandson of Charles Stoneham, principal owner of New York Giants (1919–36), and nephew of Horace Stoneham, Giants owner from 1936–76
- Started with Giants as batboy, but joined team after World War II as vice president at age of 24 in 1946; though not always officially titled general manager, served as head of baseball operations for most of his full-time tenure with Giants
- Under his leadership, Giants were first MLB team to sign players from Dominican Republic and first to sign a player from Japan (Masanori Murakami, debut in 1964)
- Leading candidate to replace William Eckert as MLB commissioner in 1969, but after 17 deadlocked ballots, Bowie Kuhn chosen as compromise candidate
- As NL president, regarded holding the line against the designated hitter as the main achievement of his league presidency

FEHR, DONALD (July 18, 1948–)
- Graduate, University of Missouri–Kansas City Law School, 1973
- Lawyer at Jolley, Moran, Walsh, Hager and Gordon, Kansas City law firm representing MLBPA
- Labor Attorney and Union Official: MLBPA general counsel (1977–82); MLBPA Executive Director, 1983–2009; National Hockey League Players Association, Executive Director (2010–present)
- As outside counsel for MLBPA, handled Messersmith free agency case
- Negotiated a new CBA following the season-ending strike in 1994

FRANK, JEROME (September 10, 1889–January 13, 1957)
- Graduate, University of Chicago Law School, 1912
- Private practice, Chicago, 1912–30; NYC, 1930–33
- General Counsel, Agriculture Adjustment Administration, 1933–35
- SEC commissioner, 1937–41
- Judge, U.S. Court of Appeals, 2nd Cir., 1941–57
- Joined with Judge Learned Hand to render 2–1 decision in *Gardella v. Chandler*, 172 F.2d 402 (2d Cir. 1949), ruling that baseball's connection with radio/TV gave game an interstate character that might be sufficient to bring it within purview of antitrust laws and thus allow distinguishing of *Federal Baseball Club v. National League*, 259 U.S. 200 (1922)
- Wrote: "[I]f the players be regarded as quasi-peons, it is of no moment that they are well paid; only the totalitarian-minded will believe that high pay excuses virtual slavery." (at 410)
- In litigation over rights to photos of baseball players for chewing gum cards, *Haelan Laboratories Inc. v. Topps Chewing Gum, Inc.*, 202 F.2d 866 (2d Cir.1953), he created right of publicity ("a man has a right in the publicity value of his photograph")

FUCHS, EMIL ("JUDGE") (April 17, 1878–December 5, 1961)
- Graduate, New York University Law School
- Began practicing law in 1899
- Assistant District Attorney, NY, 1902–10
- Magistrate Judge, New York City, 1915–18
- Owner, Boston Braves, 1923–35
- Manager, Boston Braves, 1929 (record of 56–98, .364 W-L %)
- Attorney, N.Y. Giants
- Bought Babe Ruth's contract from Jacob Ruppert, brought him back to Boston in 1935 as player, assistant manager, and vice-president
- Ruth retired on May 27, 1935; Fuchs, in dire financial straits, forced to sell Braves to minority partner Charles Adams on July 31, 1935
- "He gained the title of judge during an interim appointment as a police magistrate in New York. When he ran unsuccessfully for a judgeship in 1921 he gave up politics for baseball." "Emil E. Fuchs, Former Owner of Boston Braves, Dies at 83," *New York Times*, Dec. 6, 1961, 47.

FULTZ, DAVID LEWIS (May 29, 1875–October 29, 1959)
- Graduate, New York University Law School, 1904
- Admitted, New York, 1905
- Law practice, NYC, 1905–47
- Major League Player: Phillies, 1898–99; Orioles, 1899; Athletics, 1901–02; New York Highlanders, 1903–05
- Sports attorney and labor union official: Organizer and president of the Fraternity of Professional Baseball Players of America (AKA Players' Fraternity), chartered in New York in September 1912; in 1914, negotiated "Cincinnati Agreement" with National Commission and minor-league executive board
- League Official: President, International League, 1919–20
- All-American football player at Brown; played professional football, 1900–01; college head football coach, 1898–99 (Missouri), 1902–04

McKenna, Brian. "Dave Fultz." Society for American Baseball Research, SABR Baseball Biography Project. Accessed March 9, 2013. http://sabr.org/bioproj/person/1857946b.

FURST, WILLIAM
- Negro Leagues attorney; attorney for Effa Manley, owner of the Newark Eagles

GARAGIOLA, JOE, JR. (1952–)
- Graduate, Georgetown University Law Center
- General Manager, Arizona Diamondbacks, 1998–2005; during this period, the team won NL 3 West division titles (1999–01), one NL pennant (01), and the franchise's only World Series title (01)
- MLB Official: Senior Vice-President, Baseball Operations, 2005–11; Senior Vice-President, Standards and On-Field Operations, 2011–present

GATES, EDWARD E. (August 23, 1871–April 21, 1935)
- Indiana University Law School; New York University, 1895
- Lawyer: Baker and Daniels, Indianapolis; Matson, Gates and Ross (predecessor of Ice, Miller); Henley, Matson and Gates; Myers and Gates

- General Counsel for Federal League
- Represented owners of Chicago Whales of Federal League in *Weegham v. Killefer*, 215 F. 168 (W.D. Mich. 1914)

GILL, LEWIS M. (1912–January 1, 2002)
- Graduate, University of Pennsylvania Law School, 1936
- Staff Attorney, NLRB
- Chairman, Cleveland Regional War Labor Board, 1942–43
- Member, National War Labor Board, 1944–45
- Practicing Attorney, 1946–?
- Permanent Arbitrator, 1970–72: Oct. 5, 1970, named by MLBPA and the clubs of the AL and NL as first permanent impartial grievance arbitrator under Article X of Basic Agreement
- President, National Academy of Arbitrators, 1971

GOLDBERG, ARTHUR J. (August 8, 1908–January 19, 1990)
- Graduate, Northwestern University School of Law, 1929
- U.S. Secretary of Labor, 1961–62
- Justice, U.S. Supreme Court, 1962–65
- U.S. Ambassador to United Nations, 1965–68
- Partner, Paul, Weiss, Rifkind, Wharton and Garrison, New York, 1968–?
- In 1972, presented oral arguments on behalf of Curt Flood before U.S. Supreme Court in *Flood v. Kuhn*

Stebenne, David. *Arthur J. Goldberg: New Deal Liberal.* New York: Oxford University Press, 1996.

GOLDBERG, STEPHEN B. (1932–)
- Graduate, Harvard Law School, 1959
- Admitted to practice: California, 1961; Illinois, 1967
- Supervisory Attorney, NLRB, 1961–65
- Professor of Law: Illinois, 1965–73; Northwestern, 1974–present (emeritus since 2004)
- Stands as the most prolific salary arbitrator for MLB and MLBPA, having arbitrated 53 cases

GOLENBOCK, PETER (July 19, 1946–)
- Graduate, New York University School of Law, 1970
- Legal Department, Prentice-Hall, Inc.
- Author of various baseball-related books, including:
    Dynasty: The New York Yankees, 1949–1964 (Englewood Cliffs, N.J.: Prentice-Hall, 1975)
    The Bronx Zoo (New York: Crown Publishers, 1979)
    Number 1 (New York: Delacorte Press, 1980)
    Bums: An Oral History of the Brooklyn Dodgers (New York: Putnam, 1984)
    Balls (New York: Putnam, 1984)

GOULD, WILLIAM B., IV (July 16, 1936–)
- Graduate, Cornell Law School, 1961
- Assistant General Counsel, United Auto Workers, 1961–62

- NLRB Attorney, 1963-65
- Attorney, Battle, Fowler, Stokes and Kheel (New York), 1965-68
- Professor of Law: Wayne State, 1968-71; Harvard, 1971-72; Stanford, 1972-present
- Chairman, National Labor Relations Board, 1994-98
- Arbitrated salary disputes between MLB Player Relations Committee and MLBPA in 1992 and 1993
- Author of *Bargaining with Baseball: Labor Relations in an Age of Prosperous Turmoil* (Jefferson, NC: McFarland, 2011)

GREENBERG, CHARLES M. ("CHUCK")
- Team Executive: Owner, CEO and Managing General Partner, Texas Rangers, 2010-11

HAND, LEARNED (January 27, 1872-August 18, 1961)
- Graduate, Harvard Law School, 1896
- Practiced law in Albany, NY, and NYC, 1896-1909
- Judge, U.S. District Court, Southern District of New York, 1909-24
- Judge, U.S. Court of Appeals, 2d Circuit, 1924-61
- Joined with Judge Jerome Frank to render 2-1 decision in *Gardella v. Chandler*, 172 F.2d 402 (2d Cir. 1949), ruling that baseball's connection with radio/TV gave game an interstate character that might be sufficient to bring it within purview of antitrust laws and thus allow distinguishing of *Federal Baseball Club v. National League*, 259 U.S. 200 (1922)

HAYES, J. WILLIAM (?-March 30, 1992)
- Founding Partner, Hayes and Humes
- Founder, Executive Business Management, Inc.
- Represented Sandy Koufax and Don Drysdale during their joint contract holdout in 1966
- Served as legal counsel and business manager to many notables in the entertainment industry (e.g., Aaron Spelling, David Wolper, Robert Stack, Lloyd Bridges)

HENDRICKS, JOHN CHARLES ("JACK") (April 9, 1875-May 13, 1943)
- Graduate, Northwestern University Law School
- Admitted to practice, Illinois, 1897
- Major League Player: New York Giants and Chicago Cubs, 1902; Washington Senators, 1903
- Minor League Manager: for Denver Grizzlies, he won 3 consecutive Western League championships, 1911-13. Also led Indianapolis Indians to American Association pennant in 1917.
- Major League Manager: St. Louis Cardinals, 1918; Cincinnati Reds, 1924-29
- One of only 8 major league managers to have earned a law degree or passed a state bar exam: Hendricks, Huggins, Jennings, La Russa, O'Rourke, Rickey, Ruel, Ward

HODGES, RUSSELL P. ("RUSS") (June 18, 1910-April 19, 1971)
- Graduate, University of Cincinnati College of Law, 1933

- Broadcast games for Cincinnati Reds, Chicago Cubs, Chicago White Sox, Washington Senators, New York Yankees, and, most notably, as lead announcer for New York and San Francisco Giants (1949–70)
- Best remembered for his radio call of Bobby Thomson's 1951 playoff walk-off home run ("The Giants Win the Pennant! The Giants Win the Pennant!) and his home run catch phrase ("Bye, Bye, Baby!")
- Fourth recipient of Ford C. Frick Award, 1980 (preceded by Mel Allen, Red Barber, and Bob Elson) from the National Baseball Hall of Fame
- Inducted into National Sportscasters and Sportswriters Association's Hall of Fame, 1975

Hodges, Russ. "All the Way with Willie." In *Voices of Sport*, edited by Marv Albert, 146–57. New York: Grosset & Dunlap, 1971.

Hodges, Russ. With Al Hirshberg. *My Giants*. Garden City, NY: Doubleday, 1963.

Smith, Curt. "Russ Hodges." In *The Team That Time Won't Forget: The 1951 New York Giants*, edited by Bill Nowlin and C. Paul Rogers III, 265–68. Phoenix: Society for American Baseball Research, 2015.

HOFHEINZ, ROY MARK ("THE JUDGE") (April 10, 1912–November 22, 1982)

- Graduate, Houston Law School, 1931
- Member, Texas House of Representatives, 1934–36
- Judge, Harris County (Texas), 1936–44
- Private law practice
- Owner, Houston Colt .45s (later Astros), 1960–76
- Co-creator and driving force of Houston Sports Association, which received major league expansion franchise in October 1960
- Conceived and gained funding to build Houston Astrodome, world's first multipurpose, air-conditioned, domed sports stadium, which opened in 1965 as Harris County Domed Stadium and was nicknamed the "Eighth Wonder of the World"; it served as home of Houston Astros, (1965–1999) and Houston Oilers (1968–97)
- Mayor, Houston, Texas, 1953–55
- Inductee, Texas Baseball Hall of Fame, 2006

Ray, Edgar W. *The Grand Huckster: Houston's Judge Roy Hofheinz, Genius of the Astrodome*. Memphis: Memphis State University Press, 1980.

HOLMES, OLIVER WENDELL, JR. (March 8, 1841–March 6, 1935)

- Graduate, Harvard Law School
- Admitted, Massachusetts, 1866
- author of *The Common Law* (1881)
- Assoc. and Chief Justice, Mass. Supreme Judicial Court (1882–1902)
- Justice, U.S. Supreme Court (1902–32)
- Author of unanimous majority opinion in *Federal Baseball Club v. National League*, 259 U.S. 200 (1922), in which baseball held not to be interstate commerce for purposes of Sherman Antitrust Act, thereby establishing what came to be viewed as the sport's exemption from antitrust

Baker, Liva. *The Justice From Beacon Hill: The Life and Times of Oliver Wendell Holmes*. New York: HarperCollins, 1991.

Novick, Sheldon M. *Honorable Justice: The Life of Oliver Wendell Holmes.* Boston: Little, Brown, 1989.

White, G. Edward. *Justice Oliver Wendell Holmes: Law and the Inner Self.* New York: Oxford University Press, 1993.

HOYNES, LOUIS L., JR.
- Graduate, Harvard Law School, 1962
- Willkie, Farr and Gallagher, New York City
- Served as legal counsel for National League and MLB
- Argued on behalf of Chub Feeney and the National League before U.S. Supreme Court in *Flood v. Kuhn* case
- Represented MLB in Messersmith-McNally arbitration hearing before Peter Seitz in late 1975

HUDNALL, GEORGE B. (January 8, 1864–October 1, 1936)
- Graduate, University of Wisconsin Law School, 1891
- City Attorney, Superior, Wisconsin, 1900–02
- Wisconsin State Senate, 1903–11
- President, State Bar of Wisconsin, 1915–16
- Lead lawyer for White Sox owner Charles Comiskey in 1924 Milwaukee suit by Joe Jackson for back wages; he brought forth grand jury confessions of players which had disappeared four years earlier during Chicago trial in which Black Sox players were acquitted

HUGGINS, MILLER (March 27, 1878–September 25, 1929)
- Graduate, University of Cincinnati Law School, 1902
- Admitted, Ohio
- Major League Player (1904–16); Manager: St. Louis Cardinals, 1913–17; New York Yankees, 1917–29
- As manager, he won 6 pennants and 3 World Series championships
- One of only 8 major league managers to have earned a law degree or passed a state bar exam: Hendricks, Huggins, Jennings, La Russa, O'Rourke, Rickey, Ruel, Ward
- Inducted into the National Baseball Hall of Fame (as manager), 1964

Steinberg, Steve, and Lyle Spatz. *The Colonel and the Hug: The Partnership that Transformed the New York Yankees.* Lincoln: University of Nebraska Press, 1975.

JENNINGS, HUGHIE (April 2, 1869–February 1, 1928)
- Attended Cornell Law School (did not graduate)
- Admitted to practice, Maryland, 1905; Pennsylvania, 1907
- Successful trial lawyer, Scranton, PA
- Major League Player (1891–1903, 1907, 1909–10, 1912, 1918), Career BA of .312
- Manager, Detroit Tigers (1907–20) and New York Giants (1924–25); won three pennants as manager
- One of founders of Players Protective Association, formed in 1900 by players in reaction to reduction of teams by National League, causing loss of 60 player jobs
- One of only 8 major league managers to have earned a law degree or passed a state bar exam: Hendricks, Huggins, Jennings, La Russa, O'Rourke, Rickey, Ruel, Ward

- Inducted into the National Baseball Hall of Fame (as player), 1945

Smiles, Jack. *"Ee-Yah": The Life and Times of Hughie Jennings, Baseball Hall of Famer.* Jefferson, NC: McFarland, 2005.

JOHNSON, FREDERIC A. (?–February 7, 1985)
- Graduate, Harvard Law School, 1924
- Attorney for individual players
- Author of articles challenging validity of baseball's reserve clause; e.g., "Baseball Law," 73 U.S. Law Rev. 252–70 (1939)
- represented plaintiff in *Gardella v. Chandler*, 172 F.2d 402 (1949)
- represented several plaintiffs (Kowalski, Corbett) in consolidated cases listed as *Toolson v. N.Y. Yankees*, 346 U.S. 356 (1953)
- classmate of A.B. "Happy" Chandler at Harvard Law School

KAPSTEIN, JERRY (1943–)
- Graduate, Boston College Law School, 1968
- Player Agent, 1973–88?
- Team Executive: San Diego Padres, President and CEO, 1988–90; Boston Red Sox, Senior Advisor, Baseball Projects, 2002–present
- After 1973 season, represented 3 Oakland A's players (Holtzman, Knowles and Fingers) in first salary arbitration cases to be heard after system added to baseball's CBA; going against Charlie Finley, won each by using substantial statistical evidence; he represented players in 10 of the 29 cases heard that winter, winning all of them
- Of the 12 players who wound up signing million-dollar contracts after 24 players granted free agency following 1976 season, Kapstein represented seven of them (Fingers, Grich, Rudi, Tenace, Gullett, Bando, Baylor)
- 1974, capitalizing on Finley's contract breach, achieved free agency for client Jim "Catfish" Hunter

KUHN, BOWIE KENT (October 28, 1926–March 15, 2007)
- Graduate, University of Virginia Law School, 1950
- Lawyer with Willkie, Farr and Gallagher (NYC) for 19 years
- Legal Counsel for MLB
    Represented baseball as outside counsel in numerous matters, including successful representation of NL in defending suit to prevent Braves from moving to Atlanta
- Commissioner of Baseball (5th), February 4, 1969–September 30, 1984:
    Baseball experienced dramatic increases in attendance, salaries, revenue and franchise values" during tenure; pioneered night baseball for World Series; divisions created during tenure as commissioner; supported inclusion of baseball in Olympic Games
- Inducted into National Baseball Hall of Fame (as Pioneer/Executive), 2008

Gietschier, Steven P. "Bowie Kuhn: Towards a Reassessment," *NINE: A Journal of Baseball History and Culture* (Spring 1999), 102–115.

Kuhn, Bowie, with Martin Appel. *Hardball: The Education of a Baseball Commissioner.* New York: Times Books, 1987.

LANDIS, KENESAW MOUNTAIN (November 20, 1866–November 25, 1944)

- Graduate, Union Law School (now Northwestern), 1891
- Admitted to practice, Illinois, 1891
- Judge, U.S. District Court (N.D. Ill), 1905–22
- As federal judge, presided over Standard Oil antitrust trial and a series of trials accusing union leaders from the Industrial Workers of the World of espionage
- First Commissioner of Baseball, November 12, 1920–November 25, 1944
- As trial judge in case involving Federal League, delayed ruling from hearing in January 1915 until parties settled in December 1915, leading to disbanding of FL
- As commissioner, banned Black Sox players despite acquittal in court, and cracked down on gambling in baseball
- Inducted into National Baseball Hall of Fame (as Executive), 1944

Pietrusza, David. *Judge and Jury: The Life and Times of Judge Kenesaw Mountain Landis*. South Bend, IN: Diamond Communications, 1998.

Sigman, Shayna M., "The Jurisprudence of Judge Kenesaw Mountain Landis." *Marquette Sports Law Review* 15 (2005): 277–330.

Spink, J.G. Taylor. *Judge Landis and Twenty-Five Years of Baseball*. New York: Thomas Y. Crowell, 1947.

LA RUSSA, ANTHONY ("TONY") (October 4, 1944–)
- Graduate, Florida State Law School, 1978
- Admitted to practice, Florida, 1979
- Practiced for Thorp, Reed, Conley and Dooley, Sarasota, FL
- Major League Player (1963, 1968–71, 1973) and Manager (1979–2011)
- As manager: won Manager of the Year Award four times (1983, 1988, 1992, 2002); 12 division titles, 6 pennants, 3 World Series titles; only manager to win World Series in three decades; 2728 wins, 3rd all-time (behind Mack and McGraw)
- One of only 8 major league managers to have earned a law degree or passed a state bar exam: Hendricks, Huggins, Jennings, La Russa, O'Rourke, Rickey, Ruel, Ward
- Inductee: National Italian American Sports Hall of Fame (1998); Hispanic Heritage Baseball Museum Hall of Fame (2008); National Baseball Hall of Fame (as Manager) (2014)

Bissinger, Buzz. *3 Nights in August: Strategy, Heartbreak, and Joy, Inside the Mind of a Manager*. Boston: Houghton Mifflin, 2005.

La Russa, Tony, with Rick Hummel. *One Last Strike: Fifty Years in Baseball, Ten and a Half Games Back, and One Final Championship Season*. New York: William Morrow, 2012.

Rains, Rob. *Tony La Russa: Man on a Mission*. Chicago: Triumph Books, 2009.

Will, George F. "Tony La Russa, On Edge." In *Men at Work: The Craft of Baseball*, chap 1. New York: Macmillan, 1990.

LEWIS, J. NORMAN
- Partner, Lewis & Mound, New York City
- Legal Counsel, MLBPA, 1953–59
- During tenure as legal counsel: minimum salary increased $5K to $7K

MacPHAIL, LELAND STANFORD ("LARRY") (February 3, 1890–October 1, 1975)

- Graduate, George Washington University Law School, 1910
- Lawyer, Columbus, Ohio
- Team Executive: Cincinnati Reds, 1933–36; Brooklyn Dodgers General Manager, 1938–42; New York Yankees, 1945–47
- Pioneered night baseball in MLB, televising games, flying between games
- Recipient of *Sporting News* Executive of the Year Award (1939)
- Son Lee was Yankees general manager and president of AL; grandson Andy was general manager of 1987 World Champion Twins; Lee elected to HOF in 1998, making Larry and Lee only father and son inductees
- Inducted into National Baseball Hall of Fame (as Executive), 1978

McKelvey, G. Richard. *The MacPhails: Baseball's First Family of the Front Office*. Jefferson, NC: McFarland, 2000.

MANFRED, ROBERT D., Jr. ("ROB") (September 28, 1958–)

- Graduate, Harvard Law School, 1983
- Clerk to U.S. District Court Judge Joseph L. Tauro
- Partner, Morgan, Lewis and Bockius, LLP, Washington, D.C., 1992–98
- Outside Counsel for MLB: participated directly in formulation and negotiation of economic and non-economic proposals for MLB in two separate rounds of collective bargaining (1990 and 1994–96); also represented teams in salary and grievance arbitrations, provided advice to teams on salary negotiations
- MLB League Official: Executive Vice-President of Labor Relations, 1998–2013; Executive Vice-President, Economics and League Affairs; Chief Operating Officer, Sept. 2013–Dec. 2014
- As MLB VP: responsible for major economic matters such as revenue sharing and the debt service rule, as well as franchise-specific matters involving all MLB clubs; lead negotiator for MLB in talks that resulted in new collective bargaining agreements in 2002, 2006 and 2011
- As COO: oversaw all of the traditional functions of the Commissioner's Office, including labor relations, baseball operations, finance, administration and club governance
- MLB Commissioner (10th), Jan. 2015–present

MILLS, ABRAHAM G. (March 12, 1844–August 26, 1929)

- Graduate, Columbian Law School (now George Washington University), 1869
- 1876, admitted to practice in District of Columbia (never practiced law)
- President, National League, 1882–84 (4th president)
- Chairman, Mills Commission, 1905
- Serving as advisor to NL President William Hulbert, offered advice on solution to problem of league teams raiding non-league teams of players under contract; this resulted in "League Alliance" (1877)
- As NL president, organized meeting of National League, American Association, and Northwestern League (the "Harmony Conference") which resulted in National Agreement of Professional Base Ball Clubs (aka Tripartite Agreement) that allowed every league team to reserve 11 players at end of a season to play for their current team throughout the next year
- As chair of Mills Commission, wrote 8-paragraph memo on 12/30/1907 which

became known as the "Mills Commission Report" and proclaimed Abner Doubleday the inventor of the game of baseball
- Charter member of American Olympic Committee

Mallinson, James. "A.G. Mills." Society for American Baseball Research, SABR Baseball Biography Project. Accessed May 21, 2014. http://sabr.org/bioproj/person/abcceflb.

MINOR, BENJAMIN SANDERS (July 21, 1865–September 27, 1946)
- Graduate, University of Virginia
- Team Executive, Washington Senators: Minority owner, 1905–19; Secretary, 1905–12; President, 1912–19; Lawyer, 1912–19
- April 19, 1922: presented oral argument to U.S. Supreme Court on behalf of defendant National League of Professional Base Ball Clubs in *Federal Baseball Club v. National League*, 259 U.S. 200 (1922)
- Served on American League Board of Directors, under Ban Johnson

MITCHELL, GEORGE J. (August 20, 1933–)
- Graduate, Georgetown University Law Center, 1960
- Trial attorney, Antitrust Division, U.S. Department of Justice, 1960–62
- Practiced law, Portland, Maine, 1965–77
- U.S. Attorney, Maine, 1977–79
- Judge, U.S. District Court for Maine, 1979–80
- U.S. Senator from Maine, 1980–95 (Senate Majority Leader, 1989–95)
- Chairman, Global Board of DLA Piper
- Member, Florida Marlins Board of Directors, 2000–01
- Consultant ("director"), Boston Red Sox, 2002–?
- As independent investigator, conducted 21-month investigation (2006–07) that led to 409-page report (December 2007) regarding use of performance-enhancing drugs by MLB players (identified 89 players for whom, the report claims, evidence exists for use of steroids or other PEDS)

MOORAD, JEFFREY S. (1955–)
- Graduate, Villanova University School of Law, 1981
- Independent Player Agent
- Partner, Steinberg & Moorad, 1985–2003
- Founder, Moorad Sports Partners, 2013–
- Minority Owner, General Partner, and CEO, Arizona Diamondbacks, 2004–2011
- Minority Owner, Vice Chair, and CEO, San Diego Padres, 2009–2012

MORTON, FERDINAND QUINTON (September 9, 1881–November 8, 1949)
- Boston University, bachelor of laws, 1909
- Admitted to practice, New York, 1910
- Wheaton and Curtis, NYC, 1910–16
- Assistant attorney general for New York County, 1916–22?
- Commissioner, Negro National League, 1935–39
- Headed United Colored Democratic Association ("Black Tammany Hall") in NYC, 1916
- NYC Civil Service Comm'n., 1922–48 (first African American member)

MOSS, RICHARD M. ("DICK")
- Graduate, Harvard Law School, 1955
- Private practice
- Assistant attorney general, Pennsylvania
- Assistant and associate general counsel, United Steelworkers
- General Counsel, MLBPA, 1967–77
- Player agent
- For MLBPA, involved in all collective bargaining negotiations and contract administration; argued all of MLBPA's legal and arbitration cases, including Messersmith
- As agent, negotiated 1st $1 million/year contract (Nolan Ryan, 1979); tried and won 1st $1 million salary arbitration (Fernando Valenzuela, 1983)
- Served as adjunct professor at USC Law Center, teaching "Sports and the Law"
- Member of Board of Directors of NAACP Legal Defense Fund and Sports Lawyers Association
- Recipient of Sports Lawyers Association Award of Excellence, 2012

MURPHY, ROBERT F.
- Graduate, Northeastern Law School
- Examiner, National Labor Relations Board
- Private practice
- Labor Attorney and Union Official: formed American Baseball Guild, 1946, which lost close strike vote against Pirates on June 7, 1946 (20–16 favored, but needed ⅔), leading to downfall of Guild
- After failure of Guild, owners made several concessions to players, including payment of spring training per diem expenses, thereafter called "Murphy Money"

NICOLAU, GEORGE (February 14, 1925–)
- Graduate, Columbia University School of Law, 1951
- Labor relations attorney, Sheehan and Harold, 1951–54, and Cooper, Ostrin and DeVarco, 1954–63
- Independent arbitrator for MLB/MLBPA, 1986–95
- ruled in favor of players on collusion cases in 1988 and 1990; rescinded the lifetime suspension of Steve Howe
- Also served as arbitrator for NBA, NHL, Major Indoor Soccer League

NUTTER, ISAAC
- Attorney, Atlantic City
- In 1927, became first elected president of the Eastern Colored League, which was formed in December 1922 and played its first season in 1923

O'MALLEY, WALTER (October 9, 1903–August 9, 1979)
- Graduate, Fordham University Law School, 1930
- Chief Legal Counsel, Brooklyn Dodgers
- Owner, Brooklyn and LA Dodgers, 1950–79
- Member, MLB Executive Council (28 years)
- Along with Horace Stoneham, pioneered move of MLB to West Coast
- Recipient of *Sporting News* Executive of the Year Award, 1955

- Inducted into National Baseball Hall of Fame (as Pioneer/Executive), 2008

D'Antonio, Michael. *Forever Blue: The True Story of Walter O'Malley, Baseball's Most Controversial Owner, and the Dodgers of Brooklyn and Los Angeles*. New York: Riverhead Books, 2009.

McCue, Andy. *Mover and Shaker: Walter O'Malley, the Dodgers, & Baseball's Westward Expansion*. Lincoln: University of Nebraska Press, 2014.

O'ROURKE, JAMES ("ORATOR") (September 1, 1850–January 8, 1919)
- Graduate, Yale Law School, 1887
- Admitted to practice, Connecticut, 1887
- Major League Player and Player/Manager
- Recorded 1st hit in NL history, with Boston Red Caps, on April 22, 1876; first person to play ML ball in four different decades, 1870s, 1880s, 1890s, 1904
- Assisted John Montgomery Ward in establishment of Brotherhood of Professional Base Ball Players (1885) and Players' League (1889)
- Helped found National Association of Professional Base Ball Leagues, a minor-league protective organization, 1901
- Minor League Executive: President, Connecticut State League, 1895, 1902, 1904–06, 1909, 1911–12
- Inducted into National Baseball Hall of Fame (as a player), 1945

Roer, Mike. *Orator O'Rourke: The Life of a Baseball Radical*. Jefferson, NC: McFarland, 2005.

PADOVA, JOHN R. (1935–)
- Graduate, Temple University Law School, 1959
- Admitted to practice, Pennsylvania
- Private practice, Pa., 1960–92
- Judge, U.S. District Court, E.D. Pa., 1992–present (Senior judge status since 2008)
- Author of opinion in *Piazza v. Major League Baseball*, 831 F. Supp. 420 (E.D. Pa. 1993), which held baseball's antitrust exemption limited to reserve clause and not applicable to "business of baseball" generally

PEPPER, GEORGE WHARTON (March 16, 1867–May 24, 1961)
- Graduate, University of Pennsylvania Law School, 1889
- Admitted to practice, Pennsylvania, 1889
- Founded Philadelphia law firm of Pepper Hamilton, 1890; now one of largest firms by revenue in U.S.
- Professor, University of Pennsylvania School of Law, 1893–1910
- Attorney for Organized Baseball in *Weegham v. Killefer*, 215 F. 168 (W.D. Mich. 1914); represented American, National, and Federal League owners in *Federal Baseball Club v. National League*, 259 U.S. 200 (1922)
- U.S. Senator, Pennsylvania, 1922–27

Pepper, George Wharton. *Philadelphia Lawyer: An Autobiography*. Philadelphia: J.B. Lippincott, 1944.

PHILLIPS, RICHIE (August 24, 1940–May 31, 2013)
- Graduate, Villanova Law School, 1966
- Philadelphia Public Defender's Office
- Philadelphia District Attorney's Office, chief of homicide and organized-crime units

- Private practice
- General Counsel and Executive Director, Major League Umpires Association, 1978–99, leading work stoppages in 1978, 1979, and 1984, 1991, and 1995
- Negotiated $1.5 million contract in 1970 for Howard Porter, future NBA star, opening door to player contracts negotiated by lawyers instead of agents
- Represented National Association of Basketball Referees, 1976–84, forcing NBA to recognize referees as a collective-bargaining unit

REINSDORF, JERRY M. (February 25, 1936–)
- Graduate, Northwestern University School of Law, 1960
- Certified Public Accountant; Registered Mortgage Underwriter; Certified Review Appraiser
- Attorney, U.S. Internal Revenue Service, 1960–64
- Private Practice, 1964–73
- Owner, Chicago White Sox, 1981–present; longest ownership tenure in history of White Sox franchise; moved White Sox from Comiskey Park to New Comiskey Park (renamed U.S. Cellular Field; now Guaranteed Rate Field)
- Member, MLB Executive Council
- Owner, Chicago Bulls, 1985–present
- Member, Board of Directors, National Baseball Hall of Fame and Museum, 2008–present
- Only third owner in history of North American sports to win a championship in two different sports (Chicago White Sox and Chicago Bulls)
- 2012 Recipient of Barnes and Thornburg Jackie Robinson Award for diversity in the workplace
- Together with Eddie Einhorn, launched SportsVision, a subscription TV service to broadcast live sporting events, in 1982

REYNOLDS, JOHN J. (?–March 31, 1997)
- Graduate, Loyola University of Chicago Law School, 1955
- General Counsel, Hotel Employees and Restaurant Employees International Union
- Partner, Rock, Fusco, Reynolds, Crowe and Garvey, Chicago
- In 1963, helped organize and served as bargaining representative for the National League Umpires Association, first umpires union

RICKEY, BRANCH (December 20, 1881–December 9, 1965)
- Graduate, University of Michigan Law School, 1911
- Major League Player (Browns, 1905–06; Highlanders, 1907) and Manager (Browns, 1913–15; Cardinals, 1919–25)
- Team Executive: General Manager, St. Louis Browns, 1913–15, 1919; General Manager, St. Louis Cardinals, 1919–42; President and General Manager, Brooklyn Dodgers, 1943–50; General Manager, Pittsburgh Pirates, 1951–55
- Baseball innovator: Developed concept of baseball farm system; helped end color line in organized professional baseball; 1954, championed use of new statistics to evaluate baseball; co-founder, with William Shea, of Continental League in 1959

A Selective List of Lawyers Involved with Baseball

- Three-time recipient of *Sporting News* Executive of the Year Award (1936, 1942, 1947)
- One of only 8 major league managers to have earned a law degree or passed a state bar exam: Hendricks, Huggins, Jennings, La Russa, O'Rourke, Rickey, Ruel, Ward
- "Bill James ... asserts that Ruth, Jackie Robinson, Branch Rickey and [Marvin] Miller form the Mount Rushmore of baseball." Jon Wertheim, "Marvin Miller Changed Players' Union—and Baseball—Forever," SI.com, Nov. 27, 2012
- Inducted into National Baseball Hall of Fame (as Pioneer/Executive), 1967

Breslin, Jimmy. *Branch Rickey*. New York: Viking, 2010.
Frommer, Harvey. *Rickey and Robinson: The Men Who Broke Baseball's Color Barrier*. New York: Macmillan, 1982.
Lowenfish, Lee. *Branch Rickey: Baseball's Ferocious Gentleman*. Lincoln: University of Nebraska Press, 2007.
O'Toole, Andrew. *Branch Rickey in Pittsburgh: Baseball's Trailblazing General Manager for the Pirates, 1950-1955*. Jefferson, NC: McFarland, 2000.
Polner, Murray. *Branch Rickey: A Biography*. rev. ed. Jefferson, NC: McFarland, 2007.

ROBERTS, THOMAS T. (1923–February 13, 2008)

- Graduate, Loyola University of Los Angeles Law School, 1957
- Mediator/Arbitrator, 1958–2008
- Baseball's Permanent Arbitrator, 1974–87: awarded Dodgers pitcher Fernando Valenzuela first $1 million contract through arbitration, 1983; ruled that teams could not negotiate drug-testing clauses with players individually, had to deal with MLBPA under CBA, 1986; ruled owners had colluded following 1985 season, to prevent free-agent players from obtaining richer contracts, 1987
- Hired by MLBPA to oversee distribution of $280 million owners agreed to pay to players to settle collusion cases in 1990
- Also arbitrator in automotive, airline, entertainment, and educational labor-management disputes
- From 1987–2000, mediated between General Motors Corp. and the United Auto Workers during their national collective bargaining agreement

ROGERS, JOHN IGNATIUS ("COLONEL") May 27, 1844–March 13, 1910)

- Graduate, University of Pennsylvania Law School
- Admitted to practice, Pennsylvania, 1864 or 1865
- Private practice, Philadelphia
- Owner, Philadelphia Phillies, 1883–1903
- With Al Reach, sporting goods magnate and former player, acquired the franchise of the Worcester Worcesters which was dropped from the National League after the 1882 season; they moved it to Philadelphia as a National League expansion franchise called the Quakers in 1883, later changing name to Phillies in 1890
- As lawyer, drafted NL's original reserve clause and uniform player's contract [Roger Abrams, *Legal Bases: Baseball and the Law* (Philadelphia: Temple University Press, 1998), 30]
- Served as Judge Advocate of Pennsylvania National Guard, giving him rank of Colonel

RUEL, HEROLD D. ("MUDDY") (February 20, 1896–November 13, 1963)
- Graduate, Washington University (St. Louis) Law School
- Admitted to practice, Missouri, 1923
- Major League Player (St. Louis Browns, 1915, 1933; New York Yankees, 1917–20; Boston Red Sox, 1921–22, 1931; Washington Senators, 1923–30; Detroit Tigers, 1931–32; Chicago White Sox, 1934)
- Manager, St. Louis Browns (1947); Pitching Coach, Chicago White Sox (1935–45)
- Special Assistant to Commissioner A.B. (Happy) Chandler (1945–46)
- August 16, 1920: behind the plate as catcher for New York Yankees when pitch thrown by Carl Mays kills Cleveland Indians shortstop Ray Chapman, only time a major-league player has died on the field
- One of only 8 major league managers to have earned a law degree or passed a state bar exam: Hendricks, Huggins, Jennings, La Russa, O'Rourke, Rickey, Ruel, Ward

Isgrig, Dwayne. "Muddy Ruel." Society for American Baseball Research, SABR Baseball Biography Project. Accessed March 2, 2013. http://sabr.org/bioproj/person/cd44a05b.
Jarvis, Robert M. "And Behind the Plate.... Muddy Ruel of the U.S. Supreme Court Bar." *Journal of Supreme Court History* (2011): 1–10.

SCOTT, ELISHA (1890–1963)
- Graduate, Washburn College of Law, 1916
- Practice of law, Topeka, KS
- In 1920, reviewed and finalized the working draft of constitution and by-laws for Negro National League which had been prepared by several sportswriters, particularly Dave Wyatt
- Argued *Webb v. School Dist. No. 90* in Kan. S. Court, one of cases that precipitated Topeka case which became *Brown v. Board of Education*

SEITZ, PETER (May 17, 1905–October 17, 1983)
- Public member of National Wage Stabilization Board
- Counsel and assistant to director of Federal Mediation and Conciliation Service
- Director of industrial relations for the Defense Department
- Permanent Arbitrator for MLB; owners terminated his services as impartial arbitrator following Messersmith-McNally decision in 1975
- "His rulings in the cases of Andy Messersmith ... and Dave McNally ... revolutionized the way major league baseball clubs signed their players." ["Peter Seitz, 78, the Arbitrator In Baseball Free-Agent Case," *New York Times*, Oct. 19, 1983, D25]
- Also permanent arbitrator for NBA and Basketball Players Association

Abrams, Roger I. "Arbitrator Seitz Sets the Players Free." *Baseball Research Journal* 38 (Fall 2009): 79–85.

SHACKELFORD, JOHN (July 17, 1905–June 27, 1964)
- Attorney in Cleveland
- Player, Negro Leagues
- President of United States Negro Baseball League, 1945–46 [league founded by Gus Greenlee with support of Branch Rickey]

SHAPIRO, RON (March 29, 1943–)
- Graduate, Harvard Law School, 1967
- 1972, founded Shapiro Sher Guinot and Sandler (Baltimore law firm)
- 1976, founded Shapiro, Robinson and Associates, a sports management firm
- As player agent, list of clients includes more Hall of Famers than any other agent, including Cal Ripken, Jim Palmer, Brooks Robinson, Kirby Puckett, and Eddie Murray
- Maryland State Securities Commissioner, 1972–74
- Son Mark Shapiro is president of the Cleveland Indians
- Has taught at the Johns Hopkins University, the University of Maryland School of Law, and the University of Baltimore School of Law

SHEA, WILLIAM (June 21–1907–October 2, 1991)
- Graduate, Harvard Law School, 1931
- Admitted to practice, District of Columbia, 1931; New York, 1932
- Partner at NYC firm of Shea and Gould
- Chaired committee formed by New York mayor to return National League team to NYC, which eventually was accomplished with Mets in 1962
- Co-founder, with Branch Rickey, of Continental League in 1959
- Shea Stadium in Flushing Meadows, NY, named in his honor in 1964 (only MLB park named after a lawyer)
- April 8, 2008, Mets retired name "Shea" alongside other retired numbers of the team

SOTOMAYER, SONIA (June 25, 1954–)
- Graduate, Yale Law School, 1979
- Judge: U.S. District Court (SDNY), 1992–98; U.S. Court of Appeals, 2d Cir, 1998–2009; U.S. Supreme Court, 2009–present
- Author of *Silverman v. Major League Baseball Player Relations Committee, Inc.*, 880 F. Supp. 246 (S.D.N.Y. 1995) [issued preliminary injunction against MLB, preventing it from unilaterally implementing new CBA and using replacement players; effectively ended 1994–95 baseball strike after 232 days]

STERRY, NORMAN SEDGWICK (July 8, 1878–February 3, 1971)
- Graduate, University of Michigan Law Department, 1903
- Admitted to practice, Michigan, May 1903; California, October 1903
- Partner, Gibson, Dunn and Crutcher, Los Angeles
- At age 75, successfully argued on behalf of client New York Yankees before the U.S. Supreme Court in *Toolson v. New York Yankees*, 346 U.S. 356 (1953), a case in which the Court upheld an exemption from the antitrust laws for Major League Baseball
- Played for University of Michigan "Point a Minute" football teams coached by Fielding Yost, 1901 and 1902, that compiled a 22–0 record and outscored opponents 1,197 to 12

TAFT, WILLIAM HOWARD (September 15, 1857–March 8, 1930)
- Graduate, Cincinnati Law School, 1880
- Admitted to Ohio Bar, 1880
- Held positions as county prosecutor, state judge, 1887–90

- U.S. Solicitor General, 1890–92 (at 32, youngest appointed)
- Judge, U.S. Court of Appeals, 6th Cir., 1892–1900
- Law Professor, Yale
- Governor-General of the Philippines, 1901–03
- 1904–08, Secretary of War
- President of the United States (27th), 1909–13
- Chief Justice, U.S. Supreme Court, 1921–30 (10th)
- First U.S. president to throw ceremonial first pitch at a baseball game (April 14, 1910, Washington, D.C.)

TAYLOR, HARRY L. (April 4, 1866–July 12, 1955)
- Graduate, Cornell Law School, 1893
- Law practice, Buffalo, NY, 1894–1906
- Judge: New York Supreme Court, Erie Co., 1906–24; New York Appellate Division, 1924–36
- Major League player: Louisville (AA, NL), 1890–92; Baltimore (NL), 1893
- Union official: Lawyer for Players Protective Association
- Team official: President, Buffalo team (Eastern League), 1905
- League official: President, Eastern League, 1906
- Chief strategist and lawyer of Players Protective Association formed in 1900 under leadership of Hughie Jennings, as result of reduction of teams by NL; PPA folded in 1903
- "Taylor issued the crucial legal opinion to his ballplayer constituents that it was his belief that the reserve clause in the NL's standard player contract had 'no legal value.' Taylor's legal analysis set the stage for Napoleon Lajoie, Jimmy Collins, and dozens of other ballplayers to jump from the NL and establish the AL as a serious competitor to the then-monopoly NL." (Charlie Bevis, "Harry Taylor," SABR Baseball Biography Project, December 16, 2011, http://sabr.org/bioproj/person/f5f468a1).

VINCENT, FRANCIS T. ("FAY") (May 29, 1938–)
- Graduate, Yale Law School, 1963
- Associate, Whitman and Ransom (NYC); Partner, Caplin and Drysdale (Wash., DC), 1968–78
- President and CEO, Columbia Pictures, 1978–82
- Executive Vice President, Coca-Cola Company
- Associate Director, Division of Corporate Finance, Securities Exchange Commission
- First-ever Deputy Commissioner of MLB; played pivotal role in investigation of gambling allegations against Pete Rose
- Commissioner (9/13/89–9/7/92) (8th); Expansion major focus during his term, with NL adding 2 teams (Rockies and Marlins), bringing MLB franchises to 28
- author of three well received oral histories of MLB: *The Only Game in Town* (2006); *We Would Have Played for Nothing* (2008); *It's What's Inside the Lines that Counts* (2010)

Vincent, Fay. *The Last Commissioner: A Baseball Valentine.* New York: Simon & Schuster, 2002.

A Selective List of Lawyers Involved with Baseball

WARD, JOHN MONTGOMERY (March 3, 1860–March 4, 1925)
- Graduate, Columbia Law School, 1885
- Major League Player (pitcher and SS), 1878–94; pitched 2d perfect game in MLB history, June 17, 1880; only player to win over 100 games as pitcher and collect over 2,000 hits
- Major League Manager (1880, 1884, 1890–94)
- President and Part-Owner, Boston Braves (1912)
- Inducted into National Baseball Hall of Fame (as player), 1964
- Led formation of Brotherhood of Professional Base Ball Players, first professional sports players union, 1885
- Staunch opponent of reserve clause, he led creation of Players' League, 1890
- Defendant in *Metropolitan Exhibition Co. v. Ward*, 9 N.Y.S. 779 (Sup. Ct. 1890) [Giants fail in effort to enjoin Ward from playing for another team]
- Author of *Base-Ball: How to Become a Player, with the Origin, History, and Explanation of the Game* (1888)
- One of only 8 major league managers to have earned a law degree or passed a state bar exam: Hendricks, Huggins, Jennings, La Russa, O'Rourke, Rickey, Ruel, Ward

Abrams, Roger I. "The Legal Process at the Birth of Baseball: John Montgomery 'Monte' Ward." In *Legal Bases: Baseball and the Law*, 1–25. Philadelphia: Temple University Press, 1998.

Di Salvatore, Bryan. *A Clever Base-Ballist: The Life and Times of John Montgomery Ward.* New York: Pantheon, 1999.

Lamb, Bill. "John Montgomery Ward." Society for American Baseball Research, SABR Baseball Biography Project. Accessed April 28, 2015. http://sabr.org/bioproj/person/2de3f6ef.

Stevens, David. *Baseball's Radical for All Seasons: A Biography of John Montgomery Ward.* Lanham, MD: Scarecrow Press, 1998.

WEINER, MICHAEL (December 21, 1961–November 21, 2013)
- Graduate, Harvard Law School, 1986
- Law Clerk, Judge H. Lee Sarokin, U.S. District Court, District of NJ, 1986–88
- MLBPA, staff lawyer, 1988–2004
- MLBPA general counsel, 2004–Feb. 2013
- MLBPA Executive Director, Dec. 2009–Nov. 2013
- MLBPA's chief negotiator for labor agreements with MLB in 2002, 2006, and 2011
- As Executive Director, MLBPA signed agreement in November 2011 for 5-year contract, which ensured that at its conclusion there would have been 21 consecutive years of labor peace
- Also served as counsel NHL Players' Association in salary arbitrations

WHEATON, WILLIAM RUFUS (May 7, 1814–September 11, 1888)
- Union Hall Academy, Jamaica, Long Island, NY
- Read law with attorney John Leveridge
- Admitted to practice, New York, 1836; Practiced law in New York City in 1830s and 1840s, and in San Francisco in 1850s
- Founding member of New York Knickerbockers in September 1845

- Helped draft first formal rules of baseball (September 1845) which became foundation of "New York Game"
- Umpired 1st recorded baseball match in U.S. on October 6, 1845
- Authored account of early baseball in New York: "How Baseball Began: A Member of the Gotham Club of Fifty Years Ago Tells About It," *San Francisco Daily Examiner*, November 27, 1887, 14, available at *Our Game* (blog), February 12, 2012, http://ourgame.mlblogs.com
- Served in California State Assembly in 1862 and 1871
- Appointed by President U.S. Grant as Register of the General Land Office of the United States, serving from 1876 to 1886

WILLIAMS, EDWARD BENNETT (May 31, 1920–August 13, 1988)
- Graduate, Georgetown University Law Center, 1944
- Admitted to practice, District of Columbia, 1945
- Lawyer, Hogan and Hartson, 1945–49; solo practice, 1949–67; founder, Williams and Connolly, 1967–88
- Taught Criminal Law and Evidence at Georgetown Law School, 1946–58
- Owner, Baltimore Orioles, 1979–88; Owner and President, Washington Redskins, 1965–85
- In 1983, his two professional teams, the Baltimore Orioles and Washington Redskins, both won their respective championships

WOOLF, BOB (February 15, 1928–November 30, 1993)
- Graduate, Boston University School of Law, 1952
- U.S. Army Judge Advocate General Corps, 1952–54
- Private practice, 1954–93
- As player agent, he "created" modern role of sports agent after Red Sox pitcher Earl Wilson hired him to manage his off-field activities and endorsements following Wilson's 1962 no-hitter; in 1964, Woolf became 1st lawyer to represent an athlete in contract negotiations, negotiating Wilson's Red Sox contract
- Baseball clients included Carl Yastrzemski, Thurman Munson, Tom Glavine, Ruben Sierra

Woolf, Bob. *Behind Closed Doors*. New York: Atheneum, 1976.
Woolf, Bob. *Friendly Persuasion: My Life as a Negotiator*. New York: Putnam, 1990.

Appendix B: A Selective Chronology of the Black Sox Scandal

September 29, 1919 ... Encountering Hugh Fullerton of the *Chicago Herald Examiner* in the telegraph room of the Sinton Hotel in Cincinnati, former major leaguer William "Sleepy Bill" Burns assures him that "the Reds are already in."[1]

October 1, 1919 ... The first game of a best-of-nine World Series match between the Chicago White Sox and Cincinnati Reds is played at Cincinnati's Redland Field. In the 4th inning, a "sure" double play is lost when Cicotte hesitates on the throw to second and Risberg stumbles over the bag before throwing to first. The Reds score 5 runs in the inning and go on to easily win the game by a score of 9–1.[2]

October 1, 1919 ... After game 1, former world boxing champion Abe Attell who claimed he acted as an intermediary for New York gambler Arnold Rothstein, does not pay the Black Sox players the $20,000 installment due them for delivering the victory to the Reds, claiming the money is "out on bets" for the next game.[3]

October 2, 1919 ... In game two, the home team Reds score 3 runs in the 4th inning when Lefty Williams, a 21-game winner in the regular season and normally a master of control (58 walks in 297 innings in 1919), gives up 3 walks (and a total of 6 for the game), a single, and a triple. The Reds win 4–2, taking a 2–0 lead in the Series after beating both aces of the White Sox staff.[4]

October 2, 1919 ... At a meeting in room 702 of the Sinton Hotel in the evening after game two, Burns provides the Black Sox players with a partial fix installment payment of $10,000, substantially less than the $40,000 they had been promised. Attell claims that is all he has because rumors of a fix have made it difficult to get good odds on the Reds. Angered, the players reject the gamblers' request that they try to win the next game so that the odds will improve, refusing to win for a "busher" (rookie pitcher Dickie Kerr).[5]

October 3, 1919 ... In game three at Comiskey Park in Chicago, Kerr gives the White Sox their first victory in the Series by subduing the Reds, 3–0, on three hits. Gandil provides a two-run single in the 2nd inning, and a Risberg triple and single by Ray Schalk in the 4th accounts for the Pale Hose's other run.[6] After the game, Chick Gandil tells Bill Burns that the Sox won the game because the players felt that they had been double-crossed. As a consequence, the fix was off as far as they were concerned. Swede Risberg later confirms this in a separate meeting with Burns.[7]

October 4, 1919 ... Despite surrendering only 5 hits and no walks in game four at Comiskey Park, Cicotte loses his second game of the World Series when his two errors in the 5th inning lead to the only runs scored in a 2–0 victory for the Reds, giving them a 3–1 edge in the Series.[8]

October 4, 1919 ... After the game, Boston gambler Joseph "Sport" Sullivan, involved in a separate second attempt to fix the Series, provides $20,000 for the players. It is split evenly between Risberg, Felsch, Jackson, and Williams (the starting pitcher in game 5).[9]

October 6, 1919 ... Game 5, Comiskey Park, Reds 5, White Sox 0 (Reds lead Series, 4–1).[10]

October 7, 1919 ... Game 6, Redland Field, White Sox 5, Reds 4, in 10 innings (Reds lead Series, 4–2).[11]

October 8, 1919 ... Game 7, Redland Field, White Sox 4, Reds 1 (Reds lead Series, 4–3).[12]

October 9, 1919 ... In game eight, the Reds defeat the White Sox, 10–5, at Chicago's Comiskey Park, winning the World Series, 5 games to 3.[13]

October 10, 1919 ... In a syndicated column initially published in the *Chicago Herald Examiner*, newspaper reporter Hugh Fullerton becomes the first to publicly raise concerns about tampering of the just completed World Series. He also asserts that seven unnamed White Sox players will not return to the team in 1920. Fullerton will later claim that Comiskey gave him the names of seven of the eight accused players, minus Buck Weaver.[14]

August 31, 1920 ... The last-place Philadelphia Phillies defeat the 5th-place Chicago Cubs, 3–0, in a game at Cubs Park. Rumors abound of attempts to bribe several Chicago players so that the Cubs will lose the game on which gamblers had bet large amounts on the Phillies to win. Concerns raised by this game will serve as a catalyst for the convening of a grand jury by Chicago's Cook County.[15]

September 7, 1920 ... Cook County Judge Charles A. McDonald convenes a grand jury to investigate allegations that a game involving the Chicago Cubs and Philadelphia Phillies in late August was fixed.[16]

September 19, 1920 ... The *Chicago Tribune* publishes an open letter reputedly from local businessman and White Sox fan Fred M. Loomis which questions the legitimacy of the 1919 World Series, referring to widespread reports of a conspiracy between players and gamblers to manipulate results in favor of the Reds. The letter is actually written by *Tribune* sportswriter James Cruisinberry who, according to his later account, overheard a conversation in late July between White Sox manager Kid Gleason and Abe Attell in which the latter confirmed the conspiracy's existence. Cruisinberry hopes the "Loomis" letter will goad the Cook County grand jury into investigating the 1919 Series.[17]

September 27, 1920 ... Based on an interview with former prizefighter and fix insider William "Billy" Maharg, sportswriter James Isaminger provides the first detailed account of the 1919 World Series scandal in an article published in the *Philadelphia North American* but quickly picked up by the Associated Press and other wire services. In the article, Maharg claims that games one, two, and eight of the Series were rigged.[18]

September 28, 1920 ... In testimony under oath before the Cook County Grand Jury, Eddie Cicotte and Joe Jackson admit accepting payments to fix the 1919 World Series. Earlier in the morning the players had made the same admission to White Sox legal counsel Alfred Austrian and Assistant State's Attorney Hartley Replogle during separate meetings in Austrian's law office. Neither confesses to making a deliberate misplay, however, despite press reports to the contrary.[19]

September 28, 1920 ... White Sox owner Charles A. Comiskey indefinitely suspends seven of the eight players accused of fixing the 1919 World Series: Cicotte, Felsch, Jackson, McMullin, Risberg, Weaver, and Williams. The eighth, Chick Gandil, was already suspended for failing to report to the team in the spring.[20]

September 29, 1920 ... Like Cicotte and Jackson the previous day, Claude "Lefty" Williams, the White Sox hurler who was the losing pitcher in 3 of the games, admits his part in the conspiracy to fix the 1919 World Series, first to Austrian and then in testimony before the grand jury. Also like his teammates, he claims not to have done anything wrong on the diamond. Unlike Cicotte and Jackson, however, he also identifies the gamblers who were at the meetings at which the fix was discussed prior to the series by name.[21]

October 29, 1920 ... The Cook County Grand Jury returns indictments against eight White Sox players and five others for their alleged role in conspiring to fix the 1919 World Series between the White Sox and the Cincinnati Reds.[22]

November 12, 1920 ... In the wake of the growing scandal over allegations of a 1919 World Series fix, Kenesaw Mountain Landis, a federal judge for the Northern District of Illinois, accepts the offer by Major League team owners to become the first commissioner of baseball.[23]

March 12, 1921 ... In light of reports that the criminal trial of those alleged to have fixed the 1919 World Series will be delayed beyond the beginning of the 1921 season, Commissioner Landis places the indicted players on the "Ineligible list," stating that "baseball is not powerless to protect itself."[24]

April 7, 1921 ... Commissioner Landis indefinitely suspends Giants outfielder Benny Kauff pending resolution of criminal charges against him for car theft and receiving stolen property. Although he will be acquitted by a jury on May 13, 1921, Landis still refuses to reinstate him, setting a precedent he will follow a few months later when dealing with the eight players found not guilty in the Black Sox criminal trial.[25]

June 27, 1921 ... The case of *State of Illinois v. Cicotte et al.* commences in the Chicago court room of Judge Hugo Friend.

July 5, 1921 ... Jury selection begins. It will conclude on July 16, resulting in a panel of 12 "mostly working class white men, ... none of whom professed to being much of a baseball fan."[26]

July 18, 1921 ... The indictments against William "Sleepy Bill" Burns, a former major league pitcher turned gambler who is alleged to have helped arrange the World Series fix and is expected to be an important prosecution witness, are dismissed and he is granted immunity from prosecution for any Black Sox-related charges.[27]

July 18, 1921 ... State's Attorney George Gorman delivers the prosecution's opening statement in which he details the plot to fix the 1919 World Series and describes the role of the indicted Black Sox figures, both players and gamblers, as well as others who were involved but not defendants in the current prosecution (such as Arnold Rothstein and Abe Attell).[28]

July 19, 1921 ... After the appearance of several preliminary witnesses on the second day of the Black Sox criminal trial, Bill Burns takes the witness stand to begin testimony that will encompass parts of three days. He confirms the existence of a plan to fix the 1919 World Series and identifies the individuals involved.[29]

August 2, 1921 ... After deliberating for less than three hours and taking a single ballot, a Chicago jury returns a verdict of not guilty for each defendant on all charges in the Black Sox criminal trial.[30]

August 3, 1921 ... Despite their acquittal the previous day, Commissioner Landis announces that he is banishing eight White Sox players involved in the 1919 World Series scandal from baseball for life: Eddie Cicotte, Oscar "Happy" Felsch, Arnold "Chick" Gandil, "Shoeless" Joe Jackson, Fred McMullin, Charles "Swede" Risberg, George "Buck" Weaver, and Claude "Lefty" Williams. They will never be reinstated.[31]

October 18, 1921 ... Buck Weaver, represented by attorneys Charles A. Williams and Julian C. Ryer, files suit in Chicago Municipal Court against the Chicago White Sox, requesting damages of $20,000 for the team's failure to pay his salary for the 1921 season.[32]

October 22, 1921 ... Municipal Court Judge George B. Holmes grants the White Sox petition to remove the suit filed by Weaver to federal court on diversity of citizenship grounds since the team is incorporated in Wisconsin. All further proceedings will be conducted in the U.S. District Court for the Northern District of Illinois.[33]

April 26, 1922 ... Oscar "Happy" Felsch, represented by Milwaukee attorney Raymond J. Cannon, files a civil suit against the Chicago White Sox in the Circuit Court of Wisconsin, Milwaukee County, seeking back pay and bonuses withheld by the team. He will later amend the complaint to specify four claims: balance due on his 1920 contract; a withheld World Series bonus from 1917; injury to his

A Selective Chronology of the Black Sox Scandal 203

professional reputation; and restraint on his livelihood caused by conspiracy to blacklist him.[34]

May 12, 1922 ... Attorney Raymond J. Cannon files civil actions against the White Sox on behalf of two more Black Sox players, Swede Risberg and Joe Jackson, in the Milwaukee circuit court. Risberg's claims are the same as those raised in the Felsch suit, but Jackson alleges breach of contract based on the three-year, $8,000 per-season pact he signed with the club in February 1920 and for which he had not been paid since owner Charles Comiskey voided it in March 1921. In addition to the unpaid wages and 1917 World Series bonus, Jackson also asks for the same $100,000 defamation and restraint on livelihood damages sought by Felsch and Risberg.[35]

July 1, 1922 ... An Illinois sports anti-corruption statute adopted in the wake of the Black Sox scandal becomes effective. The new statute makes it illegal to accept money, a bribe, or anything of value in return for failing to use one's best efforts in a professional or amateur athletic contest. Unfortunately, the prosecution in the Black Sox criminal trial had been unable to apply it retroactively to establish that the object of the alleged conspiracy—fixing the World Series—was an unlawful act in itself. Consequently, the prosecution had to "shoehorn" the fix charges into "some form of criminal fraud, such as obtaining money by false pretenses or via a confidence game," a gambit which was attacked by defense lawyers but eventually allowed by trial court judge Hugo Friend.[36]

October 5, 1922 ... Bill Burns, former White Sox pitcher and star prosecution witness at the 1921 Black Sox criminal trial but now a confectioner running a chocolate shop in Texas, is deposed by the defense in conjunction with the civil suits brought by former players against the White Sox seeking back pay and damages for injury to reputation.[37]

May 12, 1923 ... Milwaukee Circuit Judge John J. Gregory dismisses both the 1917 World Series bonus and restraint on livelihood caused by conspiracy to blacklist counts in the civil damage suits of Oscar Felsch and Swede Risberg. He lets stands the claims of injury to reputation by the two and the entire complaint of Joe Jackson.[38]

January 28, 1924 ... The civil suit brought by Joe Jackson against the Chicago White Sox seeking payment of his salary for the 1921 and 1922 seasons begins in Wisconsin Circuit Court in Milwaukee, Judge John J. Gregory presiding. Raymond J. Cannon serves as Jackson's lead counsel, while George B. Hudnall represents the White Sox as its trial counsel.[39]

May 27, 1924 ... Judge John J. Gregory signs the formal order nullifying the 11 1 jury verdict in favor of Joe Jackson in his suit against the White Sox. Citing the lack of credible evidence to support the jury's answers to ten special interrogatories he had posed, Gregory vacates the jury's $18,000 damages award and dismisses Jackson's complaint with prejudice.[40]

October 28, 1924 ... Milwaukee attorney Raymond Cannon files a declaration of intent to bring suit on behalf of Oscar Felsch and Joe Jackson against Baseball

Commissioner Kenesaw Mountain Landis to recover the players' share of the White Sox' second-place money for the 1920 season—$685.79—plus interest. The suit notice also includes the requirement that Landis submit to immediate deposition, which he does on November 3. Cannon will question Landis for two hours, during which time the commissioner asserts that the decision to withhold the money from the Black Sox players was proposed by team owners, not him, and endorsed by league presidents John Heydler and Ban Johnson.[41]

February 1925 ... The civil suits brought by Oscar Felsch and Swede Risberg are settled out of court for much less than either sought in damages from the White Sox. Felsch receives a total of $1,575.35, comprised of his two remaining paychecks for 1920, with interest and costs incurred. Risberg, who had sought $3750, receives only $401.31.

October 20, 1925 ... The Wisconsin Supreme Court dismisses an appeal filed on behalf of Joe Jackson on the basis of procedural deficiencies.[42]

March 13, 1927 ... Commissioner Landis sends a letter to George "Buck" Weaver denying the Black Sox player's request for reinstatement which was contained in a letter he sent to Landis on January 10, 1927. Landis bases his decision on Weaver's grand jury testimony in which he admitted that after Eddie Cicotte invited him to participate in the plot to throw the World Series, he "kept still."[43]

February 3, 1936 ... Joe Jackson receives 2 votes (0.8% of the 226 votes cast) in the first election to select members of the new National Baseball Hall of Fame. None of the other banned players receive a vote, although Hal Chase, frequently cast as a game-fixer, receives 11. At the time of the election, individuals expelled from the game were not formally excluded from consideration. In fact, it won't be until February 1991 that the Hall of Fame will add a clause to its voting regulations which declares that "persons on the ineligible list cannot be eligible candidates."[44]

September 17, 1956 ... After many years of silence, banned Black Sox first baseman Chick Gandil, reputed to be the player mastermind of the World Series fix, tells his version of the story in an article published in *Sports Illustrated*. The same issue contains an article by James Crusinberry, identified as "the first reporter to break the details of the Black Sox scandal."[45]

August 1963 ... Eliot Asinof's classic *Eight Men Out: The Black Sox and the 1919 World Series* is published, reviving interest and attracting widespread attention to the scandal. Black Sox center fielder Oscar "Happy" Felsch is the author's primary source.[46]

October 13, 1975 ... Charles "Swede" Risberg dies on his 81st birthday at a nursing home in Red Bluff, California. He is the last surviving member of the banned Black Sox eight.[47]

September 2, 1988 ... *Eight Men Out*, a film directed and written by John Sayles and starring David Strathairn as Eddie Cicotte, D.B. Sweeney as Joe Jackson, John Cusack as Buck Weaver, Charlie Sheen as Happy Felsch, and Clifton James as

Charles Comiskey, is released. Baseball scenes for the movie were filmed at Bush Stadium in Indianapolis.[48]

January 19, 1998 ... Hall of Famer members Ted Williams and Bob Feller submit a petition to acting commissioner Bud Selig in which they request that Shoeless Joe Jackson be removed from the list of ineligible players so that he may be considered for the National Baseball Hall of Fame by the hall's Veteran's Committee (of which Williams is a member).[49]

July 20, 2015 ... Commissioner Rob Manfred indicates that he will not "overrule Commissioner Landis' determinations" by granting the request of the Shoeless Joe Jackson Museum in Greenville, South Carolina, to remove the banned Black Sox player from MLB's ineligible list.[50]

Appendix C: A Selective Black Sox Bibliography

In General

Books and Chapters

Anderson, Wayne. *The Chicago Black Sox Trial: A Primary Source Account.* New York: Rosen Publishing, 2004.

Asinof, Eliot. *Eight Men Out: The Black Sox and the 1919 World Series.* New York: Holt, Rinehart and Winston, 1963.

Carney, Gene. *Burying the Black Sox: How Baseball's Cover-up of the 1919 World Series Fix Almost Succeeded.* Washington, D.C. : Potomac Books, 2006.

Cook, William A. *The 1919 World Series: What Really Happened?* Jefferson, NC: McFarland, 2001.

Cottrell, Robert C. *Blackball, the Black Sox, and the Babe: Baseball's Crucial 1920 Season.* Jefferson, NC: McFarland, 2002.

Dellinger, Susan. *Red Legs and Black Sox: Edd Roush and the Untold Story of the 1919 World Series.* Cincinnati: Emmis Books, 2006.

Deveney, Sean. *The Original Curse: Did the Cubs Throw the 1918 World Series to Babe Ruth's Red Sox and Incite the Black Sox Scandal?* New York: McGraw-Hill, 2010.

Farrell, James T. "I Remember the Black Sox." In *My Baseball Diary*, 99–108. Reprinted with foreword by Joseph Durso. Carbondale: Southern Illinois University Press, 1998. First published 1957 by A.S. Barnes.

Fountain, Charles. *The Betrayal: The 1919 World Series and the Birth of Modern Baseball.* New York: Oxford University Press, 1915.

Gaughran, Richard. "Saying It Ain't So: The Black Sox Scandal in Baseball Fiction." In *Cooperstown Symposium on Baseball and the American Culture (1990)*, edited by Alvin L. Hall, 38–56. Westport, CT: Meckler, 1991.

Hornbaker, Tim. *Turning the Black Sox White: The Misunderstood Legacy of Charles A. Comiskey.* New York: Sports Publishing, 2014.

Huhn, Rick. "The 1919 World Series: A Recap." In *Scandal on the South Side: The 1919 Chicago White Sox*, edited by Jacob Pomrenke, 281–88. Phoenix, AZ: Society for American Baseball Research, 2015.

Lamb, William F. *Black Sox in the Courtroom: The Grand Jury, Criminal Trial and Civil Litigation.* Jefferson, NC: McFarland, 2013.

A Selective Black Sox Bibliography

_____. "The Black Sox Scandal." In *Scandal on the South Side: The 1919 Chicago White Sox*, edited by Jacob Pomrenke, 298–309. Phoenix, AZ: Society for American Baseball Research, 2015.
Luhrs, Victor. *The Great Baseball Mystery: The 1919 World Series*. South Brunswick, NJ: A.S. Barnes, 1966.
Lynch, Michael T. *It Ain't So: A Might-Have-Been History of the White Sox in 1919 and Beyond*. Jefferson, NC: McFarland, 2010.
Nathan, Daniel A. *Saying It[apost]s So: A Cultural History of the Black Sox Scandal*. Urbana: University of Illinois Press, 2003.
Pietrusza, David. *Rothstein: The Life, Times, and Murder of the Criminal Genius Who Fixed the 1919 World Series*. New York: Carroll & Graf, 2003.
Platt, George M. "Claude Hendrix: Scapegoat or the Ninth Man Out?" In *Cooperstown Symposium on Baseball and American Culture, 2001*, edited by William M. Simons, 276–90. Jefferson, NC: McFarland, 2002.
Pomrenke, Jacob. "1919 American League Salaries." In *Scandal on the South Side: The 1919 Chicago White Sox*, edited by Jacob Pomrenke, 294–97. Phoenix, AZ: Society for American Baseball Research, 2015.
_____. "Epilogue: Offseason, 1919–20." In *Scandal on the South Side: The 1919 Chicago White Sox*, edited by Jacob Pomrenke, 310–14. Phoenix, AZ: Society for American Baseball Research, 2015.
_____, ed. *Scandal on the South Side: The 1919 Chicago White Sox*. Phoenix, AZ: Society for American Baseball Research, 2015.

Periodical Articles

Allardice, Bruce S. "'Playing Rotten, It Ain't That Hard to Do': How the Black Sox Threw the 1920 Pennant." *Baseball Research Journal* 45 (Spring 2016): 59–65.
Bachin Robin F. "At the Nexus of Labor and Leisure: Baseball, Nativism, and the 1919 Black Sox Scandal." *Journal of Social History* 36 (2003): 941–62.
Carney, Gene. "Comiskey's Detectives." *Baseball Research Journal* 38 (Fall 2009): 108–16.
_____. "Eddie Cicotte on the Day that Shook Baseball." *Base Ball, A Journal of the Early Game* 3 (Fall 2009): 99–104.
_____. "New Light on an Old Scandal." *Baseball Research Journal* 35 (2006): 74–81.
_____. "Uncovering the Fix of the 1919 World Series: The Role of Hugh Fullerton." *Nine: A Journal of Baseball History and Culture* 13 (Fall 2004): 39–49.
Cruisinberry, James. "A Newsman's Biggest Story." *Sports Illustrated*, September 17, 1956, 69–71.
Goler, Robert I. "Black Sox." *Chicago History* 17 (Fall/Winter 1988–89): 42–69.
Green, Paul. "The Later Lives of the Banished Sox." *Sports Collectors Digest*, April 22, 1988, 196–97.
Hoie, Bob. "1919 Baseball Salaries and the Mythically Underpaid Chicago White Sox." *Base Ball: A Journal of the Early Game* 6, no. 1 (Spring 2012): 17–34.
Lamb, William F. "A Black Sox Mystery: The Identity of Defendant Rachael Brown." *Base Ball, A Journal of the Early Game* 4 (Fall 2010): 5–11.
_____. "Jury Nullification and the Not Guilty Verdicts in the Black Sox Case." *Baseball Research Journal* 44 (Fall 2015): 47–56.
_____. "The People of Illinois v. Edward V. Cicotte, et al.: The Initial Grand Jury Proceedings in the Black Sox Case." *Base Ball: A Journal of the Early Game* 6 (Spring 2012): 86–101.
Lardner, John. "Remember the Black Sox?" *Saturday Evening Post*, April 30, 1938, 14–15, 82–85.

Newman, Timothy, and Bruce Stuckman. "They Were Black Sox Long Before the 1919 World Series." *Base Ball: A Journal of the Early Game* 6 (Spring 2012): 75–85.
Pomrenke, Jacob. "Bringing Home the Bacon: How the Black Sox Got Back into Baseball." *National Pastime* 26 (2006): 45–53.
_____. "No 'Solid Front of Silence': The Forgotten Black Sox Scandal Interviews." *Baseball Research Journal* 45 (Spring 2016): 51–58.
Swaine, Rick. "Ninth Man Out." *National Pastime* 20 (2000): 87–89.
Voigt, David Quentin. "The Chicago Black Sox and the Myth of Baseball's Single Sin." *Journal of the Illinois State Historical Society* 62, no. 3 (Autumn 1969): 293–306. Reprinted in *America through Baseball*, 65–76. Chicago: Nelson-Hall, 1976.

Banned Players

Eddie Cicotte

Sandoval, Jim. "Eddie Cicotte." In *Scandal on the South Side: The 1919 Chicago White Sox*, edited by Jacob Pomrenke, 16–21. Phoenix, AZ: Society for American Baseball Research, 2015.

Oscar "Happy" Felsch

Nitz, James R. "Happy Felsch." In *Scandal on the South Side: The 1919 Chicago White Sox*, edited by Jacob Pomrenke, 51–66. Phoenix, AZ: Society for American Baseball Research, 2015.

Arnold "Chick" Gandil

Gandil, Arnold (Chick), with Melvin Durslag. "This is My Story of the Black Sox Series." *Sports Illustrated*, September 17, 1956, 62–68.
Ginsburg, Daniel. "Chick Gandil." In *Scandal on the South Side: The 1919 Chicago White Sox*, edited by Jacob Pomrenke, 67–70. Phoenix, AZ: Society for American Baseball Research, 2015.

"Shoeless" Joe Jackson

Fleitz, David L. *Shoeless: The Life and Times of Joe Jackson*. Jefferson, NC: McFarland, 2001.
_____. "Joe Jackson." In *Scandal on the South Side: The 1919 Chicago White Sox*, edited by Jacob Pomrenke, 71–77. Phoenix, AZ: Society for American Baseball Research, 2015.
Frommer, Harvey. *Shoeless Joe and Ragtime Baseball*. Dallas, TX: Taylor Pub. Co., 1992.
Gropman, Donald. *Say It Ain't So, Joe! The Story of Shoeless Joe Jackson*. Boston: Little, Brown, 1979.
Herzog, William R., II. "From Scapegoat to Icon: The Strange Journey of Shoeless Joe Jackson." In *The Faith of 50 Million: Baseball, Religion and American Culture*, edited by Christopher H. Evans and William R. Herzog, 97–141. Louisville, KY: Westminster John Knox, 2002.
Jackson, Joe, with Furman Bisher. "This Is the Truth!" *Sport Magazine*, October 1949, http://www.blackbetsy.com/theTruth.html.

Fred McMullin

Pomrenke, Jacob. "Fred McMullin." In *Scandal on the South Side: The 1919 Chicago White Sox*, edited by Jacob Pomrenke, 142–55. Phoenix, AZ: Society for American Baseball Research, 2015.

Charles "Swede" Risberg

Muchlinski, Alan. *After The Black Sox: The Swede Risberg Story*. Bloomington, IN: AuthorHouse, 2005.

Sagert, Kelly Boyer, and Rod Nelson. "Swede Risberg." In *Scandal on the South Side: The 1919 Chicago White Sox*, edited by Jacob Pomrenke, 171–76. Phoenix, AZ: Society for American Baseball Research, 2015.

George "Buck" Weaver

Fletcher, David. "Buck Weaver." In *Scandal on the South Side: The 1919 Chicago White Sox*, edited by Jacob Pomrenke, 213–18. Phoenix, AZ: Society for American Baseball Research, 2015.

Stein, Irving M. *The Ginger Kid: The Buck Weaver Story*. Dubuque, Iowa: Elysian Fields Press, 1992.

Claude "Lefty" Williams

Flagler, J.M. "Requiem for a Southpaw," *The New Yorker*, December 5, 1959.

Pomrenke, Jacob. "Lefty Williams." In *Scandal on the South Side: The 1919 Chicago White Sox*, edited by Jacob Pomrenke, 232–42. Phoenix, AZ: Society for American Baseball Research, 2015.

Fiction

Boyd, Brendan. *Blue Ruin: A Novel of the 1919 World Series*. New York: Norton, 1991.

Greenberg, Eric Rolfe. *The Celebrant: A Novel*. New York: Everest House, 1983.

Kinsella, W.P. *Shoeless Joe*. Boston: Houghton Mifflin, 1982.

Stein, Harry. *Hoopla!* New York: Knopf, 1983.

Chapter Notes

Chapter 1

1. The bylaw proposed "for the Preservation of the Windows in the New Meeting House" provides that "no Person ... shall be permitted to play at any Game called Wicket, Cricket, Baseball, Batball, Football, Cat, Fives or any other Game or Games with Balls within the Distance of Eighty Yards from said Meeting House—And every such Person who shall play at any of the said Games or other Games with Balls within the Distance aforesaid, shall for any Instance thereof, forfeit the Sum of five schillings...." Josh Leventhal, *A History of Baseball in 100 Objects: A Tour through the Bats, Balls, Uniforms, Awards, Documents and Other Artifacts that Tell the Story of the National Pastime* (New York: Black Dog & Leventhal Publishers, 2015), 21.

2. Associated Press. "Pittsfield Uncovers Earliest Written Reference to Game," ESPN.com, May 11, 2004, espn.go.com [search "pittsfield"]; John Thorn, "The Pittsfield 'Baseball' Bylaw of 1791: What It Means," *Base Ball: A Journal of the Early Game* 5 (Spring 2011): 46–49.

3. Act of April 22, 1794, 15 Pa. Statutes at Large, ch. 1758 (1794); John A. Lucas, "The Unholy Experiment—Professional Baseball's Struggle Against Pennsylvania Sunday Blue Laws 1926–1934," *Pennsylvania History* 38 (1971), 164–65.

4. Bob Warrington, "The Fight for Sunday Baseball in Philadelphia," *Baseball History Blog*, Philadelphia Athletics Historical Society, July 30, 2001, http://philadelphiaathletics.org/the-fight-for-sunday-baseball-in-philadelphia/.

5. *Otsego Herald*, no. 1107, June 6, 1816, 3.

6. Dennis Corcoran, *Induction Day at Cooperstown: A History of the Baseball Hall of Fame Ceremony* (Jefferson, NC: McFarland, 2010), 30–37.

7. John Shiffert, *Base Ball in Philadelphia: A History of the Early Game, 1831–1900* (Jefferson, NC: McFarland, 2006), 13–20.

8. *The Constitution of the Olympic Ball Club of Philadelphia* (Philadelphia: John Clark, 1838), reprinted in part in Dean A. Sullivan, ed., *Early Innings: A Documentary History of Baseball, 1825–1908* (Lincoln: University of Nebraska Press, 1995), 6.

9. Richard Hershberger, "In the Beginning: Olympics of Philadelphia, Pa. vs. Camdens of Camden, N.J.," in *Inventing Baseball: The 100 Greatest Games of the 19th Century*, ed. Bill Felber (Phoenix: Society for American Baseball Research, 2013), 2n; Rich Westcott, "The Early Years of Philadelphia Baseball," *National Pastime: From Swampoodle to South Philly—Baseball in Philadelphia and the Delaware Valley* (SABR 43 Convention Issue, 2013): 136 (electronic ed.).

10. 259 U.S. 200 (1922).

11. Liva Baker, *The Justice From Beacon Hill: The Life and Times of Oliver Wendell Holmes* (New York: HarperCollins Publishers, 1991), 47; Sheldon M. Novick, *Honorable Justice: The Life of Oliver Wendell Holmes* (Boston: Little, Brown, 1989), 7; G. Edward White, *Justice Oliver Wendell Holmes: Law and the Inner Self* (New York: Oxford University Press, 1993), 7.

12. Stuart Banner, *The Baseball Trust: A History of Baseball's Antitrust Exemption* (New York: Oxford University Press, 2013), 82.

13. "Knicks Adopt Playing Rules on September 23," Protoball, accessed October 8, 2014, http://protoball.org/1845.1; Randall Brown, "How Baseball Began," *National Pastime* 24 (2004): 53–54; John Thorn, *Baseball in the Garden of Eden: The Secret History of the Early Game* (New York: Simon & Schuster, 2011), 37, 69–77 (providing rule-by-rule discussion).

14. Thorn, *Baseball in the Garden of Eden*, 37. A 74-year-old Wheaton provided a personal

reminiscence of his involvement in early baseball to a reporter in 1887. William R. Wheaton, "How Baseball Began: A Member of the Gotham Club of Fifty Years Ago Tells About It," *San Francisco Daily Examiner*, November 27, 1887, 14, available at http://ourgame.mlblogs.com/2012/02/12/how-baseball-began-william-r-wheaton-tells-his-story.

15. Thorn, *Baseball in the Garden of Eden*, 77; John Thorn, "The First Recorded Games," in Felber, *Inventing Baseball*, 6–7; Brown, "How Baseball Began," 54.

16. Mike Roer, *Orator O'Rourke: The Life of a Baseball Radical* (Jefferson, NC: McFarland, 2005), 8. For additional details on O'Rourke's birth and early life, see Bill Lamb, "Jim O'Rourke," SABR Baseball Biography Project, accessed March 23, 2016, http://sabr.org/bioproj/person/b7e9aba2#_edn1.

17. Neil W. Macdonald, *The League That Lasted: 1876 and the Founding of the National League of Professional Base Ball Clubs* (Jefferson, NC: McFarland, 2004), 96–97.

18. Roer, *Orator O'Rourke*, 132; David Arcidiacono, *Major League Baseball in Gilded Age Connecticut: The Rise and Fall of the Middletown, New Haven, and Hartford Clubs* (Jefferson, NC: McFarland, 2010), 200.

19. Revolving is defined as the process of "moving from one league or team to another without regard to one's contract or club agreement, in search of better salaries, better teams or changes of scenery." Paul Dickson, *The Dickson Baseball Dictionary*, 3rd ed. (New York: W. W. Norton & Co., 2009), 704.

20. "Our National Sports," *Spirit of the Times*, January 31, 1857, reprinted in Sullivan, *Early Innings*, 22–24.

21. Harold Seymour and Dorothy Seymour Mills, *Baseball: The Early Years* (New York: Oxford University Press, 1960), 35–36; Thorn, *Baseball in the Garden of Eden*, 113; Leventhal, *A History of Baseball in 100 Objects*, 37.

22. Leonard Koppett, *Koppett's Concise History of Major League Baseball* (Philadelphia: Temple University Press, 1998), 8–9.

23. Warren Goldstein, *Playing for Keeps: A History of Early Baseball* (Ithaca, NY: Cornell University Press, 1989), 44, 84; Robert B. Ross, *The Great Baseball Revolt: The Rise and Fall of the 1890 Players League* (Lincoln: University of Nebraska Press, 2016), 7–8.

24. Robert Schaefer, "The Great Base Ball Match of 1858: Base Ball's First All Star Game," *Nine: A Journal of Baseball History and Culture* 14 (Fall 2005): 47–58. As to the cost of baseball's first "ticket," historian John Thorn explains: "Although it is frequently written that the admission charge was fifty cents, in fact it was ten cents to watch the game, with optional transportation and livery costs making up the rest, to a higher level at thirty cents and another at fifty." Thorn, *Baseball in the Garden of Eden*, 117. The surplus collected after expenses—$71.10—was equally divided by the clubs for the benefit of the widows and orphans funds of the fire departments of the two respective cities. Schaeffer, "The Great Base Ball Match of 1858," 55.

25. John Zinn, "July to September, 1858: The Rivalry Begins—Brooklyn vs. New York," in Felber, *Inventing Baseball*, 10–12; Melvin L. Adelman, *Sporting Time: New York City and the Rise of Modern Athletics, 1820–70* (Urbana: University of Illinois Press, 1986), 131–32.

26. For more information about Ward, see David Stevens, *Baseball's Radical for All Seasons: A Biography of John Montgomery Ward* (Lanham, MD: Scarecrow Press, 1998); Bryan Di Salvatore, *A Clever Base-Ballist: The Life and Times of John Montgomery Ward* (New York: Pantheon, 1999).

27. Tony Morante, "Baseball and Tammany Hall," *Baseball Research Journal* 42 (Spring 2013), 30.

28. Philip H. Dixon, "The First Fixed Game: Mutuals of New York vs. Eckfords of Brooklyn," in Felber, *Inventing Baseball*, 46. The incident also has been variously described as "baseball's first scandal," Daniel E. Ginsburg, *The Fix Is In: A History of Baseball Gambling and Game Fixing Scandals* (Jefferson, NC: McFarland, 1995), 5; "organized baseball's first betting scandal," Goldstein, *Playing for Keeps*, 90; "the first reported incident of throwing a game," Roger I. Abrams, *The Dark Side of the Diamond: Gambling, Violence, Drugs and Alcoholism in the National Pastime* (Burlington, MA: Rounder Books, 2007), 25; and the "first punished instance of game fixing," John Thorn, "Shoeless Joe, the Bambino, the Big Bankroll, and the Jazz Age," *Our Game* (blog), June 15, 2015, http://ourgame.mlblogs.com/2015/06/15/. A contemporary account labeled it "the first and last instance of selling a game of ball." "'Hippodrome' Tactics in Base Ball; How to 'Heave a Game,'" *New York Clipper*, November 11, 1865, reprinted in Sullivan, *Early Innings*, 49–53.

29. Dixon, "The First Fixed Game," 46–47; Ginsburg, *The Fix Is In*, 6.

30. For the complete text of Devyr's confession, see "'Hippodrome' Tactics in Base Ball; How to 'Heave a Game,'" reprinted in Sullivan, *Early Innings*, 51–52.

31. Ginsburg, *The Fix Is In*, 6–7; Goldstein, *Playing for Keeps*, 90–92.

Chapter 2

1. Lee Allen, *The Cincinnati Reds* (New York: G.P. Putnam's Sons, 1948; repr., Kent: Kent

State University Press, 2006), 3–4; Greg Rhodes and John Snyder, *Redleg Journal: Year by Year and Day by Day with the Cincinnati Reds Since 1866* (Cincinnati: Road West, 2000), 16; Patrick Mondout, "Cincinnati Red Stockings," *Baseball Chronology*, accessed June 13, 2014, http://www.baseballchronology.com/Baseball/Leagues/NABBP/Clubs/Cincinnati-Red-Stockings.asp; Charles F. Faber, "Aaron Burt Champion," SABR Baseball Biography Project, accessed March 23, 2016, http://sabr.org/node/24735.

2. David Pietrusza, *Judge and Jury: The Life and Times of Judge Kenesaw Mountain Landis* (South Bend, IN: Diamond Communications, 1998), 2; J.G. Taylor Spink, *Judge Landis and Twenty-Five Years of Baseball* (New York: Thomas Y. Crowell, 1947), 1.

3. Lincoln Landis, *From Pilgrimage to Promise: Civil War Heritage and the Landis Boys of Logansport, Indiana* (Westminster, MD: Heritage Books, 2007), 38.

4. Nathaniel Grow, *Baseball on Trial: The Origin of Baseball's Antitrust Exemption* (Urbana: University of Illinois Press, 2014), 68; Spink, *Judge Landis and Twenty-Five Years of Baseball*, 20.

5. John Drebinger, "Baseball Pays Tribute to Landis By Picking Him for Hall of Fame," *New York Times*, December 11, 1944, 18; Pietrusza, *Judge and Jury*, 451.

6. In recognition of his contributions to the profession, including his work as an appellate lawyer, the Philadelphia Bar Association included Pepper on its list of "legends of the Philadelphia Bar" which it compiled for the association's 200th anniversary. "Turbulent Times, 1902–1952," *Philadelphia Lawyer* 64 (Winter 2002), 84.

7. George Wharton Pepper, *Philadelphia Lawyer: An Autobiography* (Philadelphia: J.B. Lippincott, 1944), 16.

8. *Ibid.*, 53.

9. *Ibid.*, 356–60.

10. Grow, *Baseball on Trial*, 206–07. The seat became available when Boies Penrose died. Pepper retained the seat by winning a special election later in the year.

11. Stephen Van Dulken, *Inventing the 19th Century: 100 Inventions That Shaped the Victorian Age, From Aspirin to the Zeppelin* (New York: New York University Press, 2001), 138; "A Brief History of Tabletop Baseball," *Baseball Games*, last modified April 2011, http://baseballgames.dreamhosters.com/BbHistory.htm.

12. John Thorn, "The Fathers of Fantasy Baseball," *Our Game* (blog), October 17, 2011, http://ourgame.mlblogs.com/2011/10/17/fathers-of-fantasy-baseball.

13. Jerrold Casway, "Philadelphia's Pythians," *National Pastime* 15 (1995), 120.

14. Harold Seymour and Dorothy Seymour Mills, *Baseball: The People's Game* (New York: Oxford University Press, 1990), 537–38; Shiffert, *Base Ball in Philadelphia*, 55–57; David Kenneth Wiggins and Patrick B. Miller, *The Unlevel Playing Field: A Documentary History of the African American Experience in Sport* (Urbana: University of Illinois Press, 2003), 34–36.

15. Seymour and Mills, *Baseball: The Early Years*, 42. Shiffert points out that this action "marked the first drawing of a color line in baseball. And, unlike the unwritten rule ... that governed organized baseball from the last years of the nineteenth century until 1945, this was a written injunction, at least written into the rules of the NABBP." Shiffert, *Base Ball in Philadelphia*, 55.

16. Casaway, "Philadelphia's Pythians," 123; Seymour and Mills, *Baseball: The People's Game*, 537; Shiffert, *Base Ball in Philadelphia*, 61.

17. Robert M. Jarvis & Phyllis Coleman, "Early Baseball Law," *American Journal of Legal History* 45 (2001): 118 n3.

18. *Watson v. Avery*, 65 Ky. 332, 383 (1867) (Williams, J., dissenting).

19. Henry A. Alden, Improvement in the Manufacture of Base-Balls, U.S. Patent 72,355, issued December 17, 1867. One commentator has pointed out that the fact "the patent was assigned to the New York Rubber Company: suggests the business motive" behind Alden's new manufacturing technique. Van Dulken, *Inventing the 19th Century*, 138.

20. Van Dulken, *Inventing the 19th Century*, 138.

21. The other seven are Jack Hendricks, Miller Huggins, Tony La Russa, James "Orator" O'Rourke, Branch Rickey, Herald "Muddy" Ruel, and John Montgomery Ward. J. Gordon Hylton, "Maybe the Brewers Should Hire a Lawyer as Their Next Manager," *Marquette University Law School Faculty Blog*, November 1, 2011, http://law.marquette.edu/facultyblog/2011/11/01/maybe-the-brewers-should-hire-a-lawyer-as-their-next-manager.

22. We have followed the lead of most standard sources in using 1869 as Jennings's year of birth. E.g., C. Paul Rogers III, "Hugh Ambrose Jennings," in *Deadball Stars of the American League*, ed. David Jones (Washington, DC: Potomac Books, 2006), 555; "Hughie Jennings," National Baseball Hall of Fame and Museum, accessed July 29, 2015, http://baseballhall.org/hof/jennings-hugh. However, we also acknowledge that there is some dispute regarding the year in which Jennings was born. For instance, a recent biographer indicated that Jennings was born in 1871, albeit without providing any source for that conclusion. Jack Smiles, *Ee-Yah: The Life and Times of Hughie Jennings, Baseball*

Hall of Famer (Jefferson, NC: McFarland, 2005), 7 ("Though his mine bosses thought Hughie was born in 1869, he was really born two years later, on April 2, 1871"). And to further complicate matters, his obituary in the *New York Times* stated that he was born on April 2, 1870. "Hugh Jennings Dies After Long Illness," *New York Times*, February 1, 1929, 1.

23. Rogers, "Hughie Jennings," 557.

24. The Red Stockings actually began the 1869 season with a 24–15 victory over a "picked nine" of local players on April 17, 1869, a date often given as the team's initial foray as professionals, but the May 4 engagement constituted their first game against an NABBP opponent. Thorn, *Baseball in the Garden of Eden*, 145; "Reds Timeline," Cincinnati Reds website, accessed June 13, 2014, http://cincinnati.reds.mlb.com/cin/history/timeline1.jsp; Mondout, "Cincinnati Red Stockings."

25. For a list of the ten members of the Red Stockings, including their craft or profession, baseball position, and annual salary, see Robert P. Gelzheiser, *Labor and Capital in 19th Century Baseball* (Jefferson, NC: McFarland, 2006), 175.

26. The Red Stockings season was so successful that club president Aaron Champion is reputed to have said near its end, "I'd rather be president of the Cincinnati Base Ball Club than president of the United States." Allen, *The Cincinnati Reds*, 5; Harvey Frommer, "First Professional Baseball Team: Flashback," Dr. Harvey Frommer on Sports, accessed June 15, 2014, http://www.travel-watch.com/twhtml4/firstprobaseballteam.htm. But just a year later, in November 1870, "an aura of gloom pervaded the annual meeting of the Red Stocking club directors.... Champion was ousted by a conservative regime that was angered by the treasurer's report that the club had only broken even over the two years [1869–70].... [Soon thereafter, it was announced] that the Reds would return to amateurism for 1871." David Quentin Voigt, *American Baseball: From Gentleman's Sport to the Commissioner System* (Norman: University of Oklahoma Press, 1966), 33–34. Champion "never returned to the business of baseball." Rhodes & Snyder, *Redleg Journal*, 16.

27. "A Novel Game in Philadelphia—A Negro Club in the Field—The White Club Victorious," *New York Times*, September 5, 1869, 1; Casway, "Philadelphia's Pythians," 122.

28. Lawrence D. Hogan, *Shades of Glory: The Negro Leagues and the Story of African-American Baseball* (Washington, D.C.: National Geographic, 2006), 16.

29. Jerrold Casway, "Inter-Racial Baseball: Pythians of Philadelphia vs. Olympics of Philadelphia," in Felber, *Inventing Baseball*, 69; Hogan, *Shades of Glory*, 15–16.

30. Casway, "Philadelphia's Pythians," 122.

31. Goldstein, *Playing for Keeps*, 5, 134; Koppett, *Koppett's Concise History of Major League Baseball*, 17; Voigt, *American Baseball: From Gentleman's Sport to the Commissioner System*, 36. Despite its significant role in baseball history, the National Association was not one of the six leagues defined as "major" by the Special Baseball Records Committee in its rulings of 1968–69. Included were the National League (1876–present), American League (1901–present), American Association (1882–91), Federal League (1914–15), Players' League (1890), and Union Association (1884). According to the committee, the National Association was not a major league "due to its erratic schedule and procedures." Joseph L. Reichler, ed., *The Baseball Encyclopedia: The Complete and Official Record of Major League Baseball* (New York: Macmillan, 1969), 2327–28. For contrary views, see David Q. Voigt, "Fie on Figure Filberts: Some Crimes Against Clio," *Baseball Research Journal* 12 (1983), 35–36 (questioning the committee's criteria and motives in selecting which leagues should be characterized as major); William Ryczek, "Why the National Association Was a Major League," *National Pastime Museum*, accessed October 23, 2015, http://www.thenationalpastimemuseum.com/article/why-national-association-was-major-league.

32. John Helyar, *Lords of the Realm* (New York: Villard Books, 1994), 3.

33. Michael Haupert, "William Hulbert and the Birth of the National League," *Baseball Research Journal* 44 (Spring 2015), 84.

34. Helyar, *Lords of the Realm*, 3; "The Formation of the National Association of Professional Base Ball Players," *New York Clipper*, March 25, 1871, reprinted in Sullivan, *Early Innings*, 83–88. Haupert reports that over the five-year history of the National Association, only 19 percent of the 138 players who played for more than one season remained on the same team throughout their career. And "half of the players changed teams three or more times...." Haupert, "William Hulbert and the Birth of the National League," 85.

35. "The White Stockings Gathering For the Fray: What Will be Done With Force—The Spring Programme," *Chicago Tribune*, March 14, 1875, reprinted in Sullivan, *Early Innings*, 90–92; Ed Edmonds, "Arthur Soden's Legacy: The Origins and Early History of Baseball's Reserve System," *Albany Government Law Review* 5 (2012), 41–42; John Shiffert, *Base Ball in Philadelphia: A History of the Early Game, 1831–1900* (Jefferson, NC: McFarland, 2006), 85–86; William A. Cook, *The Louisville Grays Scandal of 1877: The Taint of Gambling at the Dawn of the National League* (Jefferson, NC: McFarland, 2005), 22.

36. David Nemec, *The Great Encyclopedia of Nineteenth Century Major League Baseball* (Tuscaloosa: University of Alabama Press, 2006), 67 ("Hulbert inwardly vowed that the power in professional baseball would soon be shifted from east to the west and from players such as Force—who for the moment could revolve almost totally unrestrained from team to team— to men like himself who handled the pursestrings."); Andrew J. Schiff, *"The Father of Baseball": A Biography of Henry Chadwick* (Jefferson, NC: McFarland, 2008), 143 ("Hulbert was secretly appalled over the eastern control of the National Association and how it handled the Force case.").

37. Paul Batesel, *Players and Teams of the National Association, 1871–1875* (Jefferson, NC: McFarland, 2012), 154; David Pietrusza, *Major Leagues: The Formation, Sometimes Absorption, and Mostly Inevitable Demise of 18 Professional Baseball Organizations, 1871 to Present* (Jefferson, NC: McFarland, 1991), 21. For a detailed review of this historic transaction, see David Ball, "The Bechtel-Craver Trade and the Origins of Baseball's Sales System," *Base Ball: A Journal of the Early Game* 1 (2007), 36–55.

38. Ginsburg, *The Fix Is In*, 41–42; Steven A. Riess, *Sport in Industrial America, 1850–1920*, 2nd ed. (Malden, MA: John Wiley & Sons, 2013), 169.

39. Dan Gutman, *Banana Bats and Ding-Dong Balls: A Century of Unique Baseball Inventions* (New York: Macmillan, 1995), 142–43.

40. John Giblin, Improvement in Base-Balls, U.S. Patent 165,994, filed June 25, 1875, issued July 27, 1875.

41. J.C. O'Neill, Base-Ball Base, U.S. Patent 171,038, filed June 19, 1875, issued December 14, 1875.

42. Gutman, *Banana Bats and Ding-Dong Balls*, 90.

43. Haupert, "William Hulbert and the Birth of the National League," 86. For the text of the letter sent by Hulbert and his St. Louis associate, Charles A. Fowle, to the four National Association teams (the Bostons, the Hartfords, the Athletics, and the Mutuals of New York), see Sullivan, *Early Innings*, 95–96.

44. Goldstein, *Playing for Keeps*, 147; "'A Startling Coup d'état': The National League is Formed," *New York Clipper*, February 12, 1876, reprinted in Sullivan, *Early Innings*, 96–99; Koppett, *Koppett's Concise History of Major League Baseball*, 29; Seymour and Mills, *Baseball: The Early Years*, 80; Jon David Cash, *Before They Were Cardinals: Major League Baseball in Nineteenth-Century St. Louis* (Columbia: University of Missouri Press, 2002), 30. For in-depth coverage of the birth of the National League, see Macdonald, *The League That Lasted: 1876 and the Founding of the National League of Professional Base Ball Clubs*.

45. Koppett, *Koppett's Concise History of Major League Baseball*, 29; Seymour and Mills, *Baseball: The Early Years*, 80; Voigt, *American Baseball: From Gentleman's Sport to the Commissioner System*, 63.

46. Cash, *Before They Were Cardinals*, 30; Macdonald, *The League That Lasted*, 35. Campbell Orrick Bishop was "an attorney [and later a judge] who played with the St. Louis Unions in the 1860s.... [He] drew up a constitution for a new league based upon a draft submitted to him by Hulbert." Seymour and Mills, *Baseball: The Early Years*, 79.

47. Koppett, *Koppett's Concise History of Major League Baseball*, 28; Seymour and Mills, *Baseball: The Early Years*, 82. "Although no reserve clause was added yet, a strong effort was made to curb revolving by forbidding players to negotiate with another club until the playing season was over." Voigt, *American Baseball: From Gentleman's Sport to the Commissioner System*, 64.

48. Koppett, *Koppett's Concise History of Major League Baseball*, 29.

49. Voigt, *American Baseball: From Gentleman's Sport to the Commissioner System*, 66. At the time of the formation of the National League, Bulkeley had already served on the Hartford, Connecticut, Common Council and as a city alderman. He would go on to become the city's mayor in 1880, governor of Connecticut in 1888, and a U.S. senator, serving from 1905 to 1911. In 1879, he also would become the leader of the Aetna Life Insurance Company, founded by his father in 1853. Haupert, "William Hulbert and the Birth of the National League," 87.

50. An Act in Relation to Bets, Wagers, and Pools, ch. 178, 1877 Laws of New York 192; Stephen A. Riess, *The Sport of Kings and the Kings of Crime: Horse Racing, Politics, and Organized Crime in New York, 1865–1913* (Syracuse: Syracuse University Press, 2011), 177; Voigt, *American Baseball: From Gentleman's Sport to the Commissioner System*, 73.

51. Pietrusza, *Major Leagues*, 33; Thorn, *Baseball in the Garden of Eden*, 169.

52. Pietrusza, *Major Leagues*, 33.

53. Roger I. Abrams, *The Dark Side of the Diamond*, 83; Ginsburg, *The Fix Is In*, 47; J.E. Findling, "The Louisville Grays' Scandal of 1877," *Journal of Sports History* 3 (1976), 184. To help combat the unethical practices that had threatened the integrity of the professional game, not to mention its popularity, the founders of the National League gave to the directors of each club "considerable police authority..., including the power to expel from baseball for

life any player found engaging in dishonest acts." *Ibid.*, 177.

54. Abrams, *The Dark Side of the Diamond*, 82–84; Bob Bailey, "August 20, 1877: Gray Outcomes—Louisville Grays vs. Hartford Dark Blues," in Felber, *Inventing Baseball*, 106. Haldeman presented his evidence to the public in the form of a lengthy exposé published several days after the action taken by Louisville's directors. John Haldeman, "Cussed Crookedness, A Complete Exposé of How Four Ball Men Picked Up Stray Pennies," *Louisville Courier-Journal*, November 3, 1877, reprinted in Sullivan, *Early Innings*, 102–10.

55. Abrams, *The Dark Side of the Diamond*, 84.

56. Albert Spalding, *America's National Game* (New York: American Sports Publishing Co, 1911), 227. For a comprehensive treatment of the entire event, see Cook, *The Louisville Grays Scandal of 1877*.

57. Frederick W. Thayer, Masks, U.S. Patent 200,358, filed January 15, 1878, issued February 12, 1878.

58. Stephen Eschenbach, "Home-Plate Security," *Harvard Magazine* 106 (July–August 2004), 73. Although there is no dispute about Thayer's role in developing and patenting the first catcher's mask, conflicting reports surfaced in the late 19th century as to who first wore the mask in a game. Spink's *The National Game* reprinted accounts first proffered in the *New York Sun* in 1896 from Howard K. Thatcher, a Maine physician and former Harvard catcher, and James A. Tyng, who followed Thatcher as Harvard's catcher, with both claiming to have first worn the new device. Alfred H. Spink, *The National Game*, 2d ed. (St. Louis, Mo.: National Game Pub. Co., 1911; repr., Carbondale, Il.: Southern Illinois University Press, 2000), 384–85. While recognizing the impossibility of reconciling the contradictory accounts, Morris speculates that Thayer may have forgotten and Tyng never known about Thatcher's "brief experiment with the mask" which he claimed had occurred in early games of 1876. Peter Morris, *A Game of Inches: The Game on the Field—The Stories Behind the Innovations That Shaped Baseball* (Chicago: Ivan Dee, 2006), 433.

59. Chuck Rosciam, "The Evolution of Catcher's Equipment," *Baseball Research Journal* 39 (Summer 2010), 105; Leventhal, *A History of Baseball in 100 Objects*, 80. Inclusion in the Spalding catalog occurred only after Thayer prevailed in his patent infringement suit against A.G. Spalding for selling a copy of his patented safety mask. *Thayer v. Spaulding*, 27 F. 66 (C.C. N.D. Ill. 1886). For more on this case, including an explanation of how Spalding became Spaulding in its caption and throughout the decision, see John H. Minan and Kevin Cole, "The Player in the Iron Mask," in *The Little White Book of Baseball Law* (Chicago: American Bar Association, 2009), 27–35.

60. Thorn, *Baseball in the Garden of Eden*, 185.

61. Peter Morris and Stefan Fatsis, "Baseball's Secret Pioneer," *Slate*, February 4, 2014, http://www.slate.com [search "william edward white"].

62. John Husman, "June 21, 1879: The Cameo of Bill White—Cleveland at Providence," in Felber, *Inventing Baseball*, 116–17.

63. For the text of the "secret and unpublished" first reserve agreement, including the names of the players reserved by each of the teams, see Gelzheiser, *Labor and Capital in 19th Century Baseball*, 176.

64. Red Caps owner Arthur Soden hastened O'Rourke's action by threatening to charge him for the cost of his uniform, a move designed to cut costs that backfired because the star outfielder considered it an insult. Wright was motivated not only by his desire to manage a team but also by his interest in establishing a sporting goods business. Edmonds, "Arthur Soden's Legacy," 46–47. According to Kaese, the Boston club "taxed" its players $20 per season for their uniforms. Harold Kaese, *The Boston Braves, 1871–1953* (New York: G. P. Putnam's Sons, 1948), 29.

65. Lee Lowenfish, *The Imperfect Diamond: A History of Baseball's Labor Wars* (Lincoln: University of Nebraska Press, 2010), 41; Al Kermisch, "From A Researcher's Note Book: First Reserve Clause Enacted 100 Years Ago," *Baseball Research Journal* 8 (1979): 9–10.

66. Helyar, *Lords of the Realm*, 4; Andrew S. Zimbalist, *Baseball and Billions: A Probing Look Inside the Big Business of our National Pastime* (New York: Basic Books, 1992), 4; "The NL Adopts a Player Reservation System," *Buffalo Commercial Advertiser*, September 30 and October 3, 1879, reprinted in Sullivan, *Early Innings*, 113–15.

67. J. Gordon Hylton, "The Historical Origins of Baseball Grievance Arbitration," *Marquette Sports Law Review* 11 (2001), 177; Preston D. Orem, *Baseball (1845–1881) From the Newspaper Accounts* (Altadena, CA: published by author, 1961), 332–33.

68. Orem, *Baseball (1845–1881) From the Newspaper Accounts*, 333.

69. Bob McConnell, "Whatever Happened to Charley Jones?" *Baseball Research Journal* 30 (2001), 90–91; Hylton, "The Historical Origins of Baseball Grievance Arbitration," 178–79.

70. Allen, *The Cincinnati Reds*, 20–21; "Kicked Out; Were the Cincinnati Club by the League," *Cincinnati Daily Enquirer*, October 7, 1880, 6;

Seymour and Mills, *Baseball: The Early Years*, 92; Voigt, *American Baseball: From Gentleman's Sport to the Commissioner System*, 105.

71. Edward Achorn, *The Summer of Beer and Whiskey: How Brewers, Barkeeps, Rowdies, Immigrants, and a Wild Pennant Fight Made Baseball America's Game* (New York: PublicAffairs, 2013), 24. However, Lee Allen, historian at the Baseball Hall of Fame from 1959 until his death in 1969, argues that despite the National League's stance against liquor sales, "the real reason appears to be that ... Kennett, unique among the magnates, was vigorously opposed to the reserve clause." Lee Allen, *The National League Story*, rev. ed. (New York: Hill & Wang, 1965), 32.

72. Haupert, "William Hulbert and the Birth of the National League," 90–91; Koppett, *Koppett's Concise History of Major League Baseball*, 39.

73. Seymour and Mills, *Baseball: The Early Years*, 137–38; Voigt, *American Baseball: From Gentleman's Sport to the Commissioner System*, 122–24; Achorn, *The Summer of Beer and Whiskey*, 25; "Formation of the American Association," *Cincinnati Enquirer*, November 3, 1881, reprinted in Sullivan, *Early Innings*, 119–21.

74. Koppett, *Koppett's Concise History of Major League Baseball*, 40; Jerold J. Duquette, *Regulating the National Pastime: Baseball and Antitrust* (Westport, CT: Greenwood, 1999), 6.

75. Haupert, "William Hulbert and the Birth of the National League," 91; Zimbalist, *Baseball and Billions*, 4. For more information on the American Association, see David Nemec, *The Beer and Whisky League: The Illustrated History of the American Association—Baseball's Renegade Major League*, rev. ed. (Guilford, CT: Lyons Press, 2004).

76. Achorn, *The Summer of Beer and Whiskey*, 25–27; Koppett, *Koppett's Concise History of Major League Baseball*, 40.

77. Murray Polner, *Branch Rickey: A Biography*, rev. ed. (Jefferson, NC: McFarland, 2007), 16; Lee Lowenfish, *Branch Rickey: Baseball's Ferocious Gentleman* (Lincoln, University of Nebraska Press, 2007), 14.

78. "Branch Rickey to Bow Out Nov. 1," *Chicago Tribune*, October 20, 1955, F3; "Pirates Name Joe L. Brown to Rickey's Post," *Chicago Tribune*, October 26, 1955, C3; Lee Lowenfish, *Branch Rickey: Baseball's Ferocious Gentleman*, 531 ("The 1955 season was the last one on Rickey's five-year contract, and though owner John Galbreath publicly stated his continuing support for his fellow Ohioan, it was no secret that a change was being contemplated when the contract ended.... On October 19, 1955, the changing of the guard was officially announced. Joe L. Brown was brought in as the new general manager."); Murray Polner, *Branch Rickey: A Biography*, 218 ("The long and dreary season of 1955 dragged on for the Pirates until the autumn, when Rickey decided that for the moment he had had enough.... By resigning, he appeared to his critics to have acknowledged defeat, even though he had long intended to leave following the end of five years of active service.").

79. See generally Lee Lowenfish, "When All Heaven Rejoiced: Branch Rickey and the Origins of the Breaking of the Color Line," *NINE: A Journal of Baseball History and Culture* 11, no. 1 (2002): 1–15.

80. For more information about Rickey, see Lowenfish, *Branch Rickey: Baseball's Ferocious Gentleman*; Polner, *Branch Rickey: A Biography*; Jimmy Breslin, *Branch Rickey* (New York: Viking, 2011).

81. "Sam Wise Deserts Cincinnati for Boston," *Boston Daily Globe*, January 22, 1882, 8 (quoting from the *St. Louis Globe-Democrat*); Edmonds, "Arthur Soden's Legacy, 51–52.

82. Seymour and Mills, *Baseball: The Early Years*, 141.

83. Richard McBane, *A Fine Looking Lot of Ball-Tossers: The Remarkable Akrons of 1881* (Jefferson, NC: McFarland, 2005), 68.

84. Thorn, *Baseball in the Garden of Eden*, 174; MacDonald, *The League that Lasted*, 219; Michael Haupert, "William Hulbert," SABR Baseball Biography Project, accessed March 23, 2016, http://sabr.org/bioproj/person/d1d420b3.

85. David Fleitz, *Cap Anson: The Grand Old Man of Baseball* 99 (Jefferson, NC: McFarland, 2005).

86. For one version of the Hulbert Hall of Fame story, see Glenn Stout & Richard A. Johnson, *The Cubs: The Complete Story of Chicago Cubs Baseball* (New York: Houghton Mifflin, 2007), 18.

87. Di Salvatore, *A Clever Base-Ballist*, 294.

88. Richard L. Irwin, "A Historical Review of Litigation in Baseball," *Marquette Sports Law Journal* 1 (1991): 284.

89. *Allegheny Base-Ball Club v. Bennett*, 14 F. 257 (C.C.W.D. Pa. 1882).

90. Ibid., 259. For additional information about the decision, see Edmonds, "Arthur Soden's Legacy, 53–56.

91. Neil J. Sullivan, *The Minors: The Struggles and the Triumph of Baseball's Poor Relation from 1876 to the Present* (New York: St. Martin's Press, 1990), 17–18; James Mallinson, "A.G. Mills," SABR Baseball Biography Project, accessed March 23, 2016, http://sabr.org/bioproj/person/abccef1b.

92. Robert Fredrick Burk, *Never Just a Game: Players, Owners, and American Baseball to 1920* (Chapel Hill: University of North Carolina

Press, 1994), 73; Koppett, *Koppett's Concise History of Major League Baseball*, 45.
93. Zimbalist, *Baseball and Billions*, 4; Koppett, *Koppett's Concise History of Major League Baseball*, 41; "The Tripartite Agreement," reprinted in Sullivan, *Early Innings*, 128–30; Francis Richter, *Richter's History and Records of Base Ball* (Philadelphia: Dando, 1914), 209–10; Gelzheiser, *Labor and Capital in 19th Century Baseball*, 48–50; Duquette, *Regulating the National Pastime*, 6. According to Seymour, the number of reserved players was increased to twelve in 1886 and to fourteen in 1887. Seymour and Mills, *Baseball: The Early Years*, 108–09.
94. Eric M. Leifer, *Making the Majors: The Transformation of Team Sports in America* (Cambridge: Harvard University Press, 1995), 71.
95. Allen, *The National League Story*, 41.
96. Pietrusza, *Major Leagues*, 82; Koppett, *Koppett's Concise History of Major League Baseball*, 45.
97. Gelzheiser, *Labor and Capital in 19th Century Baseball*, 31; "Formation of the Union Association," *Sporting Life*, September 17, 1883, reprinted in Sullivan, *Early Innings*, 130–32; Cash, *Before They Were Cardinals*, 76 (the Association's constitution "condemned the reserve clause for making 'the player almost the slave to the club'"); Nemec, *The Beer and Whisky League*, 60.
98. David George Surdam, *The Ball Game Biz: An Introduction to the Economics of Professional Team Sports* (Jefferson, NC: McFarland, 2010), 170; Pietrusza, *Major Leagues*, 83.
99. Di Salvatore, *A Clever Base-Ballist*, 168.
100. Zimbalist, *Baseball and Billions*, 4; Gelzheiser, *Labor and Capital in 19th Century Baseball*, 31.
101. Bill James, *The New Bill James Historical Baseball Abstract* (New York: Free Press, 2001), 22. James counters the traditional view with a compelling analysis that concludes "it is a farce to allow the Union Association to continue to masquerade in the records as a major league." Ibid., 21–34.
102. Peter Morris, *Catcher: How the Man Behind the Plate Became An American Folk Hero* (Chicago: Ivan R. Dee, 2009), 136.
103. William Gray, Body-Protector, U.S. Patent 295,543, filed October 18, 1883, issued March 25, 1884.
104. Morris, *Catcher*, 138; Rosciam, "The Evolution of Catcher's Equipment," 108.
105. Ross E. Davies, "A Crank on the Court: The Passion of Justice William R. Day," *Baseball Research Journal* 38 (Fall 2009): 94 n.4 (listing the few baseball-related cases heard by the U.S. Supreme Court prior to its 1922 decision in *Federal Baseball v. National League*).

106. 112 U.S. 354 (1884).
107. James H. Osgood, Improvement in Modes of Covering Rounded Articles with Leather, U.S. Patent 127,098, issued May 21, 1872.
108. Josh Gilliland, "Bases Loaded: Baseball Patents and Player Contracts in the 19th Century," *The Legal Geeks* (blog), March 31, 2015, http://thelegalgeeks.com/blog/?p=8082.
109. Stevens, *Baseball's Radical for All Seasons*, 39; Di Salvatore, *A Clever Base-Ballist*, 183.
110. John Montgomery Ward, "Is the Base-Ball Player a Chattel?" *Lippincott's Magazine* 40 (August 1887), 310–19, reprinted in Sullivan, *Early Innings*, 161–70, as "John Ward Attacks the Reserve Clause (1887)."
111. George H. Rawlings, Glove, U.S. Patent 325,968, filed March 23, 1885, issued September 8, 1885; Gutman, *Banana Bats and Ding-Dong Balls*, 196.
112. See, for example, Morris, *A Game of Inches: The Game on the Field*, 289 (citing evidence for use as early as 1858, but suggesting that "the first baseball player to wear gloves regularly may have been a catcher named Ben Delavergne, around 1860"); James R. Tootle, *Vintage Base Ball: Recapturing the National Pastime* (Jefferson, NC: McFarland, 2011), 154 (noting that the "story of the development of the glove is one of evolution, not a magic day or year when all players suddenly began to wear gloves in the field").
113. Austin C. Butts of Newark, New Jersey, patented a glove for "sporting and general use" in 1878, but the patent issued to Rawlings in 1885 was the first specifically designed for a baseball player. Gutman, *Banana Bats and Ding-Dong Balls*, 195–96; Austin C. Butts, Improvement in Gloves, U.S. Patent 198,921, filed May 15, 1877, issued January 1, 1878.
114. "It was not until 1877 that I overcame my scruples against joining the 'kid-glove aristocracy' by donning a glove. When I did at last decide to do so, I did not select a flesh-colored glove, but got a black one, and cut out as much of the back as possible to let the air in. Happily, in my case, the presence of a glove did not call out the ridicule that had greeted Waite [sic] [referring to Charlie Waitt of the St. Louis Brown Stockings, the first player Spalding had seen wearing a glove in 1875]. I had been playing so long and had become so well known that the innovation seemed rather to evoke sympathy than hilarity." Spalding, *America's National Game*, 476.
115. Kelsey Campbell-Dollaghan, "The Forgotten History of Baseball's Most Iconic Objects," *Gizmodo* (blog), July 16, 2013, http://gizmodo.com/the-forgotten-history-of-baseballs-most-iconic-objects-792812600.

116. "New National Agreement Signed," *New York Times*, October 18, 1885, reprinted in Sullivan, *Early Innings*, 139–40.

117. For a near contemporaneous account of the creation and early goals of the Brotherhood, see T.J. Keefe, "The Brotherhood and Its Work," in *Players' National League Base Ball Guide* (Chicago: F.H. Brunell, 1890), 7–10, reprinted in Sullivan, *Early Innings*, 196–98. New York Giants pitcher Tim Keefe, who will be inducted into the Baseball Hall of Fame in 1964, was elected secretary of the Brotherhood, a reasonable choice given his self-taught skills in shorthand which he practiced in off hours during the season. He hoped to use this skill professionally once he completed his baseball career. Charlie Bevis, *Tim Keefe: A Biography of the Hall of Fame Pitcher and Player-Rights Advocate* (Jefferson, NC: McFarland, 2015), 92, 94.

118. Duquette, *Regulating the National Pastime*, 6.

119. Gelzheiser, *Labor and Capital in 19th Century Baseball*, 85; Ross, *The Great Baseball Revolt*, 53.

120. *Detroit Base-Ball Club v. Deppert*, 27 N.W. 856, 858 (Mich. 1886).

121. Randy J. Maniloff, "I Paid for That Rooftop Seat," *Wall Street Journal*, April 29, 2013, A17; Richard Bak, *A Place for Summer: A Narrative History of Tiger Stadium* (Detroit: Great Lakes Books, 1998), 107–09.

122. Peter Morris, *A Game of Inches: The Game Behind the Scenes—The Stories Behind the Innovations That Shaped Baseball* (Chicago: Ivan R. Dee, 2006), 25.

123. Andrew Shinkle, "A Storied Rivalry, Part I," *SB Nation* (blog), March 8, 2014, http://www.redreporter.com/2014/3/8/5481770/a-storied-rivalry-part-i; L.M. Sutter, *Arlie Latham: A Baseball Biography of the Freshest Man on Earth* (Jefferson, NC: McFarland, 2012), 62.

124. John Marsh, "On the Genealogy of Trades, Part I," *The Hardball Times* (blog), June 25, 2015, http://www.hardballtimes.com [search "genealogy"].

125. Paul Batesel, *Players and Teams of the National Association, 1871–1875* (Jefferson, NC: McFarland, 2012), 109.

126. Robert Reach, Base-Ball Mask, U.S. Patent 364,543, filed March 2, 1887, and issued June 7, 1887.

127. Heck, "Evolution of the Mask," *Eephus League of Baseball Minutiae*.

128. "The Millennium—Details of the Sporting Life Plan," *Sporting Life*, December 7, 1887, 1–2, reprinted in Sullivan, *Early Innings*, 170–71, as "Francis Richter Proposes a Player Reservation System for the Minor Leagues."

129. Rosciam, "The Evolution of Catcher's Equipment," 105.

130. George Barnard, Base-Ball Mask, U.S. Patent 376,278, filed August 29, 1887, issued January 10, 1888.

131. *Ibid*.

132. Gelzheiser, *Labor and Capital in 19th Century Baseball*, 44–45; Lee Lowenfish & Tony Lupien, *The Imperfect Diamond* (New York: Stein and Day, 1980), 30; "The Brush Salary Classification Plan," *New York Clipper*, December 1, 1888, reprinted in Sullivan, *Early Innings*, 171–73.

133. Burk, *Never Just a Game*, 102.

134. Ross, *The Great Baseball Revolt*, 82–83; William F. Lamb, "The Ward v. Johnson Libel Case: The Last Battle of the Great Baseball War," *Base Ball: A Journal of the Early Game* 2 (Fall 2008), 49.

135. "Baseball War Declared," *New York Times*, November 5, 1889, 8; "In Hostile Array; The Brotherhood Takes the Great Plunge," *Sporting Life*, November 13, 1889, 1; Di Salvatore, *A Clever Base-Ballist*, 273–79.

136. William B. Gould IV, *Bargaining with Baseball: Labor Relations in an Age of Prosperous Turmoil* (Jefferson, NC: McFarland, 2011), 58.

137. Zimbalist, *Baseball and Billions*, 5; "The Ball Players Meet," *New York Times*, December 17, 1889, 3, reprinted in Sullivan, *Early Innings*, 193; Lee Lowenfish & Tony Lupien, *The Imperfect Diamond: The Story of the Baseball's Reserve System and the Men Who Fought to Change It* (New York: Stein & Day, 1980), 35. For a thorough examination of the Players League, see Ross, *The Great Baseball Revolt*; Ed Koszarek, *The Players League: History, Clubs, Ballplayers and Statistics* (Jefferson, NC: McFarland, 2006).

138. Ross, *The Great Baseball Revolt*, 123–24.

139. 9 N.Y.S. 779 (Sup. Ct. 1890).

140. Gelzheiser, *Labor and Capital in 19th Century Baseball*, 182–83; "Ward Wins His Fight," *New York Times*, January 29, 1890, 2, reprinted in Sullivan, *Early Innings*, 201–04.

141. "Beginning to Reap the Whirlwind," *Sporting Life*, February 5, 1890, 4. Commentators continue to note the importance of the case. See, e.g., Ross, *The Great Baseball Revolt*, 126 ("With the ruling, … the new league was effectively open for business. The players who had delayed signing PL contracts until after Ward's case largely signed on in the following weeks and months."); Jarvis & Coleman, "Early Baseball Law," 125 ("Because of the defendant's fame, as well as the accompanying circumstances, it is this case that claims the honor of being the most important early baseball case.").

142. G. Richard McKelvey, *The MacPhails: Baseball's First Family of the Front Office* (Jefferson, NC: McFarland, 2000), 1. Larry MacPhail was named for the MacPhail's family friend Leland Stanford, the California governor,

railroad tycoon, and founder of the university named for their son who died in Italy as a teenager. MacPhail's mother promised the Stanfords that she would name their first son in his honor. *Ibid.*, 2.

143. Koppett, *Koppett's Concise History of Major League Baseball*, 189–90; Leventhal, *A History of Baseball in 100 Objects*, 189.

144. *Phila. Ball Club, Ltd. v. Hallman*, 8 Pa. C. 57, 63 (C.P. 1890).

145. *Ibid.*

146. *Metro. Exhibition Co. v. Ewing*, 42 F. 198, 199 (C.C.S.D.N.Y. 1890).

147. *Ibid.*, 204; Roy Kerr, *Buck Ewing: A Baseball Biography* (Jefferson, NC: McFarland, 2012), 112–13.

148. "Players' League; The First Campaign of the New League Fairly Started," *Sporting Life*, April 26, 1890, 3.

149. John W. Bauer, "Debut of the Players League," in Felber, *Inventing Baseball*, 224. The PL has similar success in the competition for players. Of the 72 players who appear in the box scores of the four opening games, all but two played in either the National League or the American Association in 1889. *Ibid.*, 222.

150. Burk, *Never Just a Game*, 112–15; Voigt, *American Baseball: From Gentleman's Sport to the Commissioner System*, 165–69; "Players' League; Still Awaiting the Final Settlement of Its Affairs," *Sporting Life*, November 29, 1890, 4.

151. Di Salvatore, *A Clever Base-Ballist*, 320.

152. *Am. Ass'n Base-Ball Club of Kansas City v. Pickett*, 8 Pa. County Ct. 232 (Ct. Com. Pl. 1890). The arguments in the case can be found in two *Sporting Life* articles, "Pickett's Case: A Full Statement From the Kansas City Club," *Sporting Life*, April 12, 1890, 10; "Pickett Enjoined: The Kansas City's Rights to His Services Recognized," *Sporting Life*, May 10, 1890, 5.

153. *Am. Ass'n Base-Ball Club of Kansas City v. Pickett*, 233; Burk, *Never Just a Game*, 110–11; Seymour and Mills, *Baseball: The Early Years*, 237.

154. "Pickett Buys His Release," *Philadelphia Times*, June 5, 1890, 2.

155. *Harrisburg Base-Ball Club v. Athletic Ass'n*, 8 Pa.C.C. 337 (Ct. Com. Pl. 1890); "Over Fifty Years Before Jackie Robinson Broke Major League Baseball's Color Barrier, an Integrated Minor League Team Battled for the Rights to Future Hall of Fame Black Ballplayer Frank Grant," *Baseball Law Reporter* (blog), December 14, 2013, http://baseballlawreporter.blogspot.com [search "Frank Grant"].

156. Sol White, *Sol White's History of Colored Base Ball, with Other Documents on the Early Black Game, 1886–1936*, rev. ed. of *Sol White's Official Base Ball Guide* (1907; rev. with preface and notes by Jerry Malloy, Lincoln: University of Nebraska Press, 1995), 110.

157. "Frank Grant," National Baseball Hall of Fame, accessed October 1, 2014, http://baseballhall.org/hof/grant-frank ("perhaps the best of the African-American players who played in white organized baseball in the 1880s, before the color line was drawn"). For more information on White, see Jerry Malloy, "Frank Grant," in *Nineteenth Century Stars*, Robert L. Tiemann, ed. (Phoenix: Society for American Baseball Research, 2012), 110–11.

158. Act of July 2, 1890, ch. 647, 26 Stat. 209 (1890).

159. "Big Deals in Base-Ball; End of the Long War Between Rival Organizations," *Chicago Daily Tribune*, January 17, 1891, 6. For the text of the agreement, see "The New Agreement; Full Text of the New Supreme Law of Base Ball," *Sporting Life*, January 24, 1891, 5.

160. Frederick G. Lieb, *The Pittsburgh Pirates* (New York: G. P. Putnam's Sons, 1948), 21; Norman L. Macht, *Connie Mack and the Early Years of Baseball* (Lincoln: University of Nebraska Press, 2007), 84–85.

161. Macht, *Connie Mack and the Early Years of Baseball*, 85; Frederick G. Lieb, *Connie Mack: Grand Old Man of Baseball* (New York: G.P. Putnam's Sons, 1945), 36.

162. Charles C. Alexander, *Turbulent Seasons: Baseball in 1890–1891* (Dallas: Southern Methodist University Press, 2011), 120–22.

163. Burk, *Never Just A Game*, 118; "A Gigantic Revolt; The Presidency," *Sporting Life*, February 21, 1891, 2–3.

164. Seymour and Mills, *Baseball: The Early Years*, 253.

165. Bill Kelly, "Arrested for Playing Baseball! How the National Pastime Became a Church and State Battleground in Nebraska," NET News, June 6, 2013, http://netnebraska.org/article/news/arrested-playing-baseball-how-national-pastime-became-church-and-state-battleground.

166. *State v. O'Rourk*, 53 N.W. 591, 592 (Neb. 1892).

167. *Ibid.*, 595.

168. Burk, *Never Just a Game*, 121; Gelzheiser, *Labor and Capital in 19th Century Baseball*, 161–63.

169. "Enjoyed the Sport—President Harrison Flees from Politics to Baseball," *Washington Post*, June 7, 1892, 1; William B. Mead and Paul Dickson, *Baseball: The Presidents' Game* (New York: Walker and Company, 1997), 13; Morris, *A Game of Inches: The Game on the Field*, 333.

170. "President Benjamin Harrison Baseball Game Attendance Log," Baseball Almanac, accessed July 29, 2013, http://www.baseball-almanac.com/prz_cbh.shtml.

171. "1892 Washington Senators," Baseball-Reference.com, accessed July 29, 2013, http://www.baseball-reference.com.

172. *Russell v. Nat'l Exhibition Co.*, 69 N.Y.S. 732, 733 (App. Div. 1901).
173. Arthur R. Ahrens, "Fred Pfeffer, Stonewall Second Baseman," *Baseball Research Journal* 8 (1979), 49–50; Di Salvatore, *A Clever Base-Ballist*, 368.
174. Di Salvatore, *A Clever Base-Ballist*, 368.
175. Rick Huhn, *The Chalmers Race: Ty Cobb, Napoleon Lajoie, and the Controversial 1910 Batting Title That Became a National Obsession* (Lincoln: University of Nebraska Press, 2014), 68–69.
176. Bill Felber, "Arrested on a Day of Rest: Washington Senators vs. Cleveland Spiders," in Felber, *Inventing Baseball*, 255.
177. *Ibid.*; Bill Felber, *A Game of Brawl: The Orioles, the Beaneaters, and the Battle for the 1897 Pennant* (Lincoln: University of Nebraska Press, 2007), 129–31; Charlie Bevis, *Sunday Baseball: The Major Leagues' Struggle to Play Baseball on the Lord's Day, 1876–1934* (Jefferson, NC: McFarland, 2003), 121–25.
178. *State v. Powell*, 50 N.E. 900 (Ohio 1898).
179. "Cleveland v. Pittsburg at Cleveland, June 19," *Sporting Life*, June 25, 1898, 3.
180. Bevis, *Sunday Baseball*, 126–27.
181. "Cleveland Chatter," *Sporting Life*, July 2, 1898, 8.
182. Bevis, *Sunday Baseball*, 128–29.
183. Gai Ingham Berlage, *Women in Baseball: The Forgotten History* (Westport, CT: Praeger, 1994), 45–46; Daniel R. Levitt, *Ed Barrow: The Bulldog Who Built the Yankees' First Dynasty* (Lincoln: University of Nebraska Press, 2008), 34.
184. The Reading *Eagle* noted that "[s]he went about it like a professional even down to expectorating on her hands," while the Hartford *Courant* stated that "[s]he plays just like a man ... and if it was not for bloomers she would be taken for a man on the diamond." "Women Players in Organized Baseball," *Baseball Research Journal* 12 (1983), 160–61.
185. Jean Hastings Ardell, *Breaking into Baseball: Women and the National Pastime* (Carbondale: Southern Illinois University Press, 2005), 105; Levitt, *Ed Barrow.*
186. Burk, *Never Just a Game*, 125–26; Seymour and Mills, *Baseball: The Early Years*, 270; "Gumbert Decision Upheld Reserve Clause in 1898," *Sporting News*, May 16, 1951, 7.
187. "Ad Gumbert," Baseball-Reference.com, accessed July 25, 2013, http://www.baseball-reference.com.
188. "Importance of Gumbert Case," *Chicago Daily Tribune*, August 18, 1898, 4.
189. Despite Clark Griffith's position as vice president of the Protective Association and the strong labor sentiments he harbored as a player, in the future both Clark Griffith and his successor, Calvin Griffith, will exhibit strong anti-union attitudes as owners of the Washington Senators and Minnesota Twins from 1920 to 1984. Daniel R. Levitt, *The Battle that Forged Modern Baseball: The Federal League Challenge and Its Legacy* (Chicago: Ivan R. Dee, 2012), 69.
190. Burk, *Never Just a Game*, 143–44; Seymour and Mills, *Baseball: The Early Years*, 309–10. As the association's legal counsel, "Taylor issued the crucial legal opinion to his ballplayer constituents that it was his belief that the reserve clause in the National League's standard player contract had 'no legal value.' Taylor's legal analysis set the stage for Napoleon Lajoie, Jimmy Collins, and dozens of other ballplayers to jump from the National League and establish the American League as a serious competitor to the then-monopoly National League." Charlie Bevis, "Harry Taylor," SABR Baseball Biography Project, December 16, 2011, http://sabr.org/bioproj/person/f5f468a1.
191. Scott Longert, "The Players' Fraternity," *Baseball Research Journal* 30 (2001), 40.
192. Burk, *Never Just a Game*, 154–55; Seymour and Mills, *Baseball: The Early Years*, 323–24.
193. Leventhal, *A History of Baseball in 100 Objects*, 116.
194. Koppett, *Koppett's Concise History of Major League Baseball*, 88–89; Lee Allen, *The American League Story*, rev. ed. (New York: Hill & Wang, 1965), 12.
195. James P. Quigel, Jr., and Louis E. Hunsinger, Jr., *Gateway to the Majors: Williamsport and Minor League Baseball* (University Park: Pennsylvania University Press, 2001), 25.
196. Burk, *Never Just a Game*, 151–52.
197. *Phila. Ball Club, Ltd. v. Lajoie*, 51 A. 973 (Pa. 1902).
198. David L. Fleitz, *Napoleon Lajoie: King of Ballplayers* (Jefferson, NC: McFarland, 2013), 78–79.
199. *Phila. Ball Club, Ltd. v. Lajoie*, 974. For analyses of the court's opinion, see G. Edward White, *Creating the National Pastime: Baseball Transforms Itself, 1903–1953* (Princeton, NJ: Princeton University Press, 1996), 55–57; Roger I. Abrams, *Legal Bases: Baseball and the Law* (Philadelphia: Temple University Press, 1998), 34–36.
200. Fleitz, *Napoleon Lajoie*, 81–84.
201. C. Paul Rogers III, "Napoleon Lajoie, Breach of Contract, and the Great Baseball War," *SMU Law Review* 55 (2002), 335.

Chapter 3

1. William A. Cook, *August "Garry" Herrmann: A Baseball Biography* (Jefferson, NC: McFarland, 2008), 44–53; "Baseball War Ends,"

Washington Post, January 11, 1903, 8; Francis C. Richter, "Settlement Procured; Peace Proclaimed," *Sporting Life*, January 17, 1903, 4, reprinted in Sullivan, *Early Innings*, 262–65; "Sweeping Peace Pact Is Signed," *Chicago Tribune*, January 11, 1903, 9.

2. "The New National Agreement," in *Reach's Official American League Base Ball Guide for 1904*, ed. Francis C. Richter (Philadelphia: A.J. Reach Co., 1904), 115–23 (contains complete text of agreement).

3. *Ibid.*, 116; Grow, *Baseball on Trial*, 13.

4. Charles Jacobson, "The Supreme Court of Baseball," *Case and Comment* 23 (1916), 665.

5. Louis P. Masur, *Autumn Glory: Baseball's First World Series* (New York: Hill and Wang, 2003), 13–15.

6. Burton Alan Boxerman and Benita W. Boxerman, *Ebbets to Veeck to Busch: Eight Owners Who Shaped Baseball* (Jefferson, NC: McFarland, 2003), 36.

7. Leventhal, *A History of Baseball in 100 Objects*, 121–22. Harshly criticized when he and manager John McGraw refused to allow the Giants to take on the American League champion Boston Americans after the 1904 season, Brush later became a proponent of the World Series and submitted a plan for its conduct to National League President Harry Pulliam. Harold Seymour and Dorothy Seymour Mills, *Baseball: The Golden Age* (New York: Oxford University Press, 1971), 14–15.

8. Bill Shaikin, "O'Malley's Long Road to the Hall of Fame," *Los Angeles Times*, December 4, 2007, 1; Andy McCue, *Mover and Shaker: Walter O'Malley, the Dodgers, and Baseball's Westward Expansion* (Lincoln: University of Nebraska Press, 2014), 6.

9. McCue, *Mover and Shaker*, 19, 23.

10. In late May 1957, National League owners granted permission for the Dodgers and Giants, owned by Horace Stoneham, to move to Los Angeles and San Francisco, respectively, if they requested permission by October 1. Joseph M. Sheehan, "Dodgers, Giants Win Right To Shift if They So Desire," *New York Times*, May 29, 1957, 1; Neil J. Sullivan, *The Dodgers Move West* (New York: Oxford University Press, 1987), 113.

11. "O'Malley, Westward Pioneer, Dies," *Sporting News*, August 25, 1979, 12.

12. Bevis, *Sunday Baseball*, 156; *People v. Poole*, 89 N.Y.S. 773 (1904).

13. "Sunday Baseball Hearing: Justice Gaynor Says Complaint Is Weak, but Takes Case Under Advisement," *New York Times*, June 8, 1904, 7.

14. *People v. Poole*, 773.

15. Bevis, *Sunday Baseball*, 157.

16. Frank Pierse Mogridge, Head-Protector. U.S. Patent 780,899, filed August 6, 1904, issued January 24, 1905 ("The use of my invention will not only insure the batter against injury to the head from being struck by the ball, but will give the batter confidence and prevent him from being intimidated by the pitcher and rendered fearful of being injured by the ball pitched."); Mike Sowell, *The Pitch that Killed* (New York: Macmillan, 1989), 288.

17. Gutman, *Banana Bats and Ding-Dong Balls*, 211.

18. On opening day, April 11, 1907, Giants catcher Bresnahan took his position at the Polo Grounds in New York wearing cricket-style shin guards, the first major leaguer to wear such equipment openly. A few others had tried pads to protect their legs, but only under their uniforms, fearing the kind of reaction that initially greeted Bresnahan, who recalled receiving "an awful razzing" and taunts of "Sissie" and "Cream Puff" from fans. Morris, *Catcher*, 229–30.

19. Robert M. Gorman & David Weeks, *Death at the Ballpark: A Comprehensive Study of Game-Related Fatalities of Players, Other Personnel and Spectators in Amateur and Professional Baseball, 1862–2007* (Jefferson, NC: McFarland, 2009), 10; Dickson, *The Dickson Baseball Dictionary*, 3rd ed., 90.

20. Roger I. Abrams, "Liberation Arbitration: The Baseball Reserve Clause Case," in *Proceedings of the 55th Annual Meeting of the National Academy of Arbitrators* (Washington, DC: Bureau of National Affairs, 2003), 192.

21. Charles Leerhsen, *Ty Cobb: A Terrible Beauty* (New York: Simon & Schuster, 2015), 122; John D. McCallum, *Ty Cobb* (New York: Praeger Publishers, 1975), 32; "Acquitted of Killing Husband," *Washington Post*, April 2, 1906, 2. Leerhsen and McCallum, quoting the *Royston Record*, state that Amanda was indicted for voluntary manslaughter, but the *Atlanta Constitution* and *Washington Post* accounts of the trial state that she was tried for murder. Leerhsen, *Ty Cobb*, 92; McCallum, *Ty Cobb*, 32; "Amanda Cobb Now Facing Jury," *Atlanta Constitution*, March 31, 1906.

22. Charles C. Alexander, *Ty Cobb* (New York: Oxford University Press, 1984), 21; Tim Hornbaker, *War on the Basepaths: The Definitive Biography of Ty Cobb* (New York: Sports Publishing, 2015), 18; Al Stump, *Cobb: A Biography* (Chapel Hill, NC: Algonquin Books, 1994), 90–91.

23. *See, e.g.*, Ty Cobb, "Batting Out Better Boys," *Rotarian* 71 (July 1947), 11; Leerhsen, *Ty Cobb*, 65, 103–04; Hornbaker, *War on the Basepaths*, 14; Alexander, *Ty Cobb*, 6, 12–17.

24. W.S. Titus, Base Ball Back Stop, U.S. Patent 849,941, filed December 20, 1906, issued April 9, 1907; Peter Morris, *Level Playing Fields*:

How the Groundskeeping Murphy Brothers Shaped Baseball (Lincoln: University of Nebraska Press, 2007), 114; Morris, *A Game of Inches: The Game Behind the Scenes*, 79–80.

25. Ken Tillman, "The Portable Batting Cage," *Baseball Research Journal* 28 (1999), 24.

26. Seymour and Mills, *Baseball: The Early Years*, 9–10; Peter Levine, *A.G. Spalding and the Rise of Baseball* (New York and London: Oxford University Press, 1985), 114.

27. Mallinson, "A.G. Mills," SABR Baseball Biography Project; Thorn, *Baseball in the Garden of Eden*, 275–81. For the text of Mills's letter to the *Beacon Journal*, dated April 3, 1905, and a second letter he wrote to Spalding, dated November 17, 1905, see David Block, *Baseball Before We Knew It: A Search for the Roots of the Game* (Lincoln: University of Nebraska Press, 2005), 252–56.

28. For a plausible speculation on the "kernel of truth" in Graves's account, involving not the Abner Doubleday of Cooperstown who had already departed for West Point by September 1838 and who would become a Civil War general, but rather his cousin, Abner Demas Doubleday, who was 11 years old in spring 1840, see Mark Pestana, "The Legendary Doubleday Game," in Felber, *Inventing Baseball*, 3–5.

29. White, *Creating the National Pastime*, 124; A.G. Mills, "Final Decision of the Baseball Commission," in *Spalding's Official Baseball Guide 1908*, ed. Henry Chadwick (New York: American Sports Publishing Co., 1908), 45–48. In addition to Mills and Sullivan, the other members of the special commission were Arthur Pue Gorman, Maryland senator and former president of the Washington Nationals; George Wright, future Hall of Fame player and a sporting goods magnate; Alfred J. Reach, another former player and sporting goods entrepreneur; Morgan Bulkeley, first president of the National League in 1876 and subsequently a Connecticut politician; and Nicholas E. Young, first secretary and fifth president of the National League. Thorn, *Baseball in the Garden of Eden*, 274.

30. Amy Whorf McGuiggan, *Take Me out to the Ball Game: The Story of the Sensational Baseball Song* (Lincoln: University of Nebraska Press, 2009), 49.

31. *Ibid.*, 71.

32. Matthew G. Doublestein, "American Song, America's Game," *National Pastime* 24 (2004), 57; Andy Strasberg, Bob Thompson, and Tim Wiles, *Baseball's Greatest Hit: The Story of Take Me Out to the Ball Game* (New York: Hal Leonard Pub., 2008), 55.

33. Strasberg, Thompson, and Wise, *Baseball's Greatest Hit*, 63–65.

34. Dave Itzkoff, "Famous Recordings to Join National Registry," *New York Times*, April 6, 2011, C2; "Complete National Recording Registry Listing," Library of Congress, accessed June 26, 2015, http://www.loc.gov/programs/national-recording-preservation-board/recording-registry/complete-national-recording-registry-listing/.

35. David W. Anderson, *More Than Merkle: A History of the Best and Most Exciting Baseball Season in Human History* (Lincoln: University of Nebraska Press, 2000), 211, 214. Undeterred by these events, the game will be played the next day, with the Cubs winning 4-2 behind the pitching of Mordecai "Three Finger" Brown. G.H. Fleming, *The Unforgettable Season* (New York: Holt, Rinehart and Winston, 1981), 306–21.

36. Francis C. Richter, "Majors Meet," *Sporting Life*, December 19, 1908, 4; Anderson, *More Than Merkle*, 212–13.

37. Harvey T. Woodruff, "Bar Dr. Creamer from All Ball Parks," *Chicago Tribune*, April 24, 1909, 8; Anderson, *More Than Merkle*, 218–20.

38. Tinsley E. Yarbrough, *Harry A. Blackmun: The Outsider Justice* (New York: Oxford University Press, 2008), 5; Linda Greenhouse, *Becoming Justice Blackmun: Harry Blackmun's Supreme Court Journey* (New York: Times Books, 2005), 2.

39. Greenhouse, *Becoming Justice Blackmun*, 42–51.

40. Roger Abrams, "Blackmun's List," *Virginia Sports and Entertainment Law Journal* 6 (2007), 186–87. Justice Blackmun's failure to include Mel Ott on the list prompted his clerks to give him an official Ott bat with a plaque inscribed, "I'll Never Forgive Myself." Yarbrough, *Harry A. Blackmun*, 163. For a fascinating look at Justice Blackmun, including a discussion of the Ott incident, see Harry A. Blackmun, interview by Harold Hongju Koh, July 6, 1994, sess. 1, pt. 1, video tape, Justice Harry A. Blackmun Oral History Project, Library of Congress, accessed July 21, 2015, http://lcweb2.loc.gov/diglib/blackmun-public/series.html?ID=D10.

41. Four other former Major League players have served in Congress: Fred Brown (Senate, 1933–39, representing New Hampshire); Jim Bunning (House of Representatives, 1987–99; Senate, 1999–2011, representing Kentucky); Wilmer "Vinegar Bend" Mizell (House of Representatives, 1969–75, representing North Carolina); and Pius L. "Pi" Schwert (House of Representatives, 1939–41, representing New York). Three Major League executives have served in Congress: Yankees Owner Jacob Ruppert (House of Representatives, 1899–1907); National League President Morgan Bulkeley (Senate, 1905–11); and Baseball Commissioner A.B. "Happy" Chandler (Senate, 1939–45). "Category: Politi-

cians," BR Bullpen, last modified September 27, 2013, http://www.baseball-reference.com/bullpen/Category:Politicians; Marty Appel, "Service of a Different Kind: Several Ballplayers Established a Second Career in Politics," *Memories and Dreams* (Winter 2008): 17–19.

42. Robert C. Gallagher, "John Tener's Brilliant Career," *Baseball Research Journal* 19 (1990): 36–38; Dan Ginsburg, "John Kinley Tener," in *Deadball Stars of the National League*, ed. Tom Simon (Dulles, VA: Brassey's, 2004), 28.

43. Benjamin F. Shibe, Base-Ball. U.S. Patent 924,696, filed August 26, 1908, issued June 15, 1909.

44. Ibid. (Specification of Letters Patent); *Our National Pastime in Our National Archives* (Washington, DC: National Archives and Records Admin., 2013), 3–4.

45. Dickson, *The Dickson Baseball Dictionary*, 3rd ed., 216.

46. Stuart Schimler, "Ben Shibe," in Jones, *Deadball Stars of the American League*, 594; Alan Schwarz, *The Numbers Game: Baseball's Lifelong Fascination with Statistics* (New York: Thomas Dunne Books, 2004), 37.

47. "An Annual Outing: The Congressional Baseball Game," U.S. House of Representatives, accessed March 29, 2016, http://history.house.gov [search "baseball"].

48. One commentator will note that for Tener, who only served in Congress from March 4, 1909, to January 16, 1911, organizing the first Congressional baseball game was his "most lasting contribution as a Congressman." Gallagher, "John Tener's Brilliant Career," 37.

49. "An Annual Outing: The Congressional Baseball Game—Statistics," U.S. House of Representatives, accessed March 29, 2016, http://history.house.gov [search "baseball"].

50. "Taft Pitches First Ball," *Chicago Daily Tribune*, April 15, 1910, 13; Christine L. Putnam, "A President Inaugurates a Remarkable Tradition," *Baseball Almanac*, April 2003, http://www.baseball-almanac.com/articles/president_taft_opening_day.shtml. For a full account of the game, played before what "was believed to be the largest crowd ever to see a baseball game in Washington," see Stephen V. Rice, "April 14, 1910: Walter Johnson Impresses President Taft on Opening Day, SABR Baseball Games Project, accessed May 7, 2015, http://sabr.org/gamesproject.

51. "Ask Taft to Act as Baseball Head," *New York Times*, November 24, 1918, 1; Davies, "A Crank on the Court, 97.

52. Lamb, "The Ward v. Johnson Libel Case: The Last Battle of the Great Baseball War," 53–55; R.W. Lardner, "Ward's Election Will Start War," *Chicago Tribune*, November 28, 1909, C1.

53. "Says Signature is a Forgery," *Boston Daily Globe*, May 12, 1911.

54. Di Salvatore, *A Clever Base-Ballist*, 375–76; Lamb, "The Ward v. Johnson Libel Case: The Last Battle of the Great Baseball War," 57–59; "Ward Given a $1000 Verdict," *Boston Daily Globe*, May 13, 1911, 6.

55. Although it was commonly believed that Lajoie's eight hits had allowed him to pass Cobb for the title, on October 15, 1910, American League President Ban Johnson announced that official season records indicated Cobb had a batting percentage of .384944, Lajoie, .384084. Cobb was declared the batting champion for 1910, but, given the closeness of the race, not to mention the questions still swirling around the Browns' performance, Hugh Chalmers agreed to present automobiles to both Cobb and Lajoie. Huhn, *The Chalmers Race*, 141.

56. David L. Fleitz, *Silver Bats and Automobiles: The Hotly Competitive, Sometimes Ignoble Pursuit of the Major League Batting Championship* (Jefferson, NC: McFarland, 2011), 184.

57. Huhn, *The Chalmers Race*, 111–14; Seymour and Mills, *Baseball: The Golden Age*, 285–86; Koppett, *Koppett's Concise History of Major League Baseball*, 111; Schwarz, *The Numbers Game*, 29 (noting publication of a poem by the *Chicago Tribune* which pondered whether the Browns performance was just the tip of the iceberg:

What must a meek outsider think.
When tricks like that they put across?
When at one frameup they will wink.
How do we know what games they toss?).

58. This wasn't the hard-drinking O'Connor's first problem with baseball management. On July 3, 1891, the American Association expelled him from its Columbus Solons club "for habitual drunkenness, disorderly conduct and insubordination." But the catcher joined the National League's Cleveland Spiders in 1892 and went on to a 21-year major league career which he completed by playing for the Browns on the fateful last day of the 1910 season. Ginsburg, *The Fix Is In*, 78–79.

59. For a detailed account of the trial, see Huhn, *The Chalmers Race*, 160–87.

60. *O'Connor v. St. Louis American League Baseball Co.*, 181 S.W. 1167, 1173 (Mo. Ct. App. 1916); Huhn, *The Chalmers Race*, 191–93.

61. Ardell, *Breaking into Baseball*, 162–63; Berlage, *Women in Baseball*, 65–67; Leslie Gibson McCarthy, "Lady B," *Cardinals Gameday Magazine* (2014, no. 2): 81–82.

62. Banner, *The Baseball Trust*, 40.

63. H.R. Res. 450, 62nd Cong. (1912), reprinted in Dean A. Sullivan, ed., *Middle Innings: A Documentary History of Baseball, 1900–1948*

(Lincoln: University of Nebraska Press, 1998), 64.

64. John Montgomery Ward, "Base Ball A Beneficent Trust," in Francis Richter, *Richter's History and Records of Base Ball* (Philadelphia: Sporting Life, 1914), 224, reprinted in Sullivan, *Middle Innings*, 64.

65. George Gipe, "Ty Cobb's Anger Led to Baseball's First Strike, A Comedy of Errors," *Sports Illustrated*, August 29, 1977, W5–6.

66. Alexander, *Ty Cobb*, 105; McCallum, *Ty Cobb*, 82–83. The subject of Cobb's attack is identified listed as "Luekers, the Fan Whom Cobb Assaulted," in "Ty Cobb vs. Ban Johnson," *Baseball Magazine* 9, no. 3 (July 1912), 11.

67. For a description of the 12 players who played as "Tigers" on May 18, see Joe Naiman, "The First Replacement Players: The 'Tigers' of May 18, 1912," *Baseball Research Journal* 25 (1996), 121–23.

68. Alexander, *Ty Cobb*, 106; McCallum, *Ty Cobb*, 85.

69. McCallum, *Ty Cobb*, 85 (misidentified as "McHarg"); William A. Cook, *August "Garry" Herrmann: A Baseball Biography* (Jefferson, NC: McFarland, 2008), 141.

70. "Johnson gave no indication of what action he would take, but the impression was gained that he had a considerable measure of sympathy with the player [Cobb].... It is a fact that crowds have been misbehaving at Mr. Farrell's Park. American League partisans say the bad actors are Polo Grounds fans who have brought their methods to the Hilltop with them." Mack, "Inclined to Cobb, New York Sentiment Was With Georgian in Row," *Sporting News*, May 23, 1912, 1.

71. Alexander, *Ty Cobb*, 107; "Cobb Case Concluded," *Sporting Life*, June 1, 1912, 1.

72. Mark Stang, *Cardinals Collection: 100 Years of St. Louis Cardinals Images* (Wilmington, OH: Orange Frazer Press, 2002), 15; Bill Borst, "The Matron Magnate," *Baseball Research Journal* (1977), 26.

73. Frederick G. Lieb, *The St. Louis Cardinals: The Story of a Great Baseball Club* (New York: G.P. Putnam's Sons, 1947), 45–46; "Mrs. Britton Wins in Suit to Control Club," *Sporting News*, May 23, 1912, 1.

74. Ross E. Davies, "Along Comes the Players Association: The Roots and Rise of Organized Labor in Major League Baseball," *New York University Journal of Legislation and Public Policy* 16 (2013): 328; Burk, *Never Just a Game*, 188–89; Brian McKenna, "Dave Fultz," SABR Baseball Biography Project, accessed March 23, 2016, http://sabr.org/bioproj/person/1857946b.

75. David L. Fultz, "The Baseball Players Fraternity and What It Stands For," *Baseball Magazine* 10 (November 1912): 29–31, 124–26, reprinted in Sullivan, *Middle innings*, 66–68.

76. H. Addington Bruce, "Baseball and the National Life," *Outlook* (May 17, 1913), 104. Ross Davies suggests that perhaps this wasn't so unprecedented, noting that Justice Day received similar updates while on the bench during the 1910 World Series. In fact, there is evidence suggesting "that at least during Day's tenure on the Court such updates became a tradition and even that reporters themselves were sometimes the sources of Day's on-the-bench reports." Davies, "A Crank on the Court," 98.

77. Davies, "A Crank on the Court," 98; "News in Highest Court: Bathtub Case Waits While Jurists Read Bulletins from Boston," *New York Times*, October 17, 1912, 1.

78. *Standard Sanitary Manufacturing Co. v. United States*, 226 U.S. 20 (1912).

79. Bruce, "Baseball and the National Life," 104.

80. "News in Highest Court," 1.

81. "I would like to know what the hell any goddamned woman can tell me about baseball." Boxerman and Boxerman, *Ebbets to Veeck to Busch*, 61–62.

82. Boxerman and Boxerman, *Ebbets to Veeck to Busch*, 60; Seymour and Mills, *Baseball: The Golden Age*, 136; Lieb, *The St. Louis Cardinals*, 48.

83. "Roger Bresnahan," Baseball-Reference.com, accessed July 30, 2013, http://www.baseball-reference.com. Bresnahan spent the next two years, 1913–14, as both a second-string and starting catcher, before the Cubs signed him on November 18, 1914, to serve as their player-manager. Joan M. Thomas, "Roger Bresnahan," in *Deadball Stars of the National League*, ed. Tom Simon (Washington, DC: Brassey's, 2004), 350.

84. David L. Fleitz, *Ghosts in the Gallery at Cooperstown: Sixteen Little-Known Members of the Hall of Fame* (Jefferson, NC: McFarland, 2004), 41; Bill Borst, "The Matron Magnet," *Baseball Research Journal* (1977), 27.

85. Although Huggins graduated from the University of Cincinnati Law School in 1902 and passed the Ohio bar, he never practiced law. The "Mighty Mite" did, however, play 13 major league seasons as a 5-foot, 6-inch second baseman and lead the New York Yankees to six pennants and three World Series titles as their manager from 1918 to 1929. He was elected to the Hall of Fame in 1964. "Huggins, Miller," National Baseball Hall of Fame and Museum, accessed July 30, 2013, http://baseballhall.org/hof/huggins-miller.

86. *Crane v. Kansas City Baseball & Exhibition, Co.*, 153 S.W. 1076 (Mo. Ct. App. 1913).

87. J. Gordon Hylton, "A Foul Ball in the Courtroom: The Baseball Spectator Injury as a

Case of First Impression," *Tulsa Law Review* 38 (2003), 486.
  88. Grow, *Baseball on Trial*, 5–6; Hugh S. Fullerton, "Federal League Organizes Today, Magnates of Six Cities Hold First Meeting in Hoosier Capital," *Chicago Daily Tribune*, March 8, 1913, 10.
  89. Grow, *Baseball on Trial*, 7–11.
  90. Longert, "The Players' Fraternity," 42–43; David L. Fultz, "Status of the Players' Petition," *Baseball Magazine* 12 (February 1914), 69.
  91. Burk, *Never Just a Game*, 197–98; Levitt, *The Battle That Forged Modern Baseball*, 72–74; Davies, "Along Comes the Players Association," 328–29. For the text of the 17 recommendations, accompanied by a full explanation of each, see David L. Fultz, "The Ball Players' Requests," *Baseball Magazine* 12 (January 1914), 81–85. For a contemporary analysis of the National Commission's actions, see David L. Fultz, "The Cincinnati Conference and Its Results," *Baseball Magazine* 12 (March 1914), 80–81.
  92. R.F. Potts, "The Great Cincinnati Meeting," *Baseball Magazine* 12 (March 1914), 37.
  93. "Club Owners Deaf to Players' Body: National Abrogates Past with Fraternity and Bars All Future Relations," *New York Times*, February 14, 1917, 6; Longert, "The Players' Fraternity," 45.
  94. *Weegham v. Killefer*, 215 F. 168, 170 (W.D. Mich. 1914).
  95. *Ibid.*, 173.
  96. Patrick E. Mears, "The Catcher, 'The Quick Lunch King' and Baseball's Reserve Clause: Major League Litigation in Grand Rapids," *Stereoscope* (Historical Society of the U.S. District Court for the Western District of Michigan) 1 (Winter 2003), 6; Banner, *The Baseball Trust*, 28–29.
  97. Deputy sheriffs served the papers on Johnson after he completed pitching the second inning of the Packers game against the Chicago Whales (or Chi-Feds) at Weeghman Park. Johnson was tagged for three earned runs and one unearned run in his two innings against the Whales. He was replaced by Dwight Stone who did not fare much better in an eventual 9–1 Chicago victory. "Tinker's Feds on Jump," *New York Tribune*, April 24, 1914, 9.
  98. Judge Foell also granted a second preliminary injunction which restrained Packers President C. C. Madison from inciting any current Reds to jump the team. Handy Andy, "Enjoins Johnson and K.C. Federals," *Chicago Tribune*, April 24, 1914, 15; "'Red' Pitcher Restrained," *New York Times*, April 24, 1914, 11; Levitt, *The Battle That Forged Modern Baseball*, 117.
  99. Authors Daniel Levitt and Sean Devaney argue that Foell's decision was of critical importance to the Federal League because players were ready to jump to the new league if the opinion had gone in its favor. Levitt, *The Battle that Forged Modern Baseball*, 125; Sean Devaney, *Before Wrigley Became Wrigley: The Inside Story of the First Years of the Cubs' Home Field* (New York: Sports Publishing, 2014), 132. For an excellent contemporary discussion of the case, see "A Surprising Decision; A Chicago Judge Makes a Unique Ruling," *Sporting Life*, June 13, 1914, 3.
  100. *Cincinnati Exhibition Co. v. Johnson*, 190 Ill. App. 630 (1914).
  101. Robert Peyton Wiggins, *The Federal League of Base Ball Clubs: The History of an Outlaw Major League, 1914–1915* (Jefferson, NC: McFarland, 2009), 76.
  102. *Cincinnati Exhibition Co. v. Marsans*, 216 F. 269 (E.D. Mo. 1914); Peter T. Toot, *Armando Marsans: A Cuban Pioneer in the Major Leagues* (Jefferson, NC: McFarland, 2004), 104–06.
  103. *Cincinnati Exhibition Co. v. Marsans*, 269.
  104. Toot, *Armando Marsans*, 107; Eric Enders, "Armando Marsáns," in *Deadball Stars of the National League*, 257; "St. Louis Federals Win Marsans Case," *New York Times*, August 20, 1915, 8.
  105. Toot, *Armando Marsans*, 145–49.
  106. *Am. League Baseball Club of Chicago v. Chase*, 149 N.Y.S. 6 (N.Y. Sup. Ct. 1914); Donald Dewey and Nicholas Acocella, *The Black Prince of Baseball: Hal Chase and the Mythology of Baseball* (Toronto: Sport Classic Books, 2004), 204–10; Levitt, *The Battle That Forged Modern Baseball*, 130–31.
  107. *Am. League Baseball Club of Chicago v. Chase*, 465.
  108. *Ibid.*, 459–60.
  109. Irwin, "A Historical Review of Litigation in Baseball," 290.
  110. Bill of Complaint, Federal League of Professional Baseball Clubs v. National League of Professional Baseball Clubs, Equity No. 373 (N.D. Ill. Jan. 5, 1915), available in 1915 Federal League Case Files, Document 18, Society for American Baseball Research, accessed October 19, 2014, http://sabr.org/research/1915-Federal-League-case-files. For an enlightening discussion of the Federal League's 92-page complaint, see Grow, *Baseball on Trial*, 65–68. For a contemporary account, see "The Famous Federal Suit," *Baseball Magazine* 14 (March 1915): 65–68.
  111. Transcript of Hearing, Federal League of Professional Baseball Clubs v. National League of Professional Baseball Clubs, Equity No. 373 (N.D. Ill. Jan. 20–23, 1915), available in 1915 Federal League Case Files, Document 119, Society for American Baseball Research, ac-

cessed October 19, 2014, http://sabr.org/research/1915-Federal-League-case-files.
112. On the three-man National Commission, National League president John Tener favored the NL's Pirates and American League president Ban Johnson voted for the AL's Browns, leaving the decision to Herrmann, the commission's chairman. Despite his position with the NL's Cincinnati Reds, Herrmann's vote resulted in a decision which ultimately favored the Browns. Despite his ownership of the NL's Cincinnati Reds, Dreyfuss's vote resulted in a decision which ultimately favored the Browns. For an insightful discussion of the possible motivations behind his action and the rift it caused between Dreyfuss and Herrmann, see Cook, *August "Garry" Herrmann*, 190–91.
113. Rick Huhn, *The Sizzler: George Sisler, Baseball's Forgotten Great* (Columbia: University of Missouri Press, 2013), 21–26, 45–47; Seymour and Mills, *Baseball: The Golden Age*, 259–61; Bill Lamberty, "George Sisler," in Jones, *Deadball Stars of the American League*, 796. For a contemporary account of the Sisler-Dreyfuss-Rickey imbroglio, see John J. Ward, "The Famous Sisler Case," *Baseball Magazine* 17 (October 1916), 33–37.
114. "Peace Seems to be Near for Organized Baseball; Agreement is Drafted," *Atlanta Constitution*, December 18, 1915, 12; Grow, *Baseball on Trial*, 104; Levitt, *The Battle that Forged Modern Baseball*, 230–31.
115. For an original typescript copy of the agreement reached on December 22, 1915, see "Cincinnati Peace Agreement," 1915 Federal League Lawsuit Case Files (document 120), Society for American Baseball Research, http://sabr.org/research/1915-Federal-League-case-files.
116. Grow, *Baseball on Trial*, 102–06; Levitt, *The Battle that Forged Modern Baseball*, 228–43; Burk, *Never Just A Game*, 208–09.
117. Grow, *Baseball on Trial*, 107; Levitt, *The Battle that Forged Modern Baseball*, 243.
118. Banner, *The Baseball Trust*, 61; Grow, *Baseball on Trial*, 110; Levitt, *The Battle That Forged Modern Baseball*, 245–46. For the complete typewritten transcript of the dismissal hearing, see Transcript of Proceedings, Federal League of Professional Baseball Clubs v. National League of Professional Baseball Clubs, Equity No. 373 (N.D. Ill. Feb. 7, 1916), available in 1915 Federal League Case Files, Document 121, Society for American Baseball Research, accessed October 19, 2014, http://sabr.org/research/1915-Federal-League-case-files.
119. I.E. Sanborn, "Roger May Sue New Cub Boss For Damages," *Chicago Tribune*, January 27, 1916, 15.
120. "Roger Settles With Cub Boss for $10,000 Sum," *Chicago Tribune*, March 5, 1916, B1.

121. Devaney, *Before Wrigley Became Wrigley*, 237–38.
122. Grow, *Baseball on Trial*, 114; Levitt, *The Battle that Forged Modern Baseball*, 255; "Ask Huge Damages of Ball Magnates," *New York Times*, March 30, 1916, 10.
123. Levitt, *The Battle that Forged Modern Baseball*, 255; Grow, *Baseball on Trial*, 121–34.
124. Robert F. Burk, *Marvin Miller: Baseball Revolutionary* (Urbana: University of Illinois Press, 2015), 3; Marvin Miller, *A Whole Different Ball Game: The Sport and Business of Baseball* (New York: Carol Publishing Group, 1991), 12.
125. Burk, *Marvin Miller*, 8–35.
126. Ibid., 46–57; Miller, *A Whole Different Ball Game*, 19–20.
127. Burk, *Marvin Miller*, 73–96.
128. Ibid., 70–71.
129. Norman L. Macht, *Connie Mack: The Turbulent and Triumphant Years, 1915-1931* (Lincoln: University of Nebraska Press, 2012), 156–58; David M. Jordan, *The A's: A Baseball History* (Jefferson, NC: McFarland, 2014), 34; Boxerman and Boxerman, *Ebbets to Veeck to Busch*, 48.
130. Cook, *August "Garry" Herrmann*, 226.
131. Henry D. Fetter, *Taking on the Yankees: Winning and Losing in the Business of Baseball, 1903-2003* (New York: W.W. Norton, 2003), 128–34.
132. Martin Donell Kohout, *Hal Chase: The Defiant Life and Turbulent Times of Baseball's Biggest Crook* (Jefferson, NC: McFarland, 2001), 191.
133. J.V. Fitzgerald, "Baseball Players Must Work or Fight, Baker Rules, Dooming National Sport," *Washington Post*, July 20, 1918, 8.
134. Patricia L. Bryan and Thomas Wolf, "On the Brink: Babe Ruth in Dennis Lehane's *The Given Day*," in *The Cooperstown Symposium on Baseball and American Culture, 2009-2010*, ed. William M. Simons (Jefferson, NC: McFarland, 2011), 44–45.
135. Jackie Robinson, with Alfred Duckett, *I Never Had It Made* (New York: G. P. Putnam's Sons, 1972), 15–16; David Falkner, *Great Time Coming: The Life of Jackie Robinson, From Baseball to Birmingham* (New York: Simon & Schuster, 1995), 16.
136. Arnold Rampersad, *Jackie Robinson: A Biography* (New York: Alfred A. Knopf, 1997), 36–82; Falkner, *Great Time Coming*, 49–64.
137. Jules Tygiel, *Baseball's Great Experiment: Jackie Robinson and His Legacy* (New York: Oxford University Press, 1983), 60; Dave Greenwald, "Alumnus Jackie Robinson Honored by Congress," UCLA Spotlight, February 1, 2005, http://spotlight.ucla.edu/alumni/jackie-robinson/.
138. Act of April 19, 1919, ch. 260, 1919 N.Y. Laws 865; Bevis, *Sunday Baseball*, 194; "Signs

Sunday Movie Bill: Sunday Baseball Measure Also Approved by Gov. Smith," *New York Times,* April 20, 1919, 10.

139. Bevis, *Sunday Baseball,* 174–94; Steve Steinberg and Lyle Spatz, *The Colonel and Hug: The Partnership that Transformed the New York Yankees* (Lincoln: University of Nebraska Press, 2015), 100.

140. Bevis, *Sunday Baseball,* 194; "Advent of Sunday Baseball Draws 60,000 Persons to Polo Grounds and Ebbets Field," *New York Times,* May 5, 1919, 14.

141. "Red Sox Trail in Hitting Carnival," *Boston Daily Globe,* July 14, 1919, 4; Ed Edmonds, "Cornering the Market: The Yankees and the Interplay of Labor and Antitrust Laws," in *Courting the Yankees: Legal Essays on the Bronx Bombers,* ed. Ettie Ward (Durham, NC: Carolina Academic Press, 2003), 310; Michael T. Lynch, Jr., *Harry Frazee, Ban Johnson and the Feud That Nearly Destroyed the American League* (Jefferson, NC: McFarland, 2008), 74–75; Sowell, *The Pitch That Killed,* 41 (describing discussion with Burt Whitman of the *Boston Herald*).

142. Lynch, *Harry Frazee,* 75; Kenneth D. Richard, "Remembering Carl Mays," *Baseball Research Journal* 30 (2001), 124.

143. The Yankees gave pitchers Allen "Rubberarm" Russell and Bob McGraw and $40,000 to Boston to acquire Mays. James C. O'Leary, "Yankees Get Mays in Red Sox Deal," *Boston Daily Globe,* July 31, 1919, 1 ("also a cash consideration, the amount of which Pres Frazee declined to state, but which is said to be about $25,000"); Lynch, *Harry Frazee,* 76; Sowell, *The Pitch That Killed,* 48.

144. Lynch, *Harry Frazee,* 78; Sowell, *The Pitch That Killed,* 50.

145. Lynch, *Harry Frazee,* 81; Sowell, *The Pitch That Killed,* 52–53; Bill Felber, *Under Pallor, Under Shadow: The 1920 American League Pennant Race That Rattled and Rebuilt Baseball* (Lincoln: University of Nebraska Press, 2011), 7.

146. *Am. League Baseball Club of New York v. Johnson,* 179 N.Y.S. 498 (Sup. Ct. 1919); Lynch, *Harry Frazee,* 94; Sowell, *The Pitch That Killed,* 56.

147. "American League Strife is Ended," *New York Times,* February 11, 1920, 18; Wiggins, *The Federal League of Base Ball Clubs,* 303; Burk, *Never Just a Game,* 227.

148. Edmonds, "Cornering the Market," 312–13.

149. Adrian Burgos, Jr., *Cuban Star: How One Negro League Owner Changed the Face of Baseball* (New York: Hill and Wang, 2011), 47.

150. Richard Bak, *Turkey Stearnes and the Detroit Stars: The Negro Leagues in Detroit, 1919–1933* (Detroit: Wayne State University Press, 1994), 67–68; Christopher Hauser, *The Negro Leagues Chronology: Events in Organized Black Baseball, 1920–1948* (Jefferson, NC: McFarland, 2006), 5; Leslie A. Heaphy, *The Negro Leagues: 1869–1960* (Jefferson, NC: McFarland, 2003), 41; Robert Peterson, *Only the Ball Was White* (Englewood Cliffs, NJ: Prentice Hall, 1970), 84.

151. Kohout, *Hal Chase,* 228–29; William F. Lamb, *Black Sox in the Courtroom: The Grand Jury, Criminal Trial and Civil Litigation* (Jefferson, NC: McFarland, 2013), 25.

152. Charles Fountain, *The Betrayal: The 1919 World Series and the Birth of Modern Baseball* (New York: Oxford University Press, 2015), 149–50; Brian McKenna, *Early Exits: The Premature Endings of Baseball Careers* (Lanham, MD: Scarecrow Press, 2007), 29.

153. Kohout, *Hal Chase,* 232–33; Lamb, *Black Sox in the Courtroom,* 26.

154. David Pietrusza, *Rothstein: The Life, Times, and Murder of the Criminal Genius Who Fixed the 1919 World Series* (New York: Carroll & Graf, 2003), 175.

155. Mark L. Armour and Daniel R. Levitt, *In Pursuit of Pennants: Baseball Operations from Deadball to Moneyball* (Lincoln: University of Nebraska Press, 2015), 41–43; Lyle Spatz and Steve Steinberg, *1921—The Yankees, the Giants, and the Battle for Baseball Supremacy in New York* (Lincoln: University of Nebraska Press, 2010), 20.

156. "Babe Ruth's Hits Are News: Home-Run King Denied Injunction Against His Portrayal in Films," *New York Times,* September 16, 1920, 4.

157. "Babe Ruth Loses Suit to Enjoin 'Outlaw' Film," *Chicago Daily Tribune,* September 16, 1920, 19; Patrick Trimble, "Babe Ruth: The Media Construction of a 1920's Sport Personality," *Colby Quarterly* 32 (March 1996), 50–51; Ken Sobol, *Babe Ruth & the American Dream* (New York: Ballantine, 1974), 121.

158. *Ruth v. Educ. Films,* 184 N.Y.S. 948 (App. Div. 1920) (mem.).

159. Trimble, "Babe Ruth," 50, 52; Marshall Smelser, *The Life That Ruth Built: A Biography* (New York: Quadrangle, 1975), 201.

160. Pietrusza, *Rothstein,* 178; Thorn, "Shoeless Joe, the Bambino, the Big Bankroll, and the Jazz Age," *Our Game* (blog).

161. Leigh Montville, *The Big Bam: The Life and Times of Babe Ruth* (New York: Doubleday, 2006), 118; Smelser, 201.

162. Trimble, "Babe Ruth," 53.

163. "Two Sox Confess; Eight Indicted; Inquiry Goes On," *Chicago Daily Tribune,* September 29, 1920, 1. For the text of Jackson's grand jury testimony, see Harvey Frommer, *Shoeless Joe and Ragtime Baseball* (Dallas, TX: Taylor Pub. Co., 1992), 191–215.

164. William F. Lamb, "The Black Sox Scandal," in *Scandal on the South Side: The 1919 Chicago White Sox*, ed. Jacob Pomrenke (Phoenix: Society for American Baseball Research, 2015), 303–04.
165. "Eight Fired by Comiskey; Wrecks Team," *Chicago Daily Tribune*, September 29, 1920, 1.
166. Lamb, "The Black Sox Scandal," 304; William Lamb, "Jury Nullification and the Not Guilty Verdicts in the Black Sox Case," *Baseball Research Journal* 44 (Fall 2015), 48.
167. Lamb, *Black Sox in the Courtroom*, 74.
168. Pietrusza, *Judge and Jury*, 169–72.

Chapter 4

1. David Quentin Voigt, *American Baseball: From the Commissioners to Continental Expansion* (Norman: University of Oklahoma Press, 1970), 139; "Something More than Mere Name to Organized Ball Now," *Sporting News*, January 20, 1921, 1.
2. Spink, *Judge Landis and Twenty-Five Years of Baseball*, 75.
3. "Major League Agreement of January 12, 1921," in *Professional Baseball in America: A Compilation of the Agreements and Rules which Define the Relations of Leagues, Clubs and Players* (Chicago: H.G. Adair, 1921), 8.
4. "We ... pledge ourselves loyally to support the Commissioner...; and we assure him that each of us will acquiesce in his decisions, even when we believe them mistaken, and that we will not discredit the sport by public criticism of him or of one another." "Pledge to Support the Commissioner," in *Professional Baseball in America*, 15; Pepper, *Philadelphia Lawyer*, 358.
5. *Conduct of Judge Kenesaw Mountain Landis: Hearings Before the House Comm. on the Judiciary*, 66th Cong. 3 (1921) (statement of Rep. Benjamin F. Welty).
6. Ross E. Davies, "The Sport of Courts: Baseball and the Law," *Baseball Research Journal* 38 (Fall 2009): 62–63.
7. Christy Walsh, *Adios to Ghosts!* (New York, 1937), 11–12; Montville, *The Big Bam*, 127–29; Robert W. Creamer, *Babe: The Legend Comes to Life* (New York: Simon and Schuster, 1974), 271–72; Kal Wagenheim, *Babe Ruth: His Life and Legend* (New York: Praeger, 1974), 82–83; Mark Ahrens, "Christy Walsh—Baseball's First Agent," *Books on Baseball* (blog), August 4, 2010, http://www.booksonbaseball.com [search "Walsh"].
8. Montville, *The Big Bam*, 129.
9. Craig Burley, "Free Benny Kauff (Part Two)," *The Hardball Times* (blog), April 19, 2004, http://www.hardballtimes.com [search "Kauff"].
10. Michael Santa Maria and James Costello, "Thrown Out Stealing," in *In the Shadows of the Diamond: Hard Times in the National Pastime* (Dubuque, IA: Elysian Fields Press, 1992), 159.
11. David Jones, "Benny Kauff," in Simon, *Deadball Stars of the National League*, 86; Wiggins, *The Federal League of Base Ball Clubs*, 326–27.
12. David Mandell, "Reuben Berman's Foul Ball," *National Pastime* 25 (2005), 106–07; Berman v. Nat'l Exhibition Co., No. 46447 (N.Y. Sup. Ct. 1923).
13. Peter Segroie, "Reuben's Ruling Helps You 'Have a Ball,'" *Baseball Research Journal* 20 (1991), 85.
14. Lamb, *Black Sox in the Courtroom*, 106.
15. *Ibid.*, 111.
16. "Jury Frees Baseball Men; All Black Sox Acquitted on Single Ballot," *Chicago Daily Tribune*, August 3, 1921, 1; Lamb, *Black Sox in the Courtroom*, 141–42.
17. In his statement to the press, Landis said: "Regardless of the verdict of juries, no player that throws a ball game, no player that undertakes or promises to throw a ball game, no player that sits in a conference with a bunch of crooked ballplayers and gamblers where the ways and means of throwing a game are discussed and does not promptly tell his club about it, will ever play professional baseball." "Baseball Leaders Won't Let White Sox Return to the Game," *New York Times*, August 4, 1921, 1; "Crooks Scared Out of Baseball, Says M'Donald," *Chicago Daily Tribune*, August 4, 1921, 21.
18. Montville, *The Big Bam*, 144–45; Smelser, *The Life That Ruth Built*, 227–31.
19. Seymour and Mills, *Baseball: The Golden Age*, 392; Smelser, *The Life That Ruth Built*, 229.
20. Charles A. Palmer, "The Czar's Court: The Commissioner of Baseball and the New York Yankees," in Ward, *Courting the Yankees*, 245.
21. Lamb, *Black Sox in the Courtroom*, 151; "Hap Felsch Sues Sox for Back Pay," *Chicago Tribune*, April 27, 1922, 17. The conspiracy and World Series bonus claims are dismissed early in the proceedings, but the claim of injury to reputation is allowed to stand. "Suits by Risberg and Felsch Ruled Out in Wisconsin Court," *New York Times*, May 13, 1923, S3; Lamb, *Black Sox in the Courtroom*, 162. Although the suits are ultimately unsuccessful, Risberg's son will later tell of Swede's claims that he made more money during his subsequent 11-year "outlaw" ballplaying career than he ever had as a member of Comiskey's White Sox. Jacob Pomrenke, "Swede Risberg: More Educated Than You Think," *SABR Black Sox Scandal Research Committee*

Newsletter 4 (June 2012), 4. For more information about Risberg's post–Black Sox career, see Alan Muchlinski, *After The Black Sox: The Swede Risberg Story* (Bloomington, IN: AuthorHouse, 2005).

22. Lamb, *Black Sox in the Courtroom*, 152; "Two More Players Sue the White Sox," *New York Times*, May 13, 1922, 11.

23. For detailed discussions of the Supreme Court's *Federal Baseball* decision, see Grow, *Baseball on Trial*, 188–218; Banner, *The Baseball Trust*, 63–89; Gary Hailey, "The Anatomy of a Murder: Federal League and the Courts," *National Pastime* 4 (1985), 62–73.

24. E.g., J. Gordon Hylton, "Why Baseball's Antitrust Exemption Still Survives," *Marquette Sports Law Journal* 9 (1999), 395; Dickson, *The Dickson Baseball Dictionary*, 3rd ed., 21; Abrams, *Legal Bases*, 58–60.

25. *Fed. Baseball Club of Balt., Inc. v. Nat'l League of Prof'l Baseball Clubs*, 259 U.S. 200, 209 (1922).

26. Pepper, *Philadelphia Lawyer*, 59.

27. Francis C. Richter, "Casual Comment," *Sporting News*, June 8, 1922, 4.

28. Act of July 13, 1921, 1921 Ill. Laws 400.

29. Lamb, "Jury Nullification and the Not Guilty Verdicts in the Black Sox Case," 48; Lamb, *Black Sox in the Courtroom*, 102.

30. William L. Doak, Fielder's Glove. U.S. Patent 1,426,824, filed April 18, 1921, issued August 22, 1922.

31. Gutman, *Banana Bats and Ding-Dong Balls*, 201; Kelsey Campbell-Dollaghan, "The Forgotten History of Baseball's Most Iconic Objects," *Gizmodo* (blog).

32. Steve Steinberg, "William Leopold Doak," in Simon, *Deadball Stars of the National League*, 358–60.

33. "Ball Players Seek to Secure Reforms," *New York Times*, October 12, 1922, 30.

34. Seymour and Mills, *Baseball: The Golden Age*, 355.

35. Davies, "Along Comes the Players Association," 333.

36. Hauser, *The Negro Leagues Chronology*, 15; Roger A. Bruns, *Negro Leagues Baseball* (Santa Barbara, CA: Greenwood, 2012), 27; Hogan, *Shades of Glory*, 165–66.

37. Burgos Jr., *Cuban Star*, 49.

38. Larry Lester, *Baseball's First Colored World Series: The 1924 Meeting of the Hilldale Giants and Kansas City Monarchs* (Jefferson, NC: McFarland, 2006), 29–33; Hogan, *Shades of Glory*, 173–78.

39. "'Babe' Ruth Is Sued by Girl for $50,000," *New York Times*, March 14, 1923, 4; "Girl to Accuse Babe Ruth Today," *New York Times*, March 15, 1923, 40.

40. Michael T. Flannery, "Affairs of the Heart," in Ward, *Courting the Yankees*, 187; Montville, *The Big Bam*, 178; Marshall Smelser, *The Life That Ruth Built: A Biography* (New York: Quadrangle/New York Times Book Co., 1975), 269 ("The girl appeared in court on March 16 and testified that Ruth had promised marriage, was guilty of statutory rape, and had fathered her child."); Wagenheim, *Babe Ruth: His Life and Legend*, 121.

41. "Withdraws Her Case Against 'Babe' Ruth," *Boston Daily Globe*, April 27, 1923, 1; Montville, *The Big Bam*, 178; Smelser, *The Life That Ruth Built*, 270 ("Bushel was not surprised. He had talked with Dolores Dixon who admitted the suit was a scheme to extort money from Ruth. And it turned out that 'Dolores Dixon' was a false name assumed by a girl never heard of before or since."). Although the final resolution may be seen as a favorable outcome for Ruth, one commentator noted of the Dixon affair that "despite Ruth's legendary reputation for carousing and womanizing, there was really only one paternity suit that amounted to any scandal." Flannery, "Affairs of the Heart," 187.

42. James E. Johnstone, Baseball Mask. U.S. Patent 1,449,183, filed July 23, 1921, issued March 20, 1923.

43. David W. Anderson, "Jim Johnstone," SABR Baseball Biography Project, accessed March 23, 2016, http://sabr.org/bioproj/person/e51cb9e8.

44. Rosciam, "The Evolution of Catcher's Equipment," 105.

45. Lamb, *Black Sox in the Courtroom*, 186.

46. "Black Sox Star's Varied Testimony Brings His Arrest," *Washington Post*, February 15, 1924, S1.

47. Lamb, *Black Sox in the Courtroom*, 189–90. Judge Gregory signed a formal order nullifying the jury verdict on May 27, 1924, citing a lack of credible evidence to support the jury's answers to the interrogatories. The order dismissed Jackson's complaint with prejudice. *Ibid.*, 190.

48. *Ibid.*, 191–92; "Jackson Loses in High Court to White Sox," *Chicago Tribune*, October 21, 1925, 29.

49. The real fan in the White House was First Lady Grace Coolidge. According to Senators owner Clark Griffith, Grace kept score of games she attended, apparently relying on experience she gained as official scorer of her college's games. Fred Stein, *A History of the Baseball Fan* (Jefferson, NC: McFarland, 2005), 167. Bucky Harris, manager of the Senators, called her "the most rabid baseball fan I ever knew in the White House," while baseball historian David Pietrusza referred to her as "the first lady of baseball." Ardell, *Breaking into Baseball*, 35; David Pietrusza, "Grace Coolidge—The First

Lady of Baseball," *Elysian Fields Quarterly* 12, no. 2 (1993), 36–39.

50. Frederic J. Frommer, *You Gotta Have Heart: A History of Washington Baseball from 1859 to the 2012 National League East Champions* (Lanham, MD: Taylor Trade Publishing, 2013), 66; Reed Browning, *Baseball's Greatest Season, 1924* (Amherst: University of Massachusetts Press, 2003), 133.

51. John Milton Cooper, Jr., *Woodrow Wilson: A Biography* (New York: Alfred A. Knopf, 2009), 258.

52. Larry Lester, *Rube Foster in His Time: On the Field and in the Papers with Black Baseball's Greatest Visionary* (Jefferson, NC: McFarland, 2012), 120–21.

53. Bowie Kuhn, *Hardball: The Education of a Baseball Commissioner* (New York: Times Books, 1987), 14.

54. Ibid., 16–17. Nathan Miller, a former governor of New York, started Willkie Farr's baseball practice in 1933, providing advice to National League President Ford Frick regarding broadcasting issues. Willkie Farr & Gallagher LLP, Firm History, accessed July 31, 2015, http://www.willkie.com/about-us/firm-history.

55. Joseph Durso, "Kuhn Is Voted Out as Baseball Commissioner," *New York Times*, November 2, 1982, A1; Murray Chass, "Kuhn Steps Aside to Put an End to Acrimony," *New York Times*, August 4, 1983, A1.

56. Irving Vaughan, "Cub Moguls Sing Praises in Ears of Mr. McCarthy," *Chicago Daily Tribune*, December 4, 1926, 21; "New Cubs Secretary," *Chicago Daily Tribune*, December 14, 1926, 23.

57. Jack Bales, "Baseball's First Bill Veeck," *Baseball Research Journal* 42 (Fall 2013), 11–12.

58. David Fletcher and George Castle, "Margaret Donahue—Pioneering Female Cubs Executive Left Her Mark on the '29 Cubs and MLB," in *Winning on the North Side: The 1929 Chicago Cubs*, ed. Gregory H. Wolf (Phoenix: Society for American Baseball Research, 2015), 206; John Owens, "Female Cubs Exec Changed the Ballgame," *Chicago Tribune*, July 22, 2013, 1:6; "For the Record," *Sports Illustrated*, February 13, 1978, 69.

59. *Commonwealth v. Am. Baseball Club of Phila.*, 138 A. 487, 499 (Pa. 1927).

60. Macht, *Connie Mack: The Turbulent and Triumphant Years, 1915–1931*, 423–26; Bevis, *Sunday Baseball*, 205; Lucas, "The Unholy Experiment," 167–68.

61. William H. Whitmore, *The Colonial Laws of Massachusetts* (Boston: Rockwell and Churchill, 1890), 1: 132–34.

62. Bevis, *Sunday Baseball*, 226; Albert J. Menendez, "The Battle for Sunday Baseball," *Liberty* (September–October 2007), http:// www.libertymagazine.org/article/the-battle-for-sunday-baseball.

63. Bevis, *Sunday Baseball*, 237. Two of the original 12 requirements concerning limits on concessions and ticket prices were struck before the final vote. William E. Brown, Jr., "Sunday Baseball Comes to Boston," *National Pastime* 14 (1994), 85.

64. The Unitarian Church of the Disciples at 60 Peterborough Street was within the proscribed thousand feet of Fenway Park. The Red Sox were forced to play Sunday games at Braves Field until the ordinance was amended in May 1932. Bevis, *Sunday Baseball*, 240–44.

65. "Two Killed, 62 Hurt in Yankee Stadium as Rain Stampedes Baseball Crowd; Victims Are Crushed at Bleacher Exit," *New York Times*, May 20, 1929, 1.

66. "Clears Ball Club in Stadium Deaths," *New York Times*, May 21, 1929, 30.

67. Tom Pettey, "Ruth's Failure to Hit Homer Leads to Suit," *Chicago Tribune*, February 11, 1932, 23.

68. "Verdict Is Set Aside in Stadium Suits," *New York Times*, February 17, 1932, 17.

69. Gorman and Weeks, *Death at the Ballpark*, 180–81.

70. Robert M. Jarvis, "And Behind the Plate … Muddy Ruel of the U.S. Supreme Court," *Journal of Supreme Court History* 36 (2011): 1, 4.

71. Charles A. Poekel, Jr., "Babe Ruth vs. Baby Ruth: The Quest for a Candy Bar," in *The Cooperstown Symposium on Baseball and American Culture, 2009–2010*, ed. William M. Simons (Jefferson, NC: McFarland, 2011), 225–26.

72. *Curtiss Candy Co. v. George H. Ruth Candy Co.*, 1930 WL 23279, 4 U.S.P.Q. 103 (Com'r Pat. & Trademarks Feb. 11, 1930).

73. *George H. Ruth Candy Co. v. Curtiss Candy Co.*, 49 F.2d 1033 (C.C.P.A. 1931); Andrew F. Smith, *Encyclopedia of Junk Food and Fast Food* (Westport, CT: Greenwood Press, 2006), 17.

74. William E. Brandt, "Babe Ruth Accepts $160,000 for 2 Years," *New York Times*, March 9, 1930, 161; Montville, *The Big Bam*, 299–301; Smelser, *The Life That Ruth Built*, 410–14.

75. Creamer, *Babe: The Legend Comes to Life*, 350–51. In 1931, Ruth led the American League in home runs with 46, slugging at .700, OPS at 1.195, walks with 128, and had a batting average of .373, while America suffered through another year of the Great Depression, so he was probably correct in his assessment.

76. Marilyn Cohen, *No Girls in the Clubhouse: The Exclusion of Women from Baseball* (Jefferson, NC: McFarland, 2009), 38–39.

77. Adam Doster, "The Myth of Jackie Mitchell, the Girl Who Struck Out Ruth and Gehrig," *The Daily Beast*, May 18, 2013, http://

www.thedailybeast.com [search "jackie mitchell"]; Ardell, *Breaking into Baseball*, 109.
78. Berlage, *Women in Baseball*, 74.
79. Pietrusza, *Judge and Jury*, 374; Ardell, *Breaking into Baseball*, 109; Cohen, *No Girls in the Clubhouse*, 39.
80. Berlage, *Women in Baseball*, 76–77; Cohen, *No Girls in the Clubhouse*, 40.
81. *Milwaukee American Association v. Landis*, 49 F.2d 298 (N.D. Ill. 1931); Pietrusza, *Judge and Jury*, 349–50.
82. *Milwaukee American Association v. Landis*, 299. One commentator has noted that "[t]his favorable ruling is credited with empowering future commissioners of baseball with generous internal authority over the organization." Irwin, "A Historical Review of Litigation in Baseball," 293.
83. *State v. Reed*, 44 S.W.2d 31, 32 (Mo. 1931); Robert M. Jarvis, "Babe Ruth as Legal Hero," *Florida State University Law Review* 22 (1995), 888n12 (providing cost of Ruth's Home Run candy bar).
84. *Hornsby v. Comm'r*, 26 B.T.A. 591, 592–93 (1932).
85. *Ibid.*, 593.
86. John Theodore, *Baseball's Natural: The Story of Eddie Waitkus* (Carbondale, IL: Southern Illinois University Press, 2002), 43–44.
87. "Letter Solves the Shooting of Billy Jurges," *Chicago Tribune*, July 7, 1932, 1.
88. Paul Geisler, Jr., "Billy Jurges," SABR Baseball Biography Project, accessed March 24, 2016, http://sabr.org/bioproj/person/aada6293.
89. "Girl Who Shot Cubs' Player Goes Free," *Chicago Tribune*, July 16, 1932, 3.
90. Geisler, "Billy Jurges."
91. As the result of a temporary restraining order preventing city police from making any arrests, the Athletics had faced off against the Chicago White Sox in a test game on Sunday, August 22, 1926, with the Philadelphia squad winning 3–2 behind the pitching of Lefty Grove. However, no additional Sunday games were played under the temporary injunction and the case eventually found its way to the Philadelphia Supreme Court which ruled in 1927 against the playing of professional baseball on Sunday (see entry for June 25, 1927).
92. W. Harrison Daniel, *Jimmie Foxx: The Life and Times of a Baseball Hall of Famer, 1907–1967* (Jefferson, NC: McFarland, 1996), 71; Bob Warrington, "The Fight for Sunday Baseball in Philadelphia," *Baseball History Blog*, Philadelphia Athletics Historical Society, July 30, 2001, http://philadelphiaathletics.org/the-fight-for-sunday-baseball-in-philadelphia/. Even though the National League allowed Sunday baseball as a result of its merger with the American Association in 1892, local laws prohibited most teams from playing Sunday games for many years, with the state of Pennsylvania the last holdout. Morris, *A Game of Inches: The Game on the Field*, 344.
93. An Act Relating to Baseball and Football on Sunday, No. 49, 1933 Pa. Laws 74.
94. The ballots used in local referenda during the statewide November election asked: "Do you favor the conduct, staging and playing of baseball and football games ... between the hours of two and six p.m. on Sunday?" Professional football did not waste any time in taking advantage of Philadelphia's vote in support of Sunday commercial sporting events; on November 12, 1933, 17,850 fans at the Baker Bowl watched the Chicago Bears and Philadelphia Eagles battle to a 3–3 tie. Lucas, "The Unholy Experiment," 174.
95. Other "judges" in major league baseball include Walter "Judge" McCredie, a right fielder who played 56 games for the Brooklyn Superbas in 1903; Judge Nagle, a pitcher who played a total of five games for the Pirates and Red Sox in 1911; Emil "Judge" Fuchs, owner of the Boston Braves from 1923 to 1935, who gained the title of judge during an interim appointment as a police magistrate in New York; and Hall of Famer Frank "The Judge" Robinson, who gained his nickname as the arbiter of the Orioles' kangaroo court in the late 1960s. Maxwell Kates, "Frank Robinson," SABR Baseball Biography Project, accessed March 23, 2016, http://sabr.org/bioproj/person/c3ac5482.
96. Joseph Wancho, "Joe Judge," SABR Baseball Biography Project, accessed March 23, 2016, http://sabr.org/bioproj/person/e7eab9b6.
97. Douglass Wallop, *The Year the Yankees Lost the Pennant: A Novel* (New York: Norton, 1954).
98. Mark Gauvreau Judge, *Damn Senators: My Grandfather and the Story of Washington's Only World Series Championship* (San Francisco: Encounter Books, 2003), 149–50.
99. Pietrusza, *Judge and Jury*, 375–77; Hank Utley and Josh Davlin, "Alabama Pitts," SABR Baseball Biography Project, accessed March 23, 2016, http://sabr.org/bioproj/person/d7db6951. Pitts was 19 at the time of his conviction for stealing $72.50. He served five-and-a-half years before his parole. McKenna, *Early Exits*, 72–73.
100. Gary Cieradkowski, *The League of Outsider Baseball: An Illustrated History of Baseball's Forgotten Heroes* (New York: Touchstone, 2015), 110.
101. "Alabama Pitts," Baseball-Reference.com, accessed June 2, 2015, http://www.baseball-reference.com.
102. *Hanna Manufacturing Co. v. Hillerich & Bradsby Co.*, 78 F.2d 763, 763 (1935).
103. *Ibid.*, 765.

104. *Ibid.*, 767.
105. *Ibid.*, 768; Robert F. Krause, "Unfair Trade—Right of Privacy—Right of Manufacturer Who Has Contracted for Use of Celebrity's Name to Injunction Against Competitor Using Such Name," *Michigan Law Review* 34 (1936): 588.
106. Spink, *Judge Landis and Twenty-Five Years of Baseball*, 226.
107. Edward Burns, "Landis Awards Pitcher Feller to Indians," *Chicago Tribune*, December 11, 1936, 33 ("Commissioner K.M. Landis decided in 1,650 polysyllabic words that Bob Feller, the boy wonder pitcher, is to go right on striking 'em out in behalf of the Cleveland Indians."); Pietrusza, *Judge and Jury*, 356–58.
108. John Sickels, *Bob Feller: Ace of the Greatest Generation* (Dulles, VA: Brassey's, 2004), 50.
109. *Ibid.*, 53; Pietrusza, *Judge and Jury*, 354.
110. Pietrusza, *Judge and Jury*, 361–67. Contemporary news accounts list the number of players as 100. "Breadon Accepts Edict," *New York Times*, March 27, 1938, 63; "Cardinals' Farms Rapped by Landis," *New York Times*, March 24, 1938, 28; "Landis Flays Cardinals, Frees 100 Players," *Washington Post*, March 24, 1938, 27. At least one set of commentators felt that Landis's actions in support of players he believed to be "ill-used" by the farm system regime was a "rearguard" one at best and that, taken together, they actually equated to "defeat on the principal issue of his twenty-four-year administration." Seymour and Mills, *Baseball: The Golden Age*, 420.
111. "Landis Flays Cardinals, Frees 100 Players."
112. Sidney Jacobson, *Pete Reiser: The Rough-and-Tumble Career of the Perfect Ballplayer* (Jefferson, NC: McFarland, 2004).
113. For more information about Giamatti and selections from his writings, see Robert P. Moncreiff, *Bart Giamatti: A Profile* (New Haven: Yale University Press, 2007); A. Bartlett Giamatti, *A Great and Glorious Game: Baseball Writings of A. Bartlett Giamatti*, ed. Kenneth S. Robson (Chapel Hill, NC: Algonquin Books, 1998). For a profile of Giamatti upon his elevation to the commissioner's position, see Frank Deford, "A Gentleman and a Scholar," *Sports Illustrated*, April 17, 1989, 86–100.
114. James R. Walker, *Crack of the Bat: A History of Baseball on the Radio* (Lincoln: University of Nebraska Press, 2015), 163–65; Ronald T. Waldo, *Pennant Hopes Dashed by the Homer in the Gloamin': The Story of How the 1938 Pittsburgh Pirates Blew the National League Pennant* (Jefferson, NC: McFarland, 2013), 157–58.
115. *Pittsburgh Athletic Co. v. KQV Broad. Co.*, 24 F. Supp. 490, 492 (W.D. Pa. 1938); Robert Alan Garrett and Philip R. Hochberg, "Sports Broadcasting and the Law," *Indiana Law Journal* 59 (1984), 158.
116. *Ibid.*
117. Marjori Bennett, Baseball Centennial, 1839–1939. Copyright G 31040, issued November 28, 1938. Copyright Office, Library of Congress, *Catalog of Copyright Entries, Part 4*, vol. 33, new series (Washington, DC: Govt. Printing Office, 1939), 179.
118. Jim Gates, "Patch Puzzle—Designer of Baseball Centennial Logo A Lost Figure in History," *Memories and Dreams* 36 (Summer 2014): 22; Todd Radom, "In 1939, Every MLB Team Wore This Logo," *Radom Thoughts: A Blog*, April 2, 2014, http://toddradom.com/in-1939-every-mlb-team-wore-this-logo.
119. The presidents of the Dodgers, Giants, and Yankees—Stephen McKeever, Horace Stoneham, and Jacob Ruppert, respectively—had signed a five-year pact in 1932 in which they agreed to refrain from broadcasting their teams' games. Once it ended after the 1938 season, current Dodger president Larry MacPhail refused to renew the agreement and, on December 6, 1938, he announced that the team would broadcast all of its 1939 games over radio station WOR. McKelvey, *The MacPhails*, 32–33; "Dodger Baseball to Be Broadcast," *New York Times*, December 7, 1938, 29; "$75,000 Lures Dodgers to Radio, Giants and Yankees Due to Follow," *Boston Globe*, December 7, 1938, 20.
120. Chuck Hildebrandt, "Here is the Actual 1939 Contract that Ended the Baseball Broadcast Moratorium for Good," SABRMedia Blog, November 24, 2015, http://sabrmedia.org [search "1939 contract"].
121. Corcoran, *Induction Day at Cooperstown*, 31.
122. "855 Baseball Centennial Stamps—First Day Covers," 1939Baseballwww, accessed March 23, 2016, http://www.1939baseball.com/first_day_of_issue.html.
123. Robert A. Moss, "Generations: Baseball on U.S. Postage Stamps," *American Philatelist* 127 (2013), 930; Jim Reisler, *A Great Day in Cooperstown: The Improbable Birth of Baseball's Hall of Fame* (New York: Carroll & Graf, 2006), 18–19.
124. "Landis Lays Down Law for Farms, Working Agreements; Detroit Loses Title to 91 Players, Must Pay 15 Others," *Sporting News*, January 18, 1940, 1; Pietrusza, *Judge and Jury*, 367–64. Detroit controlled both Beaumont and Fort Worth in the Texas League and Alexandria and Lake Charles in the Evangeline League. Gene Elston, *A Stitch in Time: A Baseball Chronology*, 3rd ed. (Houston: Halcyon Press, 2006), 11.
125. "Landis Declares Ninety-One Tigers Free Agents," *Detroit News*, January 16, 1940,

reprinted in Sullivan, *Middle Innings*, 178–79; Frederick G. Lieb, *The Detroit Tigers* (New York: G.P. Putnam's Sons, 1946), 241; Spink, *Judge Landis and Twenty-Five Years of Baseball*, 237–38.

126. "Jack Zeller Takes Full Blame for Detroit's Minor Loop Woe," *Los Angeles Times*, January 16, 1940, A9; Pietrusza, *Judge and Jury*, 367.

127. Lieb, *The Detroit Tigers*, 241.

128. Norman L. Macht, *The Grand Old Man of Baseball: Connie Mack in His Final Years, 1932-1956* (Lincoln: University of Nebraska Press, 2015), 237.

129. "Lou Gehrig Files Million-Dollar Suit," *Washington Post*, September 10, 1940, 17; William Juliano, "Libeling Lou: Iron Horse Sues to Restore His Name 90 Years Ago Today," *The Captain's Blog*, http://www.captainsblog.info [search "libel"].

130. Grantland Rice, "Lou Gehrig Denies His Disease Is Contagious; Says People Run From Him: Files Suit Against Paper for a Million Dollars," *Atlanta Constitution*, August 25, 1940, 3B.

131. Jonathan Eig, *Luckiest Man: The Life and Death of Lou Gehrig* (New York: Simon & Schuster, 2005), 346–48.

132. Henry W. Thomas, *Walter Johnson, Baseball's Big Train* (Washington, DC: Phenom Press, 1995), 336–39; "Byron Reelected By 6,000 Votes Over 'Big Train,'" *Washington Post*, November 6, 1940, 1.

133. Maryland 6th Congressional District, Western Maryland Historical Library, accessed July 14, 2015, http://www.whilbr.org/itemdetail.aspx?idEntry=6447.

134. Thomas, *Walter Johnson*, 339.

135. *Our National Pastime in Our National Archives*, 22; Richard Goldstein, *Spartan Seasons: How Baseball Survived the Second World War* (New York: Macmillan, 1980), 19. Although Landis's handwritten note is usually credited for prompting Roosevelt's Green Light Letter, others have argued that "Roosevelt's letter was a coup engineered behind the scenes by two astute baseball lobbyists," Clark Griffith, owner of the Washington Senators, and Robert E. Hannegan, postmaster general and chairman of the Democratic National Committee. William B. Mead, *Even the Browns* (Chicago: Contemporary Books, 1978), 35–38.

136. Goldstein, *Spartan Seasons*, 20.

137. "Baseball Policy Rapped," *New York Times*, February 3, 1943, 25; Chris Lamb, *Conspiracy of Silence: Sportswriters and the Long Campaign to Desegregate Baseball* (Lincoln: University of Nebraska Press, 2012), 105.

138. "Keep Going! Landis Tells Wartime Baseball; Game Will Ask No U.S. Favors to Stay Alive," *Chicago Tribune*, February 8, 1943, 19; Pietrusza, *Judge and Jury*, 436.

139. Jules Tygiel, "The Court-Martial of Jackie Robinson," *American Heritage* 35 (August/September 1984): 34–39; Rampersad, *Jackie Robinson: A Biography*, 102–09.

Chapter 5

1. Jerome Holtzman, *The Commissioners: Baseball's Midlife Crisis* (New York: Total Sports, 1998), 45; William Marshall, *Baseball's Pivotal Era, 1945-1951* (Lexington: University Press of Kentucky, 1999), 17–22.

2. Holtzman, *The Commissioners*, 45–46.

3. Andrew R. Dodge and Betty K. Koed, eds., *Biographical Directory of the United States Congress, 1774-2005* (Washington, DC: United States Printing Office, 2005), 805; Marshall, *Baseball's Pivotal Era, 1945-1951*, 41–42.

4. 91 Cong. Rec. 3904 (1945); Harry S. McAlpin, "Bill Asks Probe of Ball Jim Crow," *Atlanta Daily World*, April 27, 1945, 1; Lamb, *Conspiracy of Silence*, 244–45; Heaphy, *The Negro Leagues, 1869-1960*, 187.

5. See, e.g., Alan Schaffer, *Vito Marcantonio, Radical in Congress* (Syracuse, NY: Syracuse University Press, 1966), 151 ("Since not a single Negro was then under contract to any of the sixteen clubs in question, it is safe to assume that Marcantino was more interested in frightening organized baseball into action than he was in any inquiry."); James Edmund Boyack, "Marcantonio Hits Major Leagues Ban," *Pittsburgh Courier*, April 28, 1945, 4 ("Baseball is not the property of an individual or group of individuals. It is the heritage of all the people, and rightfully belongs to all the people….").

6. Chris Lamb, *Blackout: The Untold Story of Jackie Robinson's First Spring Training* (Lincoln: University of Nebraska Press, 2004), 8; John Thorn and Jules Tygiel, "Jackie Robinson's Signing: The Real, Untold Story," *National Pastime* 10 (1990): 7–12.

7. Lowenfish, *Branch Rickey: Baseball's Ferocious Gentleman*, 382–83; Hogan, *Shades of Glory*, 343–45.

8. Rebecca S. Kraus, *Minor League Baseball: Community Building Through Hometown Sports* (New York: Haworth Press, 2003), 17; Neil J. Sullivan, *The Dodgers Move West* (New York: Oxford University Press, 1987), 90.

9. John Drebinger, "Big League Status Is Denied to Coast," *New York Times*, December 12, 1945, 37.

10. Carl T. Felker, "Coast Writers Split on Big League Rating; Most View Step-Up as Premature," *Sporting News*, December 13, 1945, 2.

11. Robert F. Burk, *Much More than a Game: Players, Owners, & American Baseball Since 1921* (Chapel Hill: University of North Carolina Press, 2001), 88; Charles P. Korr, *The*

End of Baseball As We Knew It: The Players Union, 1960–1981 (Urbana: University of Illinois Press, 2002), 15; Lowenfish, *The Imperfect Diamond*, 141; "Seeks To Organize Baseball Players," *New York Times*, April 18, 1946, 32.

12. "Yank Star Sought For Mexican Loop," *New York Times*, May 4, 1946, 18.

13. *Am. League Baseball Club of New York v. Pasquel*, 63 N.Y.S.2d 537 (Sup. Ct. 1946); "Mexican Case Won By Yanks Says Judge," *Christian Science Monitor*, May 21, 1946, 14.

14. *Brooklyn Nat'l League Baseball Club v. Pasquel*, 66 F. Supp. 117, 118–19 (E.D. Mo. 1946); G. Richard McKelvey, *Mexican Raiders in the Major Leagues: The Pasquel Brothers vs. Organized Baseball, 1946* (Jefferson, NC: McFarland, 2006), 74–75.

15. *Brooklyn Nat'l League Baseball Club v. Pasquel*, 121.

16. After meeting with player representatives in late July, the owners promised a minimum salary of $5,500, but they later reduced it to $5,000. Lowenfish, *The Imperfect Diamond*, 151.

17. Burk, *Much More than a Game*, 89–93; Helyar, *Lords of the Realm*, 11; Korr, *The End of Baseball As We Knew It*, 15–17; John Virtue, *South of the Color Barrier: How Jorge Pasquel and the Mexican League Pushed Baseball Toward Racial Integration* (Jefferson, NC: McFarland, 2008), 161; McKelvey, *The MacPhails*, 71–72; "Majors Meet All Player Demands And Set Up New Executive Council," *New York Times*, August 29, 1946, 31. In addition to addressing issues that would assuage the players, the Steering Committee warned owners that "[i]n the well-considered opinion of counsel for both Major Leagues counsel, the present reserve clause could not be enforced in an equity court in a suit for specific performance, nor as the basis for a restraining order to prevent a player from playing elsewhere, or to prevent outsiders from inducing a player to breach his contract." It then proposed that two new clauses be added to the standard player contract to address concerns regarding a fixed salary for the reserved year and the timing of a club's exercise of its rights. Major League Steering Committee, *Report for Submission to the National and American Leagues at their Meetings in Chicago*, August 27, 1946, Society for American Baseball Research, Business of Baseball Committee, http://research.sabr.org/business (follow link to documents).

18. Because the details of Berg's work for the OSS, predecessor to the CIA, was classified, they were omitted from the citation. Instead, it merely stated that "[i]n a position of responsibility in the European Theater, he [Berg] exhibited analytical abilities and a keen planning mind. He inspired both respect and constant high level of endeavor on the part of his subordinates, which enabled his section to produces studies and analyses vital to the mounting of American operations." Nicholas Dawidoff, *The Catcher Was A Spy: The Mysterious Life of Moe Berg* (New York: Pantheon Books, 1994), 233. Although a few sources describe the award as the Medal of Merit, see, e.g., Dave Anderson, "Mysterious Moe is De-Classified," *New York Times*, January 28, 1975, 21, Truman's creation of the Medal of Freedom by executive order in 1945 supports the majority of sources which identify it as the award proffered by the president to Berg. Exec. Order No. 9586, 10 Fed. Reg. 8523 (July 10, 1945).

19. Louis Kaufman, Barbara Fitzgerald, and Tom Sewell, *Moe Berg: Athlete, Scholar, Spy* (Boston: Little, Brown, 1974), 233.

20. Gary Bedingfield, "Moe Berg," *Baseball in Wartime*, last updated January 22, 2007, http://www.baseballinwartime.com [link to player biographies]; Josh Renaud, "Learn About Baseball Players Who Have Won Medal of Freedom," *St. Louis Post-Dispatch*, March 30, 2011, http://www.stltoday.com/sports/baseball/professional/learn-about-baseball-players-who-have-won-medal-of-freedom/html_53efc5fc-330d-11e0-8777-0017a44a78c22.html.

21. "Advertising News and Notes," *New York Times*, March 1, 1947, 26; Robert J. Newman, "Advertising and the Dodgers in 1947," in *The Team That Forever Changed Baseball and America: The 1947 Brooklyn Dodgers*, ed. Lyle Spatz (Lincoln: University of Nebraska Press; Phoenix: Society for American Baseball Research, 2012), 303; McCue, *Mover and Shaker*, 55.

22. "Television for Dodger Games," *New York Times*, November 8, 1946, 33; "Home Games of Dodgers to Be Televised Next Year," *Sporting News*, November 13, 1946, 10.

23. McCue, *Mover and Shaker*, 55.

24. Louis Effrat, "Chandler Bars Durocher for 1947 Baseball Season," *New York Times*, April 10, 1947, 1. Chandler also suspends coach Charlie Dressen thirty days for signing with the Yankees while still under contract with the Dodgers; fines both the Dodgers and Yankees $2,000 each for "engaging in a public controversy damaging to baseball"; and fines Dodger publicist Harold Parrott $500 for ghostwriting a "Durocher Speaks" column in the *Brooklyn Daily Eagle* which criticized Yankee owner Larry MacPhail. Lowenfish, *Branch Rickey: Baseball's Ferocious Gentleman*, 425; Leo Durocher, with Ed Linn, *Nice Guys Finish Last* (New York: Simon & Schuster, 1975), 258; Jeffrey Marlett, "The Suspension of Leo Durocher," in *The Team that Forever Changed Baseball and America*, 55.

25. Durocher, *Nice Guys Finish Last*, 235 ("To this day, if you ask me why I was sus-

pended, I could not tell you. Neither could any sportswriter who followed the case.").

26. Marlett, "The Suspension of Leo Durocher," 50; "Catholics Quit Dodgers Knothole Club Over In Protest Over the Conduct of Durocher," *New York Times*, March 1, 1947, 17.

27. Marlett, "The Suspension of Leo Durocher," 54–55; Lowenfish, *Branch Rickey: Baseball's Ferocious Gentleman*, 421–24. There also was considerable tension between Durocher and MacPhail, who had a long and tenuous relationship stretching back to the latter's days as president of the Dodgers. For a discussion of how the Durocher-MacPhail dynamic contributed to Chandler's suspension of "the Lip," see David Mandell, "The Suspension of Leo Durocher," *National Pastime* 27 (2007), 101–04.

28. On the 50th anniversary of his debut, Robinson's number 42 was permanently retired by all Major League teams in a ceremony at Shea Stadium, about 15 miles from the site of Ebbets Field. Calling the action "unprecedented," Commissioner Bud Selig said that "[n]umber 42 belongs to Jackie Robinson for the ages." And in speaking of the game in which "the 28-year-old rookie changed the face of baseball and the face of America forever," President Bill Clinton told the crowd of about 35,000 that "Jackie Robinson scored the go-ahead run that day, we've all been trying to catch up ever since." Bob Nightengale, "Here's to You, Jackie: No. 42 Retired," *Los Angeles Times*, April 16, 1997, C6.

29. Rampersad, *Jackie Robinson: A Biography*, 166–67; Louis Effrat, "Royals' Star Signs with Brooks Today," *New York Times*, April 11, 1947, 20.

30. For a thorough account of Robinson's experience on this historic day, see Jonathan Eig, "Opening Day," chap. 5 in *Opening Day: The Story of Jackie Robinson's First Season* (New York: Simon and Schuster, 2007). For a contemporary reflection on the game and Robinson's debut, see Arthur Daley, "Opening Day at Ebbets Field," *New York Times*, April 16, 1947, 32. For an extensive time line of baseball's "color line," a segregation practice dating from the 19th century, see "Baseball, the Color Line, and Jackie Robinson," American Memory, Library of Congress, accessed March 29, 2016, https://www.loc.gov/collections/jackie-robinson-baseball [link to articles and essays].

31. Rick Swaine, "Jackie Robinson," in Spatz, *The Team that Forever Changed Baseball and America*, 11–12, 14.

32. Joseph Thomas Moore, *Pride Against Prejudice: The Biography of Larry Doby* (New York: Praeger, 1988), 49–50.

33. *Ibid.*, 40–41. Manley and her husband Abe, co-owner of the Eagles, thought the offer well below Doby's value, but felt they had to accept it lest they be criticized for preventing him from reaching the majors. Paul Dickson, *Bill Veeck: Baseball's Greatest Maverick* (New York: Walker & Co., 2012), 126–27.

34. Dave Nightingale, "Sox Fire Bob Lemon, Name Doby," *Chicago Tribune*, July 1, 1978, 1; Moore, *Price Against Prejudice*, 151–53; Claire Smith, "Larry Doby, Who Broke a Color Barrier, Dies at 79," *New York Times*, June 20, 2003, C15.

35. "Finally a Hankering to Honor Doby: Aaron Says Thanks to Barrier-Breaker on 50th Anniversary of His AL Debut," *Newark Star Ledger*, July 6, 1997, sec. 5, 8; Jerome Holtzman, "Doby's Rightful Recognition," *Chicago Tribune*, March 4, 1998, 2.

36. Rory Costello, "Dan Bankhead," in Spatz, *The Team that Forever Changed Baseball and America*, 235–36.

37. Lowenfish, *Branch Rickey: Baseball's Ferocious Gentleman*, 433.

38. Joseph M. Sheehan, "Long Blows Help Beat Brooks, 16–3," *New York Times*, August 27, 1947, 27.

39. "Dan Bankhead, 54, Ex-Dodger, Is Dead," *New York Times*, May 7, 1976, 95.

40. Korr, *The End of Baseball As We Knew It*, 160 ("Fehr's familiarity with the situation in the Eighth Circuit and the characteristics of its judges proved useful to Moss and Miller during the trial.").

41. Alan Schwarz and Michael S. Schmidt, "After 26 Years, Fehr Says He Will Retire as Union Chief," *New York Times*, June 23, 2009, B15.

42. Roger Abrams, *The Money Pitch: Baseball Free Agency and Salary Arbitration* (Philadelphia: Temple University Press, 2000), 28; Tom Clavin, *The DiMaggios: Three Brothers, Their Passion for Baseball, Their Pursuit of the American Dream* (New York: HarperCollins, 2013), 214; Richard Ben Cramer, *Joe DiMaggio: The Hero's Life* (New York: Simon & Schuster, 2000), 258 ("It was Toots [Shore] who cornered Topping and Webb in his saloon one day, and convinced them to make it an even six figures—*the first hundred-thousand-dollar man!* That would be history! That was promotion! Wasn't that worth an extra ten large?").

43. John Drebinger, "DiMaggio Reported All-Time Top-Salaried Player With $90,000 Contract," *New York Times*, February 8, 1949, 33.

44. A number of publications list Hank Greenberg as the first $100,000 player, including the enlarged edition of Larry Ritter's iconic book, *The Glory of Their Times*. In his interview, Greenberg states that John Galbreath, the owner of the Pittsburgh Pirates, agreed to pay the recently traded star of the Detroit Tigers a $100,000 salary for the 1947 season. Lawrence

S. Ritter, *The Glory of Their Times: The Story of the Early Days of Baseball Told by the Men Who Played It*, New enl. ed. (New York: William Morrow, 1984), 326. Other sources for the claim include "Hank Greenberg, First $100,000 Player, Dies," *Los Angeles Times*, September 5, 1986, C1; Hank Greenberg, with Ira Berkow, *Hank Greenberg: The Story of My Life* (New York: Times Books, 1989), 181; John Rosengren, *Hank Greenberg: The Hero of Heroes* (New York: New American Library, 2013), 304. However, the authors of this book reviewed the contract cards on file at the National Baseball Hall of Fame and Museum for both DiMaggio and Greenberg. They confirm that DiMaggio was paid $100,000 for both the 1949 and 1950 seasons, while Greenberg's salary never reached that amount.

45. *Gardella v. Chandler*, 172 F.2d 402 (2d Cir. 1949).

46. David Mandell, "Danny Gardella and the Reserve Clause," *National Pastime* 26 (2006), 41.

47. Charles Weatherby, "Danny Gardella," in *Van Lingle Mungo: The Man, The Song, The Players*, ed. Bill Nowlin (Phoenix: Society for American Baseball Research, 2014), 41–42.

48. Mandell, "Danny Gardella and the Reserve Clause," 42.

49. Responding to the defendants' suggestion that "'Organized Baseball' … will be unable to exist without the 'reserve clause,'" Judge Frank writes, "Whether this is true, no court can predict. In any event, the answer is that the public's pleasure does not authorize the courts to condone illegality, and that no court should strive ingeniously to legalize a private (even if benevolent) dictatorship." *Gardella v. Chandler*, 415.

50. Burk, *Much More than a Game*, 106; Lowenfish, *The Imperfect Diamond*, 155–68. Years later, Gardella said of the settlement: "'In some ways, I considered the settlement a sell-out, a moral defeat. I think they would have lost if the case went all the way to the Supreme Court.… But my lawyer told me they would delay it for years, and still find a way to keep me out of the game.'" Jim Callaghan, "Baseball Rebel: Ex-Giant Took On Owners in '40s," *New York Daily News*, September 18, 1994.

51. Burk, *Much More Than a Game*, 106; "In Surprise Here; Happy Chandler Lifts Ban on All 'Jumpers,'" *Washington Post*, June 6, 1949, 1; Virtue, *South of the Color Barrier*, 190.

52. Wayne Stewart, *Stan the Man: The Life and Times of Stan Musial* (Chicago: Triumph Books, 2010), 121.

53. "Lanier and Martin of Cards Drop Suit Against Baseball," *New York Times*, August 28, 1949, S1.

54. Theodore, *Baseball's Natural*, 1–5.

55. *Ibid.*, 17–18.

56. C. Paul Rogers III, "Eddie Waitkus," in *Van Lingle Mungo: The Man, The Song, The Players*, ed. Bill Nowlin (Phoenix: Society for American Baseball Research, 2014), 70–71, 73.

57. Bob Goldsborough, "Baseball Stalker Inspired 'The Natural,'" *Chicago Tribune*, March 15, 2013, 1:1; Bruce Weber, "Ruth Ann Steinhagen at 83; Shot A Ballplayer," *New York Times*, March 23, 2013, A22.

58. Bernard Malamud, *The Natural* (New York: Farrar, Straus and Giroux, 1952); *The Natural* (Tri-Star Pictures, 1984).

59. Christian H. Brill and Howard W. Brill, "Take Me Out to the Hearing: Major League Baseball Players Before Congress," *Albany Government Law Review* 5 (2012): 110. Robinson is not only the first Major League player to testify before Congress, he is the most prolific, appearing on nine occasions between 1949 and 1970. *Ibid.*, 111, 120–21.

60. *Hearings Regarding Communist Infiltration of Minority Groups, Part 1: Hearings Before the House Committee on Un-American Activities*, 81st Cong. 479–83 (1949) (testimony of Jack Roosevelt "Jackie" Robinson, Player, Brooklyn Dodgers).

61. Robinson, with Duckett, *I Never Had It Made*, 94–98. For a review of the context surrounding Robinson's testimony, see Ronald A. Smith, "The Paul Robeson—Jackie Robinson Saga and a Political Collision," *Journal of Sports History* 6 (1979): 5–27.

62. Rampersad, *Jackie Robinson: A Biography*, 213–14.

63. Cieradkowski, *The League of Outsider Baseball*, 123; Eric Stone, *Wrong Side of the Wall: The Life of Blackie Schwamb, The Greatest Prison Baseball Player of All Time* (Guilford, CT: Lyons Press, 2004), 165–72.

64. Stone, *Wrong Side of the Wall*, 178–85.

65. Cieradkowski, *The League of Outsider Baseball*, 123; Stone *Wrong Side of the Wall*, 285–86 (noting that the information "seems(s) reasonable projecting from the incomplete reporting in the prison newspapers—the *San Quentin News* and the *Folsom Observer*. He also played nearly one-third of his prison games at shortstop and led his league in batting three times.").

66. "Casey Held to be Father," *New York Times*, December 30, 1950, 28; Russell Wolinsky, "Hugh Casey," in Spatz, *The Team that Forever Changed Baseball and America*, 118.

67. "Hugh Casey, of Relief Pitching Fame, Kills Self With Shotgun," *Reading* (Pa.) *Eagle*, July 3, 1951, 12.

68. Wolinsky, "Hugh Casey," 118.

69. "Casey, Ex-Dodger, Is Atlanta Suicide," *New York Times*, July 4, 1951, 18.

70. Holtzman, *The Commissioners*, 82–84; Marshall, *Baseball's Pivotal Era, 1945–1951*, 389–

90; John P. Rossi, *A Whole New Game: Off the Field Changes in Baseball, 1946-1960* (Jefferson, NC: McFarland, 1999), 80.

71. Larry Moffi, *The Conscience of the Game: Baseball's Commissioners from Landis to Selig* (Lincoln: University of Nebraska Press, 2006), 214.

72. Marshall, *Baseball's Pivotal Era, 1945-1951*, 398; Andrew O'Toole, *Branch Rickey in Pittsburgh: Baseball's Trailblazing General Manager for the Pirates, 1950-1955* (Jefferson, NC: McFarland, 2000), 20.

73. Joseph A. Loftus, "Wage Board Sets Baseball Ceilings; Ruling Halts Musial's $35,000 Rise," *New York Times*, April 11, 1951, 33; "Wage Ruling Affects Few, Baseball View," *Chicago Daily Tribune*, April 11, 1951, F1. After Musial won his fourth batting title in 1950, the Cardinals agreed to pay him $75,000 in 1951, plus $5,000 if the team exceeded 900,000 in attendance, and an additional $5,000 if it exceeded 1.2 million. Michael Haupert to SABR-L mailing list, "Musial 1951 Contract," December 6, 2015, http://APPLE.EASE.LSOFT.COM/archives/SABR-L.html; James N. Giglio, *Musial: From Stash to Stan the Man* (Columbia: University of Missouri Press, 2001), 188.

74. Luther A. Huston, "Stabilization Board's New Ruling Yields Rises to Musial, Robinson," *New York Times*, January 17, 1952, 33; "Musial Gets Pay Delayed by W.S.B.," *New York Times*, February 13, 1952, 39.

75. Tepler v. Frick, 204 F.2d 506 (2d Cir. 1953). *See also* Boyd Tepler, *In Cub Chains* (Pittsburgh: Dorrance Pub. Co., 1993).

76. Years later, still continuing the fight against baseball's immunity as chairman of the House Judiciary Committee, Celler will say about organized baseball: "They want exemption from antitrust laws. Well, they're not going to get it. I am going to fight them tooth and nail." "They Said It," *Sports Illustrated*, February 2, 1959, 18.

77. *Study of Monopoly Power: Hearings Before the Subcommittee on Study of Monopoly Power of the House Committee on the Judiciary*, pt. 6, *Organized Baseball*, 82nd Cong. 16-18, July 30-October 24, 1951 (Washington, DC: U.S. Govt. Print. Off, 1952); Lowenfish, *The Imperfect Diamond*, 174; White, *Creating the National Pastime*, 299-309.

78. Paul Dickson, *Bill Veeck: Baseball's Greatest Maverick* (New York: Walker & Co., 2012), 191-92; Eldon Ham, *Larceny & Old Leather: The Mischievous Legacy of Major League Baseball* (Chicago: Academy Chicago Publishers, 2005), 66-67.

79. Brian McKenna, "Eddie Gaedel," SABR Baseball Biography Project, accessed March 23, 2016, http://sabr.org/bioproj/person/fa5574c8.

For a discussion of Veeck's inspiration for sending a midget to bat—was it James Thurber's 1941 baseball short story for the *Saturday Evening Post*, "You Could Look It Up," or overhearing John McGraw tell Veeck's father about his desire to use the Giants' hunchbacked good luck charm, Eddie Morrow, as a batter just one time before retiring—see Jim Tootle, "Bill Veeck and James Thurber: The Literary Origins of the Midget Pinch Hitter," *Nine: A Journal of Baseball History and Culture* 10 (Spring 2002), 110-19.

80. Gaedel is the only player in Major League history to wear a fraction as a uniform number. Jim Reisler, "Eddie Gaedel: The Sad Life of Baseball's Midget," *National Pastime* 6 (Winter 1987), 9.

81. Frederick J. Day, *Clubhouse Lawyer: Law in the World of Sports* (New York: iUniverse Star, 2004), 11-12; Bob Broeg, *The 100 Greatest Moments in St. Louis Sports* (St. Louis: Missouri Historical Society Press, 2000), 93. When Gaedel dies on June 18, 1961, after a drunken altercation in a bowling alley which left him severely injured, Bob Cain drives 300 miles to attend the funeral; he is the only person there with any connection to baseball. Eric Robinson, "The Peculiar Professional Baseball Career of Eddie Gaedel," *National Pastime: North Side, South Side, All Around the Town* (SABR 45 Convention Issue, 2015), 73.

82. Dickson, *Bill Veeck*, 193.

83. *Study of Monopoly Power: Hearings Before the Subcommittee on Study of Monopoly Power of the House Committee on the Judiciary*, 1049-57. For a discussion of his role on the subcommittee, see John Paul Stevens, Remarks at the Sports Lawyers Association 41st Annual Conference Luncheon, Baltimore, MD, May 15, 2015, http://www.supremecourt.gov/publicinfo/speeches/JPS_SportsLawyersAssociation_05-15-15.pdf.

84. *Study of Monopoly Power: Hearings Before the Subcommittee on Study of Monopoly Power of the House Committee on the Judiciary*, 1049-50.

85. Ibid., 1054.

86. Bowley Crowther, "'The Winning Team,' Story About Grover Cleveland Alexander, Arrives at the Mayfair," *New York Times*, June 21, 1952, 12; Hal Erickson, *The Baseball Filmography, 1915 through 2001*, 2nd ed. (Jefferson, NC: McFarland, 2002), 475.

87. Jan Finkel, "Grover Cleveland Alexander," in Simon, *Deadball Stars of the National League*, 209.

88. Joe Posnanski, "Monitoring the Hall of Fame Monitor," *NBC SportsWorld*, accessed February 15, 2016, http://sportsworld.nbcsports.com/baseball-hall-of-fame-monitor-bill-james/. But for Jack Warner's decision to star

Jimmy Stewart, rather than Reagan (who had pleaded for the role) in *The Stratton Story*, another baseball biopic, this would be a triple-threat trivia question. The full name of Monty Stratton, who pitched for the Chicago White Sox from 1934 to 1938, was Monty Franklin Pierce Stratton. Erickson, *The Baseball Filmography, 1915 through 2001*, 479.

89. McKenna, *Early Exits*, 46; J.G. Preston, "On Eleanor Engle, Who Wasn't Allowed to Play Shortstop for the Harrisburg Senators," *The J.G. Preston Experience* (blog), November 21, 2009, https://prestonjg.wordpress.com [search "engle"] (noting that Engle was 26, not 24, as reported in contemporaneous accounts).

90. "Trautman Bars Woman Players, Censures 'Travesty' on Baseball," *New York Times*, June 24, 1952, 38; Johnny Travers, "Gal Shortstop's Bid Given Short 'No' by O.B. Officials," *Sporting News*, July 2, 1952, 5; Berlage, *Women in Baseball*, 78.

91. Ardell, *Breaking into Baseball*, 118 (quoting Bulletin 639, June 24, 1952, to Club and League Presidents, from George Trautman).

92. Mike Eisenbath, *The Cardinals Encyclopedia* (Philadelphia: Temple University Press, 1999), 404–05.

93. Richard Goldstein, "Fred Saigh, Who Helped Cardinals Stay Put, Dies at 94," *New York Times*, January 2, 2000, A35.

94. *Haelan Laboratories, Inc. v. Topps Chewing Gum, Inc.*, 202 F.2d 866, 868 (2d Cir. 1953). See generally J. Gordon Hylton, "Baseball Cards and the Birth of the Right of Publicity: The Curious Case of *Haelan Laboratories v. Topps Chewing Gum*," *Marquette Sports Law Review* 12 (2001), 273–94.

95. Martin Kane, "The Baseball Bubble Trouble," *Sports Illustrated* (August 16, 1954), 38.

96. 346 U.S. 356 (1953).

97. *Ibid.*, 357.

98. *Ibid.*, 358 (Burton, J., dissenting).

99. *Subjecting Professional Baseball Clubs to the Antitrust Laws: Hearings Before a Subcommittee of the House Committee on the Judiciary*, 83rd Cong. 42–65, March 18–May 25, 1954 (Washington, DC: U.S. Govt. Print. Off, 1954).

100. *Ibid.*, 56.

101. Kate Buford, *Native American Son: The Life and Sporting Legend of Jim Thorpe* (New York: Alfred A. Knopf, 2010), 372–74; Don Jensen, "Jim Thorpe," in Simon, *Deadball Stars of the National League*, 82.

102. "Players Form Organization; Major Leaguers Seek Contract Revisions," *Chicago Tribune*, July 13, 1954, B1; "Players Organize and Retain Lewis," *New York Times*, July 13, 1954, 26.

103. Shirley Povich, "This Morning," *Washington Post*, July 15, 1955, 31.

104. Davies, "Along Comes the Players Association," 337–38; Korr, *The End of Baseball As We Knew It*, 2.

105. Cramer, *Joe DiMaggio*, 371–72.

106. James R. Devine, "Joe DiMaggio (and His Lawyer)," in Ward, *Courting the Yankees*, 10.

107. David Jones, *Joe DiMaggio: A Biography* (Westport, CT: Greenwood Press, 2004), 134.

108. "Dodgers' President Accused of Slander," *New York Times*, July 6, 1955, 18; McCue, *Mover & Shaker*, 113. New York Appellate Division Justice Charles D. Breitel identified the O'Malley comments at the heart of the litigation as: "The first is that the physician's claimed fee is exorbitant. The second is that the second operation was probably unnecessary. The third is that, by way of opinion, the medical profession believes that the first operation had been successful. The fourth is that plaintiff physician thought he was operating on the patient's bankroll, rather than on his hand." *Shenkman v. O'Malley*, 157 N.Y.S.2d 290, 294 (App. Div. 1956).

109. Neil Lanctot, *Campy: The Two Lives of Roy Campanella* (New York: Simon & Schuster, 2011), 304–06, 319.

110. "Campy and O'Malley Say No to Surgeon for $9,600 for Operation on Roy," *Sporting News*, June 8, 1955, 9.

111. "Campy's Doc Wins $5,000 Fee," *Sporting News*, February 22, 1956, 28; "O'Malley Suit Settled," *New York Times*, November 21, 1957; Lanctot, *Campy*, 327–28 (identifying Shenkman as "litigious"); McCue, *Mover and Shaker*, 113.

112. Hylton, "Baseball Cards and the Birth of the Right of Publicity," 291; *Topps Chewing Gum, Inc.*, 67 F.T.C. 744, 765 (1965).

113. The Federal Trade Commission's investigation started on January 30, 1962. The Initial Decision was rendered by hearing examiner Herman Tocker on August 7, 1964. *Topps Chewing Gum, Inc.*, 67 F.T.C. 744, 747 (1965).

114. Act of July 16, 1956, no. 579, 1956 La. Acts 1054 ("[A]ll persons ... are prohibited from sponsoring, arranging, participating in, or permitting on premises under their control any ... athletic training, games, sports or contests ... in which the participants or contestants are members of the white and negro races."); "Louisiana Draws Sport Color Line," *New York Times*, July 17, 1956, 13.

115. "Ask Veto of La. Bill Banning Mixed Sports," *Chicago Defender*, July 16, 1956, 21; Bruce Adelson, *Brushing Back Jim Crow: The Integration of Minor-League Baseball in the American South* (Charlottesville: University Press of Virginia, 1999), 208.

116. *Dorsey v. State Athletic Comm'n*, 168 F. Supp. 149, 153 (E.D. La. 1958); Adelson, *Brushing Back Jim Crow*, 227–28.

117. Adelson, *Brushing Back Jim Crow*, 220, 238; "New Orleans Quits Southern Association," *Washington Post*, March 16, 1960, D2.

118. John Drebinger, "Baseball Clubs Reject Pay Raise," *New York Times*, February 3, 1957, 159; "Major Owners Refuse Hike in Minimum Pay," *Chicago Tribune*, February 3, 1957, A2.

119. Cary S. Henderson, "Los Angeles and the Dodger War, 1957–1962," *Southern California Quarterly* 62 (1980), 278–79; "L.A. Voters Narrowly Approve Stadium in Chavez Ravine," in Dean A. Sullivan, ed., *Late Innings: A Documentary History of Baseball, 1945–1972* (Lincoln: University of Nebraska Press, 2002), 126–28. The tight battle over the referendum included a five-hour "Dodgerthon" telecast over KTTV two days before the vote. Many Hollywood notables, including Jack Benny, Danny Thomas, Dean Martin, Jerry Lewis, Ronald Reagan, Debbie Reynolds, and Joe E. Brown, appeared in support of a "yes" vote for the team. McCue, *Mover and Shaker*, 210.

120. O'Malley had purchased both Wrigley Field and the PCL's Los Angeles Angels from Cubs owner Philip Wrigley in February 1957, thereby acquiring territorial rights to the Los Angeles market. Roscoe McGowen, "Dodgers Buy Los Angeles Club, Stirring Talk of Shift to Coast," *New York Times*, February 22, 1957, 1; McCue, *Mover and Shaker*, 140–41.

121. Henderson, "Los Angeles and the Dodger War, 1957–1962," 269–74; Sullivan, *The Dodgers Move West*, 99–104.

122. Ed Edmonds, "Cornering the Market," in Ward, *Courting the Yankees*, 318. For the complete text of Stengel's testimony, see "Statement of Casey Stengel, Manager of the New York Yankees," in *Baseball and the American Legal Mind*, ed. Spencer Weber Waller, Neil B. Cohen & Paul Finkelman (New York: Garland, 1995), 103–24.

123. Bill Nowlin, "Pumpsie Green, Infield (1959–62)," in *Red Sox Baseball in the Days of Ike and Elvis: The Red Sox of the 1950s*, ed. Mark Armour and Bill Nowlin (Phoenix: Society for American Baseball Research, 2012), 190–99; "White Sox Score Over Boston, 2–1," *New York Times*, July 22, 1959, 31.

124. William A. Shea, Announcement of Formation of Continental League, news release, July 27, 1959, reprinted in Sullivan, *Late Innings*, 141–44.

125. Dan Daniel, "Majors Flash Green Light to Third League," *Sporting News*, August 26, 1959, 2; David George Surdam, *The Big Leagues Go to Washington: Congress and Sports Antitrust, 1951–1989* (Urbana: University of Illinois Press, 2015), 106–08.

126. Surdam, *The Big Leagues Go to Washington*, 110.

127. "NL Upholds Promise, Awards Franchises to Two CL Teams; AL Reneges," in Sullivan, *Late Innings*, 156.

128. "Major Leagues Sued: Portland Club Asks $1,800,000 in Antitrust Action," *New York Times*, July 31, 1959, 15.

129. *Portland Baseball Club, Inc. v. Baltimore Baseball Club, Inc.*, 282 F.2d 680, 680 (9th Cir. 1960).

130. Roger Kahn, *The Boys of Summer* (New York: Harper & Row, 1972), 327–28, 333–36; Brian M. Endsley, *Bums No More—The 1959 Los Angeles Dodgers, World Champions of Baseball* (Jefferson, NC: McFarland, 2009), 213.

131. Ted Reed, *Carl Furillo, Brooklyn Dodgers All-Star* (Jefferson, NC: McFarland, 2011), 149–53; Dan Hafner, "Furillo Fires Blacklist Charge," *Los Angeles Herald Examiner*, March 29, 1961.

132. Reed, *Carl Furillo*, 158–59; Dan Daniel, "Frick Denies Furillo Claim of Black List," *Sporting News*, January 17, 1962, 20.

133. "Vern Law is Pitcher of the Year," *New York Times*, November 4, 1940, 43.

134. One of the four is infielder Vance Law, Vern's son, who played more than 1,200 games for five teams during a career that spanned 1980 to 1991. The others are Ron Law, who appeared in 35 games for the Cleveland Indians in 1969, and Rudy Law, and outfielder who compiled a .271 lifetime batting average while playing in 749 games for four teams between 1978 and 1986.

135. Raised in a strict Mormon household, Law was a deacon in the church by the age of 12; at 19, he was an elder. C. Paul Rogers III, "Vernon Law," in *Sweet '60: The 1960 Pittsburgh Pirates*, ed. Clifton Blue Parker and Bill Nowlin (Phoenix: Society for American Baseball Research, 2013), 128; Larry Moffi, *This Side of Cooperstown: An Oral History of Major League Baseball in the 1950s* (Iowa City: University of Iowa Press, 1996), 181 ("I got the nickname Deacon because I didn't swear, didn't drink, went to church, and did quite a bit of speaking in other churches, youth groups and so forth.").

136. Moffi, *This Side of Cooperstown*, 186–87; Richard Deitsch, "Catching Up With … Vernon Law, Pirates Ace, October 10, 1960," *Sports Illustrated*, May 22, 2000, 15.

137. Frank Finch, "51,574 See Dodgers Drop Double Bill," *Los Angeles Times*, April 30, 1962, B1.

138. "Damage Suit Nets $20,000 for Roseboro," *Los Angeles Times*, October 20, 1967, B2; "Roseboro Victor in Suit," *New York Times*, October 21, 1967, 23.

139. *Roseboro v. Rawlings Mfg. Co.*, 79 Cal. Rptr. 567, 570 (Cal. Ct. App. 1969).

140. Richard Dozer, "Cubs Sign Negro Coach," *Chicago Tribune*, May 30, 1962, C1;

Steve Rushin, "A Life Well-Lived," *Sports Illustrated*, January 20, 2003, 15.

141. Lew Freedman, *African American Pioneers of Baseball: A Biographical Encyclopedia* (Westport, CT: Greenwood Press, 2007), 7–9.

142. *Ibid.*, 11–12; Buck O'Neil, with Steve Wulf and David Conrads, *I Was Right on Time* (New York: Simon and Schuster, 1996), 204–05.

143. O'Neil, *I Was Right on Time*, 15.

144. Richard Goldstein, "Buck O'Neil, Negro Leagues Pioneer, Is Dead at 94," *New York Times*, October 7, 2006, C10.

145. Brian M. Endsley, *Finding the Left Arm of God: Sandy Koufax and the Los Angeles Dodgers, 1960-1963* (Jefferson, NC: McFarland, 2015), 242–44.

146. Edward R. Ward, "Baseball and the Law," *Baseball Research Journal* 25 (1996), 154.

147. William A. Cook, *The Summer of '64: A Pennant Lost* (Jefferson, NC: McFarland, 2002), 103.

148. Richard Sandomir, "Honor for Shea at Shea: He Brought Mets Here," *New York Times*, April 8, 2008, D5.

149. Michael Shapiro, *Bottom of the Ninth: Branch Rickey, Casey Stengel, and the Daring Scheme to Save Baseball from Itself* (New York: Times Books, 2009), 279.

150. Leonard Koppett, "Shea Stadium Opens with Big Traffic Jam," *New York Times*, April 18, 1964, 1.

151. Matt Lupica, *The Baseball Stadium Insider: A Comprehensive Dissection of All Thirty Ballparks, Legendary Players, and Memorable Moments* (Kent: Black Squirrel Books, 2015), 9–10.

152. Ray Yasser, "Warren Spahn's Legal Legacy: The Right to be Free from False Praise," *Seton Hall Journal of Sports and Entertainment Law* 18 (2008), 50.

153. "Spahn Awarded $10,000 by Court," *New York Times*, May 29, 1964, 19. In particular, Shapiro exaggerated the nature of Spahn's World War II experiences, claiming he was a war hero, which Spahn insisted he was not. Yasser, "Warren Spahn's Legal Legacy," 53n27, 55–56.

154. The case was affirmed by two New York state courts before the United States Supreme Court remanded the case on May 22, 1967. Seventeen months later the United States Supreme Court agreed to consider another appeal before finally dismissing the case on January 17, 1969. Yasser, "Warren Spahn's Legal Legacy," 71–72 (providing chart which outlines complicated timeline of the lawsuit). Within the week Spahn agrees to drop the lawsuit. "Spahn Agrees to Give Up Damage Suit," *Danville Register* (Va.), January 23, 1969, 2-D.

155. Yasser, "Warren Spahn's Legal Legacy," 82–83.

156. For a description of Stotz's efforts leading up to the first game, including acquiring sponsors for three founding teams, see Lance Van Auken and Robin Van Auken, *Play Ball! The Story of Little League Baseball* (University Park: Pennsylvania State University Press, 2001), 24–34.

157. Act of July 16, 1964, Pub. L. No. 88–378, 78 Stat. 325 (1964).

158. Act of December 26, 1974, Pub. L. No. 93–551, 88 Stat 1744 (1974). The word "boy" was changed to "young people," and Little League's purpose was rewritten as "to instill citizenship and sportsmanship," with the word "manhood" removed. Berlage, *Women in Baseball*, 101; Abrams, "The Twelve-Year-Old Girl's Lawsuit that Changed America," 256.

159. Teammates had difficulty pronouncing his first name—"Masa-nori became Ma-samu-ri"—so they called him Mashi instead, a nickname with which he became comfortable. Robert K. Fitts, *Mashi—The Unfulfilled Dreams of Masanori Murakami, the First Japanese Major Leaguer* (Lincoln: University of Nebraska Press, 2015), 59.

160. Joseph Durso, "Japanese Hurler Appears in Relief: Murakami is First from Nation to Play in Majors," *New York Times*, September 2, 1954, 42; Fitts, *Mashi*, 88–96.

161. Terumi Rafferty-Osaki, "Asians and Baseball: The Breaking and Perpetuating of Stereotypes," in *The Cooperstown Symposium of Baseball and American Culture, 2007-2008*, ed. William M. Simons (Jefferson, NC: McFarland, 2009), 136.

162. Fitts, *Mashi*, 134–35.

163. Larry R. Gerlach, "Crime and Punishment: The Marichal-Roseboro Incident," *Nine: A Journal of Baseball History and Culture* 12 (Spring 2004): 4–5.

164. John Roseboro, with Bill Libby, *Glory Days with the Dodgers and Other Days with Others* (New York: Atheneum, 1978), 6.

165. Richard Goldstein, "John Roseboro, a Dodgers Star, Dies at 69," *New York Times*, August 20, 2002, C16; Gerlach, "Crime and Punishment," 20–21.

166. John Rosengren, *The Fight of Their Lives: How Juan Marichal and John Roseboro Turned Baseball's Ugliest Brawl into a Story of Forgiveness and Redemption* (Guilford, CT: Lyons Press, 2014), 184–87; Gwen Knapp, "40 Years Later, the Fight Resonates in a Positive Way," *San Francisco Chronicle*, August 21, 2005, C1.

Chapter 6

1. Frank Finch, "Koufax, Drysdale Eye $1 Million Pact; Dodger Aces Want 3-Year Package

Deal," *Los Angeles Times*, February 23, 1966; Ed Edmonds, "The Great Dodgers Pitching Tandem Strikes a Blow for Salaries: The 1966 Drysdale-Koufax Holdout and Its Impact on the Game," in *The Cooperstown Symposium of Baseball and American Culture, 2007-2008*, ed. William M. Simons (Jefferson, NC: McFarland, 2009), 248.

2. Don Drysdale, with Bob Verdi, *Once a Bum, Always a Dodger* (New York: St. Martin's, 1990), 125.

3. Cal. Lab. Code § 2855. Although the first California statute on the length of personal services contracts was passed in 1872 (two-year limit) and amended in 1931 (seven years), it is often referred to as the de Havilland Law after Academy Award winning actress Olivia de Havilland who won a lawsuit against Warner Brothers when the studio tried to lengthen her contract beyond seven calendar years due to the 25 weeks she was suspended for refusing certain roles. *De Haviland v. Warner Bros. Pictures, Inc.*, 153 P.2d 983 (Cal. Ct. App. 1944).

4. Edmonds, "The Great Dodgers Pitching Tandem Strikes a Blow for Salaries," 256-57.

5. *Ibid.*, 258.

6. Paul D. Staudohar, *Playing for Dollars: Labor Relations and the Sports Business*, 3rd ed. (Ithaca, NY: Cornell University Press 1996), 38.

7. Burk, *Marvin Miller*, 102; Korr, *The End of Baseball As We Knew It*, 28-34; Lowenfish, *The Imperfect Diamond*, 197; Miller, *A Whole Different Ball Game*, 33-35.

8. Burk, *Marvin Miller*, 108; Burk, *Much More Than a Game*, 150; Korr, *The End of Baseball* As We Knew It, 40-41; Lowenfish, *The Imperfect Diamond*, 199; Miller, *A Whole Different Ball Game*, 38.

9. Ashford gave credit to Pacific Coast League President Clarence "Pants" Rowland for his promotion to the majors. Joseph P. Murphy, Jr., "The Busher from Dubuque: Pants Rowland Wore Many Hats," *Baseball Research Journal* 24 (1995), 121. For Ashford's recollections of his long career as a barrier breaking minor league umpire, see Larry R. Gerlach, *The Men in Blue: Conversations with Umpires* (New York: Viking Press, 1980), 269-75.

10. Shirley Povich, "This Morning," *Washington Post*, April 12, 1966, C1.

11. Mark Armour, "Emmett Ashford: Entertainer and Pioneer," *National Pastime* 27 (2007), 57.

12. Eric Robinson, "Movies, Bullfights, and Baseball, Too: A Sports Stadium Built for Spectacle First and Sports Second," *National Pastime: Baseball in the Space Age* (SABR 44 Convention Issue, 2014): 12-13.

13. James M. Faria and Robert T. Wright, Monofilament Ribbon File Product, U.S. Patent 3,332,828, filed December 28, 1965, issued July 25, 1967. Even at the outset, there was disagreement over just how "useful" the product was, as evidenced by Dick Allen's oft-quoted remark, "If a horse can't eat it, I don't want to play on it." Alan Drooz, "For Better or Worse: Artificial Turf Was Introduced to Baseball 25 Years Ago and Has Taken Root in the National Pastime," *Los Angeles Times*, April 18, 1991, 6.

14. Mary Bellis, "History of Astroturf," About.com, accessed September 20, 2014, http://inventors.about.com/od/astartinventions/a/astroturf.htm.

15. *State v. Milwaukee Braves*, 144 N.W.2d 1, 7-8 (Wis. 2002).

16. Hundley received an $110,000 bonus from the San Francisco Giants payable over five years. Steve Rushin, *The 34-Ton Bat: The Story of Baseball as Told Through Bobbleheads, Cracker Jacks, Jockstraps, Eye Black, and 375 Other Strange and Unforgettable Objects* (New York: Little, Brown, 2013), 342.

17. *Hundley v. Commissioner*, 48 T.C. 339 (1967); "Hundley Beat Tax Problem, And Kept Money In Family," *Sarasota Herald-Tribune*, July 4, 1967, 22.

18. Rushin, *The 34-Ton Bat*, 340.

19. The bulk of the evidence indicates that the minimum salary was $7000 prior to the completion of the 1968 collective bargaining agreement. *E.g.*, "Major Loops Hike Pay Minimum to $7000," *Los Angeles Times*, October 1, 1957, C1 (quoting MLBPA representative J. Norman Lewis as stating that the change from $6000 to $7000 was the players' "greatest advance since the pension plan"); "Baseball Owners Raise Minimum Salary $3,000," *Chicago Tribune*, February 22, 1968, E1; Lowenfish, *The Imperfect Diamond*, 202-03. However, in his memoir, former MLBPA executive director Marvin Miller stated that the actual figure was lower when negotiations over the first CBA began in early 1967. "Twenty years earlier, in 1947, the owners set the player's minimum salary at $5,000 a year. The owners simply passed a rule to that effect. Between 1947 and 1967, a period of steep inflation, the owners generously increased the minimum salary once, by $1,000, to $6,000 a year." Miller, *A Whole Different Ball Game*, 95. Whatever the amount actually was, Miller clearly identifies MLBPA's goal regarding minimum salary: "After discussion with the players, we decided to propose that the minimum be raised to $12,000 a year." Miller, *Ibid.*

20. Lowenfish, *The Imperfect Diamond*, 202-03; Roger I. Abrams, "Liberation Arbitration: The Baseball Reserve Clause Case," in *Proceedings of the 55th Annual Meeting of the National Academy of Arbitrators* (Washington, DC: Bureau of National Affairs, 2003), 199.

21. 291 F. Supp. 242, 243 (E.D. Mo. 1968).
22. "American League Ousts 2 Umpires," *New York Times*, September 17, 1968, 54; Mark Armour, "A Tale of Two Umpires," *Baseball Research Journal* 38 (Fall 2009), 127.
23. "Comment by Cronin," *New York Times*, September 18, 1968, 37.
24. Armour, "A Tale of Two Umpires," 128–29.
25. *Salerno v. Am. League of Prof'l Baseball Clubs*, 429 F.2d 1003, 1005 (2d Cir. 1970).
26. Miller, *A Whole Different Ball Game*, 144.
27. Korr, *The End of Baseball As We Knew It*, 74; Lowenfish, *The Imperfect Diamond*, 202; Miller, *A Whole Different Ball Game*, 145–49.
28. Miller, *A Whole Different Ball Game*, 144.
29. *Ibid.*,149.
30. Jerome Holtzman, "Big Strike Fund, Collusion Judgments Give Players Leverage Over Owners," *Chicago Tribune*, November 8, 1988, B5.
31. Bowie Kuhn, *Hardball: The Education of a Baseball Commissioner* (New York: Times Books, 1987), 33–34; Leonard Koppett, "Bowie Kuhn, Wall St. Lawyer, Named Commissioner Pro Tem of Baseball," *New York Times*, February 5, 1969, 29; G. Richard McKelvey, *For It's One, Two, Three, Four Strikes You're Out at the Owners' Ball Game: Players Versus Management in Baseball* (Jefferson, NC: McFarland, 2001), 73.
32. Kuhn, *Hardball*, 400–03; Holtzman, *The Commissioners*, 206.
33. Koppett, *Koppett's Concise History of Major League Baseball*, 402–04; Kuhn, *Hardball*, 430–36.
34. *Wills v. Comm'r*, 411 F.2d 537, 539–41 (9th Cir. 1969).
35. *Ibid.*, 541–43; "U. S. Court Tags Wills 'Out' on Taxes for Prizes," *Jet*, June 29, 1967, 52 (discussing lower court ruling).
36. *Am. League of Prof'l Baseball Clubs & Ass'n of Nat'l Baseball League Umpires*, 180 N.L.R.B. 190 (1969), reprinted in Sullivan, *Late Innings*, 250–53.
37. On October 8, 1969, the Cardinals traded Flood, catcher Tim McCarver, relief pitcher Joe Hoerner, and outfielder Byron Browne, to the Phillies for three players, slugging first-baseman Dick Allen, second-baseman Cookie Rojas, and pitcher Jerry Johnson. Later, after Flood refused to report to the Phillies, the Cardinals would send Willie Montanez (April 8, 1970) and Jim Browning (August 30, 1970) to complete the trade. Kuhn, *Hardball*, 74; Albert Theodore Powers, *The Business of Baseball* (Jefferson, NC: McFarland, 2003), 156.
38. Curt Flood, with Richard Carter, *The Way It Is* (New York: Trident Press, 1971), 194; McKelvey, *For It's One, Two, Three, Four Strikes You're Out at the Owners' Ball Game*, 78. For background on Flood, discussion of his reaction to the trade, and baseball's response, see Burk, *Marvin Miller*, 138–45; Korr, *The End of Baseball As We Knew It*, 84–89; Kuhn, *Hardball*, 80–85; Lowenfish, *The Imperfect Diamond*, 207–10; Miller, *A Whole Different Ball Game*, 180–192; Brad Snyder, *A Well-Paid Slave: Curt Flood's Fight for Free Agency in Professional Sports* (New York: Viking, 2006), 69–102.
39. Kuhn, *Hardball*, 83–84.
40. Snider, *A Well-Paid Slave*, 106–07; Miller, *A Whole Different Ball Game*, 192.
41. Morton Sharnik, "Downfall of A Hero," *Sports Illustrated*, February 23, 1970, 16–21; David Condon, "Suspend Denny McLain; Detroit Pitcher Ban Is Indefinite," *Chicago Tribune*, February 20, 1970, 1; Kuhn, *Hardball*, 69; Ronald Blum, "Rose Affair Stirs Memories of McLain," *Los Angeles Times*, May 21, 1989, 3:1.
42. "Denny McLain Gets 23-Year Prison Sentence," *Los Angeles Times*, April 26, 1985, 3:1; *United States v. McLain*, 823 F.2d 1457 (11th Cir. 1987); "Court Overturns McLain Conviction," *New York Times*, August 8, 1987, 1:49; Denny McLain, with Eli Zaret, *I Told You I Wasn't Perfect* (Chicago: Triumph Books, 2007), 265; "McLain, Released After 30 Months, Rejoins Family to Await New Trial," *Los Angeles Times*, September 5, 1987, 3:1.
43. "McLain Gets Probation Instead of New Prison Term," *Philadelphia Inquirer*, December 16, 1988, C9.
44. "McLain Found Guilty," *New York Daily News*, December 14, 1996; "Another Wrong Turn for Troubled Ex-Tiger Denny McLain," *Detroit Free Press*, September 24, 2011.
45. *Flood v. Kuhn*, 309 F. Supp. 793, 798–801 (S.D.N.Y. 1970); Leonard Koppett, "Judge Says Trial Must Solve Issue," *New York Times*, March 5, 1970.
46. For a comprehensive treatment of the trial, see Neil F. Flynn, *Baseball's Reserve System: The Case and Trial of Curt Flood v. Major League Baseball* (Springfield, IL: Walnut Park Group, 2006).
47. Lowenfish, *The Imperfect Diamond*, 212; Miller, *A Whole Different Ball Game*, 200; Snyder, *A Well-Paid Slave*, 188.
48. "Federal Judge Rules Against Flood on Reserve Clause," *Washington Post*, August 13, 1970, H1; Thomas Rogers, "Lawyers to Make a Speedy Appeal," *New York Times*, August 13, 1970, 53.
49. *Flood v. Kuhn*, 316 F. Supp. 271, 276, 278 (S.D.N.Y. 1970).
50. *Flood v. Kuhn*, 443 F.2d 264 (2d Cir. 1971).
51. Staudohar, *Playing for Dollars*, 28.
52. Lee Lowenfish, *The Imperfect Diamond: A History of Baseball's Labor Wars*, rev. ed. (New York: DeCapo Press, 1991), 211; Abrams, "Liberation Arbitration," 201.

53. For a complete account of the final game, see "June 28, 1970: A Play-by-Play Account of the Final Pirate Game at Forbes Field," in *Forbes Field: Essays and Memories of the Pirates' Historic Ballpark, 1909-1971*, ed. David Cicotello and Angelo J. Louisa (Jefferson, NC: McFarland, 2007), 94-118.

54. "Forbes Field," ballparksofbaseball.com, accessed January 27, 2016, http://www.ballparksofbaseball.com/past/ForbesField.htm; Thad Mumau, *"Had 'Em All the Way": The 1960 Pittsburgh Pirates* (Jefferson, NC: McFarland, 2015), 211.

55. *Uhlaender v. Henricksen*, 316 F. Supp. 1277 (D. Minn. 1970). The named parties in the suit were Ted Uhlaender, a member of the Minnesota Twins when the case was filed, and Marvin Miller, executive director of the Major League Baseball Players Association. Uhlaender was traded to the Cleveland Indians prior to the trial, so Jim Kaat and Gaylord Perry testified for the Players Association. J. Gordon Hylton, "The Major League Baseball Players Association and the Ownership of Sports Statistics: The Untold Story of Round One," *Marquette Sports Law Review* 17 (2006): 100 (noting that Uhlaender's involvement in the litigation was a mystery).

56. Rolf Valtin, "In Memoriam, Lewis M. Gill, 1912-2002," in *Arbitration 2002—Workplace Arbitration: A Process in Evolution, Proceedings for the Fifty-Fifth Annual Meeting, National Academy of Arbitrators*, ed. Charles J. Coleman (Washington, D.C.: Bureau of National Affairs, 2003), vi-vii. Gill served as president of the National Academy of Arbitrators in 1971.

57. "Baseball Hires Arbitrator Gill," *Washington Post*, October 2, 1970, C3; Lowenfish, *The Imperfect Diamond*, 211; J. Gordon Hylton, "The Historical Origins of Baseball Grievance Arbitration," *Marquette Sports Law Review* 11 (2001): 183.

58. Burk, *Much More Than a Game*, 170-71; Ken Kaiser, with David Fisher, *Planet of the Umps: A Baseball Life from Behind the Plate* (New York: St. Martin's Press, 2003), 251; McKelvey, *The MacPhails*, 204; Benjamin G. Rader, *Baseball: A History of America's Game*, 3rd ed. (Urbana, IL: University of Illinois Press, 2008), 213.

59. Burk, *Much More Than a Game*, 169-70; David Quentin Voigt, *American Baseball: From Postwar Expansion to the Electronic Age* (University Park: Pennsylvania State University Press, 1983), 294.

60. Burk, *Much More Than a Game*, 171.

61. Bruce Markusen, *Roberto Clemente: The Great One* (New York: Sports Publishing, 2001), 232-33.

62. "Murtaugh had not planned this. To the contrary, he was totally oblivious to the milestone that resulted when he penned the names of the starting lineup on the scorecard, until he met with reporters who were standing outside his clubhouse following the game." John McCollister, *The Good, the Bad, and the Ugly Pittsburgh Pirates: Heart-Pounding, Jaw-Dropping, and Gut-Wrenching Moments from Pittsburgh Pirates History* (Chicago: Triumph Books, 2008), 204.

63. Bruce Markusen, "Remembering the All Black Lineup," *Bruce Markusen's Cooperstown Confidential* (blog), September 1, 2006, http://bruce.mlblogs.com/2006/09/01/remembering-the-all-black-lineup.

64. Miller, *A Whole Different Ball Game*, 131-41; Mark Armour, "Alex Johnson," in *The Year of the Blue Snow: The 1964 Philadelphia Phillies*, eds. Mel Marmer and Bill Nowlin (Phoenix: Society for American Baseball Research, 2013), 137; Burk, *Much More than a Game*, 168; Hylton, "The Historical Origins of Baseball Grievance Arbitration,183-84.

65. The San Diego Padres signed a membership agreement with the National League on August 15, 1968; the Seattle Pilots signed a membership agreement with the American League on October 1, 1968. *Portland Baseball Club, Inc. v. Kuhn*, 368 F. Supp. 1004, 1005 (D. Ore. 1971), aff'd, 491 F.2d 1101 (9th Cir. 1974).

66. *Ibid.*, 1007.

67. *Ibid.*, 1008-09. Judge Solomon also ruled that the Portland Baseball Club was not the real party in interest and that baseball's antitrust exemption precluded Portland Baseball Club's antitrust claim.

68. Korr, *The End of Baseball As We Knew It*, 102-10; Miller, *A Whole Different Ball Game*, 203-23.

69. Miller, *A Whole Different Ball Game*, 221-22; Robert C. Berry, William B. Gould IV, and Paul D. Staudohar, *Labor Relations in Professional Sports* (Dover, MA: Auburn House, 1986), 60.

70. Rader, *Baseball: A History of America's Game*, 214; "Talking a Walk: A Chronology of Strikes by Major Sports Leagues," *Los Angeles Times*, April 3, 1992, C2.

71. *Flood v. Kuhn*, 407 U.S. 258 (1972). For more about the case, see Alex Belth, *Stepping Up: The Story of All-Star Curt Flood and His Fight for Baseball Players' Rights* (New York: Persea Books, 2006); Snyder, *A Well-Paid Slave*; Robert Michael Goldman, *One Man Out: Curt Flood versus Baseball* (Lawrence: University Press of Kansas, 2008).

72. In particular, Blackmun proclaims that "1. Professional baseball is a business and it is engaged in interstate commerce. 2. With its reserve system enjoying exemption from the federal antitrust laws, baseball is, in a very distinct

sense, an exception and an anomaly. *Federal Baseball* and *Toolson* have become an aberration confined to baseball. 3.... [T]he aberration is an established one ... deemed fully entitled to the benefit of *stare decisis*, ... and one that has survived the Court's expanding concept of interstate commerce.... [The Court] has voiced a preference that if any change is to be made, it come by legislative action that, by its nature, is only prospective in operation." *Flood v. Kuhn*, 282–83.

73. *Ibid.*, 286 (Douglas, J., dissenting).

74. *Ibid.*, 294 (Marshall, J., dissenting).

75. *Ibid.*, 260–65. "[Blackmun's] list is the most widely known presentation of a 'who's who' in baseball. It is certainly the only one to appear in the West volumes of reported decisions." Abrams, "Blackmun's List," 188.

76. Joseph Durso, "Delay Called in Spring Training," *New York Times*, February 9, 1973, 17.

77. Murray Chass, "Baseball Peace Arrives With 3-Year Accord," *New York Times*, February 26, 1973, 39; Leonard Koppett, "6-Year-Old Union Keeps Players' Benefits in Step," *New York Times*, February 26, 1973, 39; Charles Korr, *The End of Baseball As We Knew It*, 126–30.

78. Dave Brady, "Curt Flood's Fight Was Not in Vain," *Washington Post*, February 28, 1973, D1.

79. Murray Chass, "Two Yankees Disclose Family Exchange," *New York Times*, March 6, 1973, 51; Flannery, "Affairs of the Heart," 183–84; "Trade of the Century," *Sports Illustrated*, July 31, 2000, 147.

80. Berlage, *Women in Baseball*, 99; "Girl Ballplayer Gets to First Base," *New York Times*, June 20, 1973, 46.

81. *Nat'l Organization for Women, Essex County Chapter v. Little League Baseball, Inc*, 318 A.2d 33, 35 (N.J. Super. Ct. App. Div. 1974), *aff'd summarily*, 338 A.2d 198 (N.J. 1974).

82. Douglas E. Abrams, "The Twelve-Year-Old Girl's Lawsuit that Changed America: The Continuing Impact of *Now v. Little League Baseball, Inc.* at 40," *Virginia Journal of Social Policy & the Law* 20 (2012): 251–52. Unfortunately, by the time the matter was resolved by the legal system, Maria Pepe, at age 13, was too old to play Little League baseball. Berlage, *Women in Baseball*, 101.

83. Maria Pepe, as told to Jeff Merron, "Breaking Barriers," *ESPN Page 2*, updated July 22, 2005, http://.espn.go.com [search "maria pepe"].

84. John Rosengren, *Hammerin' Hank, George Almighty & the Say Hey Kid: The Year that Changed Baseball Forever* (Naperville, IL: Sourcebooks, 2008), 306–08; "Guilty Pleas in Campaign Gift Case," *San Francisco Chronicle*, August 24, 1974.

85. Bill Madden, *Steinbrenner: The Last Lion of Baseball* (New York: HarperCollins, 2010), 64–66; Kuhn, *Hardball*, 199 ("Illegal contributions may be one thing, but obstruction of justice is quite another.... People get put in jail for obstruction of justice.").

86. Madden, *Steinbrenner*, 63–64, 102.

87. G. Michael Green and Roger D. Launius, *Charlie Finley: The Outrageous Story of Baseball's Super Showman* (New York: Walker & Co., 2010), 215; Leonard Koppett, "A's Hunter Ruled Free Agent," *New York Times*, December 16, 1974, 51; Miller, *A Whole Different Ball Game*, 233.

88. Burk, *Much More than a Game*, 191; 216; Miller, *A Whole Different Ball Game*, 235.

89. Green and Launius, *Charlie Finley*, 216; Leonard Koppett, "A's Plan Suit Today Over Hunter," *New York Times*, December 18, 1974, 59.

90. Leonard Koppett, "Backing of Hunter Arbitration Decision Called Prelude to Changing Pro Sports Setup," *New York Times*, January 5, 1975, S4; Burk, *Much More than a Game*, 191.

91. Ira Berkow, "Catfish Hunter, Who Pitched in 6 World Series for A's and Yankees, Dies at 53," *New York Times*, September 10, 1999, A1 (lists value of contract as $3.35 million); Helyar, *Lords of the Realm*, 148–50 ($3.5 million); Burk, *Much More than a Game*, 192 ($3.75 million).

92. Matt Rothenberg, "From One Robinson to Another," *Inside Pitch*, National Baseball Hall of Fame E-Newsletter, April 13, 2015, http://baseballhall.org/discover/breaking-baseball-barriers-from-one-robinson-to-another. On October 15, 1972, during a celebration of the 25th anniversary of his breaking the color line, Jackie Robinson spoke about baseball's failure to employ blacks beyond the playing field: "I'd like to live to see a black manager, I'd like to live to see the day when there is a black man coaching at third base." Rachel Robinson, with Lee Daniels, *Jackie Robinson: An Intimate Portrait* (New York: Abrams, 1996), 216. He died nine days later on October 24, 1972, and thus did not see Frank Robinson become the first black Major League manager.

93. For Robinson's first-hand account of how he became baseball's first black manager, see Frank Robinson, with Roy Blount, Jr., "I'll Always Be Outspoken," *Sports Illustrated*, October 21, 1974, 30–38.

94. Lew Freedman, *African American Pioneers of Baseball: A Biographical Encyclopedia* (Westport, CT: Greenwood Press, 2007), 231–32.

95. Kates, "Frank Robinson," SABR Baseball Biography Project, http://sabr.org/bioproj/person/c3ac5482.

Chapter Notes—6

96. Alexander Campanis, Baseball Glove, U.S. Patent 3,898,696, filed October 15, 1974, and issued August 12, 1975.

97. Roger I. Abrams, "Liberation Arbitration: The Baseball Reserve Clause Case," in *Proceedings of the 55th Annual Meeting of the National Academy of Arbitrators* (Washington, DC: Bureau of National Affairs, 2003), 192. Similarly, Richard Moss, who argued the case on behalf of the Players Association, will say of the case: "In financial impact, it was probably the biggest grievance arbitration case in the history of labor relations. Over the years, the difference between winning and losing that case can be described in billions of dollars." Julia Collins, "HLS Names in Lights: Baseball Player's Agent," *Harvard Law Bulletin* (Spring 1998), http://today.law.harvard.edu/bulletin/issue/spring-1998/.

98. Kenneth Denlinger, "If You Don't Like the Call, Then Fire the Umpire," *Washington Post*, December 25, 1975, E11.

99. "Sale of Baseball Giants to Group in Toronto Is Halted Temporarily," *Wall Street Journal*, January 14, 1976, 11.

100. Kuhn, *Hardball*, 190–91.

101. Berry, Gould, and Staudohar, *Labor Relations in Professional Sports*, 61; Kenneth M. Jennings, *Swings and Misses: Moribund Labor Relations in Professional Baseball* (Westport, CT: Praeger, 1997), 3–4.

102. "Bowie Kuhn Orders Camps to Open," *Chicago Tribune*, March 18, 1976, C1; Murray Chass, "Training Slated to Start Today: Kuhn Orders Camps to Open," *New York Times*, March 18, 1976, 64; Joseph Durso, "Baseball Clubs Begin Training 18 Days Late," *New York Times*, March 19, 1976, 1; Korr, *The End of Baseball As We Knew It*, 181; Kuhn, *Hardball*, 161–64. Although Kuhn would never admit it, many felt that Dodger owner Walter O'Malley, concerned about losing lucrative game dates, persuaded the commissioner to open the spring training camps and end the lockout. McCue, *Mover and Shaker*, 349; Helyar, *Lords of the Realm*, 175–76.

103. Richard Dozer, "Players OK New Pact," *Chicago Tribune*, July 13, 1976, C1.

104. *Kansas City Royals Baseball Corp. v. Major League Baseball Players Ass'n.*, 532 F.2d 615 (8th Cir. 1976).

105. Gould, *Bargaining with Baseball*, 53.

106. Mark Armour, "Charlie Finley," in *Mustaches and Mayhem: Charlie O's Three-Time Champions, The Oakland Athletics 1972–74*, ed. Chip Greene (Phoenix: Society for American Baseball Research, 2015), 22; McCue, *Mover and Shaker*, 349.

107. Michael Fallon, "Steve Yeager," SABR Baseball Biography Project, accessed March 23, 2016, http://sabr.org/bioproj/person/69e2594b.

108. William J. Buhler, Throat Protecting Attachment for A Baseball Catcher's Mask, U.S. Patent D258322, filed October 16, 1978, issued February 24, 1981.

109. Buhler was not the first to devise a mask with a "billy goat" extension designed to protect the catcher's neck. In the 1888 edition of *Spalding's Official Baseball Guide*, A.G. Spalding and Brothers offered for sale its "New Patented Neck-Protecting Mask" with a "peculiar shaped extension at the bottom which affords the same protection to the neck as the mask does to the face." Morris, *A Game of Inches: The Game on the Field*, 299.

110. Jason Reid, "Trainer Buhler Dies at 75," *Los Angeles Times*, May 19, 2003, D5; William J. Buhler, Baseball Player's Chest Protector, U.S. Patent 4,272,847, filed April 30, 1979, issued June 16, 1981.

111. Select Comm. on Professional Sports, *Inquiry Into Professional Sports: Final Report of the Select Committee on Professional Sports*, H.R. Rep. No. 94–1786, at 4 (1977); "Baseball's Immunity Questioned," *Los Angeles Times*, January 4, 1977, D2; "Panel Opposes Pro Baseball's Exempt Status," *Los Angeles Times*, January 3, 1977, B2.

112. Select Comm. on Professional Sports, *Inquiry Into Professional Sports*, 4; "House Asks More Study on Baseball," *New York Times*, January 4, 1977, L35; Nancy Scannell, "Panel Delays Antitrust Vote," *Washington Post*, January 4, 1977, C1.

113. *Inquiry into Professional Sports, Part 1: Hearings Before the House Select Committee on Professional Sports*, 94th Cong. (1976); *Inquiry into Professional Sports, Part 2: Hearings Before the House Select Committee on Professional Sports*, 94th Cong. (1976).

114. *Atlanta Nat'l League Baseball Club. Inc. v. Kuhn*, 432 F. Supp. 1213, 1216–17 (N.D. Ga. 1977). For more on the Kuhn-Turner litigation, see Eldon L. Ham, "The Theft of Gary Matthews," chap. 16 in Ham, *Larceny and Old Leather*; Helyar, *Lords of the Realm*, 225–26; Mitchell Nathanson, *A People's History of Baseball* (Champaign: University of Illinois Press, 2012), 48–51.

115. *Atlanta Nat'l League Baseball Club.*, 1223.

116. Deirdre Carmody, "Female Reporter Sues Over Locker-Room Ban," *New York Times*, December 30, 1977, A17.

117. *Ludtke v. Kuhn*, 461 F. Supp. 86, 98 (S.D.N.Y. 1978).

118. *Finley v. Kuhn*, 569 F.2d 527 (7th Cir. 1978).

119. Art. I, Sec. 2 of the Major League Agreement in force at the time of the litigation provided in part:

The functions of the Commissioner shall be as follows: (a) To investigate, either upon complaint or upon his own initiative, any act, transaction or practice charged, alleged or suspected to be not in the best interests of the national game of Baseball.... (b) To determine, after investigation, what preventive, remedial or punitive action is appropriate in the premises, and to take such action either against Major Leagues, Major League Clubs or individuals, as the case may be." *Finley v. Kuhn*, 533 n. 11.

120. For further discussion of the litigation and decision, see Green and Launius, *Charlie Finley*, 247–59; Kuhn, *Hardball*, 173–87; Miller, *A Whole Different Ball Game*, 377–79.

121. Robert Cover, "Your Law-Baseball Quiz," *N.Y. Times*, April 5, 1979, A23, reprinted in Waller, Cohen & Finkelman, *Baseball and the American Legal Mind*, 431–33.

122. McKelvey, *The MacPhails*, 204.

123. "Umpires Return to Work Today," *Chicago Tribune*, May 19, 1979, G1; Koppett, *Koppett's Concise History of Major League Baseball*, 405.

124. Danny Robbins, "Peace Turns Into Cold War for New Umps," *Chicago Tribune*, August 12, 1979, C3.

125. "Paul in the Hall," *Roll Call*, June 26, 2012, http://www.rollcall.com/heard-on-the-hill/paul-in-the-hall/. Massachusetts Representative Joe O'Connell hit a three-run homer in the initial 1909 game, but there is some question about whether it was an inside-the-park shot. "Solons Play Ball; Minority Shows That It Can Swat the Leather," *Washington Post*, July 17, 1909, 1 ("He was pretty groggy at the finish and stumbled near the plate, but James Francis muffed the ball and O'Connell got by."); "Rush This to Lincoln, Neb.; Democrats Win National Victory; After That the Deluge," *Chicago Daily Tribune*, July 17, 1909, 2 ("The Washington public had forgotten what a home run looked like until Representative O'Connell ... lined one out in the seventh.").

126. "Democrats in Landslide," *Washington Post*, July 27, 1979, E2.

127. Elizabeth Traynor, "Ron Paul Inducted into Congressional Baseball Hall of Fame—In Astros Garb," *Houston Chronicle* (blog), June 28, 2012, http://blog.chron.com/txpotomac/2012/06/ron-paul-inducted-into-congressional-baseball-hall-of-fame-%E2%80%93-in-astros-garb/.

128. Ginsburg, *The Fix Is In*, 238; James Tuite, "Mays Leaving Baseball," *New York Times*, October 30, 1979, B15; James S. Hirsch, *Willie Mays: The Life, The Legend* (New York: Scribner, 2010), 536–37.

129. Ginsburg, *The Fix Is In*, 239; Hirsch, *Willie Mays*, 538.

130. Rom Fimrite, "Mantle & Mays," *Sports Illustrated*, March 25, 1985, 72 (quoting Ueberroth); Michael Martinez, "Mays and Mantle Reinstated," *New York Times*, March 19, 1985, B7.

131. Murray Chass, "Ryan Going to Astros for $4 Million," *New York Times*, November 16, 1979, A25; Abrams, *The Money Pitch*, 33; Michael Haupert, "Baseball's Major Salary Milestones," *Baseball Research Journal* 40 (Fall 2011), 91.

132. Murray Chass, "Ryan Pact Reflects Splurge in Baseball," *New York Times*, November 20, 1979, B16.

133. Murray Chass, "Strike Is Authorized By Baseball Players," *New York Times*, March 5, 1980, B5.

134. Murray Chass, "Baseball Exhibition Strike In Effect Amidst Confusion," *New York Times*, April 3, 1980, A37; Korr, *The End of Baseball As We Knew It*, 198; Berry, Gould, and Staudohar, *Labor Relations in Professional Sports*, 65.

135. Jane Leavy, "Strike Is Off, Study Set on Compensation," *Washington Post*, May 24, 1980, C1; Berry, Gould, and Staudohar, *Labor Relations in Professional Sports*, 66.

136. Kostya Kennedy, *Pete Rose: An American Dilemma* (New York: Sports Illustrated Books, 2014), 231.

137. Murray Chass, "Carew, Perry and Jenkins Are Voted Into Hall of Fame," *New York Times*, January 9, 1991, B7; Ferguson Jenkins, with Lew Freedman, *Fergie: My Life from the Cubs to Cooperstown* (Chicago: Triumph Books, 2009), 159; Staudohar, *Playing for Dollars*, 55.

138. Jenkins, *Fergie*, 157.

139. Chass, "Carew, Perry and Jenkins Are Voted Into Hall of Fame."

140. H.R. 7903, 96th Cong. (1980).

141. *Excessive Violence in Professional Sports: Hearing on H.R. 7903 Before the Subcomm. on Crime of the H. Comm. on the Judiciary*, 96th Cong. 5 (1981) (statement of Rep. Ron Mottl).

142. Ibid., 204.

143. Joseph Durso, "Free-Agent Stalemate is Hinted," *New York Times*, January 4, 1981, S3; Korr, *The End of Baseball As We Knew It*, 205–07; Lowenfish, *The Imperfect Diamond*, 233.

144. Red Smith, "A Shot Heard Round Baseball," *New York Times*, February 20, 1981, B9.

145. Murray Chass, "Baseball Strike Off as Players, Owners Extend Deadline," *New York Times*, May 29, 1981, A17; Korr, *The End of Baseball As We Knew It*, 213.

146. Murray Chass, "Baseball Players Go Out on Strike After Talks With the Owners Fail," *New York Times*, June 12, 1981, A1; Korr, *The End of Baseball As We Knew It*, 213; Lowenfish, *The Imperfect Diamond*, 238; Dave Nightingale, "Miller Says Strike 'Is On' As Baseball

Talks Break Off," *Chicago Tribune*, June 12, 1981, C1.

147. Jim Kaplan, "No Games Today," *Sports Illustrated*, June 22, 1981, 17.

148. Jim Kaplan, "Let the Games Begin," *Sports Illustrated*, August 10, 1981, 14–19; Murray Chass, "Strike Over, Baseball Resumes Aug. 9," *New York Times*, August 1, 1981, 1; Lowenfish, *The Imperfect Diamond*, 245 (listing the announcement date as July 29, 1981); Robert Markus, "Both Sides Lost—Reinsdorf," *Chicago Tribune*, August 1, 1981, N1.

149. "Baseball Strike Issues," *New York Times*, August 1, 1981, 18; Berry, Gould, Staudohar, *Labor Relations in Professional Sports*, 73.

150. Robert Markus, "Split-Season Plan Goes Against Sox," *Chicago Tribune*, August 7, 1981, C1.

151. *Fleer Corp. v. Topps Chewing Gum, Inc.*, 658 F.2d 139 (3d Cir. 1981).

152. *Ibid.*, 149–50.

153. *Ibid.*, 154.

154. "Valenzuela Granted $1 Million," *New York Times*, February 20, 1983, S9; Vic Wilson, "Fernandomania," *National Pastime: Endless Seasons—Baseball in Southern California* (SABR 41 Convention Issue, 2011), 94.

155. Mark Heisler, "Fernando Hits Jackpot for Million," *Los Angeles Times*, February 20, 1983, F1; "Fernando Feels Like a Million," *Chicago Tribune*, February 20, 1983, C2.

156. "Fehr Elected by Players," *New York Times*, December 9, 1983, B5; Staudohar, *Playing For Dollars*, 29.

157. "Donald M. Fehr, Executive Director," Major League Baseball Players Association, accessed July 31, 2015, http://mlbplayers.mlb.com/pa/bios/fehr.jsp.

158. Schwarz and Schmidt, "After 26 Years, Fehr Says He Will Retire as Union Chief."

159. *Selig v. United States*, 740 F.2d 572, 575 (7th Cir. 1984).

160. *Ibid.*, 580.

161. "Brewers' Selig Gets Good News," *Sporting News*, August 13, 1984, 19.

162. Murray Chass, "Salary Arbitration Is Major Obstacle," *New York Times*, August 5, 1985, C3.

163. Kenneth Reich, "Baseball Strike Settled; Play to Resume Today," *Los Angeles Times*, August 8, 1985, A1.

164. Aaron Skirboll, *The Pittsburgh Cocaine Seven: How A Rugtag Group of Fans Took the Fall for Major League Baseball* (Chicago: Chicago Review Press, 2010), 189.

165. *Ibid.*, 170–81.

166. Ross Newhan, "Ueberroth Suspends Seven Players for Use of Drugs," *Los Angeles Times*, March 1, 1986; Michael Goodwin, "Baseball Orders Suspension of 11 Drug Users," *New York Times*, March 1, 1986, 1; Peter S. Finley, Laura L. Finley, and Jeffrey Fountain, *Sports Scandals* (Westport, CT: Greenwood Press, 2008), 29.

167. John Trechak, "The Seventh Circuit Beans Performer Publicity Rights in Baseball's Telecast Rights Rhubarb," *Loyola Los Angeles Entertainment Law Review* 8 (1988), 76.

168. David E. Shipley, "Three Strikes and They're out at the Old Ball Game: Preemption of Performers' Rights of Publicity under the Copyright Act of 1976," *Arizona State Law Journal* 20 (1988), 370–71.

169. *Balt. Orioles, Inc. v. Major League Baseball Players Ass'n*, 805 F.2d 663, 667–70 (7th Cir. 1986).

170. *Ibid.*, 674–79.

171. *Parks v. Steinbrenner*, 520 N.Y.S.2d 374, 375 (App. Div. 1987).

172. "Steinbrenner Is Disputed," *New York Times*, September 1, 1982, B8; Kirk Johnson, "Heckling Umpires: It's Legal," *New York Times*, July 24, 1987, B1.

173. *Parks v. Steinbrenner*, 376–77.

174. *Kelly v. Marylanders for Sports Sanity, Inc.*, 530 A.2d 245, 256–57 (Md. Ct. App. 1987).

175. Peter Richmond, *Ballpark: Camden Yards and the Building of an American Dream* (New York: Simon & Schuster, 1993), 127.

176. Murray Chass, "Ruling Backs Players on Collusion Charges Against Teams in '85," *New York Times*, September 22, 1987, A1.

177. Ross Newhan, "Arbitrator Rules Baseball Owners Guilty of Collusion," *Los Angeles Times*, September 22, 1987, N1; Jerome Holtzman, "Arbitrator: Baseball Owners in Collusion," *Chicago Tribune*, September 22, 1987, C1.

178. In re Arbitration Between Major League Baseball Players Ass'n & Twenty-Six Major League Baseball Clubs, Grievance No. 86-2, Panel Decision No. 76, reprinted in part in Dean A. Sullivan, ed., *Final Innings: A Documentary History of Baseball, 1972–2008* (Lincoln: University of Nebraska Press, 2010), 138.

179. *Croteau v. Fair*, 686 F. Supp. 552 (E.D. Va. 1988); Caryle Murphy and Peter Pae, "Judge Rejects Bias Claim of Girl Cut from Baseball Team," *Washington Post*, March 24, 1988, D1; Leslie A. Heaphy and Mel Anthony May, *Encyclopedia of Women and Baseball* (Jefferson, NC: McFarland, 2006), 82.

180. "Flawless At First," *New York Times*, March 19, 1989, S1; Berlage, *Women in Baseball*, 108.

181. Deirdre Fleming, "Coach Attempting to Stay Focused," *Bangor (Me.) Daily News*, April 25, 1996, C7.

182. "Casey at the Bat: A Ballad of the Republic, Sung in the Year 1888," *Examiner* (San Francisco), June 3, 1888, 4. Actor DeWolf Hopper will offer the first public recitation of the

poem on the night of August 14, 1888, at Wallack's Theatre in New York City during the intermission of the McCaull's Light Opera Company's presentation of *Prince Methusalem*. Prominent among the audience are members of the New York Giants and Chicago White Stockings, who earlier in the day had completed a historic game in which the Chicago nine beat their New York rivals, 4–2, thereby ending pitcher Tim Keefe's 19-game winning streak, still the major league single season record. By his own estimate, Hopper will go on to recite "Casey at the Bat" more than 10,000 times over the next several decades. Peter Mancuso, "Tim Keefe Finally Loses," in Felber, *Inventing Baseball*, 196–97.

183. John Evangelist Walsh, *The Night Casey Was Born: The True Story Behind the Great American Ballad "Casey at the Bat"* (Woodstock, NY: Overlook Press, 2007), 174–75; 134 Cong. Rec. 13361–62 (1988) (statement of Rep. Lantos).

184. Murray Chass, "Grievance Is Filed Over Parrish Talks," *New York Times*, February 21, 1987, 50; "Grievance Registered by Players," *Washington Post*, February 21, 1987, C5; Staudohar, *Playing For Dollars*, 38.

185. Jerome Holtzman, "Collusion II: Owners Found Guilty Again," *Chicago Tribune*, September 1, 1988, D1; Gould, *Bargaining with Baseball*, 90–91.

186. Bryan Curtis, "The Steroid Hunt," *Grantland*, January 8, 2014, http://grantland.com [search "steroid"]; Andrew S. Zimbalist, *Circling the Bases: Essays on the Challenges and Prospects of the Sports Industry* (Philadelphia: Temple University Press, 2011), 152.

187. "Report That He Used Steroids Denied by Athletics' Canseco," *St. Louis Post-Dispatch*, October 1, 1988, C3.

188. Kevin Nelson, *Baseball's Even Greater Insults* (New York: Simon & Schuster, 1993), 39. Canseco will take the vitriol with good humor, flexing his muscles in response to the chanting. Ibid.

189. Mike Penner, "Sound and Vision: If Anything, This Juicy Story Sure Has Legs," *Los Angeles Times*, February 14, 2005, D4; Curtis, "The Steroid Hunt"; José Canseco, *Juiced: Wild Times, Rampant 'Roids, Smash Hits, and How Baseball Got Big* (New York: Regan Books, 2005).

190. Michael Martinez, "Bill White a Unanimous Choice to Head National League," *New York Times*, February 4, 1989, 47.

191. Bill White, with Gordon Dillow, *Uppity: My Untold Story About the Games People Play* (New York: Grand Central Pub., 2011), 112–20.

192. Warren Corbett, "Bill White," in *Drama and Pride in the Gateway City: The 1964 St. Louis Cardinals*, ed. John Harry Stahl and Bill Nowlin (Lincoln: University of Nebraska Press and Society for American Baseball Research, 2013), 235–36; White, *Uppity*, 191.

193. John M. Dowd et al., *Report to the Commissioner: In the Matter of Peter Edward Rose, Manager, Cincinnati Reds Baseball Club* (May 9, 1989), available at http://www.thedowdreport.com.

194. Office of the Commissioner of Baseball, In the Matter of Peter Edward Rose (August 23, 1989), Baseball Almanac, accessed March 18, 2015, http://www.baseball-almanac.com/players/p_rosea.shtml; Kennedy, *Pete Rose*, 212–13.

195. James Reston, Jr., *Collision at Home Plate: The Lives of Pete Rose and Bart Giamatti* (New York: Edward Burlingame Books, 1991), 305–08. Explaining his banning of Rose from Organized Baseball, Giamatti said: "One of the game's greatest players has engaged in a variety of acts which have stained the game, and he must now live with the consequences of those acts." He then concluded his statement: "The matter of Mr. Rose is now closed. It will be debated and discussed. Let no one think that it did not hurt baseball. That hurt will pass, however, as the great glory of the game asserts itself and a resilient institution goes forward. Let it also be clear that no individual is superior to the game." Office of the Commissioner of Baseball, Statement of A. Bartlett Giamatti (August 24, 1989), Baseball Almanac, accessed March 18, 2015, http://www.baseball-almanac.com/players/p_roseb.shtml.

196. Stephen L. Willis, "A Critical Perspective of Baseball's Collusion Decisions," *Seton Hall Journal of Sports Law* 1 (1991), 109–10; Marc Edelman, "Has Collusion Returned to Baseball? Analyzing Whether a Concerted Increase in Free Agent Player Supply Would Violate Baseball's 'Collusion Clause,'" *Loyola of Los Angeles Entertainment Law Review* 24 (2004), 164.

197. In fact, soon after Roberts made his initial award of damages, the Players Association submitted additional claims for more than $16.5 million. Burk, *Much More than a Game*, 268.

198. Richard Justice, "Collusion Award Is $10.5 Million; Baseball Owners Are Wincing," *Washington Post*, September 1, 1989, H1.

199. *Pirone v. Macmillan, Inc.*, 894 F.2d 579, 582 (2d Cir. 1990); Amy Dockser Marcus and Wade Lambert, "Court Limits Superfund Pollution Liability," *Wall Street Journal*, January 30, 1990, B11; "Daughters of Babe Ruth Lose in Appeals Court Ruling," *Toledo Blade*, January 30, 1990, 21.

200. *Pirone v. Macmillan, Inc.*, 585–86.

201. Murray Chass, "Lockout's On, But Vincent Has Suggestions," *New York Times*, February 14, 1990, B9.

202. Dickson, *The Dickson Baseball Dictionary*, 3rd ed., 843.

203. Richard Justice, "Baseball Dispute Is Settled, Season to Open on April 9," *Washington Post*, March 19, 1990, A1.
204. Chass, "Lockout's On, But Vincent Has Suggestions."
205. Mike Towle, *Pete Rose: Baseball's Charlie Hustle* (Nashville, TN: Cumberland House, 2003), 217; Ginsburg, *The Fix Is In*, 252.
206. William A. Cook, *Pete Rose: Baseball's All-Time Hit King* (Jefferson, NC: McFarland, 2004), 136–42 (includes excerpts of the transcript of the proceedings, including Spiegel's questioning of Rose and his statement upon issuing the sentence).
207. Kennedy, *Pete Rose*, 221–31. Within a month, on February 4, 1991, the Hall's board of directors will unanimously approve adoption of the special committee's recommendation. Although Hall of Fame president Edward Stack will state that the new rule is not aimed specifically at Rose, the all-time career leader in hits is the only living person on the ineligible list at the time of its adoption. Murray Chass, "Board Says Rose Is Ineligible for Hall of Fame," *New York Times*, February 5, 1991, B9.
208. Steve Berkowitz, "Arbitrator Leaves Baseball Owners 0–3 Against Union in Collusion Cases," *Washington Post*, July 19, 1990, C8.
209. Ross Newhan, "Owners Take a Third Strike on Collusion," *Los Angeles Times*, July 19, 1990, 39; Staudohar, *Playing For Dollars*, 39.
210. Claire Smith, "Arbitrator Finds 3d Case of Baseball Collusion," *New York Times*, July 19, 1990, B9.
211. Anabolic Steroids Control Act of 1990, Pub. L. No. 101-647, tit. XIX, 104 Stat. 4851-54 (1990).
212. Murray Chass, "With No Ceremony, Collusion Agreement is Reached," *New York Times*, December 22, 1990, 49.
213. Murray Chass, "Players Said to Hit Collusion Jackpot," *New York Times*, November 4, 1990, S1.
214. "Baseball," *Washington Post*, December 22, 1990, F2.
215. Murray Chass, "Collusion Checks Are Signal of End Of Owners Error," *New York Times*, May 25, 2004, D4; Ross Newhan, "Around the Horn," *Los Angeles Times*, May 30, 2004, D4.
216. Mark Neuhalfen, Baseball Catcher's Chest Protector, U.S. Patent 5,020,156, filed November 14, 1989, and issued June 4, 1991; Rosciam, *The Evolution of Catcher's Equipment*, 108.
217. Memorandum from Francis T. Vincent, Jr., to All Major League Clubs, "Baseball's Drug Policy and Prevention Program," June 7, 1991, 2.
218. George J. Mitchell, *Report to the Commissioner of Baseball of an Independent Investigation into the Illegal Use of Steroids and Other Performance Enhancing Substances by Players in Major League Baseball* (December 13, 2007), 41, available at http://files.mlb.com/mitchrpt.pdf. See also entry for November 29, 1990.
219. *Postema v. Nat'l League of Prof'l Baseball Clubs*, 799 F. Supp. 1475 (S.D.N.Y. 1992), *rev'd on other grounds*, 998 F.2d 60 (2d Cir. 1993).
220. *Ibid.*, 1478. The three who proceeded Postema were Amanda Clement (semi-pro level, 1905), Bernice Gera (Class A New York-Penn League, 1972), and Christine Wren (Class A Northwest and Midwest Leagues, 1975–77). Ardell, *Breaking into Baseball*, 138–48.
221. *Postema v. Nat'l League of Prof'l Baseball Clubs*, 1479.
222. Grant Wahl, "Baseball Umpire Pam Postema—March 14, 1988," *Sports Illustrated*, April 28, 1997, [14]. According to docket information available on Westlaw, the case was closed and dismissed with prejudice and without costs on October 22, 1993. For more information about Postema's career as an umpire, although not the case since the book does not cover the litigation, see Pam Postema & Gene Wojciechowski, *You've Got to Have B*lls to Make It in This League* (New York: Simon & Schuster, 1992).
223. *Chicago Nat'l League Ball Club, Inc. v. Vincent*. The opinion was originally available at 1992 WL 179208 (N.D. Ill.) and 1992 U.S. Dist. LEXIS 14948 (N.D. Ill.). Because of Judge Conlon's order to withdraw and vacate the judgment, the opinion is no longer available on Westlaw or LexisNexis. However, an edited version of the original opinion is available in Michael J. Cozzillio et al., *Sports Law: Cases & Materials*, 2nd ed. (Durham, NC: Carolina Academic Press, 2007), 86–92.
224. Cozzillio et al., *Sports Law*, 91.
225. Ross Newhan, "Merely a Charge, or Act of Sin?" *Los Angeles Times*, August 8, 1993, C8; *Piazza v. Major League Baseball*, 831 F. Supp. 420, 422 (E.D. Pa. 1993).
226. *Piazza v. Major League Baseball*, 422–23. In January 1993, Lurie accepted a $100 million offer from a group of San Francisco-based investors headed by Peter Magowan, chairman of the Safeway supermarket chain. William Carlsen, "Giants Sale to New Owners Final," *San Francisco Chronicle*, January 15, 1993, A22.
227. *Piazza v. Major League Baseball*, 421.
228. *Ibid.*, 436.
229. Mitchell Nathanson, "Law," in *Understanding Baseball: A Textbook*, ed. Trey Strecker et al. (Jefferson, NC: McFarland, 2015), 150.
230. Dubbed the "Great Lakes Gang" by the Chicago media, the group consisted of Stanton Cook, Chairman, Chicago Cubs; Bud Selig, President, Milwaukee Brewers; Peter O'Malley;

Owner, Los Angeles Dodgers; Carl Pohlad, Owner, Minnesota Twins; Jerry Reinsdorf, Chairman, Chicago White Sox; and William Bartholomay, Chairman, Atlanta Braves. Steve Marantz, "The Great Lakes Gang," *The Sporting News*, September 19, 1994, 32; Holtzman, *The Commissioners*, 4.

231. Murray Chass, "Owners, in an 18–9 Vote, Ask Vincent to Resign," *New York Times*, September 4, 1992, B7.

232. Murray Chass, "Vincent, Bowing to Owners' Will, Resigns as Baseball Commissioner," *New York Times*, September 8, 1992, A1.

233. Rick Pearson, "'Foul Ball' Law Restricts Suits," *Chicago Tribune*, September 25, 1992.

234. 745 Ill. Comp. Stat. Ann. 38/10 (West 2010).

235. *Coronel v. Chicago White Sox*, 595 N.E.2d 45 (Ill. App. Ct. 1992); *Yates v. Chicago Nat'l League Ball Club*, 595 N.E.2d 570 (Ill. App. Ct. 1992); Ted J. Tierney, "Heads Up! The Baseball Facility Liability Act," *Northern Illinois University Law Review* 18 (1998), 610.

236. Ariz. Rev. Stat. Ann. § 12–554 (2003); Colorado Baseball Spectator Safety Act of 1993, Colo. Rev. Stat. § 13–21–120 (2014); New Jersey Baseball Spectator Safety Act of 2006, N.J. Stat. Ann § 2A:53A-43–53A-48.

237. Douglas Martin, "Historic Day at Bar: Dodger Stays in Brooklyn," *New York Times*, April 9, 1993, B1.

238. *Major League Baseball Properties, Inc. v. Sed Non Olet Denarius, Ltd.*, 817 F. Supp. 1103, 1126 (S.D.N.Y. 1993), vacated 859 F. Supp. 80 (S.D.N.Y. 1994).

239. *Ibid.*, 1127.

240. *New Orleans Pelicans Baseball, Inc. v. Nat'l Ass'n of Prof'l Baseball Leagues, Inc.*,1994 WL 631144 (U.S. Dist. Ct. E.D. La. Mar. 1, 1994).

241. 831 F. Supp. 420 (E.D. Pa. 1993).

242. *New Orleans Pelicans Baseball, Inc.*, *8.

243. "Newcombe Sues Over Beer Ad," *New York Times*, March 11, 1994, B12.

244. Freedman, *African American Pioneers of Baseball*, 106; A.S. Doc Young, "Don Newcombe: Baseball Great Wins Fight Against Alcoholism," *Ebony*, April 1976, 62.

245. *Newcombe v. Adolf Coors Co.*, 157 F.3d 686, 692 (9th Cir. 1998).

246. Gai Ingham Berlage, "The Colorado Bullets," *Baseball Research Journal* 27 (1998), 40–42; Ardell, *Breaking into Baseball*, 121–23.

247. Heaphy and May, *Encyclopedia of Women and Baseball*, 259; "Colorado Silver Bullets Live Out Their Baseball Dreams," *Santa Cruz Sentinel*, May 16, 1994, 13.

248. Mary H.J. Farrell, "Baseball's for Men Only? These Girls of Summer Say It Ain't So," *People*, June 6, 1994, 63; Christina V. Godbey, "Deputy D.A. Makes Her Case for Reviving Pro Baseball League," *Los Angeles Times*, November 21, 1993, 2; Andrea Higbie, "The Lady Is A Pitcher (and a Prosecutor)," *New York Times*, September 4, 1994, 30.

249. Murray Chass, "The Labor Negotiations: Ball's in Whose Court?" *New York Times*, July 30, 1994, 31; Duquette, *Regulating the National Pastime*, 105.

250. Murray Chass, "Mediation Is Set, But Not One Batter Comes to the Plate," *New York Times*, August 13, 1994, 1.

251. Murray Chass, "No Runs, No Hits, No Errors: Baseball Goes on Strike," *New York Times*, August 12, 1994, A1; Staudohar, *Playing for Dollars*, 22.

252. Baseball Fans and Communities Protection Act, H.R. 4994, 103rd Cong. (1994).

253. Koppett, *Koppett's Concise History of Major League Baseball*, 456–63.

254. 831 F. Supp. 420 (E.D. Pa. 1993).

255. *Butterworth v. Nat'l League of Prof'l Baseball Clubs*, 644 So. 2d 1021, 1025 (Fla. 1994).

256. *Kaplan v. Vincent*, 937 F. Supp. 307, 310 (S.D.N.Y. 1996).

257. Richard Sandomir, "In Proposal, Vincent Memoir Airs Criticisms," *New York Times*, March 4, 1994, B9; Dean Chadwin, "Writer Cries Balk, Sues to Publish the Secret Story of Fay Vincent," *Observer*, October 13, 1997.

258. *Kaplan v. Vincent*, 317–19.

259. Fay Vincent, *The Last Commissioner: A Baseball Valentine* (New York: Simon & Schuster, 2002).

260. *Silverman v. Major League Baseball Player Relations Comm., Inc.*, 880 F. Supp. 246, 258–59 (S.D.N.Y. 1995); Banner, *The Baseball Trust*, 245.

261. Tom Verducci, "Brushback," *Sports Illustrated*, April 10, 1995, 60–67.

262. The lead named plaintiff, Art Shamsky, hit .300 for the "Miracle Mets" while sharing right field with Ron Swoboda. He also worked as a Mets broadcaster for several years after retiring in 1972. In an episode ("The Dog") of the first season of television comedy *Everyone Loves Raymond*, Ray Barone gives a bulldog that followed him home to his brother Robert. Robert names the dog "Shamsky" after one that he had as a boy which he named for his favorite New York Mets player. Shamsky appeared as himself in a season three episode ("Big Shots"), along with other 1969 Met players, including Tommie Agee, Bud Harrelson, Cleon Jones, Ed Kranepool, and Tug McGraw. Eric Aron, "Art Shamsky," SABR Baseball Biography Project, accessed March 5, 2016, http://sabr.org/bioproj/person/68fc8356.

263. *Shamsky v. Garan, Inc.*, 632 N.Y.S.2d 930, 937 (N.Y. Sup. Ct. 1995).

264. *Ibid.*, 935–36.

265. *McCoy v. Major League Baseball*, 911 F. Supp. 454, 458 (W.D. Wash. 1995).
266. *Ibid.*, 458.

Chapter 7

1. *Jethroe v. Major League Baseball Props., Inc.*, No. 95-72 (W.D. Pa. September 30, 1996).
2. "Lawsuit Dismissed," *New York Times*, October 6, 1996, 13; Richard Goldstein, "Sam Jethroe is Dead at 83; Was Oldest Rookie of the Year," *New York Times*, June 19, 2001, A21.
3. Murray Chass, "Pioneer Black Players To Be Granted Pensions," *New York Times*, January 20, 1997, C9; Gould, *Bargaining with Baseball*, 246.
4. For more about the life of Curt Flood and his fight against baseball's reserve clause, see Flood, with Carter, *The Way It Is*; Belth, *Stepping Up: The Story of Curt Flood and His Fight for Baseball Players' Rights* (New York: Persea Books, 2006); Snyder, *A Well-Paid Slave*; Stuart L. Weiss, *The Curt Flood Story: The Man Behind the Myth* (Columbia: University of Missouri Press, 2007); Goldman, *One Man Out*; Abraham Iqbal Khan, *Curt Flood in the Media: Baseball, Race, and the Demise of the Activist-Athlete* (Jackson: University Press of Mississippi, 2012).
5. 407 U.S. 258 (1972).
6. *Lowe v. California League of Prof'l Baseball*, 65 Cal. Rptr. 2d 105 (1997).
7. *Ibid.*, 106.
8. Pub. L. No. 105-297, § 3, 112 Stat. 2824 (1999). For a contemporary analysis of the Act and its implications, see Symposium, "The Curt Flood Act," *Marquette Sports Law Journal* 9 (1999): 307-444.
9. Other parties are also excluded from using the act, but the most important political challenge to passage involved the minor leagues. Nathaniel Grow, "Reevaluating the Curt Flood Act of 1998," *Nebraska Law Review* 87 (2008), 751-52; Gary R. Roberts, "A Brief Appraisal of the Curt Flood Act of 1998 From the Minor League Perspective," *Marquette Sports Law Journal* 9 (1999), 416.
10. Jason Reid, "Dodgers Sign Kevin Brown for $105 Million," *Los Angeles Times*, December 13, 1998, 1.
11. Dan Rosenheck, "For Critics of Lee's Contract, Brown Deal Is Not Supporting Evidence," *New York Times*, January 3, 2011, D8.
12. Jonathan Fraser Light, *The Cultural Encyclopedia of Baseball*, 2nd ed. (Jefferson, NC: McFarland, 2005), 41; Staudohar, *Playing for Dollars*, 40.
13. Gordon Edes, "Cummings Loses Case," *Boston Globe*, February 10, 1999, C5.
14. *Minnesota Twins Partnership v. State*, 592 N.W.2d 847 (Minn. 1999).
15. 831 F. Supp. 420 (E.D. Pa. 1993).
16. *Minnesota Twins Partnership v. State*, 856.
17. Bill Shaikin, "For Some, an Outdated Ad; for Others, the Mona Lisa," *Los Angeles Times*, July 19, 2000, 7; Tom Zappala and Ellen Zappala, with Lou Blasi, *The T206 Collection: The Players and Their Stories* (Portsmouth, NH: Peter E. Randall, 2010), viii.
18. Michael O'Keeffe and Teri Thompson, *The Card: Collectors, Con Men, and the True Story of History's Most Desired Baseball Card* (New York: William Morrow, 2007), 1-2; Frank Ceresi, "Tobacco Baseball Cards and Wagner's Own Wagner Card," *Baseball Almanac*, accessed December 2, 2015, http://www.baseball-almanac.com/treasure/autont005.shtml; Zappala and Zappala, *The T206 Collection*, viii (noting that Wagner was "an avid tobacco user himself"); "Wagner A Wonder; One Player in Game Who is Not Money Mad," *Sporting News*, October 24, 1912, 2.
19. Rita Reif, "Honus Wagner Baseball Card Goes to Gretzky," *New York Times*, March 23, 1991, 16; David Zax, "A Brief History of the Honus Wagner Baseball Card," Smithsonian.com, April 30, 2007, http://www.smithsonianmag.com [search "wagner card"].
20. Ross E. Davies, "The Law Firm and the League: Morgan, Lewis and Bockius LLP, Major League Baseball, and MLB.com," *Baseball Research Journal* 39 (Fall 2010): 74-75; Ashby Jones, "Tuck in the Bullpen," *American Lawyer*, January 2002, 18.
21. Murray Chass, "Free Agency Key to Future Peace," *New York Times*, October 15, 1987, B17; Davies, "The Law Firm and the League," 75-78.
22. *United States v. Cleveland Indians Baseball Co.*, 532 U.S. 200 (2001).
23. Linda Greenhouse, "Justices Return to Commercial Speech Quandary," *New York Times*, April 18, 2001, A18; Jeffrey C. Honaker, "*United States v. Cleveland Indians*: FICA and FUTA Taxes v. the Social Security Act—Why Have Different Definitions for Identical Language?" *Akron Tax Journal* 17 (2002), 99-131.
24. *Major League Baseball Players Ass'n v. Garvey*, 532 U.S. 504 (2001).
25. *Garvey v. Roberts*, 203 F.3d 580 (9th Cir. 2000).
26. John M. Willis, "Salt Lake Stingers Stung for $600,000," *Rome News-Tribune*, October 3, 2001, 5A; Larry Bowie, "Lawsuit Over Use of Name 'Buzz' Ends with Settlement," *The Whistle* (Ga. Inst. of Technology), October 8, 2001, 1.
27. Jeff Pearlman, "It's a Wrap!" *Sports Illustrated*, October 15, 2001, 49; Light, *The Cultural Encyclopedia of Baseball*, 431.

28. *Popov v. Hayashi*, No. 400545, 2002 WL 31833731 (Cal. Super. Ct. Dec. 18, 2002).

29. Ira Berkow, "73rd Home Run Ball Sells for $450,000," *New York Times*, June 26, 2003, D4.

30. Crosetti, for instance, was a two-time All-Star who played 17 years for the New York Yankees, winning six World Series rings. Camilli also was a two-time All-Star for the Dodgers and the recipient of the Most Valuable Player Award in 1941 when he hit 34 home runs and drove in 120 runs. Though named plaintiff Al Gionfriddo was the least successful as a player, batting only .266 in 228 games over four major league seasons, he is forever known for one of the greatest defensive efforts in World Series history, a spectacular running catch of a deep drive by Joe DiMaggio in Game Six of the 1947 World Series that was captured in an iconic photograph and on video. Rory Costello, "Al Gionfriddo's Memorable Game Six Catch," in Spatz, *The Team that Forever Changed Baseball and America*, 320–22; Richard Goldstein, "Al Gionfriddo, 81; Remembered for '47 Catch," *New York Times*, March 16, 2003, N31.

31. *Gionfriddo v. Major League Baseball*, 114 Cal. Rptr. 2d 307, 317 (Ct. App. 2002).

32. *Metropolitan Sports Facilities Comm'n v. Minnesota Twins Partnership*, 638 N.W.2d 214 (Minn. Ct. App. 2002).

33. Scott R. Rosner, "History and Business of Contraction in Major League Baseball," *Stanford Journal of Law, Business & Finance* 8 (2003), 273–74; Marshall H. Tanick, "Play Ball: Minnesota Baseball Litigation Lore," *National Pastime: Short but Wondrous Summers—Baseball in the North Star State* (SABR 42 Convention Issue, 2012), 142–43.

34. Tom Verducci, "Totally Juiced," *Sports Illustrated*, June 3, 2002, 36. Caminiti also states that "[i]t's no secret what's going on in baseball. At least half the guys are using steroids." Ibid.

35. *Steroid Use in Professional Baseball and Anti-Doping Issues in Amateur Sports: Hearing before the Subcomm. on Consumer Affairs, Foreign Commerce, and Tourism of the S. Comm. on Commerce, Science, and Transportation*, S. Hrg. 107-1126, 107th Cong. Washington, DC: U.S. Govt. Print. Off., 2002; Zimbalist, *Circling the Bases*, 155.

36. Paul D. Staudohar, "Baseball Negotiations: A New Agreement," *Monthly Labor Review* 125 (December 2002), 19–20. Phil Rogers, "Players Propose Steroid Testing; Baseball Owners 'Quite Pleased,'" *Chicago Tribune*, August 8, 2002, 1:1; Jason Reid, "Players Propose Steroid Testing," *Los Angeles Times*, August 8, 2002, D1.

37. "Baseball's Labor Deal," *Los Angeles Times*, August 31, 2002, D4; Staudohar, "Baseball Negotiations," 21.

38. Major League Baseball, "Program Testing for Major Leaguers for Steroids to Commence in 2004," news release, November 13, 2003, http://www.mlb.com/news/press_releases/ [follow "archive" link].

39. David Wharton, "Baseball to Impose Penalties for Steroid Use; Stricter Rule Is Triggered after the Drugs Are Found in More than 5% of Tests on Major Leaguers," *Los Angeles Times*, November 14, 2003, A1; Jack Curry and Jere Longman, "Results of Steroid Testing Spur Baseball to Set Tougher Rules," *New York Times*, November 14, 2003, A1.

40. "Woman Hit by Chair Likely Will Sue Rangers for Injuries," *Washington Post*, September 16, 2004, D2; "Reliever Charged With Felony Battery," ESPN.com, September 15, 2004, http://espn.go.com/mlb/news/story?id=1881073.

41. "Rangers Drop Appeals, Suspensions Reduced," *USA Today*, September 22, 2004.

42. Henry K. Lee, "Rangers and A's Fan Settle Chair Lawsuit," *San Francisco Chronicle*, January 13, 2007; "Rangers Settle Lawsuit with A's Fan," ESPN.com, January 12, 2007, http://espn.go.com/mlb/news/story?id=2729391.

43. *Restoring Faith in America's Pastime: Evaluating Major League Baseball's Efforts To Eradicate Steroid Use: Hearing Before the House Committee on Government Reform*, 109th Cong., Mar. 17, 2005.

44. Ibid., 264 (statement of Mark McGwire); Dave Sheinin, "Baseball Has A Day of Reckoning in Congress; McGwire Remains Evasive During Steroid Testimony," *Washington Post*, March 18, 2005, A1.

45. Jorge Arangure, "Palmeiro Suspended For Steroid Violation," *Washington Post*, August 2, 2005, A1.

46. *Cohn v. Corinthian Colleges, Inc.*, 86 Cal. Rptr. 3d 401, 403 (Ct. App. 2008). For a poetic rendition of the facts and holding of this case, see Bob Rains, "Mama's Got a Brand New Bag," *Green Bag 2d* 12 (2009): 345–46.

47. *Confirmation Hearing on the Nomination of John G. Roberts, Jr. to Be Chief Justice of the United States: Hearing Before the S. Comm. on the Judiciary*, S. Hrg. 109-158, 109th Cong. 55 (2005) (statement of Judge John G. Roberts, Jr.).

48. Integrity in Professional Sports Act, S. 1960, 109th Cong. (2005).

49. Major League Baseball, "MLB, MLBPA Announce New Drug Agreement," news release, November 15, 2005, http://www.mlb.com/news/press_releases/ [follow "archive" link].

50. Earlier in the year, on April 25, 2005, Commissioner Selig had asked the players to accept this sanction paradigm (50–100-lifetime ban), but Fehr offered a counter-proposal on September 26 consisting of a 20-game suspension for the first offense, 75 games for the sec-

ond, and the penalty to be left up to the commissioner for a third positive test. Associated Press, "Performance-Enhancing Drugs in Baseball: A Timeline," Cleveland.com, May 9, 2009, http://www.cleveland.com/tribe/index.ssf/2009/05/performanceenhancing_drugs_in.html.

51. Tim Brown, "Baseball Adds Muscle to Steroid Punishment," *Los Angeles Times*, November 16, 2005, A1; Mark Conrad, *The Business of Sports: A Primer for Journalists* (New York: Routledge, 2011), 269.

52. Jose de Jesus Ortiz, "Astros to Fight Denial of Bagwell Disability Claim," *Houston Chronicle*, March 28, 2006; Gloria Gonzalez, "Astros, CIGNA Settle Bagwell Claim," *Business Insurance*, December 18, 2006, http://www.businessinsurance.com [search "Bagwell"].

53. Plaintiff's Original Petition, Houston McLane Co.v. Conn. Gen. Life Ins. Co., No. 06-cv-1506 (S.D. Tex. May 2, 2006), Society for American Baseball Research, Business of Baseball Committee, http://research.sabr.org/business (follow link to documents).

54. Ortiz, "Astros to Fight Denial of Bagwell Disability Claim."

55. Pete Thomas, "Newswire," *Los Angeles Times*, December 15, 2006, D6; Gonzalez, "Astros, CIGNA Settle Bagwell Claim."

56. 505 F.3d 818 (8th Cir. 2007).

57. Mitchell, *Report to the Commissioner of Baseball of an Independent Investigation into the Illegal Use of Steroids and Other Performance Enhancing Substances by Players in Major League Baseball*.

58. Duff Wilson and Michael S. Schmidt, "Report Ties Star Players to Baseball's 'Steroids Era,'" *New York Times*, December 14, 2007, A1.

59. Paul Pringle, "The Unlikely Big Man in Baseball's Drug Scandal," *Los Angeles Times*, December 15, 2007, A1; Juliet Macur, "Guilty Plea Widens Baseball's Steroids Scandal," *New York Times*, April 28, 2007, A1. Radomski would later write a book about his experiences in the PED business. Kirk Radomski, *Bases Loaded: The Inside Story of the Steroid Era in Baseball by the Central Figure in the Mitchell Report* (New York: Hudson Street Press, 2009).

60. Wilson and Schmidt, "Report Ties Star Players to Baseball's 'Steroids Era.'"

61. *Mitchell Report: Illegal Use of Steroids in Major League Baseball, Day 2: Hearing Before the House Committee on Oversight and Government Reform*, 110th Cong., February 13, 2008; Jeff Barker, "Clemens Denies Drug Use: Pitcher, Former Trainer Trade Steroid Allegations at House Hearing," *Baltimore Sun*, February 14, 2008, A1.

62. Del Quentin Wilbur and Ann E. Marimow, "Clemens Acquitted of All Six Charges," *Washington Post*, June 19, 2012, A1; Frederick C. Bush, "Roger Clemens," in Hanks and Nowlin, *Nuclear-Powered Baseball*, 46.

63. Brocail v. Detroit Tigers, Inc., 268 S.W.3d 90 (Tex. App. 2008).

64. Oliver v. National Collegiate Athletic Association, 920 N.E.2d 203 (Ohio Ct. C.P. 2009).

65. Pat Borzi, "Settlement Sheds Little Light on N.C.A.A. Rule on Agents," *New York Times*, July 24, 2010, D1; Katie Thomas, "Former Pitcher Receives Settlement From the N.C.A.A.," *New York Times*, October 9, 2009, B12.

66. Remarks on the Nomination of Sonia Sotomayor To Be a Supreme Court Associate Justice, *Public Papers of the Presidents of the United States: Barack Obama* (Washington, D.C.: Government Printing Office, 2010). For an analysis of two of Sotomayor's opinions as a federal judge which played "an important role in shaping U.S. sports law," including her determination that MLB owners could not unilaterally impose new labor conditions on players during the 1994–95 strike, see Michael A. McCann, "Justice Sonia Sotamayor and the Relationship Between Leagues and Players: Insights and Implications," *Connecticut Law Review* 42 (2010): 901–23.

67. Schwarz and Schmidt, "After 26 Years, Fehr Says He Will Retire as Union Chief." On December 18, 2010, the National Hockey League Players Association will announce that its membership has voted to appoint Fehr as its new executive director. He will start in the position immediately. National Hockey League Players Association, "NHLPA Membership Appoints Don Fehr as Executive Director," media release, December 18, 2010, http://www.nhlpa.com/news/nhlpa-membership-appoints-don-fehr-as-executive-director.

68. Richard Goldstein, "Michael Weiner, 51, Dies; Headed Baseball Union," *New York Times*, November 22, 2013, B8.

69. Eldon H. Ham, *Broadcasting Baseball: A History of the National Pastime on Radio and Television* (Jefferson, NC: McFarland, 2011), 175. Uecker, who batted exactly .200 in his six-year, 297-game Major League career, began his Brewers play-by-play career in 1971. The National Baseball Hall of Fame presented him with its Ford C. Frick Award for broadcasters in 2003. Uecker also starred in television's *Mr. Belvedere* (1985–90) and as Harry Doyle, the Cleveland Indians' broadcaster, in the *Major League* film trilogy.

70. Affidavit of Robert G. Uecker in Support of Petition for Temporary Restraining Order and Permanent Injunction, Uecker v. Ladd, No. 30711 (Wis. Cir. Ct. June 1, 2006), available at "Juuust a Bit Out There," smokinggun.com, June 2, 2006, http://www.thesmokinggun.com/documents/sports/juuust-bit-out-there; Emily

Fredrix, "Bob Uecker Files Restraining Order," *Washington Post*, June 4, 2006.

71. *Ladd v. Uecker*, 780 N.W.2d 216, 218 (Wis. Ct. App. 2010).

72. *Ibid.*, 220.

73. *Buday v. New York Yankees Partnership*, 486 F. App'x 894 (2d Cir. 2012).

74. *Ibid.*, 897.

75. *Ibid.*, 898.

76. Susan King, "National Film Registry Selects 25 Films for Preservation," *Los Angeles Times*, December 19, 2012, D12; Library of Congress, "2012 National Film Registry Picks in A League of Their Own," news release, revised December 20, 2012, http://www.loc.gov/today/pr/2012/12-226.html.

77. Pub. L. No. 100-446, 102 Stat. 1782 (1988).

78. Official Website of the AAGBPL, accessed July 25, 2015, http://www.aagpbl.org/index.cfm.

79. *New York Yankees Partnership v. Evil Enterprises, Inc.*, 2013 WL 1305332 (Trademark Tr. & App. Bd.); Ryan Davis, "Yankees Triumph In 'Evil Empire' Trademark Battle," Law360, February 21, 2013, http://www.law360.com/articles/417427/yankees-triumph-in-evil-empire-trademark-battle.

80. "Lucchino was widely quoted as saying: 'The evil empire extends its tentacles even into Latin America.'" Ashby Jones, "New York Yankees: Yes, We're 'Evil,'" wsj.com, February 22, 2013, http://www.wsj.com/articles/SB10001424127887323549204578320531185286140; Gordon Edes, "Battle for Contreras Fuels Rivalry," *Boston Globe*, December 28, 2002, F1.

81. *New York Yankees Partnership*, *6.

82. Steve Eder and Michael S. Schmidt, "Antidoping Suit Cites Six Linked to Florida Clinic," *New York Times*, March 23, 2013, D2; Tim Elfrink, "A Miami Clinic Supplies Drugs to Sports' Biggest Names," *Miami New Times*, January 31, 2013.

83. Mike Oz, "A-Rod Ruling Explained—How Arbitrator Fredric Horowitz Decided on 162 Games," *Yahoo Sports!* January 13, 2014, https://sports.yahoo.com/ [search "horowitz"].

84. Steve Eder, "For Rodriguez, Suspended Animation: 12 Other Players Agree Not to Fight M.L.B. Punishment," *New York Times*, August 6, 2013, B8; Major League Baseball, "Discipline Issued in Biogenesis Investigation," news release, August 5, 2013, http://www.mlb.com/news/press_releases/ [follow "archive" link]; Greg Botelho and Quand Thomas, "MLB Drops Lawsuit Against Biogenesis and its Founder, Anthony Bosch," CNN, February 19, 2014, http://www.cnn.com/2014/02/18/justice/mlb-lawsuit-biogenesis-bosch/.

85. "Presidential Presence," *Memories and Dreams* 36, no. 4 (2014), 8.

86. Paul Hagen, "Obama Visits Hall, Touts Baseball's Historic Role," MLB.com, May 22, 2014; Juliet Eilperin, "Obama Visits Baseball Hall of Fame in Cooperstown to Promote U.S. Tourism," *Washington Post*, May 23, 2014; "Obama Donates Sox Jacket He Wore in '09 to Hall of Fame," *Chicago Tribune*, May 23, 2014, 9.

87. Ross H. Freeman, "The (Hot) Dog Days of Summer: Missouri's 'Baseball Rule' Takes a Strike," *Missouri Law Review* (2015), 559-61.

88. *Coomer v. Kansas City Royals Baseball Corp.*, 437 S.W.3d 184, 188 (Mo. 2014).

89. Brian Burnes, "Jury Clears Royals Once Again in Sluggerrr Hot Dog Toss That Ended Badly," *Kansas City Star*, June 17, 2015, http://www.kansascity.com/news/local/article24791023.html.

90. Sasha Goldstein, "Bryan Stow Verdict: Jury Finds Los Angeles Dodgers Negligent, Awards $18 Million," *New York Daily News*, July 9, 2014.

91. "Jury Finds Dodgers Negligent in Bryan Stow Case," *USA Today*, July 9, 2014.

92. Barry Jacobs, "Esq.," *Student Lawyer* 10 (April 1982), 56-57.

93. Paul Sullivan, "Monumental Afternoon," *Chicago Tribune*, July 28, 2014, 3:4.

94. Lawrence Baldassaro, "Tony La Russa," SABR Baseball Biography Project, April 17, 2014, http://sabr.org/bioproj/person/6dbc8b54.

95. Phil Kosin, "Diamond Classics: Baseball Lawyers Make Mark," *ABA Journal* 71 (October 1985), 34-35.

96. Michael S. Schmidt, "Baseball Promotes Selig's Deputy," *New York Times*, August 15, 2014, B9; Howard Bloom, "Who Is Rob Manfred? Man Who Should Be Next MLB Commissioner," *Sporting News*, August 14, 2014, http://www.sportingnews.com/mlb/story/2014-08-13/who-is-rob-manfred-baseball-commissioner-bud-selig-candidate-new.

97. Jim Doyle, "Jim Thorpe's Body Will Remain in Pennsylvania," *Pennsylvania Record*, October 23, 2014, http://pennrecord.com/news/14958-jim-thorpes-body-will-remain-in-pennsylvania.

98. Native American Graves Protection and Repatriation Act, Pub. L. No. 101-601 (1990) (codified as amended at 25 U.S.C. §§ 3001-3013).

99. *Thorpe v. Borough of Thorpe*, 770 F.3d 255, 266 (3d Cir. 2014).

100. Bob Goldsborough, "Really Long Road Trip," *Chicago Tribune*, December 14, 2014, 14; U.S. Department of State, "Ambassador Mark Gilbert," accessed March 29, 2016, http://www.state.gov/r/pa/ei/biog/237045.htm.

101. *City of San José v. Office of Comm'r of Baseball*, 776 F.3d 686, 692 (9th Cir. 2015).

102. *Ibid.*, 690-91.

103. "Defamation Suit vs. Clemens Settled," ESPN.com, March 18, 2015, http://espn.go.com [search "clemens settlement"].
104. Jay Schreiber, "Defamation Lawsuit by Clemens's Ex-Trainer Is Settled," *New York Times*, March 19, 2015, B15. In fact, Clemens stated after the settlement conference: "I was not present, nor would have I participated in paying one dime. Everyone knows my stance on the subject." Frederick C. Bush, "Roger Clemens," in Hanks and Nowlin, *Nuclear-Powered Baseball*, 47.
105. *Right Field Rooftops, LLC v. Chicago Baseball Holdings, LLC*, 87 F. Supp. 3d 874 (N.D. Ill. 2015).
106. Jared S. Hopkins, "Federal Judge Lets Wrigley Upgrades Continue: Rooftop Business Tried to Stop Video Board Installation," *Chicago Tribune*, April 3, 2015, 4.
107. Jared S. Hopkins and Ameet Sachdev, "Rooftops' Lawsuit Against Cubs Dismissed; 'Chapter Closed' as U.S. Judge Sides with Ballclub over Nearby Businesses," *Chicago Tribune*, October 1, 2015, 12.
108. Despite an unprecedented seven Most Valuable Player Awards and ownership of the all-time single season and career home run records, Bonds garnered the support of barely more than a third of the voters in each of the first three Hall of Fame elections in which he was eligible, 2013 to 2015. Although his percentage increased to 44.3 percent in the 2016 election, it still fell well short of the 75 percent required for election. "Hall of Fame Ballot History," Baseball-Reference.com, accessed March 4, 2016, http://www.baseball-reference.com/awards/hall-of-fame-ballot-history.shtml. For substantial accounts of performance-enhancing drugs and the public perception of Barry Bonds, see Jeff Pearlman, *Love Me, Hate Me: Barry Bonds and the Making of an Antihero* (New York: HarperCollins, 2006); and Mark Fainaru-Wada and Lance Williams, *Game of Shadows: Barry Bonds, Balco, and the Steroids Scandal That Rocked Professional Sports* (New York: Gotham Books, 2006).
109. Rob Harms, "U.S. Ends Its Long Pursuit of Bonds," *New York Times*, July 22, 2015, B13.
110. "Bonds Steroids Case Is Dropped," *Los Angeles Times*, July 22, 2015, D6.
111. *United States v. Bonds*, 784 F.3d 582, 586 (9th Cir. 2015).
112. "Yankee Fan's Defamation Suit Is Put To Sleep," *The Smoking Gun* (blog), September 29, 2015, http://thesmokinggun.com/documents/fail/judge-boots-sleepy-fan-lawsuit-674502; "Dozing Baseball Fan's $10 Million ESPN Lawsuit Is Thrown Out," *Reuters*, October 2, 2015, http://www.reuters.com [search "dozing fan"].
113. Tom Verducci, "Yogi Berra, 1925–2015," *Sports Illustrated*, October 5, 2015, 9. Berra won three Most Valuable Player awards (1951, 1954, 1955) while finishing second twice. As a player he won a record 10 World Series rings out of 14 tries, and he participated as a coach or manager in an additional seven series.
114. "The Jurisprudence of Yogi Berra," *Emory Law Journal* 46 (1997), 699.
115. Major League Baseball, "Commissioner Informs Rose of Decision," news release, December 14, 2015, http://www.mlb.com/news/press_releases/ [follow "archive" link]. Rose applied to Manfred for reinstatement on February 26, 2015. He had previously applied to Commissioner Bud Selig in 1997, but Selig never ruled on the application. Michael S. Schmidt, "Dear Pete: It's Still a No. Sincerely, Baseball," *New York Times*, December 15, 2015, B10.
116. *In the Matter of Peter Edward Rose, Decision of Commissioner Robert D. Manfred, Jr. Concerning the Application of Rose for Removal From the Permanently Ineligible List*, December 14, 2015, [2].
117. James Pilcher, "MLB Commissioner Upholds Pete Rose's Ban From Baseball," *Cincinnati Enquirer*, December 14, 2015, http://www.cincinnati.com/story/sports/mlb/reds/2015/12/14/pete-rose-reinstatement-decision-main/26319063/.
118. *In re Peter Edward Rose*, [3].

Appendix B

1. William F. Lamb, *Black Sox in the Courtroom: The Grand Jury, Criminal Trial and Civil Litigation* (Jefferson, NC: McFarland, 2013), 12–13.
2. Lamb, *Black Sox in the Courtroom*, 13–14; Rick Huhn, "The 1919 World Series: A Recap," in *Scandal on the South Side: The 1919 Chicago White Sox*, ed. Jacob Pomrenke (Phoenix: Society for American Baseball Research, 2015). 281–82; "First Crooked Play of the Series Told in Detail," *Chicago Daily Tribune*, September 29, 1920, 2.
3. William F. Lamb, "The Black Sox Scandal," in Pomrenke, *Scandal on the South Side*, 300; Gene Carney, "New Light on an Old Scandal," *Baseball Research Journal* 35 (2006), 77.
4. Lamb, *Black Sox in the Courtroom*, 14–15; Huhn, "The 1919 World Series: A Recap," 283.
5. Carney, "New Light on an Old Scandal," 77.
6. Lamb, *Black Sox in the Courtroom*, 15; Huhn, "The 1919 World Series: A Recap," 283–84.
7. Carney, "New Light on an Old Scandal," 78.
8. Lamb, *Black Sox in the Courtroom*, 15–

16; Huhn, "The 1919 World Series: A Recap," 284; Lamb, "The Black Sox Scandal," 300–01.
9. "Black Sox Scandal," Baseball-Reference.com, accessed March 28, 2016, http://www.baseball-reference.com/bullpen/Black_Sox_Scandal.
10. Huhn, "The 1919 World Series: A Recap," 284–85.
11. *Ibid.*, 285–86.
12. *Ibid.*, 286–87.
13. *Ibid.*, 287–88; Lamb, *Black Sox in the Courtroom*, 19–20.
14. Lamb, *Black Sox in the Courtroom*, 23; Jacob Pomrenke, "Epilogue: Offseason, 1919–20," in Pomrenke, *Scandal on the South Side*, 310.
15. Lyle Spatz and Steve Steinberg, *1921—The Yankees, the Giants,* and *the Battle for Baseball Supremacy in New York* (Lincoln: University of Nebraska Press, 2010), 40–41; Gene Carney, *Burying the Black Sox: How Baseball's Cover-up of the 1919 World Series Fix Almost Succeeded* (Washington, DC: Potomac Books, 2006), xi.
16. Lamb, "The Black Sox Scandal," 302–03; Rick Swaine, "Ninth Man Out," *National Pastime* 20 (2000), 88.
17. Fred M. Loomis, "Is Anything Wrong with the Sox? 1919 World Series Scandal Revived; Fan Seeks Answers to Rumors," *Chicago Tribune*, September 19, 1920, pt. 2, 1; James Crusinberry, "A Newsman's Biggest Story," *Sports Illustrated*, September 17, 1956, 69–71; Daniel A. Nathan, *Saying It's So: A Cultural History of the Black Sox Scandal* (Urbana: University of Illinois Press, 2003), 24–25.
18. Lamb, *Black Sox in the Courtroom*, 48–49; Lamb, "The Black Sox Scandal," 303; Carney, *Burying the Black Sox*, xi.
19. "Two Sox Confess; Eight Indicted; Inquiry Goes On," *Chicago Daily Tribune*, September 29, 1920, 1; Lamb, "The Black Sox Scandal," 303–04; William F. Lamb, "Jury Nullification and the Not Guilty Verdicts in the Black Sox Case," *Baseball Research Journal* 44 (Fall 2015), 48.
20. "Eight Fired by Comiskey; Wrecks Team," *Chicago Daily Tribune*, September 29, 1920, 1.
21. Lamb, "The Black Sox Scandal," 304; Lamb, "Jury Nullification and the Not Guilty Verdicts in the Black Sox Case," 48.
22. Lamb, *Black Sox in the Courtroom*, 74.
23. David Pietrusza, *Judge and Jury: The Life and Times of Judge Kenesaw Mountain Landis* (South Bend, IN: Diamond Communications, 1998), 169–72.
24. "'Indicted Players Ineligible'—Landis; Ruling by Judge Follows Report of Trial Delay," *Chicago Daily Tribune*, March 13, 1921, A1; Spatz and Steinberg, *1921—The Yankees, the Giants,* and *the Battle for Baseball Supremacy in New York*, 12–13.

25. Craig Burley, "Free Benny Kauff (Part Two)," *The Hardball Times* (blog), April 19, 2004, www.hardballtimes.com/free-benny-kauff-part-two; Michael Santa Maria and James Costello, "Thrown Out Stealing," in *In the Shadows of the Diamond: Hard Times in the National Pastime* (Dubuque, IA: Elysian Fields Press, 1992), 159.
26. Lamb, *Black Sox in the Courtroom*, 106.
27. *Ibid.*, 107; "Called 'Jumper,' Comiskey Rages at Trial of Sox," *Chicago Daily Tribune*, July 19, 1921, 2.
28. Lamb, *Black Sox in the Courtroom*, 111.
29. *Ibid.*, 112–15; "Burns Tells Story of Plot to Throw 1919 World Series," *New York Times*, July 20, 1921, 1; "How 'Black Sox' Sold Out: Burns Reveals Shame; Gives Cicotte Boost," *Chicago Daily Tribune*, July 20, 1921, 1; "Tells How Players Made Gamblers Lose," *New York Times*, July 21, 1921, 1.
30. "Jury Frees Baseball Men; All Black Sox Acquitted on Single Ballot," *Chicago Daily Tribune*, August 3, 1921, 1; Lamb, *Black Sox in the Courtroom*, 111.
31. "Baseball Leaders Won't Let White Sox Return to the Game," *New York Times*, August 4, 1921, 1; "Crooks Scared Out of Baseball, Says M'Donald," *Chicago Daily Tribune*, August 4, 1921, 21.
32. Lamb, *Black Sox in the Courtroom*, 150.
33. *Ibid.*
34. *Ibid.*, 151; "Hap Felsch Sues Sox for Back Pay," *Chicago Tribune*, April 27, 1922, 17.
35. Lamb, *Black Sox in the Courtroom*, 152; "Two More Players Sue the White Sox," *New York Times*, May 13, 1922, 11.
36. Act of July 13, 1921, 1921 Ill. Laws 400; Lamb, "Jury Nullification and the Not Guilty Verdicts in the Black Sox Case," 48; Lamb, *Black Sox in the Courtroom*, 102.
37. *Ibid.*, 156; Carney, "New Light on an Old Scandal," 76.
38. Lamb, *Black Sox in the Courtroom*, 162; "Suits by Risberg and Felsch Ruled Out in Wisconsin Court," *New York Times*, May 13, 1923, S3.
39. *Ibid.*, 167–68; Carney, "New Light on an Old Scandal," 74.
40. Lamb, *Black Sox in the Courtroom*, 191.
41. *Ibid.*, 195; Irving Vaughan, "Landis Passes Buck to Owners in Scandal Suit," *Chicago Tribune*, November 4, 1924, 16. There is no record that litigation on the matter was ever actually initiated. On December 10, 1925, major league team owners agreed to distribute the second-place shares withheld from the Black Sox players to their White Sox teammates. Lamb, *Black Sox in the Courtroom*, 195.
42. *Ibid.*; "Jackson Loses in High Court to White Sox," *Chicago Tribune*, October 21, 1925, 29.

43. "Weaver Ban Holds, Is Landis Verdict," *New York Times*, March 14, 1927, 23; "Weaver Files Plea for Reinstatement," *New York Times*, January 11, 1927, 35.
44. "Georgian Gets 222 Votes, 4 Short of Perfect Score and 7 More Than Ruth and Wagner," *New York Times*, February 3, 1936, 23; Murray Chass, "Board Says Rose Is Ineligible for Hall of Fame," *New York Times*, February 5, 1991, B9.
45. Arnold (Chick) Gandil, with Melvin Durslag, "This is My Story of the Black Sox Series," *Sports Illustrated*, September 17, 1956, 62–68; Crusinberry, "A Newsman's Biggest Story."
46. Lamb, "The Black Sox Scandal," 308–09; "Black Sox Scandal," Baseball-Reference.com, accessed March 28, 2016, http://www.baseball-reference.com/bullpen/Black_Sox_Scandal.
47. Lamb, *Black Sox in the Courtroom*, 215; Kelly Boyer Sagert and Rod Nelson, "Swede Risberg," in Pomrenke, *Scandal on the South Side*, 215.
48. "Eight Men Out," IMDb, accessed March 28, 2016, http://www.imdb.com.
49. "Two Greats Want Jackson in Hall," *Sarasota Herald Tribune*, January 20, 1998, 4C.
50. Letter from Robert Manfred, MLB Commissioner, to Arlene Marcley, President, Shoeless Joe Jackson Museum (July 20, 2015); "Say It's No: MLB denies Jackson," *Chicago Tribune*, September 2, 2015, 2; "MLB Won't Reinstate Shoeless Joe Jackson," ESPN, September 1, 2015, http://espn.go.com/mlb/story/_/id/13555698/mlb-commissioner-rob-manfred-reinstate-shoeless-joe-jackson.

Bibliography

Books

Abrams, Roger I. *The Dark Side of the Diamond: Gambling, Violence, Drugs and Alcoholism in the National Pastime.* Burlington, MA: Rounder Books, 2007.
_____. *Legal Bases: Baseball and the Law.* Philadelphia: Temple University Press, 1998.
_____. *The Money Pitch: Baseball Free Agency and Salary Arbitration.* Philadelphia: Temple University Press, 2000.
Achorn, Edward. *The Summer of Beer and Whiskey: How Brewers, Barkeeps, Rowdies, Immigrants, and a Wild Pennant Fight Made Baseball America's Game.* New York: PublicAffairs, 2013.
Adelman, Melvin L. *Sporting Time: New York City and the Rise of Modern Athletics, 1820–70.* Urbana: University of Illinois Press, 1986.
Adelson, Bruce. *Brushing Back Jim Crow: The Integration of Minor-League Baseball in the American South.* Charlottesville: University Press of Virginia, 1999.
Alexander, Charles C. *Turbulent Seasons: Baseball in 1890–1891.* Dallas: Southern Methodist University Press, 2011.
_____. *Ty Cobb.* New York: Oxford University Press, 1984.
Allen, Lee. *The American League Story.* Rev. ed. New York: Hill & Wang, 1965.
_____. *The Cincinnati Reds.* New York: G.P. Putnam's Sons, 1948. Reprinted with foreword by Greg Rhodes. Kent: Kent State University Press, 2006.
_____. *More Than Merkle: A History of the Best and Most Exciting Baseball Season in Human History.* Lincoln: University of Nebraska Press, 2000.
_____. *The National League Story.* Rev. ed. New York: Hill & Wang, 1965.
Arcidiacono, David. *Major League Baseball in Gilded Age Connecticut: The Rise and Fall of the Middletown, New Haven, and Hartford Clubs.* Jefferson, NC: McFarland, 2010.
Ardell, Jean Hastings. *Breaking into Baseball: Women and the National Pastime.* Carbondale: Southern Illinois University Press, 2005.
Armour, Mark, and Daniel R. Levitt. *In Pursuit of Pennants: Baseball Operations from Deadball to Moneyball.* Lincoln: University of Nebraska Press, 2015.
Armour, Mark, and Bill Nowlin, eds. *Red Sox Baseball in the Days of Ike and Elvis: The Red Sox of the 1950s.* Phoenix: Society for American Baseball Research, 2012.
Bak, Richard. *A Place for Summer: A Narrative History of Tiger Stadium.* Detroit: Great Lakes Books, 1998.
_____. *Turkey Stearnes and the Detroit Stars: The Negro Leagues in Detroit, 1919–1933.* Detroit: Wayne State University Press, 1994.
Baker, Liva. *The Justice From Beacon Hill: The Life and Times of Oliver Wendell Holmes.* New York: HarperCollins, 1991.
Banner, Stuart. *The Baseball Trust: A History of Baseball's Antitrust Exemption.* New York: Oxford University Press, 2013.
Batesel, Paul. *Players and Teams of the National Association, 1871–1875.* Jefferson, NC: McFarland, 2012.

Bibliography

Belth, Alex. *Stepping Up: The Story of Curt Flood and His Fight for Baseball Players' Rights.* New York: Persea Books, 2006.
Berlage, Gai Ingham. *Women in Baseball: The Forgotten History.* Westport, CT: Praeger, 1994.
Berry, Robert C., William B. Gould IV, and Paul D. Staudohar. *Labor Relations in Professional Sports.* Dover, MA: Auburn House, 1986.
Bevis, Charles W. *Sunday Baseball: The Major Leagues' Struggle to Play Baseball on the Lord's Day, 1876–1934.* Jefferson, NC: McFarland, 2003.
_____. *Tim Keefe: A Biography of the Hall of Fame Pitcher and Player-Rights Advocate.* Jefferson, NC: McFarland, 2015.
Block, David. *Baseball Before We Knew It: A Search for the Roots of the Game.* Lincoln: University of Nebraska Press, 2005.
Boxerman, Burton Alan, and Benita W. Boxerman. *Ebbets to Veeck to Busch: Eight Owners Who Shaped Baseball.* Jefferson, NC: McFarland, 2003.
Breslin, Jimmy. *Branch Rickey.* New York: Viking, 2011.
Broeg, Bob. *The 100 Greatest Moments in St. Louis Sports.* St. Louis: Missouri Historical Society Press, 2000.
Browning, Reed. *Baseball's Greatest Season, 1924.* Amherst: University of Massachusetts Press, 2003.
Bruns, Roger A. *Negro Leagues Baseball.* Santa Barbara, CA: Greenwood, 2012.
Buford, Kate. *Native American Son: The Life and Sporting Legend of Jim Thorpe.* New York: Alfred A. Knopf, 2010.
Burgos, Adrian, Jr. *Cuban Star: How One Negro League Owner Changed the Face of Baseball.* New York: Hill and Wang, 2011.
Burk, Robert F. *Marvin Miller: Baseball Revolutionary.* Urbana: University of Illinois Press, 2015.
_____. *Much More Than a Game: Players, Owners, & American Baseball Since 1921.* Chapel Hill: University of North Carolina Press, 2001.
_____. *Never Just a Game: Players, Owners, and American Baseball to 1920.* Chapel Hill: University of North Carolina Press, 1994.
Canseco, José. *Juiced: Wild Times, Rampant 'Roids, Smash Hits, and How Baseball Got Big.* New York: Regan Books, 2005.
Cash, Jon David. *Before They Were Cardinals: Major League Baseball in Nineteenth-Century St. Louis.* Columbia: University of Missouri Press, 2002.
Chadwick, Henry. *Spalding's Official Baseball Guide 1908.* New York: American Sports Publishing Co., 1908.
Cicotello, David, and Angelo J. Louisa, eds. *Forbes Field: Essays and Memories of the Pirates' Historic Ballpark, 1909–1971.* Jefferson, NC: McFarland, 2007.
Cieradkowski, Gary. *The League of Outsider Baseball: An Illustrated History of Baseball's Forgotten Heroes.* New York: Touchstone, 2015.
Clavin, Tom. *The DiMaggios: Three Brothers, Their Passion for Baseball, Their Pursuit of the American Dream.* New York: HarperCollins, 2013.
Cohen, Marilyn. *No Girls in the Clubhouse: The Exclusion of Women from Baseball.* Jefferson, NC: McFarland, 2009.
The Constitution of the Olympic Ball Club of Philadelphia. Philadelphia: John Clark, 1838. Reprinted in part in *Early Innings: A Documentary History of Baseball, 1825–1908*, edited by Dean A. Sullivan, 5–8. Lincoln: University of Nebraska Press, 1995.
Conrad, Mark. *The Business of Sports: A Primer for Journalists.* New York: Routledge, 2011.
Cook, William A. *August "Garry" Herrmann: A Baseball Biography.* Jefferson, NC: McFarland, 2008.
_____. *The Louisville Grays Scandal of 1877: The Taint of Gambling at the Dawn of the National League.* Jefferson, NC: McFarland, 2005.
_____. *Pete Rose: Baseball's All-Time Hit King.* Jefferson, NC: McFarland, 2004.
_____. *The Summer of '64: A Pennant Lost.* Jefferson, NC: McFarland, 2002.
Cooper, John Milton, Jr. *Woodrow Wilson: A Biography.* New York: Alfred A. Knopf, 2009.
Corcoran, Dennis. *Induction Day at Cooperstown: A History of the Baseball Hall of Fame Ceremony.* Jefferson, NC: McFarland, 2010.

Cozzillio, Michael J., Mark S. Levinstein, Michael R. Dimino, Sr., and Gabe Feldman. *Sports Law: Cases & Materials*, 2nd ed. Durham, NC: Carolina Academic Press, 2007.
Cramer, Richard Ben. *Joe DiMaggio: The Hero's Life*. New York: Simon & Schuster, 2000.
Creamer, Robert W. *Babe: The Legend Comes to Life*. New York: Simon & Schuster, 1974.
Dawidoff, Nicholas. *The Catcher Was A Spy: The Mysterious Life of Moe Berg*. New York: Pantheon Books, 1994.
Day, Frederick J. *Clubhouse Lawyer: Law in the World of Sports*. New York: iUniverse Star, 2004.
Devaney, Sean. *Before Wrigley Became Wrigley: The Inside Story of the First Years of the Cubs' Home Field*. New York: Sports Publishing, 2014.
Dewey, Donald, and Nicholas Acocella. *The Black Prince of Baseball: Hal Chase and the Mythology of Baseball*. Toronto: Sport Classic Books, 2004.
Di Salvatore, Bryan. *A Clever Base-Ballist: The Life and Times of John Montgomery Ward*. New York: Pantheon, 1999.
Dickson, Paul. *Bill Veeck: Baseball's Greatest Maverick*. New York: Walker & Co., 2012.
_____. *The Dickson Baseball Dictionary*. 3rd ed. New York: W. W. Norton & Co., 2009.
Dodge, Andrew R., and Betty K. Koed, eds. *Biographical Directory of the United States Congress, 1774–2005*. Washington, D.C.: United States Printing Office, 2005.
Drysdale, Don, with Bob Verdi. *Once a Bum, Always a Dodger*. New York: St. Martin's, 1990.
Duquette, Jerold J. *Regulating the National Pastime: Baseball and Antitrust*. Westport, CT: Greenwood, 1999.
Durocher, Leo, with Ed Linn. *Nice Guys Finish Last*. New York: Simon & Schuster, 1975.
Eig, Jonathan. *Luckiest Man: The Life and Death of Lou Gehrig*. New York: Simon & Schuster, 2005.
_____. *Opening Day: The Story of Jackie Robinson's First Season*. New York: Simon & Schuster, 2007.
Eisenbath, Mike. *The Cardinals Encyclopedia*. Philadelphia: Temple University Press, 1999.
Elston, Gene. *A Stitch in Time: A Baseball Chronology*. 3rd ed. Houston: Halcyon Press, 2006.
Endsley, Brian M. *Bums No More—The 1959 Los Angeles Dodgers, World Champions of Baseball*. Jefferson, NC: McFarland, 2009.
_____. *Finding the Left Arm of God: Sandy Koufax and the Los Angeles Dodgers, 1960–1963*. Jefferson, NC: McFarland, 2015.
Erickson, Hal. *The Baseball Filmography, 1915 through 2001*. 2nd ed. Jefferson, NC: McFarland, 2002.
Fainaru-Wada, Mark, and Lance Williams. *Game of Shadows: Barry Bonds, Balco, and the Steroids Scandal That Rocked Professional Sports*. New York: Gotham Books, 2006.
Falkner, David. *Great Time Coming: The Life of Jackie Robinson, From Baseball to Birmingham*. New York: Simon & Schuster, 1995.
Felber, Bill. *A Game of Brawl: The Orioles, the Beaneaters, and the Battle for the 1897 Pennant*. Lincoln: University of Nebraska Press, 2007.
_____. *Under Pallor, Under Shadow: The 1920 American League Pennant Race That Rattled and Rebuilt Baseball*. Lincoln: University of Nebraska Press, 2011.
_____, ed. *Inventing Baseball: The 100 Greatest Games of the 19th Century*. Phoenix: Society for American Baseball Research, 2013.
Fetter, Henry D. *Taking on the Yankees: Winning and Losing in the Business of Baseball, 1903–2003*. New York: W.W. Norton, 2003.
Finley, Peter S., Laura L. Finley, and Jeffrey Fountain. *Sports Scandals*. Westport, CT: Greenwood Press, 2008.
Fitts, Robert K. *Mashi—The Unfulfilled Dreams of Masanori Murakami, the First Japanese Major Leaguer*. Lincoln: University of Nebraska Press, 2015.
Fleitz, David L. *Cap Anson: The Grand Old Man of Baseball*. Jefferson, NC: McFarland, 2005.
_____. *Ghosts in the Gallery at Cooperstown: Sixteen Little-Known Members of the Hall of Fame*. Jefferson, NC: McFarland, 2004.
_____. *Napoleon Lajoie: King of Ballplayers*. Jefferson, NC: McFarland, 2013.
_____. *Silver Bats and Automobiles: The Hotly Competitive, Sometimes Ignoble Pursuit of the Major League Batting Championship*. Jefferson, NC: McFarland, 2011.

Fleming, G.H. *The Unforgettable Season*. New York: Holt, Rinehart and Winston, 1981.
Flood, Curt, and Richard Carter. *The Way It Is*. New York: Trident Press, 1971.
Flynn, Neil F. *Baseball's Reserve System: The Case and Trial of Curt Flood v. Major League Baseball*. Springfield, IL: Walnut Park Group, 2006.
Fountain, Charles. *The Betrayal: The 1919 World Series and the Birth of Modern Baseball*. New York: Oxford University Press, 2015.
Freedman, Lew. *African American Pioneers of Baseball: A Biographical Encyclopedia*. Westport, CT: Greenwood Press, 2007.
Frommer, Frederic J. *You Gotta Have Heart: A History of Washington Baseball from 1859 to the 2012 National League East Champions*. Lanham, MD: Taylor Trade Publishing, 2013.
Frommer, Harvey. *Shoeless Joe and Ragtime Baseball*. Dallas, TX: Taylor Pub. Co., 1992.
Gelzheiser, Robert P. *Labor and Capital in 19th Century Baseball*. Jefferson, NC: McFarland, 2006.
Gerlach, Larry R. *The Men in Blue: Conversations with Umpires*. New York: Viking Press, 1980.
Giamatti, A. Bartlett. *A Great and Glorious Game: Baseball Writings of A. Bartlett Giamatti*. Edited by Kenneth S. Robson. Chapel Hill, NC: Algonquin Books, 1998.
Giglio, James N. *Musial: From Stash to Stan the Man*. Columbia: University of Missouri Press, 2001.
Ginsburg, Daniel E. *The Fix Is In: A History of Baseball Gambling and Game Fixing Scandals*. Jefferson, NC: McFarland, 1995.
Goldman, Robert Michael. *One Man Out: Curt Flood versus Baseball*. Lawrence: University Press of Kansas, 2008.
Goldstein, Richard. *Spartan Seasons: How Baseball Survived the Second World War*. New York: Macmillan, 1980.
Goldstein, Warren. *Playing for Keeps: A History of Early Baseball*. Ithaca, NY: Cornell University Press, 1989.
Gorman, Robert M., and David Weeks. *Death at the Ballpark: A Comprehensive Study of Game-Related Fatalities of Players, Other Personnel and Spectators in Amateur and Professional Baseball, 1862–2007*. Jefferson, NC: McFarland, 2009.
Gould, William B., IV. *Bargaining with Baseball: Labor Relations in an Age of Prosperous Turmoil*. Jefferson, NC: McFarland, 2011.
Green, G. Michael, and Roger D. Launius. *Charlie Finley: The Outrageous Story of Baseball's Super Showman*. New York: Walker & Co., 2010.
Greenberg, Hank. With Ira Berkow. *Hank Greenberg: The Story of My Life*. New York: Times Books, 1989.
Greene, Chip, ed. *Mustaches and Mayhem: Charlie O's Three-Time Champions, The Oakland Athletics 1972–74*. Phoenix: Society for American Baseball Research, 2015.
Greenhouse, Linda. *Becoming Justice Blackmun: Harry Blackmun's Supreme Court Journey* (New York: Times Books, 2005).
Grow, Nathaniel. *Baseball on Trial: The Origin of Baseball's Antitrust Exemption*. Urbana: University of Illinois Press, 2014.
Gutman, Dan. *Banana Bats and Ding-Dong Balls: A Century of Unique Baseball Inventions*. New York: Macmillan, 1995.
Ham, Eldon H. *Broadcasting Baseball: A History of the National Pastime on Radio and Television*. Jefferson, NC: McFarland, 2011.
_____. *Larceny & Old Leather: The Mischievous Legacy of Major League Baseball*. Chicago: Academy Chicago Publishers, 2005.
Hauser, Christopher. *The Negro Leagues Chronology: Events in Organized Black Baseball, 1920–1948*. Jefferson, NC: McFarland, 2006.
Hawks, Emily, and Bill Nowlin, eds. *Nuclear-Powered Baseball: Articles Inspired by the Simpsons Episode, "Homer at the Bat."* Phoenix: Society for American Baseball Research, 2016.
Heaphy, Leslie A. *The Negro Leagues: 1869–1960*. Jefferson, NC: McFarland, 2003.
Heaphy, Leslie A., and Mel Anthony May. *Encyclopedia of Women and Baseball*. Jefferson, NC: McFarland, 2006.

Helyar, John. *Lords of the Realm*. New York: Villard Books, 1994.
Hirsch, James S. *Willie Mays: The Life, The Legend*. New York: Scribner, 2010.
Hogan, Lawrence D. *Shades of Glory: The Negro Leagues and the Story of African-American Baseball*. Washington, D.C.: National Geographic, 2006.
Holtzman, Jerome. *The Commissioners: Baseball's Midlife Crisis*. New York: Total Sports, 1998.
Hornbaker, Tim. *War on the Basepaths: The Definitive Biography of Ty Cobb*. New York: Sports Publishing, 2015.
Huhn, Rick. *The Chalmers Race: Ty Cobb, Napoleon Lajoie, and the Controversial 1910 Batting Title That Became a National Obsession*. Lincoln: University of Nebraska Press, 2014.
_____. *The Sizzler: George Sisler, Baseball's Forgotten Great*. Columbia: University of Missouri Press, 2013.
Jacobson, Sidney. *Pete Reiser: The Rough-and-Tumble Career of the Perfect Ballplayer*. Jefferson, NC: McFarland, 2004.
James, Bill. *The New Bill James Historical Baseball Abstract*. New York: Free Press, 2001.
Jenkins, Ferguson, with Lew Freedman. *Fergie: My Life from the Cubs to Cooperstown*. Chicago: Triumph Books, 2009.
Jennings, Kenneth M. *Swings and Misses: Moribund Labor Relations in Professional Baseball*. Westport, CT: Praeger, 1997.
Jones, David, ed. *Deadball Stars of the American League*. Washington, D.C.: Potomac Books, 2006.
_____. *Joe DiMaggio: A Biography*. Westport, CT: Greenwood Press, 2004.
Jordan, David M. *The A's: A Baseball History*. Jefferson, NC: McFarland, 2014.
Judge, Mark Gauvreau. *Damn Senators: My Grandfather and the Story of Washington's Only World Series Championship*. San Francisco: Encounter Books, 2003.
Kaese, Harold. *The Boston Braves, 1871–1953*. New York: G. P. Putnam's Sons, 1948.
Kahn, Roger. *The Boys of Summer*. New York: Harper & Row, 1972.
Kaiser, Ken. With David Fisher. *Planet of the Umps: A Baseball Life from Behind the Plate*. New York: St. Martin's Press, 2003.
Kaufman, Louis, Barbara Fitzgerald, and Tom Sewell. *Moe Berg: Athlete, Scholar, Spy*. Boston: Little, Brown & Co., 1974.
Kennedy, Kostya. *Pete Rose: An American Dilemma*. New York: Sports Illustrated Books, 2014.
Kerr, Roy. *Buck Ewing: A Baseball Biography*. Jefferson, NC: McFarland, 2012.
Khan, Abraham Iqbal. *Curt Flood in the Media: Baseball, Race, and the Demise of the Activist-Athlete*. Jackson: University Press of Mississippi, 2012.
Kohout, Martin Donell. *Hal Chase: The Defiant Life and Turbulent Times of Baseball's Biggest Crook*. Jefferson, NC: McFarland, 2001.
Koppett, Leonard. *Koppett's Concise History of Major League Baseball*. Philadelphia: Temple University Press, 1998.
Korr, Charles P. *The End of Baseball As We Knew It: The Players Union, 1960–1981*. Urbana: University of Illinois Press, 2002.
Koszarek, Ed. *The Players League: History, Clubs, Ballplayers and Statistics*. Jefferson, NC: McFarland, 2006.
Kraus, Rebecca S. *Minor League Baseball: Community Building Through Hometown Sports*. New York: Haworth Press, 2003.
Kuhn, Bowie. *Hardball: The Education of a Commissioner*. New York: Times Books, 1987.
Lamb, Chris. *Blackout: The Untold Story of Jackie Robinson's First Spring Training*. Lincoln: University of Nebraska Press, 2004.
_____. *Conspiracy of Silence: Sportswriters and the Long Campaign to Desegregate Baseball*. Lincoln: University of Nebraska Press, 2012.
Lamb, William F. *Black Sox in the Courtroom: The Grand Jury, Criminal Trial and Civil Litigation*. Jefferson, NC: McFarland, 2013.
Lanctot, Neil. *Campy: The Two Lives of Roy Campanella*. New York: Simon & Schuster, 2011.
Landis, Lincoln. *From Pilgrimage to Promise: Civil War Heritage and the Landis Boys of Logansport, Indiana*. Westminster, MD: Heritage Books, 2007.
Leerhsen, Charles. *Ty Cobb: A Terrible Beauty*. New York: Simon & Schuster, 2015.

Levine, Peter. *A.G. Spalding and the Rise of Baseball*. New York and London: Oxford University Press, 1985.
Lieb, Frederick G. *Connie Mack: Grand Old Man of Baseball*. New York: G.P. Putnam's Sons, 1945.
_____. *The Detroit Tigers*. New York: G.P. Putnam's Sons, 1946.
_____. *The Pittsburgh Pirates*. New York: G.P. Putnam's Sons, 1948.
Leifer, Eric M. *Making the Majors: The Transformation of Team Sports in America*. Cambridge: Harvard University Press, 1995.
Lester, Larry. *Baseball's First Colored World Series: The 1924 Meeting of the Hilldale Giants and Kansas City Monarchs*. Jefferson, NC: McFarland, 2006.
_____. *Rube Foster in His Time: On the Field and in the Papers with Black Baseball's Greatest Visionary*. Jefferson, NC: McFarland, 2012.
Leventhal, Josh. *A History of Baseball in 100 Objects: A Tour through the Bats, Balls, Uniforms, Awards, Documents and Other Artifacts that Tell the Story of the National Pastime*. New York: Black Dog & Leventhal Publishers, 2015.
Levitt, Daniel R. *The Battle that Forged Modern Baseball: The Federal League Challenge and Its Legacy*. Chicago: Ivan R. Dee, 2012.
_____. *Ed Barrow: The Bulldog Who Built the Yankees' First Dynasty*. Lincoln: University of Nebraska Press, 2008.
Light, Jonathan Fraser. *The Cultural Encyclopedia of Baseball*, 2nd ed. Jefferson, NC: McFarland, 2005.
Lowenfish, Lee. *Branch Rickey: Baseball's Ferocious Gentleman*. Lincoln: University of Nebraska Press, 2007.
_____. *The Imperfect Diamond: A History of Baseball's Labor Wars*. Bison Books ed. Lincoln: University of Nebraska Press, 2010.
Lupica, Matt. *The Baseball Stadium Insider: A Comprehensive Dissection of All Thirty Ballparks, Legendary Players, and Memorable Moments*. Kent, OH: Black Squirrel Books, 2015.
Lynch, Michael T., Jr. *Harry Frazee, Ban Johnson and the Feud That Nearly Destroyed the American League*. Jefferson, NC: McFarland, 2008.
Macdonald, Neil W. *The League That Lasted: 1876 and the Founding of the National League of Professional Base Ball Clubs*. Jefferson, NC: McFarland, 2004.
Macht, Norman L. *Connie Mack and the Early Years of Baseball*. Lincoln: University of Nebraska Press, 2007.
_____. *Connie Mack: The Turbulent and Triumphant Years, 1915–1931*. Lincoln: University of Nebraska Press, 2012.
_____. *The Grand Old Man of Baseball: Connie Mack in His Final Years, 1932–1956*. Lincoln: University of Nebraska Press, 2015.
Madden, Bill. *Steinbrenner: The Last Lion of Baseball*. New York: HarperCollins, 2010.
Malamud, Bernard. *The Natural*. New York: Farrar, Straus and Giroux, 1952.
Markusen, Bruce. *Roberto Clemente: The Great One*. New York: Sports Publishing, 2001.
Marmer, Mel, and Bill Nowlin, eds. *The Year of the Blue Snow: The 1964 Philadelphia Phillies*. Phoenix: Society for American Baseball Research, 2013.
Marshall, William. *Baseball's Pivotal Era, 1945–1951*. Lexington: University Press of Kentucky, 1999.
Masur, Louis P. *Autumn Glory: Baseball's First World Series*. New York: Hill and Wang, 2003.
McBane, Richard. *A Fine Looking Lot of Ball-Tossers: The Remarkable Akrons of 1881*. Jefferson, NC: McFarland, 2005.
McCallum, John D. *Ty Cobb*. New York: Praeger, 1975.
McCollister, John. *The Good, the Bad, and the Ugly Pittsburgh Pirates: Heart-Pounding, Jaw-Dropping, and Gut-Wrenching Moments from Pittsburgh Pirates History*. Chicago: Triumph Books, 2008.
McCue, Andy. *Mover and Shaker: Walter O'Malley, the Dodgers, and Baseball's Westward Expansion*. Lincoln: University of Nebraska Press, 2014.
McGuiggan, Amy Whorf. *Take Me out to the Ball Game: The Story of the Sensational Baseball Song*. Lincoln: University of Nebraska Press, 2009.

McKelvey, G. Richard. *For It's One, Two, Three, Four Strikes You're Out at the Owners' Ball Game: Players Versus Management in Baseball*. Jefferson, NC: McFarland, 2001.
_____. *The MacPhails: Baseball's First Family of the Front Office*. Jefferson, NC: McFarland, 2000.
_____. *Mexican Raiders in the Major Leagues: The Pasquel Brothers vs. Organized Baseball, 1946*. Jefferson, NC: McFarland, 2006.
McKenna, Brian. *Early Exits: The Premature Endings of Baseball Careers*. Lanham, MD: Scarecrow Press, 2007.
McLain, Denny. With Eli Zaret. *I Told You I Wasn't Perfect*. Chicago: Triumph Books, 2007.
Mead, William B. *Even the Browns*. Chicago: Contemporary Books, 1978.
Mead, William B., and Paul Dickson. *Baseball: The Presidents' Game*. New York: Walker and Company, 1997.
Miller, Marvin. *A Whole Different Ball Game: The Sport and Business of Baseball*. New York: Carol Publishing Group, 1991.
Moffi, Larry. *The Conscience of the Game: Baseball's Commissioners from Landis to Selig*. Lincoln: University of Nebraska Press, 2006.
_____. *This Side of Cooperstown: An Oral History of Major League Baseball in the 1950s*. Iowa City: University of Iowa Press, 1996.
Moncreiff, Robert P. *Bart Giamatti: A Profile*. New Haven: Yale University Press, 2007.
Montville, Leigh. *The Big Bam: The Life and Times of Babe Ruth*. New York: Doubleday, 2006.
Moore, Joseph Thomas. *Pride Against Prejudice: The Biography of Larry Doby*. New York: Praeger, 1988.
Morris, Peter. *Catcher: How the Man Behind the Plate Became An American Folk Hero*. Chicago: Ivan R. Dee, 2009.
_____. *A Game of Inches: The Game Behind the Scenes—The Stories Behind the Innovations That Shaped Baseball*. Chicago: Ivan R. Dee, 2006.
_____. *A Game of Inches: The Game on the Field—The Stories Behind the Innovations That Shaped Baseball*. Chicago: Ivan R. Dee, 2006.
_____. *Level Playing Fields: How the Groundskeeping Murphy Brothers Shaped Baseball*. Lincoln: University of Nebraska Press, 2007.
Muchlinski, Alan. *After The Black Sox: The Swede Risberg Story*. Bloomington, IN: AuthorHouse, 2005.
Mumau, Thad. *"Had 'Em All the Way": The 1960 Pittsburgh Pirates*. Jefferson, NC: McFarland, 2015.
Nathanson, Mitchell. *A People's History of Baseball*. Champaign, IL: University of Illinois Press, 2012.
Nelson, Kevin. *Baseball's Even Greater Insults*. New York: Simon & Schuster, 1993.
Nemec, David. *The Beer and Whisky League: The Illustrated History of the American Association—Baseball's Renegade Major League*. Rev. ed. Guilford, CT: Lyons Press, 2004.
_____. *The Great Encyclopedia of Nineteenth Century Major League Baseball*. 2nd ed. Tuscaloosa: University of Alabama Press, 2006.
Novick, Sheldon M. *Honorable Justice: The Life of Oliver Wendell Holmes*. Boston: Little, Brown, 1989.
Nowlin, Bill, ed. *Van Lingle Mungo: The Man, The Song, The Players*. Phoenix: Society for American Baseball Research, 2014.
O'Keeffe, Michael, and Teri Thompson. *The Card: Collectors, Con Men, and the True Story of History's Most Desired Baseball Card*. New York: William Morrow, 2007.
O'Neil, Buck. With Steve Wulf and David Conrads. *I Was Right on Time*. New York: Simon & Schuster, 1996.
O'Toole, Andrew. *Branch Rickey in Pittsburgh: Baseball's Trailblazing General Manager for the Pirates, 1950–1955*. Jefferson, NC: McFarland, 2000.
Orem, Preston D. *Baseball (1845–1881) From the Newspaper Accounts*. Altadena, CA: published by author, 1961.
Our National Pastime in Our National Archives. Washington, D.C.: National Archives and Records Admin., 2013.
Parker, Clifton Blue, and Bill Nowlin, eds. *Sweet '60: The 1960 Pittsburgh Pirates*. Phoenix: Society for American Baseball Research, 2013.

Pearlman, Jeff. *Love Me, Hate Me: Barry Bonds and the Making of an Antihero*. New York: HarperCollins, 2006.
Pepper, George Wharton. *Philadelphia Lawyer: An Autobiography*. Philadelphia: J.B. Lippincott, 1944.
Peterson, Robert. *Only the Ball Was White*. Englewood Cliffs, NJ: Prentice Hall, 1970.
Pietrusza, David. *Judge and Jury: The Life and Times of Judge Kenesaw Mountain Landis*. South Bend, IN: Diamond Communications, Inc. 1998.
_____. *Major Leagues: The Formation, Sometimes Absorption, and Mostly Inevitable Demise of 18 Professional Baseball Organizations, 1871 to Present*. Jefferson, NC: McFarland, 1991.
_____. *Rothstein: The Life, Times, and Murder of the Criminal Genius Who Fixed the 1919 World Series*. New York: Carroll & Graf, 2003.
Polner, Murray. *Branch Rickey: A Biography*. rev. ed. Jefferson, NC: McFarland, 2007.
Pomrenke, Jacob, ed. *Scandal on the South Side: The 1919 Chicago White Sox*. Phoenix: Society for American Baseball Research, 2015.
Postema, Pam, and Gene Wojciechowski. *You've Got to Have B*lls to Make It in This League*. New York: Simon & Schuster, 1992.
Powers, Albert Theodore. *The Business of Baseball*. Jefferson, NC: McFarland, 2003.
Professional Baseball in America: A Compilation of the Agreements and Rules which Define the Relations of Leagues, Clubs and Players. Chicago: H.G. Adair, 1921.
Quigel, James P., Jr., and Louis E. Hunsinger, Jr. *Gateway to the Majors: Williamsport and Minor League Baseball*. University Park: Pennsylvania University Press, 2001.
Rader, Benjamin G. *Baseball: A History of America's Game*. 3rd ed. Urbana: University of Illinois Press, 2008.
Radomski, Kirk. *Bases Loaded: The Inside Story of the Steroid Era in Baseball by the Central Figure in the Mitchell Report*. New York: Hudson Street Press, 2009.
Rampersad, Arnold. *Jackie Robinson: A Biography*. New York: Knopf, 1997.
Reed, Ted. *Carl Furillo, Brooklyn Dodgers All-Star*. Jefferson, NC: McFarland, 2011.
Reichler, Joseph L., ed. *The Baseball Encyclopedia: The Complete and Official Record of Major League Baseball*. New York: Macmillan, 1969.
Reisler, Jim. *A Great Day in Cooperstown: The Improbable Birth of Baseball's Hall of Fame*. New York: Carroll & Graf, 2006.
Riess, Steven A. *Sport in Industrial America, 1850–1920*. 2nd ed. Malden, MA: John Wiley & Sons, 2013.
_____. *The Sport of Kings and the Kings of Crime: Horse Racing, Politics, and Organized Crime in New York, 1865–1913*. Syracuse: Syracuse University Press, 2011.
Reston, James. *Collision at Home Plate: The Lives of Pete Rose and Bart Giamatti*. New York: Edward Burlingame Books, 1991.
Rhodes, Greg, and John Snyder. *Redleg Journal: Year by Year and Day by Day with the Cincinnati Reds Since 1866*. Cincinnati: Road West, 2000.
Richmond, Peter. *Ballpark: Camden Yards and the Building of an American Dream*. New York: Simon & Schuster, 1993.
Richter, Francis. *Richter's History and Records of Base Ball*. Philadelphia: Dando, 1914.
Ritter, Lawrence S. *The Glory of Their Times: The Story of the Early Days of Baseball Told by the Men Who Played It*. New enl. ed. New York: William Morrow, 1984.
Robinson, Jackie. *I Never Had It Made*. With Alfred Duckett. New York: G. P. Putnam's Sons, 1972.
Robinson, Rachel. With Lee Daniels. *Jackie Robinson: An Intimate Portrait*. New York: Abrams, 1996.
Roer, Mike. *Orator O'Rourke: The Life of a Baseball Radical*. Jefferson, NC: McFarland, 2005.
Roseboro, John. *Glory Days with the Dodgers and Other Days with Others*. With Bill Libby. New York: Atheneum, 1978.
Rosengren, John. *The Fight of Their Lives: How Juan Marichal and John Roseboro Turned Baseball's Ugliest Brawl into a Story of Forgiveness and Redemption*. Guilford, CT: Lyons Press, 2014.
_____. *Hammerin' Hank, George Almighty & the Say Hey Kid: The Year that Changed Baseball Forever*. Naperville, IL: Sourcebooks, 2008.

_____. *Hank Greenberg: The Hero of Heroes.* New York: New American Library, 2013.
Ross, Robert B. *The Great Baseball Revolt: The Rise and Fall of the 1890 Players League.* Lincoln: University of Nebraska Press, 2016.
Rossi, John P. *A Whole New Game: Off the Field Changes in Baseball, 1946–1960.* Jefferson, NC: McFarland, 1999.
Rushin, Steve. *The 34-Ton Bat: The Story of Baseball as Told Through Bobbleheads, Cracker Jacks, Jockstraps, Eye Black, and 375 Other Strange and Unforgettable Objects.* New York: Little, Brown, 2013.
Schaffer, Alan. *Vito Marcantonio, Radical in Congress.* Syracuse, NY: Syracuse University Press, 1966.
Schiff, Andrew J. *"The Father of Baseball": A Biography of Henry Chadwick.* Jefferson, NC: McFarland, 2008.
Schwarz, Alan. *The Numbers Game: Baseball's Lifelong Fascination with Statistics.* New York: Thomas Dunne Books, 2004.
Seymour, Harold, and Dorothy Seymour Mills. *Baseball: The Early Years.* New York: Oxford University Press, 1960.
_____. *Baseball: The Golden Age.* New York: Oxford University Press, 1971.
_____. *Baseball: The People's Game.* New York: Oxford University Press, 1990.
Shapiro, Michael. *Bottom of the Ninth: Branch Rickey, Casey Stengel, and the Daring Scheme to Save Baseball from Itself.* New York: Times Books, 2009.
Shiffert, John. *Base Ball in Philadelphia: A History of the Early Game, 1831–1900.* Jefferson, NC: McFarland, 2006.
Sickels, John. *Bob Feller: Ace of the Greatest Generation.* Dulles, VA: Brassey's, 2004.
Simon, Tom, ed. *Deadball Stars of the National League.* Washington, D.C.: Brassey's, 2004.
Simons, William M., ed. *Cooperstown Symposium of Baseball and American Culture, 2007–2008.* Jefferson, NC: McFarland, 2009.
_____, ed. *Cooperstown Symposium on Baseball and American Culture, 2009–2010.* Jefferson, NC: McFarland, 2011.
Skirboll, Aaron. *The Pittsburgh Cocaine Seven: How A Ragtag Group of Fans Took the Fall for Major League Baseball.* Chicago: Chicago Review Press, 2010.
Smelser, Marshall. *The Life That Ruth Built: A Biography.* New York: Quadrangle/New York Times Book Co., 1975.
Smiles, Jack. *Ee-Yah: The Life and Times of Hughie Jennings, Baseball Hall of Famer.* Jefferson, NC: McFarland, 2005.
Smith, Andrew F. *Encyclopedia of Junk Food and Fast Food.* Westport, CT: Greenwood Press, 2006.
Snyder, Brad. *A Well-Paid Slave: Curt Flood's Fight for Free Agency in Professional Sports.* New York: Viking, 2006.
Sobol, Ken. *Babe Ruth & the American Dream.* New York: Ballantine, 1974.
Sowell, Mike. *The Pitch that Killed.* New York: Macmillan, 1989.
Spalding, Albert. *America's National Game.* New York: American Sports Publishing Co, 1911.
Spatz, Lyle, ed. *The Team that Forever Changed Baseball and America: The 1947 Brooklyn Dodgers.* Lincoln: University of Nebraska Press; Phoenix: Society for American Baseball Research, 2012.
Spatz, Lyle, and Steve Steinberg. *1921—The Yankees, the Giants,* and *the Battle for Baseball Supremacy in New York.* Lincoln: University of Nebraska Press, 2010.
Spink, Alfred H. *The National Game.* 2d ed. St. Louis, Mo.: National Game Pub. Co., 1911. Reprinted with foreword by Steven P. Gietschier. Carbondale, Il.: Southern Illinois University Press, 2000.
Spink, J.G. Taylor. *Judge Landis and Twenty-Five Years of Baseball.* New York: Thomas Y. Crowell, 1947.
Stahl, John Harry, and Bill Nowlin, eds. *Drama and Pride in the Gateway City: The 1964 St. Louis Cardinals.* Lincoln: University of Nebraska Press and Society for American Baseball Research, 2013.
Stang, Mark. *Cardinals Collection: 100 Years of St. Louis Cardinals Images.* Wilmington, OH: Orange Frazer Press, 2002.

Bibliography

Staudohar, Paul. *Playing For Dollars: Labor Relations and the Sports Business.* 3rd ed. Ithaca, NY: Cornell University Press, 1996.
Stein, Fred. *A History of the Baseball Fan.* Jefferson, NC: McFarland, 2005.
Steinberg, Steve, and Lyle Spatz. *The Colonel and Hug: The Partnership that Transformed the New York Yankees.* Lincoln: University of Nebraska Press, 2015.
Stevens, David. *Baseball's Radical for All Seasons: A Biography of John Montgomery Ward.* Lanham, MD: Scarecrow Press, 1998.
Stewart, Wayne. *Stan the Man: The Life and Times of Stan Musial.* Chicago: Triumph Books, 2010.
Stone, Eric. *Wrong Side of the Wall: The Life of Blackie Schwamb, The Greatest Prison Baseball Player of All Time.* Guilford, CT: Lyons Press, 2004.
Stout, Glenn, and Richard A. Johnson. *The Cubs: The Complete Story of Chicago Cubs Baseball.* New York: Houghton Mifflin, 2007.
Strasberg, Andy, Bob Thompson, and Tim Wiles. *Baseball's Greatest Hit: The Story of Take Me Out to the Ball Game.* New York: Hal Leonard Pub., 2008.
Trey Strecker, Stephen P. Gietschier, Mitchell Nathanson, John A Fortunato, and David George Sudham, eds. *Understanding Baseball: A Textbook.* Jefferson, NC: McFarland, 2015.
Stump, Al. *Cobb: A Biography.* Chapel Hill, NC: Algonquin Books, 1994.
Sullivan, Dean A., ed. *Early Innings: A Documentary History of Baseball, 1825–1908.* Lincoln: University of Nebraska Press, 1995.
_____, ed. *Final Innings: A Documentary History of Baseball, 1972–2008.* Lincoln: University of Nebraska Press, 2010.
_____, ed. *Late Innings: A Documentary History of Baseball, 1945–1972.* Lincoln: University of Nebraska Press, 2002.
_____, ed. *Middle innings: A Documentary History of Baseball, 1900–1948.* Lincoln: University of Nebraska Press, 1998.
Sullivan, Neil J. *The Dodgers Move West.* New York: Oxford University Press, 1987.
_____. *The Minors: The Struggles and the Triumph of Baseball's Poor Relation from 1876 to the Present.* New York: St. Martin's Press, 1990.
Surdam, David George. *The Ball Game Biz: An Introduction to the Economics of Professional Team Sports.* Jefferson, NC: McFarland, 2010.
_____. *The Big Leagues Go to Washington: Congress and Sports Antitrust, 1951–1989.* Urbana: University of Illinois Press, 2015.
Sutter, L.M. *Arlie Latham: A Baseball Biography of the Freshest Man on Earth.* Jefferson, NC: McFarland, 2012.
Tepler, Boyd. *In Cub Chains.* Pittsburgh: Dorrance Pub. Co., 1993.
Theodore, John. *Baseball's Natural: The Story of Eddie Waitkus.* Carbondale, IL: Southern Illinois University Press, 2002.
Thomas, Henry W. *Walter Johnson, Baseball's Big Train.* Washington, D.C.: Phenom Press, 1995.
Thorn, John. *Baseball in the Garden of Eden: The Secret History of the Early Game.* New York: Simon & Schuster, 2011.
Tiemann, Robert L. *Nineteenth Century Stars.* Phoenix: Society for American Baseball Research, 2012.
Toot, Peter T. *Armando Marsans: A Cuban Pioneer in the Major Leagues.* Jefferson, NC: McFarland, 2004.
Tootle, James R. *Vintage Base Ball: Recapturing the National Pastime.* Jefferson, NC: McFarland, 2011.
Towle, Mike. *Pete Rose: Baseball's Charlie Hustle.* Nashville, TN: Cumberland House, 2003.
Tygiel, Jules. *Baseball's Great Experiment: Jackie Robinson and His Legacy.* New York: Oxford University Press, 1983.
Van Auken, Lance, and Robin Van Auken. *Play Ball! The Story of Little League Baseball.* University Park: Pennsylvania State University Press, 2001.
Van Dulken, Stephen. *Inventing the 19th Century: 100 Inventions That Shaped the Victorian Age, From Aspirin to the Zeppelin.* New York: New York University Press, 2001.
Vincent, Fay. *The Last Commissioner: A Baseball Valentine.* New York: Simon & Schuster, 2002.

Virtue, John. *South of the Color Barrier: How Jorge Pasquel and the Mexican League Pushed Baseball Toward Racial Integration*. Jefferson, NC: McFarland, 2008.
Voigt, David Quentin. *American Baseball: From Gentleman's Sport to the Commissioner System*. Norman: University of Oklahoma Press, 1966.
_____. *American Baseball: From Postwar Expansion to the Electronic Age*. University Park: Pennsylvania State University Press, 1983.
_____. *American Baseball: From the Commissioners to Continental Expansion*. Norman: University of Oklahoma Press, 1970.
Wagenheim, Kal. *Babe Ruth: His Life and Legend*. New York: Praeger, 1974.
Waldo, Ronald T. *Pennant Hopes Dashed by the Homer in the Gloamin': The Story of How the 1938 Pittsburgh Pirates Blew the National League Pennant*. Jefferson, NC: McFarland, 2013.
Walker, James R. *Crack of the Bat: A History of Baseball on the Radio*. Lincoln: University of Nebraska Press, 2015.
Waller, Spencer Weber, Neil B. Cohen, and Paul Finkelman, eds. *Baseball and the American Legal Mind*. New York: Garland, 1995.
Wallop, Douglass. *The Year the Yankees Lost the Pennant: A Novel*. New York: Norton, 1954.
Walsh, Christy. *Adios to Ghosts!* New York, 1937.
Walsh, John Evangelist. *The Night Casey Was Born: The True Story Behind the Great American Ballad "Casey at the Bat."* Woodstock, NY: Overlook Press, 2007.
Ward, Ettie, ed. *Courting the Yankees: Legal Essays on the Bronx Bombers*. Durham, NC: Carolina Academic Press, 2003.
Weiss, Stuart L. *The Curt Flood Story: The Man Behind the Myth*. Columbia: University of Missouri Press, 2007.
White, Bill, with Gordon Dillow. *Uppity: My Untold Story About the Games People Play*. New York: Grand Central Pub., 2011.
White, G. Edward. *Creating the National Pastime: Baseball Transforms Itself: 1903–1953*. Princeton, NJ: Princeton University Press, 1996.
_____. *Justice Oliver Wendell Holmes: Law and the Inner Self*. New York: Oxford University Press, 1993.
White, Sol. *Sol White's History of Colored Base Ball, with Other Documents on the Early Black Game, 1886–1936*. Rev. ed. of *Sol White's Official Base Ball Guide*, 1907. Preface and notes by Jerry Malloy. Lincoln: University of Nebraska Press, 1995.
Whitmore, William H. *The Colonial Laws of Massachusetts*. Vol. 1. Boston: Rockwell and Churchill, 1890.
Wiggins, David Kenneth, and Patrick B. Miller. *The Unlevel Playing Field: A Documentary History of the African American Experience in Sport*. Urbana: University of Illinois Press, 2003.
Wiggins, Robert Peyton. *The Federal League of Base Ball Clubs: The History of an Outlaw Major League, 1914–1915*. Jefferson, NC: McFarland, 2009.
Wolf, Gregory H., ed. *Winning on the North Side: The 1929 Chicago Cubs*. Phoenix: Society for American Baseball Research, 2015.
Yarbrough, Tinsley E. *Harry A. Blackmun: The Outsider Justice*. New York: Oxford University Press, 2008.
Zappala, Tom, and Ellen Zappala, with Lou Blasi. *The T206 Collection: The Players and Their Stories*. Portsmouth, NH: Peter E. Randall, 2010.
Zimbalist, Andrew S. *Baseball and Billions: A Probing Look Inside the Big Business of our National Pastime*. New York: Basic Books, 1992.
_____. *Circling the Bases: Essays on the Challenges and Prospects of the Sports Industry*. Philadelphia: Temple University Press, 2011.

Chapters in Books

Abrams, Roger I. "Liberation Arbitration: The Baseball Reserve Clause Case." Chap. 12 in *Proceedings of the 55th Annual Meeting of the National Academy of Arbitrators*. Washington, D.C.: Bureau of National Affairs, 2003.

Bibliography 269

Armour, "Alex Johnson." In *The Year of the Blue Snow: The 1964 Philadelphia Phillies*, edited by Mel Marmer and Bill Nowlin, 132–39. Phoenix: Society for American Baseball Research, 2013.
Armour, Mark. "Charlie Finley." In *Mustaches and Mayhem: Charlie O's Three-Time Champions, The Oakland Athletics 1972–74*, edited by Chip Greene, 14–23. Phoenix: Society for American Baseball Research, 2015.
Bailey, Bob. "August 20, 1877: Gray Outcomes—Louisville Grays vs. Hartford Dark Blues." In Felber, *Inventing Baseball*, 106–07.
Bauer, John W. "Debut of the Players League." In Felber, *Inventing Baseball*, 222–24.
Bryan, Patricia L., and Thomas Wolf. "On the Brink: Babe Ruth in Dennis Lehane's *The Given Day*." In *Cooperstown Symposium on Baseball and American Culture, 2009–2010*, edited by William M. Simons, 42–56. Jefferson, NC: McFarland, 2011.
Bush, Frederick C. "Roger Clemens." In *Nuclear-Powered Baseball: Articles Inspired by the Simpsons Episode, "Homer at the Bat,"* edited by Emily Hawks and Bill Nowlin, 35–48. Phoenix: Society for American Baseball Research, 2016.
Casway, Jerrold. "Inter-Racial Baseball: Pythians of Philadelphia vs. Olympics of Philadelphia." In Felber, *Inventing Baseball*, 68–70.
Corbett, Warren. "Bill White." In *Drama and Pride in the Gateway City: The 1964 St. Louis Cardinals*, edited by John Harry Stahl and Bill Nowlin, 232–37. Lincoln: University of Nebraska Press and Society for American Baseball Research, 2013.
Costello, Rory. "Al Gionfriddo's Memorable Game Six Catch." In Spatz, *The Team that Forever Changed Baseball and America*, 320–22.
———. "Dan Bankhead." In Spatz, *The Team that Forever Changed Baseball and America*, 235–38.
Devine, James R. "Joe DiMaggio (and His Lawyer)." In Ward, *Courting the Yankees*, 3–21.
Dixon, Philip H. "The First Fixed Game: Mutuals of New York vs. Eckfords of Brooklyn." In Felber, *Inventing Baseball*, 46–48.
Dunn, Geoffrey. "José Canseco." In *Nuclear-Powered Baseball: Articles Inspired by the Simpsons Episode, "Homer at the Bat,"* edited by Emily Hawks and Bill Nowlin, 23–34. Phoenix: Society for American Baseball Research, 2016.
Edmonds, Ed. "Cornering the Market: The Yankees and the Interplay of Labor and Antitrust Laws." In Ward, *Courting the Yankees*, 303–32.
———. "The Great Dodgers Pitching Tandem Strikes a Blow for Salaries: The 1966 Drysdale-Koufax Holdout and Its Impact on the Game." In *The Cooperstown Symposium of Baseball and American Culture, 2007–2008*, edited by William M. Simons, 248–62. Jefferson, NC: McFarland, 2009.
Enders, Eric. "Armando Marsáns." In Simon, *Deadball Stars of the National League*, 255–57.
Felber, Bill. "Arrested on a Day of Rest: Washington Senators vs. Cleveland Spiders." In Felber, *Inventing Baseball*, 254–56.
Finkel, Jan. "Grover Cleveland Alexander." In Simon, *Deadball Stars of the National League*, 209–11.
Flannery, Michael T. "Affairs of the Heart." In Ward, *Courting the Yankees*, 183–213.
Fletcher, David, and George Castle. "Margaret Donahue—Pioneering Female Cubs Executive Left Her Mark on the '29 Cubs and MLB." In *Winning on the North Side: The 1929 Chicago Cubs*, edited by Gregory H. Wolf, 206–11. Phoenix: Society for American Baseball Research, 2015.
Ginsburg, Dan. "John Kinley Tener." In Simon, *Deadball Stars of the National League*, 26–28.
Ham, Eldon L. "The Theft of Gary Matthews." Chap. 16 in *Larceny and Old Leather: The Mischievous Legacy of Major League Baseball*. Chicago: Academy Chicago Publishers, 2005.
Hershberger, Richard. "In the Beginning: Olympics of Philadelphia, Pa. vs. Camdens of Camden, N.J." In Felber, *Inventing Baseball*, 1–2.
Husman, John. "June 21, 1879: The Cameo of Bill White—Cleveland at Providence." In Felber, *Inventing Baseball*, 116–17.
Jensen, Don. "Jim Thorpe." In Simon, *Deadball Stars of the National League*, 81–82.
Jones, David. "Benny Kauff." In Simon, *Deadball Stars of the National League*, 83–86.

"June 28, 1970: A Play-by-Play Account of the Final Pirate Game at Forbes Field." In *Forbes Field: Essays and Memories of the Pirates' Historic Ballpark, 1909-1971*, edited by David Cicotello and Angelo J. Louisa, 94–118. Jefferson, NC: McFarland, 2007.

Keefe, T.J. "The Brotherhood and Its Work." In *Players' National League Base Ball Guide*, 7–10. Chicago: F.H. Brunell, 1890. Reprinted in Sullivan, *Early Innings*, 196–98.

"L.A. Voters Narrowly Approve Stadium in Chavez Ravine." In Sullivan, *Late Innings*, 126–28.

Lamb, William F. "The Black Sox Scandal." In *Scandal on the South Side: The 1919 Chicago White Sox*, edited by Jacob Pomrenke, 298–309. Phoenix: Society for American Baseball Research, 2015.

Lamberty, Bill. "George Sisler." In Jones, *Deadball Stars of the American League*, 795–97.

Malloy, Jerry. "Frank Grant." In *Nineteenth Century Stars*, edited by Robert L. Tiemann, 110–11. Phoenix: Society for American Baseball Research, 2012.

Mancuso, Peter. "Tim Keefe Finally Loses." In Felber, *Inventing Baseball*, 195–97.

Marlett, Jeffrey. "The Suspension of Leo Durocher." In Spatz, *The Team that Forever Changed Baseball and America*, 50–56.

Mills, A.G. "Final Decision of the Baseball Commission." In *Spalding's Official Baseball Guide 1908*, edited by Henry Chadwick, 45–48. New York: American Sports Publishing Co., 1908.

Minan, John H., and Kevin Cole. "The Player in the Iron Mask." In *The Little White Book of Baseball Law*, 27–35. Chicago: American Bar Association, 2009.

Nathanson, Mitchell. "Law." In *Understanding Baseball: A Textbook*, edited by Trey Strecker, Stephen P. Gietschier, Mitchell Nathanson, John A Fortunato, and David George Sudham, 143–85. Jefferson, NC: McFarland, 2015.

"The New National Agreement." In *Reach's Official American League Base Ball Guide for 1904*, edited by Francis C. Richter, 115–23. Philadelphia: A.J. Reach Co., 1904.

Newman, Robert J. "Advertising and the Dodgers in 1947." In Spatz, *The Team that Forever Changed Baseball and America*, 298–304.

"NL Upholds Promise, Awards Franchises to Two CL Teams; AL Reneges." In Sullivan, *Late Innings*, 156–59.

Nowlin, Bill. "Pumpsie Green, Infield (1959–62)." In *Red Sox Baseball in the Days of Ike and Elvis: The Red Sox of the 1950s*, edited by Mark Armour and Bill Nowlin, 190–99. Phoenix: Society for American Baseball Research, 2012.

Palmer, Charles A. "The Czar's Court: The Commissioner of Baseball and the New York Yankees." In Ward, *Courting the Yankees*, 243–58.

Pestana, Mark. "The Legendary Doubleday Game." In Felber, *Inventing Baseball*, 3–5.

Poekel, Charles A., Jr. "Babe Ruth vs. Baby Ruth: The Quest for a Candy Bar." In *Cooperstown Symposium on Baseball and American Culture, 2009–2010*, edited by William L. Simon, 225–28. Jefferson, NC: McFarland, 2011.

Rafferty-Osaki, Terumi. "Asians and Baseball: The Breaking and Perpetuating of Stereotypes." In *Cooperstown Symposium of Baseball and American Culture, 2007–2008*, edited by William M. Simons, 131–46. Jefferson, NC: McFarland, 2009.

Rogers, C. Paul, III. "Eddie Waitkus." In Nowlin, *Van Lingle Mungo: The Man, The Song, The Players*, 66–75.

_____. "Hugh Ambrose Jennings." In Jones, *Deadball Stars of the American League*, 555–58.

_____. "Vernon Law." In *Sweet '60: The 1960 Pittsburgh Pirates*, edited by Clifton Blue Parker and Bill Nowlin, 128–37. Phoenix: Society for American Baseball Research, 2013.

Santa Maria, Michael, and James Costello. "Thrown Out Stealing." In *In the Shadows of the Diamond: Hard Times in the National Pastime*, 154–59. Dubuque, IA: Elysian Fields Press, 1992.

Schimler, Stuart. "Ben Shibe." In Jones, *Deadball Stars of the American League*, 593–94.

"Statement of Casey Stengel, Manager of the New York Yankees." In *Baseball and the American Legal Mind*, edited by Spencer Weber Waller, Neil B. Cohen & Paul Finkelman, 103–24. New York: Garland, 1995.

Steinberg, Steve. "William Leopold Doak." In Simon, *Deadball Stars of the National League*, 358–60.

Swaine, Rick. "Jackie Robinson." In Spatz, *The Team that Forever Changed Baseball and America*, 6-14.
Thomas, Joan M. "Roger Bresnahan." In Simon, *Deadball Stars of the National League*, 348-50.
Thorn, John. "The First Recorded Games." In Felber, *Inventing Baseball*, 6-7.
Valtin, Rolf. "In Memoriam, Lewis M. Gill, 1912-2002." In *Arbitration 2002—Workplace Arbitration: A Process in Evolution, Proceedings for the Fifty-Fifth Annual Meeting, National Academy of Arbitrators*, edited by Charles J. Coleman, v-viii. Washington, D.C.: Bureau of National Affairs, 2003.
Ward, John Montgomery. "Base Ball A Beneficent Trust." In Francis Richter, *Richter's History and Records of Base Ball*, 224-25. Philadelphia: Sporting Life, 1914. Reprinted in Sullivan, *Middle Innings*, 64-65.
Weatherby, Charles. "Danny Gardella." In Nowlin, *Van Lingle Mungo: The Man, The Song, The Players*, 39-44.
Wolinsky, Russell. "Hugh Casey. " In Spatz, *The Team That Forever Changed Baseball and America*, 113-18.
Zinn, John. "July to September, 1858: The Rivalry Begins—Brooklyn vs. New York." In Felber, *Inventing Baseball*, 10-12.

Periodical Articles

Abrams, Douglas E. "The Twelve-Year-Old Girl's Lawsuit that Changed America: The Continuing Impact of *Now v. Little League Baseball, Inc.* at 40." *Virginia Journal of Social Policy & the Law* 20 (2012): 241-69.
Abrams, Roger I. "Blackmun's List." *Virginia Sports and Entertainment Law Journal* 6 (2007): 181-207.
Ahrens, Arthur R. "Fred Pfeffer, Stonewall Second Baseman." *Baseball Research Journal* 8 (1979): 46-52.
Alito, Samuel A., Jr. "The Origin of the Baseball Antitrust Exemption." *Journal of Supreme Court History* 34 (July 2009): 183-95, reprinted in *Baseball Research Journal* 38 (Fall 2009): 86-93.
Appel, Marty. "Service of a Different Kind: Several Ballplayers Established a Second Career in Politics." *Memories and Dreams* (Winter 2008): 17-19.
Armour, Mark. "Emmett Ashford: Entertainer and Pioneer." *National Pastime* 27 (2007): 54-58.
———. "A Tale of Two Umpires." *Baseball Research Journal* 38 (Fall 2009): 126-30.
Bales, Jack. "Baseball's First Bill Veeck." *Baseball Research Journal* 42 (Fall 2013): 7-16.
Ball, David. "The Bechtel-Craver Trade and the Origins of Baseball's Sales System." *Base Ball: A Journal of the Early Game* 1 (2007): 36-55.
Berlage, Gai Ingham. "The Colorado Bullets." *Baseball Research Journal* 27 (1998): 40-42.
Borst, Bill. "The Matron Magnate." *Baseball Research Journal* (1977): 25-30.
Brill, Christian H., and Howard W. Brill, "Take Me Out to the Hearing: Major League Baseball Players Before Congress." *Albany Government Law Review* 5 (2012): 90-122.
Brown, Randall. "How Baseball Began." *National Pastime* 24 (2004): 51-54.
Brown, William E., Jr. "Sunday Baseball Comes to Boston." *National Pastime* 14 (1994): 83-85.
Bruce, H. Addington. "Baseball and the National Life." *Outlook* (May 17, 1913): 104-07.
Casway, Jerrold. "Philadelphia's Pythians." *National Pastime* 15 (1995): 120-23.
Cobb, Ty. "Batting Out Better Boys." *Rotarian* 71 (July 1947): 10-12.
Collins, Julia. "HLS Names in Lights: Baseball Player's Agent." *Harvard Law Bulletin* (Spring 1998), http://today.law.harvard.edu/bulletin/issue/spring-1998/.
Davies, Ross E. "Along Comes the Players Association: The Roots and Rise of Organized Labor in Major League Baseball." *New York University Journal of Legislation and Public Policy* 16 (2013): 321-349.
———. "A Crank on the Court: The Passion of Justice William R. Day." *Baseball Research Journal* 38 (Fall 2009): 94-107.

_____. "The Law Firm and the League: Morgan, Lewis and Bockius LLP, Major League Baseball, and MLB.com." *Baseball Research Journal* 39 (Fall 2010): 74–80.
_____. "The Sport of Courts: Baseball and the Law." *Baseball Research Journal* 38 (Fall 2009): 59–78.
Deford, Frank. "A Gentleman and a Scholar." *Sports Illustrated*, April 17, 1989, 86–100.
Deitsch, Richard. "Catching Up With … Vernon Law, Pirates Ace, October 10, 1960." *Sports Illustrated*, May 22, 2000, 15.
Doublestein, Matthew G. "American Song, America's Game." *National Pastime* 24 (2004): 55–58.
Edelman, Marc. "Has Collusion Returned to Baseball? Analyzing Whether a Concerted Increase in Free Agent Player Supply Would Violate Baseball's 'Collusion Clause.'" *Loyola of Los Angeles Entertainment Law Review* 24 (2004): 159–84.
Edmonds, Ed. "Arthur Soden's Legacy: The Origins and Early History of Baseball's Reserve System." *Albany Government Law Review* 5 (2012): 38–89.
Eschenbach, Stephen. "Home-Plate Security." *Harvard Magazine* 106 (July–August 2004): 73–74.
"The Famous Federal Suit," *Baseball Magazine* 14 (March 1915): 65–68.
Farrell, Mary H.J. "Baseball's for Men Only? These Girls of Summer Say It Ain't So." *People*, June 6, 1994, 63.
Fimrite, Ron. "Mantle & Mays," *Sports Illustrated*, March 25, 1985, 70–84.
Findling, J.E. "The Louisville Grays' Scandal of 1877." *Journal of Sports History* 3 (1976).
"For the Record." *Sports Illustrated*, February 13, 1978, 69.
Freeman, Ross H. "The (Hot) Dog Days of Summer: Missouri's 'Baseball Rule' Takes a Strike." *Missouri Law Review* (2015): 559–78.
Fultz, David L. "The Ball Players' Requests." *Baseball Magazine* 12 (January 1914): 81–85.
_____. "The Baseball Players Fraternity and What It Stands For." *Baseball Magazine* 10 (November 1912): 29–31, 124–26. Reprinted in Sullivan, *Middle innings*, 66–68.
_____. "The Cincinnati Conference and Its Results." *Baseball Magazine* 12 (March 1914): 79–82.
_____. "Status of the Players' Petition." *Baseball Magazine* 12 (February 1914): 69–72.
Gallagher, Robert C. "John Tener's Brilliant Career." *Baseball Research Journal* 19 (1990): 36–38.
Garrett, Robert Alan, and Philip R. Hochberg. "Sports Broadcasting and the Law." *Indiana Law Journal* 59 (1984): 155–93.
Gates, Jim. "Patch Puzzle—Designer of Baseball Centennial Logo A Lost Figure in History." *Memories and Dreams* 36 (Summer 2014): 22.
Gerlach, Larry R. "Crime and Punishment: The Marichal-Roseboro Incident." *Nine: A Journal of Baseball History and Culture* 12 (Spring 2004): 1–28.
Gipe, George. "Ty Cobb's Anger Led to Baseball's First Strike, A Comedy of Errors." *Sports Illustrated*, August 29, 1977, W5–6.
Grow, Nathaniel. "Reevaluating the Curt Flood Act of 1998," *Nebraska Law Review* 87 (2008): 747–58.
Hailey, Gary. "The Anatomy of a Murder: Federal League and the Courts." *National Pastime* 4 (1985): 62–73.
Haupert, Michael. "Baseball's Major Salary Milestones." *Baseball Research Journal* 40 (Fall 2011): 89–93.
_____. "William Hulbert and the Birth of the National League." *Baseball Research Journal* 44 (Spring 2015): 83–92.
Henderson, Cary S. "Los Angeles and the Dodger War, 1957–1962." *Southern California Quarterly* 62 (1980): 261–89.
Honaker, Jeffrey C. "*United States v. Cleveland Indians*: FICA and FUTA Taxes v. the Social Security Act—Why Have Different Definitions for Identical Language?" *Akron Tax Journal* 17 (2002): 99–131.
Hylton, J. Gordon. "Baseball Cards and the Birth of the Right of Publicity: The Curious Case of *Haelan Laboratories v. Topps Chewing Gum*." *Marquette Sports Law Review* 12 (2001): 273–94.

———. "A Foul Ball in the Courtroom: The Baseball Spectator Injury as a Case of First Impression." *Tulsa Law Review* 38 (2003): 485–502.
———. "The Historical Origins of Baseball Grievance Arbitration." *Marquette Sports Law Review* 11 (2001): 175–184.
———. "The Major League Baseball Players Association and the Ownership of Sports Statistics: The Untold Story of Round One." *Marquette Sports Law Review* 17 (2006): 87–108.
———. "Why Baseball's Antitrust Exemption Still Survives." *Marquette Sports Law Journal* 9 (1999): 391–402.
Irwin, Richard L. "A Historical Review of Litigation in Baseball." *Marquette Sports Law Journal* 1 (1991): 283–300.
Jacobs, Barry. "Esq." *Student Lawyer* 10 (April 1982): 56–57.
Jacobson, Charles. "The Supreme Court of Baseball." *Case and Comment* 23 (1916): 665–67.
Jarvis, Robert M. "And Behind the Plate. .. Muddy Ruel of the U.S. Supreme Court." *Journal of Supreme Court History* 36 (2011): 1–10.
———. "Babe Ruth as Legal Hero." *Florida State University Law Review* 22 (1995): 885–97.
Jarvis, Robert M., and Phyllis Coleman. "Early Baseball Law." *American Journal of Legal History* 45 (2001): 117–31.
"The Jurisprudence of Yogi Berra." *Emory Law Journal* 46 (1997): 697–790.
Kane, Martin. "The Baseball Bubble Trouble." *Sports Illustrated*, August 16, 1954, 38.
Kaplan, Jim. "Let the Games Begin." *Sports Illustrated*, August 10, 1981, 14–19.
———. "No Games Today." *Sports Illustrated*, June 22, 1981, 17–21.
Kermisch, Al. "From A Researcher's Note Book: First Reserve Clause Enacted 100 Years Ago." *Baseball Research Journal* 8 (1979): 9–10.
Kosin, Phil. "Diamond Classics: Baseball Lawyers Make Mark." *ABA Journal* 71 (October 1985): 34–35.
Krause, "Unfair Trade—Right of Privacy—Right of Manufacturer Who Has Contracted for Use of Celebrity's Name to Injunction Against Competitor Using Such Name." *Michigan Law Review* 34 (1936): 588–90.
Lamb, William F. "Jury Nullification and the Not Guilty Verdicts in the Black Sox Case." *Baseball Research Journal* 44 (Fall 2015): 47–56.
———. "The Ward v. Johnson Libel Case: The Last Battle of the Great Baseball War." *Base Ball: A Journal of the Early Game* 2 (Fall 2008): 47–62.
Longert, Scott. "The Players' Fraternity." *Baseball Research Journal* 30 (2001): 40–47.
Lowenfish, Lee. "When All Heaven Rejoiced: Branch Rickey and the Origins of the Breaking of the Color Line." *NINE: A Journal of Baseball History and Culture* 11, no. 1 (2002): 1–15.
Lucas, John A. "The Unholy Experiment—Professional Baseball's Struggle Against Pennsylvania Sunday Blue Laws 1926-1934." *Pennsylvania History* 38 (1971): 163–175.
Mandell, David. "Danny Gardella and the Reserve Clause." *National Pastime* 26 (2006): 41–44.
———. "Reuben Berman's Foul Ball." *National Pastime* 25 (2005): 106–07.
———. "The Suspension of Leo Durocher." *National Pastime* 27 (2007): 101–04.
McCann, Michael A. "Justice Sonia Sotamayor and the Relationship Between Leagues and Players: Insights and Implications." *Connecticut Law Review* 42 (2010): 901–23.
McCarthy, Leslie Gibson. "Lady B." *Cardinals Gameday Magazine* (2014, no. 2): 80–88.
McConnell, Bob. "Whatever Happened to Charley Jones?" *Baseball Research Journal* 30 (2001): 89–91.
Menendez, Albert J. "The Battle for Sunday Baseball." *Liberty* (September–October 2007), http://www.libertymagazine.org/article/the-battle-for-sunday-baseball.
Mears, Patrick E. "The Catcher, 'The Quick Lunch King' and Baseball's Reserve Clause: Major League Litigation in Grand Rapids." *Stereoscope* (Historical Society of the U.S. District Court for the Western District of Michigan) 1 (Winter 2003): 1–12.
Morante, Tony. "Baseball and Tammany Hall." *Baseball Research Journal* 42 (Spring 2013): 30–36.
Moss, Robert A. "Generations: Baseball on U.S. Postage Stamps." *American Philatelist* 127 (2013): 930–42.

Murphy, Joseph P., Jr. "The Busher from Dubuque: Pants Rowland Wore Many Hats." *Baseball Research Journal* 24 (1995): 117–22.
Naiman, Joe. "The First Replacement Players: The 'Tigers' of May 18, 1912." *Baseball Research Journal* 25 (1996): 121–23.
Pearlman, Jeff. "It's a Wrap!" *Sports Illustrated*, October 15, 2001, 46–49.
Pietrusza, David. "Grace Coolidge—The First Lady of Baseball." *Elysian Fields Quarterly* 12, no. 2 (1993): 36–39.
Pomrenke, Jacob. "Swede Risberg: More Educated Than You Think," *SABR Black Sox Scandal Research Committee Newsletter* 4 (June 2012): 3–4.
Potts, R.F. "The Great Cincinnati Meeting." *Baseball Magazine* 12 (March 1914): 33–38.
"Presidential Presence." *Memories and Dreams* 36, no. 4 (2014): 8.
Rains, Bob. "Mama's Got a Brand New Bag." *Green Bag 2d* 12 (2009): 345–46.
Reisler, Jim. "Eddie Gaedel: The Sad Life of Baseball's Midget." *National Pastime* 6 (Winter 1987): 9.
Richard, Kenneth D. "Remembering Carl Mays." *Baseball Research Journal* 30 (2001): 122–26.
Roberts, Gary R. "A Brief Appraisal of the Curt Flood Act of 1998 From the Minor League Perspective," *Marquette Sports Law Journal* 9 (1999): 413–37.
Robinson, Eric. "Movies, Bullfights, and Baseball, Too: A Sports Stadium Built for Spectacle First and Sports Second." *National Pastime: Baseball in the Space Age* (SABR 44 Convention Issue, 2014): 10–17.
———. "The Peculiar Professional Baseball Career of Eddie Gaedel." *National Pastime: North Side, South Side, All Around the Town* (SABR 45 Convention Issue, 2015), 72–73.
Robinson, Frank, with Roy Blount, Jr. "I'll Always Be Outspoken." *Sports Illustrated*, October 21, 1974, 30–38.
Rogers, C. Paul, III. "Napoleon Lajoie, Breach of Contract, and the Great Baseball War." *SMU Law Review* 55 (2002): 325–45.
Rosciam, Chuck. "The Evolution of Catcher's Equipment." *Baseball Research Journal* 39 (Summer 2010): 104–12.
Rosner, Scott R. "History and Business of Contraction in Major League Baseball." *Stanford Journal of Law, Business & Finance* 8 (2003): 265–88.
Rushin, Steve. "A Life Well-Lived." *Sports Illustrated*, January 20, 2003, 15.
Schaefer, Robert. "The Great Base Ball Match of 1858: Base Ball's First All Star Game." *Nine: A Journal of Baseball History and Culture* 14 (Fall 2005): 47–66.
Segroie, Peter. "Reuben's Ruling Helps You 'Have a Ball.'" *Baseball Research Journal* 20 (1991): 85.
Sharnik, Morton. "Downfall of A Hero." *Sports Illustrated*, February 23, 1970, 16–21.
Shipley, David E. "Three Strikes and They're out at the Old Ball Game: Preemption of Performers' Rights of Publicity under the Copyright Act of 1976." *Arizona State Law Journal* 20 (1988): 369–421.
Smith, Ronald A. "The Paul Robeson—Jackie Robinson Saga and a Political Collision." *Journal of Sports History* 6 (1979): 5–27.
Staudohar, Paul D. "Baseball Negotiations: A New Agreement." *Monthly Labor Review* 125 (December 2002): 15–22.
Tanick, Marshall H. "Play Ball: Minnesota Baseball Litigation Lore." *National Pastime: Short but Wondrous Summers—Baseball in the North Star State* (SABR 42 Convention Issue, 2012): 141–47.
"They Said It." *Sports Illustrated*, February 2, 1959, 18.
Thorn, John. "The Pittsfield 'Baseball' Bylaw of 1791: What It Means." *Base Ball: A Journal of the Early Game* 5 (Spring 2011): 46–49.
Thorn, John, and Jules Tygiel. "Jackie Robinson's Signing: The Real, Untold Story." *National Pastime* 10 (1990): 7–12.
Tierney, Ted J. "Heads Up! The Baseball Facility Liability Act." *Northern Illinois University Law Review* 18 (1998): 601–17.
Tillman, Ken. "The Portable Batting Cage." *Baseball Research Journal* 28 (1999): 23–26.
"Trade of the Century." *Sports Illustrated*, July 31, 2000, 147.

Trechak, John. "The Seventh Circuit Beans Performer Publicity Rights in Baseball's Telecast Rights Rhubarb." *Loyola Los Angeles Entertainment Law Review* 8 (1988): 75–91.
Trimble, Patrick. "Babe Ruth: The Media Construction of a 1920's Sport Personality." *Colby Quarterly* 32 (March 1996): 45–57.
"Turbulent Times, 1902–1952." *Philadelphia Lawyer* 64 (Winter 2002): 82–92.
"Ty Cobb vs. Ban Johnson." *Baseball Magazine* 9, no. 3 (July 1912): 8–14, 94, 96, 100.
Tootle, Jim. "Bill Veeck and James Thurber: The Literary Origins of the Midget Pinch Hitter." *Nine: A Journal of Baseball History and Culture* 10 (Spring 2002): 110–19.
Tygiel, Jules. "The Court-Martial of Jackie Robinson." *American Heritage* 35 (August/September 1984): 34–39.
"U. S. Court Tags Wills 'Out' on Taxes for Prizes." *Jet*, June 29, 1967, 52.
Verducci, Tom. "Brushback." *Sports Illustrated*, April 10, 1995, 60–67.
_____. "Totally Juiced." *Sports Illustrated*, June 3, 2002, 34–48.
_____. "Yogi Berra, 1925–2015." *Sports Illustrated*, October 5, 2015, 6–11.
Voigt, David Q. "Fie on Figure Filberts: Some Crimes Against Clio." *Baseball Research Journal* 12 (1983): 32–38.
Wahl, Grant. "Baseball Umpire Pam Postema—March 14, 1988." *Sports Illustrated*, April 28, 1997, [14].
Ward, Edward R. "Baseball and the Law." *Baseball Research Journal* 25 (1996): 154.
Ward, John J. "The Famous Sisler Case." *Baseball Magazine* 17 (October 1916): 33–37.
Ward, John Montgomery. "Is the Base-Ball Player a Chattel?" *Lippincott's Magazine* 40 (August 1887), 310–19. Reprinted in Sullivan, *Early Innings*, 161–70 (as "John Ward Attacks the Reserve Clause (1887)").
Westcott, Rich. "The Early Years of Philadelphia Baseball." *National Pastime: From Swampoodle to South Philly—Baseball in Philadelphia and the Delaware Valley* (SABR 43 Convention Issue, 2013, electronic ed.): 136–40.
Willis, Stephen L. "A Critical Perspective of Baseball's Collusion Decisions." *Seton Hall Journal of Sports Law* 1 (1991): 109–48.
Wilson, Vic. "Fernandomania." *National Pastime: Endless Seasons—Baseball in Southern California* (SABR 41 Convention Issue, 2011): 94–96.
"Women Players in Organized Baseball." *Baseball Research Journal* 12 (1983): 157–61.
Yasser, Ray. "Warren Spahn's Legal Legacy: The Right to be Free from False Praise." *Seton Hall Journal of Sports and Entertainment Law* 18 (2008): 49–83.
Young, A.S. Doc. "Don Newcombe: Baseball Great Wins Fight Against Alcoholism." *Ebony*, April 1976, 54–62.

Newspaper Articles

"Acquitted of Killing Husband." *Washington Post*, April 2, 1906, 2.
"Advent of Sunday Baseball Draws 60,000 Persons to Polo Grounds and Ebbets Field." *New York Times*, May 5, 1919, 14.
"Advertising News and Notes." *New York Times*, March 1, 1947, 26.
"Amanda Cobb Now Facing Jury." *Atlanta Constitution*, March 31, 1906.
"American League Ousts 2 Umpires." *New York Times*, September 17, 1968, 54.
"American League Strife is Ended." *New York Times*, February 11, 1920, 18.
Anderson, Dave. "Mysterious Moe is De-Classified." *New York Times*, January 28, 1975, 21.
Andy, Handy. "Enjoins Johnson and K.C. Federals." *Chicago Tribune*, Apr. 24, 1914, 15.
"Another Wrong Turn for Troubled Ex-Tiger Denny McLain." *Detroit Free Press*, September 24, 2011.
Arangure, Jorge. "Palmeiro Suspended For Steroid Violation." *Washington Post*, August 2, 2005, A1.
"Ask Huge Damages of Ball Magnates." *New York Times*, March 30, 1916, 10.
"Ask Taft to Act as Baseball Head." *New York Times*, November 24, 1918, 1.
"Ask Veto of La. Bill Banning Mixed Sports." *Chicago Defender*, July 16, 1956, 21.
"'Babe' Ruth Is Sued by Girl for $50,000." *New York Times*, March 14, 1923, 4.
"Babe Ruth Loses Suit to Enjoin 'Outlaw' Film." *Chicago Daily Tribune*, September 16, 1920, 19.

"Babe Ruth's Hits Are News: Home-Run King Denied Injunction Against His Portrayal in Films." *New York Times*, September 16, 1920, 4.
"The Ball Players Meet." *New York Times*, December 17, 1889, 3. Reprinted in Sullivan, *Early Innings*, 193.
"Ball Players Seek to Secure Reforms." *New York Times*, October 12, 1922, 30.
Barker, Jeff. "Clemens Denies Drug Use: Pitcher, Former Trainer Trade Steroid Allegations at House Hearing." *Baltimore Sun*, February 14, 2008, A1.
"Baseball." *Washington Post*, December 22, 1990, F2.
"Baseball Hires Arbitrator Gill." *Washington Post*, October 2, 1970, C3.
"Baseball Leaders Won't Let White Sox Return to the Game." *New York Times*, August 4, 1921, 1.
"Baseball Owners Raise Minimum Salary $3,000." *Chicago Tribune*, February 22, 1968, E1.
"Baseball Policy Rapped." *New York Times*, February 3, 1943, 25.
"Baseball Strike Issues." *New York Times*, August 1, 1981, 18.
"Baseball War Ends." *Washington Post*, January 11, 1903, 8.
"Baseball War Declared." *New York Times*, November 5, 1889, 8.
"Baseball's Immunity Questioned." *Los Angeles Times*, January 4, 1977, D2.
"Baseball's Labor Deal." *Los Angeles Times*, August 31, 2002, D4.
"Beginning to Reap the Whirlwind." *Sporting Life*, February 5, 1890, 4.
Berkow, Ira. "73rd Home Run Ball Sells for $450,000." *New York Times*, June 26, 2003, D4.
_____. "Catfish Hunter, Who Pitched in 6 World Series for A's and Yankees, Dies at 53." *New York Times*, September 10, 1999, A1.
Berkowitz, Steve. "Arbitrator Leaves Baseball Owners 0–3 Against Union in Collusion Cases." *Washington Post*, July 19, 1990, C8.
"Big Deals in Base-Ball; End of the Long War Between Rival Organizations." *Chicago Daily Tribune*, January 17, 1891, 6.
"Black Sox Star's Varied Testimony Brings His Arrest." *Washington Post*, February 15, 1924, S1.
Bloom, Howard. "Who Is Rob Manfred? Man Who Should Be Next MLB Commissioner," *Sporting News*, August 14, 2014, http://www.sportingnews.com/mlb/story/2014-08-13/who-is-rob-manfred-baseball-commissioner-bud-selig-candidate-new.
"Bonds Steroids Case Is Dropped." *Los Angeles Times*, July 22, 2015, D6.
Borzi, Pat. "Settlement Sheds Little Light on N.C.A.A. Rule on Agents." *New York Times*, July 24, 2010, D1.
Bowie, Larry. "Lawsuit Over Use of Name 'Buzz' Ends with Settlement." *The Whistle* (Ga. Inst. of Technology), October 8, 2001, 1.
"Bowie Kuhn Orders Camps to Open." *Chicago Tribune*, March 18, 1976, C1.
Boyack, James Edmund. "Marcantonio Hits Major Leagues Ban." *Pittsburgh Courier*, Apr. 28, 1945, 1, 4.
Brady, Dave. "Curt Flood's Fight Was Not in Vain." *Washington Post*, February 28, 1973, D1.
Brandt, William E. "Babe Ruth Accepts $160,000 for 2 Years." *New York Times*, March 9, 1930, 161.
"Branch Rickey to Bow Out Nov. 1." *Chicago Tribune*, October 20, 1955, F3.
"Breadon Accepts Edict." *New York Times*, March 27, 1938, 63.
"Brewers' Selig Gets Good News." *Sporting News*, August 13, 1984, 19.
Brown, Tim. "Baseball Adds Muscle to Steroid Punishment." *Los Angeles Times*, November 16, 2005, A1.
Burnes, Brian. "Jury Clears Royals Once Again in Sluggerrr Hot Dog Toss That Ended Badly," *Kansas City Star*, June 17, 2015, http://www.kansascity.com/news/local/article24791023.html.
Burns, Edward. "Landis Awards Pitcher Feller to Indians." *Chicago Tribune*, December 11, 1936, 33.
"Byron Reelected By 6,000 Votes Over 'Big Train.'" *Washington Post*, November 6, 1940, 1.
Callaghan, Jim. "Baseball Rebel: Ex-Giant Took On Owners in '40s." *New York Daily News*, September 18, 1994.
"Campy and O'Malley Say No to Surgeon for $9,600 for Operation on Roy." *Sporting News*, June 8, 1955, 9.

"Campy's Doc Wins $5,000 Fee." *Sporting News*, February 22, 1956, 28.
Carlsen, William. "Giants Sale to New Owners Final." *San Francisco Chronicle*, January 15, 1993, A22.
Carmody, Deirdre. "Female Reporter Sues Over Locker-Room Ban." *New York Times*, December 30, 1977, A17.
"Casey at the Bat: A Ballad of the Republic, Sung in the Year 1888." *Examiner* (San Francisco), June 3, 1888, 4.
"Casey, Ex-Dodger, Is Atlanta Suicide." *New York Times*, July 4, 1951, 18.
"Casey Held to be Father." *New York Times*, December 30, 1950, 28.
"Catholics Quit Dodgers Knothole Club Over In Protest Over the Conduct of Durocher." *New York Times*, March 1, 1947, 17.
Chadwin, Dean. "Writer Cries Balk, Sues to Publish the Secret Story of Fay Vincent." *Observer*, October 13, 1997.
Chass, Murray. "Baseball Exhibition Strike In Effect Amidst Confusion." *New York Times*, April 3, 1980, A37.
_____. "Baseball Peace Arrives With 3-Year Accord." *New York Times*, February 26, 1973, 39.
_____. "Baseball Players Go Out on Strike After Talks With the Owners Fail." *New York Times*, June 12, 1981, A1.
_____. "Baseball Strike Off as Players, Owners Extend Deadline." *New York Times*, May 29, 1981, A17.
_____. "Board Says Rose Is Ineligible for Hall of Fame." *New York Times*, February 5, 1991, B9.
_____. "Carew, Perry and Jenkins Are Voted Into Hall of Fame." *New York Times*, January 9, 1991, B7.
_____. "Collusion Checks Are Signal of End Of Owners Error." *New York Times*, May 25, 2004, D4.
_____. "Free Agency Key to Future Peace." *New York Times*, October 15, 1987, B17.
_____. "Grievance Is Filed Over Parrish Talks." *New York Times*, February 21, 1987, 50.
_____. "Kuhn Steps Aside to Put an End to Acrimony." *New York Times*, August 4, 1983, A1.
_____. "The Labor Negotiations: Ball's in Whose Court?" *New York Times*, July 30, 1994, 31.
_____. "Lockout's On, But Vincent Has Suggestions." *New York Times*, February 14, 1990, B9.
_____. "Mediation Is Set, But Not One Batter Comes to the Plate." *New York Times*, August 13, 1994, 1.
_____. "No Runs, No Hits, No Errors: Baseball Goes on Strike." *New York Times*, August 12, 1994, A1.
_____. "Owners, in an 18–9 Vote, Ask Vincent to Resign." *New York Times*, September 4, 1992, B7.
_____. "Pioneer Black Players To Be Granted Pensions." *New York Times*, January 20, 1997, C9.
_____. "Player Union Sets May 29 Deadline." *New York Times*, February 26, 1981, D1.
_____. "Players Said to Hit Collusion Jackpot." *New York Times*, November 4, 1990, S1.
_____. "Ruling Backs Players on Collusion Charges Against Teams in '85." *New York Times*, September 22, 1987, A1.
_____. "Ryan Going to Astros for $4 Million." *New York Times*, November 16, 1979, A25.
_____. "Ryan Pact Reflects Splurge in Baseball." *New York Times*, November 20, 1979, B16.
_____. "Salary Arbitration Is Major Obstacle." *New York Times*, August 5, 1985, C3.
_____. "Strike Is Authorized By Baseball Players." *New York Times*, March 5, 1980, B5.
_____. "Strike Over, Baseball Resumes August 9." *New York Times*, August 1, 1981, 1.
_____. "Training Slated to Start Today: Kuhn Orders Camps to Open." *New York Times*, March 18, 1976, 64.
_____. "Two Yankees Disclose Family Exchange." *New York Times*, March 6, 1973, 51.
_____. "Vincent, Bowing to Owners' Will, Resigns as Baseball Commissioner." *New York Times*, September 8, 1992, A1.
"Clears Ball Club in Stadium Deaths." *New York Times*, May 21, 1929, 30.
"Cleveland Chatter." *Sporting Life*, July 2, 1898, 8.
"Cleveland v. Pittsburg at Cleveland, June 19." *Sporting Life*, June 25, 1898, 3.

"Club Owners Deaf to Players' Body: National Abrogates Past with Fraternity and Bars All Future Relations." *New York Times*, February 14, 1917, 6.
"Cobb Case Concluded." *Sporting Life*, June 1, 1912, 1.
"Colorado Silver Bullets Live Out Their Baseball Dreams." *Santa Cruz Sentinel*, May 16, 1994, 13.
"Comment by Cronin." *New York Times*, September 18, 1968, 37.
Condon, David. "Suspend Denny McLain; Detroit Pitcher Ban Is Indefinite." *Chicago Tribune*, February 20, 1970, 1.
"Court Overturns McLain Conviction." *New York Times*, August 8, 1987, 1:49.
Cover, Robert. "Your Law-Baseball Quiz." *N.Y. Times*, April 5, 1979, A23.
"Crooks Scared Out of Baseball, Says M'Donald." *Chicago Daily Tribune*, August 4, 1921, 21.
Crowther, Bosley. "'The Winning Team,' Story About Grover Cleveland Alexander, Arrives at the Mayfair." *New York Times*, June 21, 1952, 12.
Curry, Jack, and Jere Longman. "Results of Steroid Testing Spur Baseball to Set Tougher Rules." *New York Times*, November 14, 2003, A1.
Daley, Arthur. "Opening Day at Ebbets Field." *New York Times*, Apr. 16, 1947, 32.
Daniel, Dan. "Frick Denies Furillo Claim of Black List." *Sporting News*, January 17, 1962, 20.
_____. "Majors Flash Green Light to Third League." *Sporting News*, August 26, 1959, 2.
"Damage Suit Nets $20,000 for Roseboro." *Los Angeles Times*, October 20, 1967, B2.
"Dan Bankhead, 54, Ex-Dodger, Is Dead." *New York Times*, May 7, 1976, 95.
"Daughters of Babe Ruth Lose in Appeals Court Ruling." *Toledo Blade*, January 30, 1990, 21.
"Democrats in Landslide." *Washington Post*, July 27, 1979, E2.
"Denny McLain Gets 23-Year Prison Sentence." *Los Angeles Times*, Apr. 26, 1985, 3:1.
"Dodger Baseball to Be Broadcast." *New York Times*, December 7, 1938, 29.
"Dodgers' President Accused of Slander." *New York Times*, July 6, 1955, 18.
Doyle, Jim. "Jim Thorpe's Body Will Remain in Pennsylvania." *Pennsylvania Record*, October 23, 2014, http://pennrecord.com/news/14958-jim-thorpes-body-will-remain-in-pennsylvania.
Dozer, Richard. "Cubs Sign Negro Coach." *Chicago Tribune*, May 30, 1962, C1.
_____. "Players OK New Pact." *Chicago Tribune*, July 13, 1976, C1.
Drebinger, John. "Baseball Clubs Reject Pay Raise." *New York Times*, February 3, 1957, 159.
_____. "Baseball Pays Tribute to Landis By Picking Him for Hall of Fame." *New York Times*, December 11, 1944, 18.
_____. "Big League Status Is Denied to Coast." *New York Times*, December 12, 1945, 37.
_____. "DiMaggio Reported All-Time Top-Salaried Player With $90,000 Contract." *New York Times*, February 8, 1949, 33.
Drooz, Alan. "For Better or Worse: Artificial Turf Was Introduced to Baseball 25 Years Ago and Has Taken Root in the National Pastime." *Los Angeles Times*, April 18, 1991, 6.
Durso, Joseph. "Baseball Clubs Begin Training 18 Days Late." *New York Times*, March 19, 1976, 1.
_____. "Delay Called in Spring Training." *New York Times*, February 9, 1973, 17.
_____. "Free-Agent Stalemate is Hinted." *New York Times*, January 4, 1981, S3.
_____. "Japanese Hurler Appears in Relief: Murakami is First from Nation to Play in Majors." *New York Times*, September 2, 1954, 42.
_____. "Kuhn Is Voted Out as Baseball Commissioner." *New York Times*, November 2, 1982, A1.
Eder, Steve. "For Rodriguez, Suspended Animation: 12 Other Players Agree Not to Fight M.L.B. Punishment." *New York Times*, August 6, 2013, B8.
Eder, Steve, and Michael S. Schmidt. "Antidoping Suit Cites Six Linked to Florida Clinic." *New York Times*, March 23, 2013, D2.
Edes, Gordon. "Battle for Contreras Fuels Rivalry." *Boston Globe*, December 28, 2002, F1.
_____. "Cummings Loses Case." *Boston Globe*, February 10, 1999, C5.
Effrat, Louis. "Chandler Bars Durocher for 1947 Baseball Season." *New York Times*, April 10, 1947, 1.
_____. "Royals' Star Signs with Brooks Today." *New York Times*, April 11, 1947, 20.
"Eight Fired by Comiskey; Wrecks Team." *Chicago Daily Tribune*, September 29, 1920, 1.

Elfrink, Tim. "A Miami Clinic Supplies Drugs to Sports' Biggest Names." *Miami New Times*, January 31, 2013.
"Enjoyed the Sport—President Harrison Flees from Politics to Baseball." *Washington Post*, June 7, 1892, 1.
"Federal Judge Rules Against Flood on Reserve Clause." *Washington Post*, August 13, 1970, H1.
"Fehr Elected by Players." *New York Times*, December 9, 1983, B5.
Felker, Carl T. "Coast Writers Split on Big League Rating; Most View Step-Up as Premature." *Sporting News*, December 13, 1945, 2.
"Fernando Feels Like a Million." *Chicago Tribune*, February 20, 1983, C2.
"Finally a Hankering to Honor Doby: Aaron Says Thanks to Barrier-Breaker on 50th Anniversary of His AL Debut." *Newark Star Ledger*, July 6, 1997, sec. 5, 8.
Finch, Frank. "51,574 See Dodgers Drop Double Bill." *Los Angeles Times*, April 30, 1962, B1.
_____. "Koufax, Drysdale Eye $1 Million Pact; Dodger Aces Want 3-Year Package Deal." *Los Angeles Times*, February 23, 1966.
Fitzgerald, J.V. "Baseball Players Must Work or Fight, Baker Rules, Dooming National Sport." *Washington Post*, July 20, 1918, 8.
"Flawless At First." *New York Times*, March 19, 1989, S1.
Fleming, Deirdre." Coach Attempting to Stay Focused." *Bangor (Me.) Daily News*, April 25, 1996, C7.
"Formation of the American Association." *Cincinnati Enquirer*, Nov. 3, 1881. Reprinted in Sullivan, *Early Innings*, 119–21.
"The Formation of the National Association of Professional Base Ball Players." *New York Clipper*, March 25, 1871. Reprinted in Sullivan, *Early Innings*, 83–88.
Fredrix, Emily. "Bob Uecker Files Restraining Order." *Washington Post*, June 4, 2006.
Fullerton, Hugh S. "Federal League Organizes Today, Magnates of Six Cities Hold First Meeting in Hoosier Capital." *Chicago Daily Tribune*, March 8, 1913, 10.
"A Gigantic Revolt; The Presidency." *Sporting Life*, February 21, 1891, 2–3.
"Girl Ballplayer Gets to First Base." *New York Times*, June 20, 1973, 46.
"Girl to Accuse Babe Ruth Today." *New York Times*, March 15, 1923, 40.
"Girl Who Shot Cubs' Player Goes Free." *Chicago Tribune*, July 16, 1932, 3.
Godbey, Christina V. "Deputy D.A. Makes Her Case for Reviving Pro Baseball League." *Los Angeles Times*, November 21, 1993, 2.
Goldsborough, Bob. "Baseball Stalker Inspired 'The Natural.'" *Chicago Tribune*, March 15, 2013, 1:1.
_____. "Really Long Road Trip." *Chicago Tribune*, December 14, 2014, 14.
Goldstein, Richard. "Al Gionfriddo, 81; Remembered for '47 Catch." *New York Times*, March 16, 2003, N31.
_____. "Buck O'Neil, Negro Leagues Pioneer, Is Dead at 94." *New York Times*, October 7, 2006, C10.
_____. "Fred Saigh, Who Helped Cardinals Stay Put, Dies at 94." *New York Times*, January 2, 2000, A35.
_____. "John Roseboro, a Dodgers Star, Dies at 69." *New York Times*, August 20, 2002, C16.
_____. "Michael Weiner, 51, Dies; Headed Baseball Union." *New York Times*, November 22, 2013, B8.
_____. "Sam Jethroe is Dead at 83; Was Oldest Rookie of the Year." *New York Times*, June 19, 2001, A21.
Goldstein, Sasha. "Bryan Stow Verdict: Jury Finds Los Angeles Dodgers Negligent, Awards $18 Million." *New York Daily News*, July 9, 2014.
Goodwin, Michael. "Baseball Orders Suspension of 11 Drug Users." *New York Times*, March 1, 1986, 1.
Greenhouse, Linda. "Justices Return to Commercial Speech Quandary." *New York Times*, April 18, 2001, A18.
"Grievance Registered by Players." *Washington Post*, February 21, 1987, C5.
"Guilty Pleas in Campaign Gift Case." *San Francisco Chronicle*, August 24, 1974.
"Gumbert Decision Upheld Reserve Clause in 1898." *Sporting News*, May 16, 1951, 7.

Hafner, Dan. "Furillo Fires Blacklist Charge." *Los Angeles Herald Examiner*, March 29, 1961.
Haldeman, John. "Cussed Crookedness, A Complete Exposé of How Four Ball Men Picked Up Stray Pennies." *Louisville Courier-Journal*, November 3, 1877. Reprinted in Sullivan, *Early Innings*, 102–10.
"Hank Greenberg, First $100,000 Player, Dies." *Los Angeles Times*, September 5, 1986, C1.
"Hap Felsch Sues Sox for Back Pay." *Chicago Tribune*, April 27, 1922, 17.
Harms, Rob. "U.S. Ends Its Long Pursuit of Bonds." *New York Times*, July 22, 2015, B13.
Heisler, Mark. "Fernando Hits Jackpot for Million." *Los Angeles Times*, February 20, 1983, F1.
Higbie, Andrea. "The Lady Is A Pitcher (and a Prosecutor)." *New York Times*, September 4, 1994, 30.
"'Hippodrome' Tactics in Base Ball; How to 'Heave a Game.'" *New York Clipper*, November 11, 1865. Reprinted in Sullivan, *Early Innings*, 49–53.
Holtzman, Jerome. "Arbitrator: Baseball Owners in Collusion." *Chicago Tribune*, September 22, 1987, C1.
———. "Big Strike Fund, Collusion Judgments Give Players Leverage Over Owners." *Chicago Tribune*, November 8, 1988, B5.
———. "Collusion II: Owners Found Guilty Again." *Chicago Tribune*, September 1, 1988, D1.
———. "Doby's Rightful Recognition." *Chicago Tribune*, March 4, 1998, 2.
"Home Games of Dodgers to Be Televised Next Year." *Sporting News*, November 13, 1946, 10.
Hopkins, Jared S. "Federal Judge Lets Wrigley Upgrades Continue: Rooftop Business Tried to Stop Video Board Installation." *Chicago Tribune*, April 3, 2015, 4.
Hopkins, Jared S., and Ameet Sachdev. "Rooftops' Lawsuit Against Cubs Dismissed; 'Chapter Closed' as U.S. Judge Sides with Ballclub over Nearby Businesses." *Chicago Tribune*, October 1, 2015, 12.
"House Asks More Study on Baseball." *New York Times*, January 4, 1977, L35.
"Hugh Casey, of Relief Pitching Fame, Kills Self With Shotgun." *Reading* (Pa.) *Eagle*, July 3, 1951, 12.
"Hugh Jennings Dies After Long Illness." *New York Times*, February 1, 1929, 1.
"Hundley Beat Tax Problem, And Kept Money In Family." *Sarasota Herald-Tribune*, July 4, 1967, 22.
Huston, Luther A. "Stabilization Board's New Ruling Yields Rises to Musial, Robinson." *New York Times*, January 17, 1952, 33.
"Importance of Gumbert Case." *Chicago Daily Tribune,* August 18, 1898, 4.
"In Hostile Array; The Brotherhood Takes the Great Plunge." *Sporting Life*, November 13, 1889, 1.
"In Surprise Here; Happy Chandler Lifts Ban on All 'Jumpers.'" *Washington Post*, June 6, 1949, 1.
Itzkoff, Dave. "Famous Recordings to Join National Registry." *New York Times*, April 6, 2011, C2.
"Jack Zeller Takes Full Blame for Detroit's Minor Loop Woe." *Los Angeles Times*, January 16, 1940, A9.
"Jackson Loses in High Court to White Sox." *Chicago Tribune*, October 21, 1925, 29.
Johnson, Kirk. "Heckling Umpires: It's Legal." *New York Times*, July 24, 1987, B1.
Jones, Ashby. "Tuck in the Bullpen." *American Lawyer*, January 2002, 18.
"Jury Finds Dodgers Negligent in Bryan Stow Case." *USA Today*, July 9, 2014.
"Jury Frees Baseball Men; All Black Sox Acquitted on Single Ballot." *Chicago Daily Tribune*, August 3, 1921, 1.
Justice, Richard. "Baseball Dispute Is Settled, Season to Open on April 9." *Washington Post*, March 19, 1990, A1.
———. "Collusion Award Is $10.5 Million; Baseball Owners Are Wincing." *Washington Post*, September 1, 1989, H1.
"Keep Going! Landis Tells Wartime Baseball; Game Will Ask No U.S. Favors to Stay Alive." *Chicago Tribune*, February 8, 1943, 19.
"Kicked Out; Were the Cincinnati Club by the League." *Cincinnati Daily Enquirer*, October 7, 1880, 6.
King, Susan. "National Film Registry Selects 25 Films for Preservation." *Los Angeles Times*, December 19, 2012, D12.

Knapp, Gwen. "40 Years Later, the Fight Resonates in a Positive Way." *San Francisco Chronicle*, August 21, 2005, C1.
Koppett, Leonard. "A's Hunter Ruled Free Agent." *New York Times*, December 16, 1974, 51.
———. "A's Plan Suit Today Over Hunter." *New York Times*, December 18, 1974, 59.
———. "Backing of Hunter Arbitration Decision Called Prelude to Changing Pro Sports Setup." *New York Times*, January 5, 1975, S4.
———. "Bowie Kuhn, Wall St. Lawyer, Named Commissioner Pro Tem of Baseball." *New York Times*, February 5, 1969, 29.
———. "Judge Says Trial Must Solve Issue." *New York Times*, March 5, 1970.
———. "Shea Stadium Opens with Big Traffic Jam." *New York Times*, April 18, 1964, 1.
———. "6-Year-Old Union Keeps Players' Benefits in Step." *New York Times*, February 26, 1973, 39.
"Landis Declares Ninety-One Tigers Free Agents." *Detroit News*, January 16, 1940. Reprinted in Sullivan, *Middle Innings*, 178–79.
"Landis Lays Down Law for Farms, Working Agreements; Detroit Loses Title to 91 Players, Must Pay 15 Others." *Sporting News*, January 18, 1940, 1.
"Lanier and Martin of Cards Drop Suit Against Baseball." *New York Times*, August 28, 1949, S1.
Lardner, R.W. "Ward's Election Will Start War." *Chicago Tribune*, November 28, 1909, C1.
"Lawsuit Dismissed." *New York Times*, October 6, 1996, 13.
Leavy, Jane. "Strike Is Off, Study Set on Compensation," *Washington Post*, May 24, 1980, C1.
Lee, Henry K. "Rangers and A's Fan Settle Chair Lawsuit." *San Francisco Chronicle*, January 13, 2007.
"Letter Solves the Shooting of Billy Jurges." *Chicago Tribune*, July 7, 1932, 1.
Loftus, Joseph A. "Wage Board Sets Baseball Ceilings; Ruling Halts Musial's $35,000 Rise." *New York Times*, April 11, 1951, 33.
"Lou Gehrig Files Million-Dollar Suit." *Washington Post*, September 10, 1940, 17.
"Louisiana Draws Sport Color Line." *New York Times*, July 17, 1956, 13.
Mack. "Inclined to Cobb, New York Sentiment Was With Georgian in Row." *Sporting News*, May 23, 1912, 1.
Macur, Juliet. "Guilty Plea Widens Baseball's Steroids Scandal." *New York Times*, April 28, 2007, A1.
"Major Leagues Sued: Portland Club Asks $1,800,000 in Antitrust Action." *New York Times*, July 31, 1959, 15.
"Major Loops Hike Pay Minimum to $7000." *Los Angeles Times*, October 1, 1957, C1.
"Major Owners Refuse Hike in Minimum Pay." *Chicago Tribune*, February 3, 1957, A2.
"Majors Meet All Player Demands And Set Up New Executive Council." *New York Times*, August 29, 1946, 31.
Maniloff, Randy J. "I Paid for That Rooftop Seat." *Wall Street Journal*, Apr. 29, 2013, A17.
Marantz, Steve. "The Great Lakes Gang." *Sporting News*, September 19, 1994, 32.
Marcus, Amy Dockser, and Wade Lambert. "Court Limits Superfund Pollution Liability." *Wall Street Journal*, January 30, 1990, B11.
Markus, Robert. "Both Sides Lost—Reinsdorf." *Chicago Tribune*, August 1, 1981, N1.
———. "Split-Season Plan Goes Against Sox." *Chicago Tribune*, August 7, 1981, C1.
Martin, Douglas. "Historic Day at Bar: Dodger Stays in Brooklyn." *New York Times*, April 9, 1993, B1.
Martinez, Michael. "Bill White a Unanimous Choice to Head National League." *New York Times*, February 4, 1989, 47.
———. "Mays and Mantle Reinstated." *New York Times*, March 19, 1985, B7.
McAlpin, Harry S. "Bill Asks Probe of Ball Jim Crow." *Atlanta Daily World*, Apr. 27, 1945, 1.
McGowen, Roscoe. "Dodgers Buy Los Angeles Club, Stirring Talk of Shift to Coast." *New York Times*, February 22, 1957, 1.
"McLain Found Guilty." *New York Daily News*, December 14, 1996.
"McLain Gets Probation Instead of New Prison Term." *Philadelphia Inquirer*, December 16, 1988, C9.
"Mexican Case Won By Yanks Says Judge." *Christian Science Monitor*, May 21, 1946, 14.

Murphy, Caryle, and Peter Pae. "Judge Rejects Bias Claim of Girl Cut from Baseball Team." *Washington Post*, March 24, 1988, D1.
"Musial Gets Pay Delayed by W.S.B." *New York Times*, February 13, 1952, 39.
"New Cubs Secretary." *Chicago Daily Tribune*, December 14, 1926, 23.
"The New Agreement; Full Text of the New Supreme Law of Base Ball." *Sporting Life*, January 24, 1891, 5.
"New Orleans Quits Southern Association." *Washington Post*, March 16, 1960, D2.
"Newcombe Sues Over Beer Ad." *New York Times*, March 11, 1994, B12.
Newhan, Ross. "Arbitrator Rules Baseball Owners Guilty of Collusion." *Los Angeles Times*, September 22, 1987, N1.
———. "Around the Horn." *Los Angeles Times*, May 30, 2004, D4.
———. "Merely a Charge, or Act of Sin?" *Los Angeles Times*, August 8, 1993, C8.
———. "Owners Take a Third Strike on Collusion." *Los Angeles Times*, July 19, 1990, 39.
———. "Ueberroth Suspends Seven Players for Use of Drugs." *Los Angeles Times*, March 1, 1986.
"News in Highest Court: Bathtub Case Waits While Jurists Read Bulletins from Boston." *New York Times*, October 17, 1912, 1.
Nightengale, Bob. "Here's to You, Jackie: No. 42 Retired." *Los Angeles Times*, April 16, 1997, C6.
Nightingale, Dave. "Miller Says Strike 'Is On' As Baseball Talks Break Off." *Chicago Tribune*, June 12, 1981, C1.
———. "Sox Fire Bob Lemon, Name Doby." *Chicago Tribune*, July 1, 1978, 1.
"The NL Adopts a Player Reservation System." *Buffalo Commercial Advertiser*, September 30 and October 3, 1879. Reprinted in Sullivan, *Early Innings*, 113–15.
"A Novel Game in Philadelphia—A Negro Club in the Field—The White Club Victorious." *New York Times*, September 5, 1869, 1.
"Obama Donates Sox Jacket He Wore in '09 to Hall of Fame." *Chicago Tribune*, May 23, 2014, 9.
"Obama Visits Baseball Hall of Fame in Cooperstown to Promote U.S. Tourism." *Washington Post*, May 23, 2014.
"O'Malley Suit Settled." *New York Times*, November 21, 1957.
"O'Malley, Westward Pioneer, Dies." *Sporting News*, August 25, 1979, 12.
Ortiz, Jose de Jesus. "Astros to Fight Denial of Bagwell Disability Claim." *Houston Chronicle*, March 28, 2006.
"Our National Sports." *Spirit of the Times*, January 31, 1857. Reprinted in Sullivan, *Early Innings*, 22–24.
Owens, John. "Female Cubs Exec Changed the Ballgame." *Chicago Tribune*, July 22, 2013, 1:6.
"Panel Opposes Pro Baseball's Exempt Status." *Los Angeles Times*, January 3, 1977, B2.
"Peace Seems to be Near for Organized Baseball; Agreement Is Drafted." *Atlanta Constitution*, December 18, 1915, 12.
Pearson, Rick. "'Foul Ball' Law Restricts Suits." *Chicago Tribune*, September 25, 1992.
Penner, Mike. "Sound and Vision: If Anything, This Juicy Story Sure Has Legs." *Los Angeles Times*, February 14, 2005, D4.
Pettey, Tom. "Ruth's Failure to Hit Homer Leads to Suit." *Chicago Tribune*, February 11, 1932, 23.
"Pickett Buys His Release." *Philadelphia Times*, June 5, 1890, 2.
"Pickett Enjoined: The Kansas City's Rights to His Services Recognized." *Sporting Life*, May 10, 1890, 5.
"Pickett's Case: A Full Statement From the Kansas City Club." *Sporting Life*, April 12, 1890, 10.
Pilcher, James. "MLB Commissioner Upholds Pete Rose's Ban From Baseball." *Cincinnati Enquirer*, December 14, 2015, http://www.cincinnati.com/story/sports/mlb/reds/2015/12/14/pete-rose-reinstatement-decision-main/26319063/.
"Pirates Name Joe L. Brown to Rickey's Post." *Chicago Tribune*, October 26, 1955, C3.
"Players Form Organization; Major Leaguers Seek Contract Revisions." *Chicago Tribune*, July 13, 1954, B1.

"Players' League; Still Awaiting the Final Settlement of Its Affairs." *Sporting Life*, November 29, 1890, 4.
"Players' League; The First Campaign of the New League Fairly Started." *Sporting Life*, April 26, 1890, 3.
"Players Organize and Retain Lewis." *New York Times*, July 13, 1954, 26.
Povich, Shirley. "This Morning." *Washington Post*, July 15, 1955, 31.
_____. "This Morning." *Washington Post*, April 12, 1966, C1.
Pringle, Paul. "The Unlikely Big Man in Baseball's Drug Scandal." *Los Angeles Times*, December 15, 2007, A1.
"Rangers Drop Appeals, Suspensions Reduced." *USA Today*, September 22, 2004.
"'Red' Pitcher Restrained." *New York Times*, Apr. 24, 1914, 11.
"Red Sox Trail in Hitting Carnival." *Boston Daily Globe*, July 14, 1919, 4.
Reich, Kenneth. "Baseball Strike Settled; Play to Resume Today." *Los Angeles Times*, August 8, 1985, A1.
Reid, Jason. "Dodgers Sign Kevin Brown for $105 Million." *Los Angeles Times*, December 13, 1998, 1.
_____. "Players Propose Steroid Testing." *Los Angeles Times*, August 8, 2002, D1.
_____. "Trainer Buhler Dies at 75." *Los Angeles Times*, May 19, 2003, D5.
Reif, Rita. "Honus Wagner Baseball Card Goes to Gretzky." *New York Times*, March 23, 1991, 16.
Renaud, Josh. "Learn About Baseball Players Who Have Won Medal of Freedom." *St. Louis Post-Dispatch*, March 30, 2011, http://www.stltoday.com/sports/baseball/professional/learn-about-baseball-players-who-have-won-medal-of-freedom/html_53efc5fc-330d-11e0-8777-0017a4a78c22.html.
"Report That He Used Steroids Denied by Athletics' Canseco." *St. Louis Post-Dispatch*, October 1, 1988, C3.
Rice, Grantland. "Lou Gehrig Denies His Disease Is Contagious; Says People Run From Him: Files Suit Against Paper for a Million Dollars." *Atlanta Constitution*, August 25, 1940, 3B.
Richter, Francis C. "Casual Comment." *Sporting News*, June 8, 1922, 4.
_____. "Majors Meet." *Sporting Life*, December 19, 1908, 4.
_____. "Settlement Procured; Peace Proclaimed." *Sporting Life*, January 17, 1903, 4. Reprinted in Sullivan, *Early Innings*, 262–65.
Robbins, Danny. "Peace Turns Into Cold War for New Umps." *Chicago Tribune*, August 12, 1979, C3.
"Roger Settles With Cub Boss for $10,000 Sum." *Chicago Tribune*, March 5, 1916, B1.
Rogers, Phil. "Players Propose Steroid Testing; Baseball Owners 'Quite Pleased.'" *Chicago Tribune*, August 8, 2002, 1:1.
Rogers, Thomas. "Lawyers to Make a Speedy Appeal." *New York Times*, August 13, 1970, 53.
"Roseboro Victor in Suit." *New York Times*, October 21, 1967, 23.
Rosenheck, Dan. "For Critics of Lee's Contract, Brown Deal Is Not Supporting Evidence." *New York Times*, January 3, 2011, D8.
"Rush This to Lincoln, Neb.; Democrats Win National Victory; After That the Deluge." *Chicago Daily Tribune*, July 17, 1909, 2.
"St. Louis Federals Win Marsans Case." *New York Times*, August 20, 1915, 8.
"Sale of Baseball Giants to Group in Toronto Is Halted Temporarily." *Wall Street Journal*, January 14, 1976, 11.
"Sam Wise Deserts Cincinnati for Boston." *Boston Daily Globe*, January 22, 1882, 8.
Sanborn, I.E. "Roger May Sue New Cub Boss For Damages." *Chicago Tribune*, January 27, 1916, 15.
Sandomir, Richard. "In Proposal, Vincent Memoir Airs Criticisms." *New York Times*, March 4, 1994, B9.
_____. "Honor for Shea at Shea: He Brought Mets Here." *New York Times*, April 8, 2008, D5.
"Says Signature is a Forgery." *Boston Daily Globe*, May 12, 1911.
Scannell, Nancy. "Panel Delays Antitrust Vote." *Washington Post*, January 4, 1977, C1.
Schmidt, Michael S. "Baseball Promotes Selig's Deputy." *New York Times*, August 15, 2014, B9.

_____. "Dear Pete: It's Still a No. Sincerely, Baseball." *New York Times*, December 15, 2015, B10.

Schreiber, Jay. "Defamation Lawsuit by Clemens's Ex-Trainer Is Settled." *New York Times*, March 19, 2015, B15.

Schwarz, Alan, and Michael S. Schmidt. "After 26 Years, Fehr Says He Will Retire as Union Chief." *New York Times*, June 23, 2009, B15.

"Seeks to Organize Baseball Players." *New York Times*, April 18, 1946, 32.

"$75,000 Lures Dodgers to Radio, Giants and Yankees Due to Follow." *Boston Globe*, December 7, 1938, 20.

Shaikin, Bill. "For Some, an Outdated Ad; for Others, the Mona Lisa." *Los Angeles Times*, July 19, 2000, 7.

_____. "O'Malley's Long Road to the Hall of Fame." *Los Angeles Times*, December 4, 2007, 1.

Sheehan, Joseph M. "Dodgers, Giants Win Right To Shift if They So Desire." *New York Times*, May 29, 1957, 1.

_____. "Long Blows Help Beat Brooks, 16–3." *New York Times*, August 27, 1947, 27.

Sheinin, Dave. "Baseball Has a Day of Reckoning in Congress; McGwire Remains Evasive During Steroid Testimony." *Washington Post*, March 18, 2005, A1.

"Signs Sunday Movie Bill: Sunday Baseball Measure Also Approved by Gov. Smith." *New York Times*, April 20, 1919, 10.

Smith, Claire. "Arbitrator Finds 3d Case of Baseball Collusion." *New York Times*, July 19, 1990, B9.

_____. "Larry Doby, Who Broke a Color Barrier, Dies at 79." *New York Times*, June 20, 2003, C15.

Smith, Red. "A Shot Heard Round Baseball." *New York Times*, February 20, 1981, B9.

"Solons Play Ball; Minority Shows That It Can Swat the Leather." *Washington Post*, July 17, 1909, 1.

"Something More than Mere Name to Organized Ball Now." *Sporting News*, January 20, 1921, 1.

"Spahn Agrees to Give Up Damage Suit." *Danville Register* (Va.), January 23, 1969, 2-D.

"Spahn Awarded $10,000 by Court." *New York Times*, May 29, 1964, 19.

"'A Startling Coup d'état': The National League is Formed." *New York Clipper*, February 12, 1876. Reprinted in Sullivan, *Early Innings*, 96–99.

"Steinbrenner Is Disputed," *New York Times*, September 1, 1982, B8.

"Suits by Risberg and Felsch Ruled Out in Wisconsin Court." *New York Times*, May 13, 1923, S3.

Sullivan, Paul. "Monumental Afternoon." *Chicago Tribune*, July 28, 2014, 3:4.

"Sunday Baseball Hearing: Justice Gaynor Says Complaint Is Weak, but Takes Case Under Advisement." *New York Times*, June 8, 1904, 7.

"A Surprising Decision; A Chicago Judge Makes a Unique Ruling." *Sporting Life*, June 13, 1914, 3.

"Sweeping Peace Pact Is Signed." *Chicago Tribune*, January 11, 1903, 9.

"Taft Pitches First Ball." Chicago Daily Tribune, April 15, 1910, 13.

"Talking a Walk: A Chronology of Strikes by Major Sports Leagues." *Los Angeles Times*, April 3, 1992, C2.

"Television for Dodger Games." *New York Times*, November 8, 1946, 33.

Thomas, Katie. "Former Pitcher Receives Settlement From the N.C.A.A." *New York Times*, October 9, 2009, B12.

Thomas, Pete. "Newswire." *Los Angeles Times*, December 15, 2006, D6.

"Tinker's Feds on Jump." *New York Tribune*, Apr. 24, 1914, 9.

"Trautman Bars Woman Players, Censures 'Travesty' on Baseball." *New York Times*, June 24, 1952, 38.

Travers, Johnny. "Gal Shortstop's Bid Given Short 'No' by O.B. Officials." *Sporting News*, July 2, 1952, 5.

Tuite, James. "Mays Leaving Baseball." *New York Times*, October 30, 1979, B15.

"Two Killed, 62 Hurt in Yankee Stadium as Rain Stampedes Baseball Crowd; Victims Are Crushed at Bleacher Exit." *New York Times*, May 20, 1929, 1.

"Two More Players Sue the White Sox." *New York Times*, May 13, 1922, 11.

"Two Sox Confess; Eight Indicted; Inquiry Goes On." *Chicago Daily Tribune*, September 29, 1920, 1.
"Umpires Return to Work Today." *Chicago Tribune*, May 19, 1979, G1.
"Valenzuela Granted $1 Million." *New York Times*, February 20, 1983, S9.
Vaughan, Irving. "Cub Moguls Sing Praises in Ears of Mr. McCarthy." *Chicago Daily Tribune*, December 4, 1926, 21.
"Verdict Is Set Aside in Stadium Suits." *New York Times*, February 17, 1932, 17.
"Vern Law is Pitcher of the Year." *New York Times*, November 4, 1940, 43.
"Wage Ruling Affects Few, Baseball View." *Chicago Daily Tribune*, April 11, 1951, F1.
"Wagner a Wonder; One Player in Game Who Is Not Money Mad." *Sporting News*, October 24, 1912, 2.
"Ward Given a $1000 Verdict." *Boston Daily Globe*, May 13, 1911, 6.
"Ward Wins His Fight." *New York Times*, January 29, 1890, 2. Reprinted in Sullivan, *Early Innings*, 201–04.
Weber, Bruce. "Ruth Ann Steinhagen at 83; Shot A Ballplayer." *New York Times*, March 23, 2013, A22.
Wharton, David. "Baseball to Impose Penalties for Steroid Use; Stricter Rule Is Triggered after the Drugs Are Found in More than 5% of Tests on Major Leaguers." *Los Angeles Times*, November 14, 2003, A1.
"White Sox Score Over Boston, 2–1," *New York Times*, July 22, 1959, 31.
"The White Stockings Gathering For the Fray: What Will be Done With Force—The Spring Programme," *Chicago Tribune*, March 14, 1875. Reprinted in Sullivan, *Early Innings*, 90–92.
Wilbur, Del Quentin, and Ann E. Marimow. "Clemens Acquitted of All Six Charges." *Washington Post*, June 19, 2012, A1.
Willis, John M. "Salt Lake Stingers Stung for $600,000." *Rome News-Tribune*, October 3, 2001, 5A.
Wilson, Duff, and Michael S. Schmidt. "Report Ties Star Players to Baseball's 'Steroids Era.'" *New York Times*, December 14, 2007, A1.
"Withdraws Her Case Against 'Babe' Ruth." *Boston Daily Globe*, April 27, 1923, 1.
"Woman Hit by Chair Likely Will Sue Rangers for Injuries." *Washington Post*, September 16, 2004, D2.
Woodruff, Harvey T. "Bar Dr. Creamer from All Ball Parks." *Chicago Tribune*, April 24, 1909, 8.
"Yank Star Sought For Mexican Loop." *New York Times*, May 4, 1946, 18.
"Yankees Get Mays in Red Sox Deal." *Boston Daily Globe*, July 31, 1919, 1.

Websites and Blogs

"855 Baseball Centennial Stamps—First Day Covers," 1939Baseballwww, accessed March 23, 2016, http://www.1939baseball.com/first_day_of_issue.html.
"1892 Washington Senators," Baseball-Reference.com, accessed July 29, 2013, http://www.baseball-reference.com.
"1915 Federal League Case Files," Society for American Baseball Research, accessed October 19, 2014, http://sabr.org/research/1915-Federal-League-case-files.
"Ad Gumbert," Baseball-Reference.com, accessed July 25, 2013, http://www.baseball-reference.com.
Ahrens, Mark. "Christy Walsh—Baseball's First Agent," *Books on Baseball* (blog), August 4, 2010, http://www.booksonbaseball.com [search "Walsh"].
"Alabama Pitts," Baseball-Reference.com, accessed June 2, 2015, http://www.baseball-reference.com.
"An Annual Outing: The Congressional Baseball Game," U.S. House of Representatives, accessed March 29, 2016, http://history.house.gov [search "baseball"].
Anderson, David W. "Jim Johnstone," SABR Baseball Biography Project, accessed March 23, 2016, http://sabr.org/bioproj/person/e51cb9e8.
Aron, Eric. "Art Shamsky," SABR Baseball Biography Project, accessed March 23, 2016, http://sabr.org/bioproj/person/68fc8356.

Associated Press. "Performance-Enhancing Drugs in Baseball: A Timeline," Cleveland.com, May 9, 2009, http://www.cleveland.com/tribe/index.ssf/2009/05/performanceenhancing_drugs_in.html.
Associated Press. "Pittsfield Uncovers Earliest Written Reference to Game," ESPN.com, May 11, 2004, espn.go.com [search "pittsfield"].
Baldassaro, Lawrence. "Tony La Russa," SABR Baseball Biography Project, April 17, 2014, http://sabr.org/bioproj/person/6dbc8b54.
"Baseball, the Color Line, and Jackie Robinson," American Memory, Library of Congress, accessed March 29, 2016, https://www.loc.gov/collections/jackie-robinson-baseball [link to articles and essays].
Bedingfield, Gary. "Moe Berg," *Baseball in Wartime*, last updated January 22, 2007, http://www.baseballinwartime.com [link to player biographies].
Bellis, Mary. "History of Astroturf," About.com, accessed September 20, 2014, http://inventors.about.com/od/astartinventions/a/astroturf.htm.
Bevis, Charlie. "Harry Taylor," SABR Baseball Biography Project, December 16, 2011, http://sabr.org/bioproj/person/f5f468a1.
Botelho, Greg, and Quand Thomas, "MLB Drops Lawsuit Against Biogenesis and its Founder, Anthony Bosch," CNN, February 19, 2014, http://www.cnn.com/2014/02/18/justice/mlb-lawsuit-biogenesis-bosch/.
"A Brief History of Tabletop Baseball," *Baseball Games*, last modified April 2011, http://baseballgames.dreamhosters.com/BbHistory.htm.
Burley, Craig. "Free Benny Kauff (Part Two)," *The Hardball Times* (blog), April 19, 2004, http://www.hardballtimes.com [search "Kauff"].
Campbell-Dollaghan, Kelsey. "The Forgotten History of Baseball's Most Iconic Objects," *Gizmodo* (blog), July 16, 2013, http://gizmodo.com/the-forgotten-history-of-baseballs-most-iconic-objects-792812600.
"Category: Politicians," BR Bullpen, last modified September 27, 2013, http://www.baseball-reference.com/bullpen/Category:Politicians.
Ceresi, Frank. "Tobacco Baseball Cards and Wagner's Own Wagner Card," *Baseball Almanac*, accessed December 2, 2015, http://www.baseball-almanac.com/treasure/autont005.shtml.
"Complete National Recording Registry Listing," Library of Congress, accessed June 26, 2015, http://www.loc.gov/programs/national-recording-preservation-board/recording-registry/complete-national-recording-registry-listing/.
Curtis, Bryan. "The Steroid Hunt," *Grantland*, January 8, 2014, http://grantland.com [search "steroid"].
Davis, Ryan. "Yankees Triumph In 'Evil Empire' Trademark Battle," Law360, February 21, 2013, http://www.law360.com/articles/417427/yankees-triumph-in-evil-empire-trademark-battle.
"Defamation Suit vs. Clemens Settled," ESPN.com, March 18, 2015, http://espn.go.com [search "clemens settlement"].
"Donald M. Fehr, Executive Director," Major League Baseball Players Association, accessed August 13, 2012, http://mlbplayers.mlb.com/pa/bios/fehr.jsp.
Doster, Adam. "The Myth of Jackie Mitchell, the Girl Who Struck Out Ruth and Gehrig," *The Daily Beast*, May 18, 2013, http://www.thedailybeast.com [search "jackie mitchell"].
"Dozing Baseball Fan's $10 Million ESPN Lawsuit Is Thrown Out," Reuters, October 2, 2015, http://www.reuters.com [search "dozing fan"].
Faber, Charles F. "Aaron Burt Champion," SABR Baseball Biography Project, accessed March 23, 2016, http://sabr.org/node/24735.
Fallon, Michael. "Steve Yeager," SABR Baseball Biography Project, accessed, March 23, 2016, http://sabr.org/bioproj/person/69e2594b.
"Forbes Field," ballparksofbaseball.com, accessed January 27, 2016, http://www.ballparksofbaseball.com/past/ForbesField.htm.
"Frank Grant," National Baseball Hall of Fame, accessed October 1, 2014, http://baseballhall.org/hof/grant-frank.
Frommer, Harvey. "First Professional Baseball Team: Flashback," Dr. Harvey Frommer on

Sports, accessed June 15, 2014, http://www.travel-watch.com/twhtml4/firstprobaseballteam.htm.
Geisler, Paul, Jr. "Billy Jurges," SABR Baseball Biography Project, accessed March 24, 2016, http://sabr.org/bioproj/person/aada6293.
Gilliland, Josh. "Bases Loaded: Baseball Patents and Player Contracts in the 19th Century," *The Legal Geeks* (blog), March 31, 2015, http://thelegalgeeks.com/blog/?p=8082.
Gonzalez, Gloria. "Astros, CIGNA Settle Bagwell Claim." *Business Insurance*, December 18, 2006, http://www.businessinsurance.com [search "Bagwell"].
Greenwald, Dave. "Alumnus Jackie Robinson Honored by Congress," UCLA Spotlight, February 1, 2005, http://spotlight.ucla.edu/alumni/jackie-robinson.
Haupert, Michael. "William Hulbert," SABR Baseball Biography Project, accessed March 23, 2016, http://sabr.org/bioproj/person/d1d420b3.
Hagen, Paul. "Obama Visits Hall, Touts Baseball's Historic Role," MLB.com, May 22, 2014.
"Hall of Fame Ballot History." Baseball-Reference.com, accessed March 4, 2016, http://www.baseball-reference.com/awards/hall-of-fame-ballot-history.shtml.
Hildebrandt, Chuck. "Here Is the Actual 1939 Contract That Ended the Baseball Broadcast Moratorium for Good," SABRMedia Blog, November 24, 2015, http://sabrmedia.org [search "1939 contract"].
"Huggins, Miller." National Baseball Hall of Fame and Museum, accessed July 30, 2013, http://baseballhall.org/hof/huggins-miller.
"Hughie Jennings." National Baseball Hall of Fame and Museum, accessed July 29, 2015, http://baseballhall.org/hof/jennings-hugh.
Hylton, J. Gordon. "Maybe the Brewers Should Hire a Lawyer as Their Next Manager," *Marquette University Law School Faculty Blog*, November 1, 2011, http://law.marquette.edu/facultyblog/2011/11/01/maybe-the-brewers-should-hire-a-lawyer-as-their-next-manager.
Jones, Ashby. "New York Yankees: Yes, We're 'Evil.'" wsj.com, February 22, 2013, http://www.wsj.com/articles/SB10001424127887323549204578320531185286140.
Juliano, William. "Libeling Lou: Iron Horse Sues to Restore His Name 90 Years Ago Today," *The Captain's Blog*, September 9, 2010, http://www.captainsblog.info [search "libel"].
"Juuust A Bit Out There," smokinggun.com, June 2, 2006, http://www.thesmokinggun.com/documents/sports/juuust-bit-out-there.
Kates, Maxwell. "Frank Robinson," SABR Baseball Biography Project, accessed March 23, 2016, http://sabr.org/bioproj/person/c3ac5482.
Kelly, Bill. "Arrested for Playing Baseball! How the National Pastime Became a Church and State Battleground in Nebraska." NET News, June 6, 2013, http://netnebraska.org/article/news/arrested-playing-baseball-how-national-pastime-became-church-and-state-battleground.
"Knicks Adopt Playing Rules on September 23," Protoball, accessed October 8, 2014, http://protoball.org/1845.1.
Lamb, Bill. "Jim O'Rourke," SABR Baseball Biography Project, accessed March 23, 2016, http://sabr.org/bioproj/person/b7e9aba2#_edn1.
Mallinson, James. "A.G. Mills," SABR Baseball Biography Project, accessed March 23, 2016, http://sabr.org/bioproj/person/abccef1b.
Markusen, Bruce. "Remembering the All Black Lineup," *Bruce Markusen's Cooperstown Confidential* (blog), September 1, 2006, http://bruce.mlblogs.com/2006/09/01/remembering-the-all-black-lineup.
Marsh, John. "On the Genealogy of Trades, Part I," *The Hardball Times* (blog), June 25, 2015, http://www.hardballtimes.com [search "genealogy"].
Maryland 6th Congressional District, Western Maryland Historical Library, accessed July 14, 2015, http://www.whilbr.org/itemdetail.aspx?idEntry=6447.
McKenna, Brian. "Dave Fultz," SABR Baseball Biography Project, accessed March 23, 2016, http://sabr.org/bioproj/person/1857946b.
———. "Eddie Gaedel," SABR Baseball Biography Project, accessed March 23, 2016, http://sabr.org/bioproj/person/fa5574c8.
"The Mitchell Report," MLB.com, accessed February 26, 2016, http://mlb.mlb.com/mlb/news/mitchell/coverage.jsp (follow link to "players").

"The Mitchell Report: Name by Name," NYTimes.com, July 5, 2011, http://www.nytimes.com/interactive/2007/12/13/sports/20071213_MITCHELL_FEATURE.html?_r=0#112.
Mondout, Patrick. "Cincinnati Red Stockings," *Baseball Chronology*, accessed June 13, 2014, http://www.baseballchronology.com/Baseball/Leagues/NABBP/Clubs/Cincinnati-Red-Stockings.asp.
Morris, Peter, and Stefan Fatsis. "Baseball's Secret Pioneer," *Slate*, February 4, 2014, http://www.slate.com [search "william edward white"].
Official Website of the AAGBPL, accessed July 25, 2015, http://www.aagpbl.org/index.cfm.
"Over Fifty Years Before Jackie Robinson Broke Major League Baseball's Color Barrier, an Integrated Minor League Team Battled for the Rights to Future Hall of Fame Black Ballplayer Frank Grant," *Baseball Law Reporter* (blog), December 14, 2013, http://baseballlawreporter.blogspot.com [search "Frank Grant"].
Oz, Mike. "A-Rod Ruling Explained—How Arbitrator Fredric Horowitz Decided on 162 Games," *Yahoo Sports!* January 13, 2014, https://sports.yahoo.com/ [search "horowitz"].
"Paul in the Hall," *Roll Call*, June 26, 2012, http://www.rollcall.com/heard-on-the-hill/paul-in-the-hall/.
Pepe, Maria, as told to Jeff Merron. "Breaking Barriers," *ESPN Page 2*, updated July 22, 2005, http://.espn.go.com [search "maria pepe"].
Posnanski, Joe. "Monitoring the Hall of Fame Monitor," *NBC SportsWorld*, accessed February 15, 2016, http://sportsworld.nbcsports.com/baseball-hall-of-fame-monitor-bill-james/.
"President Benjamin Harrison Baseball Game Attendance Log," *Baseball Almanac*, accessed July 29, 2013, http://www.baseball-almanac.com/prz_cbh.shtml.
Preston, J.G. "On Eleanor Engle, Who Wasn't Allowed to Play Shortstop for the Harrisburg Senators," *The J.G. Preston Experience* (blog), November 21, 2009, https://prestonjg.wordpress.com [search "engle"].
Putnam, Christine L. "A President Inaugurates a Remarkable Tradition," *Baseball Almanac*, April 2003, http://www.baseball-almanac.com/articles/president_taft_opening_day.shtml.
Radom, Todd. "In 1939, Every MLB Team Wore This Logo," *Radom Thoughts: A Blog*, April 2, 2014, http://toddradom.com/in-1939-every-mlb-team-wore-this-logo.
"Rangers Settle Lawsuit with A's Fan," ESPN.com, January 12, 2007, http://espn.go.com/mlb/news/story?id=2729391.
"Reds Timeline," Cincinnati Reds website, accessed June 13, 2014, http://cincinnati.reds.mlb.com/cin/history/timeline1.jsp.
"Reliever Charged With Felony Battery," ESPN.com, September 15, 2004, http://espn.go.com/mlb/news/story?id=1881073.
Rice, Stephen V. "April 14, 1910: Walter Johnson Impresses President Taft on Opening Day," SABR Baseball Games Project, accessed March 23, 2016, http://sabr.org/gamesproject.
"Roger Bresnahan," Baseball-Reference.com, accessed July 30, 2013, http://www.baseball-reference.com.
Rothenberg, Matt. "From One Robinson to Another." *Inside Pitch*, National Baseball Hall of Fame E-Newsletter, April 13, 2015, http://baseballhall.org/discover/breaking-baseball-barriers-from-one-robinson-to-another.
Ryczek, William. "Why the National Association Was a Major League," *National Pastime Museum*, accessed October 23, 2015, http://www.thenationalpastimemuseum.com/article/why-national-association-was-major-league.
Shinkle, Andrew. "A Storied Rivalry, Part I," *SB Nation* (blog), March 8, 2014, http://www.redreporter.com/2014/3/8/5481770/a-storied-rivalry-part-i.
Thorn, John. "The Fathers of Fantasy Baseball," *Our Game* (blog), October 17, 2011, http://ourgame.mlblogs.com/2011/10/17/fathers-of-fantasy-baseball.
_____. "Shoeless Joe, the Bambino, the Big Bankroll, and the Jazz Age," *Our Game* (blog), June 15, 2015, http://ourgame.mlblogs.com/2015/06/15/.
Traynor, Elizabeth. "Ron Paul Inducted into Congressional Baseball Hall of Fame—in Astros Garb," *Houston Chronicle* (blog), June 28, 2012, http://blog.chron.com/txpotomac/2012/06/ron-paul-inducted-into-congressional-baseball-hall-of-fame-%E2%80%93-in-astros-garb/.

Utley, Hank, and Josh Davlin. "Alabama Pitts," SABR Baseball Biography Project, accessed March 23, 2016, http://sabr.org/bioproj/person/d7db6951.
Wancho, Joseph. "Joe Judge," SABR Baseball Biography Project, accessed March 23, 2016, http://sabr.org/bioproj/person/e7eab9b6.
Warrington, Bob. "The Fight for Sunday Baseball in Philadelphia," *Baseball History Blog*, Philadelphia Athletics Historical Society, July 30, 2001, http://philadelphiaathletics.org/the-fight-for-sunday-baseball-in-philadelphia/.
Willkie Farr & Gallagher LLP, Firm History, accessed July 31, 2015, http://www.willkie.com/about-us/firm-history.
Zax, David. "A Brief History of the Honus Wagner Baseball Card," Smithsonian.com, April 30, 2007, http://www.smithsonianmag.com [search "wagner card"].

Government Documents

Congressional Bills and Resolutions

Baseball Fans and Communities Protection Act, H.R. 4994, 103rd Cong. (1994).
H.R. Res. 450, 62nd Cong. (1912).
H.R. 7903, 96th Cong. (1980).
Integrity in Professional Sports Act, S. 1960, 109th Cong. (2005).

Congressional Record

91 Cong. Rec. 3904 (1945).
134 Cong. Rec. 13361–62 (1988) (statement of Rep. Lantos).

Congressional Hearings and Reports

Conduct of Judge Kenesaw Mountain Landis: Hearings Before the House Comm. on the Judiciary, 66th Cong. Washington, D.C.: U.S. Govt. Print. Off., 1921.
Confirmation Hearing on the Nomination of John G. Roberts, Jr. to Be Chief Justice of the United States: Hearing Before the S. Comm. on the Judiciary, S. Hrg. 109-158, 109th Cong. Washington, D.C.: U.S. Govt. Print. Off., 2005.
Excessive Violence in Professional Sports: Hearing on H.R. 7903 Before the Subcomm. on Crime of the H. Comm. on the Judiciary, 96th Cong. Washington, D.C.: U.S. Govt. Print. Off., 1981.
Hearings Regarding Communist Infiltration of Minority Groups, Part 1: Hearings Before the House Committee on Un-American Activities, 81st Cong. Washington, D.C.: U.S. Govt. Print. Off., 1949.
Inquiry into Professional Sports, Parts 1 and 2: Hearings Before the House Select Committee on Professional Sports, 94th Cong. Washington, D.C.: U.S. Govt. Print. Off., 1976.
Mitchell Report: Illegal Use of Steroids in Major League Baseball, Day 2: Hearing Before the House Committee on Oversight and Government Reform, 110th Cong. Washington, D.C.: U.S. Govt. Print. Off, 2008.
Restoring Faith in America's Pastime: Evaluating Major League Baseball's Efforts To Eradicate Steroid Use: Hearing Before the House Committee on Government Reform, 109th Cong. Washington, D.C.: U.S. Govt. Print. Off, 2005.
Select Comm. on Professional Sports, *Inquiry Into Professional Sports: Final Report of the Select Committee on Professional Sports*, H.R. Rep. No. 94–1786 (1977).
Steroid Use in Professional Baseball and Anti-Doping Issues In Amateur Sports: Hearing before the Subcomm. on Consumer Affairs, Foreign Commerce, and Tourism of the S. Comm. on Commerce, Science, and Transportation, S. Hrg. 107-1126, 107th Cong. Washington, D.C.: U.S. Govt. Print. Off., 2002.
Study of Monopoly Power: Hearings Before the Subcommittee on Study of Monopoly Power of the House Committee on the Judiciary, pt. 6, Organized Baseball, 82nd Cong., July 30–October 24, 1951. Washington, D.C.: U.S. Govt. Print. Off, 1952.
Subjecting Professional Baseball Clubs to the Antitrust Laws: Hearings Before a Subcommittee of the House Committee on the Judiciary, 83rd Cong. 42–65, March 18–May 25, 1954. Washington, D.C.: U.S. Govt. Print. Off, 1954.

Copyrights and Patents

Alden, Henry A. Improvement in the Manufacture of Base-Balls, U.S. Patent 72,355, issued December 17, 1867.
Barnard, George. Base-Ball Mask, U.S. Patent 376,278, filed August 29, 1887, issued January 10, 1888.
Bennett, Marjori, Baseball Centennial, 1839–1939. Copyright G 31040, issued November 28, 1938. Copyright Office, Library of Congress, *Catalog of Copyright Entries, Part 4*, vol. 33, new series, 179. Washington, D.C.: Govt. Printing Office, 1939.
Buhler, William J. Baseball Player's Chest Protector. U.S. Patent 4,272,847, filed April 30, 1979, issued June 16, 1981.
_____. Throat Protecting Attachment for a Baseball Catcher's Mask. U.S. Patent D258322, filed October 16, 1978, issued February 24, 1981.
Butts, Austin C. Improvement in Gloves. U.S. Patent 198,921, filed May 15, 1877, issued January 1, 1878.
Campanis, Alexander. Baseball Glove. U.S. Patent 3,898,696, filed October 15, 1974, issued August 12, 1975.
Doak, William L. Fielder's Glove. U.S. Patent 1,426,824, filed April 18, 1921, issued August 22, 1922.
Faria, James M., and Robert T. Wright. Monofilament Ribbon File Product. U.S. Patent 3,332,828, filed December 28, 1965, issued July 25, 1967.
Giblin, John. Improvement in Base-Balls. U.S. Patent 165,994, filed June 25, 1875, issued July 27, 1875.
Gray, William. Body-Protector, U.S. Patent 295,543, filed October 18, 1883, issued March 25, 1884.
Johnstone, James E. Baseball Mask. U.S. Patent 1,449,183, filed July 23, 1921, issued March 20, 1923.
Mogridge, Frank Pierse. Head-Protector. U.S. Patent 780,899, filed August 6, 1904, issued January 24, 1905.
Neuhalfen, Mark. Baseball Catcher's Chest Protector. U.S. Patent 5,020,156, filed November 14, 1989, issued June 4, 1991.
O'Neill, J.C. Base-Ball Base. U.S. Patent 171,038, filed June 19, 1875, issued December 14, 1875.
Osgood, James H. Improvement in Modes of Covering Rounded Articles with Leather. U.S. Patent 127,098, issued May 21, 1872.
Rawlings, George H. Glove. U.S. Patent 325,968, filed March 23, 1885, issued September 8, 1885.
Reach, Robert. Base-Ball Mask. U.S. Patent 364,543, filed March 2, 1887, issued June 7, 1887.
Shibe, Benjamin F. Base-Ball. U.S. Patent 924,696, filed August 26, 1908, issued June 15, 1909.
Thayer, Frederick W. Masks. U.S. Patent 200,358, filed January 15, 1878, issued February 12, 1878.
Titus, W.S. Base Ball Back Stop. U.S. Patent 849,941, filed December 20, 1906, issued April 9, 1907.

Presidential Documents

Exec. Order No. 9586, 10 Fed. Reg. 8523 (July 10, 1945).
Obama, Barack. Remarks on the Nomination of Sonia Sotomayor To Be a Supreme Court Associate Justice. *Public Papers of the Presidents of the United States: Barack Obama*. Vol. 1, pp. 714–16. Washington, D.C.: Government Printing Office, 2010.

Miscellaneous

In re Arbitration Between Major League Baseball Players Ass'n & Twenty-Six Major League Baseball Clubs, Grievance No. 86-2, Panel Decision No. 76. Reprinted in part in *Final Innings: A Documentary History of Baseball, 1972–2008*, edited by Dean A. Sullivan, 138–45. Lincoln: University of Nebraska Press, 2010.
"Cincinnati Peace Agreement," 1915 Federal League Lawsuit Case Files (document 120), Society

Bibliography 291

for American Baseball Research, http://sabr.org/research/1915-Federal-League-case-files.

Dowd, John M., et al., *Report to the Commissioner: In the Matter of Peter Edward Rose, Manager, Cincinnati Reds Baseball Club* (May 9, 1989), available at www.thedowdreport.com.

Harry A. Blackmun, interview by Harold Hongju Koh, July 6, 1994, sess. 1, pt. 1, video tape, Justice Harry A. Blackmun Oral History Project, Library of Congress, accessed July 21, 2015, http://lcweb2.loc.gov/diglib/blackmun-public/series.html?ID=D10.

Haupert, Michael, to SABR-L mailing list. "Musial 1951 Contract," December 6, 2015, http://APPLE.EASE.LSOFT.COM/archives/SABR-L.html.

In the Matter of Peter Edward Rose, Decision of Commissioner Robert D. Manfred, Jr. Concerning the Application of Rose for Removal From the Permanently Ineligible List, December 14, 2015.

Library of Congress. "2012 National Film Registry Picks in A League of Their Own," news release, revised December 20, 2012, www.loc.gov/today/pr/2012/12-226.html.

"Major League Agreement of January 12, 1921." In *Professional Baseball in America: A Compilation of the Agreements and Rules which Define the Relations of Leagues, Clubs and Players*, 7–14. Chicago: H.G. Adair, 1921.

Major League Baseball, "Commissioner Informs Rose of Decision," news release, December 14, 2015, http://www.mlb.com/news/press_releases/ [follow "archive" link].

———, "Discipline Issued in Biogenesis Investigation," news release, August 5, 2013, http://www.mlb.com/news/press_releases/ [follow "archive" link].

———, "MLB, MLBPA Announce New Drug Agreement," news release, November 15, 2005, http://www.mlb.com/news/press_releases/ [follow "archive" link].

———, "Program Testing for Major Leaguers for Steroids to Commence in 2004," news release, November 13, 2003, http://www.mlb.com/news/press_releases/ [follow "archive" link].

Major League Steering Committee. *Report for Submission to the National and American Leagues at their Meetings in Chicago.* August 27, 1946. Available from Society for American Baseball Research, Business of Baseball Committee, http://research.sabr.org/business (follow link to documents).

Memorandum from Francis T. Vincent Jr. to All Major League Clubs, "Baseball's Drug Policy and Prevention Program," June 7, 1991.

Mitchell, George J. *Report to the Commissioner of Baseball of an Independent Investigation into the Illegal Use of Steroids and Other Performance Enhancing Substances by Players in Major League Baseball.* December 13, 2007. Available at http://files.mlb.com/mitchrpt.pdf.

National Hockey League Players Association, "NHLPA Membership Appoints Don Fehr as Executive Director," media release, December 18, 2010, http://www.nhlpa.com/news/nhlpa-membership-appoints-don-fehr-as-executive-director.

Office of the Commissioner of Baseball, "In the Matter of Peter Edward Rose" (August 23, 1989), Baseball Almanac, accessed March 18, 2015, www.baseball-almanac.com/players/p_rosea.shtml.

———, "Statement of A. Bartlett Giamatti" (August 24, 1989), Baseball Almanac, accessed March 18, 2015, www.baseball-almanac.com/players/p_roseb.shtml.

"Pledge to Support the Commissioner." In *Professional Baseball in America: A Compilation of the Agreements and Rules which Define the Relations of Leagues, Clubs and Players*, 8. Chicago: H.G. Adair, 1921.

Shea, William A. Announcement of Formation of Continental League, news release, July 27, 1959. Reprinted in Sullivan, *Late Innings*, 141–44.

Stevens, John Paul. Remarks at the Sports Lawyers Association 41st Annual Conference Luncheon, Baltimore, MD, May 15, 2015, www.supremecourt.gov/publicinfo/speeches/JPS_SportsLawyersAssociation_05-15-15.pdf.

Index of Cases and Statutes

Bold numbers refer to page numbers

Cases

Allegheny Base-Ball Club v. Bennett, 14 F. 257 (C.C.W.D. Pa. 1882), **29–30**.
Am. Ass'n Base-Ball Club of Kansas City v. Pickett, 8 Pa. County Ct. 232 (Ct. Com. Pl. 1890), **37**.
Am. League Baseball Club of Chicago v. Chase, 149 N.Y.S. 6 (N.Y. Sup. Ct. 1914), **57–58**.
Am. League Baseball Club of New York v. Johnson, 179 N.Y.S. 498 (Sup. Ct. 1919), **62–63**.
Am. League Baseball Club of New York v. Pasquel, 63 N.Y.S.2d 537 (Sup. Ct. 1946), **92**.
Atlanta Nat'l League Baseball Club. Inc. v. Kuhn, 432 F. Supp. 1213 (N.D. Ga. 1977), **128**.
Balt. Orioles, Inc. v. Major League Baseball Players Ass'n, 805 F.2d 663 (7th Cir. 1986), **136**.
Berman v. Nat'l Exhibition Co., No. 46447 (N.Y. Sup. Ct. 1923), **70**.
Brocail v. Detroit Tigers, Inc., 268 S.W.3d 90 (Tex. App. 2008), **162–63**.
Brooklyn Nat'l League Baseball Club v. Pasquel, 66 F. Supp. 117 (E.D. Mo. 1946), **92**.
Buday v. New York Yankees Partnership, 486 F. App'x 894 (2d Cir. 2012), **164–65**.
Butterworth v. Nat'l League of Prof'l Baseball Clubs, 644 So. 2d 1021 (Fla. 1994), **148, 150, 155**.
Cepeda v. Swift & Co., 291 F. Supp. 242 (E.D. Mo. 1968), **116**.
Chicago Nat'l League Ball Club, Inc. v. Vincent, available in Michael J. Cozzillio et al., *Sports Law: Cases & Materials*, 2nd ed., 86–92. Durham, NC: Carolina Academic Press, 2007, July 23, 1992.
Cincinnati Exhibition Co. v. Johnson, 190 Ill. App. 630 (1914), **57**.
Cincinnati Exhibition Co. v. Marsans, 216 F. 269 (E.D. Mo. 1914), **57**.
City of San José v. Office of Comm'r of Baseball, 776 F.3d 686 (9th Cir. 2015), **168–69**.
Cohn v. Corinthian Colleges, Inc., 86 Cal. Rptr. 3d 401 (Ct. App. 2008), **160**.
Commonwealth v. Am. Baseball Club of Phila., 290 Pa. 136, 138 A. 497 (1927), **76–77**.
Coomer v. Kansas City Royals Baseball Corp., 437 S.W.3d 184 (Mo. 2014), **166**.
Coronel v. Chicago White Sox, 595 N.E.2d 45 (Ill. App. Ct. 1992), **145**.
Crane v. Kansas City Baseball & Exhibition, Co., 153 S.W. 1076 (Mo. Ct. App. 1913), **55**.
Croteau v. Fair, 686 F. Supp. 552 (E.D. Va. 1988), **138**.
Curtiss Candy Co. v. George H. Ruth Candy Co., 1930 WL 23279, 4 U.S.P.Q. 103 (Com'r Pat. & Trademarks Feb. 11, 1930), **78–79**.

De Haviland v. Warner Bros. Pictures, Inc., 153 P.2d 983 (Cal. Ct. App. 1944), **245n3**.
Detroit Base-Ball Club v. Deppert, 27 N.W. 856, 858 (Mich. 1886), **33**.
Dorsey v. State Athletic Comm'n, 168 F. Supp. 149 (E.D. La. 1958), **105**.
Fed. Baseball Club of Balt., Inc. v. Nat'l League of Prof'l Baseball Clubs, 259 U.S. 200 (1922), **15, 221n105, 71–72, 73, 99, 102, 122–23, 144, 154**.
Finley v. Kuhn, 569 F.2d 527 (7th Cir. 1978), **129**.
Fleer Corp. v. Topps Chewing Gum, Inc., 658 F.2d 139 (3d Cir. 1981), **134**.
Flood v. Kuhn, 309 F. Supp. 793 (S.D.N.Y. 1970), **119**.
Flood v. Kuhn, 316 F. Supp. 271 (S.D.N.Y. 1970), **119**.
Flood v. Kuhn, 443 F.2d 264 (2d Cir. 1971), **119**.
Flood v. Kuhn, 407 U.S. 258 (1972), **50, 61, 76, 122–23, 144, 153**.
Garvey v. Roberts, 203 F.3d 580 (9th Cir. 2000), **156**.
George H. Ruth Candy Co. v. Curtiss Candy Co., 49 F.2d 1033 (C.C.P.A. 1931), **78–79**.
Gionfriddo v. Major League Baseball, 114 Cal. Rptr. 2d 307 (Ct. App. 2002), **157**.
Haelan Laboratories, Inc. v. Topps Chewing Gum, Inc., 202 F.2d 866 (2d Cir. 1953), **101–02**.
Hanna Manufacturing Co. v. Hillerich & Bradsby Co., 78 F.2d 763, 763 (1935), **82–83**.
Harrisburg Base-Ball Club v. Athletic Ass'n, 8 Pa.C.C. 337 (Ct. Com. Pl. 1890), **37**.
Hornsby v. Comm'r, 26 B.T.A. 591 (1932), **80**.
Hundley v. Comm'r, 48 T.C. 339 (1967), **115**.
Jethroe v. Major League Baseball Props., Inc., No. 95–72 (W.D. Pa. Sept. 30, 1996), **152**.
Kaplan v. Vincent, 937 F. Supp. 307 (S.D.N.Y. 1996), **148–49**.
Kelly v. Marylanders for Sports Sanity, Inc., 530 A.2d 245 (Md. Ct. App. 1987), **137**.
Ladd v. Uecker, 780 N.W.2d 216 (Wis. Ct. App. 2010), **164**.
Lowe v. California League of Prof'l Baseball, 65 Cal. Rptr. 2d 105 (1997), **153**.
Ludtke v. Kuhn, 461 F. Supp. 86 (S.D.N.Y. 1978), **128–29**.
Mahn v. Harwood, 112 U.S. 354 (1884), **31**.
McCoy v. Major League Baseball, 911 F. Supp. 454 (W.D. Wash. 1995), **149–50**.
Major League Baseball Players Ass'n v. Garvey, 532 U.S. 504 (2001), **156**.
Major League Baseball Properties, Inc. v. Sed Non Olet Denarius, Ltd., 817 F. Supp. 1103 (S.D.N.Y. 1993), *vacated* 859 F. Supp. 80 (S.D.N.Y. 1994), **145**.
Metro. Exhibition Co. v. Ewing, 42 F. 198 (C.C.S.D.N.Y. 1890), **36**.
Metro. Exhibition Co. v. Ward, 9 N.Y.S. 779 (Sup. Ct. 1890), **35, 36**.
Metro. Sports Facilities Comm'n v. Minnesota Twins Partnership, 638 N.W.2d 214 (Minn. Ct. App. 2002), **157–58**.
Milwaukee American Association v. Landis, 49 F.2d 298 (N.D. Ill. 1931), **79–80**.
Minnesota Twins Partnership v. State, 592 N.W.2d 847 (Minn. 1999), **154–55**.
Nat'l Organization for Women, Essex County Chapter v. Little League Baseball, Inc, 318 A.2d 33, 35 (N.J. Super. Ct. App. Div. 1974), *aff'd summarily*, 338 A.2d 198 (N.J. 1974), **124**.
New Orleans Pelicans Baseball, Inc. v. Nat'l Ass'n of Prof'l Baseball Leagues, Inc., 1994 WL 631144 (U.S. Dist. Ct. E.D. La. Mar. 1, 1994), **146**.
New York Yankees Partnership v. Evil Enterprises, Inc., 2013 WL 1305332 (Trademark Tr. & App. Bd.), **165**.
Newcombe v. Adolf Coors Co., 157 F.3d 686 (9th Cir. 1998), **146**.
O'Connor v. St. Louis American League Baseball Co., 181 S.W. 1167 (Mo. Ct. App. 1916), **52–53**.
Oliver v. National Collegiate Athletic Association, 920 N.E.2d 203 (Ohio Ct. C.P. 2009), **163**.
Parks v. Steinbrenner, 520 N.Y.S.2d 374 (App. Div. 1987), **136–37**.
People v. Poole, 89 N.Y.S. 773 (1904), **47**.
Phila. Ball Club, Ltd. v. Hallman, 8 Pa. C. 57 (C.P. 1890), **36**.

Phila. Ball Club, Ltd. v. Lajoie, 51 A. 973 (Pa. 1902), **43**.
Piazza v. Major League Baseball, 831 F. Supp. 420 (E.D. Pa. 1993), **144, 146, 148, 150**.
Pirone v. Macmillan, Inc., 894 F.2d 579 (2d Cir. 1990), **140–41**.
Pittsburgh Athletic Co. v. KQV Broad. Co., 24 F. Supp. 490 (W.D. Pa. 1938), **84**.
Popov v. Hayashi, No. 400545, 2002 WL 31833731 (Cal. Super. Ct. Dec. 18, 2002), **157**.
Portland Baseball Club, Inc. v. Baltimore Baseball Club, Inc., 282 F.2d 680 (9th Cir. 1960), **107**.
Portland Baseball Club, Inc. v. Kuhn, 368 F. Supp. 1004 (D. Ore. 1971), *aff'd*, 491 F.2d 1101 (9th Cir. 1974), **122**.
Postema v. Nat'l League of Prof'l Baseball Clubs, 799 F. Supp. 1475 (S.D.N.Y. 1992), *rev'd on other grounds*, 998 F.2d 60 (2d Cir. 1993), **143–44**.
Right Field Rooftops, LLC v. Chicago Baseball Holdings, LLC, 87 F. Supp. 3d 874 (N.D. Ill. 2015), **169**.
Roseboro v. Rawlings Mfg. Co., 79 Cal. Rptr. 567 (Cal. Ct. App. 1969), **108**.
Russell v. Nat'l Exhibition Co., 69 N.Y.S. 732 (App. Div. 1901), **40**.
Ruth v. Educ. Films, 184 N.Y.S. 948 (App. Div. 1920) (mem.), **64–65**.
Salerno v. Am. League of Prof'l Baseball Clubs, 429 F.2d 1003 (2d Cir. 1970), **116, 121**.
Selig v. United States, 740 F.2d 572 (7th Cir. 1984), **135**.
Shamsky v. Garan, Inc., 632 N.Y.S.2d 930 (N.Y. Sup. Ct. 1995), **149**.
Shenkman v. O'Malley, 157 N.Y.S.2d 290 (App. Div. 1956), **104**.
Silverman v. Major League Baseball Player Relations Comm., Inc., 880 F. Supp. 246 (S.D.N.Y. 1995), **149**.
Standard Sanitary Manufacturing Co. v. United States, 226 U.S. 20 (1912), **55**.
State v. Milwaukee Braves, 144 N.W.2d 1 (Wis. 2002), **115**.
State v. Powell, 50 N.E. 900 (Ohio 1898), **40–41**.
State v. O'Rourk, 53 N.W. 591(Neb. 1892), **39**.
State v. Reed, 44 S.W.2d 31 (Mo. 1931), **80**.
Tepler v. Frick, 204 F.2d 506 (2d Cir. 1953), **99**.
Thayer v. Spaulding, 27 F. 66 (C.C. N.D. Ill. 1886), **219n59**.
Thorpe v. Borough of Thorpe, 770 F.3d 255 (3d Cir. 2014), **168**.
Toolson v. New York Yankees, 346 U.S. 356 (1953), **102, 123, 144, 153**.
Topps Chewing Gum, Inc., 67 F.T.C. 744 (1965), **104**.
Uhlaender v. Henricksen, 316 F. Supp. 1277 (D. Minn. 1970), **120**.
United States v. Bonds, 784 F.3d 582 (9th Cir. 2015), **170**.
United States v. Cleveland Indians Baseball Co., 532 U.S. 200 (2001), **156**.
United States v. McLain, 823 F.2d 1457 (11th Cir. 1987), **119**.
Watson v. Avery, 65 Ky. 332 (1867), **21**.
Weegham v. Killefer, 215 F. 168 (W.D. Mich. 1914), **20, 182, 191, 225n94**.
Wills v. Comm'r, 411 F.2d 537 (9th Cir. 1969), **117**.
Yates v. Chicago Nat'l League Ball Club, 595 N.E.2d 570 (Ill. App. Ct. 1992), **145**.

Statutes and Regulations

Federal

Act of July 16, 1964, Pub. L. No. 88–378, 78 Stat. 325 (1964), **110**.
Act of December 26, 1974, Pub. L. No. 93–551, 88 Stat. 1744 (1974), **110**.
Anabolic Steroids Control Act of 1990, Pub. L. No. 101–647, tit. XIX, 104 Stat. 4851–54 (1990), **142**.
Curt Flood Act of 1998, Pub. L. No. 105–297, §3, 112 Stat. 2824 (1999), **148, 151, 153–54, 169**.
National Film Preservation Act of 1988, Pub. L. No. 100–446, 102 Stat. 1782 (1988), **165**.

Native American Graves Protection and Repatriation Act, Pub. L. No. 101-601, 104 Stat. 3048 (1990) (codified as amended at 25 U.S.C. §§ 3001-3013), **168**.

Sherman Antitrust Act, Act of July 2, 1890, ch. 647, 26 Stat. 209 (1890), **37, 45, 118, 134, 168**.

State and Local

An Act for the Prevention of Vice and Immorality, and of Unlawful Gaming, and to Restrain Disorderly Sports and Dissipation, Act of April 22, 1794, 15 Pa. Statutes at Large, ch. 1758 (1794), **14**.

An Act in Relation to Bets, Wagers, and Pools, ch. 178, 1877 Laws of New York 192, **25**.

Act of April 19, 1919, ch. 260, 1919 N.Y. Laws 865, **62**.

Act of July 13, 1921, 1921 Ill. Laws 400, **73**.

Act of July 16, 1956, no. 579, 1956 La. Acts 1054, **105**.

An Act Relating to Baseball and Football on Sunday, No. 49, 1933 Pa. Laws 74, **81**.

Ariz. Rev. Stat. Ann. § 12-554 (2003), **145**.

Baseball Facility Liability Act, 745 Ill. Comp. Stat. Ann. 38/10 (West 2010), **145**.

Cal. Lab. Code § 2855, **113**.

Colorado Baseball Spectator Safety Act of 1993, Colo. Rev. Stat. § 13-21-120 (2014), **145**.

New Jersey Baseball Spectator Safety Act of 2006, N.J. Stat. Ann § 2A:53A-43-53A-48, **145**.

Subject Index

Abbey, Bert 42
Abrams, Roger I. 47–48, 50, 126
Adams, Charles 77
admission charges 28, 76; first game with 16–17
African Americans *see* integration of baseball, Negro Leagues
A.G. Spalding and Brothers *see* Spalding, Albert G
Agee, Tommie 250*n*262
agents: CBA establishes player's right to use 120; first for player 69; NCAA rule against use of 163; Richard Moss 131, 134; Scott Boras 154, 163
Ainsworth, Eddie 61
A.J. Reach Co. *see* Reach, Alfred James
Albany Senators (Int'l League) 82
alcohol 146; sales of 27, 28l; *see also* Anheuser-Busch; Coors Brewing Co
Alden, Henry A.: first baseball-related patent 21–22
Alexander, Doyle 143
Alexander, Grover Cleveland 100
All-American Girls Professional Baseball League (AAGPBL) 147, 165; as basis for movie 165
Allen, Dick 241*n*13, 242*n*37
Altman, George 108
ambassadors, U.S.: only player to serve as 168
American Association (AA): Beer and Whiskey circuit, called 28; endorses Richter's "Millennium Plan" 34; formation and cessation of 28, 39; major league status of 217*n*31; and National Agreement of 1883 18, 30; and National Agreement of 1885 32; and National Agreement of 1891 19, 38, 38–39; and peace agreement with NL 19, 39; players jump to Players' League 35
American Baseball Guild: formation of 89, 92; strike vote in support of 93
American League (AL) 63: expansion of 126, 50th anniversary of 100; formation of 19,

42–43; integration of 89, 94–95; major league status of 42, 217*n*31; and National Agreement of 1903 19, 44, 45–46; and National Agreement of 1921 68; and peace agreement with NL 19, 45; sued—by FL 58, by female umpire 143–44, by fired umpires 118
American Shipbuilding Co. 125
Americana Hotel (Bal Harbour, FL) 117
amyotrophic lateral sclerosis 86
Andujar, Joaquin 136
Angel Stadium (Anaheim, CA) 160
Anheuser-Busch 101, 102
Anson, Adrian "Cap" 42
Ansonio Hotel (NYC) 69
antitrust 102–103, 116
antitrust, baseball's exemption from: applicability—to entirety of baseball business 146, 149–50, 154–55, 168–69, created by *Federal Baseball* 71–72, to reserve system only 144, 148, upheld by *Flood* 112, 119, 122–23, 153, upheld by *Toolson* 90, 102; court challenges—over baseball cards 134, by FL against O.B. 44, 45, 58, 59, 60, first use of 58, over franchise movement 115, 144, 146, 148, 154–55, 168–69, over reserve clause 90, 96, 118, 119, 122–23, 153, over stadium expansion 169, over televising MLB games 107; federal legislative action regarding—Curt Flood Act of 1998, 148, 151, 153–54, exemption from—bill to eliminate 148, hearings on 106, report on elimination of 128, hearings on 90, 99, 100, 106, resolution on "Baseball Trust" 53, Sherman Antitrust Act 37
Appling, Luke 109
arbitration: arbitrator's jurisdiction upheld 127; and collusion by owners 113, 137–38, 138–39, 140, 141–42, 156; of expansion compensation to PCL 122; free agency created by 112, 126; of grievances 115, 120; in minor leagues 43; of salaries—American Baseball Guild proposal for 92, creation and expan-

297

sion by CBAs 123, 127, 131, 141, 154, eligibility for 141, first million-dollar award 134, first woman to serve as arbitrator 154, as strike cause 135
arbitrators, individual: Elizabeth Neumeier 154; Frederic Horowitz 166; George Nicolau 138–39, 141–42; Lewis M. Gill 120, 121–22; Peter Seitz 47–48, 125, 126, 126–27, 127; Raymond Goetz 131; Tom Roberts 134, 137–38, 140, 156
Arlington, Lizzie 41
Ashburn, Richie 102
Ashford, Emmett 114
Association of Major League Umpires 121
Astrodome (Houston) 114–15
Atlanta Braves (NL) 128; *see also* Boston Beaneaters (NL); Boston Braves (NL);Boston Red Stockings (NL); Milwaukee Braves (NL)
Atlanta Crackers (So. Ass'n.) 61
Atlantan Hotel (Atlanta) 98
Atlantic City Bacharach Giants (ECL) 74
Attell, Abe 65, 70; Black Sox grand jury indicts 66
Austrian, Alfred 65

Baby Ruth candy bar: trademark dispute over 78–79
Bagwell, Jeff: insurance claim for disability of 161
Baird, Thomas 91
Baker, Newton D. 61
Baker Bowl (Philadelphia) 75
Ball, Philip: purchases St. Louis Browns (AL) after FL peace agreement with O.B. 59
ballparks: disputes over building or expansion of 105, 137, 169; enclosed grounds first used 17; owner liability for foul ball injuries limited 145; giveaways, discriminating between recipients of 160; lawsuit to prevent erection of grandstands overlooking 33; *see also* Angel Stadium, Astrodome; Baker Bowl; Candlestick Park; Citi Field; Dodger Stadium; Fenway Park; Forbes Field; Griffith Stadium; Metrodome; Milwaukee County Stadium; Oakland Coliseum; Oriole Park at Camden Yards; Shea Stadium; Shibe Park; Three Rivers Stadium; Wrigley Field (Los Angeles); Yankee Stadium
Bally's Park Place Casino 130
Baltimore Black Sox (ECL) 74
Baltimore Orioles (AA) 28; purchased by NL as part of peace agreement 19, 39
Baltimore Orioles (AL) 44, 126
Baltimore Terrapins 59; and antitrust suit against O.B. 45, 60, 72
Bando, Sal 132
Bankhead, Dan 95
Banks, Ernie 108
Barber, Walter L. "Red" 35

Barnard, George 34
Barrow, Ed 41, 79
Bartholomay, William 250n230
Baseball (television program) 109
"Baseball and the Law" (poem) 109
baseball cards: and antitrust 134; first card sold for $1 million 155; litigation over use of photos on 101–02, 104; MLBPA agreement with Topps 116–17
Baseball Encyclopedia 50
Baseball Magazine 54
Baseball Research Journal 109
Baseball-themed games: license for use of names and statistics in fantasy baseball 161; license for use of names and statistics in video games 120; patents for 20–21, 21
basic agreement: first-ever 112, 115–16; of 1968 112, 115–16; of 1970 119–20; of 1973 123; of 1976 127; of 1980 131; of 1981 133; of 1985 135; of 1990 141; of 1996 154; of 2002 158, 159; of 2011 164; and Rob Manfred 168; owners enjoined from implementing new CBA during strike 149
Bathtub Trust case 55
Bauer, William J. (Judge) 135
Bavasi, Emil J. "Buzzie": and Furillo contract dispute 107; and Koufax/Drysdale contract dispute 113–14
Beaver, Donald 155
Bechtel, George 24
Beer and Whiskey Circuit *see* American Association
Bennett, Charlie 29–30
Bennett, Fred 79–80
Bennett, Marjori 84
Benny, Jack 239n119
Berg, Moe: Medal of Freedom awarded to 93
Berman, Reuben 70
Berra, Dale 136
Berra, Lawrence Peter "Yogi" 149, 170; comment on Koufax by 109; compared to Earl Warren 129; "Jurisprudence of Yogi Berra" (article) 170–71
Bierbauer, Louis: contract with Pittsburgh Alleghenys approved 38
Billington, James H. 49
Biltmore Hotel (NYC) 59
Biogenesis 152, 165–66
Bishop, C. Orrick 25
Black, Hugo (Justice) 129
Black Sox Scandal 45; civil trials by expelled players 71, 75; criminal trial 70; grand jury—confessions by players 65, indictments of 66; Illinois sports anti-corruption statute 73; Landis expels players 67, 70
blacklisting of players 27; allegations of—by Carl Furillo 107, by Oscar Felsch 71; National Agreement of 1891 abolishes 38; used against—Fred Pfeffer 40, players jumping to Union Association 31

Subject Index

Blackmun, Harry (Justice) 50; opinion in *Flood v. Kuhn* 50, 122–23, 153
Blue, Vida 127, 129
Bluege, Ossie 82
Bolden, Ed: and formation of Eastern Colored League 74
Bonds, Barry: criminal trials of 152, 170; disputed ownership of home-run ball 157; and PEDs—HOF impact of 170, 255n108, named in Mitchell Report 151, 162
Boone, Bob 132
Boras, Scott 154, 163
Bosch, Anthony 166
Boston Americans *see* Boston Red Sox (AL)
Boston Beaneaters (NL) 38, 40; *see also* Atlanta Braves (NL); Boston Braves (NL); Boston Red Stockings (NL); Milwaukee Braves (NL)
Boston Braves (NL) 64, 77, 89, 90, 94, 152–53; and dispute over sale of Scott Perry 61; *see also* Atlanta Braves (NL); Boston Beaneaters (NL); Boston Red Stockings (NL); Milwaukee Braves (NL)
Boston Daily Globe 29
Boston Red Sox (AL) 42, 54–55, 62–63, 63, 77, 81, 93, 127, 129, 154, 165; last team to integrate 81, 106; World Series, agreement to play in first 46
Boston Red Stockings (NL) 27; and Sam Wise revolving dispute 29; *see also* Atlanta Braves (NL); Boston Beaneaters (NL); Boston Braves (NL); Milwaukee Braves (NL)
Boston Reds (AA) 38
Boston Reds (PL) 36
Boston University 154
Boswell, Tom 139
Bowman Co.: and litigation over baseball cards 101–02, 104
Boyd, Willaim 64
Boyle, Jack 33
Bradford (PA) Phillies (Pony League) 130
Bramham, W.G. 82
Braun, Ryan: suspended for PED use 152, 166
Breadon, Sam 101
Bresnahan, Roger: dispute over contract to manage Cubs 60; first to use batting helmet and shin guards 47; sues Cardinals' owner over firing 55
bribery *see* gambling and game fixing
Briggs, Walter 85
Britton, Helene: fires Cardinals' manager 55; first female owner of team 53, 54
broadcasters: Bill White as first black 139; Bob Uecker as 164; Joe Garagiola as 102–103; sleeping fan sues TV announcers for defamation 170; *see also* radio, television
Brocail, Doug: sues Tigers over arm injury 162–63
Brock, Lou 108

Brooklyn Atlantics 28
Brooklyn Dodger Sports Bar and Restaurant 145
Brooklyn Dodgers (NL) 35, 46–47, 47, 73, 83, 85, 90, 91, 94, 98, 104, 126, 146; and Dan Bankhead 95; and first legal Sunday game in NY 62; and Jackie Robinson 89, 94; and Mexican League 92; televising games of 93–94; trademark dispute over use of name by bar 145
Brooklyn Eckfords (NABBP): and first fixed game 14, 17
Brooklyn Royal Giants (ECL) 74
Brooklyn Tip Tops (FL) 64
Brooklyn Wonders (PL) 36
Brosnan, Jim 119
Brotherhood Manifesto 34–35
Brotherhood of Professional Base Ball Players 40; formation of 18, 32–33; Players' League, formation of 18, 34–35, 36–37
Brouthers, Dan 33
Brown, Bobby 139
Brown, Fred 222n41
Brown, Joe E. 239n119
Brown, Kevin: and $105 million contract 154; named in Mitchell Report 151, 162
Brown, Mordecai "Three-Finger" 56, 222n35
Brown, Rachael: Black Sox grand jury indicts 66
Brown University 26
Browne, Byron 242n37
Browning, Jim 242n37
Brush, John T.: and attempt to bribe umpires 50; salary classification scheme of 18, 34; and World Series rules 46
Buckley, William 20–21
Budit, Tanit 164–65
Bueno, Jennifer 159
Buffalo Bisons (NL) 23
Buffalo Blues (FL) 58
Buge, Donald 98
Buhler, Bill: patent for "billy goat" catcher's mask 127, patent for lightweight chest protector 128
Bulkeley, Morgan 226n29; Congress, one of 3 MLB executives to serve in 223n41; first president of National League 25
Bunning, Jim: Congress, one of 5 players to serve in 222n41; co-sponsor of antitrust exemption bill 148; PEDs—legislation introduced by 160, testimony about 159
burial sites: of Jim Thorpe 103, 168; of William Hulbert 29
Burns, Bill "Sleepy": Black Sox grand jury indicts 66
Burns, Ken 109
Burton, Harold (Justice) 102
Busch, August, Jr., "Gussie" 101
Bush, George H.W. 142
Bushel, Hyman 74

Butler, Dick 105
Butterworth, Robert 148
Buzas, Joe 157
Byron, William 86

Cabell, Enos 136
Cain, Bob 100
California Angels (AL) 130, 160; and Alex Johnson suspension 121–22; see also Los Angeles Angels (AL)
Camilli, Dolph 157
Caminiti, Ken: admits PED use 151, 158
Campanella, Roy 104
Campanis, Al: catcher's glove patented by 126
Candlestick Park 126, 147
Cannon, Raymond J.: and civil suits by Black Sox players 71; National Baseball Players Association, formed by 73–74
Cannon, Robert C. 73; as legal advisor of MLBPA 114
Canseco, José 151, 158; PED testimony of 159; steroid use, first player publicly accused of 139
Caray, Harry 49
Carey, Max 109
Carson, Johnny 164
Carter, Joseph 77–78
Casey, Hugh 98
"Casey at the Bat" (Ernest Thayer) (poem): in *Congressional Record* 138; paraphrased or mentioned in court decision 135, 168
Cash, Dave 121
Cashen, Frank 132
catchers: lawsuit over defective mask 108; patents for equipment of—chest protectors 31, 128, 143, glove 126, mask 26, 33, 34, 74–75, 127
Catholic Youth Organization 94
Catto, Octavious V. 21
Caylor, Oliver Perry 28
Cedar Rapids Raiders (WL-A) 83
Celler, Emanuel 90, 99
centennial of baseball: commemorative stamp for 85; copyright of logo for 84
Cepeda, Orlando: and dispute over licensing agreement 116
Chadwick, Henry: and Mills Commission 48–49
Chalmers Motor Co.: and 1910 AL batting race 52
Champion, Aaron Burt 19
Chandler, Albert B. "Happy" 78; Congress, one of 3 MLB executives to serve in 223n41; election and resignation as commissioner 89, 90–91, 98; and Mexican League 96, 96–97; and suspension of Leo Durocher 94
Charlotte Knights (So. League) 146
Chase, Charles 25
Chase, Hal: accused of game-fixing 64; Black Sox grand jury indicts 66; jumps from AL to FL 57–58
Chattanooga Lookouts (So. Ass'n) 33, 79
Chavez Ravine (Los Angeles) 105
Chicago Bears (NFL) 235n94
Chicago Cubs (NL) 49–50, 50, 60, 64, 64, 81, 85, 97, 102, 103, 115, 120, 134, 138, 145, 165; first black coach 108–09; first female front-office executive 76; injunction prevents division shift of 144; lawsuits against—by Ad Gumbert over reserve clause 41–42, by Boyd Tepler for negligence 99; and Wrigley Field expansion dispute 169
Chicago Defender (newspaper) 63
Chicago Pirates (PL) 36
Chicago Tribune (newspaper) 52, 227n57
Chicago Whales (FL) 60; and Bill Killefer litigation 56–57
Chicago White Sox (AL) 42–43, 58, 62, 77, 78, 93, 95, 106, 145, 166, 168; and civil suits by Black Sox players 71, 75; and World Series of 1919 (Black Sox scandal) 45, 65, 66
Chicago White Stockings (NAPBBP): contractual dispute over Davy Force 23
Chicago White Stockings (NL) see Chicago Cubs (NL)
Cicotte, Eddie: acquitted in Black Sox criminal trial 70; Black Sox grand jury 65, 66; expelled from baseball 70; suspended by Comiskey 65
"Cincinnati Agreement" (1914) 56
Cincinnati Red Stockings 22, 27, 28, 33; first openly all-professional team 18, 19; and Sam Wise revolving dispute 29
Cincinnati Reds (NL) 35, 44, 57, 64, 70, 171; expelled from NL 27–28; reserve clause ruled unenforceable 57; and World Series of 1919 (Black Sox scandal) 66
Citi Field (NY) 109–10
City Item (Phil. newspaper) 23
Civil War 13–14, 18, 20, 44, 49
Claridge Casino Hotel (Atlantic City) 130
Clark, Jack 142–43
Clark, Stephen C. 20
Clarke, Bill 42
Clemens, Roger: Congressional testimony of 162; and McNamee defamation suit 169; named in Mitchell Report 152, 162; perjury trial of 162
Clement, Amanda: first woman to umpire professional game 249n220
Clemente, Roberto 121, 129
Cleveland, Grover 78
Cleveland Blues (NL) 26
Cleveland Broncos see Cleveland Indians (AL)
Cleveland Buckeyes (NAL) 153
Cleveland Indians (AL) 43, 81, 114, 122, 124; and Chalmers batting race 52; first black manager in MLB 113, 125–26; and integra-

Subject Index 301

tion of AL 89, 94–95; Napoleon Lajoie plays for 43; and signing of Bob Feller 68, 83; and tax case over collusion settlement 156
Cleveland Naps (AL) *see* Cleveland Indians (AL)
Cleveland Spiders (NL): and Sunday baseball law 40–41, 41
Clines, Gene 121
Clinton, Bill: remarks about Jackie Robinson by 235n28
Cobb, Amanda 48
Cobb, Ty 67, 69, 86; and 1910 AL batting race 52–53; Congressional testimony on reserve clause by 99; father, relationship with and shooting of 48; suspension of, leads to first-ever player strike 53–54
Cobb, W.H. 48
Cochrane, Mickey 77
Cohn, Michael 160
collective bargaining agreement (CBA) *see* basic agreement
collusion: by owners—Collusion I 137–38, 140, Collusion II 138–39, Collusion III 141–42, damages settlement 142–43, 156; CBA provision against 112, 114, 125, 138, 139; and Donald Fehr 95–96, 142; tax treatment of settlement damages 156
Colorado Silver Bullets 138, 147
Columbia Broadcasting System (CBS) 93–94
Columbia Law School 31–32, 93
Columbian League 55
Columbus Red Birds (AA, minor) 35
Comeback Player of the Year 108
Comiskey, Charles A.: and civil suits by Black Sox players 71, 75; suspends Black Sox players 65
commissioner of baseball: election and resignation of—A. Bartlett Giamatti 84, 139–40, Albert B. "Happy" Chandler 89, 90–91, 98, Bowie Kuhn 76, 117, Fay Vincent 145, Kenesaw Mountain Landis (first) 45, 66, Peter Ueberroth 117, Rob Manfred 152, 156, 167–68, William Eckert 117; first to testify before Congress 100; powers of—best interests of baseball 100, 127, 127, 128, 129, established by National Agreement of 1921, 68, grievance resolution removed as 120, interpreted by court 79–80, 144; William Howard Taft, refuses offer to become 51; *see also* names of commissioners
Congress, U.S. 73; A.B. "Happy" Chandler, remains senator after elected commissioner 91; "Casey at the Bat" in *Congressional Record* 138; confirmation of player as U.S. ambassador by 168; Congressional Baseball Game 51, 130, 246n125; firsts—player to be member of 50, testimony by player 97, by commissioner 100; hearings conducted by—antitrust exemption (Estes Kefauver) 106, monopolies and antitrust exemption (Emmanuel Celler) 90, 99, PEDs 151, 158, 159–60, 162, Supreme Court confirmation of Roberts 160, Supreme Court confirmation of Sotomayor 163, violence in professional sports 132; Kenesaw Mountain Landis impeachment attempt by 67, 68–69; Little League chartered by 110; players serving in 222n41; report on antitrust exemption by 128
Congress, U.S., statutes and resolutions of: Anabolic Steroids Control Act 142, 143; "Baseball Trust" resolution 53; Clayton Act 96, 148, 168; Curt Flood Act of 1998, 148, 151, 153–54, 169; Integrity in Professional Sports Act (proposed) 160; Labor-Management Relations Act 162; Native American Graves Protection and Repatriation Act 168; Sherman Antitrust Act 37, 72, 118, 134, 168; Sports Violence Act 132
Congress, U.S., witnesses testifying before: Brian McNamee 162; Casey Stengel 106; Curt Schilling 160; Donald Fehr 158; Ford Frick 100; Frank Thomas 160; Hank Peters 132; Jackie Robinson 97; Jim Bunning 159; Joe Garagiola 102–103; John Roberts 160; José Canseco 159; Mark McGwire 160; Rafael Palmeiro 160; Rob Manfred 158; Roger Clemens 162; Sammy Sosa 159
Congress Hotel (Chicago) 63
Connecticut General Life Ins. Co. 161
Connelly Containers 104
Connor, John 33
Constitution, U.S.: Commerce & Supremacy clauses—dispute over Braves move to Atlanta 115; Due Process clause—dispute over purchase of Giants 144, female reporter in locker room 128–29; First Amendment—fantasy baseball use of names and stats 161, right of publicity defeated by 157, 13th Amendment—Curt Flood suit over reserve clause 118, 119
Continental League 90, 106–07, 109
contracts: action for breach of—Brocail 162–63, Finley 125, Furillo 107, Jackson 71, 75, Magee 64, Ruth 65, Vincent 148–49; disputes over "revolving" players—Force 23, Lajoie 112, 113–14, Pickett 37; of Eddie Gaedel 100; George Sisler contract signed as minor voided 58–59; Koufax/Drysdale joint holdout over 112, 113–14; standard player contract, revised by Cincinnati Agreement 56; unenforceable for lack of mutuality—Bennett 29–30, Chase 57–58, Ewing 36, Hallman 36, Grant 37, Ward 35; *see also* licensing
Contreras, José 165
Conyers, John 132
Cook, Stanton 250n230
Coolidge, Calvin: first president to attend opening game of World Series 75

Coolidge, Grace: interest in baseball 229n49
Cooper, Irving Ben (Judge) 119
Cooperstown, NY 48–49, 85; ordinance prohibits ball playing in 14–15
Coors Brewing Co.: and Newcombe suit over beer ad 146; sponsorship of Colorado Silver Bullets 147
Copley Plaza Hotel (Boston) 77
copyright and trademark: copyright dispute over—game telecasts 136, Yankees top hat logo 164–65; copyright of—centennial logo 84, "Take Me Out to the Ballgame" 49; preemption of publicity rights by 136, 149; trademark dispute over—autograph bats 82–83, Baby Ruth candy bar 78–79, Brooklyn Dodger name 145, "evil empire" phrase for Yankees 165, name of mascot 156–57, Ruth's image 140–41
Corriden, John 52
courts see judicial system
Cover, Robert 129
Crane, S.J. 55
Craver, William (Bill): first sale of player, involvement in 24; and Louisville Grays scandal 25–26
Creamer, Joseph 50
cricket 13, 16, 21, 21, 214n1, 221n18
criminal trials and convictions of: Alabama Pitts 82; Amanda Cobb 48; Barry Bonds 152, 170; Benny Kauff 69; Black Sox players 67, 70; Blackie Schwamb 98; Curtis Strong (Pittsburgh Drug Trials) 135–36; Denny McLain 118–19; Ferguson Jenkins 131–32; Frank Francisco 159; Fred Saigh 101; George Steinbrenner 124–25; John McGraw 64; Kirk Radomski 162; Pete Rose 141; Ruth Ann Steinhagen 97; Violet Popovich [Valli] 81
Cronin, Joe: sued by fired umpires 116, 121
Crosby, Bing 108
Crosetti, Frankie 157
Croteau, Julie 147; first woman player and coach in NCAA 138; and sex discrimination lawsuit 138
Cullenbine, Roy 85
Cummings, Midre 154
Curt Flood Act of 1998 148, 151, 153–54, 169
"Curt Flood Rule" (5- and10-year rule) 123
Curtiss Candy Co. 78–79
Cy Young Award see pitchers

Dalton, Harry 132
Damn Yankees (motion picture) 82
Davis, Geena 165
Dawson, Andre 166
Day, Doris 100
Day, Larraine 94
Day, William R. (Justice) 54–55
defamation 64–65; Bob Uecker sued for 164; Brian McNamee sues Clemens for 169; Campanella doctor sues O'Malley for 104; fired umpires sue MLB for 116; Gehrig sues Jimmy Powers for 86; George Steinbrenner sued for, by umpire 136–37; Newcombe suit over beer ad 146; sleeping fan sues TV announcers for 170; Ward sues Ban Johnson for 52
DeMarco, Tony 134
Denver Zephyrs (Int'l League) 146
Deppert, John, Jr. 33
Des Moines Demons (WL-A): and signing of Bob Feller 68, 83
Detroit Tigers 22, 43, 99, 118, 160; Doug Brocail sues for arm injury 162–63; free agency granted minor league players of 68, 85–86; players strike over Cobb suspension 53–54
Detroit Wolverines (NL) 28, 29, 30, 33
Devlin, James A.: and Louisville Grays scandal 25–26
Devyr, Thomas: and first fixed game 17
DiMaggio, Joe: first $100,000 annual player contract 96; and marriage to Marilyn Monroe 103–04
discrimination in baseball: racial—first recorded act of segregation 21, La. antimixing statute 105, NABBP rejection of black teams 21, NY legislative resolutions regarding 87, 91, pension benefits for Negro League players 152–53; sexual—high school baseball 138, Little League baseball 113, 124, 147, and stadium giveaways 160, professional baseball 143–44; see also integration of baseball
divorce see family law
Dixon, Delores 74
Doak, William L. 73
Doby, Larry: AL integrated by 89, 94–95; second African American manager 95
Dodger Stadium (Los Angeles): acquisition of property for 105
Donahue, Margaret 76
Dorsey, Joe 105
Doubleday, Abner 44, 48–49, 84
Doubleday, Abner Demas 222n28
Douglas, William O. (Justice) 123, 129
Dowd, John: and Pete Rose investigation 140, 171
Dressen, Charlie 234n24
Dreyfuss, Barney: and first World Series 46; and George Sisler contract 58–59
drugs: amphetamines, random testing for 161; and Ferguson Jenkins 131–32; joint prevention and treatment program 158; Pittsburgh drug trials 113, 135–36, 136; steroids included in policy about 143; see also performance enhancing drugs
Drysdale, Don: and contract holdout 112, 113–14, 138
Drysdale, Ginger 113
Duffy, Edward: and first fixed game 17

Subject Index   303

Durocher, Leo: suspended by Happy Chandler 94

Eastern Colored League *see* Negro Leagues
Eastern League 43
Ebbets, Charles 46
Ebbets Field 235n28
Eckert, William D. 117
Edgewater Beach Hotel (Chicago) 97
Elberfeld, Kid 79
elections 86
Ellis, Dock 121
Engel, Joe 79
Engle, Eleanor 79, 101
equipment: baseballs—cork-centered, first patent for 51, first manufacturers of 24; batting cage, first patent for 48; bats—dispute over use of player names on 82–83; catcher's glove with fluorescent stripe, patent for 126; catcher's mask—first patent for 26, suit over defective 108, with horizontal crossbars, patent for 74–75; with inflatable padding, patent for 33, with "open view" patent for 34, with throat protector, patent for 127; chest protector—inflatable and padded, patent for 31, lightweight, patent for 128, with hinged shoulder flap, patent for 143; fielder's glove with webbing, patent for 73; head protector for batters, first patent for 47; shin guards, use pioneered by Bresnahan 47
ESPN 170
Evans, Billy 51
Everyone Loves Raymond (television program) 250n262
Ewing, William "Buck" 57; reserve clause in contract unenforceable 18–19, 36
expansion: of AL—Angels and Senators 107, Blue Jays 126, Pilots 122; compensation to PCL for dispute over 122; Congressional report in response to 128; and Continental League 90, 106–07; of NL—Colt .45's and Mets 106, Padres 122; PCL seeks to become major league 91–92

Faber, Red 109
Fallon, William 64
family law: marriage and divorce of DiMaggio and Monroe 103–04; paternity suit against—Babe Ruth 74, Hugh Casey 98; wife swap by Yankee pitchers 123–24
fans *see* spectators and fans
fantasy baseball *see* baseball themed games
Fargo-Moorhead Twins (Northern League) 83
Faria, James 114
Farley, James 85
Farmer, Walter M. 75
Fashion Race Course (NY) 16–17
Fed. Baseball Club of Balt., Inc. v. Nat'l League of Prof'l Baseball Clubs 15, 144, 154; and antitrust exemption 45, 71–72; Congressional hearing on 99; Francis Richter critique of 72–73; upheld by—*Flood* 112, 119, 122–23, 153, *Toolson* 102
Fed. League of Prof'l Baseball Clubs v. Nat'l League of Prof'l Baseball Clubs: FL antitrust suit against O.B. 58
Federal courts *see* judicial system
Federal League (FL) 60, 69, 72; antitrust suit against O.B. 44, 58, 59; Armando Marsans enjoined from jumping to 57; formation and cessation of 44, 45, 55–56, 56; Hal Chase allowed to jump to 57–58; major league status of 217n31; and peace agreement with O.B. 59
Federal Trade Commission 104
Feeney, Charles "Chub" 121
Fehr, Donald: birth and career of 95–96, 163–64; and collusion settlement 142; and testimony on drug testing 158; as MLBPA executive director 134–35, 163–64; and stiffer penalties for PED use 160
Fehr, Steve 134
Feinberg, George 74
Feller, Bob 105; dispute over signing of 68, 83
Felsch, Oscar "Happy": acquitted in Black Sox criminal trial 70; Black Sox grand jury indicts 66; civil suit against White Sox 71; expelled from baseball 70; suspended by Comiskey 65
Fenway Park (Boston) 55, 77
Fifth Avenue Hotel (NYC) 34
Fingers, Rollie 127, 129
Finley, Charles O. 76; and Hunter grievance over contract 125; Kuhn voids sale of players by 127, 129
First Amendment *see* Constitution, U.S
firsts: all-star game 16–17; base hit in NL 16; baseball card sold for $1 million 155; known mention of baseball 14; manufacturer of baseballs 24; openly all-professional team 19; postage stamp related to baseball 85; written constitution for club team 15; *see also* agents; Congress, U.S.; gambling and game fixing; integration of baseball; judicial system; leagues; motion pictures; patents; president, U.S.; salaries; unions in baseball; women in baseball; work stoppages
Fisk, Carlton 140
Fitzgerald, Thomas 23
Flood, Curt 76, 153; and suit against MLB 118, 119, 122–23
Flood v. Kuhn 50, 112, 118, 119, 122–23, 144, 151
Florida: and dispute over Giants move to 148
Florida State University 168
Forbes Field (Pittsburgh) 84, 120
Force, Davy 23

Ford Motor Co. 93
Fordham Law School 46
Foster, Andrew "Rube": and Negro National League 63, 75
Foster, Willie 75
foul balls: injuries from *see* spectators and fans; retention by spectators 70
franchise movement: and antitrust 144, 148, 154–55, 168–69; Curt Flood Act does not cover 169; minor league rule regarding 146; specific moves or proposed moves: Athletics—toKansas City 90, to San José, 168–69; Braves—to Milwaukee 90, to Atlanta 115; Dodgers to Los Angeles 47, 90, 105; Giantsto—Florida 144, 148, to San Francisco 90, 225n10, to Toronto 126; Pilots to Milwaukee 135; Twins to North Carolina 154–55
Francisco, Frank 159
Frank, Jerome (Judge) 96, 102
Frank H. Fleer Corp. 104
Frankfurter, Felix (Justice) 129
Fraternity of Professional Baseball Players of America (Players' Fraternity) 54; and Cincinnati Agreement with National Commission 56
fraud 149, 162
Frazee, Harry 62–63
free agency: arbitration ruling creates 126; and collusion cases 137–38, 138–39, 140, 141–42, 142–43, 156; compensation for signing of 131, 131–32, 133; granted by CBA 127; and Hunter-Finley grievance 125; joint committee to study 131, 132; and Landis rulings 68, 83, 85–86; *see also* Flood v. Kuhn, Messersmith-McNally case
Freedman, Andrew 40
Frick, Ford 87, 90, 91, 100, 101, 107; and Furillo contract dispute 107
Friend, Hugo (Judge) 70, 73
Frisch, Frank 109
Fuchs, Emil "Judge" 77, 231n95
Fuller, Jenny 124
Fultz, David L. 54
Furillo, Carl: and contract dispute with Dodgers 107

Gaedel, Eddie 99–100
Gaetti, Gary 142
Gallagher, Thomas 53
Gamble, Oscar 137
gambling and game fixing 45, 67; bribery of umpires 49–50; Chalmers batting race dispute 52; first—fixed game 14, 17, player permanently banned for 24; Louisville Grays scandal 25–26; Magee claim about 1918 game 64; statutes about—Illinois sports anti-corruption 73, New York anti-pooling 25; suspensions and expulsions for—Denny McLain suspended for bookmaking 118–19, first player permanently banned for 24, Mays and Mantle banned for casino jobs 130, Pete Rose for gambling 113, 140, 171; *see also* Black Sox scandal
Gandil, Chick 65; acquitted in Black Sox criminal trial 70; Black Sox grand jury indicts 66; expelled from baseball 70
Garagiola, Joe 102–03
Gardella, Danny: and antitrust suit against baseball 90, 96, 97
Garvey, Steve 143; and collusion settlement claim 156
Gates, Edward 57
Gehrig, Lou 69, 79, 141; sues Jimmy Powers for defamation 86
Geisler, Jerry 104
General Foods 93
General Mills 84
George H. Ruth Candy Co. 78–79
George Washington University 35
Georgetown University 82
Georgia Tech 156–57
Gera, Bernice: first woman umpire at Class A 249n220
Giamatti, A. Bartlett 139; birth, death, and career of 84, 140; and Pete Rose 113, 140
Giambi, Jason 151, 162
Giblin, John 24
Gibson, Kirk 138, 140
Gilbert, Mark 168
Giles, Warren 101
Gill, Lewis M. 120; and Alex Johnson case 121–22
Gillespie, Ray 92
Gilmore, James A. 59, 60
Gionfriddo, Al: and right of publicity action 157
Goetz, Raymond: Alex Johnson suspension overturned by 131
Goldberg, Arthur 61, 118
Gonzaga University 108
Gorman, Arthur Pue 226n29
Gorman, George 70
Graceland Cemetry 29
Grand Central Hotel (NYC) 25
Grant, Ulysses "Frank" 37
Graves, Abner 49
Gray, William 31
Grebey, Ray: and Basic Agreement of 1980 131; of 1981 133; and 1981 strike 132, 133
Green, Elijah "Pumpsie" Jr.: integrates Boston Red Sox 81, 106
"Green Light Letter" 68, 86–87
Greenberg, Hank 96, 119
Gregg, Hal 95
Gregory, John J. (Judge) 75
Gretzky, Wayne 155
Griffith, Calvin 220n189
Griffith, Clark 63, 233n135; and Protective Association of Professional Baseball Players 42
Griffith Stadium (Washington, D.C.) 75

Subject Index

Grimes, Burleigh 109
Grove, Robert "Lefty" 77
Gumbert, Addison "Ad": reserve clause upheld in suit for lost wages 41–42

Haelan Laboratories 102, 104
Haldeman, John A. 25
Haldeman, Walter 25
Hall, George: and Louisville Grays scandal 25–26
Hall of Fame *see* National Baseball Hall of Fame and Museum
Hallman, Bill: contract lacks mutuality, unenforceable 19, 36
Hand, Learned (Judge) 52, 96
Hanks, Tom 165
Hanlon, Edward "Ned" 33, 137
Hanna Manufacturing Co. 82–83
Hannagan, Steve 84
Hannegan, Robert E. 101, 233n135
Harding, Warren G. 69
Harmony Conference: leads to first National Agreement 30
Harrelson, Bud 250n262
Harridge, William 87, 91; Gaedel contract voided by 100
Harris, Bucky 229n49
Harrisburg Senators (Interstate) 101
Harrison, Benjamin: first president to attend MLB game 40; signs Sherman Antitrust Act 37
Hart, James A. 42
Harvard University 26, 50
Hawaii Islanders (PCL) 98
Hayashi, Patrick: and dispute over Bonds home-run ball 157
Hayes, J. William 113–14
Hayhurst, E. Hicks 21
Headin' Home (motion picture) 65
Hearst, William Randolph 138
Hedges, Robert Lee: owner sued for firing manager 52
Hendricks, Jack 212n21
Henricksen, Keith, and Kent 120
Hernandez, Jackie 121
Hernandez, Keith 136
Herrmann, August "Garry": and George Sisler contract 58; and NL/AL peace agreement 44, 45; and World Series of 1919 (Black Sox scandal) 66
Heydler, John 50, 52, 64
Hickok Belt 117
Hickory Rebels (Tar Heel League) 82
Hilldale Daisies (ECL) 74
Hillerich and Bradsby Co. 82–83
Hodges, Gil 110
Hoerner, Joe 242n37
Holland, John 108
Holmes, Oliver Wendell, Jr. (Justice) 15; decision in *Federal Baseball* 71–72

Hoover, Herbert 68, 79
Hopper, DeWolf: "Casey at the Bat" first public recitation by 138
Horner, Bob 143
Hornsby, Rogers: tax case of 80
Horowitz, Frederic 166
Hotel Carlos (Chicago) 81
Hotel Commodore (NYC) 105
Houston Astros (NL; AL) [Colt .45's] 130, 134, 162, 163; and Astroturf 114–15; and Bagwell disability insurance claim 161; as expansion franchise 106; first million-dollar player contract 130–31
Houston Oilers (NFL) 115
Huggins, Miller: lawyer-manager 167, 212n21; replaces Roger Bresnahan as Cardinals' manager 55
Hulbert, William A. 27, 29; and Davy Force contractual dispute 23; and formation of NL 18, 24–25
Hundley, Cecil 115
Hundley, Randy: tax case of 115
Hunter, Jim "Catfish": and grievance over Finley breach of contract 125
Hurley, Ed 100
Hurst, Tim 40
Huston, Tillinghast L'Hommedieau 62–63, 63

Idelson, Jeff 166
Indianapolis Defender (newspaper) 63
Indianapolis Freeman (newspaper) 63
injuries: Boyd Tepler suit against Cubs for 99; Carl Furillo salary claim for 107; Doug Brocail suit against Tigers for 162–63; Jeff Bagwell disability insurance claim for 161; John Roseboro suit for defective mask 108; *see also* negligence, spectators and fans
insurance: Bagwell disability claim 161
integration of baseball: African American major league firsts—in American League 89, 94–95, broadcaster 139, coach 108–09, league president 139–40, lineup 121, manager 113, 125–26, pitcher 95, player 26, player in 20th century (J. Robinson) 89, 94, umpire 114; first game between black and white teams 22–23; first Japanese player in MLB 110–11; Frank Grant plays for integrated team 37; Pumpsie Green integrates Boston Red Sox 106; Jackie Robinson signs with Montreal Royals 89, 91
internet: use by Major League Baseball Advanced Media 152; mlb.com domain name acquired by MLB 155; and statute of limitations 164

Jackson, Joe "Shoeless Joe": acquitted in Black Sox criminal trial 70; Black Sox grand jury 65, 66; civil suit against White Sox 71, 75; expelled from baseball 70; perjury of 75; suspended by Comiskey 65

Jackson, Thomas 74
Janney, Stuart 60
Japanese players and teams: first player in MLB 110–11
Jenkins, Ferguson: criminal conviction and suspension of 131–32
Jennings, Hughie: birth and career of 22; forms substitute team when Tigers strike 53; lawyer-manager in HOF 167; and Protective Association of Professional Baseball Players 42
Jethroe, Sam: and pension benefits for Negro Leaguers 152–53
Jim Thorpe (PA) 103, 168
Jobe, Frank 128
John, Tommy 128, 140
Johnson, Alex: suspension by Angels overturned by arbitrator 121–22
Johnson, Byron Bancroft "Ban" 45, 61; and Carl Mays suspension 63; and Chalmers batting race 52; criticism of Kenesaw Mountain Landis by 67; and formation of AL 19, 42; and George Sisler contract dispute 226n112; Ty Cobb suspension leads to first player strike 53–54; Ward's defamation suit against 52; and World Series of 1919 (Black Sox scandal) 66
Johnson, Edwin C. 102–103
Johnson, Frederic A. 96
Johnson, George H. "Chief": reserve clause in contract unenforceable 57
Johnson, Jerry 242n37
Johnson, Lyndon 110
Johnson, Walter 51
Johnstone, James: attempt to bribe as umpire 50; patent for catcher's mask 74–75
Jones, Charley: suit for back pay 27
Jones, Cleon 250n262
Jones, James C. 68
Judge, Joe 81–82
judicial system: baseball references in court opinions 50, 123, 135; first decision—about injury from foul ball 55, with reference to baseball 21, of U.S. Supreme Court related to baseball 31; first litigation—challenging action of National Commission 61, use by O.B. to settle dispute 29; judges compared to umpires 160
Julian Messner, Inc. 110
Jurges, Billy: and shooting incident 81

Kansas City Athletics (AL) *see* Oakland Athletics (AL); Philadelphia Athletics (AL)
Kansas City Blues (AA) 55
Kansas City Cowboys (AA) 37
Kansas City Monarchs (NNL, NAL) 74, 91, 108
Kansas City Packers (FL) 57
Kansas City Royals (AL) 134; and injury to fan from hot dog toss 166
Kaplan, David 148–49
Kauff, Benny: suspended by Landis 69–70
Keefe, Tim 138, 218n117
Keenan, James 74
Kefauver, Estes 106
Kekich, Mike 123–24
Kennett, William H. 27–28
Keyser, Lee 83
Killefer, William: reserve clause in contract unenforceable 56–57
Killilea, Henry 46
Kiner, Ralph 103
Klein, Lou 108
Klem, Bill: attempt to bribe as umpire 50
Knickerbocker Base Ball Club of New York 13, 15, 123
Koufax, Sandy 111; and contract holdout 112, 113–14, 138; poem inspired by 109
Kozinski, Alex (Judge) 170
KQV Broadcasting Co.: and dispute over broadcasting Pirates games 84
Kramer, Louis 39
Kranepool, Ed 250n262
Krauthoff, Louis C. 38
Kruk, John 170
Kubek, Tony 109
Kuhn, Bowie 122; birth and career of 76, 117; and female reporter in locker room 128; Finley player sale voided by 127, 129; Flood suit against 118, 119, 122–23; and Hunter-Finley arbitration decision 125; lockout ended by 126–27; suspensions—Alex Johnson 121–22, Denny McLain 118–19, Ferguson Jenkins 131, George Steinbrenner 125, Mickey Mantle 130, Ted Turner 128, Willie Mays 130

La Russa, Tony: lawyer-manager 167, 212n21
Labatt Brewing Co. 126
Ladd, Ann 164
Lajoie, Napoleon 57; and Chalmers batting race 52–53; enjoined from playing for Athletics 43
Landes, Stan 121
Landis, Kenesaw Mountain 46, 63, 87; birth, career & death of 19–20, 66, 68, 89, 90; Bob Feller, signing dispute resolved by 68, 83; and centennial postage stamp 85; commissioner of baseball—first 45, 66, powers established 45, 68; Congress attempts to impeach 67, 68–69; and FL antitrust suit against O.B. 44, 58, 59; Fred Bennett, resolves dispute over rights to 79–80; free agency rulings of 68, 83, 85–86; and military service of players in World War II 68, 86–87, 87; and prisoner minor league contract 82; resignation as federal judge 69; suspensions and expulsions of—Babe Ruth 67, 71, Benny Kauff 69–70, Black Sox players 67, 70, 71, Lee Magee 64; voids contract of woman pitcher 79

Subject Index 307

Lanier, Max 97
Lanigan, Ernest 31
Lantos, Tom 138
Lardner, Ring 52
Law, John 82
Law, Ron 239n134
Law, Rudy 239n134
Law, Vance 2393n134
Law, Vernon 107–08
lawyers in baseball: Alfred Austrian, attorney for Chicago White Sox 65; C. Orrick Bishop, drafts constitution of National League 25; Christy Walsh, first player agent 69; Donald Fehr, attorney for MLBPA 95, 164; Edward Gates, attorney for FL 57; Elisha Scott, drafts NNL constitution 63; first openly all-professional team includes many 19; Frederic A. Johnson, attorney for Danny Gardella 96; George Wharton Peppe, attorney for O.B. in *Federal Baseball* case 72, drafts commissioner's powers 68; Harry Taylor, legal counsel for Protective Association of Professional Baseball Players 42; J. Norman Lewis, represents MLBPA 103; J. William Hayes, represents Koufax/Drysdale in holdout 113–14; John Dowd investigation of Pete Rose 140; John Reynolds, attorney for umpires 121; lawyer-managers 167, 212n21; Lewis M. Gill, first impartial grievance arbitrator 120; managers with JD or bar admission 22; Michael Weiner, attorney for MLBPA 164; Morgan, Lewis and Bockius firm, relationship with MLB 155–56; players and executives as, Aaron Burt Champion 19, Abraham G. Mills 49, Bowie Kuhn 76, David L. Fultz 54, Fred Saigh 101, Gina Satriano 147, Hughie Jennings 22, 167, James "Orator" O'Rourke 15–16, John Montgomery Ward 31–32, 167, Larry MacPhail 35, Miller Huggins 55, 167, Moe Berg 93, Muddy Ruel 78, Robert Manfred 152, 167, Tony La Russa 167, Walter O'Malley 46, Wesley Branch Rickey 28, 167; Raymond J. Cannon, forms National Baseball Players Association 73–74; Richie Phillips, lawyer for umpires 129; Robert C. Cannon, legal advisor of MLBPA 114; William A. Shea, stadium named for 109; William R. Wheaton, codifies Knickerbocker rules 15
Lazzeri, Tony 100
League Championship Series (LCS) 120–21
A League of Their Own (motion picture) 147, 165
leagues: contraction halted by injunction 151, 157–58; first—player to serve as president of NL 50, 51, league of professional teams 23, salary cap imposed by 32; formation and cessation of—All-American Girls Professional Baseball League 147, American Association 28, 39, American League 19, 42–43, Continental League 90, 106–07, Eastern Colored League 67, 74, Federal League 44, 45, 55–56, 59, National Association of Base Ball Players 16, National Association of Professional Base Ball Players 18, 23, National Association of Professional Baseball Leagues 43, National League 18, 24–25, Negro National League 63, 67, 75, Players' League 18, 34–35, 37, Union Association 18, 30–31; major league status of 217n31; PCL rejected as major league 91–92; peace agreement between—AA and NL 19, 39, AL and NL 44, 45, FL and O.B. 59, 60; *see also* names of individual leagues
Leland Hotel (Chicago) 43
Leonard, Jeffrey 136
Lewis, Cary B. 63
Lewis, J. Norman 103, 105, 241n19
Lewis, Jerry 239n119
Lewis, John L. 60
libel *see* defamation
licensing: and baseball cards 101–02, 116–17, 134, 155; of baseball centennial logo 84; Cepeda dispute over 116; required for using player names & stats 120; and Wrigley Field expansion dispute 169
Lippincott's Magazine 32
Little League: and Congressional charter 110; girls in 110, 113, 124, 147
lockouts *see* work stoppages
Long, Earl K. 105
Los Angeles: awarded AL expansion franchise 107; move of Dodgers to 105
Los Angeles Angels (AL) 107
Los Angeles Dodgers 47, 103, 108, 109, 111, 114, 117, 126, 126, 127, 139, 157; and Chavez Ravine site for Dodger Stadium 105; and Fernando Valenzuela salary arbitration 134; and Furillo contract dispute 107; and Kevin Brown contract 154; and Koufax/Drysdale contract dispute 113–14; and 1981 World Series 133–34; and parking lot attack on fan 167; and trademark dispute over Brooklyn Dodger name 145
Louisville Colonels (AA) [Eclipse]: and first trade between major and minor league teams 33; purchased by NL as part of peace agreement 19, 39
Louisville Eclipse (AA) *see* Louisville Colonels (AA)
Louisville Grays (NL): game fixing scandal 25–26
Lovitz, Jon 165
Lucas, Henry Van Noye: and Union Association 30–31
Lucchino, Larry 165
Ludtke, Melissa: female reporter sues for locker room access 128–29
Lueker, Frank 53

Lurie, Bob 144
Lynch, William 77

MacArthur, Douglas 137
Mack, Connie 51, 167; and challenge to Sunday baseball law 77, 81; player contract with Pittsburgh Alleghenys approved 38; and Scott Perry dispute 61
Macmillan, Inc. 140
MacPhail, Leland Stanford "Larry," Sr.: birth and career of 35–36; player pension program recommended by 93; radio broadcast moratorium 232n119; and report of Major League Steering Committee 93; and suspension of Leo Durocher 94
MacPhail, Leland Stanford, "Lee," Jr. 36, 135
Madonna 165
Magee, Lee: expelled from baseball 64
Maglie, Sal 97
Magowan, Peter 249n226
Maharg, Billy 54
Mahn, Louis H. 31
Major League (motion picture) 253n59
Major League Baseball (MLB): antitrust suit against—by Curt Flood 118, 119, 122–23, by minor league over televising games 107, by prospective Giants' buyers 144; acquires internet domain name 155; and copyright in game telecasts 136; and Curt Flood Act 153–54; franchise contraction enjoined 157–58; lockouts by owners of—of 1973, 123; of 1976, 126–27; of 1990, 141; NLRB jurisdiction, subject to 118; and pension benefits for Negro Leaguers 152–53; PED use—CBA imposes penalties for 159, joint drug agreement with MLBPA 160–61, Biogenesis investigation and suspensions for 152, 165–66; and umpires strike 129–30; *see also* basic agreement
Major League Baseball Advanced Media 152, 161
Major League Baseball Players Association (MLBPA) 73, 155, 158; and baseball cards 116–17, 134; and collusion grievances 113, 137–38, 138–39, 140, 141–42, 142–43, 156; and Curt Flood Act 153–54; executive directors of—Donald Fehr 95–96, 134–35, 163–64, Marvin Miller 114, Michael Weiner 163–64; and Flood suit 118; formation of 103; and grievances of—Alex Johnson 121–22, Andy Messersmith 112, 126, Catfish Hunter 125, Dave McNally 112, 126, Ferguson Jenkins 131; legal advisors of—J. Norman Lewis 103, Robert C. Cannon 114; and pension benefits for Negro Leaguers 152–53; PED use—CBA imposes penalties for 151, 159, drops opposition to testing for 151, 158, joint drug agreement with MLB 160–61; and rights of players over game telecasts 136; strike by—of 1972 (first) 122; of 1980 131; of 1981 133; of 1985 135; of 1994–95 113, 147, 147–48, 149; *see also* basic agreement
Major League Umpires Association: and umpires strike 129–30
Malamud, Bernard 97
Manfred, Robert "Rob": and Congressional testimony on steroids 158; elected commissioner 152, 156, 167–68; and Pete Rose request for reinstatement 171
Manley, Effa 95
Mann, Arthur 94
Mantle, Mickey 76, 109, 129, 141; banned by Kuhn 130
Manush, Heinie 109
Marcantino, Vito: and resolution to investigate baseball discrimination 91
Marichal, Juan 111
Maris, Roger 109, 129
marriage *see* family law
Marsans, Armando: enjoined from jumping to FL 57
Marshall, Penny 165
Marshall, Thurgood (Justice) 123
Martin, Dean 239n119
Martin, Fred 97
mascots: and foul ball injury caused by 153, 166; trademark dispute over name of 156–57
Massachusetts: and Sunday baseball 77
"Massachusetts Game" 13, 16
Mathews, Eddie 102
Matthews, Gary 128
Mauch Chunk and East Mauch Chunk (PA) 103
Mays, Carl: suspended by Johnson 62–63; trade to Yankees upheld by AL owners 63
Mays, Willie 76, 102, 129; banned by Kuhn 130
McCarthy, Edward 169
McCarver, Tim 242n37
McCourt, Frank 167
McCoy, Benny 85–86
McCredie, Walter "Judge" 231n95
McFarlane, Todd 157
McGeehan, John N. 77–78
McGraw, Bob 227n143
McGraw, John 22, 69, 167; and Lambs Club brawl 64
McGraw, Tug 250n262
McGwire, Mark: and HOF 152; PED testimony of 160
McKeever, Edward 46
McKeever, Stephen 232n119
McKnight, Harmer Denny 28
McLain, Denny: convictions and suspension of 118–19
McLaughlin, George V. 46
McMullin, Fred: acquitted in Black Sox criminal trial 70; Black Sox grand jury indicts 66; expelled from baseball 70; suspended by Comiskey 65

Subject Index 309

McNall, Bruce 155
McNally, Dave *see* Messersmith-McNally Case
McNamee, Brian: Congressional testimony of 162; and defamation suit against Roger Clemens 169
Medal of Freedom 93
Meeker, Edwin 49
Memphis Red Sox (NAL) 95
Merkle, Fred 50
Messersmith, Andy *see* Messersmith-McNally Case
Messersmith-McNally Case 47–48, 112, 126–27; role of Donald Fehr in 95, 135; Seitz arbitration decision 126, 127
Metro, Charlie 108
Metrodome (Minneapolis) 151, 158
Meusel, Bob 71
Mexican League 93; ban of jumpers to 96, 96–97; and injunctions 90, 92
Miami New Times (newspaper) 166
military service: Jackie Robinson, court martial of 68, 87–88; of Moe Berg 93; of Pete Reiser 83; in World War I, players not exempt from 61–62; in World War II—Landis policy 68, 87, Roosevelt's "Green Light Letter" 68, 86–87
Millennium Plan: proposal for reserving players 18, 34
Miller, Marvin J. 60–61, 95, 103, 112, 114, 245n19; and Basic Agreement of 1980 131; of 1981 133; and Hunter–Finley arbitration decision 125; licensing agreement with Topps 116–17; MLBPA executive director, elected as 114; and strike of 1981 132–33, 133
Mills, Abraham G.: and Mills Commission 48–49; and National Agreement of 1883, 30
Mills, Dorothy Seymour 29
Mills Commission: members of 25, 222n29; report of 44, 48–49
Milner, John 136
Milwaukee Brewers (AA, minor) 79–80
Milwaukee Brewers (AL 1970–97; NL 1998– date) 132, 134, 135, 164
Milwaukee Braves (NL): and move to Atlanta 115; *see also* Atlanta Braves (NL); Boston Beaneaters (NL); Boston Braves (NL); Boston Red Stockings (NL)
Milwaukee County Stadium 115
Minneapolis Millers (AA, minor) 106
Minnesota: and antitrust investigation of Twins move to NC 154–55
Minnesota Twins (AL) 163; contraction halted by injunction 151, 157–58; proposed move to NC 154–55; *see also* Washington Senators (1901–60)
Minor League Baseball *see* National Association of Professional Baseball Leagues
minor leagues: arbitration in 43; and Bob Feller contract 68, 83; and Curt Flood Act 154; and franchise movement 146; and integrated team 37, 89, 91; and Landis free agency rulings 68, 83; Millennium Plan for reserving players for minor leagues 34; and National Agreement of 1903, 45–46; and National Association of Professional Baseball Leagues 43; player trade, first between major and minor league teams 33; prisoner's contract to play in 82; televising MLB games threat to 107; and umpire's sex discrimination suit 143–44; women— barred from playing in 101, first to play in 41; *see also* names of leagues
Mr. Belevedere (television program) 253n59
Mitchell, George: and report on PED use 151–52, 161–62
Mitchell, Jackie: first woman to sign pro contract 79, 101
Mizell, Wilmer "Vinegar Bend" 222n41
MLB Network 152
Mogridge, Frank: Pneumatic Head Protector, invented by 47
Monroe, Marilyn: and marriage to Joe DiMaggio 103–04
Monsanto Industries 114
Montanez, Willie 242n37
Montreal Expos (NL) 47, 117, 126, 134, 151, 158
Montreal Royals (Int'l League) 89, 91, 94
Morgan, Lewis and Bockius, LLP 167; relationship with MLB 155–56; transfers internet domain name to MLB 155
Morris, Jack 142
Moses, Robert 47
Moss, Richard 95, 245n97; and first million-dollar player contract 131; and first million-dollar salary arbitration award 134
motion pictures: about baseball—*Damn Yankees* 82, *Headin' Home* 65, *A League of Their Own* 147, 165, *Major League* 253n59, *The Natural* 97, *The Stratton Story* 242n88, *The Winning Team* 100; and Babe Ruth— featured in *Headin' Home* 65, seeks to enjoin use of images in 64–65; first baseball movie added to National Film Registry 165
Motley, Constance Baker (Judge) 145
Mottl, Ron 130, 132
Murakami, Masanori "Mashi": first Japanese player in MLB 110–11
Murphy, Robert Francis: and American Baseball Guild 89, 92, 93
Murray Hill Hotel (NYC) 38
Murtaugh, Danny 121
Murtha, John 138
Musial, Stan: salary limited by Korean War wage controls 98–99

Nagle, Judge 231n95
National Agreement: of 1883, Harmony Conference leads to pact between NL, AA, and

Northwestern League 30; of 1885, signed by NL and AA 32; of 1891—AA withdraws from 38–39; signed by NL, AA, and WL 38; of 1901, established for minor leagues 43; of 1903, signed by AL, NL, and National Association of Professional Baseball Leagues 44, 45–46; of 1921, signed by AL and NL 68

National Association of Base Ball Players (NABBP) 22; and first fixed game 14, 17; formation of 13, 16; rejection of black teams 21

National Association of Professional Base Ball Players (NAPBBP): formation of 18, 23; not classified as major league 217n31

National Association of Professional Baseball Leagues 16, 82, 147; formation of 43; franchise movement rule of 146; Minor League Baseball, name changed to 43; and National Agreement of 1903, 45–46; women, barred from playing by 101

National Baseball Hall of Fame and Museum (HOF) 15; and Barry Bonds 152, 170, 259n108; first president in office to visit 166; Ford C. Frick Award recipients—Joe Garagiola 103, Bob Uecker 253n59; grand opening of 85; MacPhails, only father and son inductees to 36; Moe Berg's military medal, donated to 93; recognizes Pittsfield bylaw as first known reference to game 14; *see also* National Baseball Hall of Fame, individuals inducted in

National Baseball Hall of Fame, individuals inducted in: Andre Dawson 166; Bill Terry 109; Bowie Kuhn 76; Branch Rickey 28, 167; Bruce Sutter 134; Buck Ewing 36; Burleigh Grimes 109; Casey Stengel 109; Catfish Hunter 125; Dan Brouthers 33; Duke Snider 102; Eddie Mathews 102; Ferguson Jenkins 132; Frank Frisch 109; Frank Grant 37; Frank Robinson 231n95; George Wright 22; Harry Wright 22; Heinie Manush 109; Honus Wagner 155; Hughie Jennings 22, 167; ineligible list, rule about 141; Jackie Robinson 94, 102; James O'Rourke 15–16; Jim Bunning 148, 160; John Montgomery Ward 17, 167; Juan Marichal 111; Kenesaw Mountain Landis 20, 66; Larry Doby 95; lawyer-managers elected to 22, 167; Luke Appling 109; Max Carey 109; Mickey Mantle 130; Mike Piazza 144; Miller Huggins 55, 167; Morgan Bulkeley 25; Ned Hanlon 33; Nolan Ryan 131; Red Faber 109; Richie Ashburn 102; Rogers Hornsby 80; Rube Foster 63; Sam Thompson 33; Tim Keefe 222n117; Tony La Russa 167; Ty Cobb 48, 86; Walter Johnson 86; Walter O'Malley 46; Warren Spahn 110; William Hulbert 29; Willie Mays 102, 130; Zack Wheat 109; *see also* National Baseball Hall of Fame and Museum (HOF)

National Baseball Players Association (NBPA) 73–74

National Broadcasting Co. 84

National Collegiate Athletic Association: no-agent rule of 163

National Commission 46; and Cincinnati Agreement with Players' Fraternity 56; created by National Agreement of 1903 19, 45–46; and FL antitrust suit against 58; George Sisler contract voided by 58–59; Scott Perry, enjoined from acting in dispute over 61; replaced by commissioner 66

National Film and Recording Registries: first baseball movie added to 165; "Take Me Out to the Ball Game" added to 49

National Labor Relations Board (NLRB) 133; MLB subject to jurisdiction of 112, 118; and suit by fired umpires 116

National League of Professional Base Ball Clubs *see* National League

National League (NL) and Braves move to Atlanta 115; division shift of Cubs enjoined 144; FL antitrust suit against 58; formation of 24–25; and Giants failed move to Florida 148; liquor sales policy of 27–28; major league status of 217n31; and National Agreement of 1883 30; and National Agreement of 1885 32; and National Agreement of 1891 19, 38; and National Agreement of 1903 19, 44, 45–46; and National Agreement of 1921 68; and peace agreement with AA 19, 39; and peace agreement with AL 19, 44, 45; players jump to Players' League 35; president of—A. Bartlett Giamatti 84, 139, Abraham G. Mills 30, 49, Bill White 139–40, Chub Feeney 121, Ford Frick 87, 91, John Heydler 52, 64, John Tener 50–51, Morgan Bulkeley 25, Nicholas E. Young 38, William Hulbert 29; Richter's "Millennium Plan" endorsed by 34; salary classification scheme adopted by 34; Sunday baseball policy of 27–28

National Organization for Women 124

The Natural (book and motion picture) 97

Navin, Frank 54

Nebraska: and Sunday baseball 39

negligence: and foul ball injuries caused by mascot 153, 166; injured pitcher sues team for 99, 162; Newcombe suit over beer ad 146; and parking lot attack on fan 167; and suit over fan stampede 77–78; *see also* spectators and fans

Negro Leagues 91; Eastern Colored League (ECL), formation of 67, 74; major league pension benefits for former players in 152–53; museum of 109; Negro National League (NNL)—formation and dissolution of 63, 67, 74, 75; Negro World Series 67, 74

Negro National League (NNL) *see* Negro Leagues

Neuhalfen, Mark 143
Neumeier, Elizabeth: first woman to serve as arbitrator 154
New Orleans Pelicans (So. Ass'n) 105
New York: and Sunday baseball 47, 62
New York Baseball Writers Association 87
New York Cuban Stars (ECL) 74
New York Daily News (newspaper) 86
"New York Game" 13, 15, 16
New York Giants (NL) 36, 40, 47, 49–50, 54, 64, 69, 75, 80, 85, 90, 93, 96, 97, 103, 168; and first legal Sunday baseball game in NY 62; and retention of foul balls by spectators 70
New York Giants (PL) 36
New York Jets (NFL) 109
New York Knickerbockers *see* Knickerbocker Base Ball Club of New York
New York Lincoln Giants (ECL) 74
New York Mets (NL) 106, 110, 130, 132, 154; as expansion franchise 106; retired numbers of 110; and right of publicity claim 149
New York Mutuals (NABBP): and first fixed game 14, 17
New York Times (newspaper) 148
New York Yankees 35, 67, 79, 79, 84, 103, 106, 107, 125, 127, 133–34, 137, 146, 154, 162, 170; and Carl Mays trade 62–63, 63; and Catfish Hunter contract 125; copyright dispute over top hat logo 164–65; fan stampede, leads to negligence suit against 77–78; and female reporter in locker room 128–29; first $100,000 player contract in baseball 96; injunction against Mexican League 92; trademark dispute over "evil empire" 165; wife swap by pitchers of 123–24
Newark Eagles (NNL) 95
Newcombe, Don: suit over beer ad 146
Newspaper Enterprise Association (NEA) 52
Nichols, Alfred: and Louisville Grays scandal 25–26
Nicol, Hugh 33
Nicolau, George: collusion decisions of 138–39, 141–42
Niekro, Phil 140, 147
Nightwatch (television program) 139
Nixon, Richard 50, 124, 124
Northwestern League: and National Agreement of 1883, 30
Norwood, Marvin 167
Norworth, Jack 49

Oakland Athletics (AL) 76, 133, 159; and move to San José, 168–69; and sale of players 127, 129; *see also* Kansas City Athletics (AL); Philadelphia Athletics (AL)
Oakland Coliseum [Network Associates Coliseum] 159
Obama, Barack: first president in office to visit HOF 166; nominates Sotomayor to Supreme Court 163

O'Connor, Chuck 142
O'Connor, John: sues St. Louis Browns for breach of contract 52–53
O'Donnell, Rosie 165
Office of Strategic Services (OSS) 93
Ohio: and Sunday baseball 40–41, 41
Oklahoma State University 163
Oliver, Al 121
Oliver, Andy 163
Olympic Ball Club of Philadelphia 13; adopts written constitution 15; and first game between black and white teams 22–23
Olympic Games 103, 117
O'Malley, Peter 139, 250n230
O'Malley, Walter 46–47, 90, 103; and move of Dodgers to Los Angeles 105; role in ending lockout 249n102; slander suit against 104; and televising of games 94
O'Neil, John "Buck": first black coach in MLB 108–09
O'Neill, John C. 24
ordinances *see* statutes, ordinances, and resolutions
ordinances: Boston—allowing Sunday baseball 77; Cooperstown (NY)—prohibiting ball playing in village 14–15; Philadelphia—allowing Sunday baseball 81; Pittsfield (MA)—banning games near meeting house 14
Oriole Park at Camden Yards: dispute over acquisition of land for 137
O'Rourk, Tim 39
O'Rourke, James "Orator" 15–16, 26; jump to Providence prompts reserve clause 27; lawyer-manager 167, 212n21; and National Association of Professional Baseball Leagues 16
Osgood, James H.: patent for baseball cover 31
Ott, Mel 222n40
Owen, Mickey: jumps to Mexican League 92
ownership, transfer of: and blocked purchase of Giants 144; Charles Weeghman acquires Cubs in FL peace agreement 59; Fred Saigh forced to sell Cardinals 101; Helene Britton inherits Cardinals 53, 54; NL acquires AA teams in peace agreement 19, 39; Philip Ball acquires Browns in FL peace agreement 59; Roger Bresnahan purchase of Toledo (AA) 60; Walter O'Malley acquires Dodgers 46–47

Pacific Coast League (PCL) 107, 114; compensation for MLB expansion 122; rejection as major league 91–92
Palace Hotel (Buffalo) 27
Palmeiro, Rafael: named in Mitchell Report 151, 162; suspension for PED use 160; testimony of 160
Pank, J.H. 28

Parker, Dave 136
Parks, Dallas: umpire sues Steinbrenner for defamation 136–37
Parrish, Lance 143
Parrott, Harold 238n24
Pasquel brothers 90, 92
patents: Astroturf 114–15; ball 21–22; base with bell that rings 24; baseball equipment, first for 21–22; baseball—cork-centered, cover for 31, first for 51; batting cage 48; board games 20–21, 21; catcher's glove with fluorescent stripe 126; catcher's mask—first 26, with horizontal crossbars 74–75, with inflatable padding 33, with "open view" 34, with throat protector 127; chest protector—inflatable and padded 31, lightweight 128, with hinged shoulder flap 143; fielder's glove 32; head protector for batters 47
Paul, Ron 130
peace agreement: between AA and NL 19, 39; between AL and NL 19, 44, 45; between FL and O.B. 59
Pennsylvania: and Sunday baseball 14, 77, 81
Pennsylvania State Convention of Base Ball Players 21
pensions: benefits increased by owners 105; CBA increases funding for 127, 131, 141; first program for 89, 93; league-wide strike over 122, 147; Negro League players, benefits for 152–53
Pepe, Maria 124
Pepper, George Wharton 20; attorney for—O.B. in *Federal Baseball* case 72, Phillies in *Killefer* case 57; powers of commissioner, drafted by 68
performance enhancing drugs (PEDs): Anabolic Steroids Control Act becomes law 142; and Biogenesis 152, 165–66; and Barry Bonds 152, 170; and CBAs 151, 158, 164; Congressional hearings on—testimony by Clemens and McNamee 162, testimony by Manfred and Fehr 158; and Donald Fehr 96; joint MLB/MLBPA prevention and treatment program—created 151, 158, penalties increased 160–61, violations of 166; José Canseco—first player publicly accused of steroid use 139; Mitchell Report on use of 151–52, 161–62; penalties for—first inclusion in CBA of 151, 159, "3 strikes and out" imposed 160–61, steroids prohibited by drug policy 143; testing for 96, 151, 158, 159, 164
perjury: and Barry Bonds 170; and Joe Jackson 75; and Roger Clemens 162
Perry, Charles D. 87
Perry, Scott: dispute over sale of 61
Peters, Hank 132
Peterson, Fritz 123–24
Pettitte, Andy 169; Congressional testimony 162; named in Mitchell Report 151, 162

Petty, Lori 165
Pfeffer, Fred: suspended by New York Giants 40
Philadelphia Athletics (AA) 28, 38
Philadelphia Athletics (AL) 43, 51, 86, 90; Napoleon Lajoie, dispute over jump to 43; Scott Perry, dispute over sale to 61; and Sunday baseball law challenge 76–77, 81; *see also* Kansas City Athletics (AL), Oakland Athletics (AL)
Philadelphia Athletics (NAPBBP): and Davy Force contract dispute 23; and first sale of player 24
Philadelphia Athletics (PL) 36, 37
Philadelphia Centennials (NAPBBP): and first sale of player 24
Philadelphia Eagles (NFL) 235n94
Philadelphia Phillies (NL) 36, 81, 97, 121, 132, 133, 135, 139; and Curt Flood trade 118, 119, 122–23; Napoleon Lajoie, dispute over jump from 43; reserve clause in contract unenforceable 56–57
Philadelphia Quakers (NL) *see* Philadelphia Phillies (NL)
Philadelphia Quakers (PL) 36
Phillips, Horace B. 28
Piazza, Mike 144, 154
Piazza, Vince: MLB blocks purchase of Giants by 144
Piazza v. Major League Baseball 144; antitrust exemption holding of—accepted 148, rejected 146, 149–50, 154–55, 168–69
Pickett, John: enjoined from playing for PL 19, 37
Pierce, Eleanor 77–78
Piercy, Bill 71
Pirone, Dorothy Ruth 140
pitchers: Babe Ruth strikes out against woman pitcher 79; Cy Young Award for 107, 134, 146, 152, 162, 169; firsts—black pitcher in MLB 95, $100,000/year contract 114, woman pitch in major-league stadium 147; injured pitcher sues for negligence 99, 162; wife swap by Yankee pitchers 123–24
Pitts, Edwin "Alabama": as prisoner, minor league contract approved by Landis 82
Pittsburgh Alleghenys (AA) 28, 30
Pittsburgh Burghers (PL) 36, 50
Pittsburgh Drug Trials 113, 135–36, 136
Pittsburgh Pirates (NL) [Alleghenys] 41, 95, 107–08, 108, 153; adoption of Pirates nickname 38; first all-black lineup 121; Forbes Field, first and last games at 120; and George Sisler contract dispute 58–59; radio broadcasts of, dispute over 84; and strike vote in support of American Baseball Guild 93; World Series, agreement to play in first 46
Pittsburgh Rebels (FL) 59
Pittsfield, MA: bans games near meeting house 14

Subject Index 313

Player Relations Committee (PRC) 132, 135, 139, 142, 155
players: blacklisting of *see* blacklisting of players; injury to *see* injuries; license required to use names and stats in game 120; named—Judge 81–82, 231*n*95, Law 107–08, 239*n*134; pensions of *see* pensions; sales and trades of *see* sales and trades of players; *see also* military service, salaries, suspensions and expulsions
Players Association *see* Major League Baseball Players Association
Players' Fraternity *see* Fraternity of Professional Players of America
Players' League (PL): cases involving—*Am. Ass'n Base-Ball Club of Kansas City v. Pickett* 37, *Metro. Exhibition Co. v. Ewing* 36, *Metro. Exhibition Co. v. Ward* 35, *Phila. Ball Club, Ltd. v. Hallman* 36; formation and cessation of 18, 19, 34–35, 36–37, 37; major league status of 217*n*31
Players Protective Association *see* Protective Association of Professional Baseball Players
poetry and baseball: "Baseball and the Law" 109; "Casey at the Bat" 138
Pohlad, Carl 155, 250*n*230
Pompez, Alex 63, 74
Poole, Ed 47
Popov, Alex: and dispute over Bonds home-run ball 157
Popovich [Valli], Violet: and shooting of Billy Jurges 81
Portland Beavers (PCL) 157; compensation for MLB expansion to 122; sues MLB over televising of games 107
Postema, Pam: sex discrimination suit by umpire 143–44
Povich, Shirley 103
Powell, Jack 40–41
Powers, Jimmy: and Lou Gehrig suit for defamation 86
Powers, Pat 43, 45
president, U.S.: HOF, first to visit while in office 166; MLB game, first to attend 40; opening day pitch, first to throw 44, 51; and salary comparison with Ruth 68, 79; World Series game, attendance at 75; *see also* names of presidents
prisons and prisoners: Alabama Pitts on prison team at Sing Sing 82; Blackie Schwamb—prison pitching record of 98; Denny McLain in 119; Pete Rose—at Marion (IL) Prison Camp 141; Ruth Ann Steinhagen—at Kankakee State Prison 97
privacy, right to 102, 140–41; and Warren Spahn suit against publisher 110
property law: dispute over Bonds home-run ball 157
Protective Association of Professional Baseball Players 42

Providence Grays (NL) 16, 26, 27, 29
publicity, right of: and Babe Ruth's image 64–65, 140–41; copyright preemption of—commercial exploitation of identity 149; game telecasts 136; created in dispute over baseball cards 101–02; in Don Newcombe suit over beer ad 146; and fantasy baseball use of names and stats 161; and Mets dispute over team image on clothing 149; non-commercial speech protected from, in Gionfriddo suit 157; and Orlando Cepeda licensing dispute 116
Pulliam, Harry 45; and attempt to bribe umpires 50
Pythian Base Ball Club: and first game between black and white teams 22–23; NABBP denies membership to 21

radio 35; dispute over broadcasts of Pirates' games 84; unified MLB broadcasting agreement 84–85
Radomski, Kirk: as source for Mitchell Report 162
Ramsey, Thomas "Toad" 33
Rancho Cucamonga Quakes (Calif. League) 153
Rawlings, George H.: fielder's glove patent 32
Rawlings Sporting Goods: sale of fielder's glove with webbing 73; and suit over defective mask 108
Reach, Alfred James 226*n*29; sporting goods firm of, patent for batter's head protector 47
Reach, Robert: catcher's mask with inflatable padding, patent for 33
Reagan, Ronald 239*n*119; pardons George Steinbrenner 125; portrays Grover Cleveland Alexander 100
Rector, Andrew: sleeping fan sues TV announcers for defamation 170
Redford, Robert 97
Reed, Floyce 80
Reed, Stanley (Justice) 102
Reinsdorf, Jerry 250*n*230, 148
Reiser, Pete 83
relocation of franchises *see* franchise movement
Replogle, Hartley 65
reserve clause/system 43, 99; abrogated for 10 year veterans 56; American Baseball Guild's proposal regarding 92; antitrust exemption limited to 144, 148; CBA creates study committee on 115–16; Congressional testimony on—by Joe Garagiola 102–103, by Ty Cobb 99; first use of 18, 27; league policies about—AA 28, 30, Union Association 30–31; legal challenges to—*Cincinnati Exhibition Co. v. Johnson* 57, first litigation concerning 29–30, *Flood v. Kuhn* 112, 118, 119, 122–23, 153, *Gardella v. Chandler* 96,

Metropolitan Exhibition Co. v. Ward 35, upheld in Gumbert suit for lost wages 41–42, upheld in *Toolson v. New York Yankees* 102, *Weegham v. Killefer* 56–57; and MacPhail committee report on 93; and Messersmith-McNally arbitration decision 112, 126; Millennium Plan for reserving players for minor leagues 34; and National Agreement of 1883 30; and National Agreement of 1903 44, 45–46; and NL/AL peace agreement 44, 45

Resolute Base Ball Club of Cincinnati *see* Cincinnati Red Stockings

resolutions: Congress, U.S., "Baseball Trust" 53, New York, opposing baseball discrimination 87, seeking investigation of baseball discrimination 91

"revolving": litigation over players jumping leagues—Bill Hallman 36, Buck Ewing 36, Hal Chase 57–58, Napoleon Lajoie 43, John Pickett 37, Sam Wise 29; problem for NAPBBP 18, 23

Reynolds, Allie 103

Reynolds, Debbie 239n119

Reynolds, John 121

Richardson, Bobby 109

Richter, Francis: critique of *Federal Baseball* case 72–73; proposes as minor league reserve system 18, 34

Rickey, Wesley Branch 28–29, 35; and Continental League 90, 106–07; and Dan Bankhead 95; farm system developed by 83; and George Sisler contract dispute 59; and Jackie Robinson 89, 91, 94; lawyer-manager 167, 212n21; and Leo Durocher suspension 94; and televising of Dodger games 93–94

Risberg, Charles "Swede": acquitted in Black Sox criminal trial 70; Black Sox grand jury indicts 66; civil suit against White Sox 71; expelled from baseball 70; suspended by Comiskey 65

Rizzuto, Phil 139

Roach, William 85

Roberts, John 163; compares judges to umpires 160

Roberts, Tom: collusion decisions of 137–38, 140, 156; first million-dollar salary arbitration award 134

Robeson, Paul 97

Robinson, Frank 95, 231n95; first black manager 113, 125–26

Robinson, Jackie 94, 102, 106, 119, 125; birth and career of 62; color line broken by 89, 94; court martial of 68, 87–88; retired number of 110, 239n28; signs with Montreal Royals 89, 91; testifies at HUAC hearing 97

Robison, Frank: and Ohio Sunday baseball law 40, 41

Robison, M. Stanley 53

Rockefeller, John D. 20, 44

Rockne, Knute 69

Rodriguez, Alex: suspended for PED use 152, 166

Rogers, John I. 43

Rojas, Octavio "Cookie" 242n37

Rona, Barry 139

Roosevelt, Franklin D. 86; Green Light Letter 68, 86–87

Roosevelt, Theodore 20

Rose, Charlie 139

Rose, Harvey 24

Rose, Pete 84; suspension for gambling 113, 140, 171; tax conviction of 141

Roseboro, John: and Marichal incident 111; and suit over defective mask 108

Rothstein, Arnold: and World Series of 1919 (Black Sox scandal) 64, 66, 70

rounders 13, 49

Rowland, Clarence "Pants": and Emmett Ashford 241n9; and PCL's quest for major league status 91–92

Rudi, Joe 127, 129

Ruel, Herold D. "Muddy": admitted to practice before U.S. Supreme Court 78; lawyer-manager in MLB 212n21

Ruppert, Jacob 232n119; and Babe Ruth contract 79; Congress, one of 3 MLB executives to serve in 223n41; and dispute over Carl Mays sale 62–63, 63

Russell, Allen 227n143

Russell, Bill 127

Ruth, Babe: Baby Ruth Home Run candy bar—stolen in burglary 80, trademark dispute over 78–79; Christy Walsh as agent for 69; and comparison with president's salary 68, 79; *Headin' Home*, sues producer of 65; HR failure blamed for fan stampede 78; and image of—on calendar 140–41, in motion picture 64–65; Obama handles bat of 166; paternity suit against 74; salary of 79; strikes out against woman pitcher 79; suspended for post–World Series barnstorming 67, 71

Ryan, Nolan 134; first million-dollar player contract 130–31

Saigh, Fred: Cardinals owner convicted of tax evasion 101

St. Louis Brown Stockings (AA) *see* St. Louis Browns (AA)

St. Louis Browns (AA) 28, 33; purchased by NL as part of peace agreement 39

St. Louis Browns (AL) 63, 78, 84, 85, 98; and dispute over rights to Fred Bennett 79–80; and Eddie Gaedel 99–100; and George Sisler contract dispute 59; sued by John O'Connor for breach of contract 52–53

St. Louis Cardinals (NL) 73, 80, 97, 99, 102,

139; acquired by Anheuser-Busch 101; and Curt Flood trade 118, 119, 122–23; free agency granted to minor league players of 68, 83; Helene Britton first female owner of MLB team 53, 54; manager Roger Bresnahan fired by owner Britton 55; *see also* St. Louis Browns (AA)
St. Louis Star-Times (newspaper) 92
St. Louis Terriers (FL) 57, 59
St. Nicholas Hotel (Cincinnati) 45
salaries: arbitration of *see* arbitration and arbitrators; cap on—Brush salary classification scheme 18, 34, ceiling set by Wage Stabilization Board 98–99, first in O.B. 32, resistance to 32, 96, 147; of individuals—Kevin Brown 154, Joe DiMaggio 96, Don Drysdale 114, Sandy Koufax 114, Stan Musial 98–99, Mike Piazza 154, Babe Ruth 68, 79, Nolan Ryan 130–31; firsts—$100,000 annual 96, $100,000 annual for pitcher 112, 114, first $1,000,000 annual 130–31, $1,000,000 salary arbitration award 134, first $100 million contract 154; required minimum—CBA raises to $10,000 115; to $12,000 120; to $15,000 123; to $18,000 127; to $30,000 131; to $35,000 131 to $100,000 141, creation of 89, 93, owners refuse increase in 105
Salerno, Al: fired umpire sues Joe Cronin and MLB 116, 118, 121
sales and trades of players: American Baseball Guild proposal for 92; Carl Mays disputed sale 62–63, 63; Finley player sales voided by Kuhn 127, 129; firsts—sale of player 24, trade of players between major league teams 33, between major and minor league teams 33, 5-and-10-year rule for trades 123; Players Protective Association proposal for 42; Scott Perry disputed sale 61
Salt Lake Bees (PCL) [Buzz; Stingers]: trademark dispute over mascot name 156–57
San Diego Padres (NL) 122, 156
San Francisco Examiner (newspaper) 138
San Francisco Giants (NL) 111, 147, 157, 167; and contractual dispute over Masanori Murakami 110–11; and move of Athletics to San José, 169; and purchase of 144; and relocation—to Toronto 126, to Florida 148
San Quentin prison 98
Sanchez, Louie 167
Sanguillen, Manny 121
Satriano, Gina: and Colorado Silver Bullets 147; first female starting pitcher in major-league park 147; and Little League 147
Satriano, Tom 147
Saucier, Frank 99
Schang, Wally 62
Schieffer, Tom 168
Schilling, Curt 160
Schmelz, Gus 33

Schwamb, Ralph "Blackie": and minor league career after prison release 98
Schwert, Pius L. "Pi" 222n41
Scott, Elisha 63
Seattle Pilots (AL) 122, 135
Seaver, Tom 110
Sebring, Francis 21
Seitz, Peter 47–48; arbitration decisions—Hunter-Finley 125, Messersmith-McNally 126, 126–27, 127
Selig, Allan H. "Bud" 113, 148, 152, 250n230; and Mitchell Report 161; and PEDs 160; and Pete Rose 255n115; remarks about Jackie Robinson by 235n28; retires as commissioner 156, 167; tax case of 135
Seymour, Harold 29
Shamsky, Art 250n262
Shapiro, Milton 110
Shea, William 65
Shea, William A.: and Continental League 90, 106–07; stadium named for 109
Shea Stadium (NY) 109, 110, 235n28
Shenkman, Samuel 104
Sherman Antitrust Act 168; applicability to baseball 45, 72; and baseball cards 134; as basis for Flood suit 118; signed by Harrison 37
Shibe, Benjamin F.: cork-centered baseball, first patent for 51
Shibe, John 77
Shibe, Tom 77
Shibe Park (Philadelphia) 77
Shoremeade Hotel (Miami) 98
Shreveport Sports (Texas League) 105
Shulman, Dan 170
Siegel, Brian 155
Silverman, Daniel 133
Sinclair, Harry 59, 60
Sing Sing Prison 82
Sinton Hotel (Cincinnati) 56, 59
Sisk, B.F. 128
Sisler, George 83; contract signed as minor voided 58–59
60 Minutes (television program) 139
slander *see* defamation
Slavin, James 64
Smalley, Roy 137
Smith, Al 62
Smith, Lonnie 136
Snider, Duke 102
Soden, Arthur H.: and creation of reserve clause 18, 27; suspends Charley Jones over salary dispute 27
Sosa, Sammy 159
Sotomayor, Sonia (Judge) 163; enjoins owners from implementing CBA during strike 149
Souter, David (Justice) 163
Southern Association: impact of Louisiana antimixing law on 105

Spahn, Warren: and privacy suit against publisher 110
Spalding, Albert G. 32, 34, 137; A.G. Spalding and Brothers 34, 48; and Louisville Grays scandal 26; and Mills Commission 48–49; and patent for—batting cage 48, catcher's mask, assignment to 34, catcher's mask with throat protector 245*n*109
Spalding Base Ball Guide: includes Thayer's patented catcher's mask 26, Mills Commission Report published in 49
Speaker, Tris 67, 129
Special Baseball Records Committee: establishes major league status of leagues 31, 213*n*31
spectators and fans: sleeping fan sues broadcaster for defamation 170; giveaways, discriminating between recipients of 160; injury to—act limits liability of stadium for foul ball injuries 145, brawl with players causing 159, fan stampede causing 77–78, first appellate opinion to consider 55, mascot actions leading to 153, 166, stadium parking lot attack causing 167; players stalked by—Bob Uecker, by Ann Ladd 164, Eddie Waitkus, by Ruth Steinhagen 97; *see also* admission charges
Spedden, Charles 74
Spering, Charles 23
Sporting Life (newspaper) 34, 35, 72
Sporting News (newspaper) 47, 72
Sports Illustrated (magazine) 102, 128, 146; and Caminiti admission of PED use 158; and McLain gambling scandal 118
Sportswriters: female reporter in locker room 128–29; John Haldeman reveals Louisville scandal 25; Lou Gehrig sues Jimmy Powers for defamation 86; Ray Gillespie and Mexican League 92; Ring Lardner and Ward-Johnson defamation suit 52
spring training: Miller tours camps during 114; "Murphy money" for 89, 93; and strike or lockout 122, 123, 126–27, 131, 141
Springer, Dennis 157
stadiums *see* ballparks
Standard Oil 20
Stanton, Frank 93
Stargell, Willie 121
Start, Joe 26
statutes, federal: Anabolic Steroids Control Act 142, 143; Clayton Act 96, 148, 168; Curt Flood Act of 1998 148, 151, 153–54, 169; Labor-Management Relations Act 162; Native American Graves Protection and Repatriation Act 168; Sherman Antitrust Act 37, 72, 118, 134, 168; Sports Violence Act 132; *see also* Constitution, U.S
statutes, states: Illinois—Baseball Facility Liability Act 145; sports anti-corruption 73; Louisiana—antimixing 105; Maryland—authorizing acquisition of land for stadium 137; Michigan—statute of frauds 162, workers' compensation 162; New York—allowing local choice for Sunday baseball 62, anti-pooling 25; Pennsylvania—preventing Sunday baseball 14
Steinbrenner, George: defamation, sued by umpire for 136–37; suspended by Bowie Kuhn 125; Watergate conviction of 124–25
Steinhagen, Ruth Ann 81; shoots Eddie Waitkus 97
Steininger, Edward 54
Stengel, Casey 109–10; Congressional testimony by 106
Stennett, Rennie 121
Stevens, John Paul (Justice) 100
Stevens, Julia Ruth 140
Stewart, Jimmie 238*n*88
Stoneham, Horace 232*n*119, 126
Stotz, Carl E. 110
Stout, Ernest 52
Stovey, Harry 38
Stow, Brian 167
Strathairn, David 165
Stratton, Monty 242*n*88
The Stratton Story (motion picture) 238*n*88
strict liability: and suit over defective mask 108
strikes *see* work stoppages
Strong, Curtis 135–36
Strong, Nat 74
Stuart, Dick 108
Sullivan, James E. 48–49
Sunday Baseball by league 13; AA policy allows 28; NL—policy against 27–28; policy changed by merger with AA 235*n*92
Sunday Baseball by state 13; Massachusetts—Boston ordinance allows 77, referendum allows local choice 77; Nebraska—blue law upheld by Supreme Court 39, 1913 law allows local choice 39; New York—blue law upheld 47, law allows local choice 62; Ohio—blue law enforced against Cleveland Spiders 41, blue law upheld 40–41; Pennsylvania—blue law enacted 14; blue law upheld 76–77; law allows local choice 81, Philadelphia ordinance allows 81
Supreme Court, U.S. 52; antitrust exemption of created in *Federal Baseball* 71–72; antitrust exemption upheld by *Flood* 112, 122–23, antitrust exemption upheld by *Toolson* 102, baseball interest of justices—Blackmun 50, Day 54–55, *Federal Baseball v. National League* 71–72; *Flood v. Kuhn* 122–23; judges compared to umpires by Roberts 160; *Julian Messner, Inc. v. Spahn* 228*n*154; *Mahn v. Harwood* 31 (first ever); *Major League Baseball Players Ass'n v. Garvey* 156; Muddy Ruel, admitted to practice before 78; nomi-

Subject Index 317

nated to—Blackmun 50, Roberts 160, Sotomayor 163; players compared to justices of 129; *Toolson v. New York Yankees* 102; *U.S. v. Cleveland Indians Baseball Co.* 156; World Series updates for 54–55
suspensions and expulsions: Alex Johnson, by Angels 121–22; Alex Rodriguez, for PED use 152, 166; Benny Kauff, by Landis 69–70; Black Sox players 65, 67, 70; Carl Mays, by Ban Johnson 62–63; Charley Jones, by Soden over salary dispute 27; commissioner's power to impose 68; Denny McLain, by Kuhn 118–19; Ferguson Jenkins, by Kuhn 131; Frank Francisco, by Bob Watson 159; Fred Pfeffer, suspension of, leads to suit against Giants 40; George Steinbrenner, by Kuhn 125; HOF rule about players on ineligible list 141; John O'Connor, expelled from AA 227n58; Joseph Creamer, for 1908 bribe attempt 50; Lee Magee, by Landis 64; Leo Durocher, by Chandler 94; Louisville Grays, for fixing games of 25–26; Mexican League jumpers—by Chandler 96, suspension lifted 96–97; Mickey Mantle, by Kuhn 130; Pete Rose, for gambling 113, 140, 171; Pittsburgh Drug Trials players, by Ueberroth 136; Rafael Palmeiro, for failed PED test 160; Ryan Braun, for PED use 152, 166; Ted Turner, by Kuhn 128; Ty Cobb, by Johnson 53–54; Willie Mays, by Kuhn 130; Yankee players—by Landis for post–World Series barnstorming 67, 71
Sutter, Bruce 134
Sutton, Don 140
Swift and Co. 116
Synar, Mike 148

Taft, Charles 51
Taft, William Howard: opening day pitch, first to throw out 44, 51, 166; refuses offer to become 1st commissioner 51
"Take Me Out to the Ballgame" (song): copyright for 49
Tammany Hall 14, 17, 62
Tappe, El 108
taxation: collusion settlement, implications for 142, 156; tax cases of—Bud Selig 135, Fred Saigh 101, Maury Wills 117, Pete Rose 141, Randy Hundley 115, Rogers Hornsby 80; tax home of player is team's home 117
Taylor, Harry Leonard 42
Taylor, Zack 100
Television: *Baseball*, PBS documentary on 109; and copyright of game telecasts 136; first season-long sponsorship of broadcasts 93–94; minor leagues threatened by MLB use of 107; and MLB Network 152; sleeping fan sues broadcaster for defamation 170
Tener, John K.: first player to serve as NL president 50–51, 140; and George Sisler contract dispute 230n112; organizer of first Congressional Baseball Game 51; resigns as NL president 61; U.S. Congress, first player to serve in 50–51
Tepler, Boyd: sues Cubs for negligence 99
Terkel, Studs 60
Terry, Bill 109
Texas League 105
Texas Rangers (AL) 131, 159, 168; *see also* Washington Senators (1961–71)
Thayer, Ernest Lawrence: "Casey at the Bat" author of 135, 138
Thayer, Frederick W.: first patent for catcher's mask 26
Thomas, Danny 239n119
Thomas, Frank: interviewed for Mitchell Report 162; PED testimony of 160
Thompson, Russell 75
Thompson, Sam 33
Thorn, John 14
Thorpe, Jim: buried in renamed towns 103, 168
Thorpe, Patricia "Patsy" 103
Three Rivers Stadium 121
Thurman, Allan W.: and disputed contracts of AA players 38, 38–39
tickets *see* admission charges
Timur, Kenneth 164–65
Tinker, Joe 60
Tirendi, Vincent 144
Titus, Wellington Stockton 48
Toledo Iron Men (AA, minors) [Mud Hens] 60
Toole, John Conway 68
Toolson v. New York Yankees 102, 123, 144
Topping, Dan 96
Topps Chewing Gum Co., Inc.: and litigation over baseball cards 101–02, 104; MLBPA agreement with 116–17
Toronto Blue Jays (AL) 126, 137, 162
Toronto Maple Leafs (Int'l League) 153
town ball 13, 15, 16
trademark *see* copyright and trademark
Trautman, George M.: voids contract of woman player 101
Travers, Aloysius S. 53–54
Tresh, Tom 109
Tripartite Agreement *see* National Agreement (of 1883)
Truman, Harry S.: awards medal to Moe Berg 93
Turner, Ted 76; suspended by Kuhn 128
Tyng, James Alexander 26

Ueberroth, Peter: and collusion by owners 139; elected commissioner 117; lifts suspensions of Mays and Mantle 130; suspension of Pittsburgh Drug Trials players 136
umpires: attempted bribery of 49–50; catcher's mask with horizontal crossbars,

patented by 74–75; compared to judges by Roberts 160; first African American as 114; strike by 120–21, 129–30; suits by—antitrust and defamation action by fired umpires 116, 118, 121, defamation action against Steinbrenner 137, discrimination action by woman umpire 143–44; union of—Major League Umpires Association 121, 129–30, umpires allegedly fired for supporting 116

Union Association: formation of 18, 30–31; major league status of 31, 213*n*31

unions in baseball: for players—American Baseball Guild, formation and cessation of 89, 92, 93, Brotherhood of Professional Base Ball Players, formation of 18, 32–33, first 32–33, Fraternity of Professional Baseball Players of America, chartered 54; weakening of 56, Major League Baseball Players Association, formation of 103, National Baseball Players Association, formation and dissolution of 73–74, Protective Association of Professional Baseball Players, formation of 42, *see also* names of unions; for umpires—Association of Major League Umpires 121, umpires fired for supporting 116

United States League 55

United States Supreme Court *see* Supreme Court, U.S

United Steelworkers 61

University of California, Los Angeles (UCLA) 62, 88

University of Cincinnati 228*n*85

University of Massachusetts 138

University of Michigan 28, 59

University of Missouri–Kansas City 95

University of Pennsylvania 20, 120

University of Pittsburgh 120

University of Virginia 76

Valentine, Bill: fired umpire sues Cronin and MLB 116, 118, 121

Valenzuela, Fernando: first million-dollar salary arbitration award 134

Vance, Dazzy 79

Van Horn, John 24

Veeck, Bill, Jr.: and contract of midget Eddie Gaedel 99–100; and integration of baseball 95

Veeck, William L., Sr. 64, 76

Victoria Hotel (NYC) 30

Vincent, Fay 145; and Basic Agreement of 1990 141; and division shift of Cubs 144; includes steroids in drug policy 143; and suit over biography 148–49

Von der Ahe, Chris 33, 53

Von Tilzer, Albert 49

Wage Stabilization Board: Korean War salary ceiling set by 98–99

Wagner, Honus: and sale of baseball card 155

Wagner, Robert F. 63, 109

Waitkus, Eddie: and comparison with Jurges shooting 81; shot by obsessed fan 97

Walker, James J. "Jimmy" 62

Wallace, Mike 139

Walsh, Christy: agent for Babe Ruth 69

Wansley, William: and first fixed game 17

Ward, Edward R. 109

Ward, John Montgomery 17, 34, 58; article in *Lippincott's Magazine* 32; and Brotherhood of Professional Base Ball Players 32; and Congressional resolution on "Baseball Trust" 53; and defamation suit against Ban Johnson 52; lawyer-manager 31–32, 167, 212*n*21; and Players' League 34–35; represents Fred Pfeffer in suit against Giants 40; reserve clause in contract unenforceable 18–19, 35

Ward, Robert 59

Warner, Jack 238*n*88

Warren, Earl (Justice): compared to Yogi Berra 129

Washington Senators (AL 1901–60) 43, 51, 61, 75, 78, 82, 93; *see also* Minnesota Twins (AL)

Washington Senators (AL 1961–71) 107, 114; *see also* Texas Rangers (AL)

Washington Senators (NL 1891–99) 40

Washington Statesmen (AA): purchased by NL as part of peace agreement 19, 39

Washington University Law School 78

Watergate 124–25

Watson, Bob 159

Weaver, George "Buck": acquitted in Black Sox criminal trial 70; Black Sox grand jury indicts 66; expelled from baseball 70; suspended by Comiskey 65

Weeghman, Charles 60; allowed to buy Chicago Cubs by FL peace agreement with O.B. 59; injunction to force Bill Killefer to play with Whales denied 56–57; settles contract dispute with manager Roger Bresnahan 60

Weiner, Michael: replaces Donald Fehr as executive director of MLBPA 163–64

Weiss, George 96

Weissman, Hilda 98

Welker, Herman 108

Wells, George Titus 48

Welty, Benjamin 68–69

Werker, Henry F. (Judge) 133

Western Association: and National Agreement of 1891, 38

Western League (A 1900–37, 1947–58) (WL-A) 103

Western League (1885–99) (WL) 19; becomes AL 42

Wheat, Zack 109

Wheaton, William R.: role in codifying

Subject Index

Knickerbocker rules 15; umpires first recorded game using Knickerbocker rules 15
White, Bill: first black MLB broadcaster 139; first black league president 139–40
White, William Edward: first black major leaguer 26
Wilkinson, J.L. 75, 91
Williams, Billy 108
Williams, Claude "Lefty": acquitted in Black Sox criminal trial 70; Black Sox grand jury 65, 66; expelled from baseball 70; suspended by Comiskey 65
Williamsport (PA) 110
Willkie, Wendell 86
Willkie Farr & Gallagher 76, 117
Wills, Maury: tax case of 117
Wilson, Woodrow: first president to attend World Series game 75
Wilson Sporting Goods 116
The Winning Team (motion picture) 100
Wisconsin: and suit over Braves move to Atlanta 115
Wise, Samuel W. 29
women in baseball: Colorado Silver Bullets, formation of 147; and female reporters in locker room 128–29; firsts involving— coach of NCAA men's team 138, front-office executive not an owner 76. owner of MLB team 53. player in minor league game 41. player in NCAA 138. professional team of since AAGPBL 147. salary arbitrator 154. signed to minor league contract 79, 101. starting pitcher in major-league stadium 147. umpire 143–44, 249n220; Grace Coolidge rabid fan 229n49; high school sex discrimination case 138; and Little League 110, 113, 124, 147; Marjori Bennett creates centennial logo 84; and minor leagues— barred from playing in 101, first to play in 41; umpire's sex discrimination suit 143–44
Wood, John S. 97
work stoppages 112–13; American Baseball Guild's strike attempt 93; first strike by— players, in-season 133, players, league-wide 122, players, one team 53–54, umpires 120–21; licensing revenue produces strike fund for MLBPA 119; lockouts—197, 123, 197, 126–27, 199, 141; owners enjoined from implementing new CBA during strike 149; strikes of—1972 122, 1980 131, 1981 133, 133–34, 1985 135, 1994–95 113, 147, 147–48, 149, 149–50; umpire strikes 120–21, 129–30
workers' compensation 163
World Series: barnstorming after completion of, rule against 71; firsts—attendance by U.S. president 75, in modern era, agreement for 46, Negro World Series 67, 74; of 1903—agreement for 46; of 1912—Justice Day receives updates while on bench 54–55; of 1919 *see* Black Sox scandal; of 1947— right of publicity suit by Gionfriddo 147; of 1963—Koufax inspires poem 109; of 1969— right of publicity suit by Mets players 149; of 1977—female reporter in locker room 128; of 1981—after split season because of strike 134; of 1994—cancelled because of strike 148, 149; of 2005—Obama wears White Sox ring at HOF 166
Wren, Christine 249n220
Wright, George 22, 222n29
Wright, John 80
Wright, Robert 114
Wright, William Henry "Harry" 27, 29; organizer and manager of Cincinnati Red Stockings 22
Wrigley, Philip K. 165, 239n120
Wrigley, William 99
Wrigley Field (Chicago) 81; Rooftop owners and expansion of 169
Wrigley Field (Los Angeles) 105
Wyatt, Cary B. 63

Yale University 16, 84, 129, 142
Yankee Stadium: negligence suit over fan stampede at 78
Yeager, Steve 127
The Year the Yankees Lost the Pennant (book) 82
Young, Cy 55–56
Young, Nicholas E. 38, 226n29
YouTube 170

Zeller, Jack 85
Zimmer, Charley "Chief": and Protective Association of Professional Baseball Players 42

www.ingramcontent.com/pod-product-compliance
Lightning Source LLC
Chambersburg PA
CBHW051208300426
44116CB00006B/473